The Law of Higher Education

The Law of Higher Education

Second edition

D J Farrington
BSC, DPHIL, LLB, LLM, ADV DIP ED, FRSA
Deputy Secretary, University of Stirling

Butterworths
London, Edinburgh, Dublin
1998

United Kingdom	Butterworths a Division of Reed Elsevier (UK) Ltd, Halsbury House, 35 Chancery Lane, LONDON WC2A 1EL and 4 Hill Street, EDINBURGH EH2 3JZ
Australia	Butterworths, SYDNEY, ADELAIDE, BRISBANE, CANBERRA, MELBOURNE and PERTH,
Canada	Butterworths Canada Ltd, TORONTO and VANCOUVER
Ireland	Butterworth (Ireland) Ltd, DUBLIN
Malaysia	Malayan Law Journal Sdn Bhd, KUALA LUMPUR
New Zealand	Butterworths of New Zealand Ltd, WELLINGTON and AUCKLAND
Singapore	Butterworths Asia, SINGAPORE
South Africa	Butterworths Publishers (Pty) Ltd, DURBAN
USA	Michie, CHARLOTTESVILLE, Virginia

© Reed Elsevier (UK) Ltd 1998

A CIP Catalogue record for this book is available from the British Library.

First edition   1994   1 0014 1 9 422

ISBN 0 406 89635 6

Printed and bound in Great Britain by Redwood Books, Trowbridge, Wiltshire

Visit us at our website: http://www.butterworths.co.uk

Preface

The period 1994 to 1997 saw a continuation of the changes in higher education which led to the first edition of this book. The disappearance of the 'binary line' in 1992 left in its wake a highly complex and varied system of higher education governance and gave rise to continuous argument about the criteria for the use of the word 'university' in institutional titles. Funding methodologies developed further. A far-reaching and thorough review of the system was conducted by a committee chaired by Sir Ron Dearing. The boundaries between secondary, further and higher education continue to shift: the present volume therefore crosses the traditional boundaries to explore further the legal issues at the interfaces. The University of Buckingham remains the only institution which is entirely independent of government, but the dependence of the publicly-funded system on government grants has continued to decline with the development of a more market-oriented approach in the spirit of the late 1980s and early 1990s.

The complex systems for quality assurance and assessment were simplified in 1997, to the great relief of all concerned. Assessments of teaching quality are now well-established and the third research assessment exercise took place in 1996. These assessments influence funding, which itself influences what can be provided, and so the circle goes on. Charters issued under the Citizens' Charter Initiative setting out standards of service to be expected by 'customers' of higher education, including students, which first appeared in 1993, had considerable influence on the way the institution-student relationship was perceived.

These changes, which are well-documented, take place in an organisational setting which has its roots firmly embedded in a legal framework, itself changing as new policy directions require an adjustment of the respective powers and responsibilities of the actors in the play. State intervention in the way the traditional universities operate has never been greater, while the new universities and the non-university sector of higher education have seen the legal basis of their existence and the control over their activities change dramatically.

The present work aims to be a comprehensive and practical guide to the way in which the law underpins and relates to the daily work of academic and other staff, students and other customers of higher education in the United Kingdom. I should like to acknowledge the advice and support given by a number of individuals and organisations. First the CUA/CRS Legal Group which produced *Universities and the Law*: its chairman Frank Mattison, lately Registrar and Secretary of the University of Hull, Bob Seaton, Secretary of the University of Dundee, Charles Henderson of the University of Bath and Richard Farr of the University of Hull. I hope this book is a further worthy successor to their pioneering efforts. Thanks are also due to David Anderson-Evans of CVCP, and Butterworths for their enthusiastic support of the project. Institutions in membership of UCELNET (the Universities and Colleges Education Law Network, founded in 1996) provided much useful material. Special thanks go to Gill Evans, Perry Whalley, Clive Robertson, James Bracher, Rachel Woolf and Ludwig Giesecke for useful and often entertaining discussions on aspects of the work, and to James Parlour, Ian Budden and many other colleagues who have corresponded with me. I would also thank my wife, herself a practising university administrator, for her immense support and encouragement.

I gratefully acknowledge the permission given by the Higher Education Funding Council for England, the Scottish Higher Education Funding Council, the Joint Information Systems Committee, the Association of University Administrators, the Committee of Vice-Chancellors and Principals, and a number of universities and colleges, to enable me to reproduce copyright material.

Every effort has been made to state the law as at 31 December 1997 as the author understands it. I have also taken account of the introduction of the Teaching and Higher Education Bill and the Employment Rights (Dispute Resolution) Bill.

DJF

Stirling

January 1998

Foreword

We have known Dennis Farrington for several years and have been impressed both by the breadth and depth of his knowledge, and also by his enthusiasm. We know from our work as solicitors acting in the higher education sector that administrators in universities and colleges have found the first edition of this book to be a valuable item on their bookshelves, and no doubt this second, revised edition will be equally useful to them, perhaps even more so. We have ourselves turned to his book on innumerable occasions, and we would recommend this revised edition to other practitioners in this field. It offers a broad overview of legal issues affecting higher education institutions and the author's mastery of his subject is undisputed.

Clive Robertson
Lawford & Co
Watchmaker Court
65 St John Street
London EC1M 4HQ

tel: 0171 353 5099

LAWFORD & CO

SOLICITORS

The Association of University Administrators

Mission

The AUA is an open and accessible body for all those with administrative and managerial responsibilities in higher education in the UK and the Republic of Ireland among whom it seeks to promote the highest standards of professionalism.

AUA is committed to serving the aspirations of its members through:
- the provision of appropriate opportunities for professional development through its annual conference, specific training and development initiatives and publications
- the establishment of information networks through Newslink and other means and the encouragement of links between members and groups of members
- fostering links and exchanges of information with similar organisations in higher education overseas.

In furtherance of its mission, the Association seeks to enhance its status and credibility as a recognised professional and influential voice in higher education.

For more information, please contact

AUA Office
University of Manchester, Oxford Road, Manchester, M13 9PL

Tel: 0161 275 2063 **Fax:** 0161 275 2036

email: aua@man.ac.uk **Internet:** http://www.man.ac.uk/aua

 THE ASSOCIATION OF UNIVERSITY ADMINISTRATORS

Contents

Chapter 3

Funding and quality   243

Chapter 5

The employment of staff   404

Table of statutes

Table of statutory instruments

List of cases

E

PARA

Decisions of the European Court of Justice are listed below numerically. These decisions are also included in the preceding alphabetical list.

71/76:	Thieffry v Conseil de l'Ordre des Avocats à la Cour de Paris (1977), ECJ	1.114
61/81:	EC Commission v United Kingdom (1982), ECJ	5.77
107/83:	Ordre des Avocats au Barreau de Paris v Klopp (1984), ECJ .	1.114
152/84:	Marshall v Southampton and South West Hampshire Area Health Authority (Teaching) (1986), ECJ	5.97
170/84:	Bilka-Kaufhaus GmbH v Weber von Hartz (1987), ECJ	5.79
66/85:	Lawrie-Blum v Land Baden-Wurttemberg (1986), ECJ	5.104
316/85:	Centre Public d'Aide Sociale, Courcelles v Lebon (1987), ECJ	4.135
24/86:	Blaizot v University of Liège (1988), ECJ	4.135
39/86:	Lair v University of Hanover (1988), ECJ	4.135
157/86:	Murphy v Bord Telecom Eireann (1988), ECJ	5.77
197/86:	Brown v Secretary of State for Scotland (1988), ECJ	4.135
222/86:	Union Nationale des Entraîneurs et Cadres Techniques Professionnels du Football (UNECTEF) v Heylens (1987), ECJ	1.114
101/87:	P Bork International A/S v Foreningen af Arbejdsledere i Danmark (1989), ECJ	5.114
109/88:	Handels-og Kontorfunktionaerernes Forbund i Danmark v Dansk Arbejdsgiverforening (acting for Danfoss)(1989), ECJ . 5.78, 5.164
C-177/88:	Dekker v Stichting Vormingscentrum voor Jong Volwassenen (VJV - Centrum) Plus (1990), ECJ	5.164
C-179/88:	Handels-og Kontorfunktionaerernes Forbund i Danmark (acting for Hertz) v Dansk Arbejdsgiverforening (acting for Aldi Marked K/S) (1991), ECJ	5.159
C-262/88:	Barber v Guardian Royal Exchange Assurance Group (1990), ECJ	5.77
C-184/89:	Nimz v Freie und Hansestadt Hamburg (1991), ECJ	5.164
C-188/89:	Foster v British Gas plc (1990), ECJ; apld (1991), HL	2.60
C-6, 9/90:	Francovich and Bonifaci v Italy (1992), ECJ	1.58
C-30/90:	EC Commission v United Kingdom (1993), ECJ	6.68
C-29/91:	Dr Sophie Redmond Stichting v Bartol (1992), ECJ	5.114
C-200/91:	Coloroll Pension Trustees Ltd v Russell (1995), ECJ	5.78
C-209/91:	Rask and Christensen v ISS Kantineservice A/S (1993), ECJ . .	5.114
C-271/91:	Marshall v Southampton and South West Hampshire Area Health Authority (No 2) (1994), ECJ; apld (1994), HL	5.97
C-19/92:	Kraus v Land Baden-Würtemberg (1993), ECJ	1.114
C-92/92:	Collins v Imtrat Handelsgesellschaft mbH (1993), ECJ . . 6.10, 6.15
C-127/92:	Enderby v Frenchay Health Authority (1993), ECJ 5.78, 5.79
C-326/92:	Patricia Im- und Export Verwaltungsgesellschaft mbH v EMI Electrola mbH (1993), ECJ 6.10, 6.15
C-382/92:	EC Commission v United Kingdom (1994), ECJ	5.161
C-28/93:	Van den Akker v Stichting Shell Pensioenfonds (1994), ECJ . . .	5.78
C-13/94:	P v S and Cornwall County Council (1996), ECJ	5.98

Glossary of terms used in this book

1 Legislation

The word 'statute' used in this book has two entirely different meanings. The first equates to Act of Parliament, the second to a form of internal legislation used by chartered universities. The principal Acts of Parliament cited are as follows:

CDPA	Copyright, Designs and Patents Act 1988
DDA	Disability Discrimination Act 1995
E(2)A86	Education (No 2) Act 1986
EA94	Education Act 1994
EA96	Education Act 1996
EA97	Education Act 1997
ERA	Education Reform Act 1988
ESA96	Education (Scotland) Act 1996
ESLA90	Education (Student Loans) Act 1990
ESLA96	Education (Student Loans) Act 1996
EmpRA	Employment Rights Act 1996
FHEA	Further and Higher Education Act 1992
FHESA	Further and Higher Education (Scotland) Act 1992
HASAW	Health and Safety At Work, Etc Act 1974
ITA	Industrial Tribunals Act 1996
PA	Patents Act 1977
RRA	Race Relations Act 1976
SDA	Sex Discrimination Act 1975
TULRCA	Trade Union and Labour Relations (Consolidation) Act 1992
TURERA	Trade Union Reform and Employment Rights Act 1993
[THEB	Teaching and Higher Education Bill 1997 – Second Reading text]

2 Organisations

AHUA	Association of Heads of University Administrations
AUA	Association of University Administrators
BTEC	Business and Technician Education Council
COSHEP	Committee of Scottish Higher Education Principals
COSUP	Committee of Scottish University Principals
CSIC	Committee of Scottish and Irish Chairmen
CUC	Committee of University Chairmen (England & Wales)
CVCP	Committee of Vice-Chancellors and Principals of the Universities of the United Kingdom
DANI	Department of Agriculture for Northern Ireland
DENI	Department of Education for Northern Ireland
DfEE	Department for Education and Employment
DfID	Department for International Development
FEFC	Further Education Funding Council
HEFCE	Higher Education Funding Council for England
HEFCW	Higher Education Funding Council for Wales
HESA	Higher Education Statistics Agency
NIHEC	Northern Ireland Higher Education Council
QAA	Quality Assurance Agency for Higher Education
QCA	Qualifications and Curriculum Authority
SCOP	Standing Conference of Principals
SHEFC	Scottish Higher Education Funding Council
SOEID	Scottish Office Education and Industry Department
SQA	Scottish Qualifications Authority
TTA	Teacher Training Agency

3 Others

CCI	Citizens' Charter Initiative
GCE	General Certificate of Education
GNVQ	General National Vocational Qualification
HNC	Higher National Certificate
HND	Higher National Diploma
NCIHE	National Committee of Inquiry into Higher Education ('Dearing')
NVQ	National Vocational Qualification
SCE	Scottish Certificate of Education
SNVQ	Scottish National Vocational Qualification

4   Cases

Almost all cases referred to in this book are reported in one or more of the major series of law reports. Non-lawyers should refer to a standard legal directory for information on the abbreviations used.

Chapter 1

Introduction to higher education – structure and governance

A *universitas* is composed of two elements, the one external, the other internal: recognition by legitimate authority, and the common will of the members which gives their self-constituted society its solidarity and official form. *Sinibaldo de' Fieschi.*

Let us now move away from our snobbish, caste-ridden obsession with university status. *Tony Crosland.*

A definition of 'higher education'

1.1 It was almost 40 years ago that Tony Crosland promoted the dual system of higher education which was finally laid to rest in 1993 with university status granted to a large number of institutions formerly under local authority control.[1] Until relatively recently it was probably possible to identify what we 'really' meant by higher education with the universities which de' Fieschi (later Pope Innocent IV) was discussing in 1243.[2] Today, most people who have an interest in the British system of higher education probably think they know what is meant by the term, or at any rate their knowledge is adequate for their purposes. Let us put that to the test: what exactly is 'higher education'? The *Shorter Oxford English Dictionary* definition of 'higher' is 'superior to the common sort' and if we apply that to the same dictionary's definition of 'education' we find that as

1 See S Crosland *Tony Crosland* (1982) p 59.
2 See M B Hackett *The original statutes of Cambridge University* (1970) p 104 and P Michaud-Quantin *La conscience d'être membre d'une universitas* in *Beiträge zum Berufsbewusstsein des mittelalterlichen Menschen* Miscellanea mediaevalia iii (1964) p 11.

practitioners of higher education we are engaged in the business of giving 'systematic instruction, schooling or training, superior to the common sort to the young (and, by extension, to adults) in preparation for the work of life.' The section on development of higher education in the 1993 report of the National Commission on Education[3] mentions only 'universities' as having a mission to educate and train people to the highest levels:

> Universities have a mission to pursue and transfer new knowledge; to help to manage and apply the international knowledge explosion set off by modern communications and information technology; and to educate and train to the highest levels people who will, to a large extent, provide the brains and backbone of industry and commerce, the professions, service organisations and political life in this country.

In fact we deliver education and training through the medium of a wider group of distinctive higher education institutions, which also engage in fundamental and applied research, consultancy, short courses in adult and continuing education and a variety of commercial activity.

Definition in law

1.2 A definition of 'higher education' is given in section 120(1) and Schedule 6 Education Reform Act 1988 (ERA) (the definition adopted by the Further and Higher Education Act 1992 (FHEA)) and in section 38 Further and Higher Education (Scotland) Act 1992 (FHESA). The latter definition is very similar to the former:

> ... education provided by means of any of the courses falling, for the time being, within this section ...
> (a) a course at a higher level in preparation for a higher diploma or certificate;
> (b) a first degree course;
> (c) a course for the education and training of teachers;
> (d) a course of postgraduate studies (including a higher degree course);
> (e) a course at a higher level in preparation for a qualification from a professional body.

---

3 *Learning to Succeed: A Radical Look at Education Today and A Strategy for the Future* Report of the Paul Hamlyn Foundation National Commission on Education 1993 p 289.

The 'higher' nature of the courses (a term which itself requires definition) arises if they are of a higher standard than those in preparation for GCE Advanced Level, SCE Highers, BTEC and SQA[4] national certificates and diplomas other than HNC and HND, and broadly equivalent to GNVQ, NVQ or SVQ Level 3. In its report 'Higher Education in the Learning Society' the National Committee of Inquiry into Higher Education (NCIHE)[5] observed that higher education is only one part of an interdependent system of education and training and forms part of 'tertiary' education. It decided to concentrate on education above Level 3.

1.3   There have been other legal definitions, for example that given by the VAT Tribunal in *Church of Scientology v Customs and Excise Comrs.*[6] 'Education' for the purposes of exemption from value added tax is somewhat vaguely defined as 'training in any form of art' (with certain exceptions).[7] The Tribunal developed that to define education in terms of activities and processes involving learning and concerned with developing the ability of individuals to understand and articulate, to reason and make judgments and to develop sensitivity and creativity. From that case it appears that the courts consider higher education as involving 'logical reasoning, critical interpretation and research, not mere acceptance of propounded doctrine.'

The aims of higher education

The Robbins Report

1.4   The Committee which produced the 'Robbins Report' of 1963[8] thought that there were at least four objectives in higher education, expressed in no particular order and being, in balance, essential features of the system: (i) instruction in skills suitable to play a part in the general division of labour, (ii) promoting the general powers of the mind; (iii) the advancement of learning, (iv) the transmission of a common culture and common standards of citizenship.

---

4   The Scottish Qualifications Authority (SQA) took over the functions of the Scottish Examination Board (SEB) and the Scottish Vocational Educational Council (SCOTVEC) in 1997 – Education (Scotland) Act 1996.
5   Commonly known as the 'Dearing Committee' after its Chair, Sir Ron Dearing, report published in July 1997.
6   [1977] VATTR 278, 290.
7   Schedule 9 Group 6 Value Added Tax Act 1994.
8   *Report of the Committee on Higher Education* Cmnd 2154 (1963), paragraphs 22–29.

A modern re-statement

1.5 In 1994 the then Secretary of State for Education and Employment undertook a consultation exercise which invited views on what changes should be made to the Robbins' aims. The outcome, reported by NCIHE, was that there needed to be a shift in the balance between them and some development to reflect changing conditions.[9] NCIHE suggested that the four main purposes of higher education as we approach the millennium are:

- to inspire and enable individuals to develop their capabilities to the highest potential levels throughout life, so that they grow intellectually, are well-equipped for work, can contribute effectively to society and achieve personal fulfilment;
- to increase knowledge and understanding for their own sake and to foster their application to the benefit of the economy and society;
- to serve the needs of an adaptable, sustainable, knowledge-based economy at local, regional and national levels;
- to play a major role in shaping a democratic, civilised, inclusive society.

If we consider in isolation what the aims of the principal 'customers' of higher education are, then it is fairly clear that there is an increased emphasis on learning for the purpose of acquiring qualifications, illustrated by this extract from a speech given by the minister responsible for higher education in March 1993:

> What is expected? What then do [students] want? The evidence suggests that students are looking for a social as well as an academic experience, but this is less and less their major aim. They expect that their time in higher education will be a time of real learning with the benefit of interesting and challenging teaching by teachers who know their subject and can communicate it, and that it will give them good qualifications, widely respected, which will open doors to employment, self-employment or further study or research as well as to a fuller and richer life.[10]

1.6 The 'evidence' to support this statement is not cited, but it is clear from this speech, from the Citizens' Charter Initiative and other developments including an increased emphasis on assessments of quality in both teaching and research that higher education has much

9 DfEE, Scottish Office, Welsh Office and DENI (1996) *Purposes of Higher Education*. Unpublished, reported in paragraph 5.8, Main Report, NCIHE, July 1997.
10 T Boswell MP, Under-Secretary of State at the Department for Education *Quality and the Consumer* Sainsbury Seminar, 16 March 1993.

more of a market orientation than before. The old idea of the 'social club,' which is indeed how many older readers will best remember their time as students, has gone and with the change in emphasis has come a new concentration on the rights of the 'customer' or 'client' (student) to a quality education provided by bodies in a contractual relationship with the state. The language of the Further and Higher Education Acts reinforces this: they make funding available for the 'provision of education' both by recognised institutions and by 'any person.'[11] This is consistent with the former Conservative government's policy on the provision of education at school level, and the provision of health services by independent trusts. At date of publication the Labour Government elected in 1997 has made no significant changes to this system, although the prospective introduction of tuition fees following on the report of NCIHE reinforces the market culture, and the suggestions for a Virtual University[12] and a University of Industry[13] take us well away from the notion of a residential community and the social experience which this may provide.

A commodity supplied by providers

1.7   Higher education is increasingly seen as a commodity which is supplied to the state by a group of contractors, the higher education providers. There are now two main groups of providers of higher education: the universities and some non-university institutions. The proportion of students following higher education courses enrolled at universities, non-university higher education institutions and further education colleges varies across the UK. In England it is about 75% university, with the balance split roughly equally between higher and further education institutions, whereas in Scotland the corresponding proportions are 65%, 8% and 27%, in Wales 66%, 29% and 5% and in Northern Ireland 81%, 3% and 16%.[14] All universities (except the privately-funded University of Buckingham) and a number of non-university institutions receive a proportion of their public funding for teaching and research from the relevant funding agency: in England the Higher Education Funding Council for England (HEFCE), in Wales the Higher Education Funding Council for Wales (HEFCW), in Scotland the Scottish Higher

11   Section 65 FHEA; section 40 FHESA.
12   Paragraph 8.26, Report on National Consultation, NCIHE, July 1997.
13   Paragraph 8.41, Report on National Consultation, NCIHE, July 1997.
14   Charts 16.1–16.4, Main Report, NCIHE, July 1997.

Education Funding Council (SHEFC) and in Northern Ireland the relevant government departments advised by the Northern Ireland Higher Education Council (NIHEC).[15] The Funding Councils were established under the 1992 Acts to fund the provision of education and research by higher education institutions and the provision of higher education courses by other bodies or persons. SHEFC's role is to fund higher education institutions to provide higher education whereas HEFCE funds the provision of higher education by both higher education and further education institutions: this difference of approach reflects the different systems operative before April 1993.[16] The total expenditure of higher education institutions in 1995/96 was over £10 billion, representing about 1.4% of GDP.[17]

1.8 The Qualifications and Curriculum Authority (QCA)[18] has the power to operate at level 5 (degree-equivalent level) 'by consent' in respect of those degrees which confer exemption from professional body recognition. In Scotland the equivalent body is SQA.

The universities

A definition

1.9 The first group of providers is the universities. The *Shorter Oxford English Dictionary* definition of a university is:

> The whole body of teachers and students pursuing, at a particular place, the higher branches of learning; such persons associated together as a society or corporate body, having the power of conferring degrees and other privileges, and forming an institution for the promotion of education in the higher branches of learning;[19] the colleges, buildings, etc., belonging to such a body.

---

15 A Funding Council for Northern Ireland was advocated by NCIHE.
16 The Designation of Institutions of Higher Education (Scotland) Order 1992 (SI 1992/1025) as amended by The Designation of Institutions of Higher Education (Amendment) (Scotland) Order 1993 (SI 1993/424) designates those colleges eligible to receive funding from SHEFC. Funding for higher education courses in further education institutions is obtained directly from government.
17 Paragraph 3.93, Main Report, NCIHE, July 1997.
18 QCA is the successor to the National Council for Vocational Qualifications (NCVQ) – Education Act 1997.
19 As to what constitutes the 'higher branches of learning' see the judgment of Vaisey J in *St David's College Lampeter v Ministry of Education* [1951] 1 All ER 559, 561.

It is possible to apply this definition to a non-university institution with degree-awarding powers but the dictionary has not yet caught up with the 1992 changes.

1.10   There are 115[20] institutions titled universities (including the various constituent parts of the Universities of London and Wales which are federations) and three directly comparable bodies which are separately funded by HEFCE (London and Manchester Business Schools and the Royal College of Art): these are by no means a homogeneous group of institutions. Some knowledge of their history and development is needed to understand the legal framework in which they now operate, the terms of employment of their staff and the relationship of their students to the institution. It is a reflection of the changes in higher education since 1963 that Robbins recorded the existence of only 31 universities (although this figure did not include the then existing London and Wales colleges).

1.11   With the exception of the wholly new universities founded in the period 1959–64, 'traditional' UK universities, ie those constituted prior to 1992, are essentially the product of local enterprise, having been founded by private benefactors, trusts and endowments of various kinds.[21] To quote NCIHE, university distribution is 'to an extent an accident of history'[22] being the product of historical and legislative circumstances rather than of any overall rationale based on location, distribution through the UK, size or type. As elsewhere in Europe, universities first appeared in the twelfth to fifteenth centuries, essentially as places of vocational training for the clergy, their forerunners being the monastery and cathedral schools. Some of the European universities such as Paris were corporations of masters or teachers (*universitas magistrorum*), some such as Bologna were corporations of students (*universitas scholarium*) and some such as Orleans were mixed communities.[23] It is into this later category that by the later Middle Ages the United Kingdom foundations as communities of 'Doctors, Masters and Scholars' (eg St Andrews)

20 As at July 1997, according to the Higher Education Statistics Agency (HESA): the latest university to be created was The University of Abertay, Dundee in 1994. The last university to be created in England was Luton (from the former College of Higher Education) in 1993; the former Cranfield Institute of Technology (which had a Royal Charter) changed its name to become Cranfield University on the same day.
21 Eg manufacturers of biscuits (Reading), household goods (Hull).
22 Paragraph 16.32, Main Report, NCIHE, July 1997.
23 For a good account of the development of universities in Europe see B Caul *Value-Added: The Personal Development of Students in Higher Education* (1993) chapter 1.

could best be fitted. As Ronald Cant[24] explained, in a sense the first two categories of members were those fully-qualified while the scholars were the novices or apprentices: since at least some of the masters were engaged in study with the object of becoming doctors, there was no hard and fast distinction as there is today between academic staff and students. All were 'partners in the craft of scholarship and members of a single society' the formal title of which remains, at Oxford, 'Chancellor, Masters and Scholars of the University of Oxford.'[25] It is from these rather humble origins that today's higher education system has grown.

1.12 Another term commonly used in the Middle Ages was *studium generale*. This was an institution, like Bologna, which admitted students from any nation: study was undertaken in the 'lower Faculty' of Arts and at least one of the 'higher Faculties' of Law, Medicine and Theology. This hierarchical description of the Faculties, which excludes science and social sciences, management and a whole range of subjects now studied at university, has as we shall see been of legal significance almost to the present day.

Legal basis

1.13 In *British Universities and the State*[26] Robert Berdahl wrote that '... universities, like other corporate entities in the body politic, must operate in a legal and constitutional frame of reference without with their ordered existence would be impossible.' The legal nature of a university has always interested educationalists; it has most recently been examined by Clive Lewis in 1983[27] and by Charles Henderson and Frank Mattison in 1990.[28] Even at the later date chartered universities outnumbered the rest by a factor of 10. At the end of 1997 there are 30 chartered universities in England and Wales which are eleemosynary corporations, ie their purposes include the perpetual distribution of the bounty of the founder, plus Oxford and Cambridge which are civil corporations. The remaining English and Welsh universities, however, were established by a statutory process,

24 R G Cant *The University of St Andrews* (1970).
25 See eg *Malcolm v Chancellor, Masters and Scholars of the University of Oxford (t/a Oxford University Press)* [1994] EMLR 17, CA.
26 R O Berdahl *British Universities and the State* (1959).
27 C B Lewis 'The Legal Nature of a University and the Student-University Relationship' (1983) 15 Ottawa Law Review 11.
28 C L S Henderson and F T Mattison, chapter 1 in D J Farrington and F T Mattison (eds) *Universities and the Law* (1990, CUA/CRS).

mainly by statutory instruments made under the 1988–1992 legislation. The latter group are institutions conducted by higher education corporations or companies limited by guarantee but the 'statutory' group includes the University of Newcastle-Upon-Tyne. In Scotland four are chartered corporations, all charters dating from the 1960s, four are governed by nineteenth century Acts of Parliament (having been created by papal bulls and royal charters in medieval times) and five were created by subordinate legislation from pre-existing institutions of higher education as a result of the 1992 legislation. In Northern Ireland both universities are chartered corporations.

1.14 The distinction between those which are chartered and those which are not is of considerable significance, particularly in relation to the status of members of the institution and in relation to the remedies available to students against their institutions. The distinctions will be made at the appropriate points. However, it is important to recognise that, as Beetz J stated in the Canadian Supreme Court in *Re Harelkin*[29]

> '[The fact of statutory incorporation] does not alter the traditional nature of such an institution as a community of scholars and students enjoying substantial internal autonomy. While a university incorporated by statute and subsidised by public funds may in a sense be regarded as a public service ... its immediate and direct responsibility extends primarily to its present members ...'

The St David's College case

1.15 Until relatively recently it was accepted that the legal definition of a university was that adopted by Vaisey J in the classic case *St David's College Lampeter v Ministry of Education*.[30] This case was an action brought by the College[31] for a declaration that it was a university, providing a university education, for the purposes of the then current regulations for student grants.[32] The full list of essential attributes of a university put forward by the College was based on those of the *studium generale* and accepted by the judge, as follows:

---

29 [1979] 2 SCR 561, 96 DLR (3d) 14.
30 [1951] 1 All ER 559.
31 Founded in 1822 and now University of Wales, Lampeter.
32 Regulations for State Scholarships and University Supplemental Awards 1948 (SI 1948/1655).

(i)   the institution must be incorporated by the highest authority (ie the sovereign power);
(ii) it should be open to receive students from all parts of the world;
(iii) there should be a plurality of masters among the academic staff (ie there cannot be a university with only one teacher);
(iv) teaching should be carried out in at least one of the higher faculties, that is, 'of course'[33] theology ('the queen of sciences'), law (or philosophy) and medicine;
(v)   there should be residents in the institution's own buildings or near at hand;
(vi) the 'most obvious and most essential quality': the institution should have the right to confer degrees.

1.16   Vaisey J's approach to this 'admittedly ... borderline institution' was based not on what the ordinary member of society might consider to be a university, but on what conclusion would be arrived at by 'the ordinary man who does know what a university is or who has received his education at a university.'[34] St David's College failed to secure university status principally because its power to award degrees was limited to those of Bachelor of Divinity and Bachelor of Arts. This power, granted by charter in 1829, with subsequent charters in 1853, 1865 and 1896, was considered by the judge to be a limited concession of the 'royal fountain of honour and office and privilege.'[35] On these grounds it fell short of a 'university properly so called.' If these 'essential attributes' were to be applied today, a number of universities would fail the test of being 'properly so called' since they do not teach in at least one of the higher facilities and hence cannot be considered as a *studium generale*. Some institutions treated now as the equivalent of universities have limits on their degree awarding powers, some admit no overseas students and at least one (the Open University) makes no provision for residence of undergraduates. The fact that an institution teaches only a limited range of subjects does not prevent it from being classified as a [school or] university for the purposes of exemption from VAT[36] under the Value Added Tax Act 1994.

The power to award degrees

1.17   It appears that at least one principal objective of anyone entering higher education for instruction or training 'superior to the

---

33   Per Vaisey J at 561.
34   [1951] 1 All ER 559, 561.
35   Blackstone *Commentaries on the Law of England* (1765).
36   *Bell Concord Educational Trust Ltd v Customs and Excise Comrs* [1986] VATTR 165, 183; affirmed on this point [1988] STC 143, 147, CA.

common sort' is to gain a tertiary-level qualification which may be a degree, diploma or certificate, and which 'opens doors' to prospective employment by being recognised as being of value. The highest of these awards is the degree, either at first or higher level, and the ability of an institution to award degrees sets it apart from those which do not have this power. All universities have full degree awarding powers, either granted by their charter or by or under Act of Parliament. Some non-university institutions have limited degree awarding powers eg Harper Adams Agricultural College and Henley Management College, both of which have passed independent quality assurance tests. St David's University College's own degree-awarding powers were suspended in 1971, students thereafter taking degrees of the University of Wales. The College was eventually re-titled University of Wales, Lampeter in 1996.

1.18 Before the 1992 Acts gave the Secretaries of State the power to designate institutions as 'competent to grant awards,' the accepted view was that the power to grant degrees derived from the exercise of the royal prerogative[37] even though, before its incorporation into the University of London, the power granted to Heythrop College in Oxfordshire by the Holy See to confer degrees was not questioned. There is an interesting academic argument about the derivation of this part of the prerogative from the medieval powers of the Roman Catholic Church, but that is beyond the scope of this book.[38] Also in the pre-1992 universities the award of degrees and other academic distinctions is traditionally the prerogative of the sovereign academic body (eg the Senate), except in some cases the award of honorary degrees is reserved to the governing body. In the post-1992 universities and certain non-university institutions the 'royal fountain of honour, etc' has been replaced by the somewhat less mystical provisions of legislation.[39] And in some of the new institutions the degree-awarding power is no longer in the hands of academics but is that of the body corporate (the Board of Governors or Court) subject to consultation with the academic body. While this arrangement fits better with the concept of the corporation itself having the power to

---

37 A view confirmed by the then Mr St John Stevas MP, when a junior Minister, in the House of Commons on 1 December 1972: *Official Report* cols 875–878.

38 See D J Christie *The Power to Award Degrees: Public Law* (Winter 1976) pp 358–396; T A Owen *Universities Quarterly* (1972) 26 pp 271–282; and C A H Franklyn *Academical Dress from the Middle Ages to the Present Day* (1970).

39 Section 76 FHEA; section 48 FHESA: see eg The Academic Awards and Distinctions (Glasgow Caledonian University) (Scotland) Order of Council 1993.

admit new members or transfer members from one class to another, in most of these institutions neither students nor graduates are members. A Degree Awarding Powers Committee of QAA advises the Secretaries of State on applications from institutions to the Privy Council for degree awarding powers or university title.

Limitations on degree-awarding powers

1.19   Degree-awarding powers of the older universities are generally unlimited and they may create new classes and descriptions of degree at will. Apart from the general limitation which may be imposed on non-university institutions restricting them to awarding limited types of degrees, there appears also to be a limitation on the power of the post-1992 English and Welsh universities to award higher doctorates (other than honorary degrees). This arises since although degrees may be awarded both to persons completing a programme of study or supervised research or to members of staff of the institution, there is no power to award degrees to others (eg alumni) who may wish to submit published work for a higher doctorate, a common practice in the older universities.[40]

1.20   HEQC (now QAA) takes the view that degree awarding powers granted under FHESA may be removed from Scottish institutions but not powers granted under FHEA to English and Welsh institutions. There is no statutory route to removing degree-awarding powers from chartered institutions.[41]

Power to deprive

1.21   Section 76 FHEA and section 48 FHESA provide that institutions with the power to award degrees granted under the statute also have the power to take them away. It is a matter for the institution to determine the conditions under which such deprivation may occur. Many charters contain the same power and where it is not express it may possibly be implied, although deprivation of graduate status carries with it deprivation of corporator status: in such cases there is a long-established right to be heard in a fair manner.[42] In practice, holders of degrees are only deprived of them

---

40   Section 76 FHEA and section 48 FHESA.
41   HEQC submission to NCIHE, Main Report, recommendation 64, July 1997.
42   *Dr Bentley's Case* (1723) 1 Stra 557.

where it is shown that they have been obtained through fraud or other improper conduct, eg serious plagiarism in a doctoral thesis. Falsely representing oneself as a graduate is probably a fraud at common law, and forgery of degree certificates, being documents of formal character, is an offence under Part I Forgery and Counterfeiting Act 1981.

A revised definition

1.22   Vaisey J's definition, although strictly limited to the point upon which the declaration was sought, has never been overruled and it was for that reason that the government decided to put the issue of the post-1992 English and Welsh universities' status beyond doubt in section 77(4) FHEA: '... a form of insurance against the remote possibility of legal challenge ...' It was not considered necessary to extend this to the new Scottish universities, since the parallels '... were so slight ...'[43]

1.23   The definition of nearly 50 years ago is not quite the same as the set of criteria suggested by Christine Shinn[44] following an examination of the attitude of the University Grants Committee to requests for university status made over the period 1919–1946. These appeared to be that the institution should be:
(i)   a centre of academic excellence;
(ii)   have sound finances;
(iii)   have a reasonably sized body of students and faculty;
(iv)   be strongly supported by the local community;
(v)   be committed to freedom of thought;
which, with hindsight, ties in much more closely to the practice of higher education now (particularly criterion (iii)) than the *studium generale* criterion of 'teaching in at least one of the higher faculties.' It also ties in with definitions used in other countries with a similar higher education system, eg New Zealand, where among the criteria required for university status are acceptance of a role as critic and conscience of society and having a wide diversity of teaching and research.[45] However recent changes must cause us to revise our views

43   Lord Strathclyde House of Lords *Official Report* col 1466 12 March 1992.
44   C Shinn *Paying the Piper: The Development of the University Grants Committee 1919–1946* (1986).
45   In 1993 the New Zealand Vice-Chancellors' Committee sought judicial review of the New Zealand Qualifications Authority's grant of the title to one institution, on the ground that it did not meet the legally-defined criteria. The application was withdrawn when the institution concerned voluntarily relinquished the title: *The Higher* 12 November.

of what constitutes a 'university' in practice: in the House of Lords the government spokesman during the passage of FHESA identified '... what it takes to be a university ...' as

> ... to have passed tests related to the quality of the work they do and have been judged competent to award their own taught course and research degrees ...
> ... to ... [have demonstrated] that they meet the criteria related to the scale and breadth of their activities.[46]

1.24 The modern criteria for the grant of university status were originally set out in a Written Answer in the House of Commons in January 1992 and modified in June 1993.[47] In 1997 they are:

(i) that there should be at least 300 full-time equivalent students in five of HEFCE's nine Academic Subject Categories;[48]

(ii) that there should be a higher education enrolment of at least 4,000 full-time equivalent students;

(iii) that at least 3,000 full-time equivalent students should be on degree-level courses; and

(iv) that such institutions should have the power to award their own taught-course and research degrees.

NCIHE considered that the numerical criteria (i) to (iii) 'threaten to distort some aspects of institutional behaviour, as institutions seek to acquire a status they perceive to be particularly valuable.'[49] Institutions seeking university status are expected to have demonstrated their ability to maintain degree standards when using degree-awarding powers (as non-university institutions) for three years. But NCIHE recommended that while there should be no changes in the current criteria (i) to (iv) above, there should be a period of relative stability in the number of universities with the weight attached to the numerical criteria reduced and greater emphasis placed on a distinctive role and characteristics of awarding this status.[50]

1.25 The criteria by which institutions are judged to fit to be able to award degrees are different. Recent government policy has been

46 Lord Strathclyde op cit note 28.
47 House of Commons *Official Report* Vol 201 Written Answers col 582; letter to Committee of Scottish Higher Education Principals (COSHEP) from SOED 30 June 1993.
48 SHEFC uses slightly different Academic Subject Categories but these will be grouped to yield an equivalent number of categories.
49 Paragraph 16.21, Main Report, NCIHE, July 1997.
50 Recommendation 63, Main Report, NCIHE, July 1997.

that before institutions are given this power they have to demonstrate effective internal validation and review processes, among other criteria. Section 76 FHEA does not refer to such criteria, but in a written answer in the House of Commons the then Secretary of State suggested that the principal criterion for granting the power to award taught-course degrees would be that

> an institution needs to be a self-critical, cohesive academic community with a proven commitment to quality assurance supported by effective assurance and enhancement systems[51]

as to which advice is taken from the Quality Assurance Agency.

Classification of universities

1.26 It is not possible to discuss adequately the complexities of the internal organisation of universities without some broad knowledge of their foundation and current status. It is surprising how often sweeping and inaccurate statements are made about the way universities are governed and managed. This is as much a problem for the Establishment as it is for newspaper editors: for example, in the first drafts of their 'Model Statute' for the implementation of their duties under Part IV of ERA, the University Commissioners used terminology which had no meaning outside Oxford and Cambridge. Further, in the discussion of the House of Lords' judgment in a case concerning academic tenure before the 1988 Act,[52] most newspapers managed to draw general conclusions from the specific facts of the case in a totally misleading way. Finally in their 1987 VAT leaflet on education,[53] HM Commissioners of Customs and Excise stated:

> A United Kingdom university means a body providing higher education under a Charter granted by the Crown or Parliament and awarding degrees which are recognised in the professional world.

1.27 In fact it is necessary to classify universities into no fewer than 10 groups: Oxford and Cambridge, London, English foundations up to the First World War, 1918–1960 twentieth century English foundations, 1960–1970 English foundations, post-1970 English foundations, pre-1960 Scottish foundations, post-1960 Scottish foundations, Welsh and Northern Irish foundations: within these

---

51 House of Commons *Official Report* Vol 201, *Written Answers* col 31.
52 *R v Lord President of the Privy Council, ex p Page* [1993] AC 682.
53 Customs and Excise VAT leaflet 701/30/87.

groups there are sub-groups dependent on the method of creation which ranges from medieval Papal Bull to incorporation of a governing body under the Further and Higher Education Acts 1992. A vast array of private legislation complicates the picture.

Non-university institutions

1.28 By late 1997 there were 61 non-university higher education institutions of which a minority had specified degree-awarding powers. Titles include 'college of higher education' and 'institute of higher education.' There were also many further education institutions offering higher education programmes, mainly part-time sub-degree level. In 1994/95 some 13% of higher education was delivered by further education colleges across the UK (27% in Scotland). At 12 colleges in England, directly-funded higher education represented more than 1,000 student places and between 35% and 50% of the total places funded in the colleges. NCIHE recommended no growth in this area.[54] In a number of further education colleges in England and Wales, higher education provision is not directly funded but is delivered on a 'franchised' basis from a higher education institution.

1.29 Although the position changes regularly, with only a handful of exceptions those higher education institutions without degree-awarding powers have their higher education programmes validated by universities: the Open University is the largest validating body.[55] A list of colleges together with their validating body is given in the Education (Listed Bodies) Order 1997.[56] Higher education colleges and institutes are not in the 'university sector' but in the 'higher education sector' in England and Wales and in the 'college sector' in Scotland. This allocation to 'sectors' is a sharp distinction which is in a number of cases quite difficult to justify. Section 72 FHEA defines an institution in England and Wales as being within the higher education sector if more than 55% of enrolled students are following higher education courses. These institutions account for more than 20% of the total higher education student numbers.[57] Institutions may move from the further education sector to the higher education sector

---

54 Recommendation 67, Main Report, NCIHE, July 1997.
55 Universities which validate degrees at colleges have formed the Council of Validating Universities.
56 SI 1997/54.
57 Quality Support Centre (1997) *Higher Education outside the Universities.*

as did Cumbria College of Art and Design in 1997.[58] There are as yet no instances of movement in the opposite direction.

1.30 The 'higher education sector' institutions make a varied and distinctive group. Some began as teacher training colleges, others are colleges devoted to study in particular fields or subjects. The churches offer higher education through 19 institutions with almost 60,000 students.[59] Over 50 of them share with the universities a funding mechanism controlled by the relevant national funding agency. A number of them, while remaining independent higher education corporations, have formed associations with universities and adopted titles which reflect their desire to be recognised as university-equivalent. Examples include the University Colleges of Scarborough – The North Riding College, and Ripon and York St John which are constituent colleges of the University of Leeds. The University College of Stockton on Tees is a college of the University of Durham.[60] The then government announced in 1993 that it would not sanction the adoption of the title 'University College' under the relevant sections of the 1992 legislation, except where the institution formed part of a university.[61]

1.31 Whatever their title, the constitutional arrangements for these institutions are as varied as those of the universities. In England, voluntary higher education colleges formed in the mid-1970s were often legally established by deeds of trust or were companies limited by guarantee, independent of local authority funding. Other colleges, while funded by local authorities, had autonomous legal identities. The position now is governed by Education Acts from 1968 to 1992. The provisions of ERA relating to variation of trust deeds of higher education corporations and designated institutions by the Secretary of State have been replaced by equivalent powers vested in the Privy Council,[62] which is required to consult the governing body, trustees and other relevant persons before making an order of variation. In Scotland, those former central institutions which did not become universities or constituent parts of universities after 1992 are either

---

58 Cumbria College of Art and Design Further Education Corporation (Transfer to the Higher Education Sector) Order 1997 (SI 1997/91).
59 Paragraph 3.84, Main Report, NCIHE, July 1997.
60 Formerly a joint college of the Universities of Durham and Teesside.
61 Letter from Tim Boswell, Parliamentary Under-Secretary of State at the Department for Education, to Tony Wood, chairman of the Standing Conference of Principals (SCOP), reported in *The Higher* 4 June 1993.
62 Section 75 FHEA and section 157(4) ERA as modified by Schedule 8 paragraph 39 FHEA.

companies limited by guarantee or their boards of governors are incorporated by schemes made under the Education (Scotland) Act 1980, section 74 of which required regulations to be made by statutory instrument by which conditions could be attached to grants by the Secretary of State.[63]

Corporations

The nature of a corporation

> A collection of many individuals, united into one body, under a special denomination, having perpetual succession under an artificial form, and vested, by the policy of the law, with the capacity of acting, in several respects, as an individual, particularly of taking and granting property, of contracting obligations, of suing and being sued.

> [A corporation] styled by the Romans *collegium* or *universitas*, is composed of a number of men united or erected by proper authority into a body-politic, to endure in continual succession, with certain rights and capacities of purchasing, suing etc. as appear most suitable to the nature of that special community, and most necessary for answering the purposes intended by it.

1.32 The first quotation is from the leading authority on corporations in English law, William Kyd, some 200 years ago.[64] The second is from the equivalent authority in Scotland, Erskine.[65] A corporation is also described as 'an ideal and legal person, intended to perpetuate the enjoyment of certain rights and privileges for the public benefit.'[66] When such an organisation is thus established by public authority 'it has a legal existence as a person, with power to hold funds, to sue, and to defend.'[67]

The classic corporation – the borough or burgh

1.33 In both England and Scotland much of the law and practice relating to chartered corporations is derived from ecclesiastical and local government law, since it was local officials and bodies which

---

63 See also the Colleges of Education (Scotland) Regulations 1987 (SI 1987/309).
64 W Kyd *A Treatise on Corpns* Vol 1 p 13 (1793).
65 Erskine *Institute* i vii 64.
66 Bell *Principles* s 2176.
67 Bell *Commentaries* 7th ed ii 157.

were first granted rights and privileges by the church, the king and the state. Corporate bodies were formed for example as the 'dean and chapter,' the 'mayor and bailiffs' or the 'chancellor and masters.' The word 'mayor' derives from the Latin 'maior' (superior): Statute 1 of the original statutes of the University of Cambridge describes the chancellor as 'maior inter omnes.'[68] It was the right to elect a maior inter omnes which was one of the most important attributes of a corporation. The 'Mayor Aldermen and Burgesses of the Borough of X' was the corporate legal title of an English borough prior to the Local Government Act 1972. While the Mayor and Aldermen at any given time were readily identifiable persons, the Burgesses were simply the local citizens with names on the electoral roll (and including the Mayor and Aldermen). The property vested in the Mayor Aldermen and Burgesses (dustcarts for example) was held by the corporation in the same way as the books in a university library are held by the corporate body in which the university's property is vested.

1.34 There are a few exceptions to the general rule that a corporation consists of more than one person: such 'corporations sole' (invented originally to allow the conveyance of seisin in a parson's glebe[69]) of which bishops of the Church of England and government ministers are the best-known examples, also occur in higher education, an example being the Master of Pembroke College Oxford.[70] A corporation sole can however be a 'creature of its members.'[71]

Universities originally local authorities

1.35 A detailed study of the history of the forms of government of the modern higher education institution is beyond the scope of this book, but it is interesting to note that from earliest times universities on the continent of Europe and subsequently in Britain and Ireland were assimilated to local authorities, which in those times had considerably more power over local inhabitants than they do now. The offices and bodies established by charter or by royal recognition of papal bull had absolute authority over their members, who had no access to the jurisdiction of the ordinary courts. They also enjoyed considerable authority over the general public within university

---

68 M B Hackett *The original statutes of Cambridge University* (1970) p 196.
69 R W M Dias *Jurisprudence* (4th ed, 1976) p 342.
70 Sir William Wade *Administrative Law* (6th ed, 1988) p 242.
71 *Re RICS's Application* [1986] ICR 550, CA.

precincts as in *Ex p Hopkins*[72] where habeas corpus issued to release Daisy Hopkins from her detention by the Vice-Chancellor of the University of Cambridge for the offence of 'walking with a member of the University,' an offence which the court held was not recognised by law. The chief magistrate, or Lord Rector, an office preserved to the present day in Scotland, although deprived of most of its powers, had the power to determine all disputes by 'visitation.' The Lord Rector's Court in Glasgow even tried a capital offence, that of Robert Bartoune, a student acquitted of murder by a jury in 1670.[73] The similarities between the old forms of local government in Britain and the constitutions of universities are important, since they allow us to use case law and other precedents to determine the powers of university (and by implication, other higher education institutions) officers and bodies. As well as the power to settle all disputes internally, these institutions also had power to hold land and enjoyed privileges of exemption from taxation. In Glasgow, in the fifteenth century, the University was so powerful that the Provost, Bailies and other officers of the city had to swear annually before the Rector or Chancellor that they would observe and enforce its privileges.

The law of corporations

1.36 Corporations of all kinds are subject to the general law of the jurisdiction in which situated (English, Scots, plus in each case relevant European law) supplemented in some instances by private statutory legislation and in all cases by their internal rules. A corporate body has full legal personality ('an artificial person' in Scots law) independent of its members[74] as opposed to an unincorporated association which has restricted personality or no personality at all and of which examples are trades unions, students' unions and clubs and societies of various kinds. The law governing corporate bodies covers mode of creation, legal capacity, powers, rights and obligations, relationship between the corporation and its members, relations with third parties, the legal status of office-holders, committees and similar subsidiary bodies. All these aspects of corporate existence are relevant to the law of higher education.

1.37 A corporation, like the limited company in *Rolloswin Investments Ltd v Chromolit Portugal Cutelarias e Produtos*

72 (1891) 61 LJQB 240.
73 J B Hay *Inaugural Addresses by Lords Rectors of the University of Glasgow* (1839), Table annexed to p xxviii.
74 *Steward v Dunn* (1844) 1 Dow & L 642, 649.

Metalicos SARL[75] is incapable of human actions such as, to quote Mocatta J[76] 'public worship or repairing to a church or of exercising itself in the duties of piety and true religion, either publicly or privately, on any day of the week' so that a contract made between two limited liability companies was not rendered void or unenforceable under section 1 Sunday Observance Act 1677 by being made on a Sunday.[77] In Scotland, a decree cannot be enforced if the only means of doing so would be to imprison all the individual members of a corporation.[78] However, after some major disasters in the 1980s and 1990s there is more pressure to make corporations, as opposed to their officers or managers, 'personally' liable.[79]

1.38　A corporate body is separate from the physical entity, that is from its members and from the property that it holds. We are accustomed to seeing pictures of university and college campuses and identifying them as 'The University of X' but in fact they are merely part of the physical manifestation of the corporation. This distinction has arisen in arguments about the tax liability of the University of Glasgow which moved from one site to another. While it appeared from the constitutional instruments that the exemption from local taxes was granted to the corporation, it having been granted the ancient privileges of the European universities, the court held on the facts of that case that the exemption attached to the property of the corporation at the date of grant, not to its subsequently-acquired property.[80]

Constitution of corporate bodies

Constitution by Royal Charter

1.39　The oldest universities were founded by the Church; for example the University of Paris is said to have been founded in about the year 800. The oldest British universities were founded either by charter or by Papal Bull, later confirmed by charter and incorporated

75　[1970] 2 All ER 673.
76　[1970] 2 All ER 673, 675.
77　It was not drawn to the attention of the court that the 1677 Act had been repealed by the Statute Law (Repeals) Act 1969.
78　*Gall v Loyal Glenbogie Lodge* (1900) 2 F 1187.
79　See C M V Clarkson 'Kicking corporate bodies and damning their souls' (1996) 59 MLR 557.
80　*The University of Glasgow v James Dunlop Kirkwood (Inspector of Poor of the Parish of Govan), The Comrs of Police of the Burgh of Partick and The Comrs of Supply of The County of Lanark* (1872) 10 M 1000.

many of the privileges and forms of government of their European predecessors. This practice has continued almost to the present day, so that almost all English universities before 1992 have been constituted by charter, by 'virtue of the Prerogative Royal and of the special grace, certain knowledge and mere motion' of the sovereign in Council: in recent times charters have been based on a model drawn up by the Privy Council in 1963, which preserved distinctions between bodies and office-holders the true meaning of which has almost been lost in the mists of time. The second oldest educational institution in the United States, the College of William and Mary, is the only US institution with a Royal Charter (1693) and is of course named after the King and Queen who granted it.

1.40 It is a source of confusion to the general public, and perhaps also to some staff and students within institutions, that the government published in 1993 *Charters for Higher Education* under the Citizens' Charter Initiative (CCI), which are completely unconnected with charters of incorporation. The word charter can mean 'a grant of rights' or 'a declaration of rights'[81] and it is the latter category to which the CCI Charters may be considered to belong.

1.41 Some of the older chartered institutions have had several charters and supplemental charters over the years. Charters have been granted by the Crown for many centuries, the most well-known examples being the charters granted to the English boroughs (which before the Reform Acts and Municipal Corporations Acts of the 1830s were classified by such names as 'potwalloper,'[82] 'scot and lot'[83] and 'burgage tenure'.)[84] On local government reform in the 1970s the custody of the charter of a borough which ceased to exist and was not incorporated into a new one was transferred to charter trustees. There is provision for these to continue in being, to elect one of their number as city major or town mayor as appropriate and to appoint to certain ancient offices of dignity.[85]

Constitution by Act of Parliament

1.42 Corporations can also be created or, as has been the practice in higher education, reconstituted by public or private Act of

---

81 SOED.
82 Where all the male householders had a vote.
83 Where those who paid certain ancient rates could vote.
84 Where the owners of certain tenements had the vote.
85 Section 246 Local Government Act 1972; Charter Trustees Order 1974 (SI 1974/176); Charter Trustees Act 1985.

Parliament (by statute – not to be confused with university internal statutes). An Act of 1571[86] confirmed the incorporation of the University of Cambridge and all privileges then held under charter or by prescription.[87] The Universities (Scotland) Acts 1858–1966, the University of London Act 1994 and the Universities of Durham and Newcastle-Upon-Tyne Act 1963 are other examples of statutes reforming pre-existing institutions created by charter or similar instrument. ERA made provision for the creation of the higher education corporations and the creation of, or transfer from local authority control of, companies limited by guarantee as the forerunners of most of the new English universities and for the making of instruments of government, based on existing arrangements in the Education (No 2) Act 1968,[88] for these and other bodies. FHEA now prescribes the way in which the instruments of government of the higher education corporations, and other institutions designated as eligible to receive funding council support, are made and amended. FHESA makes similar provision for institutions formerly governed by the terms of the Education (Scotland) Act 1980. In most instances it is the governing body rather than the institution which is created a body corporate.

Constitution by registration

1.43 Finally there is registration as a company limited by guarantee under the Companies Acts for example that of The London School of Economics and Political Science, part of the University of London and the University of Greenwich, formerly the Thames Polytechnic. University College London (earlier known as the London University) and King's College London were both founded by a company of shareholders before receiving charters in 1826 and 1829 respectively. Some of the post-Robbins universities operated as companies before receiving their charters eg The University of Stirling Limited: when the University of Stirling was granted its charter it took over the rights, assets and liabilities of the company. The memoranda and articles of association of the new universities established in this way are subject to the approval of the Privy Council under section 129B ERA introduced by section 73 FHEA. Some institutions have taken

86 13 Eliz cap 29.
87 Like Oxford, Cambridge is a university by prescription; it is the colleges which have charters, Visitors, etc. Hubert Picarda *The law and practice relating to charities* (2nd ed, 1995) 522, says that this distinction 'is to be ascribed to history rather than to logic.'
88 See also DES Circular 7/70 and *Winder v Cambridgeshire County Council* (1978) 76 LGR 176.

advantage of the powers under section 124 ERA to 'form or take part in forming a body corporate' by forming schools of the institution into companies, thereby obtaining a registered name and pre-empting any possible confusion with similar schools in towns and cities where there is more than one.[89]

Chartered corporations in English law

The distinction between chartered and other corporations

1.44 The technical position is that there are significant differences in the scope of the powers of the three types of corporation, most clearly expressed in English law in the dictum of Luxmoore J in *A-G v Leeds Corpn*:

> The corporation was incorporated by royal charter in the year 1627 in the reign of King Charles I. The fact that it is incorporated by royal charter is of importance, because a corporation so constituted stands on a different footing from a statutory corporation, the difference being that the latter species of corporation can only do such acts as are authorised directly or indirectly by the statute creating it; whereas the former can, speaking generally, do anything that an ordinary individual can do.[90]

and the dictum of Bennett J in *A-G v Leicester Corpn* '... generally speaking, such a corporation can do anything that an ordinary individual may do ...'[91] Farwell J in *A-G v Manchester Corpn*[92] expressed the principle slightly differently: 'A corporation incorporated by Royal Charter ... can do *everything* that an ordinary individual can do' [my emphasis]. Sir William Wade has argued that as a charter confers only the powers of a natural person upon a university, it has no authority to determine the rights of anyone, just as in *Hazell v Hammersmith and Fulham London Borough Council*,[93] where the Council's assertion that its powers as a 'natural person' incorporated by charter allowed it to enter into otherwise unlawful interest rate swap contracts was described in the House of Lords as

---

89 One example is the Swansea Law School, a company formed by the Swansea Institute of Higher Education, which was concerned that a proposed new Law Faculty at University College Swansea should not become known by that name. See A Beale, N Bourne and R Geary 'What's in a Name? Protecting the Law School' (1993) Business Law Review 90.
90 [1929] 2 Ch 291, 295.
91 [1943] 1 Ch 86, 93.
92 [1906] 1 Ch 643, 651.
93 [1992] 2 AC 1.

'absurd.' Therefore the institution's regulations can acquire legal force only in so far as they are incorporated into a contract between the university and an individual, such as a student.

1.45 The Anglo-Saxon legal system had no systematic theory of rights in land and the majority of land was known as 'folkland' which the Normans converted by charter or 'land-boc' into 'bookland' which could then be alienated on systematic lines. So the earliest charters were a form of conveyance of rights over property within the feudal system. This came to be developed over the years into grants from the sovereign power of the state establishing corporate bodies with full powers. The English common law originally regarded corporations as unlawful unless a charter or other royal approbation had been given, so the presumption of a 'lost grant' had to be invented to regularise the powers of bodies which had existed over a long period.[94] Chartered corporations created by the Crown have complete legal personality with all the powers that implies, for example the power to make contracts and to hold property.[95] The terms of a charter are regarded as a kind of bargain between the Crown and the corporation[96] and even transactions unauthorised by the corporation are not void against third parties as, unless their activities are restricted by public or private statute,[97] the ultra vires rule (ie that the corporation may not act outwith its powers) does not apply to them: a restriction in a charter is, according to Baron Coke in 1612 '… simply an ordinance testifying the King's desire, but it is a precept, and it does not bind in law …'[98] and some 300 years later it was stated:

---

94 *Re Company or Fraternity of Free Fishermen of Faversham* (1887) 36 ChD 329, CA; it has been suggested that the University of Cambridge is a common law corporation by immemorial custom based on a lost grant: R W M Dias *Jurisprudence* (4th ed, 1976) p 345.
95 *Jenkins v Pharmaceutical Society of Great Britain* [1921] 1 Ch 392; *Baroness Wenlock v River Dee Co* (1883) 36 ChD 675n, 685; *Peel v London and North-Western Rly Co* [1907] 1 Ch 5, 21 (per Buckley LJ); section 1 Corporate Bodies' Contracts Act 1960. The power to perform any act which an individual could perform does not extend to certain criminal offences: *R v Birmingham and Gloucester Rly Co* (1842) 3 QB 223, 232. A corporation may be restrained from performing an act possibly leading to revocation of its charter: *Rendall v Crystal Palace Co* (1858) 4 K & J 326.
96 *Baroness Wenlock v River Dee Co* (1883) 36 ChD 675; the terms of the contract may be varied by the grant of a new charter which operates as a new grant: *R v Blunt* (1738) Andr 293; *R v Massory* (1738) Andr 295.
97 As in the private Acts limiting the rights of a municipal corporation to spend money out of its tramway undertaking reserved fund: *A-G v Leicester Corpn* [1943] 1 Ch 86, and public Acts restricting the way in which they spent borough funds: *A-G v Manchester Corpn* [1906] 1 Ch 643, another tramway case.
98 *Sutton's Hospital Case* (1612) 10 Co Rep 1a, 30b.

... not only can the chartered company bind itself by acts as to which no power is affirmatively given by the charter, but even if the charter by express negative words forbids any particular act, the corporation can nevertheless at common law do the act, and if it does, it is bound thereby, and the result is only that ground is given for a proceeding by scire facias in the name of the Crown, repealing the charter.[99]

The court 'does not entertain a general jurisdiction to regulate and control charities established by charter'[100] and can only intervene to regulate or control the activities of a chartered corporation where the governing body has management of the revenues where they are considered to be in the position of trustees and have abused that trust.[101] The relevance of charity law will be discussed later.

1.46 The latest statement of the position is that in the Opinion of the Visitor (Simon Brown LJ) in *Pearce v University of Aston in Birmingham (No 2)*:[102]

... as against the outside world the University, being a body incorporated by Royal Charter, has the capacity of a natural person: as a result even acts done in contravention of a provision of its Statutes are as against the outside world not ultra vires or void.

Scire facias

1.47 Scire facias is a prerogative writ used to revoke a charter. Its use is not unlimited[103] and the courts have otherwise no power to intervene by ordinary process except possibly where the action taken by the corporation involves mismanagement of charitable funds.[104]

99 *British South Africa Co v De Beers Consolidated Mines Ltd* [1910] 1 Ch 354, 356 per Swinfen Eady J.
100 *A-G v Foundling Hospital* (1793) 2 Ves 42, 47 per Lord Commissioner Eyre.
101 *Re Whitworth Art Gallery Trusts, Manchester Whitworth Institute v Victoria University of Manchester* [1958] 1 All ER 176, 179; *A-G v Smart* (1748) 1 Ves Sen 72; *A-G v Middleton* (1751) 2 Ves Sen 327.
102 [1991] 2 All ER 469.
103 *Gray and Cathcart v Trinity College (Provost etc)* [1910] 1 IR 370.
104 In England and Wales: *A-G v Foundling Hospital* (1793) 2 Ves 42; *A-G v Christ's Hospital (Governors)* [1896] 1 Ch 879; *Re Whitworth Art Gallery Trusts, Manchester Whitworth Institute v Victoria University of Manchester* [1958] 1 All ER 176; in Scotland there might possibly be an action for breach of trust if in some way the funds of the corporation were put at risk by an otherwise valid action: *Kemp v Glasgow Corpn* 1920 SC 73, HL but as in England the charter can only be revoked by an appropriate authority: *Thompson v Incorporation of Candlemakers of Edinburgh* (1855) 17 D 765.

It is likely that any attempt by government or anyone else to prevent a chartered body from lawfully exercising its charter powers, unless this was done by primary legislation,[105] would be struck down by the court.[106] In the pre-partition Irish case *Gray and Cathcart v Trinity College (Provost etc)*[107] the power of the Crown itself to alter or recall a charter was said to be restricted to the following:

(i)   where it has in the original charter (or in a subsequent charter made valid by acceptance) expressly reserved power to alter the charter;
(ii) where the corporation is wholly or partially morbund;
(iii) where the corporation consents to the alteration.

1.48   As the courts do not possess power to revoke a charter by ordinary process, a better course is likely to be Act of Parliament; the powers of dissolution given to the Secretaries of State by section 128 ERA and section 47 FEHSA only extend to higher education corporations and designated institutions not to chartered universities. Section 73 FHEA introduced new sections 129A and 129B of ERA. Section 129(A)10 reads: 'In this section and section 129(B) "designated institution" means an institution in relation to which a designation made, or having effect as if made, under section 129 of this Act has effect but does not include any institution established by Royal Charter.' Section 45 FHESA which transferred to the Privy Council the powers of the Secretary of State contained in section 77 Education (Scotland) Act 1980, provides in subsection (7): 'This section shall apply to a designated institution notwithstanding that its name includes, by virtue of section 49 of this Act, the word "university."'

Chartered corporations ' relationship to the Crown

1.49   As the Crown has no general right of control, except to the extent provided in the charter or by authority of Parliament, chartered corporations are not entitled to Crown immunity. In *British Broadcasting Corpn v Johns* the BBC, a body incorporated by charter, contended that it was an 'emanation' of the Crown, but the court held that since it had been set up 'precisely for the reason that it was desired to avoid any suggestion that broadcasting in this country is

---

105 Examples of primary legislation interfering with charter powers are the abolition of the Visitorial jurisdiction over staff contractual disputes by ERA and the requirements for student union constitutions in EA94.
106 See eg in Scotland *University of Glasgow v Kirkwood* (1872) 10 M 1000.
107 [1910] 1 IR 370. See also *Eastern Archipelago Co v R* (1853) 2 E & B 856, 870.

an instrument of government ...,'[108] it was impossible to hold that the corporation enjoyed Crown immunity and thereby exemption from certain taxes. The same was true of the Royal Institute of Chartered Surveyors.[109]

Protection of the rights of chartered corporations

1.50 The rights of a chartered corporation may be protected by the courts at common law. Cases before the courts have involved interference with ancient rights relating to chartered markets and ferries and by analogy the courts might be prepared to protect certain rights of chartered universities, such as the power to award degrees.[110] In that respect the 'recognised bodies' provisions of ERA, to be discussed shortly, would appear to offer a complete protection. Another area where the courts might intervene to protect chartered universities is in case of an attack on its academic reputation. It is suggested that on the basis of an analogy with a commercial company,[111] a chartered institution could sue to defend its reputation, except where the imputation was only against individual members.[112] However, in principle there is no reason to restrict this to chartered institutions.

Chartered corporations in the law of Scotland

History of charters

1.51 As in England, Scots charters were first granted in the Middle Ages, to burghs (the equivalent of English boroughs) by William I ('The Lion') 1165–1214.[113] Most subsequent litigation has been

108 [1964] 1 All ER 923, 931 per Willmer J.
109 *Re RICS's Application* [1986] ICR 550, CA.
110 The court's discretion is likely to be exercised only if there is actual injury to the corporation: see dicta of Hoffman J in *Associated Newspapers Group plc v Insert Media* [1988] 1 WLR 509, 513 and of Sir George Jessel MR in *Day v Brownrigg* (1878) 10 ChD 294, 304.
111 *Linotype Co Ltd v British Empire Type Setting Machine Co Ltd* (1899) 81 LT 331, HL. It is not now possible for a local authority to protect its reputation in this way: *Derbyshire County Council v Times Newspapers Ltd* [1993] AC 534, HL, overturning *Bognor Regis UDC v Campion* [1972] 2 QB 169.
112 *National Union of General and Municipal Workers v Gillian* [1946] KB 81.
113 As in England, it has been necessary in the past to presume the grant of a charter or a seal of cause, a subordinate charter granted by a Lord of Regality: *Skirving v Smellie* (19 January 1803, unreported). It has also been necessary to ratify an incorporation, even though the seal of cause was executed in excess of authority: *Fleshers of Canongate v Wight* (1835) 14 S 135 (11 Fac 110).

related to the powers of the various species of burghs (royal burghs, burghs of barony and burghs of regality) particularly in relation to the administration of the Common Good, a particular kind of local revenue and to the powers of the guildry, whose trade monopolies were abolished in the mid-nineteenth century. The leading cases on the burghs and the guildry form the basis of the Scots law governing the powers of chartered corporations but their application to areas outwith local authorities (where the law has in any event changed significantly) is uncertain. The ancient Scottish universities were founded by a combination of charters and papal bulls. The University of Glasgow, for example, were founded in 1451 by a papal bull, its status confirmed by Letter under the Great Seal of Scotland in 1453 and subsequently by Letters and charters of confirmation on eight occasions between 1472 and 1630. The continued existence of ancient Scots charters alongside modern legislation and the meaning of Article XVIII Act of Union 1707 'no alteration be made in laws which concern private rights except for the evident utility of the subjects within Scotland' can occasionally give rise to litigation, as in Stirling in 1997 where it was asserted, apparently unsuccessfully, that a charter of Alexander II, King of Scotland in 1226, reiterated in a charter of David II in 1360, that 'no tolls or taxes should be levied on residents' ... had the result that no parking fines could be levied on residents of Stirling.

Powers of Scots chartered corporations

1.52 In essence, the position in Scotland appears to be that a chartered body has power to enter into any contract which is not expressly forbidden by its charter or, to put it another way, any act of a chartered corporation must not be at variance with the fundamental purposes for which it was established.[114] There is no legal basis for holding the action of such bodies to be void in the same way as those of corporations founded by statute. However, the corporate property is derived from the Crown, which retains a right of oversight and control and, in the case of a royal burgh might at any time intervene 'to prevent or redress any abuse or malversation on the part of the town-council.'[115] Likewise corporations might be restrained from acting outwith their powers to the detriment of individuals.[116]

114 *Ellis v Henderson* (1844) 1 Bell's App 1.
115 *Conn v Provost, Magistrates and Councillors of Renfrew* (1906) 8 F 905.
116 Two examples taken from Stirling, where the guildry was particularly powerful, are *Dick v Fleshers of Stirling* (1827) 5 S 268 where the trade unsuccessfully sought to stop 'un-freemen' butchers selling meant on other than public holidays

1.53 Corporations in Scotland are said to have certain implied powers as *naturalia*. These include powers to sue and be sued, to elect or admit new members, to appoint officers to administer corporate affairs, to have and use a common seal,[117] to hold meetings or courts of members or managers, to hold property whether moveable or heritable and to make byelaws within the limits of the purposes and constitution of the corporation. According to the court in *Cumming v Walker*[118] a non-trading corporation may lack the power to borrow money although the body concerned in that case was a trade incorporation with a relatively limited function. A non-statutory corporation's powers may be determined by customary usage.[119]

1.54 In the 1860s, the University of Edinburgh among other bodies in the city was resisting the attempt of Mr Greig, the Inspector of Poor, to levy poor-law rates. The argument of those resisting payment was that they were Crown bodies. At first instance in 1865, Mr Greig was unsuccessful, it being said by the Lord Advocate that the decision in the University's favour expressly turned upon the fact that the funds of the University were held for State purposes, and that the Crown had a strong interest in the institution, being patron of several of its Chairs.[120] On appeal, in *Greig v Edinburgh University*, the House of Lords held that the University was liable to the rates. The Lord Chancellor said:

> The University of Edinburgh is, no doubt, a great public and national institution; but the corporation of the University of Edinburgh is a corporation independent of the Crown, no doubt originally created by, but still independent of the Crown. Its property is not Crown property, but it is property vested in the Senatus Academicus for the University purposes.[121]

Lord Cranworth, quoting the opinion of the Lord Justice-Clerk, said:

---

and market days, and *Guildry of Stirling v Weir* (1823) 2 S 531 where the trade unsuccessfully sought to stop a schoolmaster selling books to his pupils, on condition that he did not open a shop.

117 The Requirements of Writing (Scotland) Act 1995 spells out the formalities to be followed by corporations in executing certain types of document.

118 *Cumming v Walker* (1742) M 2501.

119 *Kesson v Aberdeen Wrights InCorpn* (1898) 1 F 36.

120 *Greig (Inspector of Poor for the City Parish of Edinburgh) v Heriot's Hospital* (1865) 1 SLR 27, 28.

121 (1868) 5 SLR 620, 621, HL.

... the Crown is recognised both as the fountain from which the whole rights of the University flow, and also as the visitorial authority to the control of which it is at all times subject ...[122]

but that this did not mean it was a Crown body. A few years later, the University of Glasgow was unsuccessful in resisting demands for poor law rates and similar taxes.[123]

1.55 The Scottish courts have not accepted the contention that a chartered body may do anything which an individual might lawfully do. In *Kemp v Glasgow Corpn*[124] which was about the action of the corporation in defraying certain election expenses out of the Common Good, the House of Lords, which remitted the case to the Court of Session for proof before answer, agreed that the powers of the council (formerly the magistrates) in relation to the Common Good were not entirely unfettered: at least since 1491 (Act of James IV cap 19) they had been required to make an annual report of expenditure. Restriction of the activities of a body acting under royal charter 'rests, not on any limitation of its contractual powers, but on the principle that certain applications of its funds may amount to a breach of trust.'[125]

Dissolution of a Scots chartered corporations

1.56 As in England, a chartered corporation may be dissolved only by the appropriate public authority.[126] This may be by Act of Parliament, or by forfeiture of the charter if the powers entrusted to the corporation are abused,[127] or the corporation is unable to fulfil the purposes of its institution.[128] It appears that the performance of a corporation's duties may be enforced by the Court of Session.[129] A

122 This reference to the visitorial authority in Scotland is discussed later in the section on Visitors.
123 *The University of Glasgow v James Dunlop Kirkwood (Inspector of Poor of the Parish of Govan), The Comrs of Police of the Burgh of Partick and the Commissioners of Supply of the County of Lanark* (1872) 10 M 1000.
124 1920 SC 73, HL; see also *Graham v Glasgow Corpn* 1936 SC 108.
125 W M Gloag and R C Henderson *Introduction to the Law of Scotland* (J A D Hope, A F Rodgers and A Paton, eds) (9th edn, 1987) p 75.
126 *Thomson v Incorporation of Candlemakers of Edinburgh* (1855) 17 D 765.
127 Erskine *Institute* i vii 64.
128 Bell *Principles* s 2179.
129 Section 45 Court of Session Act 1988 which repealed and replaced the somewhat more loquacious section 91 Court of Session Act 1868 quoted in Volume 19 of the *Encyclopaedia of the Laws of Scotland* (1937).

university founded by Papal Bull, confirmed by royal grants at various times, can apply to the Court of Session to protect its rights.[130]

Non-chartered bodies

The doctrine of ultra vires

1.57   In contrast to the chartered corporation a body created by or under statutory authority or under companies legislation is subject to the doctrine of ultra vires, that is it is legally incapable of doing anything outwith the objects and powers which have been granted to it, or are reasonably incidental to those objects and powers.[131] In the case of local authorities there is statutory provision to this effect in section 111 Local Government Act 1972. For example in *R v Staffordshire County Council, ex p Staffordshire Polytechnic*[132] the court held that a decision by the Council to appropriate the interest accruing to a reserve fund for the polytechnic (now Staffordshire University) under Schedule 13 of the 1972 Act (as amended) was ultra vires 'Incidental to' has the relatively narrow meaning of 'reasonable implication.'[133] In the visitorial jurisdiction case involving the University of Hull, *R v Lord President of the Privy Council, ex p Page*,[134] Lord Browne-Wilkinson made it clear that the doctrine now extends to a wide variety of errors of law. Legal action has been taken in the past in such diverse areas as provision of a serviced wash-house,[135] a parcel service operated by tram,[136] in-house printing,[137] the construction of the well-known subway across Whitehall near Parliament Square[138] and more recently, proposals for the regulation of night flying at London airports[139] and 'swap' agreements made

---

130   *The University of Glasgow v James Dunlop Kirkwood (Inspector of Poor of the Parish of Govan), The Commissioners of Police of the Burgh of Partick and The Commissioners of Supply of the County of Lanark* (1872) 10 M 1000.
131   *A-G v Great Eastern Rly* (1880) 5 App Cas 473, 478 per Lord Selborne.
132   [1992] COD 228, CA.
133   *Amalgamated Society of Rly Servants v Osborne* [1910] AC 87, 97 per Lord Macnaughten; *A-G v Crayford UDC* [1962] Ch 575.
134   [1993] AC 682 at 701.
135   *A-G v Fulham Corpn* [1921] 1 Ch 440.
136   *A-G v Manchester Corpn* [1906] 1 Ch 643.
137   *A-G v Smethwick Corpn* [1932] 1 Ch 562.
138   *Westminster Corpn v London and North-Western Rly Co* [1905] AC 426: this was a case involving the exercise of a discretionary power.
139   *R v Secretary of State for Transport, ex p Richmond upon Thames London Borough Council* [1994] 1 WLR 74.

by a local authority.[140] The principles were set out by the House of Lords in *Ashbury Rly Carriage Co v Riche*:[141]

> Now ... if that is the condition upon which the corporation is established [under the Companies Act] it is a mode of incorporation which contains in it both that which is affirmative and that which is negative. It states affirmatively the ambit and extent of the vitality and power which by law is given to the incorporation, and it states, if it were necessary to state, negatively, that nothing shall be done beyond that ambit, and that no attempt shall be made to use the corporate life for any other purpose than that which is so specified.

Although the company was registered under the Companies Acts, the same principles apply to statutory corporations.[142]

1.58   English law relating to the interaction between ordinary civil proceedings and judicial review of the exercise of statutory power whether intra or ultra vires is complex and beyond the scope of this work[143] but recent case law suggests that it is not open to a plaintiff to bring ordinary proceedings solely on the grounds that a decision of a public authority has infringed rights to which he or she was entitled to protection under public law: this is a matter for judicial review.[144] This does not prevent the defendant authority from raising ultra vires as a defence,[145] although this may act to its disadvantage, since the time-limit for bringing judicial review applications is only three months. There have been a number of mixed cases, in which it is alleged that private law rights have been affected by the negligent or ultra vires exercise of public law rights.[146] A public authority may be sued for misfeasance in public office, where acting ultra vires it causes damage to the plaintiff and either it was acting with malice or knew that the action was ultra vires and would cause him or her damage. The decision to this effect in *Bourgoin SA v Ministry of Agriculture etc*[147] has been questioned by Lord Goff in the House of Lords in *Kirklees Metropolitan Borough Council Ltd v Wickes Ltd*[148]

140   Eg *Hazell v Hammersmith and Fulham London Borough Council* [1992] 2 AC 1.
141   (1875) LR 7 HL 653, 670.
142   *A-G v LCC* [1907] AC 131.
143   See C Emery 'The Vires Defence – "Ultra Vires" as a Defence to Criminal or Civil Proceedings (1992) 51 CLJ 308 and 'Collateral Attack – Attacking "Ultra Vires" Action Indirectly in Courts and Tribunals' (1993) 56 MLR 643.
144   *O'Reilly v Mackman* [1983] 2 AC 237.
145   *Wandsworth London Borough Council v Winder* [1985] AC 461.
146   See eg *Roy v Kensington etc Family Practitioner Committee* [1992] 1 AC 624; *Lonrho plc v Tebbit* [1991] 4 All ER 973.
147   [1986] QB 716.
148   [1993] AC 227.

since in the intervening period the European Court of Justice in *Francovich and Bonifaci v Italy*[149] determined that the state is liable to pay compensation to persons whose individual rights are infringed by a breach of European Union law for which the state is responsible. Section 265 Public Health Act 1875 offers some protection to local authority members and officers but does not extend to higher education institutions.

1.59   In the field of higher education this limitation on the powers of bodies created by statute applies not just to institutions but also to such statutory bodies as the Funding Councils. Since the Universities of Oxford and Cambridge, which are corporations by prescription with statutory power to make their own statutes, it may apply to them as well.[150] In the case of bodies incorporated under the Companies Acts the validity of an act done by a company may not be called in question on the ground of lack of capacity by reason of anything in the company's memorandum.[151]

1.60   Disputes arising within such institutions which cannot be settled by internal machinery may be brought before the ordinary courts and tribunals. In order that the problem of acts being ultra vires is avoided as far as reasonably practicable, it is obviously essential that the governing instruments of the institution set out clearly all possible powers which it might wish to take. Six examples will illustrate the method adopted.

(i)   THE LONDON SCHOOL OF ECONOMICS AND POLITICAL SCIENCE (A COMPANY LIMITED BY GUARANTEE).

The objects of the School set out on its Memorandum of Association are an example of a set of rules which have stood the test of time, having been amended only slightly between 1901 and the present day. The objects start with those which are familiar to a reader of any charter of the same period, for example the organisation and promotion of research and the advancement of science and learning; they go on to set out the corporation's powers in respect of property,

---

149   C-6, 9/90: [1992] IRLR 84.
150   Sir William Wade says that the classification of Oxford and Cambridge for the purposes of administrative law is therefore uncertain: *Administrative Law* (6th ed, 1988) p 648.
151   Section 108 Companies Act 1989 which substitutes new sections 35, 35A and 35B in the Companies Act 1985, derived from section 9 European Communities Act 1972, implementing in the UK a Directive pre-dating the UK's access to the European Community (European Union).

staff, funding and so on. The School is a constituent part of the University of London, which has a Visitor and a Chancellor.

(II) THE UNIVERSITY OF GREENWICH (A COMPANY LIMITED BY GUARANTEE).

This modern (1989) constitution sets out in its Memorandum of Association all those objects commonly found in charters, expanded somewhat, for example the education of students is to be undertaken 'so that they are able to develop their abilities and aptitudes and to contribute to the industrial, commercial, scientific, technological, social, professional and artistic life of the communities.' The objects go on to give the University power to hold property, employ staff, etc., as in the other constitutions.

(III) THE UNIVERSITY OF NEWCASTLE-UPON-TYNE (ESTABLISHED BY ACT OF PARLIAMENT).

While the University has no charter, the third Schedule to the Universities of Durham and Newcastle-Upon-Tyne Act 1963 constitutes the statutes which among other provisions establish the offices of Visitor and Chancellor. In all respects, other than the absence of a charter, it should be treated as the equivalent of a chartered institution: its objects are expressed in the same language as that used in a charter. The Visitor's authority is established under the Act and thereby the jurisdiction of the ordinary courts is excluded in matters within the Visitorial power.

(IV) THE MIDDLESEX UNIVERSITY (CONDUCTED BY THE MIDDLESEX UNIVERSITY HIGHER EDUCATION CORPORATION, ORIGINALLY ESTABLISHED TO CONDUCT THE MIDDLESEX POLYTECHNIC UNDER ERA).

The powers of a higher education corporation are set out in section 124 ERA, as amended and amplified by section 71 FHEA. The Instrument and Articles of Government are made by the Privy Council under those provisions and therefore subject to them.[152] The corporation has power to provide higher and further education, to carry out research and to publish the results. It also has power to do anything necessary or expedient for the purpose of or in connection with these general powers, including a range of particular powers very similar to those which one would find in a charter.

---

152 The initial constitutions were those set out in Schedule 7 ERA, as amended by FHEA.

(v) The Glasgow Caledonian University (a designated institution the Court of which is constituted by Order of Council under FHESA).

The objects of the University are set out in Part III of the relevant Order of Council, which constitutes the governing body as the 'University Court of Glasgow Caledonian University,' with 'all the rights, powers and privileges necessary or expedient to conduct the University and to ensure its well-being' and 'to advance learning and knowledge by teaching and research and to enable students to obtain the advantages of higher education.' The Order of Council then goes on to define the constitution and powers of the University Court and under Part IV (Administration) constitutes the offices of Chancellor and Principal and Vice-Chancellor. It makes provision for a Senate (to be appointed by the Court) and a Students' Association and other matters commonly found in a charter and statutes.

(vi) The Cheltenham and Gloucester College of Higher Education (constituted by Declaration of Trust and Instrument of Government made thereunder).

The objects of the College are set out in a Declaration of Trust establishing The Cheltenham and Gloucester College of Higher Education Trust as the advancement (in accordance with a specified principle in relation to the nature of religious education to be conveyed in the College) of the higher and further education of men and women (including in particular and without prejudice to the generality of the foregoing the training of teachers) by the provision, conduct and development of the College in accordance with arrangements approved by the Secretary of State. The College is required to have in its curriculum the provision of initial teacher education and the study of Christian theology. The declaration of trust also requires that residential accommodation shall be provided at the College for as many of its students as is reasonably possible. The College is then governed by an Instrument of Government made under section 156(7) ERA, which is similar in form to that of a higher education corporation.

The advantages of a charter

The magic disappears

1.61 Despite the fact that the great majority of universities created before 1992 had to petition for a royal charter, a task which was at first an uphill struggle for the former University College at Buckingham, the government decided that it was not necessary to follow this route when the new universities were created from the former polytechnics, central institutions and colleges of higher education. This was because, to quote a government spokesman: 'There is no special magic in a Royal Charter. It is merely a means of conferring a title and constituting the body with its necessary powers.'[153]

1.62 The word 'merely' is arguably ill-chosen since it rather neatly disposes of a not inconsiderable part of the history and culture of both England and Scotland. The grant of a charter has in the past been a long drawn-out procedure involving detailed negotiations between the Privy Council Office, the petitioning body and including a wide consultation among interested parties. The procedure laid down in the College Charter Act 1871 was bypassed by the expedient of conferring upon the Privy Council the power to approve changes of name of existing institutions and to make Orders setting out the principal powers of the new institutions. Thus there was no need on this occasion to refer to the Privy Council *Memorandum of General Principles for the granting of Charters*, compliance with which had used up so much time, energy and resources in the past. The requirement that the instruments of government of all the new university institutions and changes in the domestic legislation of the ancient Scottish universities are also subject to the approval of the Privy Council may be considered technically to be the equivalent process.

Status of a charter

1.63 Are there in fact any advantages in having a royal charter in the 1990s? Before 1991, when the government's intentions to proceed to create new universities by a much more cost-effective route became obvious, it was argued that there were. For example, in 1969, when the setting up of University College Buckingham was being discussed, it could be argued[154] that

> sponsors of universities must secure a charter from the Privy Council. Nothing in the laws of the United Kingdom requires it, but the nature and structure of British society do. Many employers, particularly those

153 Lord Strathclyde *Official Report* HC 12 March 1992 Col 1467.
154 H S Fearns *Towards an Independent University* (1969) Institute of Economic Affairs Occasional Paper 25 pp 23–4.

organised as professions, will recognise the degrees of a Chartered Institution. Although the true charter of any university is the quality of its staff and students, any independent university must have the official endorsement which the charter implies.

The author may have intended to use 'English' rather than 'British' as to date the ancient Scottish universities have not exercised the right granted in 1966 to apply for charters.[155]

1.64   Even in 1993 Brian Caul[156] argued strongly in favour of charters:

> It is essential that the role of the universities in society is protected through their Charters. The Charter is the means by which the university publicly pronounces its set of guiding principles or ideals and by which it will test all its actions. These values underpin the untrammelled pursuit of knowledge and consequently universities must be protected from having to endorse the dominant party political lines, traditional ways of thinking, or fashionable modes of thought ... there must be a clear degree of independence from the wider society.

1.65   It can be argued that the Orders of Council and Memoranda of Association constitute 'official endorsement' and a guarantee of independence of the new and the ancient institutions. They are, after all, granted in pursuance of the will of Parliament, arguably more tangible in the present day and age than what Sir William Wade[157] described as a 'lingering effect of the royal prerogative.' However, it is a fact of English life that there remains a certain kudos about the possession of a charter from the Sovereign. Institutions created in pursuance of a public general statute, although for practical purposes on a generally equal footing with the others, nonetheless are as we shall see different in the scope of their legal powers and for both these reasons the new institutions (and possibly the ancients) may yet seek charters of their own.

Similarities between charters and articles of government

1.66   It is impossible for the charter and statutes of a university to be changed without the consent of the Privy Council, which Graeme

---

155   Section 1 Universities (Scotland) Act 1966.
156   B Caul *Value-Added: The Personal Development of Students in Higher Education* (1993) p 37.
157   H W R Wade *Administrative law* (4th ed, 1977) p 205.

Moodie and Rowland Eustace in their book *Power and Authority in British Universities*[158] held out as an important manifestation of state control. However, it is likewise impossible for the equivalent articles of government of a non-chartered institution to be changed without either the authority of Parliament or of the Privy Council (in the case of the new universities). As the Privy Council for this purpose consists of the responsible government ministers in any event, it is easy to see how in practice all important issues are actually decided by the State.

Statutes, ordinances and other domestic legislation

1.67 A royal charter or instrument of government is only one part of the domestic legislation of a higher education institution. In a chartered university, in descending order of importance and formality required to effect change, there are normally statutes (not to be confused with Acts of Parliament), ordinances, regulations and/or rules, although some universities use different nomenclature to describe essentially the same types of constitutional instrument. In non-chartered institutions there are articles of government, byelaws and regulations of various kinds.

1.68 The medieval universities operated somewhat informally by means of custom and practice until there was some disinclination on the part of 'progressives' to be bound by tradition and as a result, fearing a threat to their existence, the universities decided to reduce the unwritten customs to formal statutes enforceable under oath. The matters originally provided for in this way concerned academic dress and the procedures to be followed at funerals but they were gradually extended to areas such as the hours and manner of lecturing, breaches of discipline, accommodation and the 'disregard of one's obligations.' These customs were then the first to be cast as formal statutes by the University of Cambridge.[159] The phraseology, although not always the substance, has survived to the present day.

1.69 The old local government charters gave the corporations the power to make 'byelaws,' a term used in a number of modern constitutions of higher education institutions to describe the equivalent of ordinances and regulations. Indeed, corporations had,

158 R Eustace and G C Moodie *Power and Authority in British Universities* (1974) pp 20–1.
159 M B Hackett *The original statutes of Cambridge University* (1970) p 63.

and retain, an inherent power to make byelaws regulating any matter connected with the purposes for which they are established.[160] At common law, such byelaws could only bind members of the corporation and could be enforceable by appropriate penalties (just as the constitutions of the ancient universities provided for rules and regulations to be enforced against the members). The principal control by the courts was in relation to the 'reasonableness' of the byelaws.[161] Since most of the local authority byelaws are now made under the authority of Act of Parliament and carry penalties for non-compliance, the courts have intervened to review cases of vires,[162] uncertainty[163] and for conflict with statute.[164] *Bugg v DPP*[165] is important, since there it was held that the defendant could not plead ultra vires, in that there was a procedural irregularity in making the byelaw, as a defence to a criminal charge. Such a challenge would have to be mounted by application for judicial review.

1.70 The charter grants exclusive power to the corporation and makes certain general statements about its principal organs of government. The statutes, which are subject to the approval of the Privy Council and appear as a schedule to the charter, set out the basic framework for the exercise of the powers of those organs and usually on a more general level the powers of certain office-holders. The statutes or ordinances and other subsidiary legislation of the University of Newcastle-Upon-Tyne and the ancient Scottish Universities follow a similar pattern. In general terms the courts will permit corporations to lessen the extent of their authority by internal rule, but powers cannot be increased by ordinance (other than the ordinances which in some universities have a different status, for example the ordinances under the Universities of Scotland Acts) or regulation.[166]

1.71 It was not until the early twentieth century that many of the minor matters previously governed by statute at the Universities of

---

160 C Cross and S Bailey *Cross on Local Government Law* (7th ed, 1986) p 107.
161 See eg *Ipswich Tailors' Case* (1614) 11 Co Rep 53a; *Slattery v Naylor* (1888) 13 App Cas 446, 452.
162 *R v Wood* (1855) 5 E & B 49: byelaw requiring removal of snow was ultra vires a power to require removal of dust, ashes, rubbish, filth, manure, dung and soil.
163 *Nash v Finlay* (1901) 85 LT 682: 'No person shall wilfully annoy passengers in the street' invalid for uncertainty.
164 *Powell v May* [1946] KB 330: attempt to restrict betting in a public place, even though permitted by Act of Parliament.
165 [1993] QB 473.
166 *R v Weymouth Corpn* (1741) 7 Mod Rep 373; *Hoblyn v R* (1772) 2 Bro Parl Cas 329, HL.

Oxford and Cambridge were made the subject-matter of ordinances (Cambridge) or decrees and regulations (Oxford) and thus left to the institutions themselves to regulate. In the pre-1992 university sector the area into which a particular matter should fall is still very much a grey one: in some institutions, for example, the composition of Faculty Boards or equivalent is prescribed in statutes, whereas in others the detailed composition is left to ordinances. The deciding factor appears to be the extent of power exercised by the body concerned. It was therefore somewhat of a surprise when ERA provided that the arrangements for discipline of academic staff, in the minutest detail, should be spelt out in statutes; in some institutions this virtually doubled the size of the statute book overnight. There are no corresponding provisions for non-academic staff nor, in most institutions, for students. That statutes were used was a result of the government's insistence that all the pre-1992 universities should have a consistent model of discipline which could not be varied except with the consent of the Privy Council: the majority of higher education institutions have no such constraint.

The universities in detail

Oxford and Cambridge

1.72   The first institution which can historically be recognised as a university was Oxford, which formally came into existence early in the thirteenth century; the institutions which became the University of Cambridge sprang from the gathering there of some of the masters who had left Oxford at the time of the *suspendium clericorum* in 1209 and settled on Cambridge in preference to Northampton.[167] Cambridge was recognised as a *studium generale* by Pope John XXII in 1318.[168] Both universities, which are civil or common law corporations by prescription or immemorial custom,[169] consist of

---

167 Others settled at Reading, while there was a later recession to Stamford. Both Northampton and Stamford may be forgiven for regretting that the settlements there did not survive. The history of the migrations and possible reasons for them, are given by Benedict Hackett in *The Original Statutes of Cambridge University* (1970) p 44 et seq. See also Alan Cobban *The Medieval English Universities: Oxford and Cambridge to c 1500* (1988).

168 Pope Gregory IX wrote to the 'Chancellor and university of scholars at Cambridge' on 14 June 1233, thus treating it as a *universitas scholarium*.

169 The correct legal title of Oxford is 'Chancellor, Masters and Scholars of the University of Oxford' as in *Malcolm v Chancellor, Masters and Scholars of the University of Oxford (t/a Oxford University Press)* [1994] EMLR 17, CA. Statutes of Elizabeth I also describe it thus.

colleges and similar bodies, each with their own foundation[170] and constitution[171] and the right to sue and be sued in their own names as in eg *St John's College Oxford v Thames Water Authority*.[172] The college system appears in a number of later institutions in differing organisational arrangements, notably Durham, St Andrews, Kent at Canterbury, York and Lancaster. Not surprisingly, there have been a number of private Acts related to Oxford and Cambridge.[173] The right to make certain 'Regius' professorial appointments at these universities is reserved to the Crown, although some changes to the Oxford system were made in 1997 placing the leading role in the hands of the University.

The University of London

1.73   The University of London is a federal institution governed currently by statutes made under the procedures prescribed in the University of London Act 1994 and predecessor legislation.[174] The University consists of a number of colleges, schools and institutes, each with their own constitution, 16 of them in receipt of direct funding from HEFCE. Many of the constituent institutions were founded in the nineteenth century, some earlier.

1.74   University College, founded in 1826 as the University of London (but with no degree-awarding powers) was the first university institution in England to admit non-conformists, Jews and Roman Catholics. King's College was granted a charter in 1829 (but again with no degree-awarding powers). A charter giving degree-awarding powers was granted to a third body – the University of London – in 1836. On the same day a charter was granted to the former University

170 See Williams *Law of the Universities* (1910) (Butterworth).
171 At least one college was found by the University Commissioners appointed under ERA to have no valid constitution, since the medieval monarch due to sign it expired before doing so and the matter was then uncompleted by his successor. A readable account of the way Oxford worked in the 1960s, which helps to explain the very different structures of governance in the ancient English universities, is Chapter VI of Volume I of *Report of the Commission of Inquiry* (1966). See now *Report of the Commission of Inquiry* (1998).
172 [1990] RVR 84, Lands Tr.
173 Eg Oxford and Cambridge Acts 1849, 1877, 1880 and 1923; University of Oxford Act 1869.
174 There are a number of private Acts, including College-specific Acts such as the University College London Acts 1979 and 1996, Queen Mary and Westfield College Act 1995, Imperial College Act 1997, University of London Acts in 1898, 1899, 1926 and 1978 and the University of London (Medical Graduates) Act 1854.

of London, which was renamed University College London. The new University of London so established was an examining body chartered to award degrees to candidates presented by University College and King's College, the Medical Schools and other institutions recognised for the purpose. Further charters were granted to the University of London in 1837, 1858 and 1863, each revoking the former. Some provisions of the 1863 charter, including the provision incorporating the University, are still extant.[175]

1.75 There is a range of constitutional arrangements within the University at present: for example, The London School of Economics and Political Science (1895) became a company limited by guarantee in 1901. Those parts of the university which are incorporated separately are, for the purposes of litigation, separate entities.[176] Major changes in the constitution came into effect in September 1994. Among these was the delegation of the exercise of degree-awarding powers to constituent schools, now formally called colleges. The degrees of the University may also be awarded to those who have studied as external students. A Lead College is designated to provide an agreed range of academic services, with certain administrative functions for the external system undertaken centrally.

English universities outside London: nineteenth and early twentieth centuries

1.76 The English foundations of the nineteenth and early twentieth centuries constituted the first major expansion of the English university system outside Oxford and Cambridge. The University of Durham was constituted in the 1830s as a result of an initiative by the Church, an earlier attempt to found a university there having failed during the Commonwealth some 180 years earlier. Letters patent were issued for the foundation of a body corporate to be known as 'the Provost, Fellows and Scholars of the College in Durham of the Foundation of Oliver, Lord Protector' and the Provost and Fellows were nominated, but Oliver's son and successor Richard effectively put an end to the scheme by promising that the college would not be able to grant degrees, a power then reserved to Oxford and Cambridge. The University of Durham Act 1832 was '... an Act

---

175 Section 7 University of London Act 1994.
176 See eg *R v Higher Education Funding Council, ex p Institute of Dental Surgery* [1994] 1 All ER 651. The Institute is part of the British Postgraduate Medical Federation and a company limited by guarantee.

to enable the Dean and Chapter of Durham to appropriate part of the property of their church to the establishment of a University in connection therewith.' A royal charter was issued in June 1837. The university is now governed by the Universities of Durham and Newcastle-Upon-Tyne Act 1963.[177]

1.77 Today's large 'civic' universities such as Birmingham, the Victoria University of Manchester and Bristol are institutions founded originally as colleges as a result of the philanthropy of local industrialists and merchants who saw the advantage of an institution of advanced learning for the economic development of their cities. All these universities were awarded charters in the period 1900–1909, having previously offered courses validated by the older bodies. The original Victoria University, founded by royal charter in 1880, had campuses in Manchester, Liverpool and Leeds but dissolved in 1903/ 4: the coincidence of Queen Victoria's Diamond Jubilee and Joseph Chamberlain's election as Lord Rector of the University of Glasgow contributed to the establishment of the University of Birmingham which was the spur to creation of individual universities in Leeds, Liverpool, Manchester and Sheffield.[178] A number of other institutions were created university colleges during this period, for example Southampton (1902), originally Hartley College (1862). The history of the former colleges is preserved to some extent in the places reserved for representatives of the original founders or their trades on the Courts and/or Councils of the universities. Although originally founded as local institutions, the universities became established as national bodies, drawing students from all over the United Kingdom and overseas.[179]

English universities: Post-First World War

1.78 A number of towns and cities were not university sites by the post-First World War period of reconstruction, after the University Grants Committee (UGC) had been created and was supporting the universities with Treasury funding and when for the first time state scholarships and county awards were available to students. The interim solution was to create a number of University Colleges, again

---

177 Earlier private Acts were passed in 1908 and 1935.
178 Lord (Edward) Boyle: Foreword to *Studies in the History of a University* P H J H Gosden and A J Taylor (eds) (1975).
179 A range of private Acts include those relating to Bristol (1909 and 1974), Leeds (1904 and 1965), Liverpool (1904), and Sheffield (1905).

relying heavily on local support, which while not in receipt of Treasury funds initially, were able to teach at higher levels, awarding degrees usually of the University of London.

1.79 The role of the Privy Council and the University Grants Committee in the process by which these institutions secured their recognition and incorporation as university colleges and later as chartered universities has been examined by Christine Shinn as noted above.

> In 1920 the Chancellor of the Exchequer had explicitly asked the UGC to 'promote a continued advance in the standard of university teaching' and to nominate which activities undertaken by institutions were of 'university character.' For its part the Privy Council referred to the Committee every case of application for a charter or amendment to charter and statutes and the Board of Trade adopted a similar policy with regard to requests for incorporation.[180]

The University of Hull, founded as Hull University College in 1927, is one example of this. Eventually, in the 1940s and 1950s all these colleges were granted University status by charter. Reading was an exception to the general rule, becoming a University in 1926 having been a University Extension College of Oxford since 1892. These universities also became part of the national scene.[181]

English universities: The 1960s

1.80 While most of the entirely new universities of the 1960s were approved, and some granted charters, before the Robbins Report of 1963,[182] that Report and the higher education policy of the Labour Government of 1964–1970 was responsible for the creation of other universities from existing institutions (and for one new university in Scotland at Stirling.)[183] This was accompanied by an expansion of local authority higher education, the forerunner of the post-1992 universities, provision aimed at local populations. The seven completely new universities with ambitious plans to meet large projected increases in the national demand for higher education had

---

180 C Shinn *Paying the Piper: The Development of the University Grants Committee 1919–1945* (1986) p 107–8.
181 Private Acts relate to Exeter (1957), Hull (1955), Keele (1962), Leicester (1958), Nottingham (1949), Reading (1926) and Southampton (1953).
182 Eg Sussex was granted its charter in 1961, whereas Kent's was not granted until 1965.
183 Stirling's charter was the last to be granted, in 1967.

been created on 'greenfield' sites: East Anglia (at Norwich), Essex (at Colchester), Kent at Canterbury (near Canterbury), Lancaster, Sussex (near Brighton),[184] Warwick and York; and nine colleges, formerly Colleges of Advanced Technology, were given university status: Aston in Birmingham,[185] Bath, Bradford,[186] Brunel (at Uxbridge), Chelsea, City (City of London), Loughborough University of Technology, Salford[187] and Surrey (at Guildford).[188] All of these are now universities created by charter, except Chelsea College, which became a school of the University of London and later merged in a reorganisation. Also at this time the University of Newcastle-upon-Tyne was created by Act of Parliament,[189] it had formerly been King's College, the Newcastle Division of the University of Durham.

1.81 While these universities did not 'serve an apprenticeship' under London or Oxford, they were all required for the first few years of their existence to have Academic Advisory Committees made up largely of eminent academic staff of other universities and appointed by the Privy Council. The functions of these Committees were to secure academic standards by satisfying themselves on the arrangements for external examiners and to advise generally on the development of the universities.

The Open University

1.82 The last university to be created in England in the 1960s, but having a pan-UK remit, was the Open University, established by charter in 1969. Until 1993 this was funded directly by the Department for Education (DFE) but is now funded by HEFCE. With the exception of a relatively small number of full-time postgraduates, all the Open University's students are part-time, undertaking what are today called distance-learning programmes, a combination of correspondence, TV and radio broadcasts, interactive computing and face-to-face tuition. In terms of student numbers, the Open University is now the largest in the United Kingdom. It commenced a part-time route to teacher training in 1994, entering into partnership agreements with schools to provide professional training.

---

184 See University of Sussex Act 1962.
185 See University of Aston in Birmingham Act 1967.
186 See University of Bradford Act 1967.
187 See University of Salford Act 1968.
188 See University of Surrey Act 1966.
189 Universities of Durham and Newcastle-Upon-Tyne Act 1963.

English universities: Post-1970

1.83 The first of the post-1970 institutions to be accorded university status was the privately-financed University of Buckingham, which had failed to secure government recognition as a university when initially founded as University College Buckingham in 1973. It received its royal charter in 1983 and remains the only UK university whose degrees are recognised under the Education Reform Act (ERA) but which is not in receipt of grant from the Funding Councils. It has a distinctive undergraduate degree programme, students completing degrees in a shorter time than the conventional pattern.

1.84 Other than Cranfield University, which already had a Royal Charter (1969) as Cranfield Institute of Technology and changed its name in 1993, the remaining English universities were granted that status following the passage of FHEA.[190] Among other things this removed the pre-existing division confirmed by Tony Crosland in 1965 but arguably established much earlier and variously known as the dual, plural or binary system, between publicly-funded universities on the one hand and, until 1988, local authority funded higher education provision on the other. Having been freed of local authority control and becoming either

(i)   higher education corporations[191] conducting polytechnics or colleges of higher education, with instruments of government approved by the Privy Council;[192] or

(ii) companies limited by guarantee conducting polytechnics

as a result of the passage of ERA, 32 former polytechnics and three colleges of higher education (Derbyshire, Dorset and Luton) were granted university status in 1992 and 1993. Five institutions within the area of the former Inner London Education Authority were already run by companies limited by guarantee and have continued as such, now conducting universities rather than polytechnics. Unlike the new universities of the 1960s, the institutions created from former polytechnics, etc, have no Academic Advisory Committees. Cranfield University is rather different, as it had an Academic Advisory Committee, prescribed by its charter, from 1969 to 1973.

1.85 There were proposals at various stages of development in 1997 for new universities in the South-West and North-West of England,

---

190 The use of the title 'university' is governed by section 77. FHEA and FHESA spawned a large number of statutory instruments.

191 Defined in sections 121, 122 and 122A ERA.

192 Section 124A and Schedule 7A ERA; Schedule 6 FHEA.

a Virtual University and a University of Industry. At time of writing it was unclear whether the Bolton Institute would be the latest institution to be awarded university title on the recommendation of the Degree Awarding Powers Committee of QAA.

1.86 Although most of the polytechnics etc were formally constituted in the late 1960s or early 1970s, many were amalgamations of a number of existing local authority colleges and so cannot be said to be part of the tradition dating from medieval times. A few, however, share similar origins with the traditional civic universities: the University of Huddersfield, for example, traces its history to 1841. The 1992 Act added provisions to ERA relative to the instruments of government of the former higher education corporations and similar bodies and together these form the legislative framework for the operation of the new universities. It is important to note that in most cases, unlike the pre-1992 English universities, it is not the university itself which is incorporated but the body (the board of governors or equivalent) which conducts the university.

The Ancient Scottish Universities

1.87 The oldest Scottish University, St Andrews, was formally inaugurated in 1413 by Papal Bull. The three other universities collectively known with St Andrews as 'the ancients' (Aberdeen, Edinburgh and Glasgow) were created over the next 170 years. Glasgow and Aberdeen were founded by Papal Bull in 1451 and 1494 respectively, Edinburgh by royal charter in 1583 as a 'tounis colledge.' Until the 1960s these were the only universities in Scotland but now constitute a minority of Scottish higher education institutions. They are governed by the Universities (Scotland) Acts 1858–1966[193] and by private Acts.[194] Commissioners appointed under the Universities (Scotland) Acts 1858 and 1889 made Ordinances during the periods 1859–1863 and 1890–1898 respectively: all Ordinances, whether made by the those Commissioners, other bodies[195] or the universities themselves are subject to the approval of the Privy Council. The 1889 Act incorporated the University Courts and vested the university property (previously held, at least in Edinburgh, by the Senatus Academicus[196]) in them, although it appears that the universities

---

193 Earlier legislation included The Universities (Scotland) Act 1853. Acts were passed in 1858, 1859, 1862, 1889, 1922, 1932 and 1966.
194 Eg the University of St Andrews Acts 1746 and 1953.
195 Eg the Commissioners appointed under the University of St Andrews Act 1953, operating between 1953 and 1958.
196 *University of Edinburgh v Torrie Trustees* 1997 SLT 1009.

continue to exist as common law corporations.[197] It is perhaps more accurate to say that the Bulls had the force of law in Scotland at the time and consequently the universities are the equivalent of chartered corporations.[198] At St Andrews the College councils were constituted corporate bodies by the Act of 1953; the colleges themselves are 'unincorporated societies of teachers and students,'[199] having previously been common law foundations with corporate status.

1.88 If indeed the universities do exist as common law corporations or the equivalent of chartered corporations, then they have implied powers as *naturalia*, one of which would be to delegate any powers to the Court, if these were not already expressly vested in the Court as a statutory personality depending for its powers on the Acts or Ordinances made under them. The Court may be considered to be a management agent for the university to the extent of the powers, rights and duties expressly conferred on the Court by the Acts and the analogy may usefully be adopted when considering the position of the post-1992 Scottish universities. An alternative analogy is between the powers of the directors of a company (the Court) and the powers of the members of the company in general meeting (the university) which may well exceed those of the directors.[200]

1.89 The history of the establishment of the University of Glasgow was exhaustively examined by the Court of Session in 1872,[201] in connection with its unsuccessful claim that on transferring from its original site to a new one, it and its principal, professors and members should continue to be immune from local taxation (in modern terms, the council tax and business rates). Glasgow had been founded as a *studium generale* by Pope Nicholas V by bull issued at the suit of James II of Scotland, conferring on the doctors, masters and students all privileges, honours and immunities enjoyed by the *studium* founded in the Pope's city of Bologna, which possessed an immunity from all taxation. Such immunities were not unusual. For example in a decree of 12 (or 25) January 1755 Elisabeth, Empress of Russia, provided that the new University founded in Moscow was free from

---

197 McBryde on Contract, para 8.93.
198 Greens *Encyclopaedia of the Laws of Scotland* Vol 6 paragraph 240.
199 Section 1(1) University of St Andrews Act 1953.
200 In terms of the English chartered university, the analogy is with the division of powers between the court and the Council.
201 *The University of Glasgow v James Dunlop Kirkwood (Inspector of Poor of the Parish of Govan), The Commissioners of Police of the Burgh of Partick and The Commissioners of Supply of the County of Lanark* (1872) 10 M 1000.

any tax[202] and in 1804 in *The Warden and College of The Souls of all Faithful People Deceased of Oxford v Costar*[203] All Souls College Oxford failed to gain exemption from a land tax, resistance to demands for payment having resulted in the seizure by bailiffs of two reading desks, two chairs and two tables.

1.90 The court dismissed Glasgow's claim by finding that the original grant, confirmed by numerous royal grants, the last of which by Charles I had been ratified by the Parliament of Scotland in 1633,[204] had to be construed in the light of usage which pointed to the immunity being confined to the original site, which had been taken over by the City of Glasgow Union Railway under an Act[205] which recited the immunities. One of the principal factors in persuading the court appears to have been that the University had opened a new chemistry department and taken over an observatory, both off the original site, and had submitted to local taxation on these. Its immunity did not extend to a new site, in respect of a new set of taxes, and at the expense of a new set of taxpayers. The case gives rise to interesting points about the nature of corporations, to be discussed later.

Other Scottish universities

1.91 The Robbins Report recommended the creation of one wholly new university in Scotland (Stirling), granted its charter in 1967. Two former colleges were given charters as Heriot-Watt (original foundation 1821) and Strathclyde (1796) Universities. All three universities were granted charters. Dundee separated from St Andrews in 1967, as Newcastle had from Durham, to form the University of Dundee, but unlike Newcastle, Dundee was granted a charter. Previously Dundee had been the unincorporated Queen's College Dundee of the University of St Andrews, formed in 1953 from University College Dundee and the Dundee School of Economics (otherwise known as the Dundee and East of Scotland Commercial College).[206]

---

202 This immunity was, unsurprisingly, later removed. L A Verbitskaya *Academic freedom and University autonomy: a variety of concepts* (1996) Higher Education Policy 9(4) 289 at 290.
203 (1804) 3 Bos & P 635.
204 C 39.
205 City of Glasgow Union Railway Act 1864.
206 Section 7 University of St Andrews Act 1953.

1.92 Pending the proposed establishment of The University of the Highlands and Islands, the University of Stirling remains the only wholly new twentieth century foundation, and the only new university in the UK which is strictly a 'Robbins' university although James VI of Scotland had promised to found a college in Stirling in 1617. Like the new universities in England, Stirling had an Academic Advisory Committee in its early years. Its unique position in Scottish higher education enabled it to experiment with an academic structure which was until recently unique in the United Kingdom: its semester system has now been adopted wholly or partially by many other higher education institutions.[207]

1.93 The eight universities, together with the Open University in Scotland, were joined in 1992–94 by five former central institutions (CIs: Napier, The Robert Gordon, Paisley, Glasgow Caledonian and Abertay Dundee Universities, all of which are descendants of older colleges – the University of Paisley for example originated in the Paisley Technical College and School of Art opened in 1897. Each CI was incorporated separately by individual regulation or scheme or as an incorporated company limited by guarantee.[208] Section 77 Education (Scotland) Act 1980 permitted the Secretary of State to amend their constitutions by statutory instrument subject to parliamentary approval. It also allowed the Secretary of State to establish and dis-establish grant-aided colleges. These provisions have, in essence, been carried forward into FHESA. The conversion of these former CIs to 'designated institution' and thence to 'university' status was achieved following passage of FHESA[209] which forms the basic legislation under which the new Scottish universities operate. As in England, the bodies conducting the new universities are incorporated (as was the case when they were central institutions)[210] whereas, for example, it is The University of

---

207 Report of the CVCP, HEFCE, HEFCW and SCOP Committee on the Structure of the Academic Year (Flowers Report) November 1993; Report of the SHEFC and COSHEP Advisory Group on the Academic Year (SAGAY or 'Thistle' Report) November 1993.

208 The Edinburgh College of Art's Board was incorporated by a private confirmation Act.

209 See for example, in respect of the Glasgow Caledonian University, The Glasgow Polytechnic and The Queen's College Glasgow (Closure) (Scotland) Order 1993 (SI 1993/554), the Glasgow Caledonian University (Establishment) (Scotland) Order 1993 (SI 1993/423), the Academic Awards and Distinctions (Glasgow Caledonian University) (Scotland) Order of Council 1993 (SI 1993/555) and The Glasgow Caledonian University (Scotland) Order of Council 1993 (SI 1993/556).

210 The previous legislation was The Central Institutions (Scotland) Regulations 1988 (SI 1988/1715) and a number of institution-specific regulations such as the Napier College of Commerce and Technology (No 2) Regulations 1985 (SI 1985/1163).

Strathclyde itself which is incorporated by charter. Thus four of the Scottish universities are themselves corporate bodies, whereas nine have incorporated courts: some or all may have corporate personality of a different kind.

1.94 There is what was described by the government spokesman in the House of Lords during the passage of the 1992 Act as

> ... a clear and very important distinction between the existing [eight] universities and designated institutions ... That does not disadvantage the designated institutions in any way; the distinction is necessary because the constitutional and organisational arrangements for designated institutions are different from those for the existing universities.[211]

The most notable difference which was not mentioned in that section of the debate is the relative ease with which the government can close the designated institutions, a power used to effect mergers between for example Jordanhill College and the University of Strathclyde and between Craigie College and the University of Paisley in 1993.[212] It is interesting to compare the arrangements for securing individual rights on mergers to those made by section 14 University of St Andrews Act 1953 on the reorganisation of that institution. There are also a number of differences in the detail of the arrangements between the Scottish institutions on the one hand and the English and Welsh institutions on the other and all these differences will be discussed as the subject-matter is covered later in this book.

The universities of Wales

1.95 The first institution to be established in Wales was St David's College, Lampeter in 1822, receiving its first charter in 1829 and now University of Wales, Lampeter. The first independent university, the University of Wales, received its original charter in 1893,[213] taking under its wing three existing colleges based in Aberystwyth (1872, charter 1889), Cardiff (1883, charter 1884) and Bangor (1884, charter 1885), all of which had previously prepared students for

---

211 Lord Strathclyde House of Lords *Official Report* Cols 1466–76.
212 See eg the Jordanhill College of Education (Closure) (Scotland) Order 1993 (SI 1993/490) and the Craigie College of Education (Closure) (Scotland) Order 1993 (SI 1993/1701) which closed the colleges and transferred their rights, liabilities, obligations etc. to the Universities of Strathclyde and Paisley respectively.
213 See also University of Wales Act 1902 and University of Wales (Medical Graduates) Act 1911.

University of London external degrees. The federal University now has eight constituent institutions. It was the only University in Wales until the Open University started operations in 1970, followed by the University of Glamorgan, formed in 1992 from the former Polytechnic of Wales after the passage of FHEA. A University of the Valleys is being proposed as a joint venture between the University of Wales, Swansea, the University of Glamorgan and the Open University.[214]

The universities of Northern Ireland

1.96 The two Northern Ireland universities are The Queen's University of Belfast founded as Queen's College in 1845, receiving its original charter as a university in 1908 and the University of Ulster, formed by charter in 1984 by the merger of the New University of Ulster (which surrendered its 1971 charter) and the Ulster Polytechnic. The University of Ulster is the only example of a trans-binary merger in the UK while the binary line remained in being. The Education Reform (Northern Ireland) Order 1989 is the parallel legislation to the 1988 Act.[215]

University colleges

Grant of title including the word 'university'

1.97 It is generally accepted that a body wishing to call itself a 'university' may lawfully acquire that title through the grant of a Royal Charter under the prerogative (or amendment to an existing Charter), through private Act of Parliament, or through the mechanisms for change of name set out in the FHEA and FHESA, where the discretion of the Privy Council is limited to '... [having] regard to the need to avoid names which are or may be confusing.'[216] It may also be possible to apply for registration of a business name containing the word 'university' through the procedures specified in the Business Names Act 1985 (BNA).[217] The latter provisions will be discussed in more detail below.

214 Paragraph 8.25, Report on National Consultation, NCIHE, July 1997.
215 Education Reform (Northern Ireland) Order 1989 (SI 1989/2406).
216 Section 77 FHEA and section 49 FHESA.
217 This Act covers all business names, whether the name is that of a partnership, an individual or a company. It is a matter of doubt (shared by DfEE officials) that the Act could apply to institutions (or the corporations conducting them) which were not a company registered under the Companies Acts.

1.98 As explained above, while a chartered university may do anything which a natural person may do and is not otherwise prohibited by the charter itself or the general law[218] that power does not extend to the creation of universities, since (i) a natural person cannot create a university and (ii) the mechanisms set out above (charter, Act of Parliament, statutory instrument) are exclusive. It is not clear however whether that applies to the situation in which a chartered university wished to confer the title 'University College' on another entity or to create such an entity itself. Such power would be exercisable either under a specific provision for affiliation or under general provisions.

1.99 One view is that the restriction on awarding the title 'university' applies equally to any title including that word.[219] Another view is that there is nothing in the general law which prevents the exercise of a power to confer the title 'University College' on any institution of any kind, whether in the UK or not, whether in the higher education sector or not, and whether the charter *expressly* grants that power or not. If that view is correct it is unlikely that anyone can interfere other than by writ of *scire facias* to revoke the charter.[220] The University Colleges linked with the Victoria University of Manchester (eg Warrington) have acquired their names by exercise of charter powers in this way and it would appear that the grant of the title 'University College' by the University of East Anglia to part of Suffolk College was also undertaken under charter powers. Which of these two views is correct could only be determined by the courts. However, on balance the first view, which is that a chartered university cannot confer the title of 'university college' by exercise of charter powers, seems to command greater support from authority. By contrast to chartered universities, non-chartered institutions require authority from statute and/or authority derived from a Memorandum and Articles of Association. An example of a statute which appears to provide the requisite power is the Universities of

218 In England and Wales the powers of a chartered corporations are unlimited except by the charter itself and the general law, eg *A-G v Manchester Corpn* [1906] 1 Ch 643; *A-G v Leeds Corpn* [1929] 2 Ch 291; *A-G v Leicester Corpn* [1943] 1 Ch 86.

219 Support for this view may be drawn from the provisions of the College Charter Act 1871. It is also the case that 'University Colleges' created before the 1960s acquired these titles either by Royal Charter or another prerogative act, or Act of Parliament, or by registration under the then applicable companies legislation. There is no instance of the title being conferred by the exercise of charter powers by an existing chartered body.

220 See *British South Africa Co v De Beers Consolidated Mines Ltd* [1910] 1 Ch 354.

Scotland Act 1889, section 15 of which grants to the Courts of the ancient Scottish universities the power to make ordinances to extend any of the universities by affiliating new colleges to them: arrangements for affiliation can be of permanent effect.[221] In England and Wales, section 124(2) ERA, the objective of which appears to be to confer powers broadly approximating to charter powers on non-chartered institutions, provides (in subsection (f)) higher education corporations etc with the power to form bodies corporate, which power could arguably be used to create a body called 'University College of ...,' either afresh or out of an existing body. The same argument would apply as in the case of chartered bodies, if the grant of any title including the word 'university' is reserved to the Crown, or to Parliament.

1.100 Before March 1992 a body wishing to acquire the word 'university' in its name other than through the device of registering a business name (see below) could have proceeded by seeking the support of an existing university through one of the mechanisms outlined above, and these mechanisms remain open to it. That they are legally valid is open to serious doubt. However since March 1992, provisions designed to enable polytechnics and higher education colleges which meet government requirements for university status to obtain the title have provided an additional route. Section 77 FHEA (and the broadly equivalent section 49 FHESA) provide a mechanism by which an existing institution *in the higher education sector*, or any body corporate carrying it on, may acquire the word 'university' in its name. The Privy Council in exercising this power to consent to a change in name has to have regard to the need to avoid names which are or may be confusing. The principal examples of the exercise of this power have been the change of name of former polytechnics and some colleges to 'University of ...,' several of these having distinctive titles with no obvious geographical affiliation. In exercising this power the Privy Council has recourse for advice to the relevant government department which in turn is advised by the Degree Awarding Powers Committee of QAA.

1.101 Section 90(4) FHEA requires 'university' to be interpreted as including a university college, or institution in the nature of a college, in a university. In a written answer[222] it was stated that the intention was to ensure that the words 'university college' should not

---

221 *Medcalfe v Cox* [1896] AC 647, HL.
222 HC Vol 201 col 583.

be used except to designate a constituent part of a university. That does not appear to be the effect, legal or practical, of the legislation.

1.102   Once the educational institution, or body corporate carrying it on, has had its name change agreed, then in England and Wales (but not in Scotland) the institution is to be treated as a university 'for all purposes' which appears to have the effect of avoiding any such institution from being denied recognition as a university pursuant to the *Lampeter* case. This means that any institution, or body corporate carrying on an institution, which has been permitted to change its name to include the word 'university' under section 77, so far as the law is concerned is a university. It follows that the agreement of the Privy Council to the use of the phrase 'University College' in a revised name automatically means that that institution is to be treated as a university 'for all purposes.' Presumably this cannot have been the intention of the legislature and repeal or amendment of section 77(4) FHEA would be required to avoid the unintended consequence.

1.103   It is argued that section 77 has no relevance to the question of exercise of powers by existing universities to create other bodies or to confer titles on new or existing bodies, whether or not the existing body is in the higher education sector or has itself any power in its instrument of government to change its name. It does not prevent any body from coming forward with a proposal that it be granted a charter[223] or be designated as an institution in the higher education sector with a name including 'university' in its title, although it is clear that no such requests would be granted at the present time.

1.104   Before the entry into force on 1 January 1983 of the Company and Business Names (Amendment) Regulations,[224] made under section 31(1) Companies Act 1981 (later section 3 BNA) any organisation could register its company or business name as including the word 'university' without any possibility of lawful hindrance whatever.[225] Neither the Registration of Business Names Act 1916 nor the original Company and Business Names Regulations[226]

---

223 Subject to the requirements of the College Charter Act 1871 designed to prevent the Privy Council granting charters without Parliamentary scrutiny.
224 SI 1982/1653.
225 For example The University of Stirling Limited registered in 1965 as the predecessor of The University of Stirling, incorporated by Royal Charter in 1967 and The University College of Sussex, registered in 1959 as the predecessor of The University of Sussex, incorporated by Royal Charter in 1961.
226 SI 1981/1685.

mentioned the word 'university.' BNA permits the Secretary of State (in practice the President of the Board of Trade) to specify words and expressions which may only be used in a business name with his or her consent. Company names are governed by separate legislation in the Companies Act 1985[227] but between 1982 and 1985 company and business names were regulated by the 1981 Act, so that the statutory instruments prescribing the 'words and expressions' are the Company and Business Names Regulations 1981 as amended in 1982, 1992 and 1995.[228] If a company carries on business under a business name which does not consist of the corporate name (with some additions irrelevant to the present discussion) it becomes subject to BNA. For each of approximately 90 specified words or expressions the Secretary of State is required to designate a government department or other relevant body. An organisation wishing to use such a word or expression must communicate that fact to the relevant body and ask if it has any objections. It must then forward a statement that the relevant body has been approached and must include with its application to the Secretary of State a copy of the response received from the relevant body. This procedure was used, according to the Standing Conference of Principals (SCOP), on four occasions between 1982 and 1988.

1.105 The relevant body for the purpose of the word 'university' is, since 5 June 1992, the Privy Council.[229] Between 1 January 1983 and 4 June 1992 it was the Department of Education and Science[230] and on the assumption that the requirements of section 3 BNA were complied with by the institutions referred to by SCOP, the Department of Education and Science must either have had no objection to these institutions or its objection was overruled. The Privy Council has stated that it would follow the advice of DfEE which is that they would not agree to the use of the phrase 'University College' in a business name unless the entity seeking that description was an integral part of an existing university: this view is consistent with the policy stated by the Secretary of State. In fact it is not clear that BNA provides a complete protection against the use of the word 'university' since the Act is designed to deal with corporate trading names used by companies and not all aspiring 'university colleges' are companies. In *London College of Science and Technology Ltd v*

---

227 Corporate bodies using business names are also required to put their corporate name on their letterhead. The purpose of this is to ensure that those trading with businesses know their true identities.
228 See now SI 1992/1196 and SI 1995/3022.
229 SI 1992/1196.
230 SI 1982/1653.

Islington London Borough Council[231] the court confirmed that BNA is capable of applying to educational establishments.

1.106   A variant of this route would be for an institution to retain the formal title (company or corporate name) of *XYZ College* but use the business name *University College of XYZ* subject to the BNA requirements if these apply. No name change under section 77 FHEA would be required although the consent of the Privy Council (in effect DfEE) under BNA would still be required (if the institution was subject to it) and all the limitations described above would still apply. In fact the use of the word *name* in section 77 is worthy of some examination. The section is side-titled 'Use of "university" in *title* of institution.' The words *title* and *name* may be interpreted differently. A *title* is arguably rather more formal than a *name*. The latter is what the institution wishes to be recognised by. Thus the formal title of *Aston University* is *The University of Aston in Birmingham* but its common name is *Aston University*. Likewise *Royal Holloway and Bedford New College* commonly calls itself *Royal Holloway, University of London* and there are other examples of this kind. It is odd that FHEA muddles these up.[232] However the corresponding Scottish side-title is 'change of name by institutions' which is actually what the section (and section 77 of the English Act) is about. This muddle requires to be rectified.

1.107   Institutions which called themselves 'university' or used the word 'university' in their title before 1 January 1983 were not subject to the business names provisions, although the small number of 'degree mill' institutions calling themselves universities should have been effectively put out of business by the recognised and listed bodies provisions of ERA.[233]

The recognition of degrees

1.108   The importance of the test of quality in the award of degrees has long been accepted in university circles. First and postgraduate degrees awarded by universities are, at least in theory, of equal status within the UK in terms of qualification for employment, entry to the

---

231 [1997] ELR 162, QBD.
232 Although side-titles are of little if any significance in statutory interpretation.
233 These provide criminal sanctions of a consumer protection nature, prosecutions to be initiated by trading standards officers or the police.

professions or further study. This equivalence has been secured by the appointment of external examiners which is an essential feature of the universities' assessment systems. Since the late 1980s procedures for the appointment of external examiners have been strengthened as part of the move towards quality assurance and ensuring that the public have confidence in the product. Further discussion of quality assurance and its significance in the relationship between institutions and their students can be found later.

Recognised bodies

1.109 With the appearance of new powers to enable institutions to grant degrees, whether limited or not, it is essential that the awards given by an institution of higher education (which must now be taken to include credits in a national or international credit accumulation and transfer system) will be recognised for the practical purposes of employment and further study. A pragmatic approach to the long-standing problem of defining which degrees were meaningful and which not was taken by Parliament in ERA which introduced the concepts of 'recognised body' and 'listed body.' A recognised body under the Act is one which is authorised to grant degrees or one which is permitted by a body so authorised to act on its behalf in the granting of degrees. Institutions with foreign 'parents' (eg branches of US universities in Britain) are exempt.[234]

1.110 The recognised bodies now include all the universities and other degree-awarding institutions, The Archbishop of Canterbury (whose power to award 'Lambeth degrees' derives from the powers of the Holy See but is now exercised by authority of a statute of Henry VIII),[235] the Royal Colleges of Art and Music,[236] the London Business School and a variety of others. There is a further category of 'recognised awards' which are not granted by a recognised or listed body but which have the same status as a degree: the bodies awarding these qualifications are the Inns of Court and a number of learned scientific and medical societies.

---

234 Section 214(5) and (10) ERA.
235 25 Henry VIII cap 25 (1534); Royal Letters Patent are issued confirming such awards: for a full account of the process see C A H Franklyn *Academical Dress from the Middle Ages to the present day, including Lambeth Degrees* (1970).
236 The three music colleges (Royal Academy of Music, Royal College of Music and Trinity College of Music) are Associate Institutions of the University of London.

Degree mills

1.111 'Degree mills' are organisations not listed in the Education (Recognised Bodies) Order 1997[237] offering to award degrees which are effectively worthless. A number of institutions so called had been established in the UK and there was no statutory bar on their offering customers degrees, etc which might reasonably be taken as being those of a UK institution. For a non-recognised body to do so now is a criminal offence, to be enforced by local authority trading standards officers. It appears that section 214 ERA is not breached if a person or organisation advertises false but impressive-looking certificates for sale, although institutions which had registered their names, grants or arms or other logos as trademarks, as advocated over a long period by CVCP, would have an effective remedy against infringement.[238]

Listed bodies

1.112 The Education (Listed Bodies) Order 1997[239] lists those institutions which either provide any course in preparation for a degree to be granted by a recognised body and are approved by that body, or are constituent colleges, schools or halls of a university which is a recognised body. Such bodies include the 'University Colleges' which are not an integral part of an existing university: the 1997 Order states the formal legal title of the institution.

Protection of status

1.113 Bodies which pass themselves off as being part of a higher education institution when they are not may face an action for passing off at common law. It must be shown that the misuse of the name is likely to deceive the public,[240] but not necessary to show that anyone has actually been deceived.[241]

---

237 SI 1997/1.
238 Such a case arose in 1997 when fake certificates were advertised on the internet.
239 SI 1997/54.
240 See eg *Grand Hotel Co of Caledonia Springs v Wilson* [1904] AC 103, PC; *Dunlop Pneumatic Tyre Co v Dunlop Motor Co* 1907 SC 15, HL.
241 See eg *Draper v Trist* [1939] 3 All ER 513, CA; *Charles Kinnell & Co Ltd v A Ballantine & Sons* 1910 SC 246.

Recognition within the European Union

1.114   As academic qualifications granted in the UK are not national awards but granted by individual institutions, and as their status differs significantly from those of other countries, there are no bilateral agreements for mutual recognition. There are of course a number of arrangements for joint and double degree programmes.[242] The Council of Ministers of the European Union has taken steps to secure the recognition of tertiary level qualifications under Articles 48 and 52 of the Treaty of Rome which deal with the free movement of workers. Multilateral agreements of 1953, 1956 and 1959 respectively cover the equivalence of diplomas leading to admission to universities, the equivalence of periods of university study and the academic recognition of university qualifications.[243] Article 57 of the Treaty on European Union empowers the Council of Ministers to issue Directives for mutual recognition of diplomas, certificates and other evidence of formal qualifications. There are sectoral directives for doctors (1975 and 1993), nurses (1977), dental practitioners (1978), veterinarians (1978), midwives (1980), architects (1985) and dispensing chemists (1985). The Council of Ministers decided in 1985 to lay down provisions relating to comparability of vocational qualifications in some sectors. In 1989 Council Directive 89/48[244] (extended in 1992)[245] created a general system for the recognition of higher education diplomas, in broad terms requiring member states of the Community to give full recognition to professional qualifications gained in other member states.[246] However, as the decision in *Kraus v Land Baden-Würtemberg*[247] shows, it is still necessary in some jurisdictions to obtain special authorisation from national authorities for the use of a qualification obtained elsewhere in the Community or outside it, where the purpose of that authorisation is to protect the public against misuse of such qualifications.[248]

242 See Report 11: Development of a framework of qualifications: relationship with continental Europe, NCIHE, July 1997.
243 D Green 1992: *The Challenge of the Single European Market* in *Higher Education into the 1990s* (1989).
244 *Official Journal* L19, 24 January 1989, p 16.
245 EC/89/48; EC/92/51.
246 As in *Thieffry v Conseil de l'ordre des avocats à la Cour de Paris*: 71/76 [1977] ECR 765.
247 Case C-19/92, [1993] ECR I-1663, ECJ.
248 The refusal by a national authority to recognise qualifications obtained elsewhere in the Community must be reasoned and is subject to judicial review: *Union National des Entraineurs et Cadres Techniques Professionals du Football v Heylens*: 222/86 [1987] ECR 4097; restrictions which discriminate against nationals of other member states may be prohibited: *Ordre des Avocats au Barreau de Paris v Klopp*: 107/83 [1984] ECR 2971.

1.115 Also relevant is Article 126 of the Treaty of Rome as amended following the Maastricht Treaty, the establishment of the programme SOCRATES and the National Academic Recognition Centres (NARICs), established and consolidated under the ERASMUS scheme, with a pilot Europe-wide course credit transfer system (ECTS) established in 1988 and running for six years in a range of subject areas.[249] SOCRATES activities include recognition of qualifications and establishment of a joint EU/Council of Europe/ UNESCO Working Party to consider the development of a diploma supplement or transcript which might be issued to individuals to aid the recognition of qualifications for academic and professional purposes.

1.116 A Council of Europe/UNESCO Convention on recognition of qualifications adopted in 1997 not only provides a new framework for recognition but also allows a host country to ask a foreign higher education institution operating on its territory to fulfil specific requirements according to national legislation before candidates are admitted to its programmes of higher education.

Franchising and collaborative provision

1.117 Franchising of programmes both at home and abroad sometimes attracts bad press coverage. A franchise arrangement is a contractual relationship between a higher education institution and the franchisee. The contract must deal with the question of liability should a student bring a claim relating to the delivery of a course and must cover all the relevant conditions of enrolment. It should also specify under what circumstances the name of the franchising institution may be used in promotional material. It should provide clear arrangements for termination and its consequences and prohibit sub-franchising without the consent of the franchisor.

1.118 In 1997, it was reported by NCIHE that UK-franchised qualifications were causing problems in Spain, Germany and Greece. Cross-border franchising is protected by Articles 52, 57 and 60 of the Treaty on European Union and the issues are to be resolved by the European Court of Justice. A Code of Practice for Overseas

---

249 Unlike the UK CATS and SCOTCAT arrangements, which envisage the accumulation of 120 credits per annum, with 360 (SCOTCAT 480) points required for an honours degree, under ECTS a student accumulates 60 credit points per annum, with 240 credits required for a degree.

Collaborative Provision was issued by HEQC in 1996, dealing with questions of enforceability of the contract in the laws of both (or all) parties and the need to be informed about practices which while lawful in one jurisdiction may be illegal in another.

Governance

Demystifying governance

1.119 Chitty J's remark in *Re Rly Sleepers Supply Co*[250] seems to me to sum up why it is that higher education institutions so often find themselves on the wrong side of a dispute: 'It is no wonder to my mind that persons who do not read statutes with care and have not legal knowledge at their finger's end should make a mistake in a matter such as this.' An understanding of the respective powers and duties of the principal bodies, committees and officers of institutions is not only valuable in itself, but is cost-effective if such disputes can be avoided. In the past, institutions have tended to rely on directing and administrative staffs for this understanding, since it has been assumed that issues of governance and procedure are complex and difficult to interpret. Unfortunately in recent years a number of incidents have occurred in which governing bodies have been criticised for failing to take appropriate action at an appropriate time and as a result new measures of control have been imposed on universities and colleges. The aim of this section is so to demystify the system so that everyone involved is aware of precisely what is expected in higher education governance as we enter the twenty-first century.

The dying Chancellor

1.120 The benevolent but dying Chancellor, a wholly fictitious character introduced to us by Frank Mattison in *Universities and the Law*,[251] provides us with the basis for modern university charters and statutes. He seeks legal advice on making a bequest of land to the university. 'Not possible' says the learned Secretary, since a testamentary disposition only takes effect at the moment of death and when that happens, the corporation is incomplete and the bequest

---

250 (1885) 29 Ch D 204.
251 F T Mattison 'Universities and the Law' in D J Farrington and F T Mattison (eds) *Universities and the Law* (1990, CUA/CRS) p 33.

is automatically void. 'How do I ensure that does not happen?' the determined Chancellor enquires. 'Simple: you ask the corporation to enact in valid form a provision for validity of acts during vacancies in office or membership of bodies.'[252]

1.121 'I'm feeling worse' says our friend the Chancellor. 'And I'm not well enough to attend the Court meeting next week. I'll ask someone else to deputise for me.' A shaking of heads – at common law a deputy cannot be appointed to act for an officer of the corporation unless there is clear authority in the constitution.[253] 'We'll have to ask them to create a new office – shall we call it *Vice-Chancellor* – but who would want a title like that!'

1.122 Our Secretary engages in some lateral thinking: remove the Chancellor from office and appoint a new one. Another setback: the common law rules governing removal from office are strict: if a majority vote is required it must be a majority of the whole corporation, including the persons to be removed.[254] Another piece of legislation required, this time to exclude officers and members from voting on matters relating to their own position. And surely the Chancellor would be entitled to a hearing?[255] At this point the Secretary looks for a new job.

Governance of the institutions

Introduction

1.123 The dying Chancellor story gives us at least two principles to work with: a corporation being a legal substitute for a natural person, we would expect (i) that it is only complete when all its constituent parts are present and (ii) that its government is carried on by the whole corporation. These are indeed the basic principles of the law of corporations.[256] Some small corporate bodies with limited membership do conduct their business in this way and were

252 See in respect of higher education corporations section 124A(6) ERA.
253 *R v Gravesend Corpn* (1824) 4 Dow & Ry KB 117.
254 *R v Sutton* (1711) 10 Mod Rep 74, 76.
255 Quite possibly he would: *R v Saddler's Co* (1863) 10 HL Cas 404; but see obiter dicta of Megarry J in *Gaiman v National Association for Mental Health* [1970] 2 All ER 362, 381, 382.
256 See S Kyd *A Treatise on the Law of Corporations* (Butterworths, 1793, reprinted 1978) p 107; cited by F T Mattison 'University Government and Management' in D J Farrington and F T Mattison (eds) *Universities and the Law* (1990, CUA/CRS).

it not for the provisions of the charter and statutes or their equivalent, the government of an eleemosynary corporation would be carried on by the whole body of members with the Chancellor presiding.[257] This was impracticable once medieval foundations grew in size and so the earliest charters made provision for designated subordinate bodies and officers to carry on the formal business of the corporation and the maintenance of some sort of organisational coherence. They also made provision for a wide range of other procedural matters, in many ways reflecting the practices of the ecclesiastical bodies with which they had close associations. The post-1988 constitutions are different, in that the corporation constituted by the instrument of government is separate from the institution which it conducts. The membership of the corporation is coterminous with the governing body of the institution,[258] which makes for a much simpler mode of operation.

1.124 The medieval charters, papal bulls and royal letters by which the older universities were constituted are the direct ancestors of modern higher education constitutions, with modifications to reflect the passage of time. The early Cambridge constitution[259] contains *inter alia* provisions which in modern terms cover disciplinary procedures, the determination of disputes, required qualifications of staff, admissions, timetabling, meetings of governing bodies, student residence and catering and administration. Students had to be accepted by masters, have their names entered on the roll or *matricula*, and had to pay fees. Masters were obliged to give lectures and scholars were obliged, generally speaking, to attend them.

Nomenclature of governance

1.125 Before embarking on a tour of governance, it is essential to note that the map is extraordinarily confusing. There is no standard nomenclature. On a comprehensive tour we would find Courts, Courts of Governors, Councils, Congregations, Convocations, Assemblies, Congresses, Meetings, Senates, Academic Councils, Boards of Governors, Curators of Patronage, Academic Boards, Faculty Boards and more besides. Just as we have settled on a meaning for 'Court' we find that it has two distinct meanings, as does 'Court

257 *R v Westwood* (1830) 4 Bligh N S 213, HL.
258 Eg section 124A(8) ERA.
259 See M B Hackett *The Original Statutes of Cambridge University* (1970) chapter 7.

of Governors': 'Convocation' has at least three. The author hopes that what follows is clear but close attention to nomenclature is vital if the traveller is not to get hopelessly lost. It would of course be extraordinarily helpful to our understanding if the whole system could be rationalised.

The Congregation

1.126 The last vestige of government by members en masse in the pre-1988 constitutions appears in what many English chartered universities[260] call the Congregation, which in theory at least is open to all members and at which degrees and other distinctions are conferred in the name of the whole corporation: a transition from one category of membership (student) to another (graduate) or admission as a member (honorary graduate). The Congregation had little formal power and its modern equivalent has none at all. In the post-1988 constitutions, government is by the members as a whole, since the members and the governing body are coterminous.

The separation of powers: Councils and Senates

1.127 The traditional form of collective university self-government, whether under charter or under Act of Parliament, has been based on a separation of powers between the body responsible for the control of resources, usually the Council (Court in Scotland) and the sovereign academic authority, usually the Senate or its equivalent: Senatus Academicus, Academic Council and Academic Board are common alternatives, although in some institutions these titles imply different functions. The Council has a 'lay' (ie non-staff and student) majority,[261] whereas the Senate has no lay membership.[262] In the first half of the twentieth century there was a clear shift towards what Graeme Moodie and Roland Eustace called 'internal academic self-government in all major areas of decision-making'[263] but the tide has

---

260 An example of usage outside England is Heriot-Watt University, which describes the Congregation as a 'meeting of Members of the University': Statute XVII.
261 Paragraph 8.30, Report on National Consultation, NCIHE, July 1997, envisages that this will continue.
262 The Universities of Oxford and Cambridge are entirely self-governing with no lay element, but the *Report of the Commission of Inquiry* (Oxford, 1998) envisages some external membership of a new Council.
263 G C Moodie and R Eustace *Power and Authority in British Universities* (1974) p 36.

turned against that in the current emphasis on the role of lay (independent) members of governing bodies.[264]

1.128   The division of power is not always clear cut, since English Councils typically appoint external examiners, approve the award of honorary degrees, may review teaching and instruction and both these bodies and the Courts of the ancient Scottish universities may in certain circumstances disallow acts of their Senates, a power preserved in the constitutions of the post-1992 universities.[265] It is not, however, universal practice, even among those institutions founded in the 1960s.[266] In the higher education corporations, the approval of the governing body and the Vice-Chancellor or equivalent is necessary for certain actions of the Academic Board.[267] The Courts of the new Scottish universities award degrees, etc subject to consultation with the Senates.[268] The division remains, however, to a greater or lesser degree in theory and to a large extent in practice and was until the mid-1980s in the older universities (but not, of course Oxford and Cambridge) a potential cause of conflict between the academic community and the controllers of the purse strings.[269] To some extent that potential conflict has been removed by the adoption by most universities of the recommendations of the Jarratt Report[270] for a more integrated approach to academic, physical and

264   For a critique of the current system see D J Farrington *Universities and Corporate Governance: A Model for the Future* in *Corporate Governance* Hume Papers on Public Policy 3(4), EUP (1995). See also C Bargh, P Scott and D Smith *Changing Patterns of Governance in Higher Education* University of Leeds (1995); P Scott *Governing Universities: Changing the Culture?* (1996); A Pettigrew *The New Public Management in Action* (1996).

265   Eg Article 25 The Glasgow Caledonian University (Scotland) Order of Council 1993 (SI 1993/556). Under this constitution the Court must approve a scheme for regulating the proceedings of the Senate; the Senate may not, without the approval of the Court, appoint committees although once the scheme is approved, it may appoint such committees as it considers appropriate.

266   In the Charter of the University of Stirling (1967), Article 8(1) provides that the Court is the governing body '... subject to ... the rights of the Academic Council ...'.

267   Eg Article 3.4 of the Articles of Government of the Middlesex University higher education corporation, where the approval of both the Board of Governors and the Principal and Vice-Chancellor are required before the Academic Board may appoint committees or delegate any of its functions to them.

268   Eg Article 5(2)(f) The Glasgow Caledonian University (Scotland) Order of Council 1993 (SI 1993/556).

269   See generally G Lockwood and J Davies (eds) *Universities: The Management Challenge* (1985).

270   *Report of the Steering Committee for Efficiency Studies in Universities* March 1985.

financial planning and resource allocation. In the post-1988 constitutions the problem does not arise.

1.129 The Jarratt Report recommended that Councils

> should assert their responsibilities in governing their institutions notably in respect of strategic plans to underpin academic decisions and structures which bring planning, resource allocation and accountability together into one corporate process linking academic, financial and physical planning.[271]

Senates were

> to continue to play their essential role in co-ordinating and endorsing detailed academic work and as the main forum for generating an academic view and giving advice on broad issues to Council.

The Jarratt Report also attacked the prevailing practice of decision-taking by committee, particularly in non-academic areas, by recommending that institutions should

> [save] academic and other time by having few committee meetings involving fewer people, and more delegation of authority to officers of the university – especially for non-academic matters.

Governing bodies

1.130 Today's emphasis is on lay or independent members being appointed by a transparent process,[272] with a definite time-limited term of office,[273] an upper age limit and conducting business in accordance with the so-called 'Nolan' principles to be discussed later. NCIHE[274] describes systems in Australia and New Zealand where recent reviews (Hoare Committee, Australia 1995 and Education Act 1989, New Zealand) have led to smaller and therefore arguably more effective governing bodies. In Australia the members are identified by an external professional process.

---

271 The preparation of such plans by all institutions is now a requirement of the Funding Councils.
272 See CUC (1995) *Advice on University Governance* CVCP N/95/7(a).
273 Paragraph 15.45 Main Report, NCIHE, July 1997, recommends not more than two terms, usually three–four years each, unless members also hold office.
274 Appendix 5, Main Report, NCIHE, July 1997.

1.131   In the 1990s there was considerable activity in the area of governance in business and industry, resulting in the reports of the Cadbury Committee[275] and Greenbury Study Group.[276] Other reports were issued on executive pay and the need for remuneration committees.[277] In 1994 the Prime Minister established a Committee on Standards in Public Life chaired by Lord Nolan and universally known as the Nolan Committee. Its terms of reference were 'To examine current concerns about standards of conduct of all holders of public office, including arrangements related to financial and commercial activities, and make recommendations as to any changes in present arrangements which might be required to ensure the highest standards of propriety in public life.'

1.132   Nolan's first Report concentrated on Parliamentary matters, where some highly publicised personal difficulties had given rise to its creation, but its second Report entered the area of higher education. In its first Report the Nolan Committee set out seven principles of conduct in public life: selflessness, integrity, objectivity, accountability, openness, honesty and leadership. In its second Report it identified common threads as (i) use of codes of conduct (ii) encouragement of independent scrutiny (iii) availability of guidance and training for governing bodies and managers. It also set out broad themes: (i) appointment and accountability of board members (ii) the role of boards in relation to officers and staff (iii) safeguards in respect of conflicts of interest.

1.133   Unfortunately the concentrated interest on good governance in institutions of higher education has arisen mainly from a series of well-publicised institutional failings, leading to reports from the Committee of Public Accounts and the National Audit Office on such matters as severance payments.[278] One result is that institutions are

275 Report and Code of Best Practice of the Cadbury Committee on Financial Aspects of Corporate Governance (1992), succeeded by the Hampel Committee on Corporate Governance.
276 *Directors' Remuneration* – Report of a Study Group chaired by Sir Richard Greenbury (1995).
277 PRONED Guidelines on Executive Pay (1992); IoD Framework for Remuneration Committees (1995).
278 Severance Payments to Senior Staff in the Publicly Funded Education Sector (1995); Proper Conduct of Public Business (1994); Governance and Management of Overseas Courses at the Swansea Institute of Higher Education (HC 222 1996/97); Independent Inquiry Report by Mr Jeremy Lever QC – Summary of Conclusions, University of Portsmouth (1995); University of Portsmouth (HC4 1997/98): the further education sector has also been the subject of inquiry: eg FEFC Report of Inquiry into Derby Tertiary College Wilmorton (1994); FEFC Report of Inquiry into St Philip's RC Sixth Form College (1994).

now expected (and indeed may be contractually obliged by the terms of Financial Memoranda with the Funding Councils) to follow the provisions of the Guides for Members of Governing Bodies issued by CUC[279] for England and Wales and by CSIC and others[280] for Scotland. These include clear provisions for avoiding conflict of interest, including the adoption of a Register of Interests. NCIHE addressed these issues in a lengthy chapter of its Report.[281] This proposed a Code of Practice for Governance with the following components: unambiguous identity of the governing body; clarity of decision-making; appropriate membership and size of governing body; arrangements for engaging formally with external constituencies; a rolling review of the effectiveness of the governing body and institutions; reporting annually on institutional performance; arrangements to address grievances by students and staff; effective academic governance.

Other bodies

1.134 Three other types of body confuse the picture and the existence of at least one (the Court) contributed to the first element of the NCIHE's proposed Code of Practice for Governance:

(i) Most pre-1992/3 English and Welsh universities' constitutions establish a body called the Court,[282] sometimes described somewhat grandly as the 'Supreme Governing Body' with 'absolute power within the University'[283]: in some of the later English charters and the Scottish charters this body, under various names – Court, Conference, Convocation, General Convocation – has more limited powers;

(ii) In some universities the collective body of all graduates (Convocation, General Council, Graduates' Association or equivalent) or a mixed body of certain graduates and staff (Cambridge's Regent House) enjoys considerable formal authority. The General Council of an ancient Scottish university elects the Chancellor and may make observations on any resolution or ordinance promoted by the University Court: this

279 Guide for Members of Governing Bodies of Universities and Colleges in England and Wales (1995).
280 Guide for Members of Governing Bodies (1996).
281 Chapter 15, Main Report, NCIHE, July 1997.
282 Court of Governors in the constituent colleges of the University of Wales.
283 Eg *Charter of the University of Hull*, Article 10. At least one chartered university has successfully petitioned for a change in its charter to remove the 'governing' function of the Court as a potential source of conflict with the real governing body, the Council.

body did at one time have considerable importance: for example in the general congregation at Glasgow (the Comitia) '... the Rector is elected and admitted to his office; public disputations are heard; inaugural discourses are delivered; the laws of the University are promulgated, and prizes for merit distributed annually' [284]; however in many universities the alumni association, while active, has no or very limited powers, on occasion electing a member of the governing body;[285]

(iii) most of the pre-1992 universities have some form of debating forum for staff (eg Assembly, Meeting) or certain categories of staff (eg Academic Congress, Academic Assembly, Academic Council, Congregation) and in some universities this enjoys formal powers – for example the Congregation of the University of Oxford (not to be confused with a degree Congregation) made news in 1993 by overturning a decision of another body (the Council – although this is not a Council in the common usage) to create a number of additional professorships on the grounds of attempting to redress the imbalance in gender among promoted posts and in 1996/7 was once again in the news by refusing to sanction a plan for the erection of a business school on a site in central Oxford[286] and overturning an attempt to reduce the maximum voting age from 75 to 65. The new universities and other institutions have no formal requirement for bodies of this type.

The graduate and staff bodies derive their origins directly from the medieval constitutions; the Courts were established to reflect the interests of local and, to a limited extent, national organisations in the work of the universities.

The English chartered university – introduction

1.135 Although the English chartered university is now a minority species, the form of government adopted by it has stood the test of time reasonably well and many of its features have been incorporated into the new forms adopted for the post-1992/3 universities and crept north of the border into the charters and statutes of the 1960s university foundations. To illustrate the workings of the system, this section will refer to the powers and functions of the various bodies established by the charter and statutes of an existing university

284 J B Hay *Inaugural Addresses by Lords Rectors of the University of Glasgow* (1839) p xxxi.
285 Eg University of Stirling Statute 9.
286 It subsequently agreed to another site. Reforms are proposed in 1998.

founded originally as a University College in the 1920s and securing a charter in the 1950s, and having made a number of modernising amendments since then. Broadly speaking, the constitutions of the Welsh universities (except Glamorgan where the constitution follows the post-1992 pattern) and the Northern Irish universities are similar to those of the English chartered universities.

The University Court (in England)

1.136   One body which has not commended itself to later draftsmen is the Court, (sometimes called the Convocation).[287] This sits at the pinnacle of power in the typical pre-Robbins university, except where its power has been diluted by a successful petition to the Privy Council for an appropriate amendment to the charter and statutes to remove its legislative and other formal powers. It is a constituent element of all the chartered institutions. For historical or other reasons there is some variation in its constitution and powers.[288] There is no logical explanation for the difference between the limited powers of the Court in the Charter of the University of Sussex (1961),[289] where the functions were limited to appointing the Chancellor and other honorific officers and receiving reports, and the 'supreme governing' powers of the Court in the Charter of the University of Kent at Canterbury (1965) where, unusually, the Court was to appoint the Vice-Chancellor.[290]

1.137   The origin of its current form lies in the constitution of the late nineteenth century colleges which became universities at the turn of the century. One of its objectives was to keep the new universities in touch with their communities. However, its legislative power was based on the fear that when separate charters were sought by the northern universities, they would exercise their new independence in competing for students by lowering their standards. Although not many of the 300-odd members of the Court would have much understanding of the highly technical matters which degree ordinances were framed to regulate, the fact that the main rules governing the award of degrees had to be submitted to a body which held its meetings in public was calculated to restrain any attempt to

---

287 Eg University of Aston in Birmingham, Charter Article 10.
288 The last Robbins era Charter, that of Stirling, (a Scottish university) has a *sui generis* Conference with only one significant power, that of appointing a member of the governing body (the Court).
289 University of Sussex, Charter Article 10 and Statute XIII.
290 University of Kent at Canterbury, Statute VI.

lower standards. In a meeting of the Court the representatives of other universities could, if need be, voice their objections in the presence of the Press.[291]

1.138   The modern Court is the closest a chartered institution comes to what in companies limited by shares would be called a shareholder's meeting. It is not a meeting of all the members (the Congregation) but represents the interests of all classes of members and of other relevant bodies, including, often, other universities and representatives of professional bodies with an interest in the quality of its work. As an example, the Court of the specimen university consists of the following classes of members, with numbers in parentheses (avoiding double counting as far as identifiable):

Class 1:   Officers (5)
Class 2:   Life Members (donors of more than £1000 and a few others) (12)
Class 3:   Representatives of public authorities (up to 70)
Class 4:   Representatives of Churches (8)
Class 5:   Members of Parliament (up to 13)*
Class 6:   Ex Officio Members (20)
Class 7:   Representatives of the University (160)*
Class 8:   Representatives of other institutions (8)*
Class 9:   Representatives of Commercial and Trade Societies and other bodies (10)*
Class 10:   Representatives of Learned Societies and Professional Bodies (13)
Class 11:   Representatives of Colleges and Schools (15)*
Class 12:   Other persons (23)*

The numbers in asterisked categories are approximate, since the Court has considerable power to vary the numbers within them. The total membership is about 360, including all members of the Council, the Senate and the Officers. Given the nature of the Court as the 'Supreme Governing Body' it may be thought rather odd that its membership is not more strictly prescribed and that it is of such an unmanageable size.

1.139   At the annual Court meeting the principal officers (the Vice-Chancellor or Principal and Treasurer or equivalent) present reports to the Court on the work of the university and its accounts for the previous academic and financial year (which typically will have ended six to eight months earlier) and there is an opportunity to question

291 A W Chapman *The Story of a Modern University. A History of The University of Sheffield* (1955) p 198.

them on their stewardship. Typically also this will be the occasion on which Ordinances, recommended for approval by the Council, are formally enacted.[292] Some of these features are preserved in the later charters which do not accord the Court the same status as the earlier ones.

1.140 As described in the Charter, the 'Supreme Governing Body' with 'absolute power' could theoretically do whatever it wished, and it is this aspect which has concerned NCIHE, but in fact in the specimen University and in many others its powers are circumscribed in the Statutes:

> The Court shall exercise all the powers and authorities of the University except to the extent to which the exercise of the same may by the Charter or Statutes be otherwise provided for.

Somewhat watered-down 'absolute power': furthermore the Statute goes on to say:

> The Court shall exercise control over the Senate through the Council and not otherwise ... and over the Council by means of Statutes and Resolutions passed at meetings of the Court and not otherwise.

1.141 What is meant by 'Resolutions' in this context is unclear, although the intention is probably to follow the reasoning in the 1906 case *Automatic Self-cleansing Filter Syndicate Co v Cuninghame*,[293] where it was held that a general meeting could not, by simple resolution, overrule the Board of Directors in an area reserved to the Board in the company's articles. A special resolution would be required. In 1983 a Visitor was called upon to adjudicate in a dispute over the levying on students of an 'amenity fee' by the Council of a university as part of a cost-saving and income-generation package adopted following the public expenditure cuts of the early 1980s.[294] The Visitor's opinion can be summarised as being to restrict the 'Resolutions' to precisely those set out in the Statutes with a capital 'R' which relate to the making of changes to the Charter and Statutes and fixing the dates of meetings, not to 'resolutions' in the normal use of the word. Thus it was open to the Council to ignore a 'resolution' of the Court overturning its decision to introduce the fee, and it did so.

292 The universities with Courts managed without them in wartime, as the Chartered and Other Bodies (Temporary Provisions) Act 1939 enabled the Court to delegate its legislative authority to the Council.
293 [1906] 2 Ch 34.
294 *Reference to the Visitor of the University of Hull*, May 1983.

1.142 The options available to a Court aggrieved by the refusal of the Council to abide by its resolutions would be

(i) to attempt to alter the composition of the Council by Resolution amending the relevant Statute (which would be subject to the approval of the Privy Council and therefore most unlikely to succeed); and/or

(ii) to replace its appointees on the Council, where they might possibly hold the balance of power; and/or

(iii) to remove the Council from office.

None of these courses of action was adopted in the dispute over the 'amenity fee' which was settled by alternative means. The analogous situation in a limited company arose in *John Shaw & Sons (Salford) Ltd v Shaw*[295] where Greer LJ held that a special resolution removing the directors would be the only course of action available.[296] What if the Court by Resolution removed all the members of the Council? The procedure for removing individual members of the Council for 'good cause' would not apply, since only the Council itself can remove members in that way and then only for serious misbehaviour or incapability. As the power to remove the Council en bloc is not reserved to the Council or Senate and the Court has 'absolute power' then presumably there is nothing to stop it doing whatever it wishes in this respect.

1.143 It is also possible that the Court holds the equivalent of what Professor Jim Gower describes as the 'default powers of the general meeting' in a limited company.[297] The Court might have power as the 'Supreme Governing Body' to intervene in extreme circumstances such as

(i) where the Council was hopelessly deadlocked[298] – although not simply where a defined majority could not be obtained as in the common requirement for a three-fourths majority for the approval of Ordinances or the removal of certain categories of staff;[299]

(ii) where no Council members had been appointed or a quorum was unobtainable;[300]

---

295 [1935] 2 KB 113, 134.

296 An ordinary resolution is now sufficient in these circumstances: section 303 Companies Act 1985.

297 L C B Gower, *Principles of Modern Company Law* (1992) pp 152–153.

298 By analogy with *Barron v Porter* [1914] 1 Ch 895.

299 By analogy with *Quin and Axtens v Salmon* [1909] AC 442, HL and *Breckland Group Holdings v London and Suffolk Properties* [1989] BCLC 100.

300 By analogy with *Alexander Ward & Co v Samyang Navigation Co* [1975] 1 WLR 673, HL and *Foster v Foster* [1916] 1 Ch 532.

(iii) where the members of the Council were disqualified from voting,[301] perhaps by reason of civil or criminal liability or conflict of interest on a large scale.

1.144   In the course of oral argument in *Pearce v University of Aston in Birmingham (No 2)*[302] it is said that the Visitor (Lord Browne-Wilkinson) speculated that if the Council persisted in its action of making certain academic staff redundant, the Visitor might be able to remove the members from office or revoke the charter. This power has not been tested but in principle it would appear that the remarks attributed to his Lordship are in substance correct, although it may be argued that only a successful petition for a writ of *scire facias* or an exercise of the royal prerogative will revoke a charter. It is not clear, however, how such action whether by the Visitor or otherwise would be of any benefit to persons in the position of the petitioners in this or any similar case. *Scire facias* may be resorted to in order to enforce the forfeiture of a charter for misuser or nonuser where there is an existing corporate body which has abused its power, but it is not an adequate remedy for abuses, since it destroys the corporation.[303] Presumably the Visitor could also take action of this kind if the Council or Senate purported to terminate a student's registration in breach of internal procedures. It is arguably unsatisfactory that both the Court and the Visitor appear to have authority to remove the Council from office.

1.145   The possible existence of reserve powers apart, it is commonly accepted that the Court is of little if any practical value but is an important opportunity for a wide range of interests to hear about the work of the university and a firm date in the local social calendar. All of its formal powers could readily be transferred to the Council or equivalent, as is the case in Scotland in some of the newer chartered universities and in the post-1992 universities. NCIHE has recommended that any uncertainty as to the locus of executive authority should be removed. That would affect the powers of the Court, but unlikely to affect the powers of the Visitor. There is of course nothing to stop any institution without a Court from having a public meeting or establishing advisory or consultative groups with a range of members of the community, with no formal authority.

---

301 By analogy with *Irvine v Union Bank of Australia* (1877) 2 App Cas 366, PC.
302 [1991] 2 All ER 469.
303 See eg the US case *Turnpike Co v State* 3 Wall 210 (1865).

The University Council

1.146 The Council is the executive governing body: in the specimen university it is described as 'the governing body and executive.'[304] Its composition is
(i)   the Chancellor (who by convention does not attend);
(ii)   the Pro-Chancellors (one of whom is in the chair and who holds office as Chairman of Council);
(iii) the Vice-Chancellor;
(iv)   the Treasurer;
(v)   the Pro-Vice-Chancellors;
(vi)   six external members appointed by the Court;
(vii) four members appointed by local authorities;
(viii) five members of the Senate (one to be of non-professorial status);
(ix)   up to six external members appointed by the Council itself;
(x)   up to two representatives of affiliated institutions;
(xi)   two members of the non-academic staff;
(xii) one member of the academic-related staff;
(xiii) two members appointed by the Convocation (the association of graduates); and
(xiv) two student representatives.

1.147 This is somewhat larger than the 12–25 members prescribed for the governing bodies of the post-1992 universities and over the ceiling of 25 proposed by NCIHE.[305] The balance is always in favour of non-staff and student membership appointed by the various constituencies indicated. It is not normal to find arrangements for members of the Council to receive financial loss or travel allowances, although local authority nominees may be in receipt of statutory allowances from the appointing authority. Non ex-officio members of the Council may be removed from office either by the body appointing them (the Privy Council, the Senate, the local authorities, the student union) or by 'good cause' procedures specified in the statutes.

1.148 There are 27 formal powers of the Council listed in the Statutes: these relate to the management of the university's resources (staff, financial and estates), organisation, drafting legislation, making

304 This language may itself be out of line with the modern concept of separation of the governing body, acting in a supervisory role, from the executive which it supervises.
305 Paragraph 15.49, Main Report, NCIHE, July 1997. In recommendation 56 NCIHE proposes that the change to a governing body of limited size be accomplished within three years, ie by summer 2000.

regulations, formal approval of honorary degrees, the appointment of external examiners and oversight of the work of the Senate. The Council 'drafts' changes to the Statutes and Ordinances for approval by the Court but in recent times there are no instances of such drafts having been rejected by the Court. The Council is the body which is 'to carry the Charter, Statutes, Ordinances and Regulations into effect' and it is therefore the Council rather than the Court which is effectively the 'supreme governing body.' The Council is in the position of employer and is the body which has formal responsibility for contracts. It exercises the ultimate disciplinary power over both staff and students. In carrying out its work it is now expected to follow the guidance for governing bodies described earlier.

The University Senate

1.149 The Senate or its equivalent is responsible for academic affairs, sometimes described as the 'governing body of the University in all academic matters'[306] in which case the powers of the Council in this area are limited, although academic development cannot be undertaken in a resource vacuum. In many universities, the membership of the Senate, which was traditionally dominated by the professoriate, has undergone substantial revision in recent years, to make it a smaller, more cost-effective and efficient body, coming closer in this respect to the smaller Academic Boards typical of the former polytechnics. In the university chosen as an example, the Senate is 'subject to the control and approval of the Council' and its responsibility is to 'regulate and superintend the education and discipline of students and of undergraduates of the University.' It now consists of senior academic officers, representatives of school boards and students, a total of 62 members. When all professors were automatically members, the total membership was well in excess of 100.

1.150 The Senate in the specimen university has 18 formal powers concerned with the regulation of teaching (including by implication the university's responsibility for quality control), and the promotion of research and the discipline of students, other than expulsion, which is in the hands of the Council. It may appoint 'Examiners' (meaning internal examiners) and may suspend or remove them for negligence or misconduct: such powers may be delegated to the Vice-Chancellor. The exercise of powers of suspension or removal would presumably

306 Eg *Charter of the University of Surrey*, Article 13.

be subject to the rules of natural justice and could be appealed both to the Council (under its powers to entertain grievances) or to the Visitor. If a separable appointment, presumably such action could also be challenged in an employment tribunal. The Senate has power to give directions to the Schools and to overrule their decisions. It exercises the university's powers to award degrees and other academic distinctions, other than honorary degrees.[307]

Other English universities – Introduction

1.151 ERA provided the basis for the government structure of the higher education corporations and other bodies transferred from local authority control and provided these bodies, and the institutions which they now conduct as universities, with a modern, relatively straightforward and streamlined system. The other institutions which are not chartered retain forms of government very similar to the chartered institutions. As pointed out above, the University of Newcastle-Upon-Tyne may be treated as a chartered institution for the purposes of this book. The constitution of the University of London has been reviewed and a new system came into operation in 1994 but the incorporation of the University by its Royal Charter of 1863 is unaffected.[308] The Universities of Oxford and Cambridge have constitutions which are complicated by the existence of the colleges and as they constitute such a small part of the system, no attempt will be made to describe them in detail.

Higher education corporations

(i) INTRODUCTION

1.152 A higher education corporation 'conducts' the university just as it previously conducted a non-university institution. This is the precise legal term presumably meaning the management of the business of a university: an example is the Order of Council of 26 April 1993 making the instrument of government for the University of Northumbria at Newcastle higher education corporation, which then conducts the University of Northumbria at Newcastle. Therefore

---

307 Confusion sometimes arises when Senates, etc have the power to 'award' but the Chancellor has the right to 'confer' which the dictionaries define as 'grant or bestow.' It is clear that the Chancellor can only confer what the Senate has awarded.
308 Section 7 University of London Act 1994.

the form of government is that of the corporation. The principal body is commonly known as the Board of Governors or Court of Governors. For the purposes of this section, the term Board of Governors will be used.[309]

(II) THE BOARD OF GOVERNORS

1.153   The typical corporation is governed by an instrument made under section 124A(3) and (4) ERA. Section 124A and Schedules 7 and 7A ERA set out the basic requirements but under section 124A(9) the Secretary of State has specified powers to change the overall requirements of Schedule 7A for instruments of government in respect of size and membership, including the eligibility for membership of employees, students and local authority representatives, and the interpretation of the schedules. The members of the corporation which conducts the institution are the members of the Board of Governors. This body is charged with formal powers equivalent to a combination of the Court and the Council of a chartered institution. The chief executive officer (Director, Principal, Rector, Provost or Vice-Chancellor) also enjoys considerable formal powers, whereas the Academic Board is placed in a subordinate position to the Board of Governors in all respects, and to the chief executive in some respects.

1.154   The responsibilities of the Board of Governors are:[310]
(i)   the determination of the educational character and mission of the University and for oversight of its activities;
(ii)   the effective and efficient use of resources, the solvency of the institution and for safeguarding its assets;
(iii) approving the annual estimates of income and expenditure and the annual accounts;
(iv) the appointment, grading, assignment, appraisal, suspension, dismissal and determination of the pay and conditions of service of the Vice-Chancellor, the Clerk of the Board of Governors and the holders of such other senior posts as the Board of Governors may determine. The Board of Governors shall also have responsibility for setting a framework for the pay and conditions of other members of the staff;
(v)   the appointment of external auditors.

---

309 For information about the way in which polytechnics were governed before ERA see Locke, Pratt, Silverman and Travers *Polytechnic Government* (1987).
310 Article 5, Articles of Association of the Manchester Metropolitan University higher education corporation.

1.155 The Board of Governors of a typical higher education corporation is made up of between 12 and 24 members plus the Principal, unless he or she chooses not to be a member. A 'ceiling' of 25 members was commended as general practice for all institutions by NCIHE.[311] A lay majority is secured[312] and there is a reserve power under paragraph 7 of Schedule 7A ERA to ensure this. Of the appointed members

(a) up to 13 shall be independent members;

(b) up to two may be teachers at the university nominated by the Academic Board and up to two may be students of the university nominated by the students thereof; and

(c) at least one and not more than nine shall be co-opted members nominated by the members of the Board of Governors who are not co-opted members.[313]

1.156 It is the possibility that staff and students may lawfully be excluded from the governing body which has caused considerable debate. Following problems experienced with the exercise of this power at the University of Huddersfield, CUC *Advice on University Governance*[314] suggests that a governing body should approach the exclusion of such representation 'with very great care' and should record formally in its minutes the grounds for any such exclusion and should publish these grounds within the institution. It was suggested to the Nolan Committee that in some circumstances there might be 'improper collusion between a small group of lay members and the Chief Executive.'[315]

1.157 Independent members of a higher education corporation must be persons appearing to the appointing authority (in practice, the existing independent members) to have experience of, and to have shown capacity in, industrial, commercial or employment matters or the practice of any profession. In addition the co-opted member required in (c) must be a person who has experience in the provision of education. Other co-opted members may be staff, students or

311 Paragraph 15.52, Main Report, NCIHE, July 1997.
312 Article 4(3) of the Instrument of Government of the Middlesex University higher education corporation.
313 Paragraph 3 of Schedule 7A ERA; see for example Article 3 of the Instrument of Government of the Middlesex University higher education corporation, 29 March 1993 and of the Instrument of Government of the University of Northumbria at Newcastle higher education corporation, 26 April 1993.
314 (1995) CVCP N/95/7(a).
315 Statement by the University of Newcastle-Upon-Tyne, submitted to the Committee on Standards in Public Life (Nolan) and quoted in its Second Report (1996) p 31.

elected members of local authorities, but these persons are not eligible for appointment as independent members. These provisions distinguish the higher education corporations from the chartered universities since there are no equivalent provisions in charters: in fact, many charters give ex officio membership to local authority representatives. The category of independent members is, as in most of the chartered institutions, without further measures of control self-perpetuating and self-regulatory.

1.158 The instruments of government make provision for the removal of members of the Board of Governors who are either unable to unfit to discharge the functions of member or are absent for a period of 12 months.[316] By contrast, whereas most charters make provision for the removal of individuals for 'good cause' it is not usual to find provision in charters for members to be removed for failing to attend meetings.[317] It is normal to find provision for the payment of financial loss allowances and travelling expenses to members of the Board of Governors of a higher education corporation.

(III) THE ACADEMIC BOARD

1.159 A typical instrument of government makes the Academic Board responsible[318]

(a) subject to the requirements of validating and accrediting bodies, for: general issues relating to the research, scholarship, teaching and courses at the institution, including criteria for the admission of students; the appointment and removal of internal and external examiners; policies and procedures for assessment and examination of the academic performance of students; the content of the curriculum; academic standards and the validation and review of courses; the procedures for the award of qualifications and honorary academic titles; and the procedures for the expulsion of students for academic reasons;

(b) for considering the development of the academic activities of the [University] and the resources needed to support them and for

---

316 The equivalent provision in local government is for removal after six months' absence: Section 85 Local Government Act 1972.
317 The Statutes of the University of London (1994) provide an exception. Subject to provisos in the Statutes and Ordinances, there is automatic cessation of membership of a member of the Council (other than an ex-officio member) who is absent from all meetings during 12 consecutive months.
318 Article 3.3, Articles of Association of the University of Northumbria at Newcastle higher education corporation.

giving advice thereon to the [Vice-Chancellor] and, through the [Vice-Chancellor], the Board of Governors;

(c) for advising on such other matters as the Board of Governors or the [Vice-Chancellor] may refer to the Academic Board.

1.160   A typical Academic Board has up to 40 members. The Vice-Chancellor is the Chairman; Members of the Directorate, Deans, Heads of Departments and Academic Services total 21; and there are 10 members of teaching staff, three other staff, three students and up to two co-opted members. This constitution is more biased towards 'management' than the constitutions of most of the Senates of the chartered universities, some of which retain the automatic membership of the entire professoriate.

Companies limited by guarantee

(I)   INTRODUCTION

1.161   A university which is a company limited by guarantee has a somewhat different form of government based on the requirements of the Companies Acts. In this case it is the institution itself which is incorporated.[319] The number of members is limited by the instrument of government (the Articles of Association): a typical number would be 25[320] and the members of the Court of Governors may become members of the university on application. There is no other category of membership.

(II)   THE COURT OF GOVERNORS

1.162   The Court of Governors of the typical company comprises the Director (ex officio), 13 governors appointed by the governors in this category (ie independent governors), two governors appointed by local authorities, two governors who are members of the academic staff appointed by the Court on the nomination of the Academic Council, one governor who is a member of the academic staff appointed by the Court on the nomination of the academic staff, one governor who is a member of the non-academic staff appointed by the Court on the nomination of the non-academic staff, one student

---

319   An example is The University of Greenwich, originally transferred from local authority control in March 1989 as the Thames Polytechnic, with a change of name approved by the Privy Council under section 77 FHEA taking effect in June 1992.

320   Article 4, Articles of Association of the University of Greenwich.

governor (over the age of 18) appointed by the Court on the nomination of the students and four additional governors appointed by the Court: qualifications for this category may be restricted and two of them must be persons who have experience in the provision of education.[321]

1.163 As in the case of the higher education corporations, the main body of governors must be chosen from those appearing to the governors to have experience of, and to have shown capacity in industrial, commercial or employment matters or the practice of any profession.[322] They must not be members of staff or students and the Articles normally place further restrictions on membership by relations and former employees.[323] There are length of service and age restrictions and, as in the higher education corporations, governors may be removed for being unfit or unable to discharge their duties or being absent from meetings for a defined period. To comply with the provisions of the Companies Acts, governors automatically cease to hold office if they become bankrupt or make any voluntary arrangement with their creditors under the provisions of the Insolvency Act 1986. They are also subject to the régime of the Company Directors Disqualification Act 1986.

1.164 The powers of the Court of Governors are similar to those of the Council of a chartered university or the Board of Governors of a higher education corporation, with the exception that they are to be exercised 'subject to the powers of the Members in general meeting.' These powers are not the same as those of the Congregation or the Court of a chartered university but are those of the general meeting of a company limited by guarantee under the Companies Act 1985. The members may elect to dispense with the holding of an annual general meeting.[324] The Court, or in the absence of a quorum any member of the Court or any two members of the University, is empowered to call an extraordinary general meeting.[325] A general meeting has the 'default powers' which may apply to an English chartered university's Court.

---

321 In the case of The University of Greenwich, one governor out of the four is appointed after consultation with the Trades Union Congress and another after consultation with the Commission for Racial Equality.
322 Article 8(1), Articles of Association of The University of Greenwich.
323 Article 9, Articles of Association of The University of Greenwich.
324 Sections 366A and 379A Companies Act 1985.
325 Eg Article 21, Articles of Association of The University of Greenwich.

(III) THE ACADEMIC COUNCIL

1.165 While the Court of Governors has power to delegate to the Academic Council such powers and functions as the Court shall think fit including power to sub-delegate, the Articles of Association set out in a Schedule the composition and functions of the Academic Council and no changes to that may be made without the approval of the Privy Council.[326] The Schedule sets out the composition of the Academic Council as being

> ... not more than 40 members reflecting the academic structure of the [University] of whom one shall be the Director (ex officio) and of whom not less than 50% shall be appointed members, not less than 30% elected teacher members and not less than 10% student members.

The appointed members are drawn from the Deputy Directors, Assistant Directors, Deans of Faculty and Heads of academic or related departments. The Director is the Chairman. The functions of the Council, which are to be exercised 'within the general policy of the [University] and subject to the ultimate responsibility of the Court,'[327] are detailed in 17 sub-paragraphs but are in practice the same as those of the Academic Board of the higher education corporation. In this as in the majority of universities the Academic Council has the power to confer the award of academic qualifications, prizes or other distinctions as may be agreed with the Court.

1.166 The prescription of percentage membership by category totals 90% plus one (the Director) so that it would be possible for the student membership to rise to seven of a total of 40. In itself a 10% student membership is high: most constitutions, as we have seen, restrict the student membership to two or possibly three.

Scottish universities

THE UNIVERSITY COURT

1.167 The 13 Scottish universities fall into three groups, as described fully earlier. There are four ancients, four institutions with modern Royal Charters and five governed by Orders of Council made under FHESA. The forms of government differ between and within these groups and the terminology used is as confusing as in England.

---

326 Article 16(1), Articles of Association of The University of Greenwich.
327 First Schedule, paragraph 9, Articles of Association of The University of Greenwich.

Some bodies, such as the Curators of Patronage who technically recommend the appointment of the Principal of Edinburgh University to the Court, are sui generis.

1.168   All the Scottish universities are governed by Courts. In the ancient and post-1992 universities the Courts have considerable formal power over the activities of the Senate or Senatus, this body being appointed by the Court in the new universities. The four modern chartered Universities have adopted a model in which the powers of the Court are separate from those of the Senate or Academic Council. The Court has no formal power over the Senate or its equivalent other than, in exercise of its resource powers, to decline to grant resources for academic activities proposed by the Senate. The power of the English chartered university's Court to make Ordinances on the recommendation of the Council is discharged in Scotland by the Court of the chartered institutions and the equivalent power to make regulations is discharged by the governing body of the post-1992 institutions. In the ancient universities, broadly speaking, what are elsewhere in the pre-1992 system called Statutes are called Ordinances, and what are elsewhere called Ordinances are called Regulations.

1.169   There is no precise equivalent to the Court of a chartered English university: the University Court's powers in Scotland broadly approximate to those of the English Council and in the four chartered institutions the Court also possesses the legislative powers of the English Court (where that body still has such powers). The nearest approximation to the English Court is called the Conference (Stirling), the Graduates' Council (Dundee), the Convocation (Heriot-Watt) and the General Convocation (Strathclyde). All these bodies, the composition of which varies, meet annually to receive the Principal's report and the audited accounts and may discuss any matter but have no other significant powers. The University of Stirling's Conference is the body with membership categories nearest to that of the English Court, having about 120 members including the Lord Lieutenant, Sheriffs Principal, MPs, representatives of local authorities, churches, professional organisations, and all the other Scottish universities plus all members of the governing body (the Court), office holders and staff and student representatives. Its only real power is to appoint a lay member of the Court. The new universities have no equivalent body, while the ancients have General Councils which in addition to receiving the annual reports etc[328] also have the right to be

328   Section 12(1) Universities (Scotland) Act 1966.

consulted before the Court exercises prescribed powers.[329] The membership of the General Council is, in summary, the Chancellor, members of the University Court, academic staff and graduates.[330] It appoints members to the University Court.

The ancient universities

1.170 The composition of the Courts of the ancient Scottish universities is prescribed by the Universities (Scotland) Act 1966,[331] consisting largely of 'assessors.' The Rector, elected by students (except in Edinburgh where staff also have a vote), is Chairman and the Principal is Vice-Chairman. Assessors are appointed by the local authority, the Chancellor, the General Council and the Senatus Academicus. There are also student members, employee representatives and some co-opted lay members. The powers of the Courts of the ancient universities are set out in the Universities (Scotland) Acts 1858–1966. They are very similar to those of the chartered and post-1992 institutions. Schedule 2 to the 1966 Act sets out the current arrangements for the enactment of Ordinances, which are submitted to the Privy Council for approval in the same way as Statutes of the modern chartered universities.

The chartered Scottish universities

1.171 The only modern chartered universities in Scotland are those of the 1960s.[332] They are not governed by the Universities (Scotland) Acts 1858–1966, so it is not surprising to find many similarities between the composition of the Courts of these institutions and the English chartered universities' Councils. The composition of the Court in a specimen chartered Scottish university is: the Principal, one member nominated by the Chancellor, such persons not exceeding two in number from among those appointed as Deputy Principals, four members appointed by the Academic Council from its own number, two members appointed by the non-professorial members of the Academic Assembly (the general meeting of academic and related staff) from among the Academic Assembly appointees to the Academic Council, the Chairman of [the local Council] whom

---

329 Part II and Schedule 2 Universities (Scotland) Act 1966.
330 Section 6 Universities (Scotland) Act 1858.
331 Schedule 1, Part I (St Andrews), Part II (Glasgow), Part III (Aberdeen) and Part IV (Edinburgh).
332 It will be recalled that the ancient universities still exist as common law corporations founded by charter or equivalent, but they are not considered as 'chartered' in the present context.

failing, the Vice-Chairman, the President and Vice-President and Treasurer of the Students' Association, one member appointed by the Conference, one member appointed by the Graduates' Association from its own number and up to eight members co-opted by the Court.[333] As usual, a lay majority is preserved, and the Court elects a Chairman from among a defined category of members excluding staff and students, the Principal being Vice-Chairman.

1.172 This constitution, while broadly similar to the others, nevertheless has several distinct features. First, it expressly encourages local authority participation by the 'whom failing' provision for the local authority seat. Second, it includes full members drawn from a variety of categories (the Chancellor's nominee, the nominees of the Graduates' Association and Conference), in addition to those appointed by the Court itself, who may be expected to be drawn from individuals whose experience and expertise is similar to that specified for independent members in the newer constitutions, although no such criteria are specified in the relevant Statute. Following the concerns expressed about good governance by the Nolan Committee and others this Court, in common with most others, has established a Court Appointments Committee to ensure that fair and open procedures are in place for the appointment of lay members by the Court itself. Such procedures do not however apply to the selection of members by the Conference or the Graduates' Association.

1.173 The powers of the Court are very similar to those of the Council of a chartered university in England, on which they appear to be modelled, except that there is no power to interfere with the decisions of the Academic Council (Senate) in academic matters, nor does the Court have any role in the appointment of examiners or the approval of honorary degrees.

THE POST-1992 SCOTTISH UNIVERSITIES

1.174 In the post-1992 institutions the Court is created a corporate body in its own right,[334] whereas corporate status in the chartered institutions is conferred on the university itself. The Court of the post-1992 universities possesses all powers of the institution. Various words are used to describe the general power of the Court as

---

333 Statute 9 University of Stirling (1967, revised 1993, 1996 and 1997).
334 Eg The University Court of The Glasgow Caledonian University constituted under Article 3, The Glasgow Caledonian University (Scotland) Order of Council (SI 1993/556).

governing body, including 'manage' and 'administer.' Part III of the Glasgow Caledonian University (Scotland) Order of Council 1993,[335] under the rubric 'Principal functions of the University Court,' states: 'The University Court shall conduct the University and carry out and promote its objects.' (The objects are defined separately). The corresponding provision in the University of Paisley (Scotland) Order 1993[336] is

> The general functions of the Court are to manage, administer and conduct the University for the objects of providing education, undertaking and carrying out research, promoting teaching, scholarship and research ...

All the Courts of the new universities are required by the instrument of government to delegate certain academic matters to the Senate or Academic Board, but with the power to disallow any act under delegated authority.

1.175 The constitution is similar, but not identical to, that of an English higher education corporation. The ordinary membership is made up of appointed and co-opted, ex-officio and staff or elected governors.[337] The appointed governors (first appointed by the Secretary of State and subsequently by the ordinary membership) and co-opted governors, where these exist, total between nine and 17. The provisions for this category of membership vary: typically, they are persons who have experience of, and have shown capacity in, industrial, commercial or employment matters or in the practice of any profession plus in some cases persons having experience of local government and the provision of education.[338] The appointed governors constitute a majority of the Court.

1.176 The governors ex officiis are the Principal (who, unlike his or her counterpart in the higher education corporation, has no choice in the matter), one or two Vice-Principals and the President of the Students' Association. Staff governors are drawn from the Senate or Academic Board, the full-time members of academic staff and the full-time members of non-academic staff. The last of these is a departure from practice in both chartered institutions and the higher education corporations. Unlike the higher education corporation,

335 SI 1993/556.
336 SI 1993/558.
337 Members, not governors at Napier University.
338 The Napier University (Scotland) Order of Council 1993 (SI 1993/557) is slightly less directory than the others in this respect.

local authority elected members are not barred from the ordinary (independent) membership, but members of staff are barred from both appointment and co-option, other than as a governor ex-officio or a staff governor. There are limitations on the period of office and the age beyond which governors may not be re-appointed. At Napier University there is provision for a member of the Court to be appointed by the Graduates' Association.[339]

1.177 At the Glasgow Caledonian University governors may not be bound when speaking or voting by mandates given by others except when exercising a proxy under arrangements approved by the Court. They are normally able to claim financial loss and travelling allowances[340] whereas an equivalent provision does not exist in the constitutions of the chartered or ancient institutions. Like the governors of higher education corporations and companies limited by guarantee, the governors may be removed from office, in a typical case

> ... where the Court deems that his continuation would bring discredit upon the name of the University or in such other circumstances as the Court may determine and record in a standing order.[341]

THE SENATE OR ACADEMIC BOARD

1.178 The differing relationship of the Senate, Senatus Academicus, Academic Council[342] or Academic Board to the Court is one feature of the Scottish universities which it is quite difficult to understand. That this is not a new difficulty is illustrated by this extract from a speech by an Under-Secretary for Scotland in 1965:

> The Secretary of State will find himself when the [Universities (Scotland) Bill] is passed, in an anomalous position. His relationship with one group of universities, Strathclyde, Dundee, Heriot-Watt and Stirling will be in one form, while his relationship with the second group, Aberdeen, St Andrews, Edinburgh and Glasgow will be in another form ... This is not a logical or defensible position and my Right Hon Friend would like to free himself as soon as possible from

---

339 Article 3(2)(f), The Napier University (Scotland) Order of Council 1993 (SI 1993/557).
340 Eg Article 6(5), The Glasgow Caledonian University (Scotland) Order of Council 1993 (SI 1993/556).
341 Article 7(3) The University of Paisley (Scotland) Order of Council 1993 (SI 1993/558): the appearance of gender-specific language in this constitution is curious.
342 At the University of Dundee the Academic Council is a body similar to the Academic Assembly or Meeting at other universities: it is not the Senate.

the anomaly ... It is equally desirable, from the universities' point of view that the powers of each component of a university should be set out explicitly. None of the enactments sets out the powers of a senate in full, for example.[343]

The intention was that the four ancient universities should apply for modern charters, which they have not done. The difficulty is now compounded by the latest Orders of Council establishing the post-1992 universities, although at least these do spell out the functions of the Senate or equivalent in full.

1.179 Whatever the constitutional niceties, it is generally recognised that the Senate or equivalent is responsible for the academic affairs of the university, where these can be disentangled from resources issues. The body typically consists of a number of holders of offices ex officiis and staff and students appointed or elected by and from various constituencies prescribed in the governing instrument. In the post-1992 universities the Senate or Academic Board is appointed by the Court but with the exception of the ex officio members the members are elected. The practical effect appears to be the same and the constitutions broadly similar, although some universities have reserved places on the Senate for all or a specified minimum number of professors, the most senior grade of academic staff.

The non-university institutions

INTRODUCTION

1.180 The non-university institutions' systems of government are equally diverse. Many of the English colleges derive their existence from institutions originally founded by deeds of trust, then administered by local education authorities and subsequently created higher education corporations under ERA. The instruments and articles of government of these bodies require approval by the Privy Council under ERA as amended by FHEA. The typical composition of the governing body (the Council) in addition to the usual ex-officio members allows for representation of the founders (similar to the places reserved for Court and Privy Council nominations on a university Council), local authority members, staff, students and a number of lay members with a background in business or commerce. For example, the Instrument of Government of the Cheltenham and

---

343 Mrs Judith Hart, Under-Secretary of State for Scotland, Scottish Standing Committee (HC) 7 December 1965.

Gloucester College of Higher Education reserves a proportion of places for Foundation Members elected from the body of Fellows of the Cheltenham and Gloucester College of Higher Education Trust incorporating the Church of England Foundation of St Paul and St Mary. Appointment of these representatives appears to be the only power reserved to the Fellows. Institutions owing their existence to Deeds of Trust have no members, since the members of the governing body are also the charitable trustees.[344] The Scottish and Welsh colleges, though having a different history, have a very similar pattern of governance.

THE BOARD OF GOVERNORS OR COUNCIL

1.181 The powers of the Board of Governors or Council are very much the same as those of the equivalent bodies in the higher education corporations and companies limited by guarantee. The constitution of the governing body, in addition to reserving places for representatives of the founders, typically also reserves places for representatives of the local authorities which managed the college prior to ERA and for a number of business, commercial or industrial members. A lay majority is preserved.

THE ACADEMIC BOARD AND THE PRINCIPAL

1.182 The pattern of government is similar to that of a post-1992 university in that the Board of Governors or Council has general control over college activities. The Academic Board is subject to the oversight of the Council; the Principal has a number of specified powers including the determination of academic programmes, where consultation with the Academic Board is all that is required. This much greater power vested directly in the Principal contrasts sharply with the very limited formal powers of a Vice-Chancellor or Principal of a university.

SUBORDINATE BODIES

1.183 In addition to the various bodies which exist and have some formal authority, there is the usual structure of subordinate bodies, committees and officers which exist to carry on the day-to-day work of the institution, undertake its detailed planning, monitoring and development and although the picture appears complex, it is possible

---

344 See for example Clause 5 of the Declaration of Trust for the Cheltenham and Gloucester College of Higher Education Trust, 24 January 1990.

to isolate the powers of all these groups and individuals and place them in a coherent legal framework. It is interesting to note that although charters and statutes usually prescribe the subordinate structure in some detail, thereby to some extent creating tablets of stone which can only be re-hewn by the Privy Council, the post-1988 constitutions do not, leaving the governing body, the chief executive and the Academic Board or its equivalent to determine what is the best organisational arrangement at any given time. In practice decisions are effectively taken by subordinate committees and are 'rarely disturbed by the governing body.'[345]

Delegation

1.184   The mechanism for exercise of authority on behalf of the governing body or academic authority is commonly known as 'delegation' but is more appropriately described as 'arranging for discharge of functions' since true delegation carries with it certain legal incidents.[346] These will be discussed first. As in many other areas dealing with the composition, functions and powers of institutional authorities, the law and practice of local government offers considerable assistance.

1.185   Other than in limited liability companies, where normal Companies Acts limitations apply, the reason for the existence of a separate statute (or article in the instrument of government) and any provisos relating to membership appears to be that under local government practice up to fairly recent times there was considerable restriction on delegation. A function conferred on a body by Act of Parliament or subordinate legislation cannot be delegated unless the legislation so allows. This is the familiar principle known as *delegatus non potest delegare*. The English practice was governed by the Local Government Act 1933[347] and a more liberal provision was introduced only in 1972.[348] The latter avoids the use of the word 'delegate' and provides that local authorities may 'arrange for the discharge of any of their functions' by committees, sub-committees or officers, but not, apparently, by committee chairmen.[349] This terminology or the

345 J L Caldwell 'Judicial Review of the Universities: the Visitor and the Visited' (1982) 1 Canterbury Law Review 307 at 318.
346 See eg *R v Skinner* [1968] 2 QB 700.
347 Section 85 of the Act provided for local authorities to delegate functions to committees.
348 Sections 101 and 102 Local Government Act 1972.
349 See *R v Secretary of State for the Environment, ex p Hillingdon London Borough Council* [1986] 1 WLR 807n, CA.

alternative 'determine or advise' is being adopted generally. The Scottish legislation follows the same practice and the Scottish institutions follow suit.

1.186   In local government law, delegation of power to committees and officers means that decisions are effective as soon as they are made and this applies in the case of contracts made with third parties.[350] In addition, the committee to whom the task has been delegated may sub-delegate without offending against the principle *delegatus non potest delegare*.[351] Section 100(G) Local Government Act 1972 requires local authorities to maintain a list open to public inspection of powers delegated to officers: there seems no reason why higher education institutions should not do the same, at least producing a list open to their members, staff and students.

Provisions for delegation in charters, etc

1.187   The law and practice of delegation in universities has been discussed by Frank Mattison.[352] The position appears to be that in order effectively to delegate a power given to a body by the charter, statute or other relevant instrument, there must be an express or implied power of delegation which then places the delegatee in the position of agent for the delegator. This has been adopted in recent times. For example, a modern Statute, that of the University of Ulster, Statute XVI provides that:

> ... the Council may delegate, upon such conditions as it may determine, and may revoke the delegation of, any of its functions to committees of the Council, joint committees of the Council and the Senate, the Vice-Chancellor or other officers of the University. Such delegation may include delegation of powers of appointment. Any delegation of function shall be explicit and a matter of record.

Exactly the same formulation appears in the powers of the Senate mutatis mutandis in Statute XVII. There is no separate Statute governing committees. Another recently modified provision is that of the University of Hull, Section 30 of the Statutes providing:

350   *Battelley v Finsbury Borough Council* (1958) 56 LGR 165: Committee offered job under delegated powers; after the contract had been issued it changed its mind. The court held that the committee and therefore the council was in breach of contract.
351   C Cross and S Bailey *Cross on Local Government Law* (7th ed, 1986) p 71.
352   F T Mattison 'University Government and Management' in D J Farrington and F T Mattison (eds) *Universities and the Law* (1990, CUA/CRS) pp 51–6.

... the Council, Senate and Boards of Schools may, by the making of Regulations, delegate any of the powers vested in them to each other or to Standing or Special Committees appointed under the provisions of Section 29 of these Statutes, or to a Member of the University.

1.188 An equivalent provision in the instrument and articles of government of a typical higher education corporation is

Instrument: Committees
The Board of Governors may establish committees and permit such committees to include persons who are not members of the Board of Governors.

Articles:
1. Subject to the following provisions of this Article, the Board of Governors may establish a committee of the Corporation for any purpose or function, other than those assigned elsewhere in these Articles to the [Principal] or to the Academic Board, and may delegate powers to such a committee or to the Chairman of the Corporation or to the [Principal] and may grant powers of sub-delegation.
2. The Board of Governors shall establish a committee or committees to determine or advise on such matters relating to employment, finance and audit as the Board may remit to them. The members of such committee or committees shall be drawn from the Board of Governors other than staff or student Governors.
3. The Board of Governors shall not, however, delegate the following:
   (a) the determination of the educational character and mission of the [University];
   (b) the approval of the annual estimates of income and expenditure;
   (c) the approval of the annual audited accounts;
   (d) ensuring the solvency of the institution and the safeguarding of its assets;
   (e) the appointment or dismissal of the [Principal];
   (f) the varying or revoking of these Articles of Government;
   (g) the making or varying or revoking of rules and bye-laws.[353]

1.189 The articles of association of a typical company limited by guarantee provide that the Court of Governors

may delegate any of its powers to any ... committee or to the Director or the Secretary or, in any matter as the Court may by resolution specify

---

353 Section 8 of the Order of Council of 29 March 1993 making an Instrument of Government and Article 5 of the Articles of Government of the Middlesex University higher education corporation.

requiring urgent action or expedition, to the Chairman of the Court, and may confer a right of sub-delegation upon any such committee or persons upon such terms and conditions as the Court sees fit provided always that the Court shall not delegate any of ... [a specified list of matters including senior staff matters, approval of estimates and making of byelaws].[354]

1.190 The other way in which functions may be discharged is through referral to committees or officers the decisions of which are subject to confirmation by the appointing body before they come into effect. This type of committee is contemplated by the use of the word 'advise' in section 2 of the Article of the higher education corporation set out above. There are some matters which the charter, statutes or instrument of government provide cannot be delegated and these, among others, will be matters upon which the appointing body may wish to take advice. It may also be advised on matters affecting individuals: such action does not violate any rule against delegation.[355]

Requirement for specific committees to be established

1.191 Section 29 of the University of Hull Statutes provides for a Policy and Resources Committee as well as a general power to appoint committees. However, unless the statutes or their equivalent prescribe otherwise, the only committee which institutions are obliged to appoint is the Audit Committee required by the Financial Memorandum and Code of Audit Practice issued by the relevant Funding Council. The governing bodies of the pre-1992 universities are expressly prevented from delegating certain of their powers under the University Commissioners' 'Model Statute' and the higher education corporations retain to themselves certain powers which are fundamental to the operation of the corporation.

Membership of committees

1.192 On the basis of the decision in *R v Sunderland Corpn*[356] it appears that at common law a member of a body cannot be compelled to serve on a committee against his or her wish. Members can be removed at will, since the appointing body can also revoke the appointment of the committee.[357]

354 Article 15(9), Articles of Association of the University of Greenwich.
355 *Osgood v Nelson* (1872) LR 5 HL 636.
356 [1911] 2 KB 458.
357 *Manton v Brighton Corpn* [1951] 2 KB 393.

The Policy and Resources Committee

1.193   The potential conflict between the powers of the Council (Court in Scotland) and those of the Senate (or equivalent) was always a problem for universities when powers were divided, even when the Council had an overall power of control. In times of expansion and steady state this was more theoretical than practical but once the major retrenchment in resources occurred in the 1970s and particularly the early 1980s the need for a more integrated approach to government became pressing. One result of that pressure has been the creation of a joint Policy (or Planning) and Resources Committee (PRC) which reports to both Council and Senate and is in practice given a considerable degree of delegated authority to act within plans and guidelines approved by its parent bodies. It is an essential element of the overall strategic planning process required by the Funding Councils. This body is normally chaired by the Vice-Chancellor or Principal with membership consisting of senior representatives of the appointing bodies. Although the specimen English chartered university makes provision for it in its revised statutes:

> There shall be a Standing Joint Committee of Council and Senate entitled Policy and Resources Committee having a membership not exceeding 15, the Chairman of which shall be the Vice-Chancellor

this is comparatively rare and in most universities it stands in the position of any other committee which the Council and Senate may appoint or discharge at will.[358] It is however the extent of delegated authority which is important and this general issue will be addressed later.

Faculties, Schools and Departments

1.194   Below the Council and Senate, universities organise themselves in a variety of ways, some into Faculties or Schools with both academic and resource allocation responsibilities, some into Departments with similar responsibilities, while others divide the responsibilities more or less clearly between these bodies. Many have made an attempt to make radical changes in traditional forms of internal government. Given the wide variety of provisions it is not possible to make general statements about institutions: in the

---

358   An Executive Committee of the Council is established in the Statutes of the University of London to 'advise ... on the development and implementation of strategic planning and policies for the University ...'.

specimen university the powers of the Boards of Schools are essentially academic, although there is a power 'to discuss any matters relating to the School' and to express opinions to the Senate. Boards of this kind provide an opportunity for participation in wider university life by academic (and sometimes other) staff other than those with formal managerial functions. They carry out much of the day-to-day academic decision-making and express opinions on university-wide issues under discussion by senior bodies, acting as a brake on rapid decision-making.

The law governing the conduct of business

Requirement for formality

1.195 However decisions are reached, there must be some formality associated with the process. To a greater or lesser extent, this is prescribed by the governing instruments, articles of government, procedural ordinances, byelaws or regulations and standing orders. It is only when a decision is questioned that it will be necessary to show that the correct procedures have been followed but it is obviously in the interests both of the institution and individuals affected by decision-making that procedures should be correctly followed at all times. At the very least this preserves public accountability.[359]

1.196 The procedures for calling meetings, the quorum required to transact business and any special periods of notice to be given for particular business (eg for changes to be proposed to a charter and statutes) should be laid down somewhere. The extent to which fine detail is covered varies: for example there is no known equivalent in the pre-1992 university sector of the provision in the Articles of Government of the Cheltenham and Gloucester College of Higher Education for the situation arising if neither the Chair nor the Vice-Chair of a committee turn up within 10 minutes of the advertised time of the meeting.[360] In the same Articles, there is also the following provision

> The Clerk shall give a minimum of 7 days' written notice of all meetings of Council and he or she shall circulate with such written notice the

---

359 For a detailed exposition of the law relating to meetings, see Sir Sebag Shaw and D Smith *The Law of Meetings – Their Conduct and Procedure* (1974).
360 Article 5.3(c).

Agenda and all papers for the Meeting including details of any resolution to be proposed at such meetings.[361]

If adopted in other institutions, that provision would effectively prevent the common practice of tabling papers and imposes a considerable self-discipline on both the officers and the subordinate committees reporting to the Council. Whether or not it leads to the most effective conduct of business is a matter for the individual institution to determine.

1.197 If anything is uncertain or is not provided for, there are common law rules which will be of assistance, relating for example to the ejection of unruly members, the adjournment of meetings and the powers and duties of the chairman.[362]

Notice

1.198 A meeting must be convened by proper authority,[363] corporate authority if that is what is required[364] and held on notice that would give every member of a board etc an opportunity of attending.[365] This can be given by an entry in the Almanac of meetings if this can be relied upon. Normally however, specific notice is given. The common law rule as it has been applied to local authorities is that the notice period excludes the day on which notice is given and the day of the meeting itself.[366] Unless there is provision in the instrument or articles of government to the contrary, a meeting may be invalidly convened if notice is not given to all the members, even if the omission is accidental.[367] Companies limited by guarantee are in a special position since the Companies Acts prescribe the arrangements for giving notice and the consequences of accidental omission.[368] Under the Codes of Audit Practice issued by the Funding

---

361 Article 5.2
362 See C Cross and S Bailey *Cross on Local Government Law* (7th ed, 1986) p 43.
363 *Re State of Wyoming Syndicate* [1901] 2 Ch 431.
364 *Re Haycraft Gold Reduction and Mining Co* [1900] 2 Ch 230: if the vires of the calling of the meeting is questioned, action must be taken quickly: *Browne v La Trinidad* (1887) 37 ChD 1.
365 *Mayor etc and Co of Merchants of the Staple of England v Governor and Co of the Bank of England* (1887) 21 QBD 160, 165, CA per Wills J.
366 *R v Herefordshire Justices* (1820) 3 B & Ald 581. Fractions of a day do not count: *Pugh v Duke of Leeds* (1777) 2 Cowp 714, 720.
367 *R v Langhorn* (1836) 4 Ad & El 538.
368 Table A, Art 131 under section 8 Companies Act 1985.

Councils an institution's external auditors may requisition a meeting of the governing body in defined circumstances.

1.199 The important question in any dispute over notice is to what extent the procedural deficiency affected the validity of the proceedings.[369] In the normal course of institutional business one would expect the members to ratify the deficiency and thus correct the record[370] but there are certain matters, such as the declaration of a state of redundancy, that are so sensitive that it would be better to avoid disputes arising at all. The courts or Visitor would normally only intervene in cases of fraud.[371]

The business of the meeting

1.200 The notice convening the meeting should state definitely that it will be held and must contain sufficient information about the business to be transacted to enable members to decide whether or not to attend.[372] It should be frank and clear in its terms, not 'tricky.'[373] Unless the instrument of government, byelaws or standing orders provide otherwise, at common law the governing body of an institution cannot act except on a summons for the particular business to be transacted[374] and the business actually transacted must bear a reasonable relationship to that for which notice was given.[375] The commonly used phrase 'any other competent business' means just that: that additional business must be within the competence of the meeting. 'Any other business' is rather too vague for this purpose. Whether business transacted is validly transacted will depend upon the facts of each case[376] and the courts will not be unduly strict in this regard.[377] The courts of Scotland have held that a majority can only bind a minority if the proceedings are sanctioned by the

---

369 *Re West Canadian Collieries Ltd* [1962] Ch 370.
370 As in *Re Oxted Motor Co Ltd* [1921] 3 KB 32; see also *Foss v Harbottle* (1843) 2 Hare 461 and *Browne v La Trinidad* (1887) 37 Ch D 1, 17, CA per Lindley LJ.
371 *Menier v Hooper's Telegraph Works* (1874) 9 Ch App 350, CA.
372 *Peel v London and North-Western Rly* [1907] 1 Ch 5, 14, CA per Vaughan Williams LJ.
373 *R v Liverpool Corpn* (1759) 2 Burr 723, 731; see also *Kaye v Croydon Tramways Co* [1898] 1 Ch 358, CA.
375 *Torbock v Lord Westbury* [1902] 2 Ch 871.
376 Sir Sebag Shaw and D Smith *The Law of Meetings – Their Conduct and Procedure* (1974) p 149 and *Wright's Case* (1871) LR 12 Eq 331.
377 See eg *Young v Ladies Imperial Club Ltd* [1920] 2 KB 523; *Re Hector Whaling Ltd* [1936] Ch 208.

constitution[378] and then only in accordance with the purposes of the incorporation.[379]

1.201 Some constitutions contain provisions for the automatic termination of meetings if the business has not been completed by a certain time. For example the Articles of Association of the Middlesex University higher education corporation provide

> ... if at any meeting the business has not been completed by such a time (not being less than two hours from its commencement) as the Chairman may at any time during the meeting direct, the meeting shall stand adjourned sine die and another meeting shall be summoned as soon as conveniently may be.[380]

Restrictions on participation

1.202 It is common in institutional articles or ordinances to find a prohibition on students participating in the transaction of 'reserved' business. For example The University of Hull Statutes Section 30(1) provides

> Any student member or members of a statutory body of the University or a committee thereof shall be required to withdraw from a meeting when it is declared by the Chairman of the meeting that the meeting is about to discuss a reserved area of business and shall not return to the meeting until the discussion on the reserved area of business is concluded.

Often members of staff cannot vote on matters relating to their own salaries or conditions of service, and lay members who may be suppliers or contractors to the institution will commonly have restrictions placed upon them by standing orders,[381] as well as by whatever mechanisms have been put in place by the institution to comply with the terms of the relevant Code of Conduct for Governors.

---

378 *Gray v Smith* (1836) 14 S 1062.
379 *Howden v Incorporation of Goldsmiths* (1840) 2 D 996; *Rodgers v Incorporation of Tailors of Edinburgh* (1842) 5 D 295.
380 Article 7.5 (part).
381 See eg Article 7.17, Articles of Government of the University of Northumbria at Newcastle higher education corporation, in relation to Governors having any 'pecuniary, family or other personal interest in any contract, proposed contract or other matter' which seems comprehensive.

The quorum

1.203   The quorum necessary to transact business is normally prescribed in the standing orders, if not in the articles of government. In the case of the Courts of the ancient Scottish universities, it is prescribed by law.[382] If not, the common law rule is that the majority of those entitled to attend[383] (ie 50% plus 1) must be at the meeting, and any decisions are validly made by a majority of those present.[384] If non-members are present their position should be made clear in the standing orders: normally they may speak only if asked and certainly may not vote. While the presence of such persons does not at common law invalidate the proceedings[385] unauthorised participation will do so.[386]

1.204   Unless otherwise prescribed it is sufficient for there to be a quorum at the commencement of business:[387] the newer constitutions tend to be rather specific about the time allowed for a quorum to form.[388] They are also rather more specific than the older charters about the qualifications necessary to constitute a quorum at meetings of the governing body: commonly this requires a majority of the quorum to be independent members.[389] In chartered corporations, technically all members of the governing body are equal and so any specific quorum must be prescribed in the Standing Orders or other local rules.

The chair

1.205   'Chair' is often used, particularly in speech, in place of 'chairman' or 'chairperson' but for the purposes of the common law

382   Section 5(1) Universities (Scotland) Act 1889.
383   Entitlement is important: see *Re Greymouth Point Elizabeth Railway and Coal Co Ltd* [1904] 1 Ch 32. Casual vacancies are included in the calculation: *Newhaven Local Board v Newhaven School Board* (1885) 30 ChD 350.
384   *Young v Ladies Imperial Club Ltd* [1920] 2 KB 523: in Scotland *Meiklejohn v Magistrates of Culross* (1805) Mor *voce* Burgh Royal, App No 17; affd (1810) 5 Pat 298.
385   *Re Imperial Chemical Industries* [1936] Ch 587, 614, 615, CA.
386   *Leary v National Union of Vehicle Builders* [1970] 2 All ER 713.
387   For the general rule see *Re Romford Canal Co* (1883) 24 ChD 85. For the quorum at the commencement of business only see *Re Hartley Baird Ltd* [1955] Ch 143.
388   See eg Article 7.13, Articles of Government of the University of Northumbria at Newcastle higher education corporation, which allows 30 minutes for this purpose.
389   See eg Article 7.4, Articles of Government of the Middlesex University higher education corporation.

rules, the term 'chairman' is the usual one to describe the person who takes the chair and controls the meeting. A formal meeting to discharge business cannot take place unless there are at least two persons present and someone in control. In higher education institutions, at least at governing body and Academic Board or Senate level the person who takes the chair is prescribed in the governing domestic legislation, usually ex officio, so that change in the holder of the office automatically brings a change in the chair. For committees, the appointing body usually appoints and may replace the chairman. Otherwise it is the task of the committee to elect (and if necessary, remove)[390] its chair. Any irregularity in the appointment of a chairman must be the subject of an immediate challenge: tacit consent validates the appointment.[391] The chairman is exempt from personal liability in respect of the conduct of the meeting provided that he or she acts bona fide and honestly.[392]

1.206 In so far as they are not spelt out in the domestic legislation of the institution, the tasks of the chair include
(i)   determining that the meeting is properly constituted and that a quorum is present;
(ii)   being informed as to the business and objects of the meeting;
(iii)   preserving order in the conduct of those present;[393]
(iv)   confining discussion within the scope of the meeting, excluding irrelevancies, and within reasonable limits of time;
(v)   deciding whether proposed motions and amendments are in order;
(vi)   formulating for discussion and decision questions which have been moved for the consideration of the meeting;
(vii)   deciding points of order and other incidental matters which require decision at the time;
(viii) ascertaining the sense of the meeting by
        (a)   putting relevant questions to the meeting and taking a vote thereon;
        (b)   declaring the result;
        (c)   causing a count to be taken if duly demanded;
(ix)   dealing with the minutes of proceedings;

---

390 See *Booth v Arnold* [1895] 1 QB 571, 579 where Lopes LJ said that the power to remove the chairman was 'essential to the good order and management of a corporation, and without it I do not see how the business of a corporation could be carried on.'
391 *Cornwall v Woods* (1846) 4 Notes of Cases, 555.
392 *Breay v Browne* (1896) 41 Sol Jo 159.
393 Which will include those who have no right to be present, as in the case of disruption of meetings by non-members of the committee or other body which is meeting.

(x) adjourning the meeting where prevailing circumstances justify that course;[394]

(xi) declaring the meeting closed when its business has been completed.

The limits on freedom of speech by the law of defamation will be discussed in chapter 2. There are certain other restrictions, notably those relating to sedition and blasphemy, but these will not be discussed.

Motions

1.207 At common law the chair of a body can put motions to a meeting without the necessity of a seconder.[395] However it is normal practice for standing orders to require a seconder. The chair must accept every motion proposed provided that it is clear, relevant and material[396] and provided that it does not offend against standing orders. One example of this might be where the standing orders of an Academic Board provide that the same issue may not be raised more than once in each academic session. Members may propose amendments: in the English procedure only one amendment can be under consideration at any one time: under Scottish procedure more than one amendment can be considered simultaneously. Amendments can be wide-ranging, but must not have the effect of negating the original motion: that can be achieved by a negative vote on the substantive motion.

1.208 There are a number of procedural motions which may be put to a meeting. These include that the motion 'be now put,' 'be not now put,' 'lie on the table' or 'be referred back,' that the meeting proceed to the next business, that discussion be adjourned, that the meeting be adjourned[397] and that the chairman leave the chair. Such motions take precedence over substantive motions and discussion on them is either limited or excluded. Where discussion is limited a motion to adjourn will take precedence over other procedural motions.

394 It should be noted that at common law a meeting may not be postponed once called, unless that power is vested in the chair: *Smith v Paringa Mines Ltd* [1906] 2 Ch 193.
395 *Re Horbury Bridge Coal, Iron and Waggon Co* (1879) 11 ChD 109, 118.
396 *Henderson v Bank of Australasia* (1890) 45 ChD 330, CA.
397 At common law this power is vested in the meeting itself rather than in the chair: *Stoughton v Reynolds* (1736) Fortes Rep 168, except where there is disorder: *R v D'Oyly* (1840) 12 Ad & El 139, 159, per Lord Denman CJ. A motion to adjourn when the rules leave it in the hands of the chair with the consent of the members is void: *Salisbury Gold Mining Co v Hathorn* [1897] AC 268.

Voting

1.209   Although formal voting tends to be the exception rather than the rule in higher education institutions, it is necessary to be clear about the law, since occasions will arise when a formal vote is called for. At common law votes at all meetings are to be taken by a show of hands, ie by raising one hand.[398] If that does not clearly reveal the majority, or on the demand of any member present, the votes are counted. In the absence of any special provision to the contrary in the instrument or articles of government, byelaws or other regulations on the subject, the common law rule prevails.[399] Sometimes the statutes or equivalent require specified majorities for certain formal business. Such a vote should be counted formally, since the chair may be challenged over it.[400]

1.210   In chartered bodies there is no common law right to a casting vote by the chairman, so that unless there is long usage pointing to a different conclusion,[401] a regulation empowering a casting vote may be void and if voting is equal, the motion is lost.[402] This is not the case in the companies limited by guarantee, where a casting vote is provided for.[403] Under companies legislation provision exists for the exercise of a vote by proxy, but there is no right at common law to vote by proxy and indeed, the companies limited by guarantee normally exclude it.[404] It may be that the exercise of the power of delegation of functions will include delegation of the right to vote, in which case one person acting for another and sitting on a body in his or her own right will not thereby acquire two votes.[405] In higher education corporations there is a statutory right to a casting vote at a meeting of the corporation.[406]

---

398 *Ernest v Loma Gold Mines Ltd* [1897] 1 Ch 1, 6, CA per Lindley LJ.
399 *Re Horbury Bridge Coal Iron & Waggon Co* (1879) 11 ChD 109, 115, CA per Jessel MR.
400 *R v Tralee UDC* [1913] 2 IR 59.
401 *Anon* (1773) Lofft 315 per Lord Mansfield CJ.
402 *R v Ginever* (1796) 6 Term Rep 797, 798.
403 See eg Article 24 of the Articles of Association of the University of Greenwich.
404 *Harben v Phillips* (1883) 23 ChD 14: see Article 24 of the Articles of Association of the University of Greenwich.
405 *Re Prain & Sons Ltd* 1947 SC 325.
406 Paragraph 14 of Schedule 7 ERA. This does not appear to extend to committees and it is not mentioned in Schedule 7A inserted by FHEA.

Minutes

1.211 There is no obligation at common law for minutes of meetings of corporations or the authorities thereof to be kept, and the charters and statutes of the pre-1992 universities do not prescribe the keeping of minutes. This is in contrast to the articles of government of the higher education corporations, which refer to access to minutes as part of the general right to access to proceedings by staff and students[407] and the articles of association of the companies limited by guarantee, which refer to the keeping of minutes by both the governing body and the general meeting of members of the company.[408] However, it is common practice to keep minutes of the governing bodies, academic authorities and principal committees of all higher education institutions, not only so that the supervisory role of one authority in an institution over another can be exercised but also so that records are kept which will stand up to close examination when questions of the propriety of expenditure and other decisions are raised.

1.212 A minute is strictly concerned only with recording the fact that a meeting was held and that certain decisions were arrived at. In practice it will first record when a meeting was held (and sometimes where), who was present and in attendance. It will also record the full terms of any resolutions adopted, the subject matter of financial transactions considered by the meeting and all specific business upon which decisions were taken. Depending on the 'house style' of the institution, it may also record in greater or less detail any arguments advanced for or against any particular course of action, and the options considered, although as it is not a verbatim record, there may be considerable licence taken with what is included and excluded and problems may arise as a result. Although it is increasingly the case that minutes are taken electronically, many staff continue to use handwritten notes and at common law it is permissible to write up the full minutes later.[409]

1.213 Whether or not reasons for decisions should be recorded is a difficult issue. As Schiemann J put it in 1991 in *R v Poole Borough Council, ex p Beebee*[410] there are 'theoretical difficulties of

---

407 See eg Article 7.12, Articles of Government of the Middlesex University higher education corporation.
408 See eg Articles 13 and 27, Articles of Association of the University of Greenwich.
409 *Re Jennings* (1851) 1 I Ch R 236.
410 [1991] 2 PLR 27, 31.

establishing the reasoning of a corporate body which acts by resolution.' In *R v University of Cambridge, ex p Evans*,[411] Sedley J surveyed the recent cases as they applied to the situation of a lecturer rejected for promotion. In *R v Higher Education Funding Council, ex p Institute of Dental Surgery*[412] the view of the court (Mann LJ and Sedley J) was that a distinction can be drawn between collegiate and corporate decisions and in the former case it should be possible for reasons for decisions to be given, although (as in that case) there might be no legal duty to do so. A similar point was raised in *R v City of London, ex p Matson*[413] where the City's submission that to give reasons for rejecting M's candidature for election as an alderman would 'call for the articulation of inexpressible value judgments' was rejected by the court. A legal duty to give reasons only arises in certain cases, eg where personal liberty is at stake[414] or fairness to the individual requires it[415] except where there is an express statutory bar.[416]

1.214 The extent to which formality is attached to the minutes varies: in some institutions they must be signed formally by the chair after being confirmed at a subsequent meeting. This signature need not take place at the meeting itself.[417] Confirmation is almost universal practice. Unless otherwise provided in the standing orders[418] the confirmed minutes are not conclusive evidence as to what occurred at the meeting to which they relate and a resolution may be proved by other evidence, even if it is not minuted.[419]

The need for clear lines of management

> Everyone who is at all acquainted with the constitution of this government must know that all warlike preparations, every military operation and every naval equipment must be directed by a Secretary of State before they can be undertaken. Neither the Admiralty, Treasury, Ordnance, nor victualling boards can move a step without the King's command so signified.

411 (1997) unreported, CO/1031/97, QBD.
412 [1994] 1 All ER 651.
413 (1995) 8 Admin LR 49.
414 As in *R v Secretary of State for the Home Department, ex p Doody* [1994] 1 AC 531.
415 As in *R v Civil Service Appeal Board, ex p Cunningham* [1992] ICR 816.
416 As in *R v Home Secretary, ex p Fayed* [1997] 1 All ER 228.
417 *Southampton Dock Co v Richards* (1840) 1 Man & G 448.
418 *Kerr v J Mottram Ltd* [1940] Ch 657.
419 *Re Fireproof Doors Ltd* [1916] 2 Ch 142.

William Knox and the war with America

1.215 How apposite is William Knox's eighteenth century dictum.[420] We may not be fighting a war – except perhaps with the Funding Councils – but managers of higher education institutions likewise tread a careful path. The King in our case is the body charged with making a decision, be it the Council, the Senate or some subordinate authority. For anticipating 'the King's command so signified' Knox's transgressors would have faced the Tower or worse: we face less serious consequences and indeed today the consequences may be worse if we fail to anticipate the decision! Nevertheless, as a very senior administrator remarked to the author on his assuming a university administrative post for the first time

> Do nothing except what the Senate tells you to do, and before you do it, consult everyone and everything, even the mushrooms on the lawn.

It is essential that managers have a clear understanding of their legal powers, duties and responsibilities.

Secrecy and the Secretary

1.216 250 years before Knox, another King's man made another very relevant comment: 'The name of Secretary hath the foundation upon the knowledge of such things as ought to be kept secret.'[421] Although the image of the 'secretarius' as a secret agent of the King might perhaps commend itself to certain sections of the higher education community today, in fact the origins of administrators and managers go back at least to the reign of Athelstan (925–40) who was one of the first to grant charters which needed to be put into writing, a function which increased enormously after the Norman Conquest.[422]

A definition of management

Trouble at Foyle's

1.217 The word 'management' is derived from the Italian *maneggiare* – to control – and ultimately from the Latin *manus* –

420 William Knox was an Under-Secretary for the Colonies in the 1770s; quoted in D Kynaston *The Secretary of State* (1978) p 145.
421 Sir Robert Wingfield quoted by Kynaston ibid p 1.
422 Ibid.

hand. It is the description of the process by which one person controls the actions of another person or a team. The controlling aspect of management has been reinforced in decisions of the courts in the field of health and safety. In 1992 the Court of Appeal (Criminal Division) in *R v Boal*[423] quashed the conviction of Francis Boal, assistant general manager of Foyle's bookshop, for alleged offences under the Fire Precautions Act 1971. Section 23 of that Act uses the phraseology of a number of similar pieces of social legislation:

> (1) where an offence under this Act committed by a body corporate is proved ... to be attributable to any neglect on the part of any director, manager, secretary or other similar officer of the body corporate ... he as well as the body corporate shall be guilty of that offence ...

As Simon Brown J pointed out[424] the recognised textbooks did not assist in the interpretation of this section. The court accepted the definition given by Lord Denning MR in 1969 in *Registrar of Restrictive Trading Agreements v W H Smith & Son Ltd*,[425] interpreting section 15(3) Restrictive Trade Practices Act 1956 adopting dicta in earlier cases on provisions of the Companies Acts which impute liability to 'managers':[426]

> The word 'manager' means a person who is managing the affairs of the company as a whole. The word 'officer' has a similar connotation ... the only relevant 'officer' here is an 'officer' who is a 'manager.' In this context it means a person who is *managing in a governing role* the affairs of the company itself. [My emphasis]

Francis Boal's conviction was quashed because he was responsible only for the day-to-day running of the bookshop rather than enjoying any 'governing role' in respect of the affairs of the company itself. A corporate body can itself be liable under section 2(1) HASAW where there is a failure to ensure the health, safety and welfare at work of any employee. As explained in *R v Gateway Foodmarkets Ltd*,[427] the breach of duty by the corporation and its liability does not depend upon any failure of the corporation itself, meaning head office personnel or senior management who 'embody' the company: and

---

423 [1992] 3 All ER 177.
424 [1992] 3 All ER 177, 180. His Lordship referred to *Stone's Justices Manual* (1992 ed) para 7–15050, 18 Halsbury's Statutes (94th ed) para 450 and Redgrave Fife and Machin *Health and Safety* (1990) p 231 as being largely silent on the point at issue, omitting mention to the authorities cited in the instant case.
425 [1969] 3 All ER 1065, 1069.
426 *Gibson v Barton* (1875) LR 10 QB 329, 336 per Blackburn J and *Re B Johnson & Co (Builders) Ltd* [1955] 2 All ER 775, 790 per Jenkins LJ.
427 [1997] 3 All ER 78, CA.

in *R v Associated Octel Co Ltd*[428] it was made clear that this applies in respect of its duty to non-employees under section 3(1) as well. There is a duty on 'managers' who do fit the definition in the legislation under HASAW, and the Management of Health and Safety At Work Regulations 1992–94[429] define the duty of care under sections 2 and 3 HASAW more explicitly as a duty of line management.

A 'governing role' and 'line management'

1.218 It is quite clear that in the pre-1992 universities, administrative staff have no 'governing role' nor would many of them consider that they are 'line management' unless this is specifically part of their job description. Managing a budget is rather different to assuming liability for the safe working of an office. Clearly it is important for them personally if they are found wanting in any area to which individual legal liability may attach. Only the Council or its equivalent has a governing role; the only individual office-holder who may, according to the domestic legislation, have any specific responsibility for 'management' is the Vice-Chancellor or Principal and this is examined further below. As we shall see, in the higher education corporations and other institutions the powers of the chief executive officer are more explicit and 'management' is a more common expression.

1.219 Setting aside the criminal or civil liability of 'managers' the problem as we turn the millennium is to delineate the functions of managers and administrators and to help to answer the question whether there is now a difference between management and administration. The higher education system is now so diverse, however, that we must consider whether there are any general principles which can be gleaned from the governing instruments.

Officers

The Meredith case

1.220 *R v Dunsheath, ex p Meredith*[430] was a dispute between a group of members of convocation of the University of London and the chairman of the convocation. The latter declined to call a meeting

428 [1996] 1 WLR 1543.
429 SI 1992/2051; SI 1994/2865.
430 [1950] 2 All ER 741, 743.

of the convocation to discuss a motion relating to the dismissal of a lecturer. The members had obtained the required number of signatures to a requisition for a special meeting. The Divisional Court held that this was a matter for the University of London Visitor (HM The King in Council). Lord Goddard CJ said

> ... an officer of the university is alleged to have refused to perform a duty placed on him by the statutes of the university, and that seems to me to be essentially a matter for the visitor, because it is a domestic question.

Whether or not the matter was subsequently referred to and disposed of by the Visitor is not reported: the important point for 'officers' to note is that if their action is a 'duty' under the statutes it may be called in question either before the Visitor where there is such an office, or in the courts where there is not.

The Chancellor

1.221 In the medieval English universities the Chancellor who, together with the Masters formed the body corporate, was both the titular head of the university and also its chief executive. It was originally an office to which the incumbent was appointed by the bishop, since the corporation was originally an ecclesiastical one. Later it became an elected office and in time most of the functions other than chairing the congregation and inception of masters (ie the award of degrees) were handed over to another officer, the title 'Vice-Chancellor' being coined at Cambridge in about 1276. The Chancellor is now normally described as the 'Head of the University' with responsibility for presiding at congregations and conferring degrees, both ceremonial functions.

1.222 The Chancellor of an English chartered university is also normally the ex officio presiding officer at meetings of the Court. As presiding officer or chairman of the Court the Chancellor has the legal responsibilities and powers of a meeting chairman, but the exercise and performance of those powers and duties will be subject to the jurisdiction of the Visitor in respect of any complaints by members of the university, and to the courts where any plaintiff can establish locus standi sufficient to commence proceedings. In some institutions the Chancellor may be a member of the governing body. Although by convention the Chancellor may not attend, he or she will otherwise presumably have the same duties and responsibilities as other members.

1.223 A Chancellor holds office either for life, until retirement age or for a fixed term, depending on the statutes of the institution. He or she may resign by writing addressed to the appropriate authority and can only be removed from office by procedures laid down in the statutes or instrument and articles of government.

1.224 In Scotland the office of Chancellor, formerly called Lord Chancellor, was originally held by a cleric (for example at Glasgow by the Archbishop of Glasgow). The duties of the post in a chartered or 'new' university are essentially the same as in the English chartered universities, ie the Chancellor being Head of the University presides at degree ceremonies and at certain other occasions, for example the Annual Meeting of the Conference of the University of Stirling.

1.225 In the ancient Scottish universities the Chancellor has a theoretically more important role. For example under the Universities (Scotland) Act 1858 the Chancellor is President of the General Council of the University of St Andrews, which must give its sanction to all 'improvements in the internal arrangements of the University' which may be proposed by the Court (the governing body). In that capacity the Chancellor's powers and duties will be similar to those of the Chancellor presiding over a Court meeting in England.

The Scottish Rector

1.226 The distinctively Scottish office of Lord Rector was derived from the institutions on which the ancient universities were originally modelled. It was an elective office, the electoral constituency being the students who at Glasgow were divided into groups or 'Nations' depending on their geographical origin, for example *Natio Loudoniana sive Thevidaliae*, encompassing the Lothians, Stirling and all the towns east of the waters of the Urr.[431] The Lord Rector, along with the Dean of Faculties, was named in the charter *nova erectio* (1577) as a visitor. The modern form of Rector was instituted in the nineteenth century in the then four universities (St Andrews, Glasgow, Aberdeen and Edinburgh) by the Universities (Scotland) Act 1858 and still exists, having been retained by the University of Dundee when it separated from St Andrews in the 1960s, albeit in a different form. The Rector in the ancient institutions is the convenor or

---

431 J B Hay *Inaugural Addresses by Lords Rectors of the University of Glasgow* (1839), Table annexed to p xxviii.

president of the Court, a member of the Court at Dundee. The office
has been held by a wide range of people.

1.227   The Rector is elected annually either by the students alone
or by the students and staff, depending on the historical development
of the institution. The office relates back to a time when the *studium
generale* was being promoted as the ideal for a Scottish university.
Times change, however, and there is a body of opinion, supported
by the Scottish Committee of NCIHE,[432] in favour of removing the
Rector from the position of considerable authority which chairing
the Court brings. The concept is thought by that opinion to be out
of place in the modern framework of public accountability,
particularly when the post-1988 constitutions place such great
emphasis on the qualities sought in members of governing bodies.
Each of the universities has permanent student representation on its
Court. The Minister responsible for education in Scotland announced
following the report of NICHE that he rejected the proposal on the
basis that removing the Rector's right to chair the Court reduced
university democracy. The other eight universities and the remaining
higher education institutions have no exact equivalent although some
have an Honorary President of the Students' Association. This post
was abolished at Stirling in 1997 by change in Statute approved by
the Privy Council, in favour of a second full student member of the
University Court, after numerous failed attempts at securing a
candidate acceptable to the majority of students voting in the annual
elections.

The Pro-Chancellors

1.228   The office of Pro-Chancellor exists only in England, Wales
and Northern Ireland. These officers are the surviving descendants
of the Chancellor's commissary or delegate, whose functions were
largely handed over to the Vice-Chancellor by the fifteenth century.
Pro-Chancellors, in the absence of the Chancellor, exercise all the
powers of the Chancellor except that of conferring degrees. In
addition, a Pro-Chancellor may be chair of the university Council
and hence his or her powers and duties are those associated with the
chairman of a meeting. Like the Chancellor, a Pro-Chancellor may
resign by writing addressed to the appropriate authority and can
normally only be removed from office for the same reasons as the
Chancellor. Some Pro-Chancellors, however, hold office for a limited

432 Recommendation 20, Report of the Scottish Committee, NCIHE, July 1997.

term and their appointment can therefore lapse by virtue of not being re-elected by the Court.

The Chairman of the governing body

1.229   The post of Chairman of the governing body has taken on increased importance in the light of concerns about the role of the governing bodies themselves. There are organisations established to provide a framework for meetings of Chairmen and both organisations, the Committee of University Chairmen (CUC) and the Committee of Scottish and Irish Chairmen (CSIC) produce guidance for members of governing bodies, the latter in collaboration with SHEFC. In the English chartered university one of the Pro-Chancellors traditionally takes the chair at meetings of the Council, although the Chancellor is normally a member.

1.230   As already explained, the Rector chairs the Court in the ancient Scottish universities. In the other Scottish institutions, the Chairman of the Court is elected from among the lay members.[433] The Chairman, unlike the Pro-Chancellor and Chairman of Council of an English chartered university, is not an Officer with defined powers other than that of chairing meetings of the Court. The Vice-Chairman of the Court of the five post-1992 Scottish universities is appointed by the Court from among the lay members, whereas the Principal is Vice-Chairman in the other universities. It is not entirely clear that it is consistent with good governance for the chief executive to chair the governing body as Vice-Chairman.

The Treasurer

1.231   The honorary office of Treasurer, which is not known in Scotland, stems from local government practice. Not all chartered universities have provision for a Treasurer in the charter or statutes. Examples of provisions are
(i)   where the charter provides for the office and the statute provides that the Treasurer 'shall perform such duties as are determined by the Court;'[434]
(ii) where the Council may appoint a Treasurer 'in an honorary

---

433   Eg Statute 9, University of Stirling; Schedule 1 paragraph B(6) The Napier University (Scotland) Order of Council 1993 (SI 1993/557).
434   University of Exeter Charter Article 10, Statute 5.

capacity' by statute and the duties are determined by the Council.[435] Here the Treasurer has some real authority:

> The receipt of the Treasurer (if appointed) for any moneys or property payable or deliverable to the University shall be a sufficient discharge for the same to the person or persons paying or delivering the same, but the Council may appoint any person or persons to give receipts for such moneys or property and in such case a receipt given by such person or any one of such persons shall be sufficient discharge for the same.

(iii) where the charter requires the appointment of a Treasurer with similar functions as in (ii);[436]

(iv) where the charter requires the appointment of a Treasurer who, perhaps with the assistance of Deputies, is responsible to the Council for superintending the financial affairs of the University.[437]

The description 'Treasurer' is also sometimes applied to a paid official as at the University of Durham where the officer is 'responsible to the Council for the conduct of the financial business of the University and for such other business as the Council may prescribe.'[438] In such cases there is no honorary Treasurer. At the majority of universities the professional duties would be assigned to the Registrar or Secretary (who would have a qualified accountant to assist him or her); at a few they are assigned directly to a Bursar, Finance Officer, Quaestor or (latterly) 'Director of Corporate Services,' who is almost certainly a chartered accountant.

The Vice-Chancellor

1.232 By far the most important of the office-holders is the Vice-Chancellor and all recent cases of concern in institutional governance have involved the post. A number of Vice-Chancellors have resigned, retired early or been dismissed as a consequence of institutional failings. The title Vice-Chancellor was invented by the University of Cambridge in about 1276 and was assigned the Chancellor's jurisdiction *ad universitatem causarum* (in all causes) as his chosen substitute or vicar. It followed a period during which the Chancellor was able to delegate some, but not all, of his powers to a commissary. The first person to hold the title of vice-chancellor was apparently Richard de Aston, a

---

435 University of East Anglia Statute 6.
436 University of Bradford Charter Article 7.
437 Victoria University of Manchester Statute V(3).
438 University of Durham Statute 9.

doctor of canon law: the office became permanent in the fifteenth century. At the University of Cambridge, the Vice-Chancellor retains power to adjudicate in certain disputes about the application of domestic legislation and may appoint a Commissary to advise him or her. An appeal against a decision of the Vice-Chancellor can be made by any 50 members of the Regent House to the Chancellor, within one week of the decision. Though doubtless this provision is intended to avoid circumstances arising in which the Vice-Chancellor's rulings are left in suspense, as Sedley J stated in *R v University of Cambridge, ex p Evans*[439] it is arguable that where the matter relates to an individual, as an alternative to a High Court action this is not a true alternative form of recourse at all.

1.233 In discussing the role of the Vice-Chancellor, this nomenclature will be used to describe the post which is in effect the chief executive officer of the institution, known by a variety of titles. Almost all the universities outside Scotland use the title Vice-Chancellor. Fifteen institutions use the title Principal, including the Scottish universities where the Principal is also the Vice-Chancellor. Examples of rarely used titles are Rector (sometimes in addition to Vice-Chancellor), Director, Provost or Master, whereas Chief Executive is commonly used as an additional title in newer universities. Some Vice-Chancellors and/or Principals have particular additional titles eg President at Queen's University Belfast, Warden at Durham and Vice-Patron at Queen Margaret College, Edinburgh.

1.234 The role of the Vice-Chancellor in most institutions has changed considerably over the past 30 years. With the exception of those institutions where the post rotates between heads of colleges, who have similar status to a Vice-Chancellor, the post is now recognised as the equivalent of a chief executive officer, the CVCP Articles of Association going so far as to accord to the post the status of 'person who has primary responsibility for the academic and executive affairs' of the institution,[440] although this is scarcely accurate in strict legal terms. The Jarratt Report recommended this in 1985, when the wide range of management styles characterising the Vice-Chancellors of the six universities was noted. Many of these differences stemmed from the structure, history and culture of the institutions; others arose from the personalities of individuals. Nevertheless, a shift was emerging in the role of the Vice-Chancellor to the style of chief executive, bearing a responsibility for leadership and effective management of the institution. In *The Crisis of the*

439 (1997) unreported CO/1031/97, QBD.
440 Article 1, Articles of Association of CVCP, July 1990.

University,[441] Peter Scott described the 'polytechnic alternative' and the management style which has characterised the former local authority institutions and distinguished it from the traditional university approach. In formal terms at least, the Director of a polytechnic enjoyed considerably more power than did a vice-chancellor of a pre-1992 university and it is clear that this was the government's intention.[442]

1.235 The Financial Memoranda with the Funding Councils require the designation of a principal office the responsibilities of which include satisfying the governing body that the institution is complying with the conditions of funding. The holder of this post, and the officer to whom the power of dismissal is delegated under the University Commissioners' statutes made under ERA, is normally the Vice-Chancellor. The Financial Memorandum provides that if the Vice-Chancellor is instructed to take action which in his or her view is not a proper expenditure of public funds, he or she should report the matter to the Funding Council. In this respect the Vice-Chancellor is placed in an analogous position to the treasurer of a local authority: if instructed to make an illegal payment such officers should disobey the order[443] even if acting under threat of dismissal.[444] This is on the basis that the treasurer acts in a fiduciary relationship towards the members of the corporation at large (the burgesses in an English borough).[445] However, the appearance in the Financial Memoranda of a paragraph which subordinates the whole Memorandum to the governing instrument of the institution gives cause for doubt that in fact the Vice-Chancellor could act outside his or her primary responsibility to the institution and the governing body.

1.236 In August 1993 *The Times* reported on the job associated with the post of Vice-Chancellor[446] which demonstrated that the power and influence exerted by the post varies significantly from institution to institution. To a certain extent this variation is bound up with the difference in formal duties and powers laid down in the charters and statutes or their equivalent. The Vice-Chancellor is

---

441 P Scott (1984) pp 168 and 183.
442 *Government and Academic Organisation of Polytechnics: Notes for Guidance* Appendix A to Department of Education and Science Administrative Memorandum 8/67.
443 *R v Saunders* (1854) 3 E & B 763.
444 *Re Hurle-Hobbs, ex p Riley* (1944) unreported.
445 *A-G v De Winton* [1906] 2 Ch 106.
446 The feature was developed from one in *Cambridge*, the magazine of the Cambridge Society.

commonly described as the principal academic and administrative officer of the university. In most charters the formal role of the Vice-Chancellor is described in terms of keeping good order and discipline and formal powers usually relate to the admission and suspension of students. This is a direct descendant of the powers of the medieval Vice-Chancellors and of those of the Principals and Vice-Chancellors of the civic institutions of the nineteenth and early twentieth centuries who were much more directly involved with individual students than the present day chief executives. For example Frank Mattison describes how the Principal of the Yorkshire College (which became the University of Leeds) was required to keep certain office hours to give advice and information to intending students (and no doubt have absolute discretion whom to admit.)[447] Some charters granted more direct management authority to the Vice-Chancellor, for example the original Statutes of Brunel University[448] placed powers of appointment of most staff in the hands of the Vice-Chancellor and Principal, something which is common in the post-1992 institutions.

1.237 The specific powers accorded to Vice-Chancellors in relation to students vary: in some cases the power to refuse to admit as a student is unconditional, and does not have to be reported. In such cases the only remedy is by way of petition to the Visitor, but it is considered that only in exceptional cases would the Visitor intervene, by virtue of the general principle that the Visitor does not interfere in the general management of the corporation to which he or she is Visitor. In other cases there is an obligation in a Statute or Ordinance to report the refusal to the university authority which has the power to regulate admission to courses: normally the Senate. The consequence of the obligation to report is not well defined.

1.238 Vice-Chancellors also frequently have the power to suspend or exclude students from any part of the university or its precincts. As the precinct is normally expressly mentioned as a second area it is assumed that it means the environs, rather than the space defined by the boundaries of the property, ie the immediate neighbourhood of the university. In exercising these powers a Vice-Chancellor should normally apply the rules of natural justice, ie the nature of the charge which is the basis of the potential exclusion should be known to the student, and the student should be given an opportunity to answer the charge.[449] In addition the Vice-Chancellor would not exercise such

447 F T Mattison *Government and Staff* in *Studies in the History of a University 1874–1974* (1975) p 189.
448 Statute 10.
449 See *Glynn v Keele University* [1971] 1 WLR 487.

powers if he or she were personally involved in the charge, eg an assault upon him or her in his or her room.

1.239 Under the 'May' Statute imposed on the pre-1992 universities by virtue of sections 202–205 ERA, the Vice-Chancellor has the power to dismiss academic staff and others covered by the Statute on the findings of a disciplinary tribunal.[450] The Vice-Chancellor takes no part in the disciplinary procedure where a matter is referred to the tribunal but decides whether to do so in the first place and may take preliminary steps not constituting part of the formal disciplinary process, guided by the principles set out by Lord Slynn of Hadley in *Rees v Crane*.[451] The Vice-Chancellor also has a formal role in the grievance procedure for staff covered by the Statute. Issues arising from the application of the Statute are covered in detail in the relevant chapter.

1.240 In the absence of the Chancellor the Vice-Chancellor presides at congregations of the university and confers degrees. He or she is almost invariably ex officio chair of the Senate or equivalent body and major committees including a Policy (or Planning) and Resources Committee. The Vice-Chancellor is excluded from membership of the Audit Committee required to be established by the Financial Memorandum.

The Principal (in Scotland)

1.241 Appointment to the office of Principal of the ancient Scottish universities has in the past been carried out with considerable formality: for example the Principal of the University of Aberdeen used to be appointed by Royal Warrant, and the Principal of the University of Edinburgh is still appointed by the Curators of Patronage, representing the University and the City. The office of Principal of the University of St Andrews was formally constituted only in 1953,[452] when its patronage was assigned to the Crown. This, along with the power of appointment in the Universities of Glasgow and Aberdeen, was transferred to the respective University Court by section 18 Education (Scotland) Act 1981.

---

450 An Appendix to the Statute sets out the arrangements for discipline, dismissal etc of the Vice-Chancellor.
451 [1994] 2 AC 173 at 189F–196F, especially 191G–192A and 192F–G; see also *Brooks v DPP* [1994] 1 AC 568, 580F–H.
452 Section 2 University of St Andrews Act 1953.

1.242   The Principal, who is also the Vice-Chancellor,[453] has similar standing in the pre-1992 universities to that of the Vice-Chancellor in the traditional English universities so is president of the Senatus Academicus or Senate. However, unlike the position in England where the Treasurer is normally Vice-Chairman of the Council and the Pro-Chancellor is Vice-Chairman of the Court, the Principal of both the ancient and the modern chartered Scottish university is both president of the Court in the absence of the Rector or Chairman, and as Vice-Chancellor is president of the General Council or its equivalent in the absence of the Chancellor. It is a matter for debate whether this arrangement is consistent with current views on the separation of governance from executive authority. The powers of the Principal are otherwise very similar to those of the English Vice-Chancellor.

1.243   The powers of the Principal of the post-1992 institutions are derived from those of the corresponding office in the pre-1992 central institutions which they replace. The formal powers are considerably greater than those of a Principal of a pre-1992 university, except that the Principal is not Vice-Chairman of the Court. Under the Central Institutions (Scotland) Regulations 1988 the Principal's role was to carry out such functions of the governing body (other than those delegated to the Academic Council) 'relating to the organisation and management of the institution and to the discipline therein.' Such powers were to be exercised 'subject to the general control and direction of the governing body but otherwise the Principal shall have all the powers and duties of the governing body in relation to those functions,' with the powers of the Principal being discharged in his or her absence by a Vice-Principal. The Financial Memorandum issued to the central institutions by the Secretary of State, following a Financial Management Survey undertaken by the (then) Scottish Education Department constituted the Principal as the accounting officer and chief executive officer of the institution

> to exercise responsibility for the control of resources; for seeking efficiency and effectiveness in the use of the college's resources; and for ensuring that financial considerations are taken into account at all stages in framing and reaching decisions and in their implementation.[454]

453 Since 1859 in the case of the ancient universities.
454 *Grant-Aided Colleges: The Roles of Governors, Principals, Academic Council/ Board. A Discussion Paper by SED.* Letter to Principals from I W Gordon, SED, Circular Letter 6/89, 26 April 1989.

Essentially that position remains unaffected by the change from CI to university.

The Deputy and Pro-Vice Chancellors

1.244 In general terms a corporation cannot appoint deputies to act for it unless clear authority to do so exists in the charter or statutes.[455] A Pro-Vice-Chancellor is an example of such a deputy; he or she can substitute for the Vice-Chancellor. Where there is power by charter for an authority to appoint a deputy, the latter has all the powers of the principal, unless appointed as a special deputy.[456] The early Vice-Chancellors had powers to appoint substitutes and deputies of their own in order to assist them with carrying out the functions which they had themselves been delegated by the Chancellor. A modern power of delegation is

> The Vice-Chancellor's duties and powers [except those relating to the appointment of Deputy and Pro-Vice-Chancellors] may be delegated by the Vice-Chancellor to the Deputy Vice-Chancellor, the Pro-Vice-Chancellors and, subject to the concurrence of the Council, to others.[457]

1.245 The Scottish institutions do not have Pro-Vice-Chancellors but a range of Deputy, Vice- and Assistant Principals. In the new institutions it is common to find at least the latter drawn from the ranks of administrative as well as academic staff but practice varies.

1.246 Apart from the reserve duty of filling the post of Vice-Chancellor if it becomes vacant or if the Vice-Chancellor is otherwise unable to discharge the functions of the post, Deputy and Pro-Vice Chancellors are normally assigned specific areas of work within the institution and take the chair at major committees. These posts are normally held for a limited term.

The Secretary and Registrar or Registrary

1.247 The titles of the chief administrative officer under the Vice-Chancellor vary, as do the formal duties of the post. Some institutions have no chief administrative officer as such, but the importance of having someone who can ensure that the governing body acts within

455 *R v Gravesend Corpn* (1824) 4 Dow & Ry KB 117.
456 *Jones v Williams* (1825) 3 B & C 762, 771 per Holroyd J.
457 Statute 12, University of London (1994).

its powers and follows proper procedures has been stressed by the Nolan Committee[458] and in the various guides issued to governing bodies.[459] Most of the chief administrative officers are technically clerks to the governing body, and it is this aspect of their work which attracts legal interest but many of them also have line management responsibilities for a wide range of administrative services. There appears to be a real risk of conflict between the holder of this office and the Chief Executive (Vice-Chancellor or Principal) to whom he or she usually reports for management purposes, since it is possible that the former would be offering critical comment on the behaviour of the latter to the governing body. The risk can only be removed by separating out the role of clerk to the governing body and making this post directly responsible to the governing body itself. Unfortunately, in most institutions that would not be a full-time activity.

1.248   Once again, it is to local authorities that we turn for analogy, particularly since the House of Lords judgment in 1982 in *A-G (ex rel Co-operative Retail Services) v Taff-Ely Borough Council.*[460] In this case the clerk of the council had erroneously issued planning consent for a retail development. The document issued referred to a non-existent resolution which in any event would have been ultra vires. The council could not subsequently confirm what was an error. From this it would appear that if, for example, a Secretary or Registrar informs a student that he or she has been granted a degree, when that has not in fact happened, the student will have no redress, except to complain of maladministration to the Visitor where there is one.

Other officers

1.249   A variety of other officers are employed by institutions, in the majority of cases in a subordinate role to the Secretary or equivalent, forming the 'civil service' of the university or college. There is an increasing tendency to bring together the formerly separate functions of Finance Officer or Bursar and Secretary as financial planning, assisted by modern technology, becomes more a general management function: there is naturally still a need for accountants (in a bookkeeping role) and supporting staff of differing

---

458 Paragraph 104, Second Report, (1996) Committee on Standards in Public Life.
459 Eg Paragraph 2.7 and Good Practice Suggestion 6, (1996) *Guide for Members of Governing Bodies*, CSIC & SHEFC.
460 (1981) 42 P&C R 1.

professional expertise. It is rare to find any significant function formally delegated below the level of Secretary or equivalent, although professional officers in estates, finance, human resources and other functions carry out a range of day-to-day administrative and management tasks.

Indemnity of officers

1.250 Officers will assume that they are indemnified for acts done in the course of their duties. However, as explained in *Burgoine v Waltham Forest London Borough Council*,[461] a contractual indemnity granted to officers for defaults committed by them 'in or about the pursuit of their duties on behalf of their employer while acting within the scope of their authority' may not, as a matter of construction, cover defaults committed by the officers in the course of activities authorised by the employer when that authorisation is ultra vires. This is of particular relevance to the non-chartered institutions. Further, in *R v Lambeth London Borough Council, ex p Wilson*[462] officers were considered to be personally liable for wasted costs arising from an authority's decision not to contest a challenge by judicial review at the eleventh hour where the authority was not party to the proceedings.

461 [1997] BCC 347.
462 [1996] 3 FCR 146.

Chapter 2

Legal issues and the jurisdiction of the courts

The range of issues

2.1 Statutory intervention in the affairs of higher education institutions by legislation has until recently been limited, with the exception of original or amending constitutional statutes, the removal of restrictions on the management of land-owning by the older universities and their colleges, the abolition of university seats in Parliament.[1] In most cases Parliament has simply applied to the higher education system those general principles of law (eg on sex and race discrimination,[2] public health,[3] access by the disabled)[4] which apply to any large public employer or occupier of land.[5] There is some specific legislation: recent examples include that governing student fees, maintenance, loans and freedom of speech (the last in England and Wales only). The more entertaining earlier statutes such as that for 'The Reformacyon of Excesse in Apparayle' which imposed some restrictions on the material and colour of academic dress[6] and that dealing with prostitutes on university premises,[7] have been repealed.

1 Examples include the Universities and Colleges Estates Act 1925 (a consolidating Act) and 1964; the Universities (Trusts) Act 1943; the Universities Elections Acts under various guises in 1861, 1868, 1881, etc.
2 Section 22 SDA; section 17 RRA; both as amended by FHEA.
3 Section 338 Public Health Act 1936.
4 Section 8 Chronically Sick and Disabled Persons Act 1970, as amended by the Further and Higher Education Acts 1992; Disability Discrimination Act 1995. Regulation 10(2)(b) Education (Teachers) Regulations 1993 deals with the issue of student teachers who become disabled during training.
5 For a full account see F T Mattison *Universities and the Law* in *Universities and the Law* D J Farrington and F T Mattison (eds) CUA/CRS (1990) section 4.
6 24 Henry VIII c 13, repealed by section 7, 1 Jac 1 c 25.
7 Universities Act 1825 s 4, repealed by Statute Law (Repeals) Act 1989.

2.2 It is difficult to envisage the institution itself committing any civil wrong (tort in England, delict in Scotland) or criminal offence. A corporate body has 'no soul to be saved or body to be kicked.'[8] It cannot commit a criminal offence punishable only by imprisonment or which requires a physical act since this is a human characteristic. Individuals actually commit offences or wrongs or omit to do something giving rise to a legal claim. A higher education institution will have tortious or delictual liability for acts or omissions provided that the action would lie against an individual,[9] and the person by whom the tort is committed is acting within the scope of his or her authority,[10] a qualification which would have to be established.[11] Some examples of the civil wrongs which could be committed by individuals and for which the institution could be liable include assault, negligence, nuisance, infringement of intellectual property rights and defamation. A case in the education field often cited is *Smith v Martin and Hull Corpn*[12] where a child was injured when a teacher told him to make up the fire in the staff room. It is possible to envisage actions arising if a member of academic staff negligently performs or instructs a student to perform a dangerous act in a laboratory, as a result of which the student is injured.

An example: passing off

2.3 Likewise many civil wrongs would actually be committed against members of staff or students and in most such cases the institution itself would have little if any standing, although it is possible to envisage cases of infringement of intellectual property rights, passing off or defamation arising in respect of the institution itself.[13] For example, passing off is the tort which protects the plaintiff from action by the defendant in deceiving a third party into believing that the defendant's business is that of, or is connected with, that of the plaintiff where the plaintiff's business is carried on under a

---

8   Per Greer LJ in *Stepney Corpn v Osofsky* [1937] 3 All ER 289, 291; C M V Clarkson 'Kicking corporate bodies and damning their souls' (1996) 59 MLR 557.
9   *Green v London General Omnibus* (1859) 7 CBNS 290, 303.
10 *Barwick v English Joint Stock Bank* (1867) LR 2 Exch 259.
11 *Mill v Hawker* (1875) LR 10 Exch 92; *Fisher v Oldham Corpn* [1930] 2 KB 364.
12 [1911] 2 KB 775.
13 The cases *University Court of the University of Glasgow v Economist* and *University Court of the University of Edinburgh v Economist* (1990) Times, 13 July were proceedings for defamation: the report is concerned solely with questions of conflict of laws.

distinctive name.[14] A summary of Lord Oliver's opinion in the 'Jif' lemon juice dispute *Reckitt & Colman Products Ltd v Border Inc*,[15] is that the plaintiff must establish goodwill or reputation in the goods or services in the mind of the public, that there should be a demonstration of misrepresentation by the defendant leading or likely to lead the public into thinking that the goods or services offered are those of the plaintiff and that damage has been or is likely to be caused to the plaintiff as a result. There is no requirement to show any misrepresentation or fraudulent attempt on the part of the defendant. It has been suggested[16] that any action for passing off might lie against an institution which sought, deliberately or not, to use a name for its activities which was also in use by another institution with a reputation to protect. The most obvious area where this might arise is the 'Business School' appellation. Whether or not this might give rise to an action for passing off would depend on whether the terms used are an accepted trade description or ordinary English terms.[17]

2.4 The words 'Business School' or 'Law School' standing alone could presumably not secure protection, but 'Anytown Business School' could possible do so if a reputation had been built up and another body purported to use the same title. This can be avoided at institutional level through the exercise of good judgment by the Privy Council in granting new titles under the 1992 legislation. If a company is formed in order to obtain the protection of a registered business name, then it is open to the President of the Board of Trade to direct a change of name within 12 months of registration if he or she considers that the registered name is too similar to an existing name.[18] It may also be required to do so if the name gives so misleading an indication of its activities as to be likely to cause harm to the public.[19]

---

14 As in *Ewing v Buttercup Margarine Co Ltd* [1917] 2 Ch 1 'Buttercup', in *William Edge & Sons Ltd v William Niccolls & Sons Ltd* (1911) 28 RPC 582 'Dolly Blue' and most recently in the House of Lords in *Reckitt & Colman Products Ltd v Border Inc* [1990] 1 WLR 491 (the lemon-shaped plastic container or 'Jif').
15 [1990] 1 WLR 491, 499.
16 A Beale, N Bourne and R Geary 'What's in a Name? Protecting the Law School' (1993) Business Law Review 90.
17 In the 'Jif case' Lord Oliver of Aylmerton at [1990] 1 WLR 491, 505 gave three examples: 'cellular clothing' (*Cellular Clothing Co Ltd v Maxton and Murray* (1899) 16 RPC 397); 'office cleaning' (*Office Cleaning Services Ltd v Westminster Window and General Cleaners Ltd* (1946) 63 RPC 39); 'Chicago Pizza' (*My Kinda Town Ltd v Soll* [1983] RPC 407.)
18 Section 28 Companies Act 1985.
19 Section 32 Companies Act 1985.

Defamation

2.5   Defamation, the law relating to which has been changed in some
important respects by the Defamation Act 1996, is a tort (delict in
Scotland) which arises when a person makes a statement about
another which exposes the latter to hatred, ridicule or contempt,
which causes that person to be shunned or avoided, or which has a
tendency to lower that person in the estimation of right-thinking
members of society generally, or injure that person in any office, trade
or profession, for example describing an actor as 'hideously ugly'.[20]
The House of Lords has held in *Derbyshire County Council v Times
Newspapers Ltd*[21] that the 'person' being protected cannot be a
municipal corporation. The basis of this decision is the public interest
which exists in the freedom in a democratic society to criticise those
who govern. It is not clear whether this ruling applies to other forms
of corporation. It has been suggested[22] that the basis of extension of
the doctrine to other corporate bodies is that they have a socio-
economic significance comparable to government. Whether this is
true of higher education institutions remains to be seen.

2.6   Defences to defamation include justification (ie the statement
was true), fair comment on a matter of public interest (if not actuated
by malice), or that the statement was made on a privileged occasion.
Of the two kinds of privilege, that of 'absolute privilege' is irrelevant
to the higher education scene, being restricted to judicial and
parliamentary occasions. An occasion on which 'qualified privilege'
may arise is:

> ... where the person who makes a communication has an interest or a
> duty, legal, social or moral, to make it to the person to whom it is
> made, and the person to whom it is so made has a corresponding
> interest or duty to receive it.[23]

It is essential to a claim of qualified privilege that there is an absence
of malice. Occasions on which privileged occasions might arise in
higher education include external examiners' reports, references and
testimonials and written and verbal statements in committees. So long

---

20   *Berkoff v Burchill* [1996] 4 All ER 1008, CA.
21   [1993] AC 534, HL; overturning *Bognor Regis UDC v Campion* [1972] 2 QB
     169.
22   F Patfield 'Defamation, Freedom of Speech and Corporations' (1993) The Juridical
     Review p 294.
23   *Adam v Ward* [1917] AC 309, 334 per Lord Atkinson.

as the person making the statement 'honestly' believes in the truth of what he or she says it will be difficult to infer malice and thus destroy the defence of privilege. An issue of this kind arose between two members of a local authority when one made a speech defamatory of the other during a meeting of the authority[24] and in the circumstances was held to be protected by qualified privilege. However, if qualified privilege is to be preserved, it is also essential that there is a duty or interest in receiving the material alleged to be defamatory. If it is issued outwith the membership of the body due to receive it, by, for example, the common practice of placing copies in a library, the privilege will almost certainly be destroyed.[25] It is possible to defame on electronic bulletin boards and otherwise on the internet.[26]

Academic freedom

2.7 In the United Kingdom the protection of academic freedom by law is limited. By contrast to other countries with a written constitution (eg Constitution of The Russian Federation, Article 29; First Amendment to the Constitution of the United States), the source of any right to academic freedom in employment is the contract of employment itself. The right of freedom of expression granted by the 1950 European Convention on Human Rights is not yet incorporated into UK law. ERA did not establish any general principle of academic freedom but required the University Commissioners to be guided by certain principles when formulating changes to the older universities' statutes and equivalent rules.

2.8 In England and Wales only, freedom of speech within the law is protected generally by section 43(1) E(2)A86:

> Every individual and body of persons concerned in the government of any [hei] shall take such steps as are reasonably practicable to ensure that freedom of speech within the law is secured for members, students and employees of the establishment and for visiting speakers.

and by section 202(2)(a) ERA in respect of redundancy, disciplinary, dismissal, involuntary ill-health retirement and grievance procedures in the older universities to give effect to this principle:

24 *Horrocks v Lowe* [1975] AC 135.
25 *De Buse v McCarthy* [1942] 1 KB 156.
26 See eg *Rindos v Hardwick* (31 March 1994, unreported), Supreme Court of Western Australia.

... the Commissioners shall have regard to the need ... to ensure that academic staff have freedom within the law to question and test received wisdom, and to put forward new ideas and controversial or unpopular opinions, without placing themselves in jeopardy of losing their jobs or privileges they may have at their institutions ...

and similar provisions appear in the instruments of government etc of the other higher education institutions.

2.9 Freedom of speech is of course only part of what we know as academic freedom, since the latter includes freedom to pursue research and freedom to publish. The latter is particularly difficult since it brings into question the ownership of the written work of staff as employees: it requires a clear set of regulations on legal responsibility for writings.

2.10 The phrase 'within the law' requires some examination. It relates to the accepted need for a balance to be struck between the individual's right to freedom of expression and the rights of others including the rights of the state.[27] Quite where such a balance should be struck in the higher education setting is a difficult question. Possible areas where the general law might intervene include treason and treason felony,[28] incitement to racial hatred,[29] unlawful discriminatory acts,[30] offences against public order, terrorist offences,[31] common law offences such as blasphemy, incitement to commit certain statutory offences including misuse of drugs,[32] indecency with children,[33] incitement to mutiny[34] or disaffection,[35] breaking up public meetings[36] and so on. Today we must have regard to the fact that statements which are potentially unlawful can be delivered in a variety of forms: spoken, written, faxed, e-mailed, put on the World Wide Web and so on. We also have to recognise that what is lawful in one jurisdiction may be unlawful in another.

---

27 See eg ECS Wade and A W Bradley *Constitutional and Administrative Law* (1993) p 412; *R v Secretary of State for the Home Department, ex p McQuillan* [1995] 4 All ER 400 at 401.
28 Treason Acts 1351–1795; Treason Felony Act 1848.
29 Public Order Act 1986.
30 SDA and RRA.
31 Prevention of Terrorism (Temporary Provisions) Acts as current.
32 Misuse of Drugs Act 1971.
33 Indecency with Children Act 1960.
34 Incitement to Mutiny Act 1797.
35 Incitement to Disaffection Act 1934.
36 Public Meeting Act 1908.

2.11 In the United States there are constitutional guarantees of freedom of speech for all government employees, except where such potential disruption is caused as to outweigh the value of the speech and that action is taken relating to the disruption and not the speech itself.[37] Colleges are described as 'the market place of ideas where academic freedom should be protected'[38] and teachers must remain 'free to enquire.'[39] Dismissal for alleged violation of law which in effect was very similar to the Treason Felony Act (designed to deal with 'subversives') was held to be unconstitutional[40] and the courts will protect academics' rights to publish non-politically correct theories as in *Levin v Karleston*.[41] Levin's right to propound his argument that blacks are less intelligent on average than whites was upheld by the Court, attempts to control it being described as 'the antithesis of freedom of speech', the creation of an investigative committee creating a 'chilling effect' on his right to speak freely about his research. The courts will not however intervene where the reason for dismissal was in fact some form of improper behaviour which does not have an educational function.[42]

2.12 However in private universities the principle is identical to that in the UK: protection of academic freedom depends on the contract and on such statutory rights as non-governmental employees enjoy, for example in relation to sex and race discrimination. In the UK staff enjoy statutory protection against discrimination and unfair dismissal and may rely upon the 1986 Act where it applies. Our law requires that staff shall be given a statement of the principal terms of employment within a set period and this statement may refer them to other documents. In universities the statement will refer them to the charter, statutes, etc and also possibly to a staff handbook or similar document. It is essential that any limitations on the individual's freedom of expression are clearly set out so that disputes may be avoided.

2.13 It is unlikely that a corporation would itself make a defamatory statement (eg in a press release) but it may be held liable for such statements made by an officer acting within the scope of his or her

---

37 *Waters v Churchill* 114 S Ct 1878 (1994).
38 *Healy v James* 408 US 169 (1972).
39 *Sweezy v New Hampshire* 354 US 234 (1957).
40 *Keyishian v Board of Regents* 385 US 589 (1967).
41 966 F 2d 85 (1992).
42 *Martin v Parrish* 805 F 2d 583 (1986).

authority.[43] If the officers or employees of a statutory body such as a Funding Council were to make a defamatory statement, for example in a quality assessment report, it again would be protected by qualified privilege except if the report was made available to anyone who did not have a duty or interest to receive it.

2.14 Institutions may feel aggrieved at newspaper articles written about them, including the increasing practice of producing league tables based often on subjective weighting by individuals of a range of performance indicators selected, more or less at random, from published or anecdotal data. Such league tables can be damaging to those who do not appear near the top, discouraging students from applying for admission, industrial and commercial sponsors from providing funds for research and development, and forming an image in the minds of the public rather different to that which the institution genuinely believes it should have. Newspapers are subject to rather different rules of law, and it is open to them to prove both that a statement was published without actual malice or gross negligence and that the earliest opportunity was taken to publish an apology.[44] Section 7(2) Defamation Act 1952 applies to newspaper reports of the general meetings of companies incorporated by charter or under the Companies Acts. Section 1 Defamation Act 1996 has amended the law in respect of so-called 'innocent' publication.

2.15 It does not amount to slander of property for someone to state that his or her article or service is better than that of a rival and to give reasons for that statement, even though the reasons involve disparagement of the rival's product.[45]

Criminal liability

2.16 Perhaps the most obvious aspect of criminal liability is that concerned with the law of health and safety but in fact an institution can commit any offence other than those for which the sole penalty is death or imprisonment or which cannot be committed vicariously. Where a conviction for a criminal offence depends upon intent being shown, that cannot be the intent of an artificial person and must be that of those in control of what the institution does.[46] In *Re Supply*

43 This was attempted unsuccessfully in *Glasgow Corpn v Lorimer* [1911] AC 209.
44 Section 2 Libel Act 1843.
45 *White v Mellin* [1895] AC 154; *Hubbuck v Wilkinson* [1899] 1 QB 86.
46 *Tesco Supermarkets v Nattrass* [1972] AC 153.

of Ready Mixed Concrete (No 2)[47] the House of Lords held that employees and the companies employing them were separate entities but that companies were only able to carry on their business by the employees acting on their behalf. The action of those employees, in the course of their employment, constituted the company's business and, if acting contrary to a court order, could render the company liable in contempt of court.[48]

Health and safety at work

Health and Safety At Work, Etc Act and Regulations

2.17 Although laws governing aspects of health and safety in specific types of employment have existed for many years, the major reforming legislation was the Health and Safety at Work etc Act 1974 (HASAW), under which regulations have been made covering a wide variety of activity, increasingly in order that the UK may comply with European Union Directives in a field in which the Union is extremely active. The equivalent legislation in Northern Ireland is the Health and Safety At Work (Northern Ireland) Order 1978.[49] Health and safety 'scares' occur from time to time, one of the most notable and costly in higher education institutions in the past having been the asbestos problems in the 1970s and 1980s leading to a series of regulations between 1983 and 1987.[50] In 1993 the so-called 'six-pack' of major regulations, implementing the 'framework' and 'daughter' directives, all of which are of relevance to higher education institutions, came into force.

2.18 The essence of HASAW is that it allows the Health and Safety Executive established by it to bring criminal proceedings against any organisation or person for breaches of the Act, regulations issued under it and certain other pre-existing legislation which is gradually being assimilated under HASAW: section 37 Deregulation and Contracting Out Act 1994 empowers the Secretary of State to repeal or revoke pre-1974 legislation without replacement. The Health and Safety Agency has similar powers in Northern Ireland. Section 47 HASAW provides that the Act does not affect common law rights of civil action or actions for breach of statutory duty by persons injured

47 [1995] 1 All ER 135.
48 See also *Stancomb v Trowbridge UDC* [1910] 2 Ch 190.
49 SI 1978/1039.
50 Less detailed regulations had existed since 1969. There are also Codes of Practice on working with asbestos.

or affected, but they may not themselves take action under it. In practice it is not easy for anyone to prove that the statutory regulations supersede the common law duty of care.[51]

The duties of employers

2.19 Section 2 HASAW spells out the duties of employers as

(i) the provision and maintenance of plant and systems at work[52] that are, so far as is reasonably practicable, safe and without risk to health;

(ii) the making of arrangements for ensuring, so far as is reasonably practicable, safety and absence of risks to health in connection with the use, handling, storage and transport of articles and substances;

(iii) the provision of such information,[53] instruction, training and supervision as is necessary to ensure, so far as is reasonably practicable, the health and safety at work of employees;

(iv) the maintenance, so far as is reasonably practicable, of any place of work under the employer's control in a condition that is safe and without risks to health, and the provision and means of access to and egress from it that are safe and without risks;

(v) the provision and maintenance of a working environment for employees that is, so far as is reasonably practicable, safe, without risks to health, and adequate as regards facilities and arrangements for their welfare at work.

Certain requirements for consulting safety representatives, establishing safety committees, etc are set out in statutory instruments.[54] What is 'reasonably practicable' will require weighing the risk in any activity against the measures necessary to eliminate it.[55]

2.20 Some examples of this in practice are:

51 *Matuszczyk v National Coal Board* 1953 SC 8; *Bux v Slough Metals* [1973] 1 WLR 1358.

52 The expression 'at work' extends to equipment provided but not actually used: *Bolton Metropolitan Borough Council v Malrod Insulations Ltd* [1993] ICR 358, CA.

53 The Safety Signs Regulations 1980 are of particular importance in laboratories and any area in which potentially dangerous equipment is used.

54 Safety Representatives and Safety Committees Regulations 1977 (SI 1977/500) as amended by Health and Safety (Consultation with Employees) Regulations 1996 (SI 1996/1513).

55 *Edwards v National Coal Board* [1949] 1 All ER 743.

(i) Use of articles and substances: *Pape v Cumbria County Council*[56] where the employer was held liable when a cleaner contracted skin problems through failing to use rubber gloves, which although they were provided, she had not been advised to wear;

(ii) Handling: *Whitfield v H & R Johnson (Tiles)*[57] where the employer was not liable when W was injured moving objects due to congenital back trouble unknown to the employer;

(iii) Safe working environment: *McSherry v British Telecom* and *Lodge v British Telecom*,[58] a 1992 case concerned with the condition known as 'repetitive strain injury' (RSI) sustained by some employees working with keyboards, where liability was established both in negligence and in breach of statutory duty under section 14 Offices, Shops and Railway Premises Act 1963, the latter in respect of failure to provide suitable seating. In *Mughal v Reuters*[59] RSI was said to have 'no place in the medical books' and in this case the plaintiff's symptoms were held not to have been caused by physical aspects of the work in which he was employed. In *Pickford v Imperial Chemical Industries*[60] the Court of Appeal held that ICI had been negligent in failing to tell P that she should break up long periods of typing with other work.

2.21 An employer who fails to implement these requirements may incur criminal liability under section 33 and if there is an accident may be liable to claim for damages at common law or in an action for breach of statutory duty under a range of statutes including the Factories Acts, the Fire Precautions Act 1971 and the Offices, Shops and Railway Premises Act 1963. The Reporting of Injuries, Diseases and Dangerous Occurrences Regulations (RIDDOR) 1995[61] set out requirements to be followed by employers.

Non-delegable duty of care

2.22 The duty of care owed by an employer to the employee is 'non-delegable' as explained in 1987 by Lord Brandon of Oakbrook in *McDermid v Nash Dredging and Reclamation Co Ltd*[62]

56 [1992] 3 All ER 211.
57 [1990] 3 All ER 426.
58 (1992) 3 Med LR 129.
59 [1993] IRLR 571.
60 [1996] IRLR 622, CA.
61 SI 1995/3163.
62 [1987] ICR 917, 930.

The essential characteristic of the duty is that, if it is not performed, it is no defence for the employer to show that he delegated its performance to a person, whether his servant or not his servant, whom he reasonably believed to be competent to perform it. Despite such delegation the employer is liable for the non-performance of the duty.

This was further illustrated in 1993 in *Morris v Breaveglen Ltd (trading as Anzac Construction Co)*[63] where the defendants remained liable under the contract of employment to fulfil their obligation to the plaintiff to take reasonable care to see that he was not exposed to unnecessary risk while working at a site operated by a third party to whom his services had been sub-contracted. This case is of considerable importance to higher education institutions who 'lend' staff to other institutions while the staff remain on the institution's payroll. The employer's duty of care cannot be delegated to the employee himself or herself.[64]

Requirement to keep abreast of knowledge

2.23 The employer must keep abreast of contemporary knowledge, as for example in the field of noise causing damage to hearing and protection which is available.[65] Section 100 EmpRA, discussed elsewhere, sets out the circumstances in which an employee may take reasonable steps to protect him or herself and fellow employees in cases of danger, while enjoying statutory protection against discipline for doing so.

Employer's duty to other persons

2.24 Section 3 HASAW extends the employer's duties to include others who use the premises concerned. In a higher education institution this includes students, members of the public or contractors working in a building. The fact that an accident may occur during an act of trespass does not diminish the employer's responsibility to maintain a safe environment at all times.[66] CVCP

---

63 [1993] ICR 766, CA.
64 *McLaughlin v British Steel Corpn* 1978 SLT 28.
65 *Baxter v Harland & Wolff plc* [1990] IRLR 516, NI Court of Appeal: see also the summary of the employer's obligations by Swanwick J in *Stokes v Guest Keen and Nettlefold (Bolts and Nuts) Ltd* [1968] 1 WLR 1776.
66 Occupiers' Liability Act 1984, giving statutory effect to the judgment of the House of Lords in *British Rlys Board v Herrington* [1972] AC 877.

advice *Health and Safety Responsibilities of Supervisors towards postgraduate and undergraduate students*[67] provides guidance. In essence responsible staff must be able to demonstrate that they have exercised an effective supervisory role, guidance being offered by dictum of Holroyd Pearce LJ in *Moloney v A Cameron Ltd*[68] as approved by the Court of Appeal in *Owen v Evans and Owen (Builders) Ltd.*[69] Proper risk assessment must be undertaken and controls and monitoring implemented, in particular covering the arrangements for absence of designated staff.

Air pollution

2.25 Section 5 HASAW places a further duty on the employer to prevent by the best practical means any emission into the atmosphere of noxious or offensive substances and to render harmless and inoffensive such substances as may be so emitted. Both the way in which plant is used and the supervision of the operation involved are important. This is obviously relevant to the operation of fume-cupboards, where the institution's management may be held responsible for failure to ensure that equipment is operating satisfactorily. Part I Environmental Protection Act 1990 is also important in this context.

Safety of manufactured or supplied articles

2.26 Section 6 HASAW states that it is the duty of any person who designs, manufactures, supplies or imports articles to ensure that they are safe and without risks when properly used. The provision was widened by the Consumer Protection Act 1987.

Duties of employees

2.27 Section 7 HASAW places a duty on every employee while at work:
(i)   to take reasonable care for the health and safety of himself or

67   Annex 1 to CVCP Circular Letter N/93/111.
68   [1961] 2 All ER 934.
69   [1962] 3 All ER 128.

herself and of other persons who may be affected by the employee's acts or omissions at work;[70] and

(ii) as regards any duty or requirement imposed on the employer or any other person by or under any of the relevant statutory provisions, to co-operate with that person so far as is necessary to enable that duty or requirement to be performed or complied with.

2.28 In addition, employees have a duty not to interfere with or misuse anything which is provided by the employer in the interests of health, safety and welfare in the work place. Where self-sustained injuries result from an employee's conduct, civil as well as criminal proceedings may result. In such cases, the degree of contributory negligence will be assessed as between employer and employee.[71]

Liability of managers, etc

2.29 Section 37 HASAW provides

(1) Where an offence ... committed by a body corporate is proved to have been committed with the consent or connivance of, or to have been attributable to any neglect on the part of, any director, manager, secretary or other similar officer of the body corporate or a person who was purporting to act in any such capacity,[72] he as well as the body corporate shall be guilty of that offence and shall be liable to be proceeded against and punished accordingly.

(2) Where the affairs of a body corporate are managed by its members, the preceding sub-section shall apply in relation to the acts and defaults of a member in connection with his functions of management as if he were a director of the body corporate.

2.30 Consent or connivance has to be proved: a director's duty is not absolute and some act or omission constituting neglect must be shown.[73] Neglect implies a failure to perform a duty which the person knows or ought to have known.[74] Therefore those in charge of

---

70 Prior to HASAW, *Imperial Chemical Industries v Shatwell* [1964] 2 All ER 999 was an unusual case where two shotfirers were found to have voluntarily taken on a risk despite careful training by the employers, who were held not to be liable when the men were injured.

71 See eg *Ross v Associated Portland Cement Manufacturers Ltd* [1964] 2 All ER 452; *Boyle v Kodak Ltd* [1969] 2 All ER 439.

72 This covers directors etc whose appointment is irregular or defective: *Dean v Hiesler* [1942] 2 All ER 340.

73 *Huckerby v Elliott* [1970] 1 All ER 189.

74 *Re Hughes* [1943] 2 All ER 269.

'managing' an institution have considerable responsibilities for the health and safety of anyone making use of the institution's facilities or entering its buildings, residences or grounds whether employees, students, contractors or the general public. Premises, equipment and plant must be safe; construction and maintenance work must be undertaken in a safe manner, whether by the direct labour force or by contractors.[75] The duty of the institution is strict and in all on-site working, the institution must ensure that contractors' staffs are aware of safety procedures.[76] What constitutes a manager or other similar officer is obviously important. There have been two relevant cases on this. In *Armour v Skeen*[77] the Director of Roads of a Regional Council was held to fall within the definition when he along with the council was prosecuted over a fatal incident. In that case although the council had issued a statement of safety policy, the Director had issued no detailed safety instructions. In *R v Boal*[78] an assistant bookshop manager was held to fall outside the similar definition used in the Fire Precautions Act 1971, because he was not 'managing in a governing role.' This issue has been discussed further in relation to institutional management in chapter 1.

Health and safety management in higher education

2.31   The Health and Safety Commission established under HASAW has an Education Services Advisory Committee (ESAC) which has produced a text *Health and Safety Management in Higher and Further Education: Guidance on Inspection, Monitoring and Auditing*. This should be read in conjunction with the Health and Safety Executive publication *Successful Health and Safety Management*.[79] Broadly the ESAC document requires
(i)   regular scheduled departmental self-inspection to assess health and safety performance against predetermined standards;
(ii)   central monitoring of the departmental self-inspection processes; and

75   Construction (Design and Management) Regulations 1994, SI 1994/3140 have the objective of providing a certificate of what went into a building, so that problems such as those arising from use of asbestos, can in future be avoided.
76   *R v Swan Hunter Shipbuilders* [1982] 1 All ER 264. For off-site working, see *Cook v Square D Ltd* [1992] ICR 262 and the Health and Safety At Work etc Act (Application outside Great Britain) Order 1995 (SI 1995/840). When it comes into force, the Posted Workers' Directive will also be relevant.
77   1977 SLT 71.
78   [1992] 3 All ER 177, CA.
79   See also CVCP (1995) *Code of Practice for University Health and Safety Management*; CVCP (1992) *Safety in Universities: Notes for Guidance*.

(iii) regular systematic health and safety auditing by suitably qualified, experienced and competent external auditors.

2.32 Responsibilities are placed on the head of the department (or such other officer as the institution may determine) to establish a departmental safety committee and appoint a member of staff as departmental safety officer. The head of department must then ensure that

(a) safety inspections of the complete department are properly organised and carried out on schedule at least once per year;
(b) any remedial action indicated is taken;
(c) records are kept of both the safety inspections and the arrangements for remedial action and a report of the inspection and remedial action is made to the departmental safety committee and a copy sent to the institution's safety adviser for the purpose of monitoring.

It is a matter for the institution to regulate how these responsibilities are assimilated into a head of department's contract of employment.

Regulations: The 'Six-Pack'

2.33 The so-called six-pack of regulations has been described as the biggest shakeup of laws relating to health and safety at work for nearly two decades. The regulations are contained in six statutory instruments of 1992, implementing six European Union Directives:[80] Management of Health and Safety At Work;[81] Manual Handling Operations;[82] Workplace Health, Safety and Welfare;[83] Personal Protective Equipment;[84] Provision and Use of Work Equipment[85] and Health and Safety (Display Screen Equipment).[86]

2.34 The essential element of these and other recent (and prospective) regulations is the emphasis on management of risk, with a closed loop of risk assessment, establishment of standards, monitoring of performance against standards and revised assessment.

---

80 Directives 89/391/EEC, 89/654/EEC, 89/655/EEC, 89/656/EEC, 90/270/EEC, 90/269/EEC. A seventh Directive, 91/383/EEC which relates to health and safety of certain temporary workers, is outside the 'six-pack' as it has limited application.
81 SI 1992/2051, amended by SI 1994/2865.
82 SI 1992/2793.
83 SI 1992/3004.
84 SI 1992/2966.
85 SI 1992/2932.
86 SI 1992/2792.

This is already familiar to higher education institutions in the Control of Substances Hazardous to Health (COSHH) Regulations 1994.[87] The regulations cover such practical matters as provisions of facilities for non-smokers, assessment of workstations and risks associated with significant use of display screens. They are significant in higher education primarily because as employers and occupiers of property, the governing bodies are responsible for their effective implementation in respect of staff, students, visitors and contractors. Staff need to be aware of them since they may be held personally liable if things go badly wrong.[88] Like all health and safety legislation, they are arguably also of considerable educative value to all students, since most if not all of them will have some responsibility in later life for the safety of others and themselves.

2.35 Unfortunately, as in any other area which has become a specialism, like the employment legislation described elsewhere, the area of health and safety is replete with legalistic jargon. Phrases such as 'significant risk' and 'suitable and sufficient risk assessment' are liable to interpretation by the courts. Particular attention has to be paid to sport, particularly since the decision in *Smoldon v Whitworth*[89] relating to the liability of a referee. Relevant publications include *Sport in Higher Education*[90] and *Safe Sport in Universities*.[91]

2.36 The details of all the regulations are beyond the scope of this book. At present, by far the most important in higher education appear to be the Provision and Use of Work Equipment Regulations 1992 (PUWER), read together with regulation 3(1) of the Management of Health and Safety at Work Regulations 1992 (MHSWR) as amended in 1994. The latter requires all employers to assess the risks to the health and safety of workers and any others who may be affected by the works carried out, for the purposes of identifying the measures needed to be taken to comply with other legislation. Carrying out this assessment will help to identify all the protective and preventive measures needed to comply with the regulations.

---

87 SI 1994/3246.
88 The duty as employee applies to everyone; the duty as 'manager' (specifically under section 23 Fire Precautions Act 1971) appears to apply only to those who have a 'governing role': see *R v Boal* [1992] 3 All ER 177, 182.
89 [1997] ELR 249, CA: see E Grayson 'Sport and the Law Update' (1997) New Law Journal 24 January.
90 CVCP (1996)
91 British Universities and Colleges Physical Education Association (1996).

2.37   The definition of equipment is, as might be expected wide-ranging and excludes only fairly obvious items such as livestock, substances (eg acids, cement, water), parts of a building structure (walls, floor, etc) and private motor vehicles. However the House of Lords has held that for the purposes of the earlier Employers' Liability (Defective Equipment) Act 1969 it includes such items as flagstones[92] which might not immediately spring to mind. A non-exhaustive list of possible items includes such obvious items as air compressors, drills and saws, and less obvious items such as computers, overhead projectors, vacuum cleaners and smoke detectors. Equipment must be suitable by design, construction and adaptation for the actual work it is provided to do and instruction given in its use. Thus for example a ladder should always be used at the correct angle and secured or held. Machinery or other equipment which is inherently dangerous in use should be appropriately guarded or protected, as for example, by fitting an earth-leakage detector in the case of electrical equipment. The use of most equipment is controlled in some other way eg scaffolding where a licence issued by the local authority is required in connection with the erection of scaffolding to alter, repair, maintain or clean any building which obstructs the highway.[93]

Regulations governing the use of buildings for particular purposes

2.38   There is much specific legislation designed to ensure that buildings used for particular purposes are suitable and safe for those purposes. In all cases the Health and Safety At Work, etc Act is also applicable. In some cases, eg animal experimentation, liquor licensing, anatomy, the law also intervenes on grounds of public policy. For example the Anatomy Act 1832 was brought in to control unsavoury practices in the early days of development of modern surgery.

Offices and shops

2.39   Before the enactment of HASAW, the Offices, Shops and Railway Premises Act 1963 (OSRPA) provided the basis of health and safety protection of employees in offices as the Factories Act 1961 did in factories. Many of its detailed provisions have been superseded by HASAW, the Fire Precautions Act 1971 and the various regulations, but some remain in force. As its title implies, the Act

---

92   *Knowles v Liverpool City Council* [1993] IRLR 588, HL.
93   Section 169 Highways Act 1980.

covers activities in offices, defined as places where more than 20 persons (at least 10 elsewhere than on the ground floor) are employed on office work under a contract of employment for an aggregate of at least 21 hours per week. Office work is defined as administration, clerical work (writing, bookkeeping, sorting and filing papers, typing, duplicating and drawing), handling money and operating telephone or telegraph equipment. A canteen or restaurant which serves office workers is regarded as office accommodation: other legislation or regulations will also apply for example in relation to hygiene and food preparation.

2.40 OSRPA also covers shops which are a common feature of higher education campuses. A shop is a building, or part of a building, where retail or wholesale trading takes place or where goods are brought by the public for repair or treatment, and also solid fuel depots. It does not extend to railway tunnels. Like other health and safety legislation, OSRPA prescribes basic standards which a good employer should have achieved in any event: contravention is a criminal offence, normally actioned under HASAW. Examples of its scope are provisions relating to

(i)   safety and cleanliness of premises and furnishings, fittings, lifts etc within them;
(ii) avoidance of overcrowding and availability of breathing space;
(iii) heating, ventilation and lighting to minimum specific standards;
(iv) provision of sanitary conveniences and washing facilities (further prescribed in the Sanitary Conveniences Regulations and Washing Facilities Regulations 1964 respectively);
(v)   requirement for supplies of wholesome drinking water;
(vi) provision of cloakrooms;
(vii) provision of sitting facilities.

2.41 There is no doubt that the unfenced hole in the floor which was the subject of the action in *Cook v Square D Ltd*[94] would have given rise to an offence under OSRPA had it occurred in the UK in an office environment. The Offices, Shops and Railway Premises (Hoists and Lifts) Regulations 1968 give a building owner the responsibility for ensuring that all such equipment is of good mechanical construction, sound, of adequate strength and properly maintained. OSRPA requirements in respect of seating are that seats should be provided which are of suitable design, construction and dimension, including footrests if employees cannot readily and comfortably support their feet. The new Health and Safety

94 [1992] ICR 362.

Regulations expand this requirement, in particular where a major part of the work involves sitting at a computer workstation.

Day nurseries and canteens

2.42 The Children Act 1989 governs the registration of day nurseries by the local authority; registration is dependent on the authority being satisfied on staffing and accommodation provided. There is a large amount of legislation governing the health aspects of the preparation and service of food, notably the Food Safety Act 1990 and regulations made under it.

Animal houses

2.43 The protection of animals used for experimental or other scientific procedures is governed by the Animals (Scientific Procedures) Act 1986. No scientific (ie other than veterinary, agricultural or animal husbandry) procedure may take place other than at the place specified in the licence granted to a person. A personal licence granted to an individual to undertake regulated procedures therefore specifies where the procedure should be performed. A project licence, authorising a programme of specified regulated procedures also specified the place or places where the procedures will be undertaken, and any place specified in a project licence must be designated by a certificate issued by the Secretary of State as a scientific procedure establishment.

Theatres, cinemas and other entertainment

2.44 The purpose of the legislation governing use of premises as theatres or cinemas is to secure the safety of the audience. Any premises used as a theatre[95] must be licensed by the local authority for the public performance of plays, whether payment is demanded or not.[96] The local authority is not concerned with the nature of the plays or the manner of their performance. Failure to apply for a licence or to comply with its terms are criminal offences. Similarly, unless the exhibitor holds an exemption certificate, premises used for public cinematographic exhibitions for which a charge is made (or

95 Even if not described as a theatre: *Archer v Willingrice* (1802) 4 Esp 186.
96 Section 18(1) Theatres Act 1968.

there is no private gain) must (in Scotland, may) be licensed for that purpose by the local authority.[97] There is an exception where they are not used for exhibitions on more than six days in the calendar year, provided that, for the purposes of securing safety of the public, written notice is given to specified authorities not less than seven days in advance and all conditions imposed by the local authority complied with.

2.45 Public[98] contests, exhibitions or displays of boxing, wrestling, judo or karate require (in Scotland, may require) an entertainment licence[99] issued by the local authority. The same applies to hypnotism[100] unless it takes place in a licensed theatre. Premises which provide public[101] dancing, music or similar entertainment require (in Scotland, may require) an entertainments licence granted by the local authority.[102] The use of private places for entertainment may also require a licence if promoted for private gain.[103]

Laboratories used for anatomical purposes

2.46 Medical research within the meaning of the Anatomy Acts 1832 to 1984 and the Human Tissue Act 1961 can potentially be undertaken in a wide range of scientific laboratories. Under section 1 Anatomy Act 1832 the licensing is of persons, and under section 12 dissection may be undertaken by such a person on premises of which notice is given to the Secretary of State by him, her, the owner or the occupier. Section 3 Anatomy Act 1984 envisages the licensing of premises. Under the 1961 Act parts of a body may be removed for medical purposes and research, provided that the specimen remains in the possession (ie under the control) of a licensed person.

Preparation and storage of spirits

2.47 Under tax legislation licences are required for the manufacture,

---

97 Section 1 Cinemas Act 1985.
98 The test is whether the public could be present, not whether they actually are: *Beynon v Caerphilly Lower Licensing Justices* [1970] 1 All ER 618.
99 Schedule 1(1) Local Government (Miscellaneous Provisions) Act 1982.
100 Section 2 Hypnotism Act 1952; section 19 and Schedule 2 Theatres Act 1968.
101 'Public' here has the same meaning as in the previous paragraph.
102 Section 30 Local Government (Miscellaneous Provisions) Act 1982.
103 Private Places of Entertainment (Licensing) Act 1967.

rectifying and compounding of spirits (except methanol), for their storage and for the storage of methylated spirits and petroleum.[104]

Licensing for the sale of alcoholic liquor, gaming machines etc

2.48 The law relating to liquor, etc licensing is complex and varies significantly between the jurisdictions of England, Wales, Scotland and Northern Ireland. No attempt will be made to deal with it here. It is however essential that the requisite licences are obtained and their terms honoured by the licensee, who will normally be the member of professional staff in charge of catering and similar services. Thankfully, although there is still considerable restriction applied to the installation and use of gambling and gaming machines,[105] the former requirement for licensing billiards and similar games has gone.[106]

Radioactive substances

2.49 The Radioactive Substances Act 1993 provides a system of state registration for premises on which radioactive substances (with the exception of those below a specified level of activity) may be kept and the persons who handle them. The use of these substances is regulated by the Ionising Radiation Regulations 1985 made under HASAW. They require notification of any new work involving radioactive substances 28 days prior to its commencement, and notification of any material change to the type of work being carried out. They also provide a mechanism for notifying dangerous occurrences and a framework for the transport and disposal of materials and waste.

Biological hazards

2.50 Regulations under HASAW control genetic manipulation, work on which requires notification to the Health and Safety

---

104 Section 100 Customs and Excise Management Act 1979; sections 18, 81 and 90 Alcoholic Liquor Duties Act 1979; Petroleum (Regulations) Acts 1928 and 1936 (Repeals and Modifications) Regulations 1974 (SI 1974/1942).
105 Gaming Act 1968.
106 Billiards (Abolition of Restrictions) Act 1987 repealing section 10 Gaming Act 1845, another example of contemporary public policy legislation.

Executive and the Advisory Committee on Genetic Manipulation. It is necessary to establish internal monitoring machinery under the supervision of which the work is carried out. The Health and Safety (Dangerous Pathogens) Regulations 1981 control the use and movement of certain dangerous pathogens. The importation of animal pathogens is controlled by regulations made under the Animal Health Act 1981 and of plant pathogens and pests by regulations made under the Plant Health Act 1967. The holding of other pathogens may require licensing under the Pests Act 1954 or the Diseases of Fish Act 1937. Part VI Environmental Protection Act 1990 deals with protection against genetically modified organisms.

Contractors and consultants

Introduction

2.51 At some time most higher education institutions will have experience of problems arising in building work. The law relating to building contracts and the employment of consultants is a specialised part of the general law of contract. As consumers of services, institutions are entitled to expect that what they receive is fit for the intended purpose and that services engaged are performed to a reasonable standard.

2.52 In addition to the common law rules applicable to all types of contract and any action which might lie in tort or delict for negligence, the Supply of Goods and Services Act 1982[107] provides additional protection for the consumer. Part I applies to the materials used in the execution of a contract and Part II to the service element (ie standards of performance) or the work itself. Contracts covered by the Act include those related to maintenance, building and construction and installation and improvement; Part I also extends to contracts of hire and Part II includes services offered by professional consultants of various kinds. The terms implied into such contracts by the Act are similar to those contained in the Sale of Goods Act 1979 as amended by the Sale and Supply of Goods Act 1994 and cover title or ownership, description, merchantable quality, fitness for purpose and sample. Assuming that the implied terms are a condition of the contract, any breach discharges the customer from

---

107 Equivalent provision is made for Scotland by the Sale and Supply of Goods Act 1994.

the obligation to pay the agreed price, and in addition damages may be recovered.

Public Works Contracts Regulations

2.53   The Public Works Contracts Regulations 1991[108] implement EC Public Works Directive 71/305/EEC as amended by 89/440/EEC and apply to all corporations in receipt of financial support from the Funding Councils.[109] These directives, together with other European Union procurement directives, are intended to facilitate the opening up of the European market by ensuring that firms in member states are allowed to compete for major contracts (those with an estimated value of less than 5m ECU net of VAT are excluded) on equal terms. There are three main principles:
(i)   Union-wide publication of notices;
(ii) use of objective criteria when selecting participants and awarding contracts;
(iii) use of non-discriminatory specifications.

Building contracts

2.54   Contracts for building and similar work are highly complex, deriving from many different sources. Unlike staff or student contracts, which are also complex, building contracts often involve very large sums of public money so it is vital that they are as tightly drawn as possible. The documents which make up a building contract can include the enquiry, a specification, drawings, a programme, the quotation and the contract document itself which, in the case of major contracts, will usually be in an approved standard form.[110] A contract being a mutual agreement, it is important not only to ensure that the contractor understands his or her obligations and complies with them, but also that the client does not place unnecessary obstacles in the path of completion. It is not unknown for staff and students in higher education institutions to fail to comprehend this point and therefore place contracts at risk.

108 SI 1991/2680.
109 See eg Scottish Office Building Directorate Practice Note No 2, June 1993 p 4.
110 An example is The Standard Form of Building Contract JCT80 issued by the Joint Contracts Tribunal – there is a Scottish equivalent.

2.55 Major projects will be supervised by the architect, who will almost certainly have been responsible for the design of the building or refurbishment scheme. He or she is the employer's agent, with powers conferred by the contract, and he or she is both entitled and obliged to protect the interests of the employer[111] being in a contractual relationship with the employer. The contractual relationship is likely to be based on the booklet *Architect's Appointment* published by the RIBA, and, since a service is being supplied, is also subject to the Supply of Goods and Services Act 1982. Alternatively, architects and other professionals may contract on the basis of their own standard terms, producing a *contract d'adhesion* the terms of which it may be possible to vary depending upon market forces. However, he or she is also expected by the Royal Institution of British Architects' Code of Professional Conduct to act impartially in all matters of dispute between contractor and building owner.[112]

2.56 In addition to the protection offered by the contract between the parties and the 1982 Act, clients are also afforded protection by the Unfair Contract Terms Act 1977 and the Unfair Terms in Consumer Contracts Regulations 1994[113] which among other things invalidates any attempt to exclude 'business liability' for negligence which results in personal injury.

Limitation

2.57 The Limitation Act 1980 stipulates that certain types of action – which includes claims for negligence against builders, architects and consultants – cannot be brought after the expiration of six years from the date on which the cause of action accrued, which in simple terms is the time when facts first exist upon which the plaintiff has the right to sue. In turn this is dependent upon whether the action is to be based on a breach of contract or on tort. Since an action in breach of contract can only be brought by one of the parties to that contract, the only recourse for third parties is an action in tort for negligence: these issues, including the operation of the Latent Damage Act 1986 constitute a complex area of law beyond the scope of this book. The law relating to prescription and limitation in Scotland is governed by the Prescription and Limitation (Scotland) Acts 1973 and 1984.

111 *Sutcliffe v Thackrah* [1974] AC 727, HL.
112 Scotland has separate but very comparable standard terms of engagement of architects.
113 SI 1994/3159.

In general there is a prescriptive period of five years: an obligation is extinguished at the end of that period if there has been no relevant claim made nor any relevant acknowledgement of the obligation. The starting date for the prescriptive period, including cases of reparation for breach of contract, can be summarised as either the date on which the loss, injury or damage occurred or, where it was a continuing process, the date on which the act, neglect or default ceased or the date when the injured party could first, with reasonable diligence, have become aware of the loss, injury or damage.

Relationship with the state

European Union law

2.58 Although some people may find the process of definition dry and tedious, it is important, increasingly so as European law has more significance in our daily lives and can affect individual employment rights. The legal status of higher education institutions within the Union varies considerably from country to country. Whether or not the British universities (and implicitly other higher education institutions) fall within the category of a 'public body' or 'organ of the state' for the purposes of English, Scots or Union law is a difficult question to answer.

2.59 There is an obvious distinction between institutions created by charter or by statutory process. In *Philips v Bury*[114] Holt CJ contrasted private charitable bodies with public corporations in terms of the right of the former to run their own affairs without interference. 'And I think ... if the Sentence be given by the proper Visitor, created so by the Founder, or by the Law, you shall never enquire into the validity, or Ground of the Sentence ... private and particular Corporations for Charity, founded and endowed by private Persons, are subject to the private Government of those who erect them.' This is referred to in *Vaneck v Governors of the University of Alberta*[115] and *Murdoch University v Bloom and Kyle*[116] in support of the proposition that chartered universities are not public bodies. However in *R v Manchester Metropolitan University, ex p Nolan*[117] Sedley J

114 (1694) Holt KB 715 at 723–4; 90 ER 1294 at 1299–1300.
115 [1975] 5 WWR 429 at 436.
116 [1980] WAR 193.
117 [1994] ELR 380; the same is true of other statutory universities in other Commonwealth countries see eg *Re Paine and University of Toronto* (1981) 131 DLR(3d) 325 at 329.

stated clearly that the university, conducted by a higher education corporation, was 'a public institution discharging public functions' recognising in that sense that at least the 'statutory' universities are what Cook J described in *Norrie v Senate of the University of Auckland*[118] as 'large publicly-funded institutions, constituted by Acts of Parliament and discharging by delegation an acknowledged responsibility of the State' in New Zealand. In a sense, the statement that universities are 'no longer private cloisters'[119] applies as much to the chartered institutions as to the rest.

2.60 The question of whether higher education institutions are 'emanations of the state' for the purpose of the direct applicability of European Directives has been discussed (in English law terms obiter) by the European Court of Justice in the sex discrimination case *Foster v British Gas plc*[120] and directly in *Turpie v University of Glasgow*.[121] In *Turpie* an industrial tribunal held that the University of Glasgow was not an organ of the state, although some 80% of its funding came from the state. According to Mancini JR in *Foster*,[122] the tribunal based its decision on 'the considerable freedom enjoyed by universities in the organisation of their teaching and research and on their long tradition of independent thought.'

2.61 However, developments since the ruling in *Foster* suggest that the reverse is the case. In *Foster* the European Court of Justice concluded that no one criterion could be formulated which would cover all situations which might arise. Some tests, such as the extent to which the state has a legal right to control the policy of the body concerned, fails to cover, inter alia, universities. The European Commission had suggested various criteria which might bring a public body within the concept of 'the state.' The first of these was the criterion of 'carrying out a public function on behalf of the state' which, the Commission suggested, covered universities which award degrees recognised by the member states.[123] Advocate-General Van Gerven was unable to find grounds to support some category of body between 'the state' and 'the individual' into which 'state universities

118 [1984] 1 NZLR 129.
119 S McLaughlin 'Up against the Law. The University Visitor' (1983) 8 Legal Service Bulletin 140 at 141.
120 C-188/89: [1990] 3 All ER 897.
121 Glasgow Industrial Tribunal (19 September 1986, unreported).
122 [1990] 3 All ER 897, 905.
123 Ibid at 917.

or even private universities that are financed wholly or virtually wholly by the state' might fall.[124] One possible solution suggested by Advocate-General Van Gerven was to consider how far the state had taken

> a general or specific power (or is simply able as a matter of fact to give ... binding directions ... to appoint or dismiss (the majority of) its directors ... to interrupt its funding wholly or in part so as to threaten its continued existence ...

stemming otherwise than from a general legislative power.
The European Court of Justice decided that

> ... article 5(1) of Directive 76/207 may be relied on in a claim for damages against a body, whatever its legal form, which has been made responsible, pursuant to a measure adopted by the state, for providing a public service under the control of the state and which has for that purpose special powers beyond those which result from the normal rules applicable in relations between individuals.

In *National Union of Teachers v Governing body of St Mary's Church of England (Aided) Junior School*[125] the Court of Appeal held that the governing body could be regarded as an emanation of the state. The test in *Foster* was a tripartite cumulative set of criteria, not a 'definition section.' The doctrine of 'direct vertical effect' was applied.[126]

2.62 The issue is also of importance in other areas of European law which impact directly on domestic law and practice. For example, Article 1 of the Council Directive on procedures for the award of public works contracts[127] defines a 'body governed by public law' as one
(i) established for the specific purpose of meeting needs in the general interest, not having an industrial or commercial character; and
(ii) having legal personality; and
(iii) financed, for the most part, by the state, or regional or local authorities, or other bodies governed by public law; or subject

---

124 Ibid at 912.
125 [1997] ICR 334.
126 See *Direct Effect – meaning of an emanation of the state* (1997) IDS Brief 582 p 4.
127 Council Directive (EEC) 71/305 as amended by Directive (EEC) 89/440.

to management supervision by those bodies; or having an administrative, managerial or supervisory board more than half of whose members are appointed by the state, regional or local authorities or other bodies governed by public law.

It seems reasonably clear that institutions of higher education fall within the definition of bodies governed by public law for this purpose.

Legislation specific to higher education

Statutory intervention in higher education institutions before 1988

2.63   After the Second World War and always in the background, as George Taylor and John Saunders pointed out[128] were the far-reaching powers conferred on the Secretary of State for Education by the Education Act 1944, now replaced by EA96, and the corresponding legislation in other parts of the UK, although in practice no attempt was made to use them. The original drafts of both the Education Reform Bill (1987) and the two Further and Higher Education Bills (1991) attempted to give the Secretaries of State rather more power over higher education than Parliament would allow, and a further attempt in the Education Bill (1993) was similarly defeated. In each case the Bill would have permitted the Secretaries of State to intervene directly in the affairs of institutions over a very wide area of activity, whereas the provisions of the Further and Higher Education Acts 1992 (FHEA and FHESA – which in this area supersede those of ERA) strictly limit the powers of the Secretaries of State as will be shown later. As it is, section 10 EA96 simply states: 'The Secretary of State shall promote the education of the people of England and Wales.'

2.64   Generally the Government did not until 1988 use legislation as a means of exerting control over higher education. For example, in a lecture in 1968 Richard Griffiths said

> Legally speaking, universities are today completely their own masters. None of the clauses, usual in Charters and Acts of Parliament creating new semi Governmental agencies, giving Ministers power to issue directions or giving the Treasury power to control numbers and remuneration of staff, are to be found in even the newest university charters ...[129]

128   G T Taylor and J B Saunders *The Law of Education* (8th ed, 1976) p 3.
129   R Griffiths 'Are the Universities Their Own Masters?' Page Fund Lecture, University College Cardiff (1968).

The University Grants Committee

2.65   Until 1988 control was exercised through the power of the purse and in the giving of advice by the former University Grants Committee, the history of which has been described by Frank Mattison[130] and Michael Shattock.[131] The Committee had existed since 1919 on a non-statutory basis but with pressure on public expenditure from the 1970s this arrangement had come under increasing criticism. Although the principle was never tested, it could be argued that its recommendations to the Secretaries of State were amenable to judicial review, particularly having regard to the dictum of Lord Parker CJ in *R v Criminal Injuries Compensation Board, ex p Lain*[132] where he described the Board as

> a servant of the Crown charged by the Crown, by executive instruction, with the duty of distributing the bounty of the Crown ... I do not think that this court should shrink from entertaining the application merely because the board have no statutory authority; they act with lawful authority, albeit such authority is derived from the executive and not from Act of Parliament.

As the UGC was a non-statutory body its activities did not fall within the scope of the Parliamentary Commissioner for Administration (the Ombudsman). When certain universities were 'fined' by the Committee in the mid-1980s for exceeding student number targets set by a process which was never made public, there was considerable pressure for reform of the funding system, to make it more open and accountable.

The National Advisory Body for Local Authority Higher Education

2.66   In what was then the 'public sector' of higher education, the National Advisory Body for Local Authority Higher Education (NAB) was, as its name implies, a body charged with advising local authorities on the level of resources which they should commit to those institutions then under local authority control. It was a

---

130   F T Mattison 'Universities and the Law' in D J Farrington and F T Mattison (eds) *Universities and the Law* CUA/CRS (1990) section 4.3.
131   M Shattock *The UGC and the Management of British Universities* (1994).
132   [1967] 2 All ER 770, 778. The Board is now a statutory body: Part VII Criminal Justice Act 1988. See also *R v Secretary of State for the Home Department, ex p Fire Brigades Union* [1995] AC 513, HL.

company limited by guarantee and on dissolution in 1989 its property was transferred to the PCFC and subsequently to the HEFCE.[133]

The role of the Privy Council

2.67 The powers of 'The Lords of Our Most Honourable Privy Council' in relation to higher education institutions are executive powers exercised by the relevant ministers, nothing more nor less. There is a legal fiction that the chartered corporations exist by exercise of the monarch's 'mere motion' under the royal prerogative and the Privy Council is a device for taking the formal powers directly out of the hands of government departments. The powers are generally exercisable by virtue of statutory authority, such as section 76 FHEA. The Council is on its own unsurprising admission in a letter to the Association of University Teachers[134] 'part of the machinery of government.' Later[135] the AUT claimed that 'never before in granting Charters and Statutes to universities or in approving amendments has [the Privy Council] tried to impose aspects of day-to-day government policy.' The issue was the Privy Council's insistence that all new and supplemental charters should contain explicit provision for dismissal on grounds of redundancy, some six years before ERA set up the University Commissioners to revise existing statutes. Ministerial responsibility for the Council's activities has been '... obscured by the dignified facade of Privy Council formality.'[136] In practice the very small Privy Council Office consults the relevant government departments and a wide range of other interests before reaching any decisions. The expertise in drafting charters, statutes, etc certainly lies there and in British society there is a certain kudos attached to approval of one's proposals by the Privy Council, although it is unlikely that many members of the public appreciate the work it does or the technical complexities of its operations.

Orders in Council and Orders of Council

2.68 Privy Council powers are exercisable in two distinct ways: by Order *in* Council and by Order *of* Council. The first requires the

---

133 Section 136 ERA as amended by Schedule 8 paragraph 37 FHEA.
134 Extract from a letter sent by the Clerk to the Privy Council to the General Secretary of the Association of University Teachers and reproduced in the *AUT Bulletin* No 101, September 1982, p 3.
135 *Bulletin* No 106.
136 E C S Wade and A W Bradley *Constitutional and Administrative Law* (1986) p 245.

presence of The Queen (or Counsellors of State in her absence) and is reserved for such matters as approving changes in royal charters of the pre-1992 universities. By contrast, the approval of the arrangements for governance of the post-1992 universities was by Order of Council, simply two government ministers of Privy Council rank.[137] The Privy Council's powers in both modes in relation to higher education extend to:

(i)   approval of draft charters under the College Charter Act 1871: approval of changes in charters and statutes;

(ii) approval of titles including the word 'university' (except where this has been granted by the President of the Board of Trade under regulations made under section 2(1)(b) Business Names Act 1985, where the Privy Council must be consulted): approval of changes in instruments corresponding to the statutes of a chartered institution where the constituting legislation so provides; approval of arrangements for governance of the new universities (in Scotland the 'designated institutions') under the 1992 Acts.

The legislation of 1988–1992

The Education Reform Act 1988 (ERA)

2.69   Pressure from the Education Departments as providers of funds for a more open, cost-effective and accountable system of financing higher education and a desire to remove higher education entirely from direct local control led to the passage of ERA. This removed the statutory obligation on local authorities to provide higher education in their area and had the effect of placing much of the relationship between the institutions and the source of the instrument of government of most of them, the Crown, on a statutory basis.

2.70   The essence of the Act as it related to higher education was

(i)   to replace the University Grants Committee by a Universities Funding Council whose relationship with universities was prescribed by statute and which came into being formally in 1989;

(ii) to appoint University Commissioners with powers to amend university statutes so as to bring academic staff of the then universities within the operation of the general law relating to employment with some continued protection for 'academic

137   Section 124(D)2 ERA introduced by section 71 FHEA.

freedom,' a concession somewhat grudgingly wrung out of the government during the passage of the Education Reform Bill;[138]

(iii) to exclude the Visitorial jurisdiction, in those universities subject to it, in respect of any dispute relating to a member of academic staff concerning appointment or dismissal except in the hearing of appeals or grievances;

(iv) to transfer the polytechnics and certain colleges from local authority to national control while maintaining the 'binary line' and to provide for the grant of funds to them and general supervision by a Polytechnics and Colleges Funding Council which came into being formally in 1989.

The Further and Higher Education Acts 1992 (FHEA and FHESA)

2.71 Those parts of the 1988 Act listed in (i) and (iv) were superseded by the provisions of the 1992 Acts (FHEA and FHESA) which removed the 'binary line' and replaced the two sectoral Funding Councils set up in 1989 by three unitary Funding Councils covering the whole of the publicly-funded higher education system in Great Britain. The effects of (ii) and (iii) will be examined in some detail in the chapter dealing with employment.

2.72 The principal powers of the Secretaries of State are now contained in the 1992 Acts. Among powers and duties in legislation other than the 1992 Acts are:

(i) powers of approval of courses in relation to specific academic and vocational disciplines, including teaching in Scotland;[139]

(ii) power to amend university statutes to conform with changes in local government;[140]

(iii) duty to make available facilities for clinical teaching and research in medical and dental schools.[141]

2.73 The powers under the 1992 Acts are the most significant and are broadly as follows:

---

138 No such provision was necessary in the case of the 'public sector' since the concept of tenure as understood in the universities was unknown in that sector. Academic freedom is protected in the Articles of Association of the new universities. Also see s 43 E(2)A 1986.

139 Eg section 55 FHESA, amending the Teaching Council (Scotland) Act 1965 (as amended).

140 Eg section 252 Local Government Act 1972.

141 Section 51 National Health Service Act 1977.

(i)   to appoint the members of the Funding Councils;[142]
(ii) to make grants to the Councils for the purpose of providing financial support for 'eligible activities' defined in the Acts, subject to such terms and conditions as the Secretary of State may determine;[143]
(iii) to give general directions[144] to the Councils;
(iv) to require information and advice from the Councils in such manner as the Secretary of State may determine;[145]
(v)   to confer or impose on a Council such supplementary functions relating to the provision of education as the Secretary of State thinks fit;
(vi) to designate institutions as eligible to receive funds administered by a Council and to transfer farther education corporations to the higher education sector once they meet the student enrolment figures required for membership of that sector;[146]
(vii) (Scotland only) to establish new institutions 'for the provision of any form of higher education';[147]
(viii) to close designated institutions (Scotland);[148] the power to dissolve higher education corporations (England and Wales) was taken in ERA;[149]
(ix) to direct the Councils to make provision for the assessment of arrangements for maintaining academic standards [academic audit as distinguished from quality assessment];[150]
(x)   to direct that the financial year of higher education corporations should begin on a date other than 1 April.[151]

Secretaries of States' Guidance to Funding Councils

2.74 The Secretaries of State issued letters of guidance to the Funding Councils once the legislation was on the statute book. These and the subsequent 'Management Statements' set out the then

142 Section 62 FHEA; Section 37 FHESA.
143 Section 68 FHEA; Section 42 FHESA.
144 These directions and others under the Act may also be revoked or varied under section 570 EA96 (originally section 111 Education Act 1944 as applied by section 89(5) FHEA).
145 Section 69 FHEA; section 43 FHESA.
146 Sections 72 and 74 FHEA; sections 5, 25 and 44 FHESA.
147 Section 46 FHESA deriving from section 77 Education (Scotland) Act 1980.
148 Section 47 FHESA.
149 Section 128 ERA.
150 Section 70 FHEA; section 39 FHESA.
151 Section 78 FHEA: with the objective of bringing higher education corporations into line with existing universities.

government's priorities for their activities. They included emphasis on the Councils' roles in relation to quality assurance and increasing cost-effectiveness of the delivery of higher education by, for example, stimulating the availability of accelerated degree programmes. Letters of guidance are issued regularly.

Appointment of members of Funding Councils

2.75 In appointing members of the Funding Councils the Secretary of State

(a) shall have regard to the desirability of including persons who appear to have experience of, and to have shown capacity in, the provision of higher education or to have held, and to have shown capacity in, any position carrying responsibility for the provision of higher education and, in appointing such persons, he shall have regard to the desirability of their being currently engaged in the provision of higher education or in carrying responsibility for such provision, and

(b) shall have regard to the desirability of including persons who appear to him to have experience of, and to have shown capacity in, industrial, commercial or financial matters or the practice of any profession.[152]

Comparison with sections 131(3) and 132(3) ERA is interesting: there, between six and nine members of the UFC and PCFC were to be persons currently engaged in the provision of higher education and the balance of 15 members were to be those with experience of industry, commerce, etc. The members of the UGC were almost entirely academics. The trend has been progressively away from academics towards 'business' people.

General directions to the Funding Councils

2.76 It is the powers of the Secretaries of State to give general directions and to attach conditions to the grants to the Funding Councils which caused most debate during the passage of the Further and Higher Education Bills, as indeed was the case during the passage of the rather less well-defined provisions of ERA, repealed by FHEA. The terms and conditions subject to which grants are made to the Councils 'must be general and may not be expressed so as to affect

---

152 This is the language of section 62(4) FHEA: section 37(3) FHESA has slightly different phrasing but is essentially the same.

any particular institution,'[153] except where it appears to the Secretary of State that there is mismanagement of the financial affairs of an institution.[154] The latter power appears under the 'directions' sections of the Acts. Restrictions on the Secretary of State's powers in relation to terms and conditions will be discussed in more detail under the Funding Councils.

2.77 A recommendation that the Secretary of State should have a reserve power of direction was first made in the report of the review of the University Grants Committee under Lord Croham. The reserve power to make directions by order first appeared in section 134(8) ERA:

> In exercising their functions under this Part of this Act each of the Funding Councils shall comply with any directions given to them by the Secretary of State.

and was re-enacted in section 81 FHEA:

(1) In exercising their functions under this Part of this Act, each council shall comply with any directions under this section, and such directions shall be contained in an order made by the Secretary of State.
(2) The Secretary of State may give general directions to a council about the exercise of their functions.
(3) If it appears to the Secretary of State that the financial affairs of any institution within the higher education sector have been or are being mismanaged he may, after consulting the council and the institution, give such directions to the council about the provision of financial support in respect of the activities carried on by the institution as he considers are necessary or expedient by reason of the mismanagement.

and in section 54 FHESA which is expressed in the same terms.

Dealing with disasters

2.78 Explaining the need for the reserve power of direction in relation to the Further and Higher Education (Scotland) Bill, the government spokesman in the House of Lords said

---

153 House of Lords *Official Report* Vol 535 col 1453.
154 Eg section 254(3) FHESA.

Essentially, the power to make general directions to a non-departmental public body is a commonplace feature of legislation these days, reflecting modern approaches to financial and ministerial accountability. Such powers are often not subject to any parliamentary scrutiny at all, but in this case they are so because of the concern about the possible effect on academic freedom of the institution-specific power, not the general power.

He went on to say that both the general power and the specific power to direct the Councils

> ... are there to deal with unpredictable contingencies ... a form of disaster insurance. The power to attach conditions to grant ... deals with the general case and the power of direction with the unforseen exceptions.

The government declined to give any examples of instances in which the 'disaster insurance' would come into play.[155]

2.79 'Mismanagement' is not defined in the Act, but presumably extends beyond alleged defalcation to incompetence. It must extend beyond mere 'unreasonable' behaviour since paragraph 50 of Schedule 8 to FHEA removes the power of the Secretary of State under section 68 Education Act 1944, extended by section 219 ERA to higher education corporations, to intervene in cases of 'unreasonableness.' The power to give directions as the Secretary of State considers 'necessary or expedient' must be exercised according to accepted principles of administrative law, ie reasonably, on proper grounds and in good faith to achieve the purposes of the legislation.[156]

Information to be provided by the Funding Councils

2.80 The power to require information, coupled with the duty of institutions to give the Councils such information as they may in turn require for the purpose of the exercise of any of their functions, ensures that by indirect means the government has access to all the information held by institutions, not just that which institutions are required to provide to the Higher Education Statistics Agency (HESA). HESA has been engaged by the Funding Councils as their agent for the purpose of providing information required by the

155 Statements by The Paymaster-General, House of Lords *Official Report* Vol 533 col 1036; Vol 534 col 638.
156 See eg Sir William Wade *Administrative law* (5th ed, 1988) pp 445–454.

Secretaries of State:[157] the collection of information in the former UFC sector has been made easier by the implementation over a period of time of a co-ordinated system for management and administrative computing.[158] 'Knowledge is control' is a common saying and now the legal basis exists to ensure that is the case in practice.

Power to confer or impose additional functions on the Funding Councils

2.81   Under section 69(5) FHEA and section 43(5) FHESA, the relevant Secretary of State may by order confer or impose on the Funding Councils such supplementary functions relating to the provision of education as he or she thinks fit. The word 'impose' suggests a reluctance on the part of the Council, whereas 'confer' implies that it is at its request. Functions are defined in section 61 FHEA (but not in FHESA) as 'including powers and duties.' The functions which may be conferred or imposed are restricted to those which are conferred on the Secretary of State by any enactment or any other power and are not entirely new functions not so authorised. In the corresponding section 134 ERA, an order conferring supplementary functions could exclude the application of the subsection which provided that the UFC and PCFC were not to be regarded as servants or agents of the Crown, enjoying Crown immunity, etc. This provision was repealed by Schedule 8 FHEA and does not re-appear in the 1992 legislation, where the description of the status of the new Funding Councils is relegated to Schedules. The change is not explained. It is possible that the exercise of the Secretary of State's 'thinking fit' could be liable to judicial review on the basis of irrationality.[159]

2.82   In FHESA, but not in FHEA, the Secretary of State must before making an order consult SHEFC and representative organisations (presumably the Committee of Scottish Higher Education Principals).

157 HESA is a private limited company formed by subscription of over 180 institutions and is the official agency for the collection, analysis and dissemination of quantitative information about higher education. It produces three main volumes: Students, Resources and First Destinations.
158 Originally known as the MAC Initiative: this was not wholly successful in meeting projected timescales for implementation.
159 There are limited grounds for this: see *Associated Provincial Picture Houses v Wednesbury Corpn* [1948] 1 KB 223, per Lord Greene MR, as supplemented and explained by Lord Diplock in *Council of Civil Service Unions v Minister for the Civil Service* [1984] 3 All ER 935, HL.

This requirement to consult with representative organisations is one which appears frequently in modern legislation[160] and its absence from the principal Act is unexplained. In Scotland only, then, the possibility exists of a judicial review if the time allowed for consultation is manifestly insufficient.[161]

Creation of Higher Education Corporations and similar bodies

2.83   When higher education functions in England and Wales were transferred from local control under ERA, the Secretary of State established higher education corporations from those colleges whose total enrolment on relevant courses on 1 November 1985 exceeded 55% of its total enrolment and also reached a certain minimum size. The 55% figure was preserved in FHEA. It does not appear in the Scottish legislation, as the central institutions had since the modern education system was introduced been under the direct control of the Secretary of State.[162] The power of the Secretary of State to create new institutions, rather than simply to designate or convert existing ones, is confined to Scotland[163] and is a power retained from the Education (Scotland) Act 1980.[164]

Dissolution of Higher Education Corporations and similar bodies

2.84   The Secretary of State has power to dissolve institutions created as higher education corporations (and successor companies) under ERA[165] and designated institutions under FHESA.[166] There is a requirement in each case to consult the governing body of the

160 See for example the similar provision in section 3(4) Access to Personal Files Act 1987.
161 On the basis of the English case *R v Secretary of State for Social Services, ex p Association of Metropolitan Authorities* [1986] 1 All ER 164. Relief by the process of judicial review is discretionary in both England and Scotland: in the AMA case it was refused, since the regulations which were the subject of the disputed consultation had already been implemented when the case was heard.
162 Section 77 Education (Scotland) Act 1980, derived from section 81 Education (Scotland) Act 1962, originally section 77 Education (Scotland) Act 1946.
163 Section 46 FHESA.
164 Section 77(2) Education (Scotland) Act 1980 also derived from section 77 of the 1946 Act.
165 Section 128 ERA.
166 Section 47. Such closure orders have been made on the amalgamation of Glasgow Polytechnic and The Queen's College Glasgow to form the Glasgow Caledonian University, and on the merger of the former Jordanhill and Craigie Colleges of Education with universities.

institution concerned and the relevant Funding Council. This power does not extend to the universities created before 1992/3, which could only be closed by revocation of charter, legislation or de-registration, depending on mode of creation.

Academic audit

2.85 The UFC sector established a unit for conducting academic audit of universities in 1990 and subsequently the work of this unit was assumed by the Higher Education Quality Council and then in 1997, by the Quality Assurance Agency (QAA). This activity was quite separate from the assessment of quality undertaken by the Funding Councils under the 1992 Acts but the two were combined in 1997 to make a more effective use of resources. This will be discussed in detail in chapter 3.

Charitable status

Introduction

2.86 Corporate status and charitable (or 'eleemosynary') status are separate issues and it is not essential that all bodies which are, or which conduct, institutions of higher education enjoy charitable status, although in practice the benefits are such that the majority do. The precise legal nature of charitable status depends on which part of the UK they are established in. Although the detail of the law is different, both the English and Scots legal systems have recognised provision of education as a charity since the seventeenth century,[167] at a time when there was no publicly-funded education in its modern sense. A charitable corporation is one whose corporate purpose is charitable[168] and, in so far as it is charitable, is the creature of the founder.[169] It is solely because it is the founder's 'creature' that on the principle *eius est disponere* the founder has rights to determine how it shall be run, to provide for its government and administration and the application in perpetuity of its revenues and 'he and his appointees have the perpetual right of patronage and visitation.'[170] However, the absence of a Visitor, which all eleemosynary

---

167 43 Eliz cap 4.
168 5(2) *Halsbury's Laws of England* 211.
169 *St John's College Cambridge v Todington* (1757) 1 Burr 158.
170 5(2) *Halsbury's Laws of England* 219; cf *Philips v Bury* (1694) Skin 447 at 482–3; H Picarda *The law and practice relating to charities* (1995, 2nd ed) 520.

corporations must have, means that the non-chartered higher education corporations must be considered to be charitable otherwise than being eleemosynary.

2.87 The practical effects of charitable status are to simplify and lessen the taxation burden on institutions and problems should only arise at the boundary between what the law considers as the provision of education and what it considers to be commercial activity. Charitable status confers the following benefits:[171] exemption from capital gains tax and from income tax and corporation tax on income other than trading income arising outside the course of the carrying on of the primary purpose of the institution; ability to recover income tax deducted from deeds of covenant and receipts under gift aid; exemption from inheritance tax for donors to institutions; substantial relief on business rates. Vacation letting of an institution's residential property or provision of catering facilities for non-educational purposes clearly fall outside the definition of 'primary purpose' and may be subject to different tax regimes. Some training facilities and franchising operations which are commercial in nature may also be excluded.[172]

2.88 Since 1995 charitable trustees and since 1996 trustees generally have wider powers of investment of their funds than before[173] and repeal of the Trustee Investments Act 1961 under the Deregulation and Contracting Out Act 1994 is in prospect. Power to invest institutional funds on a wider basis than was generally available before 1995 is included in the charter and statutes or equivalent. It is common in charters to find a clause which prescribes that wherever possible a beneficial construction should be placed on the institution's acts, thus reversing the common law rule that a grant made by the Crown at the suit of a subject is to be taken most beneficially for the Crown.[174]

---

171 Section 505 Income and Corporation Taxes Act 1988; section 256 Taxation of Chargeable Gains Act 1992.
172 H Picarda *The law and practice relating to charities* (1995, 2nd ed) p 54.
173 Charity Trustees Investment Act 1961 Order 1995 (SI 1995/1092); Trustee Investments (Division of Trust Funds) Order 1996 (SI 1996/845), sections 33–36 Pensions Act 1995, entry into force 7 April 1997.
174 *Re Beloved Wilkes' Charity* (1851) 20 LJ Ch 588; *Eastern Archipelago Co v R* (1853) 2 E & B 856.

Value Added Tax (VAT)

2.89   Value Added Tax (VAT) was introduced in the UK on accession to the European Communities in 1973. It is a tax on supplies which may either be taxable at a standard rate, zero-rated or exempt. Its scope and operation are now governed by the highly complex Value Added Tax Act 1994 (VATA): it is administered by HM Customs and Excise, with which body CVCP and other representative bodies have agreed guidelines for use by institutions and local VAT offices. Schedule 9 Group 6 covers education.

2.90   All higher education institutions will be registered for VAT as some of their activities fall outside the scope of the exemption. Trading companies and other bodies formed by institutions having a distinct legal status may have to register in their own right. Article 13A of the European Union Sixth Directive provides that certain activities in the public interest should be exempt from the tax: these include

> Children's or young people's education, school or university education, vocational training or retraining, including the supply of services and of goods closely related thereto, provided by bodies governed by public law having such as their aim or by other organisations defined by the member state concerned as having similar objects.

It goes on to extend the exemption to tuition given privately by teachers and covering school or university education. Certain supplies of education, training and research are exempt from VAT altogether. Courses in English as a foreign language provided for payment which exceeds full cost and holiday courses of an essentially recreational or sporting nature are excluded.

2.91   VATA gives exemption to all 'eligible bodies' including higher education institutions within the meaning of the education legislation. The exemption does not extend to Open University broadcasts by the BBC.[175] Education is defined for the purposes of the tax as in *Church of Scientology of California v Customs and Excise Comrs*[176] as activities and processes involving learning and concerned with developing the ability of individuals to understand and articulate, to reason and make judgments and to develop sensitivity and creativity.

---

175 *Open University v Customs and Excise Comrs* [1982] VATTR 29.
176 [1977] VATTR 278, 290.

Customs and Excise have issued a Notice giving its interpretation of 'education.'[177]

2.92 There are some trading activities which fall outside the exemption. It is the objectives, not the budgeting policy, which determines whether activities are conducted for a profit: budgeting for a surplus does not bring the institution within the scope of VAT provided that the constitution prevents it from distributing its surplus by way of dividend or bonus to its members (as all the charters, etc of higher education institutions do)[178] and that surpluses are used to maintain and improve its facilities.[179] Grants from the Funding Councils, Research Councils, government bodies and many other sponsors are not consideration for a supply and therefore fall outside the scope of VAT, whereas any payment as consideration for a supply is potentially within its scope, as are all donations of equipment. There is a special relief for goods used for certain medical purposes. There is no definition of 'research' in VATA.

2.93 A body which makes exempt supplies only is not a 'taxable person' and cannot be registered for VAT, which means that it cannot recover tax which it pays out on supplies which it receives (the input tax). Where both exempt and taxable supplies are made, the rules as to partial exemption are applied and only part of the input tax may be recoverable. It is this inability to recover input tax on exempt supplies which is one of the principal obstacles to higher education institutions contracting out services which are exempt (eg the supply of catering to students and the cleaning of halls of residence).

2.94 Provision by the bodies themselves extends, naturally, to provision by staff employed under a contract of service or otherwise to provide tuition. In *Cant v Customs and Excise Comrs*[180] it was held that the exemption extended to a barrister employed part-time by the University of Cambridge to give supervisions to law students on Saturday mornings. In *Alberni String Quartet v Customs and Excise Comrs*[181] it was held that the services of a partnership of four

---

177 C & E Notice 701/30/95.
178 That this is not the sole criterion is illustrated by the decision in *Aberdeen Chamber of Commerce v Customs and Excise Comrs* in the VAT Tribunal EDN/ 88/115 (unreported).
179 *Customs and Excise Comrs v Bell Concord Educational Trust Ltd* [1989] STC 264, CA.
180 [1976] VATTR 237.
181 [1990] VATTR 166.

musicians giving tuition, lectures and seminars at the Universities of Cambridge and Glasgow were exempt.

Fund-raising

2.95 Member states are permitted to introduce restrictions on exemptions for fund-raising events organised for the benefit of the exempt bodies where such exemption is likely to cause distortion of competition. Special provision is therefore made for fund-raising events by charities, which include fetes, bazaars, gala shows, performances or similar events separate from and not forming any part of a series or regular run of like or similar events.[182]

Zero rating

2.96 Relief is given for buildings or parts of buildings intended for use solely for a relevant residential purpose or a relevant charitable purpose. An example of the former is residential accommodation for students, including dining-rooms and kitchens if used predominantly by students living in. The relief applies even if the buildings are let out during vacations for conference delegates, etc provided that they are constructed with the intention of providing residential facilities for students. The reverse does not qualify.[183] A relevant charitable purpose means use by a charity otherwise than in the course or furtherance of a business. Business activities are those predominantly concerned with the making of taxable supplies to consumers for a consideration.

Conferences, etc

2.97 A supply of an educational conference is exempt if it falls within the definition of education and research and is not conducted for profit. In general terms the letting of bedded accommodation and catering is taxable: the letting of rooms in conjunction with the letting of bedded accommodation is taxable: where it is not let in conjunction with letting of bedded accommodation it is exempt, unless let for the

---

182 Value-Added Tax (Fund-Raising Events and Charities) Order 1989 (SI 1989/ 470).
183 For a full description see H Scott and D McClellan *Value-Added Tax and Property* (1992) chapter 5.

purpose of a supply of catering, which itself is always taxable. Likewise the supply of educational materials and incidental goods and services to students, including catering (but not supplies of alcoholic drinks, clothing, sports equipment, laundry and hairdressing) are exempt. This includes photocopying for an educational purpose.

Inter-institutional supplies

2.98 Inter-institutional supplies are exempt to the extent that they are use by one institution's students of the facilities of another. However, exemption does not normally extend to such matters are supplies of administrative computer services not directly used by students.[184] Secondment of staff is standard rated.

Income and Corporation Taxes

2.99 Section 505 Income and Corporation Taxes Act provides that there may be exemption of tax under Schedule D in respect of the profits of any trade carried on by a charity, if the profits are applied solely to the purposes of the charity and either (i) the trade is exercised in the course of the actual carrying out of a mainly primary purpose of the charity or (ii) the work in connection with the trade is carried out by beneficiaries of the charity. The provision of education and research services as primary objects of a higher education institution will fall within this category provided the profits are ploughed back into the purposes of the charity. If trading activities are likely be taxed because they do not qualify under section 505 then consideration might be given to transferring the activities to a separate company, with covenant of profits back. Certain companies with scientific research as their objective may qualify for the same privileges under section 508 of the Act. Section 256 Taxation of Chargeable Gains Act 1992 is also relevant.

England and Wales

2.100 The English law of charities is now governed by the Charities Act 1993 and the unconsolidated sections of the Charities Act 1992.

---

184 The complexities of the 'connected persons' provisions of section 839(6) and (7) Income and Corporation Taxes Act 1988 are beyond the scope of this work.

Control of charities by the courts and the Charity Commissioners is only exercised in practice in respect of higher education establishments in unusual and specific circumstances and, in the case of chartered institutions, only where the Visitor's jurisdiction does not apply.[185] Most higher education institutions are exempt or excepted charities under this legislation and not subject to the jurisdiction of the Charity Commissioners. However, institutions established as charitable trusts and some of those which are companies limited by guarantee are registered charities and do come under that jurisdiction. There is no requirement to submit accounts to the Commissioners although their powers vary slightly between exempt and excepted charities. The unlimited powers of chartered institutions do not extend to removing charitable status from gifts given with that status and the Attorney-General or the Commissioners may intervene if that is attempted.[186] Where issues do arise they are usually concerned with charitable gifts, for example of land, works of art or scholarships.[187]

2.101   The Charities Act 1993 repealed those provisions of ERA[188] and FHEA[189] which provided that the corporations brought into existence as a result of those Acts were to be exempt charities. Schedule 2 Charities Act 1993 provides that higher education corporations are exempt charities 'so far as they are charities' ie where their purposes are charitable. These corporations hold their property 'subject to a binding legal obligation to apply it for charitable purposes only.'[190]

Scotland

2.102   In Scotland

> There is no distinction either as to construction or principles of administration between gifts to charitable trusts, properly so called, and gifts to purposes which, though not charitable, are lawful and useful. The true distinction is between private trusts or bequests, in

185   *A-G v Catherine Hall Cambridge* (1820) Jac 381, 392.
186   Part VIII Charities Act 1993.
187   Eg the controversy which arose over the sale of paintings by Royal Holloway and Bedford New College, part of the University of London, for which the consent of the Charity Commissioners was sought and obtained.
188   Schedule 12, para 4.
189   Schedule 8, para 69.
190   J Warburton *Tudor on Charities* (1995, 8th ed) 159, based on *Liverpool and District Hospital for Diseases of the Heart v A-G* [1981] Ch 193.

which only individuals named or designed can claim an interest, and those which are intended for the benefit of a section of the public, and which can be enforced by *popularis actio.*[191]

This statement was accepted by the court in *Anderson's Trustees v Scott.*[192] The use of the term 'charitable' is therefore wider than the English usage and applies to public trusts in general. However, for the purposes of taxation, the term 'charitable purposes' is given the same technical meaning as in English law[193] and the English law of charities is part of the law of Scotland.[194]

2.103 Since 1990 the Scots law of charities requires a body wishing to obtain charitable status to submit details of its constitution and accounts to the Inland Revenue, the positive decision of which is final. Only a body recognised in this way, or one recognised by the Charity Commissioners in England and Wales, may represent itself as a charity in Scotland:[195] there are no Commissioners but the Lord Advocate has extensive powers of investigation with control ultimately vested in the Court of Session. The Court of Session also has power to vary trusts extending the powers of the trustees under section 105(4A) Education (Scotland) Act 1980 as in *University of Glasgow, Petitioners.*[196] All Scottish universities are recognised charities in this way.

2.104 In *M'Caig v University of Glasgow*[197] concerned with the proposed erection of a monument and sculptures in memory of a testator on the Stuart M'Caig Tower above Oban, M'Caig's surviving relative was entitled to resile from a gratuitous promise given to the university by mistake, when it was subsequently discovered that the testator's wishes were not necessarily valid. But in *Aberdeen University v Irvine*[198] on a construction of documents, the whole rent

---

191 W M Gloag and R C Henderson *Introduction to the Law of Scotland* (J A D Hope, A F Rodger and A Paton, eds) (9th ed, 1987) p 785.); see also S R Moody, C R Barker and R C Elliott 'The Legal Regulation of Scottish Charities' (1995) Journal of the Law Society of Scotland 460.

192 1914 SC 942.

193 *Income Tax Special Purposes Comrs v Pemsel* [1891] AC 531.

194 *IRC v City of Glasgow Police Athletic Association* 1953 SC (HL) 13; *Trustees for the Roll of Voluntary Workers v IRC* 1942 SC 47; *Williams' Trustees v IRC* [1947] AC 447.

195 See Part I Law Reform (Miscellaneous Provisions) (Scotland) Act 1990.

196 1991 SLT 604.

197 (1904) 6 F 918.

198 (1868) 1 Sc & Div 289, HL.

and proceeds of certain lands were devoted to charitable purposes expressed in the will of a testator.

Cy-près

2.105   In both jurisdictions,[199] where the original intention of the benefactor cannot be continued or realised because of changed circumstances, the terms of the gift may be modified under a doctrine known as *cy-près* or approximation, ie as near to the original as possible in all the circumstances. In *Re Lysaght, Hill v Royal College of Surgeons of England*,[200] Rosalind Lysaght had left £5,000 to endow studentships in the college, the terms of her will including the direction '… and any such student must be … not of the Jewish or Roman Catholic faith.' The college felt that provision was 'so invidious and so alien to the spirit of the college's work as to make the gift inoperable in that form.' The Chancery Division (Buckley J) allowed the offending words to be omitted.[201] *Re Whitworth Art Gallery Trusts, Manchester Whitworth Institute v Victoria University of Manchester*[202] was an example of a straightforward transfer of management of a gallery to a university, in the course of which a number of interesting observations were made on the court's powers in relation to charitable corporations established by charter, as the Manchester Whitworth Institute was. These are referred to above. However in *Re University of London Medical Sciences Institute Fund, Fowler v A-G*[203] money received for a project which failed had to be given back.

Uncertainty

2.106   In *Re Gott, Glazebrook and Sheen v University of Leeds*[204] a gift was left for the benefit of one or more male postgraduate students 'of British and Christian parentage.' While such a description

---

199 In Scotland, where the trustees do not have power under the trust themselves to make a *cy-près* scheme, the power of sanctioning a scheme is part of the *nobile officium* exercisable by the Inner House of the Court of Session – section 26 Trusts (Scotland) Act 1921.
200 [1965] 2 All ER 888.
201 The studentships were also restricted to men but the college did not object to that restriction.
202 [1958] 1 All ER 176.
203 [1909] 2 Ch 1.
204 [1944] 1 All ER 293.

could objectively be considered uncertain, it was held that a charitable trust, unlike other forms of trust, cannot fail for uncertainty. The same rule applies in Scotland.[205]

2.107   Generally speaking in the English system the executors of an estate have no legally enforceable interest in the administration of charitable gifts, such rights being vested in the Attorney-General acting in the public interest, but in Scotland an heir of law or executor of the founder of the charity has an interest which entitles that individual to see that the trust is properly administered.[206] In *Bradshaw v University College of North Wales*[207] certain farmland was conveyed in 1976 to the college on charitable trusts for certain educational purposes and the general purposes of the college. A dispute arose between the donor and the college and this was taken up by her executors. In 1982 the dispute was resolved by a deed of compromise, the executors agreeing not to challenge the performance of the 1976 trusts. However in 1986 the executors sought a court order that the college should account for its administration of the trust. If this were to be found wanting, the executors sought payment of a sum to the trust and the replacement of the college by new trustees. The college, supported by the Attorney-General, had the summons struck out on the ground that the executors had no interest in the charity entitled to bring proceedings: they were neither beneficiaries nor was there any circumstance under which the land could revert to the estate. Their interest now was purely as members of the public, in whose interests the Attorney-General acts.

Rights and privileges of members of charitable non-chartered bodies

Membership of non-charter bodies

2.108   Membership for the purposes of those institutions which are companies limited by guarantee is available only to members of the governing body[208] and these individuals have the rights of company members laid down in the Companies Acts. The members of higher education corporations and other bodies conducting institutions

---

205 *Clephane v Magistrates of Edinburgh* (1864) 2 M 7, HL.
206 3 *Encyclopaedia of the Laws of Scotland* (1937) p 228 paragraph 500.
207 [1988] 1 WLR 190.
208 See eg Articles 4 and 5 of the Articles of Association of the University of Greenwich (formerly Thames Polytechnic): membership is voluntary.

following ERA are the members of the board of governors.[209] The ancient Scottish universities remain common law corporations, presumably with members, but their Courts have by statute responsibility for all their financial affairs, so only the members of the Court can be considered as 'members' for this purpose. The post-1992 Scottish universities have no members as such, since it is the Courts which are incorporated rather than the institutions. As an example, Section 4 of The Paisley Technical College Scheme 1954, made under the Education (Scotland) Acts 1939 to 1953, as amended by the Paisley College of Technology (Amendment) Scheme 1973 and by The University of Paisley (Scotland) Order of Council 1993 provides: '... a governing body shall be and is hereby constituted under the name of the "Court of the University of Paisley" and under that name shall be a body corporate with perpetual succession and a common seal. ...'

Removal from membership

2.109 As membership is such a restricted category, it follows that removal from the governing body is what is in issue here. The instrument and articles of government will prescribe in what circumstances a member may be removed. These include absence from meetings for more than a specified period without permission, or becoming unable or unfit to discharge the functions of a member of the governing body.[210] The Orders of Council establishing the new universities in Scotland vary: one example is very specific, citing sequestration of estate, bankruptcy, entering into arrangement with creditors, and physical or mental illness as reasons for removal;[211] ' another is rather vague, providing for removal if 'continuation would bring discredit on the name of the University or in such other circumstances as the Court may determine and record in a standing order.'[212] The English articles of government normally provide that the person concerned may be removed by 'notice in writing' and 'thereupon the office shall become vacant' with no mention of any

---

209 See eg Article 1.1 of the Articles of Government of The Manchester Metropolitan University higher education corporation.
210 See eg Article 12 of the Articles of Association of the University of Greenwich; paragraph 6(3) of the Instrument of Government of the University of Northumbria at Newcastle higher education corporation.
211 Article 14 of The Glasgow Caledonian University (Scotland) Order of Council 1993 (SI 1993/556).
212 Article 7(3) of The University of Paisley (Scotland) Order of Council 1993 (SI 1993/558).

particular procedure to be followed. The Scottish institutions use the phrase 'office of governor' but removal from that office is effected by '[declaring] his place vacant' which must have the same practical effect. The use of the term 'office' here is interesting, since 'removal from office' or its equivalent almost certainly carries with it the right to be heard.[213] This is the equivalent of the protection against removal from office for 'good cause' which remains applicable to most offices (but not to new or promoted employment after 20 November 1987) in the chartered universities. Such provisions invariably allow for a proper investigation and a specified majority vote in the governing body (or Court – in the English chartered sense – for some high offices such as Chancellor or Pro-Chancellor).

Powers and liabilities of members

INTRODUCTION

2.110   The potential personal liability of members of governing bodies of institutions other than chartered institutions is a matter of considerable importance, given that the majority of difficult issues in governance have arisen in that sector. The position of members of non-chartered institutions in relation to debts is different to that in chartered corporations: the number of members is much smaller in the former. In general, members' liabilities limited by guarantee extend only to the amounts not previously paid up. The subscribers of a company limited by guarantee can be personally liable to some extent for the debts of the corporation, although such a situation arising in the case of universities is, we hope, hypothetical. The Memorandum of Association of the London School of Economics and Political Science provides that if a member shall receive any dividend, bonus or other profit his (sic) liability shall become unlimited, otherwise it is restricted to £1. It is also provided that the corporation may not become a member of or affiliate to any association which pays dividends or profits to its members. Nothing is said about the liability of members in the constitutions of the higher education corporations or other bodies conducting institutions, although it appears to be the case that there may be some personal liability in some circumstances.[214] However, in all cases where

213   Holders of 'offices' have an elementary right to be heard in their own defence: *Malloch v Aberdeen Corpn* [1971] 1 WLR 1578, 1582, HL per Lord Reid.
214   See C M V Clarkson 'Kicking corporate bodies and damning their souls' (1996) 59 MLR 557.

charitable status is enjoyed, the liabilities of charitable trustees are generally unlimited and there is a potential area of doubt.

LIABILITY FOR ACTS OF THE CORPORATION

2.111 Legislation may confer specific duties on the governors as a body, for example, in the higher education corporations governors must ensure the solvency of the corporation and safeguard its assets.[215] The general principle is that individual members are not liable for corporate acts except that if the act concerned is ultra vires and proves to be tortious or delictual the members who authorised the act might themselves be sued, particularly if the act complained of was wilful and malicious.[216] Members of boards of governors may find themselves faced with proceedings for breach of duty, fiduciary or otherwise. These include, as a matter of common sense, the duty to act with due diligence and skill in the best interest of the corporation and not to allow a conflict of interest between personal and corporation business. In practice, if recommendations in the relevant Guide for Governors is followed, on for example providing individual members with sufficient and proper advice, including advice on the propriety of action given by a properly-qualified clerk, the keeping of proper minutes and a register of interests, problems should not arise. As the government has indicated in respect of board members of non-departmental public bodies, 'an individual board member who has acted honestly, reasonably, in good faith and without negligence, will not have to meet out of his [sic] own personal resources any personal civil liability which is incurred in execution or purported execution of his board function.'[217]

2.112 Whether or not individual board members can be assimilated to the position of directors (in the case of lay or independent members, as non-executive directors) is a matter of debate. A director is answerable as a trustee for any misapplication of the corporation's property in which he or she participated and which he or she knew

215 See the Model Articles of Government in SI 1992/1963.
216 *R v Watson* (1788) 2 Term Rep 199. In fact, ultra vires cannot be pleaded by a corporation as a defence to escape liability in tort, as illustrated by *Campbell v Paddington Corpn* [1911] 1 KB 869 where the erection of stands to view a royal funeral procession caused a nuisance. See also O Hyams 'The potential liabilities of governors of education institutions' (1994) 6 Education and the Law 191; O Hyams 'Higher and Further Education dismissals and redundancies – problem areas and their consequences for corporations and governors' (1996) 6 Education and the Law 137.
217 Cabinet Office (1996): *Spending Public Money: Governance and Audit Issues.*

or ought to have known to be a misapplication.[218] As Sir George Jessel MR explained in *Re Forest of Dean Coal Mining Co*[219] 'It does not matter by what title directors are known, it is the position held which is that 'they are really commercial men managing a trading concern for the benefit of themselves and all the other shareholders in it.' In practice, it is perhaps more appropriate to consider members of governing bodies as charitable trustees.

Liability of charitable trustees

2.113 Lord Hardwicke LC's dictum in *Knight v Earl of Plymouth*[220] provides a useful starting point for this discussion: 'A trust is an office necessary in the concerns between man and man, and which, if faithfully discharged, is attended with no small degree of trouble, and anxiety, it is an act of great kindness in anyone to accept it.' Charitable trustees have individual responsibility and liability for charitable funds. When managing the property of the institution they must: apply the property and income of the institution only for its defined charitable purposes; act only with their legal powers; take particular care when approving the organisation of trading activities which may not be regarded as charitable; and (where the institution is a registered charity) respond properly to the requirements of the Charity Commissioners for information and returns.

2.114 Section 97(1) Charities Act 1993 defines 'charity trustees' in terms which include directors of charitable corporations as well as trusts. It is argued with support from the decision in *Harries v Comrs for Church of England*[221] that governors of a higher education corporation clearly fall within this definition and in that capacity are subject to the jurisdiction of the courts.[222] The position of individual members is then that they are unable to claim relief from the court against personal liability in circumstances analogous to those set out in section 61 Trustee Act 1925 (which are available to trustees in the strict sense) or section 727 Companies Act 1985 (which is

---

218 See *Selangor United Rubber Estates Ltd v Cradock (No 3)* [1968] 1 WLR 1555.
219 (1878) 10 Ch D 450 at 453.
220 (1747) Dick 120, 126; 21 ER 214, 216.
221 [1992] 1 WLR 1241.
222 In Consultation Paper 146 (1997), the Law Commission discusses the position of charity trustees and directors of charitable corporations. The Law Commission argues for an extension of the powers of charitable trusts, among other things in the area of delegation, and that there is much to be said for extending the proposed powers to charitable corporations.

available to company directors). Applying this principle outside the higher education corporations may conflict with the limited liability which individuals enjoy in a company limited by guarantee. In the bodies established under declaration of trust, the members of the governing body constitute the trustees, provided they are willing to accept office. The constitution of the governing body is then dependent to some extent on nominees of those bodies which have constituted the original trust.[223] Whether or not governors can be directly assimilated to charitable trustee status, there is no doubt that they stand in the position of fiduciary towards the corporation which they serve[224] and are required to return any property obtained in breach of trust or to compensate the corporation for its loss.[225] Particular attention should be paid to conflicts of interest as in *Magistrates of Aberdeen v University of Aberdeen*[226] a dispute over fishing rights.

2.115 The courts will normally however take a lenient view of the matter where the corporation is in an analogous position[227] to a trustee[228] and the members act merely as members of the body corporate. In *A-G v Caius College*,[229] Lord Langdale MR said

> I should be sorry to say anything from which it could be inferred that corporations and colleges are not bound strictly to perform the trusts they undertake, but it is evident that, in changing corporations consisting of fluctuating members, they cannot be dealt with as individual persons, for, by so doing, we should visit the present members with the consequences of errors committed by their predecessors, whom they do not in any case represent.

2.116 It is said that where the officers or directors of a corporation or company actively participate in an act which is beyond the power of the corporation to perform, they are each, to the extent of

---

223 See clause 5 of the Declaration of Trust for the Cheltenham and Gloucester College of Higher Education Trust, 24 January 1990.
224 *A-G v De Winston* [1906] 2 Ch 106.
225 *Underhill & Clayton's Law of Trusts and Trustees* (1995, 15th ed) 826–9, disapproving *Re Leeds and Hanley Theatres of Varieties* [1902] 2 Ch 809, CA.
226 (1877) 4 R 48, HL; also *Aberdeen Town Council v Aberdeen University* (1877) 2 App Cas 544, HL.
227 *Liverpool and District Hospital for Diseases of the Heart v A-G* [1981] Ch 193; *Rabin v Gerson Berger Association Ltd* (1987, unreported), CA.
228 See eg *Flood's Case* (1616) Hob 136; *Bene't (or Corpus Christi) College, Cambridge v Bishop of London* (1778) 2 Wm Bl 1182; *Lydiatt v Foach* (1700) 2 Vern 410.
229 (1837) 2 Keen 150, 169; the College was of course a chartered corporation but the principles may be applied outside the chartered sector.

participation, personally liable for the consequences. The leading authority for this proposition is *Young v Naval Military and Civil Service Co-operative Society of South Africa*[230] where company directors whose liability was in issue acted ultra vires in voting that certain payments be made to themselves: the case may be explained by the principles governing the fiduciary duties of directors. Merely causing the corporation to act ultra vires would not create liability. There would have to be a breach of some duty owed to the corporation. Unless there could be liability as a fiduciary or by analogy with directors of companies, or if members of governing bodies are properly to be regarded as if they were trustees, or unless there is some other way in which a court might determine that the members of the governing body could be liable to the corporation, causing it to act ultra vires could not properly be said without more to give rise to potential liability to the corporation. In *Symphony Group plc v Hodgson*,[231] per Balcombe LJ, the court might order costs against a non-party company director where the latter failed to give any careful thought to the basis on which proceedings should be conducted and had behaved irresponsibly.

2.117 There may be a liability to third parties where the corporation did not have the power to enter into an agreement or alternatively that some condition binding the corporation (such as Funding Council approval) had not been complied with, for a breach of warranty of authority.[232] It seems to be indicated in *Newborne v Sensolid (Great Britain) Ltd*[233] that an action for this could not be brought in the arguably analogous situation where a person contracts ostensibly as the agent of a non-existent principal. The claim might fail on the basis that the warranty was a representation of law.[234] If the warranty were one of fact rather than of law, that would be different. That might arise if a member of the governing body impliedly warranted that a procedure required by the governing instrument of the institution to be followed had indeed been followed, when in fact it had not. On the other hand, if the warranty were that the corporation had power to enter into a contract when it did not have such power, that would be a warranty with regard to law. In an institutional setting the powers of the governing body can

---

230 [1905] 1 KB 687.
231 [1994] QB 179.
232 *Bowstead and Reynolds on Agency* (1996, 16th ed) paragraph 9-062.
233 [1954] 1 QB 45 at 47.
234 *Bowstead and Reynolds on Agency* (1996, 16th ed) para 9-063; *Firbanks Executors v Humphreys* (1886) 18 QBD 54, CA; *Chapleo v Brunswick Permanent Building Society* (1881) 6 QBD 696; *Weeks v Propert* (1873) LR 8 CP 427.

frequently be delegated expressly to committees, officers or an individual officer. In such circumstances it could be argued that there is a personal liability for actions taken under delegated powers, unless the act of delegation expressly excluded personal liability. In addition statute provides for the personal responsibility of managers and licence-holders in a variety of ways, for example in health and safety matters.

Rights and privileges of members of chartered bodies

2.118   The liability of members of the governing body of a chartered institution is quite different and can only be explained in the context of membership as a general issue. As is the case in all corporations, a chartered body has perpetual succession, so that the members are constantly changing and the corporation continues even if there are no members. Professor Jim Gower[235] mentions the occasion on which all the members of a private company were killed by a bomb while the general meeting was taking place: the company survived even though it had no members. Likewise in *Re Noel Tedman Holding Pty Ltd*[236] the only two members of a company were killed in a road accident yet the company survived.

2.119   Membership has different meanings in the different types of institution. In a modern English chartered university the members, defined in the charter and statutes typically as the officers, academic (and sometimes academic-related) staff, graduates and registered students are '... constituted and from henceforth for ever shall be one Body Politic and Corporate with perpetual succession ...'[217] ie an eleemosynary corporation headed by a Chancellor. In both England and Scotland it is evident that as Ronald Cant[238] says in respect of St Andrews in the Middle Ages, even the most junior student enjoys '... at least formal equality with the most venerable doctor in general congregations of the University. ...' There are many recorded instances of mandamus issuing to enforce the rights of members of the ancient universities and their colleges[239] and members

---

235 L C B Gower *Principles of Modern Company Law* (5th ed, 1992) p 93 n 42.
236 (1967) Qd R 561, Qd Sup C.
237 Article 1, Charter of the University of Hull.
238 R G Cant *The University of St Andrews* (1970).
239 Examples cited by Sir William Wade in *Administrative Law* (6th ed, 1988) p
      650 include *R v St John's College, Cambridge* (1693) 4 Mod Rep 233; *R v
      University of Cambridge* (1723) 1 Stra 557; *R v Cambridge University* (1765) 3
      Burr 1647; *R v Chancellor of Cambridge University* (1794) 6 Term Rep 89.

of chartered corporations may obtain an injunction to restrain any act possibly leading to the revocation of the charter.[240]

2.120 This sounds very grand but in fact the totality of rights and obligations of the different classes of members can only be deduced from a detailed examination of the relevant charter, statutes, ordinances, etc or equivalent. This quickly demonstrates that, as might be expected, a student is in a rather different position than is a member of staff. A member of staff or student seeking an authoritative definition of his or her status is well-advised to take the time to read all the documents! However, in general terms, membership per se confers no particular privileges and is of little if any practical significance. No-one can be forced to be a member of a corporation and those who object on religious grounds can be exempted from membership if the statutes allow, as many do following problems which arose in the 1960s and 1970s with objectors belonging to an exclusive sect.[241]

Members' rights in relation to documents and meetings

2.121 At common law a member of a chartered, and indeed other, corporation has the right to see such documents as are reasonably necessary to enable him or her to carry out any duties connected with membership. Most members of chartered universities have no duties related to their membership as such, so the issue will not arise. But even those members who do have duties, such as the members of Courts, Councils and Senates, have, by analogy with the members of local authorities, no common law right to see documents just out of curiosity[242] but only where there is a reasonable need to do so[243] and this is an important factor in determining whether there can be any personal liability. The same principle applies with access to meetings: a member of an appointing authority does not have the right to demand attendance at a committee of which he or she is not a member.[244] Disputes of this kind are best avoided by the adoption of standing orders on access to documents, meetings and so on.

---

240 *Rendall v Crystal Palace Co* (1858) 4 K & J 326; 70 ER 136.
241 The 1994 statutes of the University of London allow for this eventuality. It may be that a chartered corporation has a common law power to waive membership.
242 *R v Southwold Corpn, ex p Wrightson* (1907) 5 LGR 888.
243 *R v Barnes Borough Council, ex p Conlan* [1938] 3 All ER 226; *R v Lancashire County Council Police Authority, ex p Hook* [1980] QB 603. In some sensitive areas, a 'need to know' principle may be invoked: *Birmingham City District Council v O* [1983] 1 AC 578.
244 *R v Hackney London Borough Council, ex p Gamper* [1985] 1 WLR 1229.

Expulsion of members

2.122 Members of chartered institutions enjoy some common law rights in relation to expulsion. In *R v Askew*,[245] Lord Mansfield referred to a case of mandamus being issued to restore a member to Oxford as early as the reign of Edward III.[246] These include a requirement for the offence for which expulsion is proposed to be clearly specified but, in so far as the issue has been raised, the extent to which any corporation, whether chartered or not, can exclude the principles of natural justice in relation to the expulsion of members is not settled. *Gaiman v National Association for Mental Health*[247] was an application for interlocutory relief by 320 Scientologists expelled by the council of the Association, a company limited by guarantee. Megarry J held that the principles of natural justice, in particular that which would afford them the right to be heard before being expelled, did not apply in the circumstances. These included
(i) that the association's interests required the council to act speedily;
(ii) that membership of the association carried with it the possibility of termination by the council in the interests of the association;
(iii) that the wording of the relevant article of association gave the council an unrestricted power;
(iv) that membership involved no real interest in property and no question of livelihood or reputation.
The relief sought was interlocutory and discretionary and no further action in the matter was reported. This is not of practical importance for academic staff members in the pre-1992/93 universities, since the disciplinary powers in respect of this category are now clear following changes made by the University Commissioners under ERA, and the courts and Visitors in the 1970s laid down a framework of general principles relating to the discipline of student members. Removal from employment, etc now automatically removes membership. It may, however, still be of interest to other categories of member, in particular in those institutions where membership is extended to all staff.[248]

---

245 (1768) 4 Burr 2186, 2189.
246 It might be noted in passing that mandamus had also issued to order the University of Oxford to expel Lollards (the followers of John Wycliffe) in 1396: *Tapping on Mandamus* (1848) p 269.
247 [1970] 2 All ER 362, 380, 381.
248 Eg the University of Stirling, the statutes of which were amended in July 1993 to extend membership to all staff.

Members' rights to intervene: England, Wales and Northern Ireland

2.123 In England, Wales and Northern Ireland it is possible for members of a chartered corporation (or the Attorney-General) to apply to the court for an injunction or interdict to stop the corporation pursuing a particular course of action. The rationale for allowing members to do this is said to be the need to protect the royal prerogative as in *Hoblyn v R*[249] where the Mayor and Aldermen of a town had usurped the powers given to the Mayor, Aldermen and Commonalty; as it was said '... if they could make laws to alter their own constitution, the King's prerogative would be taken away, and transferred to the subject ...' and that could lead to forfeiture of the charter. The power of members to intervene does not extend to petitions relating to the adoption of a supplemental charter by due process; only the Attorney-General may proceed in such a case.[250] At common law the Attorney-General upholds the public interest[251] although this may be modified by statute, as in the case of local authorities, who are empowered by section 222 Local Government Act 1972 to bring proceedings in their own name if they 'consider it expedient for the promotion or protection of the interests of the inhabitants of their area.'

2.124 It is clear from the Opinion of the Visitor (Simon Browne LJ) in *Pearce v University of Aston in Birmingham (No 2)*[252] that where there is a Visitor that officer may grant the same remedies as the court. In that case it was decided that the university was not free at common law to commit an act contrary to its Charter and Statutes (to dismiss members of academic staff on grounds of redundancy), that the Visitor had power to restrain it from doing so and further that if the act were committed the Visitor had the power to rectify the matter.

Members' liability for debts

2.125 There is old authority to the effect that where a corporation

---

249 (1772) 2 Bro Parl Cas 329, HL; see also *Jenkin v Pharmaceutical Society* [1921] 1 Ch 392; *Pharmaceutical Society of Great Britain v Dickson* [1970] AC 403.
250 *MacCormack v Queen's University* (1867) 1 IR Eq 160.
251 *Gouriet v Union of Post Office Workers* [1977] 3 All ER 70, HL, *Ashby v Ebdon* [1984] 3 All ER 869: as in the Leicester and Manchester tramway cases discussed earlier.
252 [1991] 2 All ER 469.

has been dissolved, its members, in their natural capacities, can neither recover debts which were due to the corporation nor be charged with debts contracted by it.[253] Unless the charter provides otherwise, the members of the corporation are not liable for its debts.[254] In fact, it appears from an 1891 dictum of Lindley J in *Elve v Boyton*[255] that the Crown has no general prerogative power to incorporate persons in such a way as to make them liable for the debts of the corporation. In that case, the Crown's common law power had been extended by statute but university charters were and remain issued under the common law prerogative power. That being the case, it is not surprising to find in a typical university charter a prohibition on members sharing in any profits eg: 'The University shall not make any dividend, gift, division or bonus in money unto or between any of its members except by way of prize, reward or special grant.'[256] This prohibition extends only to the membership of the corporation which in most university charters is defined as a restricted group: there is nothing to stop the university 'making dividends, gifts, bonuses etc' to its staff who are not members, and who usually constitute the majority. Moves towards single-status employment may in due course remove this distinction.

Members' rights to intervene – Scotland

2.126   In Scotland a member may obtain an interdict to prevent the corporation or its members from acting contrary to the terms of its charter. In *Howden v Incorporation of Goldsmiths*,[257] the Lord Ordinary took the view that

> ... on general principles, the existing members of all corporations, in so far as they have any right of control over the funds of the corporation, are to be held as public administrators or *quasi* trustees ...

and interdict was granted to prevent the members from dividing up the property of the corporation amongst themselves. However, only the Crown and not individual burgesses could bring actions for

253 *Edmunds v Brown and Tillard* (1668) 1 Lev 237; *Naylor v Cornish* (1684) 1 Vern 311n.
254 9 *Halsbury's Laws of England* (4th ed) para 9-1209.
255 [1891] 1 Ch 501, 507, CA; cited in *Charlesworth's Company Law* (13th ed) G Morse, E A Marshall and R Morris (eds) (1987) p 6.
256 Charter of the University of Hull, Article 21.
257 (1840) 2 D 996.

maladministration of burgh revenues.[258] The procedure developed over time was that three or more burgesses could make a complaint to the Barons of Exchequer in Scotland: today an elector can complain to the auditors. The closest the Scottish higher education system has come to this is in the cases taken at the time of the affiliation of what was then the University College of Dundee to the University of St Andrews.[259] The courts permitted members of the University Court to argue that there were defects in the arrangements: according to the report of the second case, concerned with a stipulation in an agreement made by the University Court that the union should be permanent, and dissoluble only by Act of Parliament, the Solicitor-General for Scotland appeared for them.

Members' liability for debts – Scotland

2.127 The relation of members to the institution is governed by the Roman principle *si quid universitati debetur, singulis non debetur, nec quod universitas debet, singuli debent*.[260] This was expressly approved by the Court of Session in *Muir v City of Glasgow Bank*[261] where Lord President Inglis said

> ... the corporation being a separate person has its own estate and its own liabilities, and the corporators are not liable for the corporation, but only to the corporation within the limit of the obligation they have undertaken to subscribe to the corporate funds.

So a member cannot take action against the officers of the corporation personally, but only against the corporation itself.[262]

Conclusion

2.128 The position of members of the governing body of a chartered corporation is then clear. It is the body itself which is responsible

---

258 See Erskine, *Institute*, I iv 23, which received judicial recognition in *Burgesses of Inverury (or Mollison) v Magistrates of Inverury* (1820) December 14 FC and by Lord Kyllachy (at 911) and Lord Stormonth Darling (at 913) in *Conn v Provost, Magistrates and Councillors of Renfrew* (1906) 8 F 905, HL, where the Council had expended money on opposing a Bill in Parliament apparently without going through the statutory procedures.
259 *Metcalfe v Cox* [1895] AC 328, HL; *Medcalfe v Cox* [1896] AC 647, HL.
260 *Digest* iii 4, 7 s 1.
261 (1878) 6 R 392, 401.
262 *Thomson v Lindsay* (1825) 4 S 239.

and the members carry no individual liability or responsibility, neither in English[263] nor in Scots[264] law.

The Financial Memoranda – the Designated Officer

2.129   Under the funding arrangements prior to the creation of Funding Councils by ERA it was impossible to place responsibility for expenditure of public funds on any individual. Since then, however, the Funding Councils' Financial Memoranda require the governing body of the institution to appoint a principal officer (normally the Vice-Chancellor, Principal or equivalent chief executive officer) as the designated (accounting) officer who is personally responsible for the proper application of public funds derived from the Funding Council, and would answer to the Public Accounts Committee of the House of Commons if required. Paragraph 19 of the HEFCE Financial Memorandum (paragraph 14 of the SHEFC equivalent) requires the officer concerned to bring to the attention of the Funding Council any issue relating to the expenditure of Council funds on which he or she is in disagreement with the governing body. It is interesting to speculate how this requirement links with the contract of employment of the officer concerned and his or her common law duty to obey the orders of the employer, so long as they are not unlawful, particularly since the Financial Memoranda are expressed in such a way that nothing in them requires the institution to act in a way inconsistent with its governing instrument.[265]

Powers to enter into research and commercial activities

2.130   In a chartered institution the Charter will describe the general nature of the activities and the legal power to undertake them, for example:

> To make provision for research, design, development, testing and advisory services and with these objects to enter into such arrangements with other institutions or with public bodies as may be thought desirable and to charge to the users of such services such fees as may be thought desirable ...

---

263   See eg *Re Sheffield and South Yorkshire Permanent Building Society* (1889) 22 QBD 470, 480 per Charles J.
264   See *Muir v City of Glasgow Bank* (1878) 6 R 392, 401 per Lord President Inglis.
265   Paragraph 4, HEFCE Financial Memorandum (1996); paragraph 5, SHEFC Financial Memorandum (1996).

> To sell or provide for reward or otherwise such books, stationery and
> other goods and services as may be deemed expedient and consistent
> with the objects of the University as a place of education, learning and
> research.[266]

Charters also invariably contain a clause along these lines:

> To do all such other acts and things ... whether incidental to the powers
> aforesaid or not as may be requisite in order to further the objects of
> the University.[267]

2.131   The origin of the power to trade in the post-1992 English
universities and other higher education institutions is section 1
Further Education Act 1985 as amended.[268] This permits the supply
of goods and services through institutions which result from its
educational activities, the use of its facilities and personnel and the
exploitation of ideas by staff and students. Section 124 ERA provides
that a higher education corporation shall have power inter alia:

> to carry out research and to publish the results of the research or any
> other material arising out of or connected with it in such manner as
> the corporation think fit.

A higher education corporation also has power to do anything which
appears to the corporation to be necessary or expedient for the
purpose of or in connection with that power or the powers to provide
higher and further education. There is no further reference to powers
in the instruments or articles of government.

2.132   A company limited by guarantee conducting a higher
education institution has those powers prescribed in its memorandum
and articles of association, for example:

> To provide opportunities and facilities for development and research
> of any kind including the publication of results, papers, reports,
> treatises, theses or other material in connection with or arising out of
> such research[269]

with the usual provision:

266 Articles 3(p) and (r), Charter of The University of Stirling (1967).
267 Article 3(y), Charter of The University of Stirling (1967).
268 Schedule 12 para 92 ERA; Schedule 8 para 20 FHEA.
269 Article 3(E), Memorandum of Association of the University of Greenwich.

To do all such other lawful things as are incidental or necessary to the attainment of the above objects or any of them.[270]

2.133 In the Scottish institutions the powers of the higher and further education institutions were contained in regulations made under the Education (Scotland) Act 1980 or, in the case of those incorporated as companies, under their respective memorandum and articles of association. The Orders of Council establishing the new universities under FHESA all make appropriate provision; for example Napier University:

> To initiate and establish commercial companies in their own right or in association with other persons or institutions as they may deem appropriate, to hold or continue to hold shares and interests in such companies, and to carry on any trade or business whatsoever calculated to carry out the objects of or to be for the benefit of or to advance the interest or well being of the University.[271]

Coupled with this is the power

> Generally and without prejudice to any of the foregoing to do anything incidental to the performance of any of their functions and to the furtherance of the objects of the University.[272]

An alternative approach is taken by the University of Paisley where particular functions of the Court are:

(a) to provide research, design, development, testing, laboratory, consultancy and other services by way of extension of or in connection with any of the objects of the university; and

(b) to carry on any trade or business whatsoever calculated to carry out the objects of or to be for the well-being of the University.[273]

2.134 In pursuance of these various powers institutions may decide to adopt a variety of approaches to the exercise of their powers to trade, set up commercial subsidiaries etc. These include

---

270 Article 3(G)(14), Memorandum of Association of The University of Greenwich.
271 Schedule 1 paragraph A(15), The Napier University (Scotland) Order of Council 1993 (SI 1993/557).
272 Schedule 1(D) ibid.
273 Article 5(1), The University of Paisley (Scotland) Order of Council 1993 (SI 1993/558); a similar approach is taken by The Robert Gordon University: Article 4(3), The Robert Gordon University (Scotland) Order of Council 1993 (SI 1993/1157) and by The Glasgow Caledonian University: Article 5(2), The Glasgow Caledonian University (Scotland) Order of Council 1993 (SI 1993/556).

(i)   in-house research and development contracts for sponsorship and licensing;
(ii) technology management agreements with, for example the British Technology Group;
(iii) direct outward licensing of technology;
(iv) joint ventures;
(v)   wholly-owned or partly-owned companies;[274]
(vi) promotion through science and technology or business parks.

2.135   The CVCP issued guidance to the pre-1992 universities in April 1979 in *Legal Liability on Research Contracts and Consultancies*, taking into account the Unfair Contract Terms Act 1977 and other legislation and case law to that date. Under the heading 'envoi' the CVCP stated:

> This advice is volunteered in good faith but without responsibility and on the basis that the Committee, its members, officers and advisers accept no liability in respect thereof, however arising.

Contracts

Power to contract

2.136   The functions of the governing body of a higher education institution like that of any other corporate body include power to enter into, vary, carry out and cancel contracts on behalf of the institution. In English law by virtue of the Corporate Bodies' Contracts Act 1960 no special form is required and the Scots case *Park v University of Glasgow*[275] established the powers of governing bodies to act without special form unless statute provides otherwise. However, to avoid possible problems arising a written contract is always desirable even if it simply consists of an exchange of letters. Care should always be taken not to commit the institution verbally to any action before that is done, preferably by making all arrangements 'subject to contract.'

---

274   Which can include university departments, eg The Nottingham Law School, a department of The Nottingham Trent University, reported to be the first department to raise equity capital from the private sector (*Financial Times*, 31 January 1995).
275   (1675) M 2535.

The Supply of Goods and Services Act

2.137 The Supply of Goods and Services Act 1982[276] applies to all contracts for the supply of work and materials. It automatically implies certain conditions or warranties, for example (section 12) that suppliers of services will carry out the work with reasonable skill and care and (section 13) carry out the services in a reasonable time. Section 15 provides for a reasonable price to be paid where the contract does not fix it. It is obviously better not to have to rely on terms implied from the Act and to agree all the details in advance. Care should be taken to avoid making claims about the quality of work which can be produced, or the contract may become voidable through misrepresentation, even where the misrepresentation was wholly innocent or the aggrieved party may have a remedy in damages,[277] assessed on the basis of the application of the law of contract.

Actual and ostensible authority

2.138 A contract is always technically made under the authority of the governing body, in the form prescribed by it. Other than major contracts under seal, this will be effected through agency, which arises when one party (the principal) gives another (the agent) the power to alter the principal's legal relations with a third party. In the context of a higher education institution this may be achieved
(i) by the express appointment of the agent for the particular contract concerned or a specified range of contracts;
(ii) by virtue of the doctrine of estoppel;
(iii) by the subsequent ratification by the principal of a contract made on his or her behalf without any authorisation from him or her; and
(iv) by implication of law in cases where it is urgently necessary that one person should act on behalf of another.
In practice all institutions will have some mechanism for appointing staff to act on their behalf, for example staff appointments may be made by the Clerk to the Governors or Secretary. Alternatively, and less satisfactorily from the point of view of audit and accountability, agency by estoppel arises where a person is understood to represent and act for the person or body who or which has so placed him or

276 The principles of the Act were extended to Scotland by the Sale and Supply of Goods Act 1994: see H McQueen (1995) 63(1) Scots Law Gazette 5.
277 Misrepresentation Act 1967.

her in that position. The other incidents of agency should arise rarely, if at all, in a well-managed institution, which is guided in this area by the extent of the cover offered by its professional liability insurers. It is extremely unlikely that the agent will wish to conceal the name of the principal (the institution) and this will not be considered further here.

2.139 However, it is possible that a member of staff may deliberately or unwittingly fail to disclose the fact that he or she is undertaking a piece of work as agent for the institution on which legal liability will fall in the event of any mishap. This will happen unless the third party expressly accepts that he or she is contracting with the member of staff personally, on the assumption that that member of staff is permitted to undertake such work under his or her contract of employment. Charles Henderson[278] quotes the extreme example of a professor who telephoned an outside supplier to order large quantities of food for the institution's catering service. That individual would probably not be held, on the doctrine of ostensible authority, to be an agent of the institution because the category of contract which she purported to be authorised to make was not one which would usually be associated with the office of professor. However, since the institution's rules might impose on the head of a department the duty to organise and implement research programmes, then it could be argued that a contract for the provision of research services could be made by a professor with a third party which would be entitled to believe that she was acting with the authority of the institution.[279] The same might and indeed does apply in cases where a third party offering vending machine or photocopier hire might reasonably assume that a 'personal secretary' or 'departmental administrator' or someone with a similar important-sounding title had authority to sign contracts for their services. How often we see advertisements for senior secretaries in the private sector with powers over large budgets. Purchasing Officers have found it necessary to issue regular guidance on dubious practices of various kinds operated by some firms in the photocopying, communications and related fields.

2.140 In the law of Scotland whether or not a third party is entitled to assume that an individual has power to commit the principal will

---

278 C L S Henderson 'University Trading and Entrepreneurial Activities' D J
    Farrington and F T Mattison (eds) in *Universities and the Law* CUA/CRS (1990).
279 Guidance in these matters was offered in CVCP Memorandum N/79/40 (April
    1979).

depend whether the person manifesting the authority is employed to transact all or only a specified class of business.[280] In either jurisdiction, unless a third party knows that the professor or secretary has limited authority,[281] it is highly likely that the institution will be liable.

The Supplies and Works Directives

2.141 The EC Supplies Directive covers supplies in all contracts over a fixed sum in ECU.[282] Notification to the Commission for inclusion in the supplement to the Official Journal on form UK/2110/EN takes a considerable time. There are similar arrangements for works and services contracts[283] and utilities.[284]

Companies

Formation of companies

2.142 Institutions may decide to form limited liability companies for trading purposes to take advantage of favourable taxation and grant schemes, to avoid possible challenges to charitable status and to allow decision-making to take place in a more commercial atmosphere. The extent to which institutions are able to invest public funds in such activities is dependent upon the terms of the Financial Memorandum, and all such investments must be shown in the institution's accounts.

2.143 In principle, formation of companies is very straightforward. However, it should not be assumed that separate legal personality and limited liability provide total protection for an institution which has formed a company. The courts have developed a doctrine known as 'lifting the veil of incorporation' by which the form of a company can be cast aside to reveal the substance, behind the veil of incorporation, of directors or shareholders manipulating the company in order to avoid responsibilities to third parties. The institution's governing body may find itself regarded as a 'shadow director' for

---

280 Bell *Principles* 219.
281 *Russo-Chinese Bank v Li Yau Sam* [1910] AC 174; *Armagas Ltd v Mundogas SA* [1986] AC 717.
282 Directive 77/62/EEC; Directive 93/36/EEC from 14 June 1994; SI 1991/2679.
283 Directive 93/37/EEC (was 71/305/EEC), SI 1991/2680; Directive 92/50/EEC.
284 Directive 90/531/EEC (Directive 93/38/EEC from 1 July 1994), SI 1992/3279.

actions following from advice or direction given by it to the directors who are members of staff. It is therefore essential that potential investments should be thoroughly examined by properly qualified officers and the extent of potential liability identified.

2.144 Directors of companies are responsible, under the Articles of Association of the company, for the general management and administration of the company between general meetings. Their potential liabilities are considerable as they occupy personal offices of trust and should be fully indemnified by the institution in so far as the companies legislation permits and insurance cover taken out to protect both them and the institution.

Land and its use

The Financial Memorandum

2.145 Provision for the estate has now become an explicit part of the arrangements for funding institutions. The Financial Memorandum between the relevant Funding Council and a higher education institution requires the institution to develop a strategy for managing its capital assets.

Disasters

2.146 As in other walks of life, genuine disasters in universities and colleges tend to involve the estate and its buildings, such as the collapse of the railway tunnel at the University of Kent in July 1974, illustrated in graphic terms by the late Graham Martin.[285] The tunnel, scene of many successful student parties in the 1960s (as the author can testify), simply gave way under the weight of the academic activity above it. This event and the legal consequences flowing from it was perhaps one of the more dramatic which higher education administrators have had to deal with over the years but numerous disputes have arisen in relation to the estate and property and all staff should be aware of at least the basic principles governing land and its use.

---

285 G R Martin *From Vision to Reality* (1990) chapter 9.

Rubbish, racehorses, chattels, ironmongers, dry rot and sagas

2.147 Cases have involved the circumstances in which a local authority may charge for the collection of rubbish (University of Hull);[286] the date when construction of a building ends for VAT purposes – when the 'main structure [of the building] is complete, the windows glazed and all the essential services installed' (also Hull);[287] when a chattel becomes a fixture for VAT (University of Reading);[288] what is 'repair and maintenance' (Victoria University of Manchester);[289] the meaning of 'dwelling' and other matters related to student residences (University of Bath);[290] when a racehorse gallop is held on a tenancy or licence (University of Reading);[291] in what circumstances a university might realise the value of property secured on a loan to a saddler's ironmonger (University of Glasgow);[292] when tenement owners are liable to pay for the eradication of dry rot (University of Edinburgh);[293] the meaning of 'soil' in relation to the ownership of minerals, etc (St Catherine's College, Cambridge);[294] in what circumstances compensation might be obtained for 'injurious affection of land' caused by laying a water main (St John's College Oxford);[295] and the attribution of input tax and basis of apportionment in a contract for engineering buildings (University of Wales, Cardiff).[296] Building cases tend to be long-running sagas as very often damage is not discovered until the building has been in use for some considerable time, as at the University of Warwick where a case heard in 1988 concerned buildings constructed between 1963 and 1968[297] and at the University of Glasgow, also heard in 1988,

286 *Mattison v Beverley Borough Council* (1987) 151 JP 499, CA.
287 *University of Hull v Customs and Excise Comrs* LEE/75/31, 180.
288 *University of Reading v Customs and Excise Comrs* LON/89/235, 4209. The decision was that there are two tests: (i) the method and degree of annexation and (ii) its purpose.
289 *University of Manchester v Customs and Excise Comrs* [1982] VATTR 157.
290 *University of Bath v Customs and Excise Comrs* [1996] SW II 1492.
291 *University of Reading v Johnson-Houghton* [1985] 2 EGLR 113.
292 *University of Glasgow v Yuill's Trustees* (1882) 9 R 643.
293 *University Court of the University of Edinburgh v City of Edinburgh District Council* 1987 SLT (Sh Ct) 103.
294 *Master and Fellows of St Catherine's College Cambridge v Rosse* [1916] 1 Ch 73.
295 *St John's College Oxford v Thames Water Authority* [1990] RVR 84.
296 *Customs and Excise Comrs v University of Wales College of Cardiff* [1995] STC 611.
297 *University of Warwick v Sir Robert McAlpine* (1988) 42 BLR 1.

where the architect involved had produced the original designs in 1966, although the building was not completed until 1978.[298]

The variety of issues involved

2.148 The issues to which the railway tunnel incident relates include those concerning ownership of the land on which the university was built, ownership of the tunnel and the liabilities of its owners, legal responsibilities of the various professionals who designed and built the collapsed building, health and safety of those working in it and any compensation payable to the university for loss of use. These particular issues can be extracted from the event itself and discussed generally, with other relevant issues, in the context of higher education institutions.

The law of land

Introduction

2.149 The law relating to land, its ownership and usage in all three jurisdictions in the UK is extremely complex. There are substantial differences between English and Scots law in this area, although it is argued[299] that Viscount Dunedin's statement in 1935 that 'there is no more identity between the two systems than there is between chalk and cheese' may as we turn the millennium be in need of revision. This text will not attempt to cover the general subject in any depth, but will concentrate on those areas in which those working in higher education are most likely to need practical advice. The detailed discussion will be centred on English law, although I have attempted to draw attention to the major differences between the English and Scots systems. While the statutory basis is different and procedures vary, the practical differences between English and Northern Ireland law are relatively minor.

2.150 A chartered institution, as already explained, can generally speaking do anything that an ordinary individual can do. Thus in relation to land a chartered institution may be landowner, lessor,

---

298 *University Court of the University of Glasgow v William Whitfield and John Laing (Construction) (third party)* (1988) 42 BLR 66.
299 C F Kolbert and N A M Mackay *History of Scots and English Land Law* (1977) p 342; Lord Dunedin *English and Scottish Law* Murray Lecture 19 (1935).

landlord, lessee or tenant just as a natural person may be and will incur all the rights, liabilities, privileges and duties which apply to a natural person within the applicable jurisdiction. Institutions created by or under statute can do only those acts which are authorised directly or indirectly by the creating statute or instrument of government, but such statutes and instruments invariably permit the institution to act in relation to land in the same way as a chartered body. Either type of institution may own land and the buildings erected on it, take leases on buildings, rent buildings to third parties or to members of the institution, eg to students, student unions, shops, banks, etc, or have or be subject to rights of others over the land which they own or lease, for example rights of way, easements and wayleaves for the passage of electricity cables over, or drains under, the ground, and so on.

2.151 Perhaps in the days of expansion it would have been necessary to deal in depth with issues relating to the purchase of land, planning new buildings, roadworks and so on. At the turn of the millennium issues of disposal of property, converting and adapting buildings – subject to statutory planning and building controls – and ensuring that buildings comply with the mass of statutory regulation of use, health and safety and fire precautions are perhaps most significant. No attempt will be made to deal here with questions of conveyancing, which is best left in the hands of a professional. This includes such matters as the creation of a legally-binding contract to purchase property, which as the general reader will be aware is different in England and Scotland.

2.152 The law of water is not covered in detail, although there are a number of institutions which use rivers, streams, etc for scientific purposes and some, particularly in Scotland, which maintain freshwater or marine research stations. *University of Stirling v Central Regional Council*[300] helps to establish when it is necessary to prove fault in actions for breach of statutory duty under the Water (Scotland) Act 1980. As this Act is a direct descendant of a Clauses Consolidation Act of Victorian times, the reasoning in the judgment is relevant throughout Great Britain.[301] Part II Control of Pollution Act 1974, the Environmental Protection Act 1990 and the Environment Act 1995 are also important in this area.

300 *University of Stirling v Central Regional Council* 1992 SLT 79.
301 See also D J Farrington *Developments in the Law of Aquaculture in Scotland* Water Law (1992).

England and Wales: the law of real property

Realty and personalty

2.153   The applicable law in England (and Wales, which is treated as England for this purpose) is the law of real property (or realty), based on common law and a number of statutes, principally six Acts of 1925 and one of 1922 which all came into force on 1 January 1926 and which are referred to collectively as the '1925 property legislation.'[302] The division of property into real (realty) and personal (personalty) is based on early law. The courts would restore real property (the 'res' or thing itself) to a dispossessed owner, but give the dispossessor the choice of either returning personal property or paying the value thereof. Land was realty and could be specifically recovered; swords, gloves (typically) were personalty and were not thus recoverable. Leaseholds (or 'terms of years'), which are strictly personalty rather than realty, are nevertheless classified as 'chattels real' and the law relating to them is customarily treated along with the law of real property.

Ownership of land

2.154   The basis of the law of land in England is that all land is owned by the Crown; the majority of it is occupied by tenants holding either directly or indirectly from the Crown. In the modern law, there is only one feudal tenure, that of socage, or freehold, and one non-feudal tenure, leasehold. Discussion here will be confined to the 'estate in fee simple absolute in possession', which is what you would understand from the term 'freehold residence' used by an estate agent, and the 'term of years absolute', commonly called leaseholds. These two estates are the only ones capable of existing at law. Parallel with the legal ownership or tenancy of land there may run a beneficial ownership or tenancy based in equity and the law of trusts, relating to the rights of individuals and not attached to the land. Discussion of these issues is beyond the scope of this work but the reader should

---

302   Law of Property Acts 1922 and 1925, Settled Land Act 1925, Trustee Act 1925, Administration of Estates Act 1925, Land Registration Act 1925, Land Charges Act 1925. The Law of Property (Amendment) Act 1926 is usually added to this list for completeness. Amendments were made by Law of Property (Miscellaneous Provisions) Acts in 1989 and 1994. The Trusts of Land and Appointment of Trustees Act 1996 effected a number of reforms, in particular preventing the creation of further settlements under the Settled Land Act 1925.

appreciate that equitable interests can and do exist, for example restrictive covenants, dealt with in the next paragraph.

Easements etc

2.155   Not surprisingly, the feudal system recognised obligations between adjacent landholders or of a superior in the feudal chain over an inferior. So the law allows interests or charges in or over land to be created, including easements, rights, privileges and charges by way of legal mortgage, equivalent to one of the two permitted estates. An easement is defined as 'a right to use, or restrict the use of, the land of another person' in some way, for example rights of way, rights of light and rights of water. In each case there is a 'dominant' and a 'servient' tenement (ie parcel of land), the former having the relevant right over the latter. There are also quasi-easements, such as the right to support in certain circumstances, licences, which can only exist in equity, and restrictive covenants, the law of which is an equitable extension of the law of easements.

2.156   Restrictive covenants are often attached to property on transfer, although the burden of them runs only in equity: no inspection of the land will reveal the existence of a restrictive covenant against burning lime or keeping swine, both common restrictive covenants imposed in the Victorian era. Attention should also be drawn to 'profits à prendre', the right to take something from another person's land, eg profit of pasture, allowing the grazing of animals; profit of turbary, allowing removal of turf or peat as fuel; profit of estovers, allowing removal of wood for building or fuel; profit of piscary, the right to catch and take away fish. Subject to all these restrictions and the rights of others, if any, over the land, the owner who is seised – from 'seisin' – the symbolic transfer of a twig or clot of earth – of an estate in fee simple absolute in possession can do whatever s/he likes with the land which is otherwise consistent with the general law. The most significant right of the normal householder is to mortgage the land and its buildings in order to raise funds to acquire it.

Leases

2.157   It did not suit every feudal lord to assign freehold so the law allows a contractual relationship called a lease, in which the freehold is retained by the landlord (lessor) and the leaseholder or tenant (lessee) is given the right to occupy it for a consideration. The usual type of lease is the occupational lease, where the tenant holds at a rent and either occupies it or sub-lets it. A lease is a document creating a legal interest in land for a fixed period of certain duration: it should be distinguished from a licence to occupy premises, which is an equitable arrangement. There may be considerable formality about the creation of a legal lease for other than a short period; the complexities of conveyancing are beyond the scope of this work. Rent Acts provide for security of tenure of residential tenants, and the control or regulation of rents, but educational tenancies are excepted from protection, in common with holiday homes, public houses, etc by an amendment to the Rent Act 1971 in 1974. The position is now governed by the Housing Act 1988: if the landlord (the higher education institution) wishes to terminate the tenancy for breach of conditions, and can establish its right to possession at common law, the court has no discretion but to grant possession.[303] Agricultural leases are a special case and disputes do sometimes arise.[304]

2.158 The Leasehold Reform Act 1967, while granting certain tenants the right to purchase freehold, extended in 1993, safeguarded the position of land required for public purposes by specified authorities. This included any university body which might require the land within 10 years.[305] Local authority and university bodies were empowered to oblige tenants acquiring the freehold to accept covenants restricting the carrying out of development or clearing of land as are necessary to reserve the land for possible development by the university. Section 29(6)(b) empowered the Secretary of State to exercise compulsory purchase powers on behalf of universities. In Northern Ireland a covenant in a lease granted in 1922 for a term of 10,000 years prohibited the use of a large building for institutional, religious or educational purposes. In *Queen's University Belfast's Application*[306] it was held that this unnecessarily impeded the development of the land. There was no possible market for use as a private dwelling: the immediate neighbourhood had changed since 1922 and there was no longer any practical benefit in the covenant to any of the lessors.

---

303 Schedule 1 paragraph 8 Housing Act 1988. This exemption does not extend to head leasing schemes: see eg *St Catherine's College v Dorling* [1980] 1 WLR 66, CA.
304 A recent example was *Master and Fellows of University College Oxford v Durdy* [1982] Ch 413.
305 Section 28(5)(e).
306 R/21/1990.

Registration of title and incumbrances

2.159 The 1925 property legislation continued a system of registration of title originally introduced in 1862 and progressively extended in England and Wales. There is a separate system of registration of incumbrances, the two types of register being the central Land Charges Register and the various Local Land Charges Registries maintained by local authorities. The central register is essentially a register of private rights whereas the local registers deal with public rights such as planning, making-up of private roads, etc. The central Land Charges Register is of decreasing importance as more land is the subject of registration of title, but the local registers often contain critically important information and it is essentially that these should be 'searched' before any binding contract to purchase a property is entered into. The Land Registration Act 1997 introduced procedures to expedite the process of registration on the Land Register, which since 1995 has been 'on line.'

Scotland: the law of heritable property

Heritable and moveable property

2.160 With one exception mentioned later, Scots law shares with English law the basic theory of the universal derivative tenure of all land from the Crown: land with its pertinents is the typical instance of heritable (or immovable) property. Buildings are counted as part of the ground and rights connected with land, such as leases and servitudes, are heritable. The feudal relationships of superior and vassal still exist although major changes in conveyancing law since 1971 have meant that increasingly the relationships are of practical significance only where conditions of a feu charter control the use and future development of land.[307] Sasine, like seisin in English law, was the symbolic transfer of heritage by delivery, eg handing over earth as the symbol for transfer of land. The owner of land can use his land for any purpose which is not inconsistent with the common law, statute law, conditions of his title or rights which may have been created in favour of third parties.

2.161 There are no higher education institutions currently situated in the exceptional udal landholding of Orkney and Shetland but issues

---

307 Conveyancing and Feudal Reform (Scotland) Act 1970; Land Tenure Reform (Scotland) Act 1974; Land Registration (Scotland) Act 1979.

do arise there. For example in 1958 a team from the University of Aberdeen discovered 'The St Ninian's Isle Treasure' and the issue was whether it belonged to the Crown, despite being found on udal land. In *Lord Advocate v University of Aberdeen and Budge*[308] the Court of Session held that it did.

The Register of Sasines and land registration

2.162 The system of registration of title to heritage by registration of writs in the Register of Sasines, a register open to public inspection, is a long-standing feature of Scots conveyancing. The person who appears in the Register as the owner of the land is said to be infeft, infeftment depending on the registration of the deed transferring the land. A person owning security over land acquires his or her charge over the land by registering the appropriate deed: the current form of security over land is the standard security which has replaced earlier, more complex arrangements. Land registration in the English sense is a relatively recent appearance in Scotland and is gradually being extended after the introduction of computerisation.

Servitudes

2.163 The original concept of servitudes is a Roman one. In Scots law the land may be subject to the burden of servitudes, such as rights of way, rights of support, stillicide (the right to discharge rainfall), and light or prospect. The average member of staff of a higher education institution is unlikely to come across the servitude of fuel, feal and divot which corresponds to turbary in English law. However it is possible that in an urban situation a projected development may disturb the rights of other owners to, for example, support or light and in some scientific subjects the right of aquaehaustus, to take water from a well or stream, may be of significance. The general rule that burdens on heritage do not affect singular successors unless they appear in the Register of Sasines does not apply and there is considerable case law relating to the creation of servitudes which is beyond the scope of this work.

308 1963 SC 533.

Leases

2.164 Leases in Scots law are created by contract whereby 'certain uses, or the entire possession and control of lands, houses or other heritable subjects are given to the tenant for a return, known as rent or lordship, in money or goods.'[309] It was established in *Gray v Edinburgh University*[310] that a lease requires agreement on at least the parties, the subjects and the rent. Certain long leases may be recorded in the Register of Sasines, and there is a statutory limitation of 20 years on the term of lease of a property let as a private dwellinghouse.[311] The position in relation to the Rent Acts is the same as in England and Wales.[312]

Recovery of adverse possession

England and Wales

2.165 The one area of the law of land and procedural matters relating to its ownership and possession in which many staff of higher education institutions, certainly in the decade from 1968 onwards, were likely to come into contact was recovery of possession following a student sit-in or similar disruption. In England and Wales a number of institutions have from time to time taken steps in the courts to restrain students from disruptive activity or to regain possession of buildings unlawfully occupied. Where repossession of premises unlawfully occupied is sought, the institution may proceed under RSC Order 113 by application to a judge of the High Court. This is again a highly technical matter, the law being arguably unsuited to such cases, which now almost invariably result in substantial costs being levied on student unions. Procedure requires the service of summonses which delay recovery of the property and this can have a serious effect on the operation of an institution. Any member of staff facing such a situation must immediately consult a solicitor who is familiar with High Court procedures and take steps to ensure that careful accounts are kept of any time and other resources spent or irrecoverably lost

---

309 W M Gloag and R C Henderson in J A D Hope A F Rodger and A Paton (eds) *Introduction to the Law of Scotland* (9th ed, 1987) p 487.
310 1962 SC 157.
311 Section 8 Land Tenure Reform (Scotland) Act 1974. Whether or not student residences are private dwellinghouses for the purposes of this section is undecided.
312 Schedule 4 paragraph 7 Housing (Scotland) Act 1988; Assured Tenancies (Exemptions) (Scotland) Regulations 1988 (SI 1988/2068).

through the action so that those responsible can be properly held to account.

Scotland

2.166   In Scotland the procedure is different. An interdict may be granted against named persons where there is actual or explicit threat of trespass, but otherwise procedure should be under the criminal law of trespass.[313] According to CVCP advice of 1974[314] the category of trespassers would include persons who lawfully obtain entry to premises, eg to an examination hall or to a hall of residence, but who refuse to leave when the period for which they had express or implied permission to remain expires. The civil action of summary ejection is unsuited to most disruptive activity since

> the defender's possession … [must be] … violent, fraudulent or forcible, or precarious ie at the will of the pursuer, and he can claim no title to the occupation challenged.

and there are in-built procedural delays.

Planning, building control and public health

Planning

2.167   The Town and Country Planning Act 1990 (as amended by the Planning and Compensation Act 1991) provides the basis for planning control in England and Wales, with the Town and Country Planning (Scotland) Act 1997[315] providing a similar basis in Scotland.[316] Subject to certain exceptions for minor development and changes of use,[317] all development of higher education institution estates will require planning permission of the local authority.[318] Planning authorities are required to draw up structure plans,

313   Trespass (Scotland) Act 1865; *Paterson v Robertson* 1944 JC 166.
314   Note by Professor D M Walker of the University of Glasgow appended to letter of 4 July 1974 from the Executive Secretary of CVCP to the Principals of the then Scottish universities.
315   See also Planning (Hazardous Substances) (Scotland) Act 1997 and Planning (Consequential Provisions) (Scotland) Act 1997.
316   Northern Ireland has a separate but parallel scheme.
317   Town and Country Planning General Development Order 1988, (SI 1988/1813) (as amended).
318   See section 328 Town and Country Planning Act 1990 re disposal of land.

formulating their development policy, for approval by the Secretary of State and local plans for specific areas and purposes. This procedure enables local authorities to determine, for example, which areas are to be zoned for housing, which for commercial or industrial development and which for the purposes of the higher education institution. The control of development on a day-to-day basis is normally undertaken by a council committee with officers providing advice on whether or not applications for development are in line the approved structure and local plans. Applications are advertised, objections sought and taken into account when a decision is reached, with a right of appeal against refusal of permission to the Secretary of State. Conditions may be attached to the grant of permission.

2.168 'Development' is defined in the Acts as

the carrying out of building, engineering, mining or other operations in, on, over or under land, or the making of any material change in the use of any buildings or other land.[319]

Maintenance works, improvements and alterations are not classified as development provided that they do not materially affect the external appearance of the building. Some changes of use are permitted without formality, others require permission. The likelihood of an institution failing to obtain permission or not complying with conditions is so remote as not to justify discussion here. Some institutions may have as part of the estate buildings of special architectural or historic interest and there are special requirements to be complied with before any alteration is undertaken.[320]

Building control

2.169 Regulations made by the Secretary of State under the Building Act 1984, and in Scotland the Building (Scotland) Acts 1959 and 1970, administered and enforced by local authorities, are primarily 'to ensure the health and safety of people in or about the building.' Among other matters covered by the regulations are building structure, fire precautions, sound transmission, ventilation, drainage, stairways and fuel conservation. The regulations apply to the

319 Section 55 Town and Country Planning Act 1990.
320 In Scotland under the Planning (Listed Buildings and Conservation Areas) (Scotland) Act 1997.

construction of a new building, an extension or material alteration to an existing building, or the change of use of an existing building. There are a number of different procedures by which a builder or contractor can ensure that the regulations are complied with, without necessarily depositing complete plans with the local authority. Residential accommodation is subject to the first rights of access to goods, facilities and services in Part III DDA which came into force in December 1996; later rights of access were not in force as at 31 December 1997.

Fire precautions

2.170 The Building Regulations contain mandatory rules for means of escape in case of fire applying to all buildings likely to form part of the institution's estate. The Fire Precautions Act 1971 specifies that certain types of building use may require a fire certificate issued by the fire authority (which is required to consult the local authority) and empowers the Secretary of State to issue Orders in respect of those uses.[321] It is a criminal offence not to *either* have a fire certificate for a building which requires one *or* to have applied for one. Material alterations to a building covered by a certificate must be notified to the fire authority so that they have an opportunity to review the matter. Academic buildings, whether new or existing, only come within the scope of the Act if they contain offices as defined in the Offices, Shops and Railway Premises Act 1963 described in detail elsewhere. It is a matter of debate whether the Act extends to halls of residence or similar accommodation.

Public health

2.171 Those parts of the Public Health Act 1936 still in force and relevant to higher education institutions are mainly concerned with public sewers and discharges into them.[322] Part III Building Act 1984 replaced those parts of the 1936 Act dealing with building drainage, sanitary provision and water supply. There are stringent provisions relating to fire access and egress. The Environmental Protection Act 1990 implemented a number of European Directives and replaced a

---

321 Eg The Fire Precautions (Hotels and Boarding Houses) Order 1972 (SI 1972/238); The Fire Precautions (Factories, Offices, Shops and Railway Premises) Order 1989 (SI 1989/76); Fire Precautions (Workplace) Regulations 1997, SI 1997/1840.
322 Section 27 (discharges into public sewers), 34 (private sewers, drains and cesspools) and 262 (culverting of watercourses and ditches).

considerable amount of earlier law on control of pollution, waste disposal, statutory nuisances and clean air. It also strengthened the law on litter; section 86 requires higher education institutions, so far as is practicable, to keep their land clear of litter and refuse and makes it an offence for any person to drop litter on any part of the land open to the air.

2.172 The Control of Pollution Act 1974, now largely superseded by the Environmental Protection Act 1990 and Environment Act 1995, tightened considerably the law governing disposal of waste. Charges may be levied for the collection of certain types of waste[323] and it is clear that this extends to commercial waste (from, say a shop) and disposal of laboratory waste. Charges may not be levied for the collection of 'house waste.' In *Mattison v Beverley Borough Council*[324] the Council had advised M, Registrar and Secretary of the University of Hull, that a charge for collecting waste from halls of residence would be raised, since it was not regarded by them as 'house refuse.'[325] Although the character of the waste was such that it could in principle be so regarded, the Court of Appeal held that halls of residence were not dwelling houses, that waste from them was not, therefore, 'house refuse', and that the local authority was entitled to charge for its removal.

2.173 Higher education institutions which own or lease houses for student occupation should note that under the Housing Acts, local authorities may take action if they consider that a house is unfit for human habitation or, while still being fit, is in a state of disrepair. A notice may be served on the person controlling the building requiring repairs to be undertaken and giving a time limit for completion. Similar action may be taken in respect of houses which lack certain standard amenities or are overcrowded with the statutory regulations.

Houses in multiple occupation

2.174 Houses in multiple occupation (HMO), normally let in the private sector on assured shorthold tenancies,[326] are subject to a

---

323 The Collection and Disposal of Waste Regulations 1988 (SI 1988/819) allow local authorities to raise a charge for collecting certain types of household waste including that from 'premises forming part of a university' and indeed any other educational establishment.
324 (1987) 151 JP 499, CA.
325 Section 74 Public Health Act 1936.
326 Housing Act 1996.

special legal regime, particularly in relation to fire precautions.[327] What is or is not a HMO is a matter for the court to determine in a particular case.[328] The statutory definition is 'a house [defined by the Court of Appeal in *Reed v Hastings Corpn*[329] as a structure built or adapted for use as a dwelling house or for the purpose of human habitation which is occupied [ie lived in][330] by persons who do not form a single household'[331] so in principle it is a description applicable to most student houses. New Regulations were introduced in March 1997.[332] HMOs appear to fall within the definition of 'dwelling' for the purposes of the Noise Act 1996 (not applicable in Scotland).

2.175 In *Kingston upon Hull District Council v University of Hull*,[333] the Council considered that houses owned by the university and occupied by students who paid rent individually to the university were houses in multiple occupation. Under what was then section 16 Housing Act 1961 the Council served notices on the university in 1976. Four houses were cited in the first instance, although the university owned many more which were also used for student accommodation. The main requirements of the notices were the installation of a detection/alarm system, the provision of fire resisting, self-closing doors and the making of the understairs cupboard into a protected cupboard. The university appealed to the county court where only the fire resisting/self-closing doors of the main requirements were found to be necessary. This judgment was upheld in the Court of Appeal. In this case the university was the owner and occupier of the houses: this will be true also of institutions which operate 'head-leasing' schemes.

2.176 Where the institution simply gives advice to students as to where to seek accommodation, then its duty of care is more limited. In *Ephraim v Newham London Borough Council*,[334] a case of injury

---

327 Part III Housing Act 1988.
328 The Institution of Environmental Health Officers produces a useful guide, circulated to institutions in membership of CVCP under circular letter N/93/174 of 28 July 1993. The Chartered Institute of Environmental Health has collaborated with NUS to produce a leaflet *Home Sweet Home* (1996) relating to fire safety, overcrowding, gas and electricity safety, etc.
329 (1964) 62 LGR 588. See also *Okereke v Brent London Borough Council* [1967] 1 QB 42.
330 *Silbers v Southwark London Borough Council* (1977) 76 LGR 421.
331 What is or is not a household is a matter of fact and degree: *Simmons v Pizzey* [1979] AC 37, HL.
332 Housing (Fire Safety in Houses in Multiple Occupation) Order 1997 (SI 1997/230).
333 (1979) LAG Bulletin 191, CA.
334 (1992) 91 LGR 412, CA.

by fire, the Court of Appeal, reversing a decision at first instance, held that the council were not negligent in failing to have a system of inspecting properties in multiple occupation before advising homeless people to seek bed and breakfast there. The landlord was however liable under the Occupiers' Liability Act 1957. DfEE has drafted a model registration scheme which exempts any house where the 'responsible person' is a higher education institution. Other exemptions include houses occupied either by persons who form only two households or by no more than four people forming two households in the residence.

Utilities

2.177   There are statutory regulations and byelaws (and non-statutory codes of practice) relating to the common utilities: water, gas and electricity. The Water Act 1945 and the Water (Scotland) Act 1980 enabled the various district water authorities to introduce byelaws for the purposes of preventing waste, undue consumption, misuse or contamination of water. Standardisation has now virtually been achieved with authorities adopting the 1986 edition of the Model Water Byelaws for use in their area. The Gas Act 1986 is the principal legislation governing the gas industry and the supply of gas, enabling the Secretary of State to make regulations designed to ensure the safety of gas installations. Regulations made under this and earlier legislation are designed to ensure that all installations are safe and lay down requirements covering pipework, meters, governors, fittings, testing, gas escapes and equipment connected to the supply.[335] The Electricity Acts 1947 and 1989 enable the Secretary of State to issue regulations covering the various aspects of supplying electricity, carrying out electrical installations and ensuring that safety standards are met. Contravention of many of the utilities regulations is a criminal offence.

Neighbours

2.178   Neighbouring properties may enjoy certain legal rights and have certain obligations towards the institution's estate. There are a number of issues.

---

335 The Gas Safety (Installation and Use) Regulations 1994 (SI 1994/1886), are frequently quoted in respect of safety of houses in multiple occupation.

Fencing and boundaries

2.179   In England there is no overall requirement for an owner of land to fence it or to maintain a fence. There may however be a covenant in the title deeds relating to the type of fence or wall and responsibility for its maintenance. Frequently, particularly in older deeds, the boundary is vague and if a dispute arises which cannot be settled by agreement, the courts will have to take into account the actual usage. The Party Walls etc Act 1996 covers England and Wales only. In Scotland there may be an agreement by adjoining heritors to erect a fence at their common expense; otherwise if the land exceeds five acres in area the March Dykes Act 1661 provides for compulsory contributions.

Right to light

2.180   The rights to land in English and Scots law extend *a caelo usque ad centrum* (from the sky to the centre of the earth) but a landowner does not enjoy an automatic right to light. Thus in principle, and provided any planning restrictions have been observed, if an adjoining owner decides to erect a high building or fence, there may be no redress for any neighbours affected. In England a right to light for buildings can be acquired by agreement or by prescription;[336] in Scotland the negative servitudes *Non Aedificandi, Altius Non Tollendi and Non Officiendi Luminibus* may apply. In all cases the amount of light required will depend on the use to which the building or room affected is to be put. Prescription applies to a new building provided it has been constructed largely on the same site as an old one which has acquired the right and is not significantly different in size or character.

Subsidence

2.181   In English law, soil enjoys a right to support, but buildings do not unless they have acquired it by agreement, restrictive covenant or prescription. In Scotland the servitude *Oneris Ferendi* is the right to have a building supported.[337]

---

336 Prescription is continuous use for 20 years or more without adverse claim.
337 Erskine *Institute* II 9, 7.

Nuisances: noise and smells

2.182   Anything which interferes with a landowner's enjoyment of property may be a nuisance. Depending on the circumstances, noisy operations may be restricted by injunction (interdict).[338] An alternative procedure is to apply to the local authority for an abatement notice issued under the Control of Pollution Act 1974 and the Noise Act 1996. The effect of this is either to forbid the noise completely or restrict it to certain times. If the local authority declines to exercise this power, the aggrieved party may apply directly to the magistrates (England) or sheriff (Scotland).[339] Failure to comply with an order of this kind, or an order made under a local byelaw controlling noise pollution, is a criminal offence. Other nuisances such as offensive smells may be dealt with either by injunction (interdict) or by local authority order.

Trees

2.183   Branches or roots of healthy trees, and diseased trees, can give rise to legal disputes. Unless a tree preservation order is in force restricting pruning or lopping, it is permissible to cut down overhanging branches or permeating roots, provided that they are returned to their owner.[340] Roots can also cause damage to neighbouring buildings, but not every piece of damage so caused will necessarily be the fault of the tree owner.[341] Damage caused by falling trees or branches, where this can be attributed to negligence by failure to take care of them can be held to be the responsibility of the tree owner.

2.184   A licence is required for the felling of growing trees not included in a tree preservation order. There are however a large number of exemptions, the most relevant of which are those with a trunk diameter of less than three inches (six inches in a coppice), fruit or garden trees, to prevent danger or abate nuisance, to improve the growth of other trees (four inch diameter limit), where planning

---

338   Eg *Allison v Merton, Sutton and Wandsworth Area Health Authority* [1975] CLY 2450 in which noise from a heating plant operated by the authority interfered with the neighbour's ability to sleep.

339   The Noise Act 1996 does not apply in Scotland.

340   *Lemmon v Webb* [1895] AC 1; *Halkerson v Wedderburn* (1781) M 10495.

341   See eg *Russell v Barnet London Borough Council* (1984) 83 LGR 152. If the trees are responsible for the damage, claiming poor construction is no defence: *Bunclark v Hertfordshire County Council* [1977] 2 EGLR 114.

permission has been granted, or where the aggregate cubic content does not exceed 825 cubic feet, and not more than 150 cubic feet is sold.[342] Trees are heritable property in Scotland.[343]

Control of access to property

Rights and privileges of access

2.185 It is obvious that many categories of individual have rights or privileges of access to the property of a higher education institution, depending on the nature of the property and the purpose for which they require access. Students, for example, unless under discipline, will have a right of access to the rooms in residences which they are licensed to occupy and to the rooms in which they are required or permitted to be present for teaching and examination purposes. Members of staff likewise have reasonable right of access to property for the purposes of carrying out their duties and purposes incidental to those duties. Members of the public, unless permitted access generally or for specific purposes (eg to attend a dramatic performance) or having the right to traverse a public highway or other public right of way, have no general right of access and an institution may wish to take action to restrict them.

Common duty of care

2.186 Apart from any statutory liability, an occupier owes to a visitor a common duty of care, which is the duty to take such care as in all the circumstances of the case is reasonable, to see that the visitor will be reasonably safe in using the premises for the purposes for which invited or permitted by the institution to be there, including the degree of care to be looked for in the visitor.[344] This is a question of fact and depends on the circumstances. Examples of what might be regarded ipso facto as showing negligence would be the collapse of a chimney, a tile falling off a roof, or the glass falling out of a window, each in the absence of storms.[345] Anyone who is neither

---

342 Section 9 Forestry Act 1967.
343 *Morrison v Lockhart* 1912 SC 1017.
344 *Robert Addie & Sons (Collieries) Ltd v Dumbreck* [1929] AC 358, 365.
345 *Tarry v Ashton* (1876) 1 QBD 314.

invited nor permitted to be there is a trespasser: the duty owed to a trespasser is not to injure him or her wilfully or to act with reckless disregard of his or her presence.[346]

Trespass

2.187 In English law trespass is the tort of interference with possession of land, actionable by the occupier; it is not generally a criminal offence. Examples of acts of trespass are
(i)   entering onto land without invitation or authorisation;[347]
(ii) leaving an article (eg a car) on the land;
(iii) outstaying one's welcome;
(iv) being otherwise lawfully on land, misusing it for another purpose.
Unauthorised access to certain property, such as military establishments or prisons, is a criminal offence under the legislation governing those properties. It is possible that a trespasser will commit a criminal offence during the act of trespass. And in *Hickman v Maisey*[348] the highway was improperly used for making notes on the form of racehorses being exercised on adjacent land: this was trespass since the purpose of the highway is for 'passing and re-passing.' Again in *Harrison v Duke of Rutland*[349] the right to 'pass and repass' was abused by crossing land repeatedly.

2.188 If an article left on land causes damage, it may be possible to seize it in an action known as distress damage feasant,[350] but the courts do not encourage self-help remedies.[351]

2.189 As trespass is a tort, action to remove a trespasser must be taken within the civil law. If the trespasser refuses to leave, and the occupier does not wish to risk the possibility of action for assault by removing the offender by 'use of reasonable force,' the remedy must lie in damages, on the assumption that damage has been done or in injunction, if the trespass is persistent.

---

346 *Walker v Midland Rly Co* (1886) 55 LT 489.
347 There are specific rules relating to squatters: see Part II Criminal Law Act 1977.
348 [1900] 1 QB 752.
349 [1893] 1 QB 142.
350 *Lagan Navigation Co v Lambeg Bleaching, Dyeing and Finishing Co* [1927] AC 226.
351 *Sochacki v Sas* [1947] 1 All ER 344.

Liability towards trespassers

2.190   The Occupiers' Liability Act 1984 clarified English law so that an occupier of land has a duty to ensure that all reasonable and practicable steps are taken to warn potential trespassers of any danger which may be present, or to exclude them from the property. Where trespassers are or are likely to be children, the occupier must by means of effective warning or protection keep them from injuring themselves, for example by deterring them from playing with enticing and dangerous equipment. Under section 1 Occupiers' Liability Act 1984 an occupier may discharge his or her duty towards trespassers by taking reasonable steps to give a warning of the danger concerned, or to discourage persons from taking a risk. What is a reasonable step will depend upon the facts of the case, including for example whether an institution's campus is open or has restricted access. There is no statutory liability for the property of a trespasser.

2.191   The Occupiers' Liability (Scotland) Act 1960 by contrast provides that an occupier will automatically owe a duty to all who are not visitors who enter the land, and the content of that duty varies with the nature of that entry. In Scotland a proprietor of land is entitled to apply for interdict (approximating to the English injunction) to prohibit actual or explicit threat of trespass unless permitted by statute or public necessity.[352] While the criminal law of trespass is applied mostly in regard to poaching[353] the Trespass (Scotland) Act 1865 penalises occupation of private land or premises without the owner's permission.

Rights of way

2.192   In some cases there may be a right of way for bona fide use by the public over land occupied by the institution. Some public rights of way are marked on definitive maps prepared by the local authority. Otherwise, an individual or the public in general may achieve the right to use a footpath across private land either by being given a written deed or by using it for a period of 20 years, ie prescription. However, for prescription to apply, the person must have used the path without asking for permission or offering payment, and the landowner must have implicitly accepted his or her right to do so,

---

352 Eg *Shepherd v Menzies* (1900) 2 F 443.
353 Night Poaching Acts 1828 and 1844; Day Trespass Act [Games (Scotland) Act] 1832; Poaching Prevention Act 1862.

for example by not telling him or her to stop or challenging the right. Section 31 Highways Act 1980 provides that after 20 years' unrestricted use by the public, it is assumed that the landowner has accepted the existence of a public right of way and dedicated the land as such. Section 3(3) Prescription and Limitation (Scotland) Act 1973 has the same effect in Scotland. This is why a notice recording the fact that the land is not so dedicated is frequently observed: alternatively, closing the route for at least one day per annum will achieve the same effect.

Adverse possession

2.193   Adverse possession is a means whereby someone who is not the true owner may acquire a title. This may happen as a result of a person occupying and using land or premises for a period of 12 years or more without the actual owner's permission or any interference from him or her.[354]

Trespass to goods

2.194   'The act of handling a man's goods without his permission is prima facie tortious'[355] and even negligent damage, provided that it is direct, falls within the scope of trespass. Thus, if a porter, while applying a wheel clamp to a car improperly parked on a campus scratches a door panel, there is a prima facie liability on the part of the institution.[356] It is immaterial, however, that no damage has been done to the property.[357] According to dicta in the celebrated case *Entick v Carrington*,[358] reading papers is not a trespass but seizing them and taking them away will be actionable in other ways.

---

354   *Hayward v Challoner* [1967] 3 All ER 122; *Littledale v Liverpool College* [1900] 1 Ch 19. See in relation to the inconvenience to the occupier *Wallis's Cayton Bay Holiday Camp v Shell-Mex and BP* [1974] 3 All ER 575; *Treloar v Nute* [1977] 1 All ER 230, CA.
355   *IRC v Rossminster* [1980] AC 952, 1011 per Lord Diplock.
356   An example given by Richard Farr in R Farr, D J Farrington and F T Mattison 'The University Estate' in D J Farrington and F T Mattison (eds) *Universities and the Law* CUA/CRS (1990) p 250. Reference is made to the pre-wheel clamping cases *Leame v Bray* (1803) 3 East 593 and *Fouldes v Willoughby* (1841) 8 M & W 540, 549 per Alderson B. In some circumstances wheel-clamping, even on private land, may be a criminal offence in Scotland.
357   *William Leitch & Co v Leydon* [1931] AC 90, 106 per Lord Blanesburgh.
358   (1765) 19 State Tr 1029, 1066 per Lord Camden CJ.

Occupiers' liability for property on the premises

2.195　The Occupiers' Liability Act 1957 imposes liability on the institution as the occupier of premises for the property of a visitor or other person on the premises with permission: this may be excluded if warning has been given, the member of staff, student or visitor has accepted the risk and the property is lost or damaged through no fault of the occupier. A notice to the effect that no liability for loss of or damage to property is accepted and that property is left at owner's risk is all that is required: section 2(3) Unfair Contract Terms Act 1977 provides that where there is a contractual relationship this will not in itself absolve the occupier if negligence is shown.

Occupiers' liability for persons

2.196　The exclusion of liability for injury is much more difficult to achieve. Section 2 Occupiers' Liability Act 1957 and the Occupiers' Liability (Scotland) Act 1960 impose a high standard of care. Whether or not a person consents to run the risk of accidental harm which would otherwise be the subject of an action for negligence will depend upon whether a real assent is given to the taking of the risk, and whether that assent absolved the defendant from the duty to take care.[359] It may be possible to avoid liability for the actions of independent contractors if the occupier has reasonable belief in their competence.[360] However, the wide extent of the primary duty can be illustrated by *Mallon v Spook Erections Ltd*:[361] the operators of an open-air market were held liable when an unaccompanied child was scalded by hot soup served in an open container from a market stall.

Circumstances in which fault need not be shown

2.197　Unless there is an Act of God or some similar exception, there is strict liability for the escape of dangerous things accumulated on the premises for some non-natural purpose, but this liability does not extend to a person who is not an occupier.[362] There may also be strict liability when an occupier is vicariously responsible for the act of

359 *Seymour's Case* (1956) 2 OLR 369.
360 *Ferguson v Welsh* [1988] IRLR 112.
361 1993 SLR 845.
362 *Weller v Foot and Mouth Disease Research Institute* [1966] 1 QB 569.

another. An occupier cannot in normal circumstances however be held responsible for, for example, a fire caused by a stranger[363] or by chance or unknown cause.[364]

Duty of care to persons not on the premises

2.198 Fires caused by negligence are however the subject of liability[365] and the occupier may also have a duty of care to persons on adjoining land or on the highway.[366] This extends to snow falling from a roof, when the occupier had had sufficient opportunity to clear it.[367] Fencing may sometimes be necessary when there is a danger to passers-by whether by specific requirement of statute[368] or to discharge the duty of care under the occupiers' liability legislation,[369] particularly where children are present.[370]

Northern Ireland

2.199 The 1925 property legislation of England and Wales did not apply to Northern Ireland: the pre-1921 law of Ireland was adapted to Northern Ireland by subordinate legislation under the Government of Ireland Act 1920,[371] the provisions of which were expected to be temporary pending the re-unification of the two parts of the island of Ireland. From 1921 to 1972 Northern Ireland enjoyed a form of devolved government and these matters were within the province of the Northern Ireland Parliament, which enacted some relevant

363 *Hargrave v Goldman* (1963) 110 CLR 40; *Holderness v Goslin* [1975] 2 NZLR 46.
364 Fire Precautions (Metropolis) Act 1774.
365 *Mason v Levy Auto Parts of England* [1967] 2 QB 530; also *Musgrove v Pandelis* [1919] 2 KB 43 where a motor car caught fire and damaged property in the rooms above the garage: see also *R v Hawson* (1966) 55 DLR (2d) 583.
366 *Fay v Prentice* (1845) 1 CB 828; *Castle v St Augustine's Links* (1922) 38 TLR 615. There is an absolute liability under section 36(1)(b) Highways Act 1980 for injury caused by items overhanging the highway through lack of maintenance or other fault of the occupier.
367 *Slater v Worthington's Cash Stores (1930) Ltd* [1941] 1 KB 488.
368 Section 295(1) Highways Act 1959.
369 On defective fencing see *Indermaur v Dames* (1866) LR1 CP 274.
370 *Edwards v Rly Executive* [1952] AC 737; *Cooke v Midland Great Western Rly Co of Ireland* [1909] AC 229.
371 Government of Ireland (Adaptation of Enactments) (No 3) Order 1922 No 183. See also Northern Ireland (Land Registry) Adaptation of Enactments Order 1948 No 485; Northern Ireland (Registration of Deeds) Adaptation of Enactments Order 1948 No 487.

legislation.[372] Since 1972 however, except for brief periods Northern Ireland has been governed by 'direct rule' from Westminster and most of the legislation enacted by Order in Council under the temporary provisions for its government has echoed developments in English law.[373]

2.200 One major difference between Great Britain and Northern Ireland is the much greater concentration of power in the provincial or state government (although Northern Ireland is not constitutionally a state) as opposed to local authorities. Planning, for example, is controlled by the provincial Department of the Environment, with rights of appeal to an independent Planning Appeals Commission;[374] district councils have only a consultative role in the planning process. Public housing is controlled by a central Housing Executive.[375] The principles by which these and other functions are exercised are so similar to those of England, Wales and Scotland as not to merit any special treatment here.

2.201 Northern Ireland's liquor licensing laws are within its domestic legislation. Although procedures vary, there is now no significant relevant difference for the purposes of this work between Northern Ireland and the rest of the UK.

Dealing with 'internal' disputes – The Visitor

'Alsatia in England'

2.202 One area in which the chartered universities of England, Wales and Northern Ireland differ from the rest of the system is in the existence of the visitorial jurisdiction – a true 'Alsatia in England'[376] ie where the common law does not run and where the ordinary courts have no jurisdiction. A 'Visitation' has a distinctly medieval, ecclesiastical, ring to it, variously described as 'a ghost

---

372 Eg Registration of Deeds Act (Northern Ireland) 1970.
373 The enabling legislation is the Northern Ireland Act 1974.
374 Planning (Northern Ireland) Order 1972 (SI 1972/1634).
375 Housing Act (Northern Ireland) 1971; a number of housing orders have been made under direct rule.
376 'There must be no Alsatia in England where the King's writ does not run' *Czarnikow v Roth, Schmidt & Co* [1922] 2 KB 478, 488 per Scrutton LJ.

clanking its chains'[377] or 'an archaic functionary redolent of monarchical paternalism in an isolated, unworldly community of scholars.'[378] The power of the Visitor to determine affairs relating to an eleemosynary (charitable)[379] or ecclesiastical corporation is a direct descendant of the founder's right to determine matters relating to his or her own 'endowment' (interpreted in practice to mean the act of incorporation, since when, for example, a university is created by charter, no money actually changes hands)[380] and, originally, to ensure that it did not veer from its statutes.[381] The jurisdiction survived the general reorganisation of courts etc, effected by the Judicature Act 1873 as was swiftly recognised by the courts in 1878 in *R v Hertford College Oxford*.[382] All chartered universities and the colleges

377 P Smith 'University Visitor' (1981) 97 LQR 610; 'Visitation of the Universities: A Ghost from the Past' Parts I–IV, New Law Journal (1986) pp 484, 518, 567, 665. See also W Ricquier 'The University Visitor' (1978) 4 Dalhousie Law Journal 647; T G Matthews 'The Office of the University Visitor' (1980) 11 University of Queensland Law Journal 1652; B Hadfield 'University Lecturers, the Visitor and Judicial Review' (1986) 36 NILQ 342; C Lewis 'University Visitors and the Courts' (1987) 46 Camb LJ 384; G L Peiris 'Visitorial Jurisdiction: The Changing Outlook of an Exclusive Regime' (1987) 16 Anglo-American LR 646; A N Khan 'University Visitor Revisited Parts 1 and 2' (1990) 2 Education and the Law 163, (1991) 3 Education and the Law 179; G Pitt 'Academic Tenure and the Courts' (1991) Ind LJ 292; P Whalley *The University Visitor* (1993) Proceedings Australia and New Zealand Educational Law Association Conference; K Davies 'The justiciability question' (1993) All ER Annual Review 1; A N Khan 'British Universities: Visitor's Jurisdiction' (1993) 22 Journal of Law and Education 197; S Robinson 'The Office of Visitor of an Eleemosynary Corporation: Some Ancient and Modern Principles' (1994) 18 University of Queensland LJ 106; A N Khan and A G Davison 'University Visitor and Judicial Review in the British Commonwealth (Old) Countries' (1995) 24 Journal of Law and Education 3 457.
378 S McCaughlin 'Up against the Law. The University Visitor' (1983) 8 Legal Services Bulletin, 140.
379 Ie a corporation established for the perpetual distribution of the free alms or bounty of the founder 5(2) *Halsbury's Laws of England* 211. The chartered universities are, but Oxford and Cambridge universities are civil or lay corporations like municipal corporations, where there is no visitorial jurisdiction and hence are not eleemosynary: *Thomas v University of Bradford* [1987] AC 795 at 798; A N Khan 'University Visitor re-visited I' Education and the Law (1990) 2 163. Oxford and Cambridge Universities as such are therefore susceptible to judicial review as in *R v University of Cambridge, ex p Evans* (1997, unreported) CO/1031/97.
380 5(2) *Halsbury's Laws of England* 218.
381 See 5(2) *Halsbury's Laws of England* 219; H Picarda *The Law and Practice relating to Charities* (2nd edn, 1995) p 520.
382 (1878) 3 QBD 693. See section 19(5) Supreme Court of Judicature (Consolidation) Act 1925.

of Oxford and Cambridge Universities have Visitors[383] but the jurisdiction has largely been abolished or severely attenuated in other common law jurisdictions.[384]

Origin of the office of Visitor

2.203   John Bridge says that 'the visitor appears to have been an ecclesiastical institution for the purpose of supervising the government of the church and the correction of offences at both diocesan and parochial level'[385] although both the characteristics and the basis of authority of a lay visitor and a bishop seem rather different and the basis of authority quite different. As explained by Holt CJ in *Philips v Bury*[386] the visitorial power 'ariseth from the property which the founder had in the lands assigned to support the charity.' A bishop is a steward but not an owner of property. Both Roman law and the common law furnished analogies and in view of the medieval conception of a municipality, the authority of the common law courts to pass upon the reasonableness of municipal customs and byelaws was so like the authority of the episcopal visitor with regard to the regulations and byelaws of a college or religious foundation that as Roscoe Pound said 'there is no wonder the two things became confused.'[387] After the Reformation it was settled that ecclesiastical corporations were subject to visitation by the bishop and lay charitable corporations to visitations by the founder and his heirs unless otherwise provided by the founder.[388] The visitor's role was to ensure the maintenance of good government in corporations and to secure their adherence to the purposes of their institution. Every private corporation had a visitor[389] but other corporations were subject to the visitorial authority of the king, exercisable through his

---

383   As confirmed by Kindersley VC in *Thomson v University of London* (1864) 33 L J Ch 625.

384   See eg P Whalley *The University Visitor* Proceedings of the Australia and New Zealand Educational Law Association (1993); Schedule 1, University Legislation (Amendment) Act 1994 (New South Wales).

385   J W Bridge 'Keeping Peace in the Universities: The Role of the Visitor' (1970) LQR lxxxvi 531.

386   (1694) Skin 447; 90 ER 198.

387   The distinction is explained in R Pound *Visitorial Jurisdiction over Corporations in Equity* (1936) 3 Harvard Law Review XLIX p 369.

388   *Sutton's Hospital Case* (1612) 10 Co Rep 1a.

389   *R v Lee* (1689) 1 Show 251, 252 per Holt CJ. The act of accepting a charter from the state was enough to make the corporation subject to visitorial jurisdiction: *State v Georgia Medical Society* 38 Ga 608, 627 (1869).

courts and ordinarily exercised by mandamus and by information in the nature of *quo warranto* in the King's Bench.[390]

2.204 The Chancellors of the universities formed in Oxford and Cambridge had all the powers then customarily given to ecclesiastical courts to exercise jurisdiction over the areas under the control of the university. In the very early days at Cambridge, a scholar could sue nobody (whether fellow scholar, clerk or layman) except in the university's own tribunal which in the case of Cambridge was the Chancellor's Court.[391] However it was the Lord High Chancellor of England, who was also at the time always a clergyman, who became the Visitor of the later foundations by charter. The jurisdiction exercised by the Visitor was and is in practice meant to be an inexpensive way of resolving internal disputes between members of a corporation or between members and the corporation, where 'membership' is open to a fairly wide interpretation. In *Eden v Foster*[392] an attempt to evade the jurisdiction by claiming that the appointment by the King by letters patent of 'perpetual governors' of a school meant that they were exempted from visitation was dismissed as 'unreasonable and mischievous.' While lay members of a governing body might possibly be considered to be sufficiently independent of the management of the institution to provide a route for appeals and grievances which comply with contemporary standards of fairness, it is clear from that case and other authority[393] that they cannot act in a true visitorial role unless such an appointment is implied or expressed.

2.205 Although it now applies only to a minority of the higher education system and the jurisdiction has been significantly attenuated by ERA, some of its attributes may be worth retaining at a time when institutions are facing the prospect of increased review of their decisions by the courts, despite the apparently unanimous view of the Court of Appeal at the penultimate stage in the *Page* case[394] that the jurisdiction was anachronistic and worthy of abolition. As Lord Hardwicke LC said in *A-G v Talbot*[395] the

390   Eg *A-G v Galway Corpn* (1829) 1 Mol 95, Ir Ch; *A-G v LCC* [1901] 1 Ch 781, CA; *Newcastle-upon-Tyne Corpn v A-G* [1892] AC 568; *A-G v Norwich Corpn* (1837) 2 My & Cr 406; *A-G v Aspinall* (1837) 2 My & Cr 613.
391   See generally M B Hackett *The Original Statutes of Cambridge University* (1970).
392   (1725) 2 P Wms 325.
393   5(2) *Halsbury's Laws of England* 411; *University of New Zealand v Solicitor-General* (1917) 36 NZLR 353.
394   [1991] 4 All ER 747, CA.
395   (1748) 3 Atk 662.

existence of visitors discourages 'suits which may take off these learned bodies from their studies and ingross their time very improperly.' Unfortunately for potential claimants, it also leads to relatively few reported cases so that it is difficult to build up a corpus of case law. In cases unreported except in the press in 1995 and 1997 respectively, *Jones v University of Birmingham* and *McDougall v University of Bath* the distinguishing features which caused comment were that Jones' case lasted from 1988 to 1991 and that McDougall's case produced the comment by the Visitor 'It is unfortunate that his formal grievance was not handled expeditiously by the University ... so that he felt it necessary to petition the Visitor.'

The exclusive nature of the visitorial jurisdiction

2.206 The visitorial jurisdiction outside higher education has been reviewed in *R v Visitors to the Inns of Court, ex p Calder (and Same v Same, ex p Persaud)*[396] and *R v Honourable Society of the Middle Temple, ex p Bullock*.[397] In the course of giving the court's judgment in the first case, Mann LJ referred to a dictum of Simon Brown LJ in *R v Chief Rabbi of the United Hebrew Congregations of Great Britain and the Commonwealth, ex p Wachmann*.[398] This case concerned the Chief Rabbi's disciplinary authority:

> I prefer ... [the] submission that an Orthodox rabbi is pursuing a vocation and has no choice but to accept the Chief Rabbi's disciplinary decisions. I can see no distinction in this regard between rabbis and, for instance, members of the Bar or members of a university. So far as the Bar and universities are concerned, once the exclusive visitorial jurisdiction has been invoked and exhausted, the court can review the visitor's decision ...

The latter part of this dictum begs the question: is the visitor's jurisdiction 'exclusive' or not? Brooke J in the *Bullock* case was quite clear that the visitor had 'untrammelled jurisdiction.'

2.207 It is clear from the decision of the House of Lords in *R v Lord President of the Privy Council, ex p Page* that the ordinary courts in England can in certain circumstances exercise a supervisory jurisdiction over the Visitor by way of judicial review.[399] The majority

396 [1994] QB 1.
397 [1996] ELR 349, QBD.
398 [1992] 1 WLR 1936, 1040.
399 [1993] AC 682.

in the House of Lords (Lords Keith, Griffiths and Browne-Wilkinson) held that where a Visitor's decision is made within his [sic] jurisdiction his decision was not amenable to challenge by judicial review on the ground of error in fact or of law contained in that decision. The minority (Lords Mustill and Slynn), while dissenting on this conclusion, agreed with the majority that judicial review does lie in cases where the Visitor has acted outside his jurisdiction.[400] Examples of that would be where the Visitor did not have the power under the charter or statutes to adjudicate,[401] where he or she had abused the Visitor's powers,[402] where the Visitor had acted in breach of the rules of natural justice,[403] or where the Visitor had not exercised judgment at all.[404] However, a Visitor 'need not proceed according to the rules of common law so long as he pays regard to the positive forms proscribed by the statutes regulating the foundation.'[405] The courts do not have power to grant an interlocutory injunction to restrain action pending determination of a dispute by the Visitor.[406] Subject to all this, a determination by the Visitor is final, as is the case where it exists (or previously existed) in other jurisdictions.[407]

2.208 *R v Lord President of the Privy Council, ex p Page* was concerned with the dismissal of a member of staff but has general relevance to the role of the Visitor. Charles Henderson and Frank

---

400 Their Lordships referred to Lee CJ in *R v Bishop of Chester* (1748) 1 Wm Bl 22, 25 who said 'Certainly, if a visitor is in his jurisdiction his acts are not to be inquired into; if out of it, his acts are void.'

401 On the basis of the approval by the Privy Council in *South East Asia Fire Bricks Sdn Bhd v Non-Metallic Mineral Products Manufacturing Employees Union* [1981] AC 363, 370 (and by a majority of the House of Lords in *Re Racal Communications Ltd* [1981] AC 374, 384, 390–391) of the dissenting judgment of Geoffrey Lane LJ in *Pearlman v Keepers and Governors of Harrow School* [1979] 1 All ER 365, CA.

402 See Lord Griffiths in *Thomas v University of Bradford* [1987] AC 795, 825 '... the High Court would have power upon an application for judicial review to quash a decision of the Visitor which amounted to an abuse of his powers.'

403 *Bently v Bishop of Ely* (1729) 1 Barn KB 192 quoted by Lord Browne-Wilkinson in *R v Lord President of the Privy Council, ex p Page* [1992] 3 WLR 1112, 1120; *Philips v Bury* (1694) Holt KB 715 per Holt CJ.

404 See dictum of Grose J in *R v Bishop of Ely* (1794) 5 Durn & E 475, 477.

405 5(2) *Halsbury's Laws of England* 419. Cf Discussion in R Sadler 'The University Visitor: Visitorial Precedent and Procedure in Australia' [1981] University of Tasmania LR 2 at 19.

406 *Whiston v Dean and Chapter of Rochester* (1849) 7 Hare 532.

407 See eg *University of Melbourne, ex p De Simone* [1981] VR 378; *Nair-Marshall v Murdoch University* (1993, unreported); *University of Western Australia v Rindos* (1995) 76 WAIG 736.

Mattison[408] provide a useful overview predating that decision. Relevant cases establishing the role of the Visitor in university-student disputes include *Patel v University of Bradford Senate*,[409] *Thorne v University of London*,[410] *R v Dunsheath, ex p Meredith*[411] and, most recently *Oakes v Sidney Sussex College, Cambridge*.[412] In *Patel's* case, where Khandubhai Vanmalibhai Patel sought judicial review of the University's decision to terminate his studies, Megarry VC, citing much earlier authority,[413] confirmed that the following matters listed in the applicant's submission were exclusively within the power of the Visitor: (i) withholding examination results; (ii) appointments to university committees; (iii) dismissal of a student from the university; (iv) readmission to the university. An argument put forward in *Ktorides v University of Nottingham*[414] that the jurisdiction was not exclusive because of the 'partnership' arrangement entered into by the university with a local school regarding K's placement for a postgraduate certificate of education course, was rejected by the Court of Appeal which refused leave to apply for judicial review. However, by virtue of its essentially private nature, the court will not take notice of the visitorial jurisdiction unless its existence is brought to its attention.[415]

2.209 The basis for the jurisdiction implicit in Megarry VC's judgment is that it is a function of the Visitor to decide all questions of disputed membership, provided that there is some suggestion of illegality or corruption[416] and that the matters concerned are not expressly by statute left in the discretion of other officers or members,

---

408 D J Farrington and F T Mattison (eds) *Universities and the Law* in *Universities and the Law* CUA/CRS (1990).
409 [1979] 2 All ER 582, CA; Mr Patel did not, in fact, petition the Visitor: *Note by the Registrar and Secretary of the University of Bradford* 5 April 1979.
410 [1966] 2 QB 237.
411 [1951] 1 KB 127.
412 [1988] 1 All ER 1004.
413 *Dr Widdrington's Case* (1662) 1 Lev 23, T Raym 68; *Parkinson's Case* (1689) Carth 92; *Philips v Bury* (1694) Holt KB 715; *Ex p Buller* (1855) 3 W R 447. Other early authority is discussed by Peter Smith in 'Visitation of the Universities: A Ghost from the Past' Parts I–IV in (1986) New Law Journal 484, 518, 567 and 665. See also *Ex p McFadyen* (1945) 45 SR(NSW) 200 at 202 per Davidson J and *Bagg's Case* (1615) 11 Co Rep 93b
414 (1997) unreported, CA.
415 *Dr Walker's Case* (1736) Case Lee temp Hard 212, 218 per Lord Hardwicke CJ. In the following cases the exclusive nature of the Visitor's jurisdiction was ignored: *Tubbs v Auckland University College Council* (1907) 27 NZLR 149; *R v Aston University Senate, ex p Roffey* [1969] 2 QB 538; *Glynn v Keele University* [1971] 1 WLR 487.
416 *R v Hertford College* (1878) 3 QBD 693, 701, CA.

by which we imply freedom of academic judgment.[417] What of the determination of a dispute alleging breach of contract, rather than one based on membership governed by the statutes? The parallel case of breach of contract of employment of staff has been before Visitors on numerous occasions, culminating in the *Page* case referred to above. In *Thomas v University of Bradford*,[418] which led to legislative intervention in section 206 ERA, the House of Lords held that if a dispute arose between a university and a member over her contract of employment which involved questions relating to the internal laws of the university, or the rights and duties derived from those laws, the Visitor had exclusive jurisdiction. In the latest case involving Aston, its Visitor held that the university had no power to commit a breach of contract by making staff redundant since by doing so they might also breach members' rights under the charter and statutes.[419]

2.210   The Aston Visitor's ruling confirms what we imply from earlier cases, since it clearly separates the rights of the university to commit breaches of contract against 'persons not enjoying rights under the Charter and Statutes' from its inability to commit breaches of contract against 'its members.' One conclusion is that whatever the contractual status of the university-student relationship in a chartered English institution, there is no power to breach the contract without at the same time interfering with membership and therefore bringing the case within the jurisdiction of the Visitor. This view is repeated by Lord Browne-Wilkinson in the *Page* case[420] where he said:

> Even where the contractual rights of an individual (such as his contract of employment with the university) are in issue, if those contractual rights are themselves dependent on rights arising under the regulating documents of the charity, the visitor has an exclusive jurisdiction over disputes relating to such employment.

If the word 'right' is substituted for 'employment' at the end of that passage, as appears to be the sense of the sentence, then it is clear

---

417   As in Janaki Vijayatunga's case discussed later in this section: *R v University of London, ex p Vijayatunga* [1987] 3 All ER 204 at 213; affd sub nom *R v HH the Queen in Council, ex p Vijayatunga* [1990] 2 QB 44, [1989] 2 All ER 843, CA.
418   [1987] 1 All ER 834, HL.
419   *Pearce v University of Aston in Birmingham (No 2)* [1991] 2 All ER 469; see also *Pearce v University of Aston in Birmingham* [1991] 2 All ER 461.
420   [1992] 3 WLR 1112, 1117.

that the visitor has exclusive jurisdiction over all contractual disputes involving 'those on the foundation' where the contractual rights in dispute depend upon rights arising under the charter and statutes.[421] The terms of the contract, in particular those relating to termination of course and therefore of membership, are clearly all-important.

2.211 Schedule 3 to Regulation 4(4) Unfair Terms in Consumer Contracts Regulations 1994 contains, as one of its illustrative list of contractual terms which may be regarded as unfair, the inappropriate excluding or limiting of the legal rights of the consumer where the supplier fails to perform contractual obligations and excluding or hindering the consumer's rights to take legal action or exercise any other legal remedy. Mark Davies[422] suggests that this draws into question the viability of the Visitorial system. Students in chartered universities with a Visitor face a far less well defined system in terms of rules of procedure and opportunity for appeal than do other students. It is likely that the vast majority of university applicants will have no knowledge of the significant differences in their opportunities for legal redress dependent on the actual university they decide to contract with. Quite separately from Davies' concerns, it may be argued following the decision of the Divisional Court in *R v Lord Chancellor, ex p Witham*[423] that access to the courts is a constitutional right which can only be denied by government if it persuaded Parliament to pass legislation which by express provision permitted the executive to turn people away from the courts. It remains a possibility that persons aggrieved by the requirement to go to the Visitor may petition the European Court of Human Rights.

Appointment of the Visitor

2.212 The jurisdiction is exercised either by an individual or by a Board. In *R v University of Aston Senate, ex p Roffey*[424] Donaldson J formed the view that since no visitor had been 'appointed' the High Court had original jurisdiction: 'The charter reserves a power of appointment of a Visitor, but no such appointment has yet been made.' This case has been criticised on this ground in *Patel v*

---

421 See also *A-G v Middleton* (1751) 2 Ves Sen 327.
422 M Davies 'Universities, academics and professional negligence' (1996) 12 Professional Negligence 4 102.
423 [1997] 2 All ER 779; applying *R v Boaler* [1915] 1 KB 21.
424 [1969] 2 QB 538.

University of Bradford Senate.[425] The fact that a Visitor had not been appointed was irrelevant, since the visitorial jurisdiction then vested in the Crown and

> at common law the court has no jurisdiction to deal with the internal affairs or government of the University [of London], because these have been confided by law to the exclusive jurisdiction of the Visitor.[426]

2.213   The Visitor is normally the founder and his or her heirs. If no Visitor is named in the charter, the 'default' is Her Majesty the Queen in Council, possibly but not necessarily represented by the Lord Chancellor. In the drafting of the revised statutes of the University of London (1994), the Privy Council Office suggested that the Visitor be defined as 'The Sovereign acting through the Lord President of the Privy Council' to avoid the expensive and cumbersome process, established by convention, to convene a committee of the Privy Council chaired by a Law Lord when the Visitor is described as 'Her Majesty in Council.' The statement by Donaldson J in *Roffey* was no doubt in his Lordship's view factually correct, but in fact the Visitor had at all relevant times been Her Majesty the Queen in Council and the court's jurisdiction was undoubtedly ousted by that of the Visitor. The authority for this is the dictum of Holt CJ in his dissenting judgment in *Philips v Bury*[427] '... if there be no visitor appointed by the founder, I am of opinion that the law doth appoint the founder and his heirs to be visitors.' Holt CJ's judgment was eventually adopted by the House of Lords and Lord Browne-Wilkinson has described this case as '... the locus classicus of the law of visitors.'[428] There are other old authorities to the same effect eg Lord Romilly MR in *A-G v Dedham School*[429] '... this Court treats the Crown as the permanent authority and visitor of the charity ...' The older authorities were not cited in the *Roffey* case. The University of London has a Visitor,[430] as do certain of its constituent institutions: it is conceivable that some issues could be within the jurisdiction of both. At the Queen's University of Belfast the equivalent is a Board of Visitors, consisting of four members

---

425 [1978] 3 All ER 841; if a Visitor has not been appointed, then the Visitorial power is exercised by the Lord Chancellor or such other person as he may advise Her Majesty to nominate: *A-G v Dedham School* (1857) 23 Beav 350, and see the judgment of Megarry VC in *Patel v University of Bradford Senate*, and the comments of Kelly LJ in *Re Wislang's Application* [1984] NI 63.
426 *Thorne v University of London* [1966] 2 QB 237, 240 per Diplock LJ.
427 (1694) Holt KB 715, 723.
428 *R v Lord President of the Privy Council, ex p Page* [1992] 3 WLR 1112, 1119.
429 (1857) 23 Beav 350, 356.
430 The new statutes (1994) preserve the visitorial jurisdiction.

appointed by Her Majesty by Order in Council. In *Re Veronica C M Napier*[431] all parties agreed that since two of the appointed members had a connection with the subject matter of the dispute, the Chairman (the Rt Hon Lord Scarman) could act alone with the assistance of the remaining member as a consultant.

The extent of the visitorial jurisdiction in universities

2.214 The application of the visitorial jurisdiction to universities has been thoroughly examined by Peter Smith.[432] Among other notable cases was that of *A-G v Talbot*.[433] The relator, Robert Mapletoft, a Northamptonshire man, claimed that William Talbot should not have been elected to a fellowship at Clare College because this was restricted to natives of Northampton. Lord Hardwicke LC was clear that this dispute was a matter for the college's Visitor (somewhat confusingly, the Chancellor of the University):

> If the Chancellor of this University then is visitor, the general powers of a visitor are well known; no court of law or equity can anticipate their judgment, or take away their jurisdiction, but their determinations are final and conclusive. And it is a more convenient method of determination of controversies of this nature, it is at home, *forum domesticum*, and final in the first instance, and they should be adjudged in a short way *secundum arbitrium boni viri*: it is true this power may be abused, but if it is exercised in a discreet manner, it is a much less expence [sic] than suits at law, or in equity; and in general, I believe, such appeals have been equitably determined.

It is possible for someone to be subject to a Visitor's jurisdiction without being a corporator.[434]

2.215 The Visitor, who is treated by the law as a general Visitor rather than one appointed for a specific purpose, has 'untrammelled power to investigate and right wrongs arising from the application of the domestic laws of the chartered institution'[435] – an Ombudsman with teeth. In *Norrie v Senate of the University of Auckland*,[436] the

431 (1987) unreported.
432 P Smith 'The Exclusive Jurisdiction of the University Visitor' (1981) LQR 610.
433 *A-G v Talbot* (1748) 3 Atk 662, 674.
434 *A-G v Magdalen College Oxford* (1847) 10 Beav 402; 50 ER 637.
435 *R v University of London, ex p Vijayatunga* [1988] QB 322, 344, 345 per Simon Brown LJ, approved in *R v HH the Queen in Council, ex p Vijayatunga* [1989] 3 WLR 13, 21 per Bingham LJ.
436 [1984] 1 NZLR 129 at 135–6.

court (Woodhouse P and Cooke J) held that the Visitor 'has practical responsibilities as a kind of continuing arbitrator to deal with and resolve problems affecting the university even when the answer might involve contractual or other issues of law ... he may do so ... on the basis of an original jurisdiction or in an appellate capacity or on a supervisory basis in the administrative law sense.' Lord Hailsham LC, acting as Visitor of Brunel University, stated in 1988 that '... it is of the highest importance that the Visitor should feel it is his duty to penetrate to the realities of the case without losing himself in the mass of technicalities such as those which surround the ordinary courts ...'[437]

2.216 It has been reported that in oral argument in *Pearce v University of Aston in Birmingham (No 2)*[438] the Visitor (Lord Browne-Wilkinson) opined that in extreme circumstances he might have power to remove the University Council or revoke the charter. There is no reason to doubt that this reported view is entirely correct, given the 'untrammelled' nature of the Visitorial power. The Visitor has power both to interpret and then to apply laws.[439] 'Wrongs' may be complex and involve a number of different issues, as witness the report of the Visitor into the long-running disputes associated with a course in philosophy and health at the University College of Swansea, published in May 1993.[440] The disputes concerned had already been the subject of three separate reports by distinguished experts. In that case the Visitor was 'called in' by the Council of the College to attempt to conciliate (unsuccessfully, as it turned out) as well as to adjudicate. In *Dombey v University of Sussex*[441] the removal of an elected member from the university's Senate by the Vice-Chancellor (an action confirmed by the Senate itself and by the Council) was ruled to be invalid by the Visitor even though it appeared to be the natural consequence of the abolition of the constituency which elected the complainant. Advising the Visitor, Lord Lloyd of Berwick said 'The Senate and Council has no more power to dispense with the regulations in the name of common sense, or in the name of administrative convenience, than had the Crown to dispense with the general law in the time of James II.'

437 Note circulated by Brunel University in 1988.
438 [1991] 2 All ER 469.
439 *Ex p Kirkby Ravensworth Hospital* (1808) 15 Ves 305, 311.
440 *Report of the enquiry and advice to the Lord President of the Council acting on behalf of HM The Queen, The Visitor of the University of Wales, invited by the Council of the University College of Swansea, into various complaints made to the College and associated matters.* Sir Michael Davies, May 1993. The published report is 172 pages long.
441 (1995) unreported.

2.217   Most charters, statutes and other instruments do not prescribe the Visitor's powers: one which does, although it is unclear and untested whether this limits the visitor's 'untrammelled' powers at common law, is that of the University of Kent at Canterbury, the Visitor of which is the Lord Archbishop of Canterbury. It is suggested that named Visitors might be placed in a position of conflict of interest if they were to become corporators by for example receiving an honorary degree.[442] As against that, the whole basis of the Visitorial jurisdiction is that it is not impartial, but intended to promote the original objectives of an institution's founder. Contrary to the view that a Visitor is best placed to decide questions of interpretation of academic rules and regulations runs the fact that named Visitors (including His Grace) routinely delegate their duties to Commissaries who are lawyers. If knowledge and understanding is required, an arbitrator with experience of academia would be a much better appointment.

2.218   The duties of Kent's Visitor include adjudication on 'any matter concerning the University' referred by a simple majority of the Court where the decision is 'final and binding.' This is, at least in theory, power to decide absolutely anything, given that in many universities the Court also has theoretically unlimited powers. The relative powers of the Court and the Council (or their equivalents) in England have already been discussed in the context of the Report of NCIHE. The Visitor is also given the duty of hearing certain appeals and, most unusually, an outline procedure is prescribed which includes a requirement to hear appeals within two months. A Visitor appointed in New Zealand in 1869 had 'authority to do all things which appertain to Visitors as often as to him shall seem meet' which is fairly all-embracing.[443]

2.219   Another charter which prescribes the Visitor's duties is that of the University of Essex:

> to hear and determine all questions concerning (1) the construction of the Charter, Statutes, Ordinances and Regulations of the ... University, and (2) the due and lawful exercise by any of the Statutory Bodies named in the Statutes of the powers and duties conferred upon them by the Charter, Statutes, Ordinances or regulations of the ... University.

---

442   See eg *Rigg v University of Waikato* [1984] 1 NZLR 149 at 151.
443   Charter of the University of Otago, referred to by Woodhouse P in *Norrie v Senate of the University of Auckland* [1984] 1 NZLR 129 at 134; cf *Murdoch University v Bloom* [1980] WAR 193 at 199.

Thus the Visitor here is appointed 'to hear and determine all questions' across the whole range of university activity, from what the car parking regulations mean to the due and lawful exercise of the power of dismissal of the Chancellor. This power must in practice be exercised according to certain principles. Brooke J in *R v Honourable Society of the Middle Temple, ex p Bullock*[444] said in effect that it followed from the 'untrammelled' nature of the visitorial jurisdiction that visitors should investigate the basic facts of a grievance in whatever depth they considered appropriate but where technical matters were involved, confine themselves to enquiring whether the evidence was properly considered and that no bad faith was involved.

2.220   The visitorial procedure has been described by Lord Hailsham LC as 'self-standing, untechnical, discretionary, informal and may indeed be, or become, inquisitorial.'[445] However it clearly does not extend to matters such as health and safety regulations applicable to landowners etc as they are statutory requirements independent of the general law.[446]

The visitorial jurisdiction elsewhere in higher education

2.221   The visitorial jurisdiction is known in the educational world outside the chartered universities, in any eleemosynary (ie charitable) foundation the founder of which specified that there should be a visitor. The best-known example of this is *Herring v Templeman*,[447] the dispute in 1973 between Ivan Wynford Herring, an expelled student and Dr Geoffrey Templeman, the Chairman, and other representatives of the governing body of Christ Church College, Canterbury, at the material time a teacher-training college originally set up pursuant to charitable trusts declared by the Church of England. The trust deed under which the college then operated provided that the Archbishop of Canterbury should be the visitor and Brightman J held that in this case the dispute fell within his exclusive jurisdiction. Students of the Council of Legal Education also have to have recourse to the Visitors to the Inns of Court, as in *R v Board of Examiners of the Council of Legal Education, ex p Joseph*[448] and *R v Board of Examiners of the Council of Legal Education, ex p*

444   [1996] ELR 349, QBD.
445   Information circulated by Brunel University, 1988.
446   *Thomas v University of Bradford* 1987] AC 795 at 799.
447   [1973] 2 All ER 581.
448   [1994] COD 318, CA.

Hulse.[449] However, a suggestion made at some stage in *Thirunayagam v London Guildhall University*[450] that the former Council for National Academic Awards 'acted as visitor' in the former polytechnics prior to the 1992 legislation is clearly erroneous. Neither the predecessor polytechnic nor the London Guildhall University had or has a Visitor.

Attenuation of the jurisdiction by ERA

2.222   In the 1980s the visitorial jurisdiction was seen by the government as an outmoded method of resolving employment disputes, an appeal to the jurisdiction being one of the few remaining privileges enjoyed by 'tenured' (and indeed other staff-corporators) at the older universities. The Jarratt Report had identified tenure as an obstacle to effective management of public funds. ERA, in addition to introducing the concept of redundancy to many universities for the first time, removed the exclusive jurisdiction of the Visitor in matters relating to academic staff contracts, which had been the subject of lengthy and expensive proceedings in the courts. Now such disputes which cannot be resolved by internal management procedures may go to the courts and employment tribunals in the same way as those arising between any employee and employer, as matters of private rather than public law. The Visitor retains, with some important qualifications, exclusive jurisdiction over many other disputes, notably those involving students, acting in a sense as a private ombudsman and would be the obvious source of an 'independent person' for the purposes of the provisions of EA94 dealing with complaints against student unions. The Visitor might also act as an appeal tribunal under the new disciplinary procedures introduced by the University Commissioners under ERA.

The Visitor's power of inspection

2.223   It is often forgotten that the Visitor also has a general power of 'inspection' of the university, its academic and non-academic functions but in practice inspections today tend to arise through the activities of the Funding Councils and the Quality Assurance Agency procedures. Essentially this is another example of state control, since the Visitor, if not the Queen in Council, is normally an office closely

449   (1995) unreported.
450   [1997] 4 ELM 8, 1.

associated with the power of the state although there are some which are not directly so associated, such as the Archbishop of Canterbury (Kent at Canterbury) and the Bishop of Durham (Durham). 'Visitations' of the kind envisaged by the general power of inspection are unknown now. The original concept of a visitation appears to have been replaced by the royal commission in the nineteenth century.

The Visitor's enforcement powers

2.224 The Visitor apparently has wide powers to grant relief including ordering an institution not to breach its Charter and Statutes. According to Lord Hailsham LC representing the Visitor of the University of Aston in *Casson v University of Aston in Birmingham*[451] he or she has no power to order compensation in the nature of damages:

> ... the only substantive prayer for relief in this case is a monetary claim for compensation in the nature of damages. After considerable research I have been unable to find any precedent in the long history of visitatorial powers in which a visitor has made such an order and in my view he has no such power.

This view was accepted by Kelly LJ in *Re Wislang's Application*[452] and by Sir Michael Davies in the *University College of Swansea* case in 1993. However Lord Griffiths in *Thomas v University of Bradford*[453] disagreed with this view, preferring the approach taken by Burt CJ in *Murdoch University v Bloom*[454] who considered that if a breach of contract fell within the visitorial jurisdiction he could see no reason why the Visitor should not be able to make an award of damages. Likewise it appears from the decision in *St John's College Cambridge v Todington*[455] that there is power to award compensation to a wronged corporator. In *Bell v University of Auckland*[456] the court took the view that there could be a claim for damages if it covered that part of an agreement which did not lie within the domestic law of the university which is subject to the Visitor. Although strictly speaking, the view expressed in *Thomas* related to the right to back pay or compensation for wrongful dismissal where the former

---

451 [1983] 1 All ER 88, 91.
452 [1984] NI 63.
453 [1987] AC 795.
454 [1980] WAR 193.
455 (1757) 1 Burr 158, 202.
456 [1969] NZLR 1029.

employee had accepted the dismissal, on balance it seems that the Visitor may order any appropriate remedy including an award of damages.

The visitorial jurisdiction in Scotland

2.225   The visitorial jurisdiction in universities is also said to derive from the rectorial jurisdiction in the old European institutions, the privilege of having their causes heard by a magistrate elected by themselves being granted to the students of the University of Bologna in 1158. In 1450, when William Turnbull, Bishop of Glasgow, who was both Chancellor and Rector, divested himself of the latter title and made David Cadzow, Canon of Glasgow the Rector, he was

> ... to have jurisdiction in all civil, pecuniary and minor cases, and in all quarrels and disputes among the supposts of the University, and between any of the supposts and the citizens, or other inhabitants of the Diocese, but he was not to interfere in cases of atrocious injury or other weighty matters, all of which were specially reserved for the decision of the Bishop himself.

Anyone who sought the assistance of outside courts was liable to be expelled.[457] The Rector, who was elected by the students, and was at the time always a clergyman, became the Visitor, an office which he could not delegate. None of the Scottish universities now recognises the office: the powers of the Rector are certainly not what they were, and none of the later chartered or statutory institutions has either a Rector (in the sense of the ancients) or a Visitor.

2.226   It would appear from the common good cases discussed above that the Crown retains title to intervene in the exercise of powers over corporate property.[458] The question is further complicated by a dictum of Lord Cranworth in the House of Lords in the poor-law rates case *Greig v University of Edinburgh*.[459] His Lordship, agreeing with the opinion of the Lord Justice-Clerk, said:

> ... throughout the whole history of the University, and very specially in recent Acts of Parliament, the Crown is recognised both as the

---

457 J B Hay *Inaugural Addresses by Lords Rectors of the University of Glasgow* (1839) Table annexed to p xxviii.
458 See headnote to *Conn v Provost, Magistrates and Councillors of Renfrew* (1906) 8 F 905.
459 (1868) 5 SLR 620, 622.

fountain from which the whole rights of the University flow, and also as the visitorial authority to the control of which it is at all times subject.

In referring to recent 'Acts of Parliament' Lord Cranworth can only have had in mind the Universities (Scotland) Act 1858[460] as there do not appear to have been any others. There is no mention either of a Visitor or of a visitorial jurisdiction in the Act which reformed the government and governance of the ancient universities. In modern terms, particularly since no statutory authority can be found for it, and as it was not strictly necessary for the determination of the question of liability for the poor-law rate, Lord Cranworth's dictum can be considered obiter.

2.227 It appears, therefore, that in principle the visitorial jurisdiction in Scotland exists even though it is in desuetude. It has not yet been suggested formally that it should be reactivated or that the institution of an office equivalent to a Visitor (perhaps an Ombudsman) would assist institutions. It is more likely that arbitration agreements will accomplish the same purpose so far as student complaints go, and that if an appeal tribunal for staff is constituted, a senior legal figure will be asked to act.

2.228 In defence of the absence of a visitorial jurisdiction, it has been suggested by Charles Henderson and Frank Mattison[461] that the University Court in Scotland – that is, the governing body of the University, in many respects the equivalent of the Council of an English university – has a slightly more pronounced role in the determination of domestic disputes and grievances. In most but not all universities there is provision for the Court to be asked to review any decision of the Senate or its equivalent, although this is also true of some English chartered institutions and certainly applies in the newer institutions. However it is difficult to argue that the independent members of a governing body of an institution not subject to the visitorial jurisdiction are as yet sufficiently 'independent' of management to provide a fair hearing. In general, if a matter is not resolved internally by the constitutional bodies of the university, the only remaining recourse available to a member of the university is to take the issue to the courts. The extent to which the supervisory jurisdiction of the Court of Session in Scotland extends to the issues

---

460 21 & 22 Vict Cap LXXXIII.
461 C L S Henderson and F T Mattison 'Universities and the Law' in D J Farrington and F T Mattison (eds) *Universities and the Law* CUA/CRS (1990) p 22.

which in the rest of the UK would be dealt with by the Visitor will be discussed later.

2.229 There is no doubt that where the issues in question in disciplinary proceedings are wholly related to the internal work of the institution, the visitorial jurisdiction is useful. In relation to disciplinary proceedings, John Bridge[462] has supported the jurisdiction in terms both of case law and in terms of its 'suitability, cheapness, expedition and informality' comparing the visitor to an administrative tribunal. Maintenance of order, confined to offences against the foundation's instrument of government, is one of the branches of visitorial jurisdiction explained by Davidson J in *Ex p McFadyen*.[463]

2.230 Case law certainly supports Bridge's views. The jurisdiction was commended in *Thomson v University of London*,[464] *Thorne v University of London*,[465] *Patel v University of Bradford Senate*[466] and the staff case *Thomas v University of Bradford*.[467] Its scope is not confined to corporators but to 'all persons who can be described as members of the institution or as being on the foundation'[468] as were the individuals in *Thomson*[469] and *Oakes v Sidney Sussex College Cambridge*.[470] Bridge saw the jurisdiction as satisfying the need for disciplinary procedures to avoid excessive formalism quoting the Hart Report,[471] S A de Smith[472] and D C Holland[473] in support. Advocating the use of the Visitor rather than the courts might be seen by some as an effective denial of the right of recourse to law, which is not denied to someone in a normal contractual dispute. However, as discussed earlier, there seems now to be no dispute about the exclusivity of the Visitor's unique jurisdiction.

---

462 J W Bridge 'Keeping Peace in the Universities: The Role of the Visitor' (1970) LQR lxxxvi 531.
463 (1945) 45 SR (NSW) 200 at 202.
464 (1864) 33 LJCh 625.
465 [1966] 2 QB 237.
466 [1978] 1 WLR 1488, 1489 (affirmed [1979] 2 All ER 582, CA).
467 [1986] 1 All ER 217, 233 per Lloyd LJ; on appeal [1987] 1 All ER 834, HL.
468 *Hines v Birkbeck College* [1985] 3 All ER 156, 163 per Hoffmann J.
469 Pointed out by Peter Smith (1986) New Law Journal 568.
470 [1988] 1 All ER 1004.
471 *Committee on Relations with Junior Members* (The Hart Report) Oxford University Gazette, Supplement No VII (1969) para 65.
472 (1960) 23 MLR 428, 431, 432.
473 D C Holland 'The Student and the Law' (1969) 22 Current Legal Problems 74.

Standards of natural justice

2.231 Despite the clear jurisdiction of the Visitor in chartered institutions, some cases of alleged procedural irregularity have reached the courts, based on arguably misguided applications for judicial review. The attitude generally has been that while the principles of natural justice should be observed, unduly strict standards will not be applied. In particular, in a number of cases of which the best known is the naked sunbather case *Glynn v Keele University*[474] the courts have, while accepting jurisdiction and accepting that procedural unfairness has occurred, declined to grant discretionary remedies, an attitude which has been criticised.[475] Assuming that the courts had jurisdiction, the reason for their reluctance in non-academic offences is not readily apparent. In fact, the recourse to law by students facing disciplinary action was at that time seen as the only way to secure rights against a system that was both paternalistic and tied by archaic procedures. A quotation from the Hart Report exemplifies the former characteristic:

> To turn the hearing of every disciplinary charge into a formal public trial would be, at the best, time wasting and at the worst, might damage young mens' (sic) careers, and might sharpen and harden what has been a generally mild and even friendly attitude to those faced with disciplinary charges.

2.232 In fact as has been argued above the position in England is that the actions of a chartered institution in respect of those 'on the foundation' do not fall within the scope of administrative law at all and that there can be no judicial review of actions based purely on contract. Redress in such cases can only be through the Visitor. In the cases of non-chartered institutions, redress will lie to the relevant court by action for breach of contract or judicial review, the attitude of the English courts today being that the existence of the leave stage makes it easier to deal with cases by way of judicial review rather than by action in the county courts or High Court for breach of contract.

---

474 [1971] 1 WLR 487.
475 See C B Lewis 'Procedural Fairness and University Students: England and Canada Compared' (1985) 9 Dalhousie Law Journal 313 and Sir William Wade's implicit criticism in (1971) LQR lxxxvii 320.

Dealing with internal disputes in non-Visitorial institutions

Judicial review: laws of England and Northern Ireland

2.233   Non-chartered institutions do not have Visitors. The former polytechnics were established by act of designation by the Secretary of State under Instrument and Articles of Government approved by the relevant local education authority and the Secretary of State. The Council for National Academic Awards, although it used its good offices to attempt to resolve complaints and appeals, had no role equivalent to the Visitor, despite a recent suggestion to the contrary in *Thirunayagam v London Guildhall University*.[476] Without question the most important way in which potentially the courts can control the actions of higher education institutions not subject to the exclusive visitorial jurisdiction is by judicial review. This can arise where it is alleged that a public body (or an individual acting for it) has exceeded its powers or exercised them in a way which is irrational or unreasonable. This might be demonstrated for example if the authority takes into account matters which ought not to have been taken into account or fails to give consideration to matters which it ought to have considered. The leading case in English law is *Associated Provincial Picture Houses v Wednesbury Corpn*,[477] where a decision of the local authority not to allow Sunday opening of cinemas was within its powers and not amenable to judicial review. A decision can be so unreasonable that no reasonable authority could ever have reached it.[478] As was made clear in 1993 in *R v Higher Education Funding Council, ex p Institute of Dental Surgery*,[479] the court does not attempt to place itself in the shoes of experts in, for example, the evaluation of research, so long as the evaluation is lawfully conducted. As we shall see, the main area in which applications for judicial review have been attempted has, not surprisingly, been that of the relationship between students and the institution. Students who have been disciplined or been the subject of academic or other sanctions have, from time to time, sought to impugn the institution's action in the courts. It has to be emphasised that judicial review is not a substitute for appeal on the merits of the case: as Hirst LJ explained in *Madekwe v London Guildhall University*[480] the High Court is not to be used as a form of appeal from university bodies. The issue of judicial review of administrative

476 [1997] 4 ELM 8, 1.
477 [1948] 1 KB 223.
478 *Giddens v Harlow District Auditor* (1972) 70 LGR 485.
479 [1994] 1 WLR 242.
480 5 June 1997, unreported, CA.

action is however of more general application. In this area we now find a significant divergence between the jurisdiction of the English and Scottish courts.

2.234   For an application for judicial review to be entertained in English or Northern Ireland law, the subject-matter of the dispute must have what is described as a 'public law' element. This cannot be defined as precisely as one might imagine. It is not simply a question of whether or not the state or a state agency is involved in a dispute with a citizen. In 1963 in *Ridge v Baldwin*[481] Lord Reid said

> Apart from statute or specific contract there can be no external fetters on the exercise by the court of its jurisdiction to control the proceedings of bodies or individuals who have the power to deal with the rights or liberties or status of the subject.

In 1987 in *R v Panel on Take-overs and Mergers, ex p Datafin plc*[482] the Court of Appeal was prepared to consider an application for judicial review in respect of a body (the Panel) which was an unincorporated association monitoring a code of practice which it had promulgated itself. It had neither statutory nor contractual powers and was not governmental in character. Sir John Donaldson MR said:

> Possibly the only essential elements are what can be described as a public element, which can take many different forms, and the exclusion from the jurisdiction of bodies whose sole source of power is a consensual submission to the jurisdiction.[483]

This has also been applied to LAUTRO.[484] The other leading case in this area is *R v Disciplinary Committee of the Jockey Club, ex p Aga Khan*.[485]

---

481   [1963] 2 All ER 66, 77.
482   [1987] QB 815; a similar application, which also failed, was *R v Panel on Takeovers and Mergers, ex p Guinness plc* (1988) 4 BCC 325; see also *R v Chief Rabbi of the United Hebrew Congregations of Great Britain and the Commonwealth, ex p Wachmann* [1992] 1 WLR 1036 where the Chief Rabbi was held not to be subject to the jurisdiction.
483   [1987] QB 815, 838. In *R v Insurance Ombudsman Bureau, ex p Aegon Life Assurance Ltd* (1994) Times, 7 January, the court held that the IOB was not susceptible to judicial review since its powers were solely derived from contract.
484   *R v LAUTRO, ex p Ross* [1993] QB 17.
485   [1993] 1 WLR 909.

2.235 The controlling factor in determining whether the exercise of power is subject to judicial review is not its source but its subject-matter.[486] 'The allegation of a wrong of a kind recognised as remediable by public law is sufficient to found jurisdiction in judicial review.'[487] In the later (1992) case *R v Chief Rabbi of the United Hebrew Congregations of Great Britain and the Commonwealth*[488] the court held that for a decision of a non-governmental body to be regarded as an exercise of a public function, there had to be a potentially governmental interest in the decision-making power in question. While, as in the case of the Take-over and Merger Panel, the disciplinary procedure of the Chief Rabbi was self-regulating, unlike the Panel it was not something that would otherwise be subject to statutory regulation. In *Majid v London Guildhall University*,[489] which is a company limited by guarantee conducting a university, the newspaper report states that the Court of Appeal accepted that the university was a public body but that Dr Amir Majid's complaint of racial discrimination and victimisation was a private law matter not amenable to judicial review. Dr Majid was subsequently more successful before an industrial tribunal.[490] In *R v University College London, ex p Rineker*[491] the court re-emphasised that contractual disputes between universities and their staff were not matters for judicial review.

2.236–2.237 The scope of judicial review extends even to bodies which are directly answerable to Parliament, such as the Parliamentary Commissioner for Administration (the Ombudsman).[492] The existence of a royal charter itself is insufficient to inject a public law element sufficient to attract public law remedies[493] and employment by a public authority does not itself import elements of public law.[494] The conclusion is different where institutions are exercising powers delegated by statute, even where the relationship of the parties can be assimilated to that of the

---

486 This is the statement of Lords Scarman and Diplock most quoted from the GCHQ case *Council of Civil Service Unions v Minister for the Civil Service* [1984] 3 All ER 935, HL.
487 *Leech v Parkhurst Prison Deputy Governor* and *Prevot v Long Larton Prison Deputy Governor* [1988] 1 All ER 485, 496, HL per Lord Bridge.
488 [1992] 1 WLR 1036.
489 (1993) Higher, 12 November.
490 (1995) 25 DCLD 2 and 3.
491 16 December 1994, unreported, CA.
492 *R v Parliamentary Comr for Administration, ex p Dyer* [1994] 1 WLR 621.
493 See *Re Wislang's Application* [1984] NI 63 per Kelly LJ.
494 *R v East Berkshire Health Authority, ex p Walsh* [1985] QB 152.

contractual one between employer and employee. In *R (Snaith) v Ulster Polytechnic*[495] Professor Snaith had been declared redundant and although he had been given a hearing, the question was whether for that to be a reasonable exercise of the governors' powers it should have been conducted observing the rules of natural justice. The High Court of Northern Ireland was able to exercise jurisdiction because the decision to terminate his appointment was made in exercise of the governors' powers under statutory instrument.[496] The same principle has been held to apply in Canada and Australia. In *Re Ruiperez and the Board of Governors of Lakehead University*[497] a decision to withhold tenure of a member of staff was the exercise of a statutory function under The Lakehead University Act 1965 and therefore reviewable by the courts. In *Re Board of Education for Borough of Scarborough and Pilcher*[498] a statutory contract stemmed from the School Boards and Teachers Collective Negotiations Act 1980. *Re Schabas and Caput of the University of Toronto*[499] was a student case in a statutory institution and *Re University of Sydney, ex p King*[500] was a similar case in Australia.

2.238 The Funding Councils as statutory bodies are amenable to judicial review; the first such case was *R v Higher Education Funding Council, ex p Institute of Dental Surgery*[501] where the action was in effect against the Higher Education Funding Council for England, which had succeeded to the UFC's research selectivity exercise.

2.239 Since in the chartered institutions it is now absolutely clear that the jurisdiction of the courts is ousted by that of the Visitor, past cases which have proceeded in the courts (eg *R v University of Aston Senate, ex p Roffey*,[502] *Glynn v Keele University*[503]) may now safely be ignored. In addition, it is argued that the relationship between students and their institution should now be recognised as essentially contractual, with a right of recourse to the courts or the Visitor as appropriate in an action based on contract.

---

495 [1981] NI 28.
496 Regulation 19(3)(b) Ulster College Regulations (Northern Ireland) 1969. The court applied the decisions in *Hannam v Bradford Corpn* [1970] 2 All ER 690 and *Malloch v Aberdeen Corpn* [1971] 1 WLR 1578.
497 (1982) 130 DLR (3d) 427.
498 (1982) 134 DLR (3d) 493.
499 (1974) 52 DLR (3d) 495.
500 (1944) 44 SRNSW 19.
501 [1994] 1 WLR 242.
502 [1969] 2 QB 538.
503 [1971] 1 WLR 487.

Judicial review: law of Scotland

2.240   The appellate court decision in *West v Secretary of State for Scotland*[504] leads us to a rather different conclusion in Scotland. In that case the court traced the historical development of the supervisory jurisdiction of the Court of Session and demonstrated how the jurisdiction had developed in a different way from that of the Supreme Court in England. No distinction between 'private' and 'public' law for this purpose is recognised. As in England and Wales strictly private contractual issues, such as those arising between a private employer and employee, do not fall within the jurisdiction but those in which a tripartite relationship can be demonstrated between the party with the power to act, a party to which this power has been delegated and the party affected by the exercise of the power, may fall within it. This has obvious consequences for higher education institutions, in that it is common for the powers of the governing body to be either expressly or by implication delegated to some other body or officer.

2.241   This issue arose in *Naik v University of Stirling*[505] in which at procedure roll (a preliminary proceeding) the university argued that the court had no jurisdiction to intervene in the termination of Samantha Naik's course for alleged failure to pay required tuition fees. The Lord Ordinary (Lord MacLean) discerned a tripartite relationship, as required by *West*, between the Queen as the granter of powers to the university and the fulfilment of these powers by the respondent in relation to one of its members, namely a student. A relevant decision previous to that in *West* was *Criper v University of Edinburgh*[506] where Dr Clive Criper's petition for judicial review of a decision of the University Court not to entertain a grievance was dismissed. It was held that as the matter concerning his contract of employment was a private law issue, the plea to competency by the defenders would have been sustained had the petition not been dismissed on other grounds. The court referred to the decision in *Tehrani v Argyll and Clyde Health Board (No 2)*[507] which concerned a dispute between a doctor and his employing health authority. Consistent with the English cases, this was held to involve no public law element and hence was not susceptible to judicial review. However, Ms Naik abandoned her action: in the parallel case brought

504   1992 SLT 636.
505   1994 SLT 449.
506   1991 SLT 129n, OH.
507   1990 SLT 118.

by her colleague Alastair Joobeen, *Joobeen v University of Stirling*,[508] which went to a full hearing, Lord Prosser held the dispute between Mr Joobeen and the University was a contractual one and his petition was incompetent. His remedy, if any, lay in contractual proceedings.[509]

Judicial review or contract?

2.242   It is clear that when contemplating action against an institution which does not have a Visitor and in the absence of any contractual dispute resolution procedure, a student has at least two possible alternatives: take action for breach of contract or apply for judicial review, depending on the nature of the dispute. In *Trustees of the Dennis Rye Pension Fund v Sheffield City Council*[510] the Court of Appeal held that in considering which approach should be taken, a court should look at the practical consequences of the choice made rather than just at the technical questions concerning the distinction between public and private rights. If the choice made had no significant disadvantages for the parties, the public or the court, then it should not normally be regarded as constituting an abuse of process. In case of doubt it is safer to make an application for judicial review since there would then be no question of being treated as abusing the process of the court by avoiding the protection provided by judicial review. The court can always order that the application should continue as if begun by writ.[511] In Scotland, by contrast, the failure to secure judicial review of the university's decision in *Joobeen v University of Stirling*[512] put an end to the action unless and until it was recommenced as one for breach of contract.[513]

2.243   However if arbitration under the provisions of the Arbitration Act 1996, or the equivalent Scottish common law procedures, being developed by CVCP and based on the institution-student contract are implemented, recourse to the courts may largely become a thing of the past. Institutions have been encouraged by the

508 1995 SLT 120n.
509 See in relation to this C M G Himsworth 'Further West? More Geometry of Judicial Review' 1995 SLT (News) 127; C R Munro 'Standing in Judicial Review' (1995) SLT (News) 279; V M Smith 'The Scope of Judicial Review Determined' (1997) Juridical Review 122.
510 [1997] 4 All ER 747, CA.
511 But not the other way round: RSC Ord 53, r 9(5).
512 1995 SLT 120n.
513 The rules governing judicial review in Scotland are set out in RCS r 58.

Committee on Standards in Public Life,[514] the National Union of Students,[515] NCIHE[516] and others[517] to establish an independent external review mechanism for complaints (covering also appeals in the sense of procedural irregularity etc as defined earlier) and contractual arbitration by suitably qualified and experienced arbitrators (arbiters in Scotland) appears to offer advantages over the current arrangements. To quote from *Bell's Treatise on The Law of Arbitration in Scotland*[518] 'the evident and leading object of the contract is to exclude a court of law from the determination of some matter which is in dispute; and to take, in its place, the judgment or award of some private person or persons, selected by the parties to arbitrate between them.' Arbitrators must act honestly, impartially and fairly and not outside the terms of their commission.

514 Second Report.
515 NUS Evidence to NCIHE (1997).
516 Recommendation 20, Main Report, NCIHE, July 1997.
517 Eg D J Farrington *Handling Complaints by Students* (1997) Universities and Colleges Staff Development Agency.
518 P 20.

Chapter 3

Funding and quality

The Higher Education Councils

The Funding Councils

3.1 By far the greatest direct influence on higher education is that exercised by the Funding Councils. The 1992 legislation established the English, Welsh and Scottish Higher Education Funding Councils (HEFCE, HEFCW, SHEFC) as corporate bodies and as successors to the Universities Funding Council (UFC) and the Polytechnics and Colleges Funding Council (PCFC), although all residuary matters concerning the former bodies vest in HEFCE.[1]

Further Education Funding Councils and the Teacher Training Agency

3.2 FHEA also established Further Education Funding Councils for England and Wales;[2] in Scotland funding of further education is the direct responsibility of the Secretary of State, who took over this responsibility from the former Regional Councils in 1993. While there is provision in Part I FHESA for a Further Education Funding Council in Scotland, it has not yet been activated, although it has been

---

1 Section 63(1)(b) FHEA: in relation to the employment of staff the Education (Polytechnics and Colleges Funding Council and Universities Funding Council Staff) Order 1993 (SI 1993/434) provided for transfer of named individuals to the employment of the Higher Education Funding Council for England.

2 The Further Education Funding Council for Wales (FEFCW), while it is a separate non-departmental public body, shares a joint Executive with HEFCW and the Welsh Funding Councils (WFC) is an umbrella title for the two bodies.

suggested by NCIHE that it should be.[3] Almost four million students study at England's 450 FE Colleges. There is a legal duty on FEFC to secure facilities for different age groups which are 'sufficient' and 'adequate.'[4] No such duty is placed on the funding councils in the higher education sector. FEFC has not escaped litigation.[5]

3.3 Part I EA94 also established the Teacher Training Agency (TTA) which has similar responsibilities to the Funding Councils in relation to teacher training in England. TTA works closely with HEFCE. HEFCW is responsible under EA94 for the equivalent services in Wales.

Functions of the Higher Education Funding Councils

3.4 The functions of the higher education Funding Councils are set out in Part II FHEA and Part II FHESA as follows:
(i) to administer funds made available by the Secretary of State for the purposes of providing financial support for 'eligible activities';
(ii) to impose terms and conditions on making grants, loans or other payments to institutions;
(iii) to require information from institutions;
(iv) to provide the Secretary of State with such information or advice relating to the provision of higher education as they think fit;
(v) to secure that provision is made for assessing quality of education and to establish a 'Quality Assessment Committee' (SHEFC is required to 'have regard to' the arrangements made by HEFCE and HEFCW);
(vi) to exercise any of their functions jointly if more efficient or effective to do so;
(vii) to arrange for the promotion or carrying out of efficiency studies designed to improve economy, efficiency and effectiveness in the management or operations of an institution.

3.5 As an example of the way Funding Councils operate, SHEFC produces a *Corporate Plan*[6] which set out its *Mission Statement* reproduced as Appendix A. In the introduction to its original (1993) *Operational Plan*, the Council described its operation as a Non-

---

3 Recommendation 23, Report of the Scottish Committee, NCIHE, July 1997.
4 Sections 2 and 3 FHEA. The Secretary of State has the duty to secure adequate and efficient provision in Scotland: section 1 FHESA.
5 See *R v Further Education Funding Council, ex p Parkinson* [1997] 2 FCR 67, QBD.
6 SHEFC (1997) *Corporate Plan 1997–2000*.

Departmental Public Body (NDPB) as being on 'Next Steps' principles[7] and stated its commitment to the Citizen's Charter ideals of openness, accessibility and accountability. Although the judges' remarks in *R v Higher Education Funding Council, ex p Institute of Dental Surgery*[8] were made in relation to HEFCE, it will be interesting to see how the Funding Council's commitment to openness, etc is consistent with them: 'It would take a great deal more than this to persuade us that experienced and distinguished academics, whether individually or collectively, cannot assign reasons for their own judgment.' Each Council has established a range of committees and advisory groups to assist it in its work.

The Northern Ireland Higher Education Council

3.6   The Northern Ireland Higher Education Council (NIHEC) was established in November 1992. It is advisory rather than executive, the Department of Education for Northern Ireland (DENI) retaining responsibility which elsewhere has been placed in the hands of the Funding Councils. Its broad remit is to advise DENI and, more broadly, government, on the planning and funding of higher education in Northern Ireland. NIHEC has close links with HEFCE and employs the same funding methodology in determining the block grant of the two Northern Ireland universities. A further block of funding, known as NIDevR, is allocated in support of research work specifically undertaken by the two universities in support of the economic, social and cultural life of Northern Ireland and the Council advises DENI on the allocation of these funds.

3.7   A further responsibility is to monitor and report to DENI on the steps taken towards the achievement of a more effective working relationship between the two universities, as complementarity rather than competition is seen as a guiding principle.[9] The membership of the Council reflects academic, business, research and local community interests but there are no academic members from the two Northern Ireland universities.

3.8   Like the Funding Councils, NIHEC was issued with a letter of guidance from the relevant Minister. This sets out the role of the

7   'Next Steps' is the process by which many non-policy making functions of the executive arm of the government are being devolved to executive agencies with considerable management autonomy.
8   [1994] 1 WLR 242.
9   Letter to the author from the Acting Secretary of NIHEC, 6 July 1993.

Council and the arrangements to be made between it and HEFCE. A contract has been made under FHEA[10] whereby HEFCE advises DENI (and in certain aspects of higher education, the Department of Agriculture for Northern Ireland – DANI) on the planning, development and funding of the universities over the full range of subject disciplines and with special emphasis on the co-ordinated development of the totality of university provision in Northern Ireland. HEFCE applies the same criteria and standards to the Northern Ireland universities as to the institutions for which it has responsibility in England. Once HEFCE has given its advice on funding, the function of NIHEC is to consider whether there are any particular Northern Ireland circumstances which should be taken into account, and may seek any necessary recalculation of the effect of those changes. This then forms the basis of its advice to government.

3.9 QAA reports on the quality of provision of higher education in Northern Ireland and NIHEC is required to take account of its findings in its advice on planning and funding. It was not considered practicable to establish a separate quality assessment unit in the province.

3.10 NCIHE has recommended the establishment of a Higher Education Funding Council to replace the current funding arrangements, while retaining links with HEFCE and QAA in the interests of avoiding unnecessary duplication or unnecessary divergence from UK-wide practice.[11]

Operation of the Funding Councils in Great Britain

Power of the Secretary of State to impose conditions on grants to the Funding Councils

3.11 Section 68 FHEA and section 42 FHESA confer on the respective Secretaries of State the power to make grants to the Funding Councils 'of such amounts and subject to such terms and conditions as he may determine.' The terms and conditions mentioned

> (a) may in particular impose requirements to be complied with in respect of every institution, or every institution falling within a class or description specified in the terms and conditions, being requirements to be complied with in the case of any institution

10 Section 69(3) and Schedule 1 paragraph 1(1)(b).
11 Appendix 1 *Report on Northern Ireland*, HCIHE, July 1997.

to which the requirements apply before financial support of any
amount or description so specified is provided by the council in
respect of activities carried on by the institution, but

(b) shall not otherwise relate to the provision of financial support
by the council in respect of activities carried on by any particular
institution or institutions.

'Activities' here presumably includes all the activities of a particular
institution, whether or not these are supported financially by a
Funding Council.

The terms and conditions

may not be framed by reference to particular courses of study or
programmes of research (including the contents of such courses or
programmes and the manner in which they are taught, supervised or
assessed) or to the criteria for the selection and appointment of
academic staff and for the admission of students.[12]

'Academic staff' is not defined in these Acts but presumably excludes
academic-related and support staff: the Secretary of State is not
prevented from insisting that administrative staff appointed to a
finance function are qualified accountants or that electrical tradesmen
have served an apprenticeship.

Finally, the terms and conditions may in particular

(a) enable the Secretary of State to require the repayment, in whole
or in part, of sums paid by him if any of the terms and conditions
subject to which the sums were paid is not complied with, and

(b) require the payment of interest in respect of any period during
which a sum due to the Secretary of State in accordance with any
of the terms and conditions remains unpaid.

Clause 18 THEB adds to these provisions so as to ensure that the
Secretary of State may direct the Councils to impose conditions on
governing bodies relating to student fees from 1998 onwards. It also
removes any 'prohibition or other requirement' imposed by FHEA
or FHESA on the Secretary of State in relation to this specific power.

3.12 The Secretaries of State have made grants to the Funding
Councils accompanied by Management Statements and Financial
Memoranda, the terms and conditions of which flow through to
institutions by means of the Councils' own Financial Memoranda

12 The then Secretary of State indicated that he (unlike certain of his predecessors)
had no wish to intervene in academic matters in individual institutions. Interview
in 'The Higher' 13 December 1991, p 3.

with institutions, discussed in detail below. The terms of the Financial Memorandum between the Secretary of State for Scotland and SHEFC include, for example, a requirement for an internal audit function to be established within the Funding Council. The power to impose conditions is, according to the government '... to enable the Secretary of State to promote policy developments ...'[13] and is wider than the corresponding provision in section 134(6) ERA. This appears to be because of the narrow construction placed upon the power contained in that section by Simon Brown LJ in *R v Secretary of State for Education and Science, ex p Association of Polytechnic and College Teachers*[14] where his Lordship held that the section did not entitle the Secretary of State to make payment of part of the annual grant to the PCFC conditional upon a 'satisfactory' pay settlement. It appears that section 68 FHEA (and the corresponding Scottish provision) would now permit the Secretary of State to impose such a condition. It would also permit the Secretary of State to require Funding Councils to intervene in institutions which do not comply with the general requirements under section 68 FHEA and section 42 FHESA.

The administration of funds and funding models

3.13 The Councils differ in their approach to the administration of funds. While SHEFC funds higher education institutions (and not higher education as such),[15] in England and Wales the source of funding is based on the level of education supplied and not the institution supplying it. HEFCE and HEFCW fund higher education courses in further education colleges at the same unit of resource as they offer to higher education institutions. In 1997 HEFCE funded courses at 72 universities, 16 directly-funded Schools of the University of London, 48 higher education colleges and 74 further education colleges.[16]

3.14 The powers of the Councils are set out in section 65 FHEA and in similar terms in section 40 FHESA. The first two subsections of section 65 read:

---

13 Paymaster-General House of Lords *Official Report* Vol 534 col 638.
14 (1991) Times, 22 August.
15 See letter from SOED to the Chairman of the Committee of Scottish University Principals (COSUP), 1 February 1993.
16 HEFCE Website information, May 1997.

(1) Each council shall be responsible, subject to the provisions of this Part of this Act, for administering funds made available to the council by the Secretary of State and others for the purposes of providing financial support for activities eligible for funding under this section.

(2) The activities eligible for funding under this section are–

(a) the provision of education and the undertaking of research[17] by higher education institutions in the council's area.[18]

(b) the provision of any facilities, and the carrying on of any other activities, by higher education institutions in their area which the governing bodies of those institutions consider it necessary or desirable to provide or carry on for the purpose of or in connection with education or research.

(c) the provision–
   (i)   by institutions in their area maintained or assisted by local education authorities, or
   (ii) by such institutions in their area as are within the further education sector,
   of prescribed courses of higher education,[19] and

(d) the provision by any person of services for the purposes of, or in connection with, the provision of education or the undertaking of research by institutions within the higher education sector.

There are two points arising from this section. First, it is not clear who the 'others' referred to in subsection (1) are: there are at present no other sources of public funding available to the Councils. However, the Secretaries of States' powers to impose conditions on grants made to the Councils extends to grants made by them only (section 68 FHEA and section 42 FHESA). If the Councils secured other sources of funding no doubt these would carry conditions of their own. The second point is that in subsection (2) the activities eligible for funding include the provision of 'education,' not 'higher education' so that courses run by higher education institutions other than those covered by the definition of higher education could be funded by the Councils.

3.15   The powers of the Councils in relation to funding of higher education in the further education sector in England and Wales are inherited from the PCFC provisions of ERA:[20] FHESA is self-

---

17 In Scotland, at least, the government expects that there will be some assessment of quality before research funding is granted: First Scottish Standing Committee *Official Report* 14 January 1992 col 219.

18 'Institutions within the higher education sector' in Scotland: Section 40 FHESA.

19 The wording is slightly different for Scotland.

20 Section 132(5). There was no equivalent provision in the UFC sector: section 131(5).

contained in this respect[21] and it appears that the funding of the proposed University of the Highlands and Islands (UHI) may fall under this provision.

3.16 The power to fund the activities of 'any person' is entirely new and clearly envisages the appearance of autonomous providers of education and research. One possible source of bodies eligible for funding under this section might be those providing courses of training leading to NVQ/GNVQ/SVQ Level 5 qualifications. Latterly there have been suggestions for the establishment of a University of Industry, a Virtual University and other similar bodies.

Grants, loans and other payments

3.17 Section 65(3) FHEA[22] allows the Funding Councils to make grants, loans and other payments to institutions or other persons, subject in each case to such terms and conditions as the Council think fit. The power to make 'loans or other payments' as opposed to grants is new and not inherited from ERA.[23] While it is clear what is meant by 'loans,' there is no definition of 'other payments.' Clause 18 THEB requires the Councils, if so directed by the Secretary of State, to impose conditions on governing bodies related to the imposition of student fees.

3.18 The terms and conditions on which a Council may make any grants, loans or other payments

> may in particular–
> (a) enable the council to require the repayment, in whole or in part, of sums paid by the council if any of the terms and conditions subject to which the sums were paid is not complied with, and
> (b) require the payment of interest in respect of any period during which a sum due to the council in accordance with any of the terms and conditions remains unpaid,
> but shall not relate to the application by the body to whom the grants or other payment[24] are made of any sums derived otherwise than from the council.

---

21 Section 40(2)(d) and (e) FHESA.
22 Section 40(3) FHESA.
23 Cf sections 131(6) (UFC) and 132(7) (PCFC) ERA.
24 Not 'grants, loans or other payments': loans are omitted.

From this it appears that any attempt by a Funding Council to require certification *in advance* that none of its resources would be used to fund other activities is invalid, although enquiring after the event would be within its power. This was confirmed in connection with the 1995/96 tendering exercise for Nursing and Midwifery Education in Scotland, funding for which was to be derived from the Scottish Office, not SHEFC.[25]

3.19 There has been some debate as to whether these sections permit the Councils to suspend payment of grant rather than to require repayment of grant already distributed. Paragraphs 15 of both HEFCE and SHEFC Financial Memoranda contemplate this possibility. In SHEFC's case this may arise where its Chief Executive, after discussion with the institution's governing body, is not satisfied that appropriate action is being taken to deal with matters of serious concern. In HEFCE's case there is no requirement for consultation and the Chief Executive may act where in his opinion it is appropriate and reasonable to do so in order to safeguard public funds. In principle it is considered that these paragraphs are not in accordance with the powers of the Funding Councils under the Acts. However, when the institution accepts the terms and conditions set out in the Memorandum, it is, arguably, entering into a contract with the relevant Council, both FHEA[26] and FHESA[27] giving the Councils full power to enter into contracts. If institutions appear to agree, either expressly or impliedly, to terms and conditions in the Memorandum which might go further than the Councils had statutory power to impose upon them unilaterally, such terms and conditions might be held to be binding on the normal principles of the law of contract. It is therefore essential that governing bodies give full and detailed consideration to every paragraph in the proposed Financial Memorandum before assenting to it. In this particular instance it seems clear that institutions have conceded something which in principle they could have resisted.

3.20 Taking SHEFC as an example, its powers to attach conditions to grants, loans or other payments made by it in pursuance of section 40 FHESA (making grants, loans etc from funds provided to it by the Secretary of State 'and others') are set out in subsections 3 and 4 of section 40. Subsection 4 qualifies the last sentence of subsection 3 in that the Council may not impose such conditions to 'the application

25 COSHEP Circular Letter 38/95.
26 Schedule 1, para 1(1)(b).
27 Schedule 7, para 1(1)(3).

by the [institution] of any sums derived otherwise than from the Council.' However clause 18 THEB appears to remove any prohibition on the Councils in relation specifically to the imposition of tuition fees.

3.21 The Secretary of State's powers to impose conditions on grants to the Council are set out in section 42 and the Council can only make its own allocations subject to those conditions, section 40(1) describing the responsibility of the Council as 'subject to the provisions of this part of the Act.' The Secretary of State's powers appear to be quite wide. Section 42(2)(a) allows the Secretary of State to impose requirements to be complied with in respect of every institution [or a particular class of institution] before they are in receipt of any funds from the Council. Section 42(2)(b) prevents the Secretary of State from attaching conditions to individual institutions and subsection (3) further excludes certain areas of detailed intervention within the control of institutions considered to be matters for academic judgment. The conditions which may be imposed by the Secretary of State include those set out in subsection (4) relating to repayment of grants and payment of interest on grants not repaid but this is clearly not an exclusive list.

3.22 Although terms and conditions which could affect application of funds from other than Council sources are not fundamentally ultra vires, it is considered that the Councils could not enforce a term or condition which they sought to apply solely to non-Council funds. This would be ultra vires their powers under the Acts. In addition institutions or persons to whom moneys have been granted or loaned cannot be forced by the Council to repay them out of other income, including other sources of public funding such as tuition fees and research grants.

3.23 The Councils have discretion to impose terms and conditions, some of which merely pass on to the next level the conditions imposed on the Councils themselves by the Secretaries of State on major issues of principle such as audit, value for money and accountability. Some, however, particularly the detail in relation to limits of expenditure of various kinds which may be undertaken without the approval of the Councils, will be made in the exercise of the relevant Council's own judgment. Before exercising their discretion to impose any terms and conditions, however derived, the Councils are obliged by section 66(1) FHEA[28] to consult

---

28 Section 41 FHESA is worded slightly differently but has the same general import.

such of the following bodies as appear to the council to be appropriate to consult in the circumstances–
(a) such bodies representing the interests of higher education institutions as appear to the council to be concerned, and
(b) the governing body of any particular higher education institution which appears to the council to be concerned.

except as provided by clause 18 THEB relating to the imposition of tuition fees.

3.24 The language of section 66(1)(a) leaves a considerable discretion in the hands of the Funding Councils to consult whichever 'representative' bodies they see fit. The question of which bodies are 'representative' has no clear answer, neither is it obvious how the representative rights have been granted. For the present purposes, however, it is clear that the Funding Councils recognise the Committee of Vice-Chancellors and Principals (CVCP), the Committee of Scottish Higher Education Principals (COSHEP), the Standing Conference of Principals and Directors of Colleges and Institutions of Higher Education (SCOP) and the Conference of Scottish Centrally-Funded Colleges (CSCFC). The first of these is a company limited by guarantee with defined objects including a representational role:

> ... to represent the university sector of higher education in the United Kingdom and to conduct dealings and to liaise with the Government, any local, national or other institutions, authorities, agencies, bodies or persons, wheresoever in the world situate ...[29]

However these bodies are committees, etc not of the institutions themselves but of certain office-holders, whose powers to act on behalf of their institutions are not self-evident. It is interesting to note that the Articles of Association of CVCP define the Vice-Chancellor or Principal in terms of the person who has primary responsibility for the academic and executive affairs of the institution.[30]

3.25 There are limitations on the exercise of the Councils' discretion which the government considered to be vital if competition for resources was to be ensured[31] and, in Scotland, distinctiveness of provision maintained. Section 66(2) FHEA[32] provides:

29 Article 3(c), Memorandum of Association of CVCP, July 1990.
30 Article 1, Articles of Association of CVCP, July 1990.
31 See eg First Scottish Standing Committee *Official Report* col 281 21 January 1992.
32 Section 41(2) FHESA.

... a council shall have regard to the desirability of not discouraging any institution for whose activities financial support is provided ... from maintaining or developing its funding from other sources.

Section 41(3) FHESA obliges SHEFC to

have regard (so far as they think it appropriate to do so in the light of any other relevant considerations) to the desirability of maintaining any distinctive characteristics of any institution ...

Any term or condition sought to be imposed by a Council which had the practical effect of discouraging an institution from maintaining or developing its funding from other sources, etc might be challenged on the basis that it involved the Council having failed to have regard to the desirability of not discouraging any institution in that way.

Funding models

3.26 The Councils have adopted funding models for teaching which the government expects will be based on 'fair and objective methodologies'[33] and which depend upon the ability of institutions to recruit students at a marginal cost which is lower than the average cost. For example in 1997 the HEFCE/HEFCW funding model was based on the Average Unit of Council Funding (AUCF) within 11 Academic Subject Categories (ASC) by dividing the total public funding they receive (including tuition fees) by the total number of home and EC students. Institutions with a lower AUCF benefit more from any additional funds for teaching which the Councils are able to allocate. The model appears to be a valid exercise of the Council's powers under the Act, but there are two risks if institutions take very large numbers of marginal cost students

(i) financial exposure which could in extremis allow the Secretary of State to intervene;

(ii) unplanned additions to public expenditure through payment of tuition fees and mandatory maintenance grants, an area in which the Secretary of State might legitimately intervene by direction.

It is (ii) which led the Secretaries of State through the Funding Councils to take action to cap the increase in numbers in 1993 and has led to institutions being penalised financially for exceeding planned targets.

---

33 House of Commons *Official Report* Vol 199 col 87, 26 November 1991.

3.27 The planning and allocation systems devised by the Councils are expected in the long term to bring some financial stability to institutions. However, all depends upon the funding being made available to the Councils by the Secretaries of State, which can only be determined following the annual public expenditure decisions and may be accompanied by directions, such as the limitation on further growth ('consolidation') announced in late 1992 and the promotion of science and technology, part-time study and two-year diploma qualifications.[34] On the other hand, commitments have to be made to students some months before the start of the financial year in which they will enter the institution and staff contracts are very largely 'permanent' in nature. There are therefore difficult questions about the relationship between the Councils and the institutions and how the actions of the Councils might be challenged by a range of parties potentially affected by funding decisions. Such challenges should in principle be made easier by the public disclosure of all the methods and details of the calculation of funding allocations adopted by the new Councils, a feature missing entirely from the allocation processes adopted by the UGC and certainly less transparent in the processes adopted by the UFC and PCFC. However, paradoxically, such openness might make the process more difficult. No legal challenges to funding allocations for teaching had been made by the end of 1997.

Funding for research

3.28 Funding for research is allocated on the basis of formulae derived directly from the outcome of the research selectivity exercises, first undertaken in 1988 by the UGC, then in 1992 by the UFC (acted upon by the new Councils), then in 1996 by the Funding Councils. It appears that the exercise will be repeated at regular intervals. In this area the decisions are based on peer review of work submitted by the institutions and the possibility of potential challenges to the outcome will be discussed later.

The Financial Memoranda

Purpose of the Memoranda

3.29 The Funding Councils exercise their powers to attach conditions to payments primarily by the issue of Financial

---

34 See eg letter of 2 December 1992 from SOED to SHEFC, dealing with all of these issues.

Memoranda setting out their requirements in respect of individual institutions. The original intention when the UFC and PCFC were established was that the relationship between the Councils and the institutions should be based on negotiated contracts for the provision of teaching (and probably research) but this approach was quickly and quietly dropped when the practical problems of implementing it in a sensible planning horizon became as apparent to the Councils as it had always been to the institutions. The Financial Memorandum was seen as underpinning the contractual system,[35] prescribing the general rules governing the financial relationship between institutions and the funding bodies. The system of contracts and financial memoranda was to replace the former UGC and local authority arrangements for both recurrent and capital expenditure.

3.30   As it is, the Financial Memoranda are issued by the Councils under their statutory power to attach terms and conditions to grants. It is possible that they could be regarded as contracts made under the Councils' statutory powers to enter into contracts and this interpretation is assisted by the Councils' requirement that they be accepted formally by the governing bodies and their being expressed as memoranda 'between' the Councils and the institutions. In some institutions it appears to be unnecessary for the governing body to 'accept' the conditions since the instrument of government places a direct restriction on the powers of the governing body: eg the governing instrument of the Glasgow Caledonian University provides:

> Subject to any conditions which may be imposed on the University Court as conditions of payment of grant to it, the University Court shall make such arrangements as it thinks fit for the conduct of the financial affairs of the University.[36]

That the Memoranda constitute the imposed will of the Councils rather than the result of any form of negotiation or compromise is further borne out by the fact that the Councils are the sole judge of any question of interpretation of the Memoranda,[37] although this right is only to be exercised after consultation with the other party.

35 Department of Education and Science *Changes in Structure and National Planning for Higher Education: Contracts between the Funding Bodies and Higher Education Institutions* (1987) para 19.
36 Article 6(1) The Glasgow Caledonian University (Scotland) Order of Council 1993 (SI 1993/556).
37 See paragraph 57 SHEFC Financial Memorandum; paras 71–72 HEFCE Financial Memorandum, HEFCE Circular 5/96: see also HEFCE Circular 6/96 relating to requests for consent and the use of delegated decision-making powers.

3.31 It is the terms and conditions set out in the Memoranda which have caused the greatest concern and debate, as was also the case when similar Memoranda were issued under powers granted by ERA, by the UFC and the PCFC in 1988/9. The terms of the HEFCE, HEFCW and SHEFC Memoranda and the Codes of Audit Practice which accompany them are of far-reaching importance and a full description of them is therefore essential. Naturally they are revised from time to time: the Report of The Public Accounts Committee on Severance Payments to Senior Staff in the Publicly Funded Education Sector[38] suggested that the Funding Councils should if necessary make it a condition of grant for institutions to comply with the relevant code of conduct or guidance for governors, to establish Remuneration Committees and not to have confidentiality clauses in severance settlements except where there is commercially sensitive information. In general terms, this suggestion was incorporated into revised Memoranda in 1996.[39]

Terms of the Memorandum

3.32 The Financial Memorandum is expressed so as not to require the institution to act in a manner which would cause it to lose charitable status or act in a manner inconsistent with its charter and statutes or equivalent. It

(i) states the respective responsibilities for accounting for and securing value for money from the use of public funds between the Council and the governing body of the institution and requires the governing body to designate a principal office of the institution, the holder of which will be responsible for satisfying the governing body that the conditions have been complied with;[40]

(ii) indicates how some funds will be unearmarked and others earmarked for specific purposes and imposes restrictions on use and virement;

(iii) imposes on the institution a requirement to have sound systems of internal financial management and control, to maintain financial viability, and specifies the circumstances under which deficits may be incurred;

---

38 1995.
39 Paragraph 11, HEFCE Financial Memorandum; paragraph 17, SHEFC Financial Memorandum.
40 Normally the Vice-Chancellor or other chief executive officer.

(iv) requires the institution to develop and maintain an estate and equipment strategy, imposes restrictions on transactions over specified limits without consulting the Council and specifies the circumstances under which part or all of the proceeds of disposal of assets must be returned to the Council;[41]

(v) specifies the conditions under which borrowing and leasing arrangements may be entered into;[42]

(vi) requires the institution to keep proper accounting records and provide annual reports and financial statements in a specified form and timescale;

(vii) requires the institution in general terms to recover the full costs of research contracts and external services;

(viii) specifies the arrangements for financial audit, provision of information and insurance;

(ix) requires the institution to publish a disability statement as required by DDA95;

(x) will (assuming the enactment of THEB) require the institution to impose and collect prescribed tuition fees from defined categories of student.

The HEFCE Financial Memorandum is more detailed in some respects than its SHEFC counterpart. It also contains provisions which do not appear in the SHEFC version, for example a requirement for the institution to subscribe to QAA and HESA, and the right of HEFCE to cut off access to JANET (The Joint Academic computer Network) and its progeny SUPERJANET if the institution does not conform to 'acceptable practice.'

3.33 The following principal points arise from the Memoranda:

(i) the importance of relating the terms of the Memorandum to the charter or instrument of government of the institution and to the modus operandi and standing orders of the governing body;

(ii) the potential effect of its terms on the contracts of employment of the accounting officer (normally the Principal or Vice-Chancellor) and other 'officers' (however defined) and staff;

(iii) the need for constant vigilance on the part of the governing body that they are abiding by the terms of the Memorandum and that the Funding Council is not exceeding its statutory powers.

---

41 Who owns the assets is obviously of fundamental importance.

42 One objective of this is to ensure that institutions can readily evade short-term financial controls by borrowing long-term.

Statement of Recommended Accounting Practice (SORP)

3.34 Another document referred to in the Financial Memorandum is the SORP (Statement of Recommended Accounting Practice), the relevant current statement[43] being that 'approved and franked' by the Accounting Standards Committee, a body established by professional associations representing accountants. The SORP identifies the main groups of users of universities' accounts as the governing body, government and government agencies, staff, students, alumni, other educational institutions, industry, 'the loan/ creditor group', donors and benefactors and the public. Some of these groups are more 'main users' than others: it is most unlikely for example that many alumni will even know that the accounts are published. It is, however, certainly in the interests of staff of higher education institutions to be aware of what is being done on their behalf and the SORP provides some guidance to the understanding of the accounts.

Legal position of the Funding Councils and their members

3.35 The Funding Councils are statutory corporate bodies with powers restricted by the statutes which establish them and which they may not exceed. They are not servants or agents of the Crown, neither do they enjoy any status, immunity or privilege of the Crown.[44] There appear to be two consequences of this provision.
(i) the operations of the Councils will not be subject to the Parliamentary Commissioner for Administration;
(ii) a defence to a claim for non-performance of a contract that the Funding Council has frustrated its performance will not be available, although such a defence may be available when Crown action has frustrated a contract.[45]

3.36 On the other hand impossibility of performance arising from the actions of the Councils could discharge a contract under the doctrine of the implied term ie where the performance of the contract depended upon the continued existence of a certain state of affairs

---

43 CVCP, COSHEP and SCOP *Statement of Recommended Practice: Accounting in HEIs* June 1994.
44 Schedule 1 paragraph 17 FHEA; Schedule 7 paragraph 15 FHESA.
45 Eg *Cricklewood Property and Investment Trust Ltd v Leighton's Investment Trust Ltd* [1945] AC 221.

which fails to continue.[46] Thus contracts of service or for services could be discharged if their performance depended upon the continued existence of a certain subject at the institution in question, and the Funding Council subsequently specifically withdrew all funds for the pursuit of that subject at that institution. The emphasis on medium and long-term planning adopted by the Councils makes it unlikely that sudden withdrawals of funding could occur, thus giving the institution concerned time to mitigate the consequences of withdrawal. However, instances of withdrawal of funding have occurred under the pre-1992 arrangements, for example the cessation of dental education in 1993 at the University of Edinburgh, which was forced into declaring staff redundant as a consequence.

3.37 What seems clear is that the actions of the Councils are susceptible to judicial review. They are statutory bodies performing 'public' functions and proceedings could therefore be instituted against them. To be granted leave[47] to institute proceedings an individual or body is required to have a 'sufficient interest' in the outcome.[48] A sufficient interest does not entail a direct financial or legal interest. It appears to be a mixed question of fact and law: a question of fact and degree and the relationship between the applicant and the matter to which the application relates, having regard to all the circumstances of the case.[49] There is little doubt that a higher education institution would have a sufficient interest: there is a direct link between the relevant Council and individual institutions, and the Council has certain legal duties in relation to them. Whether an individual academic whose career is at risk of being ruined or damaged by the action of a Funding Council has an interest is a more difficult issue, since there is no direct relationship and it might be difficult to demonstrate the link.[50]

3.38 The first legal challenge to a Funding Council was mounted by the Institute of Dental Surgery (University of London) which sought judicial review of the rating awarded to the Institute by

46 See in relation to the doctrine of impossibility of performance *Krell v Henry* [1903] 2 KB 740, one of several cases arising out of contracts cancelled when King Edward VII's coronation was postponed in 1902. English law derives this doctrine from Roman Law *obligationes de certo corpore* extending it from things to events.
47 In England and Wales. Leave is not a feature of the Scottish system.
48 Order 53, r 3(7); section 31(3) Supreme Court Act 1981.
49 *IRC v National Federation of Self-Employed and Small Businesses Ltd* [1982] AC 617.
50 *Finnigan v New Zealand Rugby Football Union* [1985] 2 NZLR 159 was a case in which a chain of relationships was established between an individual player suffering loss and the supervisory body indirectly responsible.

HEFCE (UFC) under the 1992 Research Selectivity Exercise. The case was based on the composition of the panel which made a recommendation to the Council. There was, it was alleged, an 'unintentional' bias towards institutions whose members of staff were members of the panel. For its part, HEFCE argued that there was no requirement for it to give reasons for its decisions, that there was no perceptible irrationality in the decisions which were reached, that no-one could question the quality, integrity or competence of the dentistry panel and that there was no flaw in the procedure. In giving its judgment rejecting the application, the Queen's Bench Divisional Court (Mann LJ and Sedley J) held that the Funding Council was not legally required to give reasons for its decisions, but that in general public decision-making bodies should 'appreciate that ... their legal position may depend on their ability to account intelligibly for their decisions by explaining not simply how but why they have reached them.'[51]

Liability of members of Funding Councils

3.39 Members of non-departmental public bodies like the Funding Councils will be treated by the law in much the same way as members of the governing bodies of other statutory corporations. They are expected to act honestly, reasonably, in good faith and without negligence. They will not be liable for corporate acts except that if the act is ultra vires and proves to be tortious or delictual the members who authorised the act might themselves be sued, particularly if the act complained of was wilful and malicious.[52]

Other functions of the Funding Councils

3.40 The Funding Councils have a number of other functions related to their principal one of financial support for institutions. One of these, the assessment of teaching quality, has now been transferred to QAA and will be discussed separately below.

---

51 *R v Higher Education Funding Council, ex p Institute of Dental Surgery* [1994] 1 WLR 242.
52 See discussion on liability of members of non-chartered bodies in chapter 2.

Provision of information by the Funding Councils

3.41 The power to provide the Secretary of State with such information or advice as the Councils think fit is one which carries over from the UFC and PCFC[53] and as a corollary the Councils have power to require the institutions to provide information to them. There is no definition of 'information' other than it must be related in some way to the exercise of the Councils' functions. It is therefore possible to conceive of a situation in which an institution would technically be able to withhold information about matters which were not funded by the relevant Council, although such action might in practice be unwise, particularly in view of the terms of the HEFCE Memorandum which enable the Council to take action to obtain information at the institution's cost.[54]

Joint exercise of functions

3.42 The Councils have a general power to exercise any of their functions jointly where it appears to them that to do so will be more efficient or will enable them more effectively to discharge their functions. The words 'efficient' and 'effective' appear in several places in the Acts: 'efficiency' is generally regarded as 'value for money' and 'effectiveness' relates to the successful achievement of objectives. The power does, for example, allow the Councils jointly to undertake a research selectivity exercise or to require the provision of information or to fund developments such as computing networks jointly.

Economy, efficiency and effectiveness studies

3.43 The power to arrange for the promotion or carrying out by any person of studies designed to improve economy, efficiency and effectiveness in the management or operations of an institution is new in the 1992 Acts, although the UFC and PCFC had power to undertake any activities they thought necessary or expedient in the exercise of their functions.[55] The language of the sections is similar to that of the Local Government Finance Act 1982[56] in relation to

---

53 Sections 131(8)(b) and 132(10)(b) ERA.
54 Paragraph 26 HEFCE Financial Memorandum; there is no equivalent provision in the SHEFC version.
55 Sections 131(8)(d) and 132(1)(c) ERA, repealed by Schedule 8 paragraphs 35 FHEA.
56 Section 26.

the powers of the Audit Commission. Definition of the words 'economy' and 'economic' has given rise to much argument but in *Bromley London Borough Council v Greater London Council*[57] the view of the Law Lords[58] was that it depended on the circumstances in which they are used. In that case, concerned with whether or not the GLC had validly levied an additional precept on London Boroughs to finance its policy of cutting fares on London Transport, Lord Brandon of Oakbrook said

> ... the words are used in order to ensure that [the bodies concerned] have proper regard, in the performance of their functions, to the principle of cost-effectiveness or value for money ...

In the opinion of the Scottish Higher Education Funding Council, the term 'value for money'

> ... is commonly used to describe the combination of economy, efficiency and effectiveness.
> *Economy* is concerned with minimising the cost of resources used for an activity, having regard to appropriate quality;
> *Efficiency* is the relationship between output, in terms of goods, services or other results, and resources consumed;
> *Effectiveness* is the extent to which objectives are achieved and the relationship between the intended results and the actual results.[59]

3.44   In the language of the Acts under which the Funding Councils exercise their powers, 'any person' could include a government agency, a consultant or anyone at all. The person has power to require the governing body of the institution to provide him or her with any information as may reasonably required and their accounts and other documents. This is a far-reaching power to enquire into anything connected with 'management or operations', neither of which is defined and would presumably be given the widest possible interpretation.

Financial audit

3.45   The provisions for financial audit of higher education institutions are since 1992 far more complex than under the preceding legislation. Most of the changes have been effected through the Financial Memoranda, but there are a number of other provisions all of which will be discussed in this section.

57 [1983] 1 AC 768.
58 Eg Lord Scarman at 841 and 843.
59 SHEFC *Code of Audit Practice* 1993, Annex A.

Seven kinds of audit

3.46   The higher education system now faces up to seven different bodies charged with auditing its financial performance. All institutions face at least five: internal and external audit (required by the Funding Councils and, in the case of external audit, by the charter or other governing instrument); the Funding Council itself, the Education Department which audits the Funding Council (and, in Scotland, the disbursement of funds direct from the Scottish Office Education and Industry Department (eg Access Funds)); the National Audit Office which audits the function of the Education Departments and has direct access to institutions' books in defined circumstances. In addition the Audit Commission may become involved in higher education in England and Wales, and the Commission and Court of Auditors of the European Union have rights of access in certain circumstances where Union funds have been granted. Each of these forms of audit will be considered separately.

The National Audit Office

3.47   The Comptroller and Auditor-General (whose office is now commonly known as the National Audit Office (NAO)) has responsibility for public audit (economy, efficiency and effectiveness of the use of resources, but not the merits of lawful policy decisions) and NAO's powers are contained in section 135 ERA, section 53 FHESA and section 7 National Audit Act 1983. The first two of these provisions allow access to an institution's 'accounts' and the latter section empowers NAO to carry out an examination into the economy, efficiency and effectiveness with which an institution has used its resources in any particular year in discharging its functions. NAO has the right of access at all reasonable times to all such documents as it may reasonably require for carrying out its examination and to obtain information from anyone holding or accountable for any such document. However there is no general power in the legislation for NAO to conduct investigations into the financial affairs of institutions other than access to the 'accounts.' Institutions have conceded this by agreeing to a paragraph in the Financial Memorandum with the relevant Funding Council[60] which gives access to the institution's 'books and records' clearly a much

---

60   Paragraph 67, HEFCE Financial Memorandum; paragraph 49, SHEFC Financial Memorandum.

wider right of access than that to the 'accounts.' However, as NAO is not a party to the Memorandum, it is questionable whether acting alone it could use this provision, without more, to justify a unilateral investigation into anything other than the 'accounts.' There does not appear to be any statutory or other authority to justify gratuitous questioning of institutions or their employees.

3.48 NAO also audits the Funding Councils.[61] In 1993 the Comptroller and Auditor-General identified a number of common obstacles to securing value for money in public bodies: a lack of care in management of assets (failure to treat public assets with the same care as if they were the personal property of those concerned); failure to pay sufficient attention to environmental impact (the fourth 'e' to add to economy, efficiency and effectiveness); poor management of projects; poor monitoring and control of activities and failure to adopt best practice.[62] Subsequent events have shown that in some institutions there appears to have been a lack of care in management of public funds.[63] In 1997 NAO offered evidence to NCIHE on its view of the responsibilities of governing bodies for securing value for money and stewardship of public funds.

The Audit Commission

3.49 FHEA also extended the powers of the Audit Commission for Local Authorities in England and Wales, at the request of a higher education Funding Council or the governing body of an institution in the higher education sector, to promote or undertake studies designed to improve economy, efficiency and effectiveness in the management or operations of the governing body (or at the request of the Council, to promote or undertake similar studies in respect of the operations of the Council itself). This includes advice to the Funding Council on directions to be given in respect of the preparation of financial statements by institutions. There is no similar power in Scotland, since higher education establishments have not been under local authority control.

---

61 Schedule 1 paragraph 16(3) FHEA; Schedule 7 paragraph 14(3) FHESA 1992.
62 Sir John Bourn, Comptroller and Auditor-General, addressing the Royal Society of Arts, 18 May 1993.
63 Eg NAO/SHEFC reports on Glasgow Caledonian University (1998).

Audit requirements of the Funding Councils

3.50   As required by the Education Departments, the Funding Councils have produced Codes of Audit Practice. The Code produced by SHEFC embodies the Funding Council's requirements in relation to the audit function, provides guidance on good practice for audit committees, external and internal audit and sets out the framework within which the different forms of audit should operate.[64] The Codes produced by the Funding Councils are very similar to the Codes of Local Government Audit Practice[65] produced by the local government audit commissions.

3.51   The Funding Councils have established their own audit services, eg HEFCE Audit Service and SHEFC Audit Branch (SHEFCAB) which is responsible for

> evaluating all control arrangements, financial or otherwise, of the Council and of institutions funded by the Council and giving assurance to SHEFC's Chief Executive and Audit Committee on those control arrangements.[66]

The word 'evaluating' is not defined but the context appears to take it beyond the dictionary definition of attaching numerical value to making judgments on efficiency and effectiveness. The Code of Audit Practice, issued under the Financial Memorandum, sets out how the Audit Branch will proceed. The Financial Memorandum grants SHEFCAB the right of access to institutions to undertake examination of financial and management controls. It has access to

> all ... records, information and assets and can require any officer to give any explanation which it considers necessary to fulfil its responsibilities.

The word 'officer' is not defined: it has different meanings in different institutions. It is not clear that individuals who might be the subject

---

64   The Code refers institutions to relevant publications of the Auditing Practices Committee, including *Auditing Standards and Guidelines* and *Guidance to Internal Auditors* and to HM Treasury's *Government Internal Handbook*. See also *Accounting Standards SAS 120* (1996).

65   Issued eg for England and Wales under section 14 Local Government Finance Act 1982.

66   SHEFC *Code of Audit Practice* 1993, paragraph 6.2.

of such enquiries have any legal duty to comply unless their contract of employment either expressly or by implication so provides.

3.52 SHEFCAB also
(i) receives a copy of the annual report produced by the Audit Committee which each institution is required to establish;
(ii) has access to all work of, and correspondence between, an institution's internal and external auditors and may meet with the external auditors if it wishes;
(iii) receives copies of the letters of appointment of external auditors, for which the Funding Council has prescribed a model;
(iv) receives copies of external auditors' Management Letters and correspondence relating to these;
(v) must be informed by the governing body of an institution if the external auditor resigns or is removed and be supplied with a copy of any statement made by the auditor.

Audit requirements of the Education Departments

3.53 The Education Departments are required to satisfy themselves that the Funding Councils have in place effective internal audit arrangements and in turn their own audit branches (eg the Scottish Office Audit Unit SOAU) will wish to ensure that the Departments have adequate controls in place for this purpose. These audit branches may themselves accompany the Funding Council auditors on visits to institutions, but will be concerned only with the performance of those auditors, not with auditing the activities of the institution. In Scotland, the Scottish Office Education and Industry Department has direct powers of inspection in respect of funds derived directly from the Department (eg Access Funds).

The Audit Committee

3.54 The governing body of each institution is required to follow common commercial practice by appointing an Audit Committee, with specified tasks and a degree of independence from other committees and management. Both internal and external auditors should have right of access to the Committee. The requirement to appoint a Committee of this kind is a direct intervention in the internal affairs of institutions, the domestic legislation of which leaves it entirely within the discretion of the main bodies whether or not to appoint any committees at all.

External audit

3.55 A typical statute[67] contains the following provisions:

1. The [governing body] shall appoint an Auditor or Auditors who shall hold office for such period, and on such remuneration, as may be determined by the [governing body].
2. Every such Auditor shall be a member of a body of accountants established in the United Kingdom and for the time being recognised for the purposes of [the Companies Acts] ... but no person shall be appointed as Auditor who is, or any member of whose firm is, a [member of the institution].
3. The Auditor or Auditors shall audit the annual statement of income and expenditure, the balance sheet and the other accounts of the [institution] and shall make a report to the [governing body] at least once in each year.
4. The Auditor or Auditors shall have the right of access at all reasonable times to the books, records, accounts and vouchers of the [institution] and shall be entitled to require from the staff of the [institution] such information and explanations as may be necessary for the performance of his, her or their duties.
   [The word 'reasonable' is omitted from the equivalent provision in the Funding Councils' model engagement letter presumably in an attempt to avoid dispute about rights of immediate access. By accepting the terms of the Code of Audit Practice, the governing body waives this qualification. The expression is intended to give authority to current auditing.][68]
5. If the office of Auditor or Auditors shall become vacant by his, her or their death or resignation or any other cause before the expiration of his, her or their period of office, the [governing body] shall forthwith appoint an Auditor or Auditors in his, her or their place for the remainder of such period.

Some university statutes use the word 'officers' which restricts the category of individuals to which the auditors have automatic access. The model letter of engagement has no restriction of this kind so that 'staff' is probably a more appropriate term. Under the corresponding local government provisions set out in section 16(1) Local Government Finance Act 1982 (and its predecessors) it was held that the rights of the auditor to access staff, documents, etc extends to contractors.[69]

---

67 This is an adapted version of the University of Stirling Statute 7 as amended in 1993.
68 C Cross and S Bailey *Cross on Local Government Law* (7th ed, 1986) p 127.
69 *Re Hurle-Hobbs* [1944] 2 All ER 261; *R v Hurle-Hobbs, ex p Simmons* [1945] KB 165.

3.56 Section 124B(4) ERA requires audit of the accounts by a person appointed by the corporation.[70] The equivalent provision in the governing instrument of a higher education corporation is simply:

> External auditors shall be appointed, and other audit work conducted, in accordance with any requirements of the [HEFCE][71]

and for a company registered under the Companies Acts:

> Auditors shall be appointed and their duties regulated in accordance with the Companies Act.[72]

3.57 The provisions for institutions not conducted by higher education corporations are extended by the Code of Audit Practice and amplified for the higher education corporations. The Code clarifies the role of the external auditors as being not only to report on the financial statements of the institution but also on the regularity of transactions in terms of the conditions attached by the Financial Memorandum (or otherwise) to the use of Funding Council grants and loans. A model letter of engagement is prescribed, which spells out the duties of the external auditors in much greater detail than the statute or equivalent provision in the instrument of government. External auditors are required to report significant irregularities, etc to the institution's designated (accounting) officer (normally the Principal, Vice-Chancellor or equivalent), to the Chairman of the Governing Body, the Chairman of the Audit Committee and the Chief Executive of the Funding Council.[73] External auditors must be re-appointed formally each year and their performance assessed by the Audit Committee. A competitive selection process is to be held at least every five years.

3.58 One innovation in the Code is the requirement that auditors may be removed by the governing body at any time, without compensation, if there are 'serious shortcomings' in their work. If removed in this way, or if resigning, external auditors are entitled to make representations direct to the governing body, make a written

70 Section 124B(4) was introduced by section 71 FHEA and replaced paragraph 18(2) of Schedule 7 ERA.
71 Article 13.4 of the Articles of Government of the Middlesex Polytechnic HEC (now the University of Middlesex), amended by substituting HEFCE for PCFC.
72 Article 60 of the Articles of Association of the University of Greenwich.
73 The designated officer is instructed to report significant irregularities, etc, discovered otherwise than by the external auditors to the Chairman of the governing body, the Chairman of the Audit Committee and the Chief Executive of the Funding Council.

statement which must be copied by the governing body to the Funding Council and may requisition a special meeting of the governing body to consider the statement. The latter power is one which not even the members of the governing body have, otherwise than by standing order, and reflects the new emphasis on the governing body being fully informed about the financial performance and management of the institution. Institutions appear to have consented almost by default to this fundamental variation in their common law or statutory powers to regulate the conduct of business.

3.59   As the Codes of Audit Practice closely resemble those produced for local government, we may have regard to general statements in relation to local government auditors made over time by the courts. Lord Denning MR, in *Asher v Secretary of State for the Environment*,[74] referring to the role of the district auditor, a post now superseded in local government by auditor employed by the Audit Commission, said

> In some respects [the external auditor] is like a company auditor. He is a watchdog to see that the accounts are properly kept and that no-one is making off with the funds. He is not bound to be of a suspicious turn of mind[75] but if anything suspicious does turn up, it is his duty to take care to follow it up.[76]

In *West Wiltshire District Council v Garland*[77] the Court of Appeal held that district auditors employed by the Audit Commission to audit the accounts of local authorities owed both a statutory duty and, relevant here, a common law duty of care to local authorities, breach of which gave rise to a right to bring an action in negligence. The House of Lords had established in *Henderson v Merrett Syndicates*[78] that there might legitimately be coexistent remedies for negligence in contract and tort. It was equally true that there might be coexistent remedies for negligence in breach of a statutory duty and in tort.

---

74 [1974] Ch 208, 219.
75 *Re Kingston Cotton Mill Co (No 2)* [1896] 2 Ch 279.
76 *Re Thomas Gerrard & Son Ltd* [1968] Ch 455.
77 [1995] Ch 297, CA.
78 [1995] 2 AC 145.

Internal audit

3.60 A further direct intervention in the internal affairs of institutions is the Funding Council requirement of internal audit, which first appeared in the Financial Memorandum issued by the sectoral Funding Councils established under ERA. Institutions are now required, at their own expense, to establish an 'internal audit function' either on their own or in consortia, with the objective of ensuring that they have sound systems of financial and other management controls. Although the Funding Councils suggest that the internal audit function should cover all financial activities, the only areas in which they can insist on the function being operated are those in which grants or loans made by them are being applied. The Code of Audit Practice makes it clear that the effective performance of the internal audit function is to be evaluated (audited) by the external auditor.

3.61 Like the external auditors, the internal auditors have right of access to the institution's accounting officer and the governing body and unlimited access to all staff and property of the institution. The Code of Audit Practice suggests mechanisms by which 'auditees' (sic) should receive reports and be required to respond to them and means by which effective liaison should be maintained between the internal, external and Funding Council auditors.

The European Union

3.62 Both the Commission and the Court of Auditors of the European Union have access at all reasonable times to all books, documents, papers and records kept by institutions relating to costs incurred in performing contracts let by the Union. This entitlement continues for up to two years after the termination or completion of the contract.[79] The terms of the contract are discussed further supra.

Academic audit and assessment of teaching quality

3.63 The earliest reference in law reports to the concept of 'quality' in higher education appears to be contained in the opinion in 1890 of Lord Kyllachy in *Cadells v Balfour*[80] where two medical students

---

79 Model Contract for Research and Development, September 1995.
80 (1890) 17 R 1138, 1149.

were involved in a dispute over the syllabus of a course. In his Lordship's view students were 'entitled ... to express their dissatisfaction' with the arrangements for tuition.[81] No doubt that was also a feature of the intervening years, but the Robbins Report of 1963 laid stress on the maintenance of standards as an essential part of the fabric of higher education;[82] its emphases on 'achievement and quality' and 'high excellence' have recently been viewed with renewed interest. The terms of reference of NCIHE in 1996/97 stated that 'standards of degrees and other higher education qualifications should be at least maintained, and assured.'[83] As a result of continuing concern about quality in the provision of higher education, pre-1992 universities had collectively established the CVCP Academic Audit Unit (AAU), one function of which was

> to consider and review universities' mechanisms for monitoring and promoting the academic standards which are necessary for achieving their stated aims and objectives.[84]

3.64 The Conservative government's White Paper on Higher Education of May 1991[85] and the subsequent Further and Higher Education Acts led to the formation of two entirely separate organisational structures with different functions. The Higher Education Quality Council (HEQC) established and funded by the institutions themselves covered the whole of higher education with similar terms of reference to those of the former CVCP Unit (ie concerned with mechanisms) and the quality assessment units responsible to and funded by the Funding Councils carried out the statutory duties imposed on the Councils under the Acts in England, Scotland and Wales (ie concerned with quality of provision).[86] It was suggested on a number of occasions since 1992 that the functions should be combined under one authority, and this was effected in 1997 by the establishment of the Quality Assurance Agency for Higher Education (QAA) which NCIHE envisaged would have a key role in producing clear 'threshold' standards for degrees, a national

81 These students were supervised by Dr Jex-Blake of the 'women into medicine' campaign.
82 Committee on Higher Education (Chairman Lord Robbins) *Higher Education* Cmnd 2154 paragraph 40.
83 See Chapter 10, Main Report, NCIHE, July 1997.
84 CVCP, 1990. The concept of Total Quality Care is discussed by R Barnett in *Improving Higher Education* SRHE (1992).
85 Cm 1541.
86 HEFCE also carried out the quality assessment function in Northern Ireland by arrangement with the Northern Ireland authorities: this arrangement is now taken over by QAA.

system of external examiners and codes of practice in every institution.[87]

The Quality Assurance Agency for Higher Education (QAA) – quality audit

3.65 The Secretary of State has power under section 82(2) FHEA to direct any two or more of the Funding Councils (including SHEFC) to make joint provision for

> the assessment by a person appointed by them of matters relating to the arrangements made by each institution in Great Britain which is within the higher education sector for maintaining academic standards in the institution.

This power is held in reserve in case the institutions themselves are jointly unable to carry out this function[88] but in fact the representative bodies of the institutions established the HEQC as a non-statutory body for this purpose, subsuming the work of the former Academic Audit Unit established by the CVCP. QAA is expected to review and report on the mechanisms and structures which individual institutions of higher education have in place to assure themselves of the quality of their own educational provision. HEQC carried out that function by undertaking a cycle of visits to institutions, using panels of senior staff seconded for this purpose and producing a report which was published and QAA established a series of 'continuation audits' as the first cycle ended. The CCI Charters require institutions to make available details of the last such visit and arrangements for access to the report. HEQC produced a number of papers to assist the process of audit.[89]

3.66 Basic quality controls are built into the teaching and learning process typically through requirements for the appointment of external examiners and for the approval of courses, syllabi, examination arrangements and the award of qualifications to be the ultimate responsibility of the senior academic body – the Senate or its equivalent, which in many institutions is subject to the control of the governing body. Normally these provisions for quality control may not be changed without the approval of the Privy Council. There

87 Recommendations 23–25, Main Report, NCIHE, July 1997.
88 House of Lords *Official Report* Vol 534, col 715.
89 Eg *Improving Institutional Capacity for Self-Regulation* (1996); *Guidelines on Quality Assurance* (1996).

is no direct relation between these provisions and the typical charter object which provides that the institution may act as it thinks fit; realistically of course it must temper its discretion with the need to ensure that its qualifications are recognised externally.

3.67 'Fitness for purpose,' the commonly accepted definition of quality, implies a comparison with the needs of the user, the 'purpose' for which the product or process is designed. Richard Freeman[90] defines quality as a characteristic that a product or service has in more or less quantity. If we take quality as 'fitness for purpose' then quality is the end that we are trying to achieve. The issues it raises are about how to identify, define and measure this end. Measurement in particular is difficult in education. The 1991 White Paper on Higher Education defined quality audit as '... a means of checking that relevant systems and structures within an institution support its key teaching mission ...' although it is unclear from what source the government deduced that universities have a 'key teaching mission.'

3.68 Quality measurement does not have to be norm-referenced and accountability to students is just one aspect of the quality debate. Academics must also be accountable to their subject (the knowledge, skills and attitudes which comprise each subject must not be distorted, suppressed or misused) and to their professional colleagues that the integrity of their discipline is upheld and that students develop positive, if critical, attitudes towards the subject and its use in society.

QAA – quality assessment

3.69 The statutory requirement for quality assessment was new in FHEA and FHESA[91] and implemented the policy on quality assurance in the White Paper *Higher Education*. The White Paper identified two ways in which the quality assessment element of quality assurance could be developed: the identification of relevant performance indicators including measures of added value[92] and direct observation of practice by external review. Under the Acts the Funding Councils are required to secure that provision is made for assessing the quality of education provided in institutions for whose activities they provide,

90 R Freeman *Quality Assurance in Learning Materials Production: Open Learning* (1991) 24.
91 Section 70 FHEA; section 39 FHESA.
92 In the House of Lords the Paymaster-General said 'Higher education institutions educate students, and it is right that performance indicators should include data showing how well they do it.' House of Lords *Official Report* Vol 535 col 678.

or are considering providing, financial support. The Councils are not required to conduct the assessments themselves but each is required to establish a Quality Assessment Committee (QAC) to give them advice on the discharge of this duty and with such other functions as the Council may confer.[93] The independence of the committee is secured by the requirement that the majority of its members must not be members of the Council and its competence by the requirement that members must have experience of, and have shown capacity in, the provision of higher education. So that those involved are reasonably acceptable to their peers, the Council must have regard to the desirability of such persons being actively involved in higher education or carrying responsibility for it. SHEFC is required to have regard to provision in England and Wales: 'having regard to' in this context does not imply rigid conformity but, as in the duty imposed on the Secretary of State to have regard to certain matters when appointing the members of the Councils, it is an 'obligation on a person under a duty not to overlook the matter.'[94]

3.70 The assessment process prior to the establishment of QAA was not carried out by the Committees but by panels of academics and others, for example HM Inspectors with experience in further and higher education. The initial steps taken in 1993 to implement the quality assessment process were not universally welcomed: legal action was threatened on the grounds of unfairness, the use of dubious statistics and the inexperience of inspectors.[95] No action of this kind had actually been taken by the end of 1997, although some of the language used in the reports is highly critical. NCIHE called upon QAA to develop a fair and robust system for dealing with complaints relating to educational funding, with Funding Councils enabled to withdraw funding if a complaint is upheld and appropriate remedial action is not forthcoming.[96]

3.71 As an operational definition of what is meant by quality in higher education, a typical Quality Framework has 11 aspects: aims and curricula; curriculum design and review; teaching and learning environment; staff resources; learning resources; course organisation; teaching and learning practice; student support; assessment and monitoring; students' work; output, outcomes and quality control.[97]

93 There is no restriction on the functions which may be conferred on a QAC but presumably it is intended that these will be related to quality assurance.
94 First Scottish Standing Committee *Official Report* 10 December 1991 col 57.
95 Report in *The Higher* 4 June 1993.
96 Paragraph 84, Main Report, NCIHE, July 1997.
97 SHEFC (1993).

Legal entitlement to quality of provision

3.72   The issue of the extent to which students are legally entitled to 'quality' in teaching or supervision is a difficult one, since it depends upon the ability of the law to recognise objectively some measurement of quality either through application of common law principles or using the measurements which are arrived at by the statutory process. Clearly, many institutions hold themselves out as offering a 'quality' product – indeed, in a highly competitive market it would be the height of folly not to do so. The courts, however, would wish to go behind the sales 'puff' and examine to what extent institutions are legally bound to provide a quality service and how this can be measured.

Commitment to quality in governing instruments

3.73   It is difficult to find a contractual commitment to quality in the charter or instrument of government of a typical modern institution. In fact, while 'attainment of expressed goals' is undoubtedly one general measure of the effectiveness of an institution,[98] institutions are not required by the operation of law to have the 'stated aims and objectives' which the CVCP Academic Audit Unit assumed, other than those laid down in their charters or other instruments of government. There has of late been a variety of statements of aims, 'mission statements' and statements of intent produced as part of an institution's public relations strategy or accompanying planning statements made to the Funding Council.

3.74   A typical 1960s charter defines the relevant object of the University as being:

> to provide instruction in such branches of learning as the University may think fit, ... and to make provision for research and for the preservation, advancement and dissemination of knowledge in such manner as the University may determine[99]

whereas the 1997 mission statement includes the objective '[to] undertake high quality teaching whilst researching at the highest level'[100] and the more detailed objectives include 'to enhance the

---

98   D M Yorke *Indicators of Institutional Achievements: Some Theoretical and Empirical Considerations: Higher Education* 16-1 (1987).
99   University of Stirling Charter (1967).
100 *Strategic Plan 1993–98*: University of Stirling (1993).

quality and effectiveness of teaching and learning' and '... to position itself in the top quartile of UK institutions for research as a centre of excellence in both research and teaching.' The last statement is the only quantitative, objectively measurable aim assuming that there is a nationally-agreed way of placing institutions in league tables; 'high quality' and 'enhanced quality' are relative terms; the latter in particular begs the question of the quality present prior to the enhancement. There is a difference between 'instruction' in the charter and 'teaching and learning' in the objectives: teaching is, it is argued by Martin Trow[101] 'not an action but a transaction; not an outcome but a process; not a performance, but an emotional and intellectual connection between teacher and learner.'

3.75 Martin Trow also discusses the process of 'deprofessionalization under way as a natural and inevitable consequence of the withdrawal of trust by government in the universities and their guilds of academics,' giving as an example the assessment of teaching by the Funding Councils. The central criterion, according to one senior official in a Funding Council was

> whether the teacher 'delivers the course the customer (ie the student) expected to get.' In this conception of the academic's role, the teacher produces a product which the customer buys, and expects to get what he paid for ... there is no provision in this conception of 'teaching to expectations' for the possibility that the teacher does not want to meet the students' expectations, but wants rather to modify these expectations, and more broadly, to modify (and enlarge) the student's mind, character and sensibility.[102]

Practical guides to the meaning of quality

3.76 A useful practical guide to what we think we mean by quality in post-compulsory education, although not specifically higher education, is the Jordanhill College publication *The Quality of Learning and Teaching Handbook*.[103] This proposed a set of Quality Statements (QS): in the context of the student's expectations of the institution and the course (the 'purpose'), those most relevant are

101 *Managerialism and the Academic Profession: The Case of England* Paper presented to a conference on 'The Quality Debate' sponsored by *The Higher* September 1993, p 10.
102 Trow, ibid p 15.
103 Curriculum Advice and Support Team (CAST) Jordanhill College, Glasgow 1990.

QS2: The overall content of each individual programme is suited to its aims and purposes;

QS3: Programme content is accurate and up-to-date in its treatment of employment practice and new technology;

QS4: Potential clients receive clear, accurate and comprehensive information about programmes on offer and have the opportunity to clarify their goals in order that students enrol on a suitable programme;

QS9: Students have access to sources of information, advice and support which assist them to meet their learning needs, cope with difficulties, and progress satisfactorily from a programme;

QS13: There is a climate of purposefulness and rapport, and a concern for individual student achievement;

QS14: The learning resources and environment are well planned and organised with regard to the accomplishment of learning outcomes;

QS15: Learning and teaching methods are appropriate to learning outcomes, emphasise student activity and responsibility, and are varied;

QS16: Assessment approaches cover all the learning outcomes and performance criteria and are applied to the work of all students;

QS17: The standards, as set out in descriptors, are correctly applied and systematically moderated.

3.77 None of these statements appears to be incorporated into any institution's charter or instrument of government, although the articles of association of the higher education corporations normally contain a clause requiring the governing body to establish procedures to ensure that students can raise matters of concern at all levels[104] and the 1993 Higher Education Charters include reference to such procedures.

3.78 The word 'standards' was defined by the CVCP Academic Audit Unit as:

[describing] the levels students are expected to reach in each course and ... defined by the university in consultation with others. External examiners are used to make sure that standards are even across higher education. It is possible to have high standards but low quality.

In *Freedoms, Rights and Accountability*[105] Donald Bligh refers to students being offered a certificate or formal award if their academic

104 See eg Article 12.2 of the Articles of Association of The Manchester Metropolitan University.
105 In D A Bligh (ed) *Accountability and Freedom for Teachers* (1982).

performance is of a certain (usually unspecified) standard. Of course, the institution does not guarantee that a student enrolled on a particular programme will complete it successfully. Admission implies that, on the evidence available at the time, the student is considered capable of doing the work of the course and is likely to complete it successfully. It is arguably the responsibility of the institution to let the student know if subsequently there is reason to believe that he or she will not be successful so that appropriate action can be taken. There is also an implicit promise to teach effectively but there are important questions about the criteria of effective teaching and what standard of teaching a court would hold it reasonable to expect in order to discharge the institution's obligations.

3.79 In 1970, the NUS/NCCL Report *Academic Freedom and the Law*[106] concluded that students might wish to criticise the teaching of a member of staff with regard to
(i)   the clarity and coherence of his [sic] exposition;
(ii) the relevance of what he teaches to the published syllabus;
(iii) his factual accuracy;
(iv) his interpretation of the subject.
The standards expected by today's students (of both male and female teachers!) are arguably higher, with the emphasis today more on the learning process as a whole than on teaching alone. This is so particularly when students are paying economic or quasi-economic fees as is the case with overseas students, who may also have cultural reasons for high expectations of their own performance or at least of rewards for it. The course and their performance on it are of paramount importance to many students, although there may be some who view the name of the university or college from which they will graduate as more significant, as has been suggested is the experience in the United States.[107]

3.80 In some cases there is in addition a contractual commitment to a third party, for example a governmental agency or an industrial sponsor, which expects that the course contracted for will be provided to professional standards. This could be extended by analogy to the authorities which pay students' fees (local education authorities in England and Wales, the Scottish Office Education Department and

106 *Academic Freedom* in *Academic Freedom and the Law* NUS/NCCL Commission on Academic Freedom and the Law 1970, chapter 2.
107 M Trow *Higher Education and the Comparative Study of Unique Traditions* Anglo-American Conference on 'Access and Quality in Higher Education' New Jersey (1987), referred to in S Franke-Wikberg 'Evaluating Educational Quality on the Institutional Level' in Higher Education Management (1990) 271.

the Northern Ireland Education and Library Boards). Renewal of such awards is normally dependent on the institution certifying that the student remains in good academic standing but the funding bodies have no direct input into quality assurance of the courses which they are partially funding. Ultimately, all such funds are derived from the relevant Education Department, which does of course have an input through the Funding Council. The real test, of course, comes when students have to pay the fees themselves.

3.81 In *A Bill of Rights for Students* Brad Imrie[108] describes certain 'rights' identified by a Students' Representative Council as a useful starting point for their work in representing students on formal staff/ student committees. These include:
(1) equality of opportunity and equity of educational experience;
(2) professional standards of capability from teaching staff;
(3) sufficient information to make informed choices about course options;
(4) coursework that provides opportunity for practice and prompt feedback to improve subsequent performance;
(5) knowledge of what is required for assessment of performance and how to succeed;
(6) a grading system which is consistent, fair and clearly explained;
(7) knowledge of the processes and assumptions that are involved when judgments are made about performance.
These are similar in concept to the Jordanhill Quality Statements and could form the basis of a definition of quality in contractual terms. Most of them can be achieved by administrative means.

The charters for higher education

3.82 The *Citizen's Charter Initiative – Raising the Standard* (CCI) was launched by the then Prime Minister in July 1991[109] and survived the change of government in 1997. CCI is 'about giving more power to the citizen...[it is] not a recipe for more state action...[it is] a testament of our belief in people's right to be informed and choose for themselves...[it] sets out the mechanism for improving choice, equality, value and accountability.' It is conceded that not all these apply to every public service but there is a common objective: 'To

108 B W Imrie *Papers of the SCED National Conference 'Putting Students First: improving the experience of higher education'* Standing Conference on Educational Development (SCED) May 1990.
109 Cm 1599, 22 July 1991.

raise the standard of public services, up to and beyond the best at present available.' The main CCI themes are

Quality: a sustained new programme for improving the quality of public services;

Choice: choice, wherever possible between competing providers, is the best spur to quality improvement;

Standards: the citizen must be told what service standards are and be able to act where service is unacceptable;

Value: the citizen is a taxpayer; public services must give value for money within a tax bill the nation can afford.

3.83 The principal charters in higher education issued in the autumn of 1993 were
* the Charter for Higher Education ('Higher quality and choice') published by the Department for Education and covering higher education in England
* the Further and Higher Education Charter for Scotland ('Raising the standard') published by the Scottish Office Education Department and covering further and higher education in Scotland.

There is also a Charter for Further Education in England and Charters covering Wales and Northern Ireland.

3.84 The author of the Student Charter Project Report commissioned by the Department of Employment under the EIHE initiative[110] defined a charter as

a statement of rights, or rights and responsibilities, between an institution and a group of students: an 'agreed statement' or one imposed by Government or by institutions.

He distinguished this from a contract, an agreement between an individual student and the institution and which is intended to be legally binding. Nevertheless, the two are linked. 'Agreed statement' charters are not new and predate CCI. The Student Charter Project Report gives examples and traces the idea at least to the 1940s. A major contribution was made by the NUS/NCCL Report *Academic Freedom and the Law* published in 1970 when student unrest and

110 B Davey, The Student Charter Project Report, University of Kent (1992).

dissatisfaction with the education system had peaked.[111] In some cases
the terms of a public service charter issued under the initiative have
become incorporated into the express terms of contracts – for example
those concerned with standards of service in the privatised utilities
and transport undertakings, where compensation is offered if set
objectives are not achieved.

3.85   The first relatively modern statement of the 'rights' of students
dates from 1940[112] followed later by a concordat in 1968 between
CVCP and the National Union of Students, but education charters
as such first appeared in the Conservative Party manifesto for the
October 1974 general election. Although those proposals related to
secondary education – a Parents' Charter – the themes were similar
to those of the 1993 CCI higher education charters: quality of
information to enable informed choice to be exercised, prospectuses
to contain material about institutional performance, rights of appeal.
Bryan Davey's report shows that in 1992, across the whole higher
education sector, just over half of institutions were either not
interested in or were opposed to the introduction of a student charter,
with former polytechnics and the colleges of higher education being
more pro-charter than the traditional universities, reflecting perhaps
the former public sector's greater familiarity with external monitoring
and evaluation of quality. This statistic did not stop government
departments from issuing charters in September 1993.[113] Although
revisions were mooted at various times, by the end of 1997 the
charters issued in 1993 remained unchanged.

3.86   The two principal charters are not 'student charters' as such
but cover a range of relationships which institutions have with the
public at large: potential students and their parents, registered
students, employers, sponsors of research or consultancy and the
public who use institutional facilities such as the Library, sports,
cultural and recreational facilities. However, they are directed
primarily at students as the major users of higher education services.
They have a similar approach to quality issues, although they treat
the relationship which gives rise to such questions in very different
ways. The English Charter describes the relationship between
institutions and their students as one of provision of services to

111 D Christie 'The Legal Basis of Student Tenure at Colleges and Universities' in
     Academic Freedom and the Law NUS/NCCL (1970).
112 British Students' Congress Leeds.
113 See D J Farrington *The Higher Education Charters: Implications for Universities
     and their Staff* (1994) CVCP/Universities and Colleges Staff Development Agency.

customers, with the focus on meeting customers' legitimate needs. If that is so, failure to provide the 'high standards' required by the charter may have implications in law.[114] Reasonably professional standards are probably already implied terms of the contract, as the discussion of quality has shown, so the issue is one of degree.

3.87   The term 'customers' also extends to employers of graduates, sponsors of research and consultancy and members of the public wishing to use institutional facilities. The Charter promotes high standards of service in all areas, including teaching, guidance, counselling and research supervision, as does the Scottish Charter which however avoids the institution-customer terminology, preferring the word 'user' to 'customer' and describing the 'complex' institution-student relationship in terms of a partnership between 'teachers'[115] and students.

3.88   A number of institutions have issued their own charters, codes of practice or expressions of intent as to the standard of service which they will offer. Whether or not these have any legal effect will depend upon the extent to which they are expressly or by implication terms of any contract between the student and the institution. Bryan Davey quotes one (unidentified) university charter as stating the responsibilities of students inter alia 'to arrive punctually at lessons' and '[to prepare] themselves appropriately for their learning as their course progresses.' An example from the further education sector states that students should 'refrain from dropping litter.'[116] The possibility of confusion between what are expected to be legally binding rights and obligations and expressions of intent is obvious. Bryan Davey's research discovered fear of litigation if charters were expressed in mandatory or directory language so that some institutional charters or codes of practice which predated the CCI charters had been 'watered-down' in effect.

3.89   It is perhaps easier to compare the impact of the Charters with that of the statutory Codes of Practice issued by the Advisory Conciliation and Arbitration Service, the Equal Opportunities Commissions and the Commission for Racial Equality. Although these have no specific legal force, they are examples of good practice

114   See J W Parlour 'Student Charters in Higher Education' (1996) 8(3) Education and the Law 229.
115   The use of the word 'teacher' in a higher education context is obviously wrong and reflects the fact that until 1993 the SOED had no major role in this area.
116   Probably now an offence under section 86 et seq Environmental Protection Act 1990.

which courts and tribunals (and no doubt the Visitor) will take into account when determining the reasonableness of employers' and others' behaviour in certain circumstances.

Exercise of professional duty

3.90   However the Charters describe it, the relationship between institutions and their students is one in which issues of quality are of fundamental importance. The leading cases in this area are not particularly helpful in determining questions of quality. As the discussion of the student-institution relationship will show, some students have raised questions about the content of the course which they might have expected to receive from a study of the prospectus. In *D'Mello v Loughborough College of Technology*[117] there is specific reference in the report to there being no breach of the college's duty to exercise professional skill and judgment. A student based overseas had joined a postgraduate course on the basis of information contained in the prospectus. The court, hearing the case some years after the event, held that although the college was bound to provide a course according to the syllabus set out in the prospectus, it was free to determine how to teach it and there could be no complaint even if the emphasis differed from the expectations of the student. The course was, according to the report, being given for the first time and it 'had some teething troubles,' although O'Connor J held that there was 'no breach of the duty the college owed to Mr D'Mello to exercise professional skill and judgment in conducting the course.' The distinction has to be drawn between the course itself and the way in which it is delivered. In cases arising in the United States, departmental and college programmes have been held to be a contractual inducement to enrol: where students can be said to have reasonably relied upon these contractual terms in undertaking a field of study, students may sue to enforce specific compliance with the proposed programme or seek an award of monetary damages for their reliance on the contract. In other situations, students given inaccurate or improper advice about degree and programme requirements, in either oral or written form, have sued for award of the degree or for modifications to the programme consistent with the alleged contractual obligation.[118]

---

117   (1970) Times, 17 June.
118   See *Behrend v State* 379 NE 2d 617 (1977) (Ohio Ct App); *Olsson v Board of Higher Education* 426 NYS 2d 249 (1980); *Craft v Board of Trustees of the University of Illinois* 516 Fed Supp 1317 (1981).

3.91 However no decisions have turned precisely on questions of professional competence of staff engaged to teach a particular course and where the issue has been raised, as in *Wong v University of Toronto*,[119] the court has held that there is no generalised wrong of 'educational malpractice' other than as associated with a specific breach of contract. Attempts to create a generalised tort have also been rejected in the United States, in such cases as *Ross v Creighton University*,[120] *Moore v Vanderloo*,[121] *Donohue v Copiague Union Free School District*[122] and *Finstand v Washburn University of Topeka*.[123] In *Moore* the court gave four reasons for rejecting the claim: there is no satisfactory standard of care by which to measure an educator's conduct; the cause of the student's failure to learn is inherently uncertain, as is the nature of damages; permitting such claims would flood the courts with litigation and would thus place a substantial burden on educational institutions; the courts are not equipped to oversee the day-to-day operations of educational institutions. In itself this seems to supply an answer to the question raised by Kirby J in 1994:[124] why should 'teachers' like other professionals, not be found liable for failure to reach a proper and satisfactory professional standard in the intellectual care of a student? As His Lordship accepted, the dearth of cases reflects difficulties for litigants in establishing, in particular, causation which is a fundamental requirement of a successful suit in negligence. It is obviously easier to establish this in a non-teaching context as for example in *Phelps v Hillingdon London Borough Council*[125] where an educational psychology service failed to diagnose dyslexia. In secondary education, in *X(Minors) v Bedfordshire County Council*[126] Lord Browne-Wilkinson said:

> In my judgment a school which accepts a pupil assumes responsibility not only for his physical well-being but also for his educational needs. The education of a pupil is the very purpose for which a child goes to school. The head teacher, being responsible for the school, himself comes under a duty of care to exercise the reasonable skills of a headmaster in relation to such educational needs.

119 (1989) 79 DLR (4th) 652.
120 740 F Supp 1319 (1990) (ND Ill).
121 386 NW2d 108 (1986) (Iowa).
122 391 NE2d (1979) 1352.
123 845 P2d 685 (1993) (Supreme Court of Kansas).
124 Keynote address to 3rd Annual Conference of the Australia and New Zealand Educational Law Association.
125 [1997] 3 FCR 621.
126 [1995] 2 AC 633, 766.

3.92 Further, while the decision in *Kantor v Schmidt*[127] where the University of New York at Stony Brook failed to inform students periodically of their progress and remaining academic obligations, was based on the interpretation of a code, Mark Davies[128] has argued that any university which did not have sufficient feedback during the academic year to allow a student to best prepare for assessment would fail to satisfy either a tortious duty of care or an implied contractual obligation to deliver its education service with reasonable skill and care.

Reasonable skill and care

3.93 If there is no generic tort of educational malpractice, and we rely on an implied term of the contract that reasonable skill and care must be taken to provide the necessary facilities, we must turn to *The Moorcock*[129] doctrine for guidance as to whether such a term can indeed be implied. Put simply, it is that one cannot imply a term purely because it is reasonable to do so but only when it is necessary to give 'business efficacy' to the contract. Examples of the application of the *Moorcock* principles in areas concerned with the standard of care and skill required of professionals are in medicine,[130] dentistry,[131] carpet-laying,[132] car repairs,[133] hair dyeing,[134] building,[135] carpet cleaning[136] and house removal.[137] Further examples are cited by Mark Davies. It seems evident that it must be an implied term of the contract between a higher education institution and its students that it will employ a team of reasonably competent professionals, including academic staff to teach its courses and supervise them. That is probably the extent of the institution's responsibility: applying the

---

127 73 AD 2d 670 (1979); 423 NYS 2d 208.
128 M Davies 'Universities, academics and professional negligence' (1996) 12(4) Professional Negligence 102.
129 (1888) 13 PD 157; affd (1889) 14 PD 64, CA: see also *McWhirter v Longmuir* 1948 SC 577, 589 per Lord Jamieson, concerned with a written contract.
130 *Eyre v Measday* [1986] 1 All ER 488, CA (a failed vasectomy).
131 *Samuels v Davis* [1943] KB 526, expressly approved in *Independent Broadcasting Authority v EMI Electronics and BICC Construction* (1980) 14 BLR 1, HL.
132 *Kimber v William Willett Ltd* [1947] 1 All ER 361.
133 *Stewart v Reavell's Garage* [1952] 2 QB 545.
134 *Ingham v Emes* [1955] 2 QB 366.
135 *Gloucester County Council v Richardson (t/a W J Richardson & Son)* [1969] 1 AC 480.
136 *Levison v Patent Steam Carpet Cleaning Co Ltd* [1978] QB 69, CA.
137 *Lally and Weller v George Bird (a firm)* (23 May 1980, unreported), QBD.

'horse to water' principle, one of the reasons given in *Moore v Vanderloo* for rejecting the claim in tort, ie what is actually learned cannot be measured in the same way as the outcome of a faulty operation, car repair or hair colouring. However, this has never explicitly been questioned or decided: it would presumably be more appropriate to make such a duty an express rather than an implied term of the contract.

3.94 In the UK there might, in addition to action in tort or contract at common law, be the possibility of action under section 13 Supply of Goods and Services Act 1982. Section 12(4) of the Act allows the Secretary of State to make an order that sections 13–15 shall not apply to services of a description specified in that order. Among services that have been excluded are arbitrators[138] and advocates.[139] However, no order has been made to exclude services which might be provided by institutions of higher education.

Distinctions between professionals and others

3.95 Du Parcq LJ in *Carr v IRC*[140] considered that occupational groups which constituted professions were those so defined by the ordinary reasonable man. In the context of higher education that must include at least academic staff. The respective roles in the public service of professionals responsible for delivering particular services and managers having more general responsibilities were considered by Christopher Pollitt[141] who suggested that an effective quality assurance system must reconcile as closely as possible the potentially conflicting demands of public accountability and professional autonomy, the managers' role being limited to requiring professionals to develop and maintain a quality assurance system operating within a common framework. Professionals should be responsible for designing the detail, running the system and implementing changes called for by the quality assurance process, which should itself involve not simply minimum quality assurances within a given institution, but also comparative quality judgments across sets of institutions. Pollitt emphasised the importance of appropriate and widescale training, for both managers and professionals, if quality is not to fall 'between the stools of financial management on the one hand and

138 SI 1985/1.
139 SI 1982/1771.
140 [1944] 2 All ER 163.
141 C Pollitt *Doing Business in the Temple? Managers and Quality Assurance in the Public Sector: Public Administration* 68(4) (1990) pp 435–52.

staff appraisal on the other' to the detriment of the service users. Public accountability seems to be less important than professional development in current efforts, which also ignore user-participation in the design and operation of quality assurance systems. Public accountability and participation in quality assurance are common in the established systems found in the United States.

3.96 The individual member of academic staff who is the professional in Pollitt's terminology is obliged to practise his/her profession using a fair and reasonable standard of competence. This obligation stems from a number of nineteenth century cases concerned with the practice of the medical profession.[142] The headnote to *Harmer v Cornelius*[143], taken from the words of Willes J, spells out the doctrine thus:

> The public profession of an art is a representation and undertaking to all the world that the professor possesses the requisite skill and ability. – When a skilled labourer, artisan or artist is employed, there is on his part an implied warranty that he is of skill reasonably competent to the task he undertakes.

and in *Lanphier v Phipos* it reads, in part, taken from the words of Tindal CJ:

> Every person who enters into a learned profession undertakes to bring to the exercise of it a reasonable degree of care and skill... he undertakes to bring a fair, reasonable and competent degree of skill...

3.97 NCIHE recommended the establishment of arrangements in higher education to secure academic teaching as a profession in its own right.[144] Of course, academic staff do not just 'teach' students; they are also involved in professional guidance and counselling. The risk of liability in tort for inadequate professional skill can be reduced by adequate training, in particular knowing when to refer a student for specialist advice. Where organisations like higher education institutions are engaged in deploying various professional skills it has been suggested that they should be 'judged by the standard of skill and care appropriate to the professional staff who ought to have been undertaking the work in question' in terms of professional

142 *Lanphier v Phipos* (1838) 8 C & P 475; *Harmer v Cornelius* (1858) 5 CBNS 236; *Rich v Pierpoint* (1862) 3 F & F 35; see also *Bolam v Friern Hospital Management Committee* [1957] 2 All ER 118.
143 (1858) 5 CBNS 236.
144 Recommendation 14, Main Report, NCIHE, July 1997.

competence.[145] Where academic staff undertake work which lies within the boundaries of another profession, then their performance should be judged not against the standards of their own profession (as academics) but against the standards of skill and care appropriate to the other profession (eg careers adviser, accredited student counsellor). Similarly administrative staff giving 'academic' advice would be judged by the standard of skill and care appropriate to academic staff. This is in accordance with the common law approach of measuring the duty of care in relation to the standard appropriate to the profession.[146]

'Academic judgment'

3.98   One problem facing any student complaining of lack of quality is the consistent line of Visitors' and court rulings that the professional academic judgment of examiners will not be impugned. For example, the Visitor's refusal to get involved in these matters was upheld in the House of Lords in 1989 in Janaki Vijayatunga's case:[147]

> If the Visitor declines to interfere with [the examiners'] decisions on matters which depend on scientific or other technical judgment then it seems to me quite impossible to say that he has committed any error of law, unless the decisions in question are so plainly irrational or fraught with bias, or some other obvious irregularity that they clearly cannot stand.

In such a case in Canada, the court in *Doane v Mount St Vincent University*[148] held that where the requirements of a university course were adequately conveyed to a student, and the student failed to achieve a passing mark in the course, it would not intervene unless the student could show fraud, malice or bad faith on the part of the university or a denial of natural justice. This would seem to be an extraordinarily difficult barrier for the aggrieved student to surmount.

---

145   R M Jackson and J L Powell *Professional Negligence* (1992) p 42.
146   *Caparo Industries plc v Dickinson* [1990] AC 605.
147   [1987] 3 All ER 204 at 213; affd sub nom *R v HM the Queen in Council, ex p Vijayatunga* [1990] 2 QB 444, [1989] 2 All ER 843, CA: see also *Saleh v University of Dundee* (1992) Times, 23 December, Ct of Sess (OH) unreported where the court would not interfere with a decision of the University Senate, acting in accordance with procedure over the appointment of external examiners for Ahmed Saleh.
148   (1977) 74 DLR (3d) 297.

It would be much better to base an action in breach of contract on failure to abide by a contractual term which can be proved objectively.

3.99 Of the contractual terms the only one which would undoubtedly cause difficulty is the assessment of fair and reasonable standards of competence. It is possible for a court to decide what is a fair and reasonable standard of competence in the practice of medicine and dentistry and so it ought prima facie to be possible to determine what is a fair and reasonable standard of teaching and supervision by a member of the academic staff of a higher education institution. Obviously it is more problematic when the measurement of what has gone wrong is in terms of lost mental value-added than in terms of lost physical movement or missing teeth. The same difficult arises with contractual claims as with tort claims: proving a link between the professional standard of teaching which is impugned and the individual student's learning. Failure of a whole or a substantial part of a class might be more readily identified with poor teaching than failure of a single student.

3.100 The quality assessment exercises being undertaken by QAA assign ratings to subjects taught at institutions on a scale ranging from 'excellent' to 'unsatisfactory' and institutions are invited to assess their performance on this scale in a number of areas. The quality of the teaching itself, which as we have seen is difficult to assess objectively, is only one part of the assessment, which also covers the general environment for teaching and learning, advice to students, the extent to which student feedback is encouraged and brought to bear on curriculum development, etc. It must be a factor in the implied terms governing quality in the contract of matriculation that the facilities available to students to support their education should be of a reasonable and appropriate standard. This might on the one hand render an institution liable under this heading (regardless of any other liability) if it did not heat classrooms during cold weather and on the other if its library facilities were grossly inadequate to support the course. How far, if at all, an institution is subject to legal action for these deficiencies is as yet unanswered: the effect of the quality assessments is likely to be of much greater practical significance.

Professional and product liability

Professional advice and services

3.101 The report of the CVCP Working Group in 1992 identified the area of professional liability in respect of negligent advice or negligent performance of a professional duty connected with specialised tasks as something which must be addressed in all research, consultancy and other commercial arrangements. The working group recommended[149] that

(i)   the matter of which party should bear the liability for work performed in relation to particular projects be addressed in all contracts. In particular, the terms should be such that the university is absolved from liability, within the limits of the law, notably the Unfair Contract Terms Act 1977; universities should not be expected to give indemnities;

(ii) within those permitted limits, the terms of the contract should state that the university will not be held responsible for any consequences arising out of any inaccuracies or omissions (unless they are the result of negligence) and that no liability attaches for the effects of any product or process that may be produced or adopted by the sponsor, notwithstanding that the formulation of such product or process may be based on the findings of the project.

It is clear also that the laws and jurisdictions of other countries, particularly in North America, can prove expensive. Some insurers will not accept the risks associated with work in these areas. The working group therefore recommended that contracts entered into with parties in other countries should whenever possible be subject to the law of the institution's domicile and the jurisdiction of its courts, unless an acceptable arbitration clause was included.

Sale of goods

3.102   Institutions may on occasion be in the position of selling goods and services rather than buying them. The Sale of Goods Act 1979, which re-enacted with amendments the Sale of Goods Act 1893, and as amended by the Sale and Supply of Goods Act 1994 and the Sale of Goods (Amendment) Act 1995, is an important piece of legislation. Probably of equal importance is the Unfair Contract Terms Act 1977 (as amended by a number of subsequent Acts and the Unfair Terms in Consumer Contracts Regulations 1994), which restricted the rights of suppliers of goods to limit liability by inserting exclusion clauses. There is also a considerable corpus of legislation relating to consumer contracts and safety. However, the common law

149 Paragraph 48.

of contract remains very important: section 62(2) Sale of Goods Act 1979 provides

> The rules of the common law, including the law merchant, except in so far as they are inconsistent with the provisions of this Act, and in particular the law of principal and agent and the effect of fraud, misrepresentation, duress or coercion, mistake or other invalidating cause, apply to contracts for the sale of goods.

3.103 The terms implied into a contract by the Sale of Goods Act 1979, as amended by the Sale and Supply of Goods Act 1994, relate to the seller's title to the goods, their description, quality and fitness for purpose. There is strict liability for breach of these terms. Common law proceedings for breach of contract including terms implied by the Sale of Goods Act, etc. are readily available. If for some reason they are not, for example because there is no contractual relationship between the user of the product and the manufacturer, there may be liability in tort or delict for breach of a duty of care owed by the manufacturer to the user. In delict, the best-known case is that of the decomposing snail in ginger beer, *M'Alister (or Donoghue) v Stevenson*,[150] where the House of Lords affirmed

> the proposition ... that a manufacturer of products, which he sells in such a form as to show that he intends them to reach the ultimate consumer in the form in which they left him with no reasonable possibility of intermediate examination, and with the knowledge that the absence of reasonable care in the preparation or putting up of the products will result in an injury to the consumer's life or property, owes a duty to the consumer to take reasonable care.

3.104 There is also a complex corpus of law relating to consumer protection,[151] which is under continuous development and interpretation by the courts. Detailed examination of this aspect of the law is beyond the scope of this work.

Insurance cover

3.105 Given the nature of protection of the user or consumer of goods and services which has developed over the past 20 years or so and the liability of the corporation towards its 'customers,' it is not surprising that a great deal of attention is paid to the extent of

---

150 [1932] AC 562, HL.
151 Eg Consumer Protection Act 1987.

professional indemnity and other forms of insurance. The essence of professional indemnity cover is that it extends to negligence on the part of the institution and individual members of staff whether in contract or tort, including infringement of third party intellectual property rights, with appropriate exceptions or greatly enhanced premiums for operations in particularly risky areas (eg medical, veterinary, drugs-related or aerial devices) or where foreign jurisdictions are likely to award much higher damages than the British courts in proven cases of negligence. It is obviously important that members of staff embarking on anything out of the ordinary should take advice on the insurance cover available.

3.106 Where possession of a degree gives automatic entry to a profession, it is common for there to be statutory authority for the relevant professional body to oversee the work of institutions to the extent of attending examinations and/or seeing examination scripts, in addition to the arrangements for quality audit and assessment and supervision by external examiners.[152] They include the relevant bodies in the medical,[153] dental,[154] veterinary surgery,[155] optical,[156] nursing,[157] osteopathic[158] and chiropractic[159] professions plus those supplementary to medicine.[160]

3.107 In some other professions, notably law and accountancy, additional professional training and qualifications are required for entry. In these cases, the professional bodies do not have statutory powers in relation to examinations but their influence on courses is considerable, since admission to the further stages of training will depend on certain subjects having been studied and completed successfully. Other bodies, such as those concerned with housing and town and country planning, exercise non-statutory influence by a system of 'visitations' prior to recognition or renewal of recognition

---

152 This assumes that 'examinations' take place: presumably if competence testing and periodic assessment were to replace formal unseen examinations the legislation would require amendment, since 'examination' is not defined and presumably has its commonsense meaning.
153 Section 6(3) Medical Act 1983.
154 Section 10(1) Dentists Act 1984.
155 Section 5(3) Veterinary Surgeons Act 1966.
156 Section 6 Opticians Act 1958.
157 Section 2 Nurses, Midwives and Health Visitors Act 1997.
158 Section 12 Osteopaths Act 1993.
159 Section 12 Chiropractors Act 1994.
160 Professions Supplementary to Medicine Act 1960, covering chiropodists, dieticians, medical laboratory technicians, occupational therapists, physiotherapists, radiographers and remedial gymnasts.

of courses. The Central Council for Education and Training in Social Work (CCETSW) has statutory power to approve courses as suitable for training social workers.[161] In Scotland, the General Teaching Council has certain functions in relation to initial teacher education (ITE).[162] The Teaching and Higher Education Bill 1997 proposes the establishment of general teaching councils in England and Wales.

3.108 Increasingly, professions are seeking chartered status: here, as in universities, the possession of a charter is seen as conferring the 'ultimate' respectability. The terms chartered chemist, physicist, biologist and engineer are in common use. Chartered member status is normally granted to persons holding a relevant degree or equivalent qualification and having had a specified period of approved practical experience. Since the title 'chartered' is of such significance, the bodies which award it themselves have some influence over courses, since they have the power to recognise qualifications for the purposes of granting membership at the relevant level: on the other hand, of course, they are membership organisations funded by subscription. A recent development is the appearance of 'European' designations such as *Eur chem*[163] awarded to chemists who have satisfied the conditions of the parent body.

Research Councils and other sponsors

3.109 All university charters or instruments of government include the promotion of research as a main objective of the institution and other higher education institutions also undertake research to some extent. Although the funding derived directly from the Funding Councils contains an element for research, allocations depending on the performance of the institution in the research selectivity exercises, a substantial part of research income is derived by competitive bidding for funds held by the Research Councils and other sponsors in the public and private sector.

3.110 There are six Research Councils established by Royal Charter under the provisions of the Science and Technology Act 1965:

161 Section 10 Health and Social Services and Social Security Adjudication Act 1983.
162 Section 7 Teaching Council (Scotland) Act 1965, as amended by section 55 FHESA.
163 The title *Eur chem* (European Chemist) is awarded by the European Communities Chemistry Council (EC3), established by the national professional societies. The title *Eur ing* (European Engineer) is similarly available in the engineering profession.

Biotechnology and Biological Sciences (BBSRC); Engineering and Physical Sciences (EPSRC); Economic and Social (ESRC); Medical (MRC); National Environment (NERC); Particle Physics and Astronomy (PPARC), and a Council for the Central Laboratory of the Research Councils. NICHE recommended the establishment of a new Arts and Humanities Research Council replacing the Humanities Research Board of the British Academy.[164]

3.111 The Research Councils and other sponsors impose on the institutions conditions under which grants and contracts will be offered and payment made. In the case of the Research Councils, these conditions relate mainly to financial control and use of resources. While commercial organisations are also concerned that resources should be properly applied to their intended purposes, they are often less concerned about the financial detail than about quality assurance, the ownership of intellectual property and the commercial application of results of sponsored research and consultancy. These issues are discussed elsewhere.

3.112 The Research Councils support research in higher education institutions by means of grants given on specified conditions which are not normally negotiable. A research contract entered into with the Research Councils, in addition to the accounting and reporting requirements, places express obligations on the contractor in respect of the employment of staff, use of equipment acquired with research funds and exploitation of results. The Councils accept no responsibility, financial or otherwise, for expenditure or liability arising out of the work (including that arising as a result of purchase of equipment and/or consumable items) during the final six months of the research grant other than that arising solely and necessarily for the purposes of the research. They reserve the right to revise the grant, or to terminate it at any time subject to reasonable notice and the payment of any final instalment which may be necessary to cover outstanding and unavoidable commitments.

Research supported by government departments

3.113 Like the Research Councils, government departments and executive agencies supporting research in higher education will only contract on their own terms. Major players in this field include the Ministry of Defence, the Department of Health, the Department for

164 Recommendation 29, Main Report, NCIHE, July 1997.

International Development, the Home and Scottish Offices. Contracts contain provisions about access, intellectual property, and termination. In some circumstances provision is made for a 'hearing' before termination: such a hearing should be fair and if not could be amenable to judicial review.

Research supported by international bodies

3.114 The main organisations falling under this heading are the various United Nations agencies and the European Union. Again these bodies will only contract on their own terms. A research contract entered into with the European Union (on the 'cost reimbursement' basis)[165] is a highly complex document which in general terms places express obligations on contractors, who are jointly and severally liable to the Commission for any failure on the part of any of them to discharge their responsibilities. The obligations include those normally associated with Research Council and government contracts and requirements to provide the proper facilities etc, but also provide for access to the work by the awarding authority and the Court of Auditors.

3.115 The European Union contract specifies that any dispute shall fall within the sole jurisdiction of the European Court of Justice. The contract itself and any liability for loss, damage or injury arising from the performance of the work under it is to be determined in accordance with the applicable law, which is left open in the model. Either the Commission or the contractor (if more than one, acting jointly and unanimously) may terminate the research on giving two months' notice that they consider no useful purpose would be served by continuing it. The Commission may terminate the contract for a number of other reasons, including bankruptcy, etc of the contractor, non-performance of obligations other than for reasonable and justifiable technical or economic reasons, the giving of false or incomplete statements by the contractor to secure financial or other advantage or where force majeure (a favourite European term) intervenes for more than a specified period.

---

165 *Model Contracts for Research and Development, 1995:* see N Byrne 'The EC's Model Research and Development Contract' [1996] 3 ICCLR 82.

Research and development sponsored by industry and commerce

3.116   When research and development is sponsored by industry or commerce, each sponsor will suggest a form of contract and it is for the higher education institution to attempt to negotiate the terms. The institution might attempt to impose its own standard terms: in this context the CCI Charters take the somewhat unrealistic view that it is the sponsor which 'asks for a contract' setting out how much the work will cost, the responsibilities of the parties and the use of the results. As the pre-1992 university system was increasingly faced with a bewildering array of draft contracts, the CVCP established a working group the main task of which was to assist institutions by proposing a model set of contract terms which institutions could use as a basis for negotiation. In fact the working group proposed a model based on work carried out in the United States.[166] The Universities Review Board Coordinating Committee published guidance on Pricing and Costing of Research and other Projects in October 1996.

3.117   The model, which, adapted for use in England, appears as Appendix B to this chapter, is intended to deal with the following issues identified by the working group as important in this area:

(i)   a clear description of the work and requirements for reporting;
(ii) avoiding giving a guarantee of specific outcomes inappropriate to a research programme;
(iii) need for agreement of both parties to variations from the original contract;
(iv) proper arrangements for termination, including arrangements for non-cancellable commitments;
(v)   avoiding excessive delays in publication while recognising sponsor's right to withhold permission for publication for a reasonable period.

The Working Group made a number of other suggestions for improvements in arrangements for sponsored research, including internal procedures for securing intellectual property rights in the work of staff and students.

---

166 CVCP *Sponsored University Research: Recommendations and Guidance on Contract Issues* Report of a Working Group (J V Reed, R D Handscombe, G M Maclean, A M A Powell and D C Young) (1992) Annex III.

Quality assurance

3.118 In the light of increased emphasis on quality assurance, some sponsors of research and consultancy now require the completion of a Vendor Quality Assurance Evaluation Questionnaire, to enable the firm to decide on the suitability of the supplying institution and the level of assessment required. The procedure requires the relevant quality approval certificates to be forwarded, together with summaries of the institution's technical ability and competence, its staff, its organisation and its quality manual. The procedure also requires that a certificate of conformity should be provided, signed by an appropriate authorised officer, which certifies that the supplies have been inspected and tested to conform with the requirements of the order. This is a new area of activity for institutions accustomed to having their technical and professional expertise accepted without detailed questioning.

Appendix A

Scottish Higher Education Funding Council Mission Statement (1997)

The mission of the Scottish Higher Education Funding Council is to promote the quality and encourage the expansion of teaching and research in Scottish higher education institutions through the efficient and effective use of public funds allocated by the Secretary of State for Scotland to support these activities.

In pursuit of this mission the Council will seek to:

*   reinforce the distinctive strengths of Scottish higher education and its international status while encouraging greater diversity, greater flexibility and responsiveness in the system;
*   help institutions to meet the needs of students and the Scottish and United Kingdom economy;
*   establish constructive working relationships with higher education institutions, other national funding councils and other education, training and research organisations;
*   consult its partners in these working relationships in order to inform its funding decisions and its advice to the Secretary of State for Scotland on policies, priorities and resource needs for higher education in Scotland;
*   promote healthy competition among institutions by being transparent in its funding decisions and by improving the availability of information about the quality of teaching and research;
*   encourage collaboration as appropriate among institutions and other education, training and research agencies;
*   within the broad framework of Government policy, balance the need to achieve accountability for the most effective use of Council funds with a recognition of institutional autonomy.

Appendix B

Model research agreement

Research Agreement with ....

THIS IS AN AGREEMENT BETWEEN:

(1)

of   ('the Sponsor')

and

(2)   ('the Institution')

WHEREAS: the research programme contemplated by this Agreement is of mutual interest and benefit to the Institution and to the Sponsor, will further the instructional and research objectives of the Institution in a manner consistent with its status as an educational institution, and may result in benefits for both the Sponsor and the Institution through inventions, improvements, and/or discoveries.

NOW THEREFORE IT IS HEREBY CONTRACTED AND AGREED BETWEEN THE PARTIES AS FOLLOWS: –

Article 1 – Definitions

The following terms shall have the following meanings:
1.1 'Project' shall mean the description of the Project as described in Appendix A, under the direction of the person designated therein as Principal Investigator or of such other member of staff

as the Sponsor and the Institution shall mutually agree. The Principal Investigator will have the assistance of a research worker who will be supported from the funds made available by the Sponsor under this Agreement.

1.2 'Contract Period' is [   ] 199[   ] until [   ] 200[   ]

1.3 'Resulting Intellectual Property' shall mean individually and collectively all inventions, improvements and/or discoveries which are conceived and/or made by one or more members of staff of the Institution acting either on their own or jointly with one or more employees of the Sponsor in performance of the Project.

Article 2 – Research Work

2.1 The Institution shall commence the performance of the Project promptly after the commencement date of the Contract Period and shall use reasonable endeavours to perform such Project substantially in accordance with the terms and conditions of this Agreement. The Sponsor and the Institution may however at any time amend the Project by mutual written agreement.

2.2 In the event that the Principal Investigator becomes unable or unwilling to continue the Project, and a mutually acceptable substitute is not available, the Institution and/or the Sponsor shall have the option to terminate the Project.

Article 3 – Reports and Conferences

3.1 Written programme reports shall be provided by the Institution to the Sponsor every [ ] months, and a final report shall be submitted by the Institution within [ ] of the conclusion of the Contract Period, or of early termination of this Agreement.

3.2 During the term of this Agreement, representatives of the Institution will meet with representatives of the Sponsor at times and places mutually agreed upon to discuss the progress and results, as well as ongoing plans, or changes therein, of the Project.

Article 4 – Costs, Billings and Other Support

4.1 Subject to Article 2 hereof, total costs to the Sponsor hereunder shall not exceed the sum of [£]. Payment shall be made by the

Sponsor according to the following schedule:
[...........]
4.2 The Sponsor shall [loan/donate] the equipment described in Appendix B to the Institution under the following conditions:
[............]
The Institution shall retain title to any equipment purchased with funds provided by the Sponsor under this Agreement.
4.3 In the event of early termination of this Agreement by the Sponsor pursuant to Article 9 hereof, the Sponsor shall pay all costs incurred and falling due for payment up to the date of termination and also all expenditure falling due for payment after the date of termination which arises from commitments reasonably and necessarily incurred by the Institution for the performance of the Project prior to the date of termination.

Article 5 – Publicity

5.1 The Sponsor will not use the name of the Institution, nor of any member of the Institution's staff, in any publicity, advertising or news release without the prior written approval of an authorised representative of the Institution. The Institution will not use the name of the Sponsor, nor any employee of the Sponsor, in any publicity without the prior written approval of the Sponsor.

Article 6 – Publications

6.1 The Sponsor recognises the principle that the results of university research should be publishable and agrees that staff and students of the Institution engaged in the Project shall be permitted to present at symposia, national, or regional professional meetings, and to publish in journals, theses or dissertations, or otherwise of their own choosing, methods and results of the Project, provided however that the Sponsor shall have been furnished copies of any proposed publication or presentation at least [ ] months in advance of the submission of such proposed publication or presentation to a journal, editor, or other third party. The Sponsor shall have [ ] months, after receipt of said copies, to object to such proposed presentation or proposed publication because there is patentable or commercially sensitive subject matter which needs protection. In the event that the Sponsor makes such objection, the said staff or students shall refrain from making such publication or presentation for a maximum of [ ] months from date of receipt of such objection in order for the Institution to file UK and/or other patent application(s) directed to the patentable or commercially sensitive subject matter contained in the proposed publication or presentation.

Article 7 – Intellectual Property

7.1 For the avoidance of doubt all background information and know-how used in connection with the Project shall remain the property of the party introducing the same.

7.2 All rights to Resulting Intellectual Property under the Project shall belong in the first instance to the Institution.

7.3 Rights to inventions, improvements and/or discoveries, whether or not patentable or capable of other intellectual property protection, relating to the Project made solely by employees of the Sponsor shall belong to the Sponsor.

7.4 The Institution will promptly notify the Sponsor of any Resulting Intellectual Property conceived and/or made during the Contract Period under the Project. If the Sponsor directs that a patent application or application for other intellectual property protection be filed, the Institution shall promptly prepare, file, and prosecute such UK and/or other application in the Institution's name. The Sponsor shall bear all costs incurred in connection with such preparation, filing, prosecution, and maintenance of UK and/or other application(s) directed to the said Resulting Intellectual Property. The Sponsor shall cooperate with the Institution to ensure that such application(s) will cover, to the best of the Sponsor's knowledge, all items of commercial interest and importance. While the Institution shall be responsible for making decisions regarding scope and content of application(s) to be filed and prosecution thereof, the Sponsor shall be given an opportunity to review and provide input thereto. The Institution shall keep the Sponsor advised as to all developments with respect to such application(s) and shall promptly supply to the Sponsor copies of all papers received and filed in connection with the prosecution thereof in sufficient time for the Sponsor to comment thereon.

7.5 If the Sponsor elects not to exercise its option to apply for protection or decides to discontinue the financial support of the prosecution or maintenance of the protection, the Institution shall be free to file or continue prosecution or maintain any such application(s) and to maintain any protection issuing thereon in the UK and/or other country at the Institution's sole expense.

Article 8 – Grant of Rights

8.1 Pursuant to Article 7.4 the Institution grants to the Sponsor the first option, at the Sponsor's sole selection, for either a non-exclusive, royalty-free licence or alternatively (for a negotiated consideration) a sole licence with a right to sub-licence on terms and conditions to be mutually agreed upon. The option shall extend for a time period of [.....] from the date of termination of the Agreement.

8.2 If the Sponsor exercises such option and requires for the purpose access to background Intellectual Property owned by the Institution in order to exploit effectively Resulting Intellectual Property, the Institution will grant a royalty-free non-exclusive licence to the Sponsor to any such background Intellectual Property that the Institution is free to license for this specific purpose.

8.3 If the Sponsor requires for any other purpose access to background Intellectual Property owned by the Institution, the Institution expresses its willingness to grant a separate licence for the purpose upon fair and reasonable commercial terms.

Article 9 – Term and Termination

9.1 This Agreement shall become effective upon the date subscribed by the parties and shall continue in effect for the full duration of the Contract Period unless sooner terminated in accordance with the provisions of this Article. The parties may, however, extend the term of this Agreement for additional periods as desired under mutually agreeable terms and conditions which the parties reduce to writing and sign. Either party may terminate this agreement upon ninety (90) days prior written notice to the other where it considers termination justified on the grounds that no further purpose would be served by continuing with the Project. Such notice of termination will only be given by either party after full discussion with the other party of the reasons for the proposal to give such notice.

9.2 If either party hereto shall commit any breach of or default in any of the terms or conditions of this Agreement, and also shall fail to remedy such default or breach within ninety (90) days after the receipt of written notice thereof from the other party hereto, the party giving notice may, at its option and in addition to any other remedies which it may have at law, terminate this Agreement by sending notice of termination in writing to the other party to such effect, and such termination shall be effective as of the date of the receipt of such notice.

9.3 Subject to Article 8, termination of this Agreement by either party for any reason shall not affect the rights and obligations of the parties accrued prior to the effective date of termination of this Agreement. No termination of the Agreement, however effected, shall affect the Sponsor's rights and duties under Article 7 hereof, or release the parties hereto from their rights and obligations under Articles 4, 5, 6, 7, 8, and 10.

Article 10 – Independent Contractor

10.1 In the performance of all services hereunder the Institution shall be deemed to be and shall be an independent contractor.

10.2 Neither party is authorised to act as agent for the other for any purpose and shall not on behalf of the other enter into any contract, warranty, or representation as to any matter. Neither shall be bound by the acts or conduct of the other.

Article 11 – Liabilities

11.1 While the Institution will use all reasonable endeavours to ensure the accuracy of the work performed and any information given, the Institution makes no warranty, express or implied, as to accuracy and will not be held responsible for any consequence arising out of any inaccuracies or omissions unless such inaccuracies or omissions are the result of negligence on the part of the Institution or its agents.

11.2 The parties agree and declare that the obligations of the Institution and its agents shall cease upon delivery of the reports and that no liability whatsoever either direct or indirect shall rest upon them for the effects of any product or process that may be produced or adopted by the Sponsor or any other party, notwithstanding that the formulation of such product or process may be based upon the findings of the Project.

11.3 Neither party shall be liable to the other for any death or injury unless it is caused by the negligence of that party or its agents, nor shall it be liable to the other for any other loss or damage whatsoever unless it is caused by its wilful default or that of its agents.

Article 12 – Governing Law

12.1 This Agreement and all terms, provisions and conditions of the Project and all questions of construction, validity and performance under this Agreement shall be governed by the Law of England and shall be subject to the exclusive jurisdiction of the English courts.

Article 13 – Assignment

13.1 This Agreement shall not be assigned by either party without the prior written consent of the parties hereto, provided that it shall be assignable to any division of the Sponsor, any majority shareholder of the Sponsor, and/or any subsidiary of the Sponsor in which 51 or more percent of the shareholding is owned by the Sponsor.

Article 14 – Agreement Modification

14.1 Any agreement to change the terms of this Agreement in any way shall be valid only if the change is made in writing and approved by mutual agreement of authorised representatives of the parties hereto.

IN WITNESS WHEREOF this page and the preceding six pages are subscribed by the parties hereto on the   day of   199 .

SIGNED on behalf of the Sponsor:

SIGNED on behalf of the Institution:

Chapter 4

Students: scholars, clients and customers

A change of status

The student contract

4.1   The principal message of this chapter will be that the status of students has changed irrevocably. The change has been from one of being in a subordinate role in the *studium generale* to one of a consumer of services. While a minority of students not in receipt of state funding for tuition have in practice been in that position prior to 1998, the changes made in student financing for the majority of new undergraduate students from autumn 1998 by Part II Teaching and Higher Education Bill 1997, following the Report of NCIHE in July 1997, now remove any doubt. All students are in effect consumers contracting with an institution to purchase those services which are themselves provided under a separate contract with the state. The UK is acquiring what has been called in Australia 'The Loose Cannon Syndrome.'[1] As there are now over 1.7 million students in higher education[2] this is a large customer base. As Martin Cave[3] has suggested 'if students did pay tuition, it is reasonable to expect that they would impose their own discipline as purchasers on institutions.'

---

1   D Considine 'The Loose Cannon Syndrome: Universities as Businesses and Students as Consumers' (1993) Australian Universities Law Review 36.
2   *Students in Higher Education Institutions 1995/96* (1997) HESA.
3   M Cave (1996) *The Impact on Higher Education of Funding Changes and Increasing Competition* Higher Education and Lifelong Learning Conference, July 1996, quoted in paragraph 16.14, Main Report, NCIHE, July 1997.

4.2 In 1989, when the Association of University Teachers threatened industrial action over a pay claim, the pre-1992 universities began to appreciate the importance of defining the terms of the institution-student contract. The advice given by leading counsel to one university[4] was crystal clear:

> In my opinion ... there is no doubt that the failure by the University to provide each student with the examination system described in the Faculty Handbook in accordance with the Regulations would amount to a breach of contract for which the student would be entitled to claim damages.

The existence of contractual relationships at both applicant and matriculated stages was confirmed by the Court of Appeal in 1993 in *Moran v University College Salford (No 2)*,[5] discussed later and in legal advice on 'The University-Student Contract' obtained by CVCP in 1996 (an Opinion of Counsel in 1997 in Scotland) when institutions, prior to the Report of NCIHE, were considering the imposition of 'top-up' fees on first registration. It also underlies the concept of using binding arbitration as a means of resolving disputes between students and institutions.[6]

4.3 Since the publication of the CCI Charters the notion of a student being a customer or consumer has developed steadily. Complaints by students about the services provided by institutions have increased: procedures designed to improve the way in which they are handled internally and thus reduce the likelihood of litigation have been proposed.[7] The basis for such procedures, whether or not they involve the Visitor as the ultimate decision-maker, is the existence of some defined obligations on both parties which taken together can in effect be considered to be a contract.

---

4   Private communication.
5   [1994] ELR 187.
6   Interim Report of a CVCP Working Group, 1997, chaired by Professor Clive Booth.
7   D J Farrington *Student Complaints* (1996) Report for the Higher Education Quality Council; D J Farrington *Handling Student Complaints* (1997) CVCP Universities and Colleges Staff Development Agency; recommendation 60, Main Report, NCIHE, July 1997; (1997) Interim Report of a CVCP Working Group chaired by Professor Clive Booth, following on recommendations contained in the Second Report of the Committee on Standards of Conduct in Public Life (the Nolan Committee).

Facilitating a quality learning experience

A change of emphasis

4.4   In considering this relationship today there is a new emphasis on the student being a party to a learning experience and there is less emphasis on disciplinary rules, constraints and controls. Both institutions and students are more concerned now with what can be done rather than with what cannot be done. Flexibility of choice, wider access to higher education and the reasonable expectations of the 'customers' make this inevitable and welcome. This discussion will therefore take a positive approach to the question: 'how does the law of higher education facilitate a quality learning experience?' There are of course bound to be constraints and controls, since no civilised community can exist without them, but these should be seen as subordinate to the main objective. Unfortunately, most of the law in this area relates to controls, for it is an area where there is relatively little legislation other than domestic rules: the cases which have come before the courts and Visitors have necessarily been about disputes. It is clear also that boundaries are shifting between full-time and part-time study, with mixed-mode attendance becoming more popular. The concept of the course may require redefinition to fit in with these changes.

Quality of service

4.5   Over 100 years after the decision of the Court of Session in *Cadells v Balfour*[8] the system seems finally to have accepted the concept of the student as consumer or customer. The rights which an individual in that position has to a 'quality service' have become of increasing importance, although as yet largely untested in the courts. The CCI Charters are specifically concerned with this, drawing the attention of potential customers to the quality audit and assessment procedures so that the customer can take these aspects of an institution's performance (along with other indicators such as graduate employment rates, wastage rates and success in attracting research funds) when making his or her choice. So we must inevitably deal with issues of quality assurance.

4.6   The various procedures established by the Funding Councils and other bodies to deal with these issues on an institutional and

8   (1890) 17 R 1138.

subject basis have already been discussed. We have also seen how individual students (customers) may acquire a right to a quality service and the obligations on the institution and its staff to provide it. What is the limit of the expectation of the customer in this context and what is the extent of the obligation of the provider? These matters are directly relevant to the institution-student relationship. There will be further discussion of the specific terms of the contract later: first, some history.

The naked sunbather (1)

A student is found sunbathing in the nude in a publicly accessible part of the institution's campus. Outraged members of the public complain to the Vice-Chancellor who, without giving him an opportunity to explain, fines the student and bans him from residence for the rest of the year. What rights does the student have in the matter?

4.7 A number of higher education institutions came under the public gaze in the late 1960s and early 1970s for student-related issues which most would probably rather have avoided. It was a very sensitive time for higher education nationally and internationally. One such was the University of Keele, which took action in the summer of 1970 against Simon Glynn, found with others sunbathing in the nude on university property, to the evident distaste of some personnel. He was disciplined by the university and after an internal appeal failed he took legal action to have part of the disciplinary sanction overturned. *Glynn v Keele University*[9] should never have reached the courts but it did and, together with a number of other cases involving other institutions, contributed to a complex debate about the nature of the institution-student relationship, which was starting to go through a transitional period. It also brought home to institutions the extent to which the supervisory jurisdiction of the English High Court could be brought to bear on the internal procedures of higher education institutions, previously considered more or less sacrosanct. Today, non-court based arbitration seems to offer students many advantages over court proceedings, notably that the person appointed as arbitrator (arbiter in Scotland) is likely to be someone with an expert knowledge of the field.

4.8 The fact that Glynn's case was brought at all tells us something about the state of university-student relationships in those days and indicates that students have a relationship with the institution which

9   [1971] 1 WLR 487.

has some legal status recognised by the courts. Although this may appear obvious today, it has not always been so. There is continued debate about the extent of the respective legal rights and obligations of the parties to that relationship, which is complicated by there being several different types of institution with distinctive legal characters.

The meaning of student

4.9 The nature of a higher education institution is that there is always a corporate body which can be identified as a party to a contract.[10] However there appears to be no legal definition of a student outwith the definitions for internal purposes in charters, statutes etc. The legislation which provides for student awards[11] and student loans,[12] although it uses the word 'student', is concerned only with defining which classes of person pursuing which type of course are eligible for the awards or loans concerned. 'Student' may be defined for other specific purposes, eg for social security.[13] The Council Tax Regulations define a student and a course for the purposes of exemption from local taxation.[14]

4.10 The *Shorter Oxford English Dictionary* definition of student is

(1) A person who is engaged in or addicted to study;
(2) A person who is undergoing a course of study and instruction at a university or other place of higher education or technical training;
(3) (a) At Christ Church Oxford: A member of the foundation, corresponding to the 'fellow' or 'scholar' at other colleges (now restricted to the senior members) (1651);
(b) A person who receives emolument, during a fixed period, to enable him to pursue his studies and as a reward of merit (1800).

4.11 Some of the pre-1992 universities spell out the status of persons as 'in statu pupillari' ie students, not members of staff: this phrase

---

10 They are '... legal corporations capable of entering into contractual relationships with ... students': G H L Fridman 'Judicial Intervention into University Affairs' (1973) Chitty's Law Journal xxi 181.
11 Education (Fees and Awards) Act 1983; Education (Grants and Awards) Act 1984; Education (Mandatory Awards) Regulations (annual).
12 Education (Student Loans) Acts 1990–1996.
13 Social Security (Miscellaneous Provisions) Act 1974.
14 See eg Council Tax (Discount Disregards) Amendment Order 1996 (SI 1996/636).

was used as a term of art in 1991 by Watkins LJ in *R v University of Liverpool, ex p Caesar-Gordon*[15] (concerned with a dispute over the University's handling of a 'free speech' issue under section 43 E(2)A86) and previously in *Oakes v Sidney Sussex College Cambridge*[16] (an attempt to invoke the jurisdiction of the ordinary courts in place of the Visitor) where the expression had a substantive meaning in the rules of the College. For the purposes of this chapter, we should include all persons who are undertaking a course of study or research, including those absent on work placements, on study abroad and those who are not registered for teaching, but are undertaking work-based training assessed by an institution for an award of eg an NVQ.

The institution-student relationship

4.12 The student is arguably the raison d'etre of the higher education institution, at least in carrying out its teaching mission. In a coda to his 1993 report on the problems which arose in the University College of Swansea, Sir Michael Davies said:

> ... The standing of the Department and the Centre matters more than that of individuals; above all the education and qualifications of their students. I do not forget the importance of research, but in the last analysis it is the students, whether they be in their first year or post-graduates, that the University, the College, the Department and the Centre are there to serve. All those mentioned in this report would do well to remember this; they have not always done so.[17]

4.13 It is of crucial importance that the relationship of the student with the institution at all stages from application to graduation or other termination of the course be clearly understood. Analysis of this relationship includes issues such as the rights of the prospective student, the status of registered student, academic matters including quality assurance, discipline and fees. These will give the reader a global view of the subject, but although it is possible to draw out a number of general themes, this process is difficult when the constitutions and domestic legislation of institutions vary as widely

15 [1991] 1 QB 124.
16 [1988] 1 All ER 1004.
17 *Report of enquiry and advice to the Lord President of the Council acting on behalf of HM The Queen the Visitor of the University of Wales invited by the Council of the University College of Swansea into various complaints made to the College and associated matters* Sir Michael Davies, May 1993.

as we have seen earlier in this book. No sensible legal analysis of an individual institution's relationship to its students can be made without an in-depth study of the domestic legislation, which includes statutes, ordinances, byelaws, regulations and rules of many kinds. As will be seen, cases in the courts have turned upon the precise wording of regulations drafted by administrators and approved and implemented by the responsible authority. Thus what is written here is a general, although hopefully useful, guide to the principles.

The concept of an institution-student contract

4.14 The concept of an institution-student contract attracted renewed attention in the light of the appearance of the CCI Charters and ideas put forward by the National Union of Students for a learning contract between institutions and individual students. Clive Lewis[18] in a review to 1983 of the theories which had been developed in the UK and Canada to describe the legal nature of the university-student relationship, concluded that it was a complex hybrid of contract and status. Some aspects of the relationship were clearly contractual and enforceable as such in private law whereas certain aspects had a public law character. This restates the view of D Christie and the National Union of Students/National Council for Civil Liberties Commission on Academic Freedom and the Law, the report of which was published in 1970.[19] The Commission's intention to examine this question was criticised in 1969 in a leading article in *The Times*[20] on the basis that neither it nor the increasing resort by both students and universities to the law would 'mark an improvement on the relaxed and informal relationship which they are superseding.'

4.15 Arguably that may have been the case in 1969: *The Times* leader was written following the case of *R v University of Aston Senate, ex p Roffey*,[21] discussed in detail later. In this case Blain J took the view that the students' status was '... akin to membership of a social body, a club with perhaps something more than mere social status attached to it ...'[22] but events since then suggest that the days

---

18 C B Lewis 'The Legal Nature of a University and the Student-University Relationship' (1983) Ottawa Law Review xv.
19 D Christie *The Legal Basis of Student Tenure at Colleges and Universities* in *Academic Freedom and the Law, Report of the NUS/NCCL Commission* (1970).
20 'Ex Statu Pupillari' *The Times* 31 March 1969.
21 [1969] 2 QB 538.
22 [1969] 2 QB 538, 556.

of the relaxed and informal relationship were numbered. As the cases are reviewed it will become clear that the attitude of the courts has moved considerably towards the point at which most problems arising in the relationship can be viewed in terms of a contract.

History of the institution-student relationship

4.16 The history of the institution-student relationship is as old as the history of higher education. In the medieval universities and colleges there was no hard and fast distinction as there is today between academic staff and students. All were 'partners in the craft of scholarship and members of a single society.'[23] The situation later at Oxford was described by M Pattison[24] as akin to 'a Lacaedaemonian regiment ... all were students alike, only differing in being at different stages of their progress ...'. Oxford started as a body of masters, students being both men and boys, as young as 15, occasionally even younger. These students attached themselves to particular masters. Student numbers increased and it was only when they formed a sizeable proportion of the inhabitants of the city, with frequent, sometimes violent squabbles between town and gown, that efforts were made to exert some authority over the whole academic community. Constitutions were developed which, as we have seen earlier, were the forerunners of modern charters and instruments of government.

Contract and status

4.17 The formal equality between members of chartered bodies and their actual status in practice are rather different: as we have seen, the rights and duties of the various different categories of members of the modern chartered university have been developed over time and are now spelt out in its statutes and ordinances. When chartered universities constituted the majority of the English higher education institutions, there was much academic discussion about the legal relationship between individual student members and the corporation

---

23 See generally (i) M B Hackett *The Original Statutes of Cambridge University* (1970); R G Cant *The University of St Andrews* (1970); J Brothers and S Hatch *Residence and Student Life* (1971); F M Powicke and A B Emden (eds) *The Universities of Europe in the Middle Ages* (1936).

24 M Pattison, in evidence to the *Commissioners appointed to inquire into the State, Discipline, Studies and Revenues of the University and Colleges of Oxford* Appendix 1852 (1482) xxii.

largely in the context of disciplinary proceedings. In those institutions where students enjoy the privileges of corporator, their status as members probably gives them rights independent of any contractual rights against the institution.[25] Sir William Wade[26] was being quite revolutionary when he suggested in 1969 that such students in chartered institutions have contracts of membership: it is implied that in return for their fees they will be treated in accordance with the university's rules. Up to fairly recent times English judges held that the university-student relationship was not contractual, relying instead on the concept of membership, disputes as to which would be settled internally by the Visitor. The leading cases on this date from 1757 to 1896, concerned with a failure to attend chapel and a subsequent disciplinary committee,[27] expulsion for assault[28] and disputes about elections to fellowships.[29]

4.18 In *Green v Master and Fellows of St Peter's College Oxford*,[30] Wills J stated the 'obvious' fact that the relationship was not contractual; indeed he could think of 'nothing more fatal to discipline' and this seems to have been assumed in the other cases. In *Thomson v University of London*,[31] Kindersley VC felt that the relationship was not a legal contract and to describe it as such was a misnomer. In Scotland it was argued that the relationship was not contractual but was regulated by public law, the student making use of a 'public facility.'[32]

The Law Quarterly Review debate

4.19 In 1974 there was a celebrated debate between William Wade[33] (as he then was) and John Garner[34] in the pages of the *Law Quarterly*

---

25 It should be remembered that even in chartered corporations students are not always corporators: for example in *Oakes v Sidney Sussex College Cambridge* [1988] 1 All ER 1004 Mr Oakes was in statu pupillari, not a member of the corporation.

26 (1969) lxxxv Law Quarterly Review 470.

27 *Green v Master and Fellows of St Peter's College Oxford* (1896) Times, 10 February.

28 *R v Grundon* (1775) 1 Cowp 315.

29 *R v Hertford College, ex p Tillyard* (1878) 3 QBD 693; *St John's College v Todington* (1757) 1 Burr 158.

30 (1896) Times, 10 February.

31 (1864) 33 LJ Ch 625.

32 8 *Stair Memorial Encyclopaedia* para 1024.

33 (1974) xc Law Quarterly Review 154.

34 (1974) xc Law Quarterly Review 6.

Review. Garner's view was that the student by entering into a contract with the chartered university acquired a status as a member of the university. He pointed out that status, such as that of a police constable or a member of the armed forces, is normally acquired by contract and in such instances the individual became liable to certain duties and entitled to certain rights, not forming part of the contract whereby he acquired the status. Wade discounted the suggestion that a student might possess a non-contractual status, as unlike the police officer or soldier, the student had no independent powers or duties. The student might have status in a chartered corporation as a member, protected by injunction or declaration;[35] such status carried with it the benefit of the principles of natural justice, like a member of a trade union or club. The rights are contractual but none the less effective on that account. Wade's article referred to Lord Devlin's statement in his report on the Cambridge sit-in,[36] where he said

> Contract is the foundation of most domestic or internal systems of discipline ... The power to discipline should be derived from the acceptance of it by the student in the contract of matriculation.

In a sense, Lord Devlin was putting the student in a similar position to a footballer who in contracting to join a club affiliated to the Football Association agrees to be subject to the FA's disciplinary rules. There has been no shortage of such cases in recent years and that of *Finnigan v New Zealand Rugby Football Union*[37] illustrates how the courts have been drawn into disputes in the parallel sport.

Non-chartered institutions

4.20 This debate is of no relevance to the former public sector of higher education and the other non-chartered institutions, where the position is relatively straightforward. Students are not members of the corporation conducting the institution, nor for that matter are most of the staff. Both categories are represented among the governing body which constitutes the corporation's membership. Students and staff of these institutions, which constitute the majority of the higher

35 This must be doubtful in view of the exclusive jurisdiction of the Visitor.
36 *Report of the Sit-In in February 1972 and its Consequences* (Devlin Report), Vol ciii Cambridge University Reporter, Special, No 12, 14 February 1972. See also L N Brown 'Student Protest in England' (1969) xvii 'American Journal of Comparative Law; L A Sheridan (1967) 'Sacking Professors and Sending Down Students – Legal Control Law, Justice and Equity.
37 [1985] 2 NZLR 159.

education system, may be forgiven for jumping to the conclusion that most of this debate is as relevant to their situation as the arcane rituals of dining in an Oxbridge college. However, the relevance will become apparent: certainly Wade's suggestion that students have 'contracts of membership' may be adapted to general relevance by substituting 'contracts with the institution' despite the lack as yet of an explicit recognition by the High Court that the relationship between a non-chartered 'statutory' institution and a student is one to be regulated by private law. Nevertheless, it is now generally accepted that a contract exists at all stages.[38] Whether or not that implies that all disputes must be litigated as contractual ones will be explored.

A contractual relationship varying with time

4.21 In principle there must be at least two contractual relationships to be considered, that of the applicant and that of the person who has matriculated. In *Moran v University College Salford (No 2)*[39] Glidewell LJ appeared to support the proposition that there are separate contracts of admission and matriculation. A third, that between the institution and an alumnus, who in many cases remains a member in a chartered institution, relates to the role of graduates' associations in the governance of institutions, although there may also be an express or implied obligation on the institution to provide references, testimonials, transcripts or at the very least confirmation of the member's status. It can be argued as an alternative that there is a continuous relationship in which the agreed terms vary as different stages are passed. Whatever the theoretical model which best describes the relationship, we must examine the position from the earliest contact between potential student and institution.

The prospective student

Application procedures

4.22 One of the areas covered by the CCI Charters is that of application procedures and the standard of information given to prospective students. The relationship between the institution and

---

38 CVCP/UCAS (1996) *The terms of The University-Student Contract*; UCAS (1997) *Opinion of (Scottish) Counsel*. See also *Bayley-Jones v University of Newcastle* (1990) 22 NSWLR 425; *Rajah v Royal College of Surgeons in Ireland* [1994] 1 IRLM 233; *Joobeen v University of Stirling* 1995 SLT 12012.
39 [1994] ELR 187 at 194.

the applicant who is not yet a student (a member in a chartered university) can only be founded on contract.[40] *Moran* establishes that the legal relationship between an individual prospective student, or applicant, and an institution is formed when a contract is entered into between legally competent parties (the institution and the applicant) for the admission of the applicant either unconditionally or on satisfaction of certain conditions, whether to the institution itself, or a faculty, department or other division.

4.23 The formation of this contract on the institution's part is normally undertaken by a duly authorised officer and it is important for institutions to establish who has that authority. So far as admission through an agent is concerned, that should not give rise to any problems, since all offers and acceptances will pass through the approved channels, often electronically.

4.24 Most prospective undergraduate students are admitted through the Universities and Colleges Admissions Service (UCAS), a company limited by guarantee formed in 1993. Some teacher training courses in Scotland remain outside this system as do all postgraduate courses. There are additional requirements for admission to the colleges of the universities of Oxford and Cambridge. There are also provisions at most institutions for non-graduating and occasional students: the extent to which they enjoy the rights and owe the duties of students will depend upon the nature and terms of the contract with the institution.

The contract of admission

4.25 The language of 'offer and acceptance' imported from the common law of contract ties in with current concepts of the student as a consumer, shopping around for a degree course using the currency of qualifications, actual or anticipated, and the differential fee levels now attached to each student client. The inception in 1998 of fees representing part of the full cost of tuition reinforces this concept, although the majority of full-time EC undergraduate fees remain to be paid by the state.

4.26 It appears that in other Commonwealth jurisdictions, in cases turning on the existence of a contractual relationship with a student,

40 Except possibly where an undergraduate student who is a member of a university applies for admission to a postgraduate course at the same institution, where there may also be a question of status.

it has been suggested that the applicant makes an offer on the basis of an invitation to treat set out in the prospectus and that the contract is concluded by acceptance by the institution.[41] An alternative view advocated in 1993 by the College in *Moran v University College Salford (No 2)*[42] was that the offer through PCAS was a mere invitation to Paul Moran to enter into discussions which might lead to an agreement to accept him on a particular course and provide him with appropriate instruction, in return for his promise to arrange for fees to be paid. The Court of Appeal did not accept this ingenious argument and held that a contract existed which was an agreement to enrol the student on the course.[43] The institution makes an offer for acceptance by the candidate. The necessary consideration required in English law for the existence of a contract is the promise by the applicant, in accepting the offer, to pay the appropriate fee or, as in the *Moran* case, the applicant acting to his detriment by giving up his chance to enter the clearing scheme when he was wrongfully informed, due to a clerical error, that he had a firm offer of a place which he had firmly accepted. Consideration is not a requirement of contract in Scotland so that acceptance of the offer of a place clearly leads to the formation of a contract. In *Burns v University of Edinburgh*[44] the court ruled for the purposes of section 17(a) RRA that an 'action letter' notifying the University's decision to hold B's application for further consideration did not amount to an 'offer.' The Minors' Contracts Act 1987 and the Age of Legal Capacity (Scotland) Act 1991 remove earlier objections that the applicant may be under the age of 18 at the material time.

Information available to applicants

4.27 Whether as an undergraduate applicant through UCAS or as a candidate making direct application for undergraduate or postgraduate study, the applicant makes an approach to individual

---

41 See eg *Pecover v Bowker* (1957) 8 DLR (2d) 20; *Re University of Sydney, ex p Forster* (1963) 63 SR (NSW) 723; *Sutcliffe v Governors of Acadia University* (1978) 95 DLR (3d) 95. See also *Steinberg v University of Health Sciences/Chicago Medical School* 354 NE 2d 586 (1976) (Ill App Ct) where this analysis was accepted by the court.

42 [1994] ELR 187.

43 The breach of contract by the College was recognised by the court which would not grant Paul Moran an order requiring the College to accept him, unlike the court in *Eden v Board of Trustees of the State University* 374 NYS2d 686 (1975) (NYAppDiv). In *Université Laval v Carrière* (1987) 38 DLR (4th) 503 the plaintiff was awarded $C10,000 damages in circumstances not dissimilar to that of Moran.

44 (26 March 1996, unreported), Sheriff Court, Edinburgh.

institutions on the basis of information supplied by the institution to him/her directly or indirectly through, for example, the school. The documents commonly issued to schools and individual applicants to assist this process include general prospectuses setting out the courses offered by the institution and the conditions for admission together with leaflets with more detailed information about specific subjects. To what extent the prospectus is 'sales puff' and to what extent contractual is illustrated by cases from the private university sector in the United States. In *University of Texas Health Science Center at Houston v Babb*[45] the court held that 'a school's catalog constitutes a written contract between the educational institution and the patron' but this is generally held to be subject to the ability of the institution to modify its offering to properly exercise educational responsibility and not be too strictly tied down by the law of contract.[46]

Disclaimers and unfair contract terms

4.28 The parties to the student-institution contract are obviously unequal. John Bridge[47] suggested that the contract of matriculation (and, for that matter, the contract of admission) is closer to a *contrat d'adhesion* ('take it or leave it') than to one based on *consensus ad idem* (where the parties negotiate an agreement). Even in medieval times scholars could only be admitted by the masters if they accepted the rules of the foundation; in the words of Holt CJ:

> I am far from being a judge as shall lay an intolerable yoke upon anyone's neck: but I must say, if the head and members of a college will receive a charity with a yoke tied to it by the founder, they must be contented to enjoy it in the manner they received it from him. If they will have one they must submit to the other.[48]

A modern statement to the same effect is found in *R v Chief Rabbi of the United Hebrew Congregations of Great Britain and the Commonwealth, ex p Wachmann*[49] where Simon Brown LJ was faced

45 646 SW 2d 502 (1982) (Texas Court of Appeal).
46 Eg *Foley v Benedic* 55 SW2d 805 (1932); *Slaughter v Brigham Young University* 514 F2d 622 (1975): see discussion on these cases in W A Kaplin and B A Lee *The Law of Higher Education* (1995, 3rd ed, Jossey-Bass), p 469.
47 (1970) lxxxvi Law Quarterly Review 531: for a discussion of the *contrat d'adhesion* see F Kessler 'Contracts of Adhesion: Some Thoughts about Freedom of Contract' (1943) Columbia Law Review xliii.
48 *Philips v Bury* (1694) 2 Term Rep 346, 358.
49 [1992] 1 WLR 1036, 1040.

with the argument that an orthodox rabbi had no choice but to accept the chief Rabbi's disciplinary authority, ie there was the relationship of a *contrat d'adhesion.* He said

> I can see no distinction in this regard between rabbis and, for instance, members of the Bar and members of a university. So far as the Bar and universities are concerned, once the exclusive visitorial jurisdiction has been invoked and exhausted, the court can review the visitor's decision; it does not decline such review on the footing that those aggrieved chose rather than were compelled to go to the Bar or university.

His Lordship can strictly only have been referring to those universities subject to the visitorial jurisdiction (which at the material time constituted the majority in England): the dictum would also now be regarded as rather too broad in its statement of the court's powers to intervene.

4.29 As they are published some 15 months before the date of entry to which they refer, prospectuses normally carry disclaimer notices indicating that the institution reserves the right to modify or cancel, without notice, any information or statement contained in the document and accepts no liability for the consequences of that action.[50] It may also refer to the possibility of additional fees being charged, although this was immediately ruled out by the government following the Report of NCIHE in July 1997. Another disclaimer may state that the contents of a particular document are not to be regarded as incorporated in the formal relationship between a student and the institution. Quite how the existence of disclaimers can be reconciled with the requirement of the CCI Charters that potential students should receive 'clear and accurate information' is unclear.

4.30 On the other hand, the appearance in a prospectus of an insurance disclaimer is clearly intended to be incorporated in the contract. The extent to which the pre-1992 universities could use disclaimers of liability was addressed by CVCP in 1992[51] taking account of the provisions of the Unfair Contract Terms Act 1977. The English common law, developed from cases heard in the early development of the railways[52] and later extended to car parking,[53] developed the concept that any liability can be excluded provided

50 The UCAS Handbook for 1998 entry carries a similar disclaimer in section 55.
51 CVCP Note N92/112, May 1992; adapted for Scotland in September 1992.
52 Eg *Parker v South-Eastern Rly Co* (1877) 2 CPD 416, CA.
53 *Thornton v Shoe Lane Parking* [1971] 1 All ER 686, CA.

that adequately clear words are used to achieve this end. In addition, the principle was established that notice of a disclaimer should be given before or at the time when the contract is concluded, which for our purposes means before or at the time of acceptance of offer of a place (with the necessary consideration required in English law being as developed in *Moran v University College Salford (No 2)*).[54]

4.31   It has never been absolutely clear that the 1977 Act applies to higher education institutions as currently constituted (although it did apply to those which were emanations of central or local government prior to the 1988–1992 legislation). The CVCP advice was that it would be prudent to assume that the Act does extend to universities (and therefore, by implication, to all higher education institutions) and the same applies to the Unfair Terms in Consumer Contracts Regulations 1994.[55] Prior to the enactment of the Regulations, the Court of Appeal held that particularly onerous or unusual terms should be fairly and reasonably brought to the other party's attention.[56] Pre-formulated terms attract the protection of the Act.[57]

4.32   The Regulations impose a requirement of 'good faith' on the terms of contracts to which they relate and state that an 'unfair term' means a term which, contrary to the requirement of good faith, causes a 'significant imbalance' in the parties' rights and obligations under the contract to the detriment of the consumer. Account has to be taken of the nature of the services being provided, the circumstances attending the conclusion of the contract and all the other terms of the contract. Particular attention is paid to whether the supplier has dealt fairly and equitably with the consumer. Contracts must be expressed in plain, intelligible language and where there is any doubt about the meaning of a term, the interpretation most favourable to the consumer prevails. An 'unfair' term is not binding on the consumer. In Schedule 3 to the Regulations there is a non-exhaustive list of terms which may be regarded as unfair. Among them are: terms which bind the consumer even though he or she has had no real opportunity to become acquainted with them before the conclusion of the contract; terms which allow unilateral alteration of the provisions of the contract, or characteristics of the services to be provided, by the supplier without a valid reason which is stated in the contract; terms obliging the consumer to fulfil his/her obligations where the supplier does not perform its side of the contract.

54   [1994] ELR 187.
55   SI 1994/3159.
56   *Interfoto Picture Library Ltd v Stiletto Visual Programmes Ltd* [1988] 1 All ER 348.
57   *McCrone v Boots Farm Sales* 1981 SLT 103.

4.33 It is easy to see how these Regulations impact on the student admissions process. A student cannot possibly be expected to be familiar with all the terms of the contract with the institution when these are not clearly spelt out in any single readily-accessible document. It is far from certain that university and colleges regulations forming part of the contract are expressed in plain and intelligible language. It is customary for institutions to reserve the right to make changes in the services offered for any reason they think fit, whether or not it is to the benefit of the students. To date no case has been brought under the 1994 Regulations, but institutions have been urged to word their prospectuses, calendars etc carefully in general and to pay particular attention to the wording of disclaimers. They also have to pay attention to policies. Universities and colleges which entice applicants with prospectus promises of a range of exciting-sounding subject options knowing that a number are not likely to be available due to staff changes, or saying that the system provides reasonable examination revision time when this has not been possible in the past due to late changes, may have difficulty arguing that they are acting in good faith for the purposes of the Unfair Contract Terms Act and Regulations.

Entry requirements, prospectuses etc

4.34 The entry requirements of universities are summarised in the Compendium of University Entrance Requirements produced annually by CVCP 'by and for the Universities as the recognised source of information on entrance requirements to first degree courses.' There are other official and unofficial guides to university and college entrance, including for Scotland the official guide produced by the Committee of Scottish Higher Education Principals (COSHEP). Prospectuses also contain information about non-academic matters such as accommodation and welfare facilities. The extent to which the contract between the institution and the applicant may import the content of prospectuses and other documents will be considered later in this chapter: no legal duty arises merely as a result of the potential applicant having received the prospectuses: it is not even in the nature of an 'invitation to treat' since the offer is made by the institution, not by the applicant.[58] In fact between publication of the prospectus and an offer of admission being made,

---

58 The distinction between a contract and an invitation to treat is most clearly understood from the judgment of Lord Goddard CJ in *Pharmaceutical Society of Great Britain v Boots Cash Chemists (Southern) Ltd* [1952] 2 QB 795; affd [1953] 1 QB 401, CA.

it is quite possible for course details to change, so that an applicant may find that a course is offered other than that applied for.

The Universities and Colleges Admissions Service (UCAS)

4.35 UCAS is 'the central agency which acts on behalf of UK universities and colleges of higher education to process applications for entry to their first degree, DipHE, HND and some university diploma courses.'[59] Lest it might be thought that UCAS simply publishes a handbook, sends out and processes application forms, it has published a Mission Statement,[60] reproduced here in full:

> The mission of UCAS is to promote a partnership between applicants on the one hand and universities and colleges on the other so as to provide applicants with equal opportunities to achieve a place in higher education, where they may fulfil their full potential, and to enable institutions to admit committed students who have the ability to benefit.
>
> To this end UCAS will:
> (a) preserve the right of each institution to choose its own students;
> (b) give all applicants, irrespective of gender, age, religion, ethnicity or educational background, the opportunity to choose courses in an informed manner;
> (c) offer a caring support for the users of the application system with due emphasis on the importance of the individual;
> (d) engage in research, consultancy, publication and other advisory activities to enable all parties to make the most of the system;
> (e) promote awareness of the opportunities available in higher education;
> (f) be responsive to changes in secondary, further and higher education and to the needs of society;
> (g) engage in appropriate agency work;
> (h) make its full contribution culturally, commercially and educationally to the environment, both local and national, in which it is rooted; and
> (i) promote the welfare of its staff and their motivation and commitment towards the mission of UCAS.

59 UCAS Handbook 1998 Entry, UCAS, Cheltenham (1997) p 61. Applicants are able to apply to a single institution; the first drafts of the CCI Charters suggested that this could be done outside the UCAS system, apparently in the belief that this would promote choice. This proposal, which was guaranteed to cause chaos, was not pursued.
60 Ibid p 82.

4.36   Setting the Mission Statement and all its good intentions aside, UCAS is simply an administrative device established by institutions to enable applications to be made more easily and to enable easier handling of them by the institutions. It is not itself a recruiting agency: recruitment is the responsibility of the institutions themselves. The relationship between the applicant and UCAS, which is assumed to be contractual, in that there is an intention to create legal relations, is confined to the principal service which UCAS advertises: that is that in return for a fee the applicant will have his or her application forwarded to each of the (up to six) institutions listed on the UCAS application form and that UCAS will handle the necessary paperwork. UCAS is a company limited by guarantee with exclusively charitable objects and therefore has the privileges and liabilities of incorporation and charitable status. Like its predecessors it is an agent for the institutions and as such is not liable for the acts or omissions of its principals unless it were expressly or implicitly to warrant that it had authority to make decisions on their behalf. UCAS publishes a clear disclaimer in its Handbook,[61] refers potential applicants to university and college publications and has adopted as a company object:

> providing and maintaining an organisation to facilitate the consideration by ... [higher education institutions] of applications for admission to and to assist applicants in gaining access to ... [institutions].[62]

If the procedures are not followed according to the information supplied to the applicant by UCAS it is possible that an action might lie against the corporation for breach of contract or negligence, but there are no recorded instances. In recent years there have been problems with computer system faults causing delays, but it is unlikely that these could have been a cause of action unless the corporation or its staff had been grossly negligent, of which there is no evidence.

4.37   UCAS is in fact careful to define the extent of its own liability:

> While UCAS makes every effort to process applications and convey decisions efficiently and accurately, it will not be liable for any mistakes which may occur,[63] or for any decisions communicated to you in good

61 Ibid p 52.
62 Article 3, Memorandum of Association of The Universities and Colleges Admissions Service, registered 27 July 1993.
63 In *Moran v University College of Salford*, the applicant had been admitted through PCAS, when a clerical error at the college caused an unconditional offer to be transmitted instead of a rejection.

faith on behalf of universities and colleges which may subsequently be amended.

and that of the institutions whose agent it is:

> The contents of this handbook do not impose a contractual obligation on any institution to provide any of the courses listed.[64]

4.38 In a section headed 'False statements/omissions' UCAS places liability on the applicant:

> You should understand that when you sign the application form you are confirming that the information you have given is correct and complete. All decisions by universities and colleges are taken in good faith on the basis of the statements you have made in your form. If an institution discovers that you have made a false statement, or have omitted significant information from your application form, eg in examination results, it has the right to withdraw or amend its offer, or terminate your registration at that institution, according to the circumstances.[65]

The Handbook refers to the 'conditions of acceptance'[66] as follows:

> Any offer of a place you may receive from a university or college is made on the understanding that in accepting it you undertake to observe the rules and regulations of the institution and undertake to observe the terms and conditions contained in the prospectus of the university or college concerned. You **must** read these terms and conditions before accepting any offer.[67]

4.39 It is of course these rules and regulations which the prospective student will have difficulty in assimilating at this stage. The Handbook continues with the statement :

> If you become a student at a university or college, it will be a term of your contract with that institution that it will take all reasonable steps to provide the educational services described in its prospectus and other promotional material. However, the institution cannot guarantee to

---

64 UCAS Handbook 1998 p 62.
65 Ibid p 73, a slightly strengthened version of the earlier wording emphasising the right of the institution.
66 In view of the contractual position a better expression would be 'conditions of offer': this suggestion was made in D J Farrington and F T Mattison (eds) *The law governing students* in *Universities and the Law* CUA/CRS (1990) but was not taken up.
67 UCAS Handbook 1998, p 74.

provide those services to you since industrial action or circumstances beyond the control of the institution may from time to time interfere with its ability to provide educational services. In such circumstances the institution will take all reasonable steps to minimise any disruption to your education.[68]

This statement did not appear in the former UCCA handbook. It is assumed that the institutions listed in the UCAS Handbook have consented to this form of disclaimer (and, indeed, agree that there is a contract between the institution and the student). While it is clear that the form of disclaimer used here is virtually identical with that common in the prospectuses of the post-1992 universities and other colleges, it is not clear whether it overrides or is itself overridden by the disclaimers set out in some of the pre-1992 university prospectuses, particularly those which recite that the content of the prospectus does not form part of any contract.

Recruiting agencies – (i) liability for acts of agents

4.40 Higher education institutions employ a variety of agencies to help in the recruitment of overseas students, normally on a fee commission basis. Such arrangements are the subject of a contract between the institution and agency concerned and in all cases it is the institution, not the agency, which has the power to decide whether or not to admit a particular applicant. Two interesting questions arise. The first is about the liability of the institution for the acts of its agents overseas. An agent could deliberately or negligently make a misleading statement in an attempt to sway a student into accepting an offer from a particular institution (eg its proximity to a major city, the number of fellow students of the same nationality, the cost of living).[69] Subject to the terms of the specific agency contract, it is clear according to both the English and Scots laws of agency that the principal is liable where the agent acts within his or her authority[70] and institutions should take all reasonable steps to satisfy themselves of the bona fides, competence and contemporary knowledge of overseas agents.

---

68 UCAS Handbook 1998 p 74.
69 See P Kaye 'Colleges in Court' (1993) Sol Jo 816.
70 See F M B Reynolds *Bowstead on Agency* (15th ed, 1985).

Recruiting agencies – (ii) conflict of laws

4.41 The second question also applies to overseas agents but is of wider importance: it is concerned with the law applicable to the formation of the contract of admission. Where a prospective student is domiciled outside the legal jurisdiction in which the institution is domiciled there may be doubts both about the applicable law and about the courts which would have jurisdiction over any dispute about the contract of admission. The law which governs procedural problems of this kind is called private international law or conflict of laws. Domicile is not the same as nationality or residence. It may be defined in the common law system as the equivalent of a person's permanent home[71] ie the place in which a person has the intention to reside indefinitely.[72] A corporation is always domiciled in the country of incorporation.[73] An offer of admission by an institution domiciled in England made to and accepted by a student domiciled in Scotland constitutes a contract formed on acceptance and prima facie subject to the jurisdiction of the Scottish courts.[74] In general terms, the law applicable to a contract is that specified by the parties or otherwise that of the jurisdiction in which the transaction contemplated by the contract is to be performed,[75] ie with which the contract has the closest and most real connection.[76] The best way to avoid difficulties of this kind is to insert in the offer an express term that any dispute about its terms which cannot be resolved by the institution's internal procedures is subject to the law of the institution's domicile.[77]

Consideration of applications

4.42 Applications to institutions are received from UCAS (or directly from candidates not applying through UCAS) and processed

71 *Whicker v Hume* (1858) 7 HL Cas 124, 160 per Lord Cranworth.
72 *Re Fuld's Estate (No 3)* [1968] P 675, 684 per Scarman J.
73 *Gasque v IRC* [1940] 2 KB 80.
74 Civil Jurisdiction and Judgments Act 1982 giving effect to the Brussels Convention on Jurisdiction and Enforcement of Judgments in Civil and Commercial Matters (1968).
75 The Contracts (Applicable Law) Act 1990 gives effect to most of the terms of the European Community Convention on the Law Applicable to Contractual Obligations (1980).
76 *The Assunzione* [1954] P 150.
77 There is, as CVCP Note N92/112 states, an obvious exception where a foreign court will have jurisdiction in matters wholly within its domestic law, as for example a motor accident during a field trip.

by academic selectors. It is an essential element of the UCAS procedure and good administrative practice that all applications are considered fairly on their merits. 'Offers of admission' may be made on the basis of formal application alone, or on formal application supplemented by interview or examination. They may be either unconditional, in which case a contract of admission is made when the unconditional offer is accepted by the applicant,[78] or conditional (eg on the acquisition of a specified number and grade of passes at GCE or SQA (Higher Grade), BTEC or SQA (vocational) qualifications or a specified class of degree), in which case the contract is made when the conditions are fulfilled and the offer then accepted by the applicant.

Rejection of applications

4.43 There is a corpus of decided cases in Commonwealth jurisdictions relating to the admission of students and in particular an institution's discretion to admit without giving reasons. Apart from any explanations which might be required by a court as part of a proceeding under anti-discrimination legislation or otherwise, English law upholds the principle that no higher education institution is obliged to give reasons for rejecting an application for admission. An institution must have the right to regulate admission, otherwise as surmised by Johnson J in the Canadian case *Pecover v Bowker*[79] it could be compelled to admit students irrespective of its ability to provide adequate tuition and facilities and that might itself constitute grounds for breach of contract, misrepresentation, etc.

4.44 Chartered universities are bound, as against their members,[80] to act in accordance with their Royal Charters, Statutes and other 'domestic' rules. Royal Charters commonly contain provisions designed to secure equality of opportunity on grounds of gender, race and political belief.[81] The CCI Charters reinforce the first two of these, although only the Scottish Charter makes reference to equality of treatment on grounds of sexual orientation.

78 As in *Moran v University College Salford (No 2)* [1994] ELR 187.
79 (1957) 8 DLR (2d) 20.
80 The possibility of a non-member bringing an action for breach of the provisions of a Royal Charter appears to be remote: see later discussion. Universities founded by or under the authority of statute law are in a different position.
81 The reason for these provisions is historical, reflecting the emancipation of the university system starting with the foundation of the original London University in the 1820s, the first to admit Jews; see also s 3 Sex Disqualification (Removal) Act 1919.

4.45 Subject to the supervening provisions of a Royal Charter, in many universities the power to refuse candidates is expressly stated, eg 'The Vice-Chancellor may without assigning any reason refuse to admit any person as a Student'[82] or 'The Vice-Chancellor may refuse to admit any person as a Student without disclosing any reason to that person.'[83] The power given to the Vice-Chancellor[84] to refuse admission is often linked with powers to suspend or exclude existing students and it appears to be both a vestige of the powers vested in the authorities of the medieval institutions to refuse to admit those who had been outlawed[85] and a power inherited from days when administration as such had not been invented.[86] It appears to be the case that a rejected applicant cannot pursue any contractual remedy against a university, since there is no contractual relationship between them. An applicant to a university with a Visitor may possibly have the right to petition that officer[87] but otherwise any remedy for a rejected applicant would have to be found in an application for judicial review.

4.46 A number of cases progressively established the reluctance of the courts to interfere in questions of admission to an essentially private organisation: to an Inn of Court,[88] to the Stock Exchange,[89] to a trainer's licence for horse racing from the Jockey Club,[90] and to a manager's licence by the British Boxing Board of Control.[91] Each of the circumstances concerned the effective deprivation of a perceived 'right' or 'liberty' to work and admission to the status was essential

82 University of Surrey, Statute 5A.
83 Loughborough University of Technology, Statute V(4).
84 One assumes it may be delegated.
85 See M B Hackett *The Original Statutes of Cambridge University* (1970) p 210: The Constitutions of the University of Cambridge XI(iii).
86 See the discussion in Chapter 1 on the powers and duties of the Principal of the Yorkshire College, the progenitor of the University of Leeds.
87 John Bridge seems to suggest this may be possible in (1970) lxxxvi Law Quarterly Review 531. In *R v Visitors to the Inns of Court, ex p Calder* and *R v Same, ex p Persaud* [1994] 3 WLR 994, Mann LJ referred to the historical account by W C Bolland 'Two problems in Legal History' (1908) 24 LQR 392. The dispute in those cases was about the discipline of existing barristers, but the jurisdiction of the Visitors over the admission, conduct and discipline of would-be 'inner' and 'utter' barristers was discussed. It is clear that the Visitorial jurisdiction extended to the selection of persons for admission (*Re S (a barrister)* [1970] 1 QB 160, 170 per Paull J) but also that the role of judges in this capacity was a statutory power totally different to that of the role of Visitors to universities: [1992] 3 WLR 994, 1007 per Mann LJ.
88 *R v Benchers of Lincoln's Inn* (1825) 4 B & C 855.
89 *Weinberger v Inglis (No 2)* [1919] AC 606.
90 *Nagle v Feilden* [1966] 2 QB 633.
91 *McInnes v Onslow Fane* [1978] 3 All ER 211.

to professional practice. If there is any enforceable 'right' of a candidate for admission it probably lies somewhere between an application to join a club ('If a man applies to join a social club and is blackballed he has no cause of action'[92]) and an application for a licence to practice.

4.47   In *R v Benchers of Lincoln's Inn*[93] both Abbott CJ and Bayley J adverted to the concept of an inchoate right to be admitted a member of a college 'in either of the universities' (ie Oxford and Cambridge). Bayley J's obiter dictum that '... [these societies] make their own rules as to the admission of members, and even if they act capriciously upon the subject, this Court can give no remedy ...' was disapproved by both Lord Denning MR and Salmon LJ in the more recent case *Nagle v Feilden*[94] and apparently also by Lord Atkinson, Lord Parmoor and Lord Wrenbury in *Weinberger v Inglis (No 2)*.[95] However, Bayley J's later statement that '... an individual has no inchoate right to be admitted as a member of a college and there is no obligation upon the college to admit him ...' has survived criticism. The *Lincoln's Inn* and similar cases[96] were reviewed by the Queen's Bench Divisional Court in 1992 in *R v Visitors to Inns of Court, ex p Calder* (and *R v Same, ex p Persaud)*.[97] In an earlier review of the admission cases by Megarry VC in *McInnes v Onslow Fane*[98] it was established that no reasons for rejection of an applicant need be given, for to do otherwise would supply the applicant with material which would assist him or her in engaging the organisation in litigation. Megarry VC asked but did not answer the question 'Is a university when selecting candidates for admission acting unfairly when it gives no reasons to the unsuccessful?'

4.48   Indeed there appeared until recently to be no requirement to comply with the rules of natural justice, although in the former polytechnic case *CCETSW v Edwards*,[99] where the provision of a diploma was vital to the potential student's career, it was held that where an interview is given it must be conducted fairly. And Blain J's dictum in *R v University of Aston Senate, ex p Roffey*,[100] where

---

92   *Nagle v Feilden* [1966] 2 QB 633, 639 per Lord Denning MR.
93   (1825) 4 B & C 855, 859.
94   [1966] 2 QB 633, 644, 654.
95   [1919] AC 606, 632, 636, 642.
96   Eg *R v Benchers of Gray's Inn* (1780) 1 Doug 353.
97   [1992] 3 WLR 994, 1000, 1002. See note 12.
98   [1978] 3 All ER 211, 222.
99   (1978) Times, 5 May.
100 [1969] 2 QB 538, 556.

he stressed the significance of possession of a degree to the job market, is also of significance. The acquisition of graduate status is no doubt of economic and social significance, but an individual institution is not generally a monopoly supplier. It is argued that the only right, if one exists at all, is to be dealt with fairly and for the application to be determined honestly, without bias and caprice, however difficult that might be to prove.[101] A rejection by a university does not cast a slur on an applicant, unlike rejection of an application for membership of certain clubs and societies. The principle that a candidate should be treated fairly and not subjected to any unreasonable undisclosed criteria appears to lie at the heart of the decision of the Court of Session in the recent case *Reilly v University of Glasgow*[102] where the unsuccessful candidate failed to show that he had the required commitment to a career in medicine. In that case the court made it clear that it was not concerned with the merits of the criteria adopted by Glasgow. It was concerned with whether Glasgow had acted illegally by imposing an unstated criterion for admission. The court found neither the intention to impose, nor the actual imposition, of a requirement that candidates should have work experience before they were entitled to admission to the medical faculty.

Discrimination on grounds of race, etc

4.49 The principle of fairness also appears in the pre-1976 case *Cumings v Birkenhead Corpn*.[103] There was no provision for discrimination in education in the Race Relations Act 1968 but the court in that case clearly expressed its right to intervene where a policy excluding pupils of one racial group from a particular school was unreasonable, capricious or irrelevant. However in that case it was demonstrated that the policy was adopted for sound educational reasons. Following the *Cumings* case, RRA which replaced the Race Relations Act 1968 introduced provisions to outlaw discrimination in the educational setting in Great Britain.[104] Section 17 (as amended

---

101 See *Barber v Manchester Regional Hospital Board* [1958] 1 WLR 181, 193 per Barry J; *Greater Lonon Council v Connolly* [1970] 1 All ER 870, 875 per Lord Denning MR.
102 [1996] ELR 394: see in respect of alleged arbitrary and subjective admissions criteria decisions in favour of the institutions in *Grove v Ohio State University* 424 FSupp 377 (1976); *Arizona Board of Regents v Wilson* 539 P2d 943 (1975).
103 [1971] 2 All ER 881.
104 The Conservative Government (prior to May 1997) announced its intention to extend RRA to Northern Ireland.

by the 1988–92 education legislation) makes it unlawful for a governing body to discriminate on grounds of race, etc against a person in the conditions of an offer[105] for admission, refusing or deliberately omitting to accept an application for admission, or in the way of affording that person as a student access to any facilities of the institution or excluding that person. It is unlawful to refuse to admit a person on racial grounds (direct discrimination) or to impose requirements or conditions which can only be complied with by a considerably smaller proportion of that racial group as opposed to others (indirect discrimination). Racial grounds means colour, race, nationality or ethnic or national origin. Section 41 RRA provides for exclusions in some instances, notably where legislation (eg Education (Fees and Awards) Act 1983) renders lawful what would otherwise be unlawful under RRA.

4.50   It appears to be settled in English law that only a member of the corporation or the state may intervene to enforce a Royal Charter, normally by writ of *scire facias* initiated by the Attorney-General; and in Scotland by proceedings exclusively initiated by the Crown (*Conn v Provost, Magistrates and Councillors of Renfrew).*[106] Thus enforcement of Charter provisions by a non-student or a person or organisation acting on his or her behalf seems a remote possibility. Judicial review as in the *Reilly* case seems possible but the technical procedures are unlikely to be appreciated fully by an overseas applicant. In any event higher education institutions may take a very much more cautious approach to volunteering reasons for refusing admission than the University of Glasgow did in *Reilly*. It is much more likely that if the issue of a personal complaint arises, action would be taken under RRA. Action under the Act must be initiated in the courts (the Sheriff Court in Scotland) within six months (eight months in certain circumstances where CRE is involved). A complainant normally issues a questionnaire to the institution with the objective of clarifying the reasons for the action taken.

4.51   On finding an allegation of discrimination to be proved, the court has all the powers to take whatever action is appropriate in the circumstances but it seems highly unlikely that any court would

105 As to the meaning of 'offer' see the recent case *Burns v University Court of the University of Edinburgh* (26 March 1996, unreported) Sheriff Court Edinburgh.
106 (1906) 8 F 905.

order an institution to admit a student which it had rejected.[107] In addition no award of damages may be made where the institution proves that the action it took by way of alleged indirect discrimination was not done with the intention of treating the claimant unfavourably on racial grounds.[108]

4.52　Section 36 RRA permits an institution to do anything *for the benefit of* persons not ordinarily resident in Great Britain in affording access to facilities for education and training or any ancillary benefits, where it appears to the institution that the persons in question do not intend to remain in Great Britain after their period of education or training here. In other words, one may discriminate in favour of overseas students. It appears that this does not prevent an institution doing something which is *adverse* to a person from outwith Great Britain but this interpretation is untested. Separately the CRE has the power under the Act to initiate an inquiry and to issue a non-discrimination notice.[109] In principle this would seem to pose a more obvious threat to an institution's position if it became apparent that it was in fact following a policy which was discriminatory on grounds of race.

Educational reasons distinguished from racial grounds

4.53　The question is how this apparently all-embracing prohibition on discriminating against nationalities etc squares with the ability of an institution to reject applicants so as to apply educational criteria to form a class which does not consist exclusively or largely of a particular nationality. It is after all overtly educational criteria which are being applied, not racial criteria, either overtly or covertly. No assistance can be found from reading the debates which took place in the House of Commons and House of Lords on the clause in the Bill which became RRA. There is no mention of overseas students and no mention of reasons other than racially-motivated reasons for

---

107　In *Moran v University College Salford (No 2)* [1994] ELR 187, the Court of Appeal allowed an application for leave to appeal against the refusal by a deputy High Court judge to grant a mandatory injunction on an interlocutory application to compel the college to admit the applicant, but dismissed the appeal in discretion, leaving the applicant to pursue damages for breach of contract. M would clearly have been unsuited to the course on ground of educational attainment.

108　Section 57(3) RRA.

109　Section 58 RRA: in the 1980s an investigation by the CRE found evidence of racial bias at an institution which used an excessively mechanical selection process.

declining admission. It appears to have been assumed that what is being prohibited by the legislation is discrimination against persons within the jurisdiction, and the appearance of section 36 reinforces that view. Against that it may be argued that, particularly where students are being recruited from within the EU and therefore pay the same fees as and have the same rights of abode as, UK citizens, it is difficult to draw a distinction between, say, a Spaniard living in London and one living in Spain. An attempt must be made to define the educational grounds upon which institutions might reasonably and lawfully discriminate against candidates from a particular overseas country in order to ensure that the quality of the programme is maintained.

4.54 While no assistance can be found from domestic law, some US cases provide some quotations which might be applied here. In the 'affirmative action' case *McDonald v Hogness*[110] the court quoted Frankfurter J in the landmark case *Sweezy v New Hampshire*[111] 'It is the business of a university to provide that atmosphere which is most conducive to speculation, experiment and creation. It is an atmosphere in which there prevail "the four essential freedoms" of a university – to determine for itself on academic grounds who may teach, what may be taught, how it shall be taught and who may be admitted to study.' The Washington Supreme Court went on to say: '... we believe that the atmosphere of "speculation, experimentation and creation" is promoted by a diverse student body.' It acknowledged that while the university must be viewed as seeking to achieve that goal that is of paramount importance in the fulfilment of its mission, constitutional limitations protecting individual rights must not be disregarded. The US courts have, surprisingly given the volume of litigation in higher education there, not been asked to consider cases of discrimination against non-US citizens other than on issues concerned with financial aid.[112] Hence the relevant case law relates only to discrimination against or in favour of (positive action) US citizens.

Guaranteed places

4.55 It has become common for institutions to guarantee places to certain categories of student, notably those undertaking access

---

110 598 P2d 707 (Wash 1979).
111 354 US 234, 263 (1957).
112 For example *Nyquist v Jean-Marie Mauclet* 432 US 1 (1977); *Toll v Moreno* 458 US 1 (1982).

courses, coming into the institution from an associated college or from a particular group of schools. All such guarantees are dependent upon performance in the qualifications required for entry, so remain conditional until those qualifications are obtained. Once the conditions are met, however, the contract becomes binding on both parties. It is not always clear that an institution gives as much attention to these candidates as it does to those applying in the normal way through UCAS and if this is so difficulties may arise later.

Conclusion of the contract of admission

4.56 When offers are accepted the institution and the applicant are contractually committed either conditionally or unconditionally, except where an 'insurance offer' (ie a fall-back position in case the necessary conditions for the principal offer are not met) is held in accordance with UCAS procedures. Once an applicant has been admitted, ie has accepted a place unconditionally or has satisfied the conditions precedent, he or she is outside UCAS's sphere. The necessary consideration in English law for the existence of the contract of admission is the promise by the applicant, in accepting the offer, to pay (or have paid by the appropriate authority) the fees demanded by the institution or, as in the *Moran* case, a detriment in that Paul Moran had given up his accommodation etc and was unable to re-enter via clearing.

4.57 At the point of formation of this preliminary contract, the terms are as follows:
- On the institution's part, to admit the applicant (i) on his/her payment of fees and otherwise complying with the relevant rules of the institution; (ii) on the basis of the offer of admission for the course or programme of study specified or agreed variation, subject to any disclaimer and including any provisos which may allow further variation in the availability of certain subjects or courses from year to year.
- On the applicant's part, to enter the institution and to (i) abide by the institution's rules; (ii) to pay or cause to be paid all relevant fees and charges at the appropriate time.

4.58 It is often forgotten that the applicant is as much bound by the contract to take up the place as the institution is bound to admit him or her, although it is highly unlikely that an institution would take action to enforce that part of the bargain. The institution's rules to which the applicant is subscribing, including the charter or instrument of government, statutes or articles, ordinances or byelaws, rules, regulations, etc, so far as they are not set out in the prospectus, may only be found in the institution's calendar or rulebook, a document unlikely to be readily accessible outside the institution. However, it is clear that the applicant is bound by them, even if he or she has not seen them, subject to the application of the Unfair Contract Terms Act and the Consumer Contract Regulations.

Quality

4.59 The question arises whether there is at this stage any warranty as to the quality of the instruction and facilities which the institution will provide to enable the course to be followed. Questions of quality assurance have been discussed earlier: if there is an implied term relating to quality in the institution-student contract it could also be implied in the contract of admission. The CCI Charters set out the right of applicants to be given full information about courses (amongst other things) so that at the pre-contract stage an informed choice can be made: this includes information derived from the quality audits and assessments to which all institutions are now subject and for which information is published by QAA. The CCI Charter for England states that universities and colleges can be expected to include in their prospectuses information on when an audit by HEQC (now QAA) last took place and on the availability of recent or forthcoming audit reports but there is no reference to inclusion in prospectuses of material about the Funding Council quality assessments, no doubt to avoid the possibility of selective quotation. All the relevant material is however available on the internet for potential students to browse.

Attempts to vary the terms of the contract of admission

4.60 Problems can arise when for strategic reasons, mainly due to changes in the financing of the institution, it seeks to make major changes in its academic programme, for example the elimination of a subject. This may occur either before or after admission. Two questions arise: (i) to what extent the institution is compelled by the operation of law to offer the course for which a potential student has applied and has accepted an unconditional or conditional offer; and (ii) where an existing student has already embarked on a course with reasonable expectation of being able to complete a specified programme of study, what are the institution's obligations. The first of these will be tackled here, whereas post-entry changes will be dealt with later.

4.61 The UCAS Handbook[113] deals with the situation in which a course is discontinued after application, but before a contract is formed. In such cases it is UCAS policy that wherever possible applications should not be disadvantaged by the discontinuation of a course, but there appears to be no remedy available either to UCAS or the disaffected applicant in these circumstances.

4.62 The position in which an offer and acceptance have been validly exchanged seems clear. Both parties have entered into a contract, the terms of which are set out above. Although the courts would expect a student whose offer had been withdrawn after acceptance to seek to mitigate the loss by finding an alternative course, it would also expect the institution to make every reasonable endeavour either to accommodate the student on another course or to find that student a place at another institution, no matter how widely drawn the institution's prospectus disclaimer might be. In the last resort, when no reasonable alternative was available, the institution would be liable to action for breach of contract with damages quantified according to the general principles of the law of contract, including the lost opportunity of one year's work in the student's life and any other detriment suffered as a consequence of, and attributable to, the breach.

Doctrine of supervening impossibility

4.63 Although largely unheard of in the past, there were reports of some institutions threatening to renege on accepted offers in the aftermath of the Government's u-turn on expansion in 1993.[114] In practice, although there were some courses withdrawn for reasons of financial exigency, the institutions concerned stated that they would apply offer conditions strictly, thus reducing the prospect of legal action. The problem largely evaporated. However, the legal issue remains: possibly the institutions could rely on the doctrine of frustration or supervening impossibility, ie that cuts in funding through the mechanism of tuition fees had made it impossible to run

---

113 Paragraph 14 in the 1998 edition.
114 The *Moran* case can be distinguished since it arose due to a clerical error in informing PCAS that the candidate had been admitted, whereas he had in fact been rejected.

the courses and therefore impossible to perform the contract. The best-known examples of this argument in the law of contract are where a major public event (eg a royal funeral) fails to take place resulting in loss to those hiring viewing space,[115] a music venue burns down[116] or a star performer is ill[117] or is called up for military service for an indefinite period.[118] A contract to write a book would be frustrated if the author went mad.[119]

4.64 The doctrine, which in Latin is *non haec in foedera veni* (it was not this that I promised to do) is best expressed in the dictum of Lord Radcliffe in *Davis Contractors Ltd v Fareham UDC*:[120]

> Frustration occurs whenever the law recognises that without default of either party a contractual obligation has become incapable of being performed because the circumstances in which performance is called for would render it a thing radically different from that which was undertaken by the contract.

However, a contract providing for alternative methods of performance is not frustrated merely because one of them becomes impossible.[121] In Scotland the court in the exercise of equitable jurisdiction will order what seems just in the circumstances.[122] It is clear that a contract for the export of goods is dissolved if their export is prohibited by statute[123] although not necessarily if by Order in Council of uncertain duration.[124] If therefore the Secretary of State or the Funding Council in exercise of statutory authority were to withdraw funding in particular areas, it may be argued that this action discharges any contract for provision of teaching in such areas. On the other hand institutions are probably bound by contracts which provided for no tuition fees to be charged even though the Government sought to impose them on students accepted in 1996 for deferred-entry places in 1998, which are otherwise subject to fees.

115 *Krell v Henry* [1903] 2 KB 740.
116 *Taylor v Caldwell* (1863) 3 B & S 826.
117 *Robinson v Davison* (1871) LR 6 Exch 269; *Poussard v Spiers* (1876) 1 QBD 410.
118 *Morgan v Manser* [1948] 1 KB 184.
119 *Jackson v Union Marine Insurance Co Ltd* (1874) LR 10 CP 125.
120 [1956] AC 696, 729.
121 *Cornelius v Banque Franco-Serbe* [1942] 1 KB 29.
122 Lord Cooper (1946) 28 J Comp Leg 1, 5.
123 *Re Anglo-Russian Merchant Traders and Batt* [1917] 2 KB 679.
124 *Andrew Millar & Co Ltd v Taylor & Co Ltd* [1916] 1 KB 402.

4.65 Similar problems may arise in taught postgraduate courses or with research students whose offers of admission to work with a particular member of staff have been accepted and the member of staff, by analogy with the star performer in the supervening impossibility case, then leaves, falls seriously ill or dies before the student actually starts work. Unless the doctrine of frustration can be called in aid, the institution might be obliged to try to find an alternative supervisor from within its existing staff or find a suitable place for the student at another institution. Otherwise it is possible, albeit unlikely, that a court (or Visitor, if there was jurisdiction, for example if the prospective graduate student was already an undergraduate member of the university) would order the institution to hire a suitably qualified member of staff. Tentative authority for this may be found in *Tsakiroglou & Co Ltd v Noblee und Thorl GmbH*.[125] In this case a cargo of nuts was to be delivered by a vessel due to travel via the Suez Canal. The canal having been closed, the ship had to take a longer route. The House of Lords held that the contract was not frustrated, since it did not expressly provide a route and since the route was immaterial to the buyer. In the case of the research student, the identification of the supervisor will almost certainly be material and the application form may specify who the supervisor is to be.

Transition to matriculation

4.66 A new contractual relationship, or phase in the continuing contractual relationship, called matriculation, registration or enrolment, is formed when the applicant completes the institution's registration procedures and becomes a student.[126] This change in the relationship generally requires the production of proof that the applicant has satisfied any conditions attaching to the offer of admission and the payment of any fees and charges due on registration. From *Orphanos v Queen Mary College*,[127] referred to by Glidewell LJ in *Moran v University College Salford (No 2)*,[128] it is clear that the 'vital question of fees' needs to be resolved before the contract is concluded and this lies at the heart of the advice given by CVCP to universities and colleges in 1996 and 1997 prior to the introduction of undergraduate tuition fees in the UK. The contract

125 [1961] 2 All ER 179, HL.
126 'Matriculation' is derived from 'matricula' or roll of members of the institution.
127 (1984) unreported, CA. The appeal to the House of Lords is reported at [1985] AC 761.
128 [1994] ELR 187.

also requires formal subscription by the applicant to the rules of the institution: a contract of admission through UCAS or directly through the institution[129] contains an express term to that effect which presumably remains in force, although this proposition has not been tested in the courts. When this contract has been entered into, the applicant becomes a registered student, who in a chartered institution is normally a corporator with all the associated rights, privileges and obligations attaching to that status, or at least is 'on the foundation' for the purposes of the visitorial jurisdiction. It is at this point that the individual in the chartered institution acquires two distinct but related relationships with the institution, contractual and that derived from status.

The contract of matriculation

Introduction

4.67 The term 'contract of matriculation' used by Lord Devlin[130] is interchangeable in the case of chartered bodies with 'contract of membership' used by Sir William Wade. It is the contract made between the institution and the student, the terms of which are similar to those of the contract of admission (including that related to equality of opportunity), except that the condition requiring admission has been performed and it may be that there is a new implied term relating to quality. A contract of this type is a bundle of obligations attaching to both parties.

Duration of contract

4.68 It is assumed that the contract is one for the whole course, subject to early termination if for example there is failure to meet the academic requirements of programmes. It is however arguable that on registration at the beginning of each session (or each semester for those institutions adopting a self-contained semester-module system) a new contract is entered into, it being an implied term of the previous contract that a new one will be made, provided any academic prerequisites have been met and consideration is received

---

129 It is interesting to note that a sample of postgraduate application forms, even in 1997, showed little evidence of this requirement being imposed on applicants.
130 *Report of the Sit-In in February 1972 and its Consequences* (Devlin Report) Vol C111, *Cambridge University Reporter*, Special, No 12, 14 February 1972, paragraph 154.

in the form of fees. It may be that a self-standing credit accumulation system would have various different contractual obligations associated with it. An implied term to continue registration would no doubt be argued on the same basis as that put forward for the unsuccessful aspiring female doctors in *Jex-Blake v Senatus Academicus of the University of Edinburgh*[131] ie that the institution could not arbitrarily exclude a student from a course for which she was properly qualified in terms of the academic and other regulations. Had she been male, the argument would probably never had arisen.

4.69 In such cases as *Akhtar v Dalhousie University*[132] and *Tuttle v Edinburgh University*[133] the courts have recognised obligations which can only be founded in contract. Contract has also been used as a basis for the decisions in *London School of Economics and Political Science v Adelstein*[134] and *University of Essex v Ratcliffe*,[135] both disciplinary cases and *Fox v Stirk, Ricketts v Registration Officer for Cambridge*,[136] on the right to be entered on the electoral roll. It was relied upon by the university in *University of Hull v Fawthrop*[137] where Tom Fawthrop was sued for breach of contract when he allegedly created a disturbance by inter alia tearing up his examination papers in an examination hall.

4.70 In *Joobeen v University of Stirling*[138] Lord Prosser held that although membership of a university (in this case a chartered university) could produce situations where judicial review was appropriate the issue in this case, failure to pay fees, being a purely contractual one, judicial review was incompetent.[139] In *Rajah v Royal*

131 (1873) 11 M 784. Women were seriously disadvantaged in higher education, as in other fields, until well into the 20th century. In Scotland, the University of St Andrews offered an external degree level qualification for women between 1877 and 1931 but only men could be admitted to degrees. The notable exception was the University of London, where women were admitted to 'special certificates of proficiency' in 1867 and to degrees in all faculties in 1876.
132 (1977) 21 NSR (2d) 593.
133 1984 SLT 17212: this case concerned the contractual duty of care to a student injured falling from a tree during supervised practice. CVCP has issued a *Code of Practice for Safety in Fieldwork* (1995) which advises higher education institutions of their duty of care '..to those they supervise ...' It goes on to state (p 1) that 'There is, of course, also the moral duty that the teacher has towards the pupil.' See also *Guidance Note on Tree Climbing* (1989) NERC.
134 (1969) Guardian, 31 January and 8 February.
135 (1969) Times, 28 November.
136 [1970] 2 QB 463.
137 (1969) Daily Telegraph, 25 January.
138 1995 SLT 120n.
139 In fact, as fees had not been paid in full, Mr Joobeen had never become a member of the university as he had never matriculated.

College of Surgeons in Ireland[140] Keane J held that the College derived its jurisdiction solely from the contract between itself and its students. This was a private law arrangement and as such not amenable to judicial review.[141] In Keane J's view it was not sufficient that the College had a statutory underpinning or a charter[142] to bring its academic decisions within the ambit of judicial review. In any event, the appeals committee which heard Ms Rajah's academic appeal had heard it in a fair and reasonable manner.[143] As was made clear by the Judicial Committee of the Privy Council in *Vidyodaya University Council v Silva*[144] a remedy through judicial review would be refused to a university lecturer who had been dismissed from his post without a hearing, since the law would not restore employment specifically in a relationship which the Board judged to be purely contractual, a point recently reinforced in *R v University College London, ex p Rinneker*.[145] The same must be true of the student contract of membership – in support of which proposition may be cited the decision in *Fekete v Royal Institution for the Advancement of Learning*.[146] However, as Sedley J put it quite simply in *R v Manchester Metropolitan University, ex p Nolan*[147]: 'The respondent is a body corporate by virtue of Chapter II of the Education Reform Act 1988. As a public institution discharging public functions, and having no Visitor, it is subject to judicial review of its decisions on conventional grounds' ie generally on grounds of illegality, irrationality or procedural impropriety.[148] The concept of a contract existing between Manchester Metropolitan University and Damian Nolan was not even raised.

---

140 [1994] 1 IRLM 233.
141 His Lordship applied *Murphy v Turf Club* [1989] IR 171, *Beirne v Comr of An Garda Síochána* [1993] IRLM 1 and earlier cases.
142 The Charter was granted originally by George III in 1784, with repeals/ amendments in 1828 and 1844.
143 Also, although not strictly relevant to the decision, the court took the view that the appeal committee's decision not to allow Ms Rajah to repeat her failed year, which she had asked for on grounds of personal circumstances and illness, was not of a nature as to necessitate the giving of reasons, applying *State (Creedon) v Criminal Injuries Compensation Tribunal* [1988] IR 51; *International Fishing Vessels v Minister for Marine* [1989] IR 149.
144 [1965] 1 WLR 77.
145 (16 December 1994, unreported), CA.
146 (1969) BR 1.
147 [1994] ELR 380, DC.
148 *Council of Civil Service Unions v Minister for the Civil Service* [1985] AC 374 per Lord Diplock at 410D–411B.

Agreement to terms

4.71 By registering and matriculating the student must 'be taken to have agreed ... to be bound by the statutes of the university ...'[149] and agreed to provisions relating to 'dismissal, discipline, regulations respecting examinations, re-reading of examination papers and so on,'[150] again probably without knowing what they are.[151] In *R v University of Aston Senate, ex p Roffey*[152] it was held that the University's regulations only took effect by way of contract, ie the students accepted them by becoming a party to a contractual relationship.

The institution's obligations

4.72 Certain obligations of institutions have been recognised for over a century. This can be illustrated by the 1890 case *Cadells v Balfour*[153] where two medical students averred that as they had attended college on the basis of its prospectus and had paid fees for a course of lectures they had established a contract by which the college was obliged to provide them with the course. It was held that such a contract was established. Although the college concerned was a voluntary medical school (run by Dr Jex-Blake who had unsuccessfully sought to compel the University of Edinburgh to provide the lectures necessary for her and other women to complete a medical degree),[154] arguably in a weaker position than an institution founded by charter or similar instrument, the general principle that students cannot ex post facto be deprived of rights for which they have contracted would apply to all institutions.

4.73 The contract in Ms Cadell's case was held not only to consist of written materials but also other facts and circumstances. Lord Kyllachy[155] identified two obligations on the part of the students: to

149 *Ceylon University v Fernando* [1960] 1 WLR 223, 231 per Lord Jenkins.
150 *Sutcliffe v Governors of Acadia University* (1978) 95 DLR (3d) 95, 101 per Cooper JA.
151 James Parlour and L R V Burwood 'Student Rights' (1995) 7(2) Education and the Law 63, suggest that there is extreme variation in both the quality and quantity of information given to students regarding the internal rules and procedures of the institution.
152 [1969] 2 QB 538.
153 (1890) 17 R 1138; see also *Lyall v Service* (1863) 2 M 115.
154 *Jex-Blake v Senatus Academicus of the University of Edinburgh* (1873) 11 M 784, referred to above.
155 (1890) 17 R 1138, 1149.

pay fees and to conform in all respects to the regulations in force from time to time. Authority for the second of these obligations was found in *Fitzgerald v Northcote*[156] where Lord Cockburn said of the relationship between a school and its scholars:

> I hold that there is an implied contract between the parent and the preceptor that the latter will continue to educate the child so long as his conduct does not warrant his expulsion from the school.[157]

4.74 A number of twentieth century cases have highlighted particular terms of the contract of matriculation. Among these are *D'Mello v Loughborough College of Technology*[158] and *Sammy v Birkbeck College*[159] in which the contractual relationship was admitted.

> Edmund D'Mello who was working for an oil company overseas had joined a postgraduate course in economics and administration of petroleum technology on the basis of information contained in the prospectus. The court, hearing the case some years after the event, held that although the college was bound to provide a course according to the syllabus set out in the prospectus, it was free to determine how to teach it and there could be no complaint even if the emphasis differed from the expectations of the student. In fact the course was taught in a general manner first of all, with the intention of applying the principles learnt to the petroleum industry in due course. Mr D'Mello did not remain on the course long enough for this to happen. The course was, according to the report, being given for the first time and like many courses of this type it had some 'teeting troubles' although O'Connor J held that there was no breach of the duty the college owed to Mr D'Mello to exercise professional skill and judgment in conducting the course.
>
> Mr Sammy had been given a third class honours degree and brought an action for mandamus to compel the award of the first class degree to which he felt he was entitled. He also sued for damages for breach of contract, fraud and professional negligence. The college admitted the existence of a contract.

4.75 In *Sammy's* case the outcome was reported in the NUS/NCCL report *Academic Freedom and the Law*:

---

156 (1865) 4 F & F 656.
157 See in relation to the contractual nature of a private school's relationship with its pupils *R v Fernhill Manor School, ex p B* [1994] 1 FCR 146, DC.
158 (1970) Times, 17 June: the College was the predecessor of the present Loughborough University of Technology.
159 (1964) Times, 3 November.

Broadly speaking, on accepting the place as a student – he having paid the recognised fee – the college were contractually bound to provide proper tuition and laboratory facilities ... There was, too, an implied term that the college had the facilities and staff with necessary professional skill to carry out the tuition required for the internal degree examination of the University of London.[160]

4.76 In the US, courts have considered college bulletins, programme guides, brochures and oral representations of faculty advisers, deans and chairpersons all as having contractual effect, resolving ambiguities largely in favour of the institution[161] and applying considerations of custom and tradition in interpreting respective rights and obligations in the contract.[162] Oral representations which contradict formal university requirements can give rise to estoppel[163] although erroneous statements will not always lead to intervention[164] especially where the statements clearly contradict written information.[165]

4.77 The institution's obligations, as has already been pointed out in relation to the contract of admission, include a requirement to treat students equally regardless of gender, race, ethnic or national origin or marital status. The Disability Discrimination Act 1995 extends this principle so far as is reasonably practicable to facilities for disabled students. Some institutions' policies go further than this and may become incorporated in the contract of matriculation by implication: for example a requirement not to discriminate on ground of sexual orientation, a right to which the Scottish but not the English CCI Charter makes express reference. Like applicants, matriculated students may also take action under the relevant provisions of the anti-discrimination legislation, whether or not the institution is subject to the Visitorial jurisdiction, although failure to comply with the anti-discrimination provisions of Charters and Statutes would lie within that jurisdiction. Even the purely statutory route can lead to

---

160 See *Academic Freedom and the Law* Report of the NUS/NCCL Commission (1970) p 59.
161 A Tucker *Avoiding Legal Pitfalls: Sensitivity to Faculty and Student Concerns* in *Chairing the Academic Department* (1984).
162 See *Greene v Howard University* 412 Fed Supp 2d 1128 (1969); *Koblitz v Western Reserve University* 21 Ohio CCR 133 (1901); see also cases referred to in T A Schweitzer 'Academic Challenge Cases: Should Judicial Review extend to Academic Evaluations of Students?' (1992) The American University Law Review , Winter, 264.
163 Eg *Blank v Board of Higher Education* 273 NYS 2d 796 (1966).
164 Eg *Olsson v Board of Higher Education* 402 NE 2d 1150 (1980).
165 Eg *Wilson v Illinois Benedictine College* 445 NE 2d 901 (1983).

complicated and therefore potentially lengthy and expensive procedures as illustrated by *Olaleye-Oruene v London Guildhall University*[166] where the alleged discrimination occurred in 1990 and 1991 but the matter was not finally disposed of (against the applicant) until 1997.

4.78 Protection of students against sexual harassment, where this can be distinguished from agreement to participate in consensual relations,[167] is attracting increasing attention[168] and most institutions have equal opportunities codes of practice to deal with this and the related issue of racial harassment. The issue of sexual harassment in employment as discrimination under SDA will be discussed. In the US, sexual harassment is a violation of Title IX of the Educational Amendments Act of 1972:

> No person in the United States shall, on the basis of sex, be excluded from participation in, be denied the benefit of, or be subject to discrimination under any education program or activity receiving Federal assistance ...

Sexually harrassed students can sue schools and colleges for unlimited damages.[169] As yet, this is not the case in the UK.

4.79 There may however be another and rather delicate issue not unrelated to this which an institution may have to act upon. This requires the implication into the contract of a duty of care both to the individual student and the rest of the institution's community, arising when a student is known by the institution (as opposed to a medical practitioner) to be a carrier of an infectious disease (for example the HIV virus) although he or she may in every other way comply with the institution's regulations. The issue is legally relatively simple: the institution does not stand in loco parentis, does not warrant that all its students, staff and visitors are physically and mentally fit, and owes to its staff, students and visitors only the common law duty of care and the statutory duty under the health and safety at work legislation. While in the case of smoking a duty may be implied under health and safety at work legislation to provide adequate facilities for non-smokers, there is no authority for the

---

166 [1997] 4 All ER 181, CA.
167 See in this connection the AUT *Code of Conduct on Personal Relations between Staff and Students in Universities* (1993).
168 See eg D Middlemiss and R Stewart 'Sexual harassment in education' in (1993) 5(41) Education and the Law p 189.
169 *Franklin v Gwinnet County Public Schools* 112 S Ct 1028 (1992).

suggestion that an institution which allows an HIV-positive carrier to remain in its employment or as a student is failing in these duties, nor for the further extension of the duty of care to those with whom the student comes into contact outside the institution. However, in providing a professional standard of service of guidance and counselling it may have a duty to warn the student that the condition concerned may effectively debar certain career avenues and that he or she would be advised possibly to change academic direction in order to keep other avenues open. The overriding principle is that the institution must do what can reasonably be expected of it in the circumstances. A parallel can be drawn between an institution's duty of care towards people who can be expected to exercise reasonable care themselves and that of a housing authority towards its tenants, where there is no absolute guarantee that lifts in a high rise block and other facilities will be working.[170]

4.80   Not every action or omission of the institution will give rise to a successful breach of contract claim. In *McBeth v Governors of Dalhousie College and University*[171] M brought an action for breach of contract when the University failed to schedule a replacement examination after he missed the regular one due to illness. The court held that while damages may be available for mental distress in some cases (eg where holidays were not of the quality contracted for) a case of this type did not fall into this category.

The student's obligations

4.81   In the early 1970s questions arose about the extent to which institutions could exercise their rights under the contract of matriculation against students who took part in 'rent strikes' and therefore failed to honour the terms of separate contracts entered into in respect of the occupation of residential property. That such contracts exist is illustrated by *Smith v Nottinghamshire County Council*,[172] where the court recognised a student's right to reasonable quiet enjoyment of residential facilities when the student took action to restrain noisy building operations, and *Bowden v University of East Anglia*,[173] where the University closed down the heating system in residences for annual repairs and the (cold) student was awarded

170   *Liverpool City Council v Irwin* [1977] AC 239.
171   (1986) 26 DLR (4th) 321.
172   (1981) Times, 13 November.
173   (1997) unreported, County Court.

£10 compensation in the county court. The view taken by counsel acting for the Committee of Vice-Chancellors and Principals[174] was that other than in cases where institutions had express provision in their rules permitting them to take such action, it was doubtful that any power to act could be implied. Counsel took the view that the accommodation contract was separate from the contract of matriculation, even though there were obvious overlaps, for example in the area of indiscipline in student residences. But failure to pay rent would not generally speaking be regarded as a breach of the contract of matriculation, or alternatively not so serious a breach as to amount to a repudiation of the contract. There might be exceptions to that general principle where, for example, it was a requirement of the contract of matriculation that a student must spend a certain number of nights in residence: failure to observe that requirement by repudiating the contract for occupation of the room might then render the contract of matriculation either impossible to perform or possible only if the institution exercised some discretionary relief.

4.82 That specific point aside, if there is to be a true learning relationship or what the Scottish CCI Charter describes as a 'partnership between teachers and students' there must be obligations on the student other than purely financial ones. In the medieval universities, scholars had particular obligations to fulfil if they were to remain matriculated. For example, at Cambridge scholars were obliged to attend the schools of their masters at least three days every week and to hear not less than three ordinary lectures. Today, that is translated into an obligation expressed in a variety of ways. Some institutions prescribe attendance at a set proportion of classes, etc before a grade can be given for the course or unit. That in itself is sufficient to cause most students to attend. It does not, however, prevent the individual remaining as a student until the end of the academic year, term or semester, whenever the grade is awarded, or possibly longer, if the grade is not a formal prerequisite for continued progress.

4.83 Setting up and running classes for students who do not turn up, or whose absence damages the dynamics of the class, can be both wasteful of resources and have an adverse effect on the learning processes of other students. The question therefore arises as to at what point the institution can be considered to be relieved of its obligation under the contract of matriculation to provide teaching, supervision and other facilities, both academic and non-academic, to students

174 CVCP Circular VC/75/95.

who behave in this way, for other than reasons which can be verified objectively, eg medical problems. The answer to that lies in the regulations and the importance of clear, intelligible and widely-publicised rules cannot be over-emphasised.

Variation of contract

Post-registration changes

4.84 A student may enter an institution on the faith of the prospectus and other publications and/or discussions with staff or admissions tutors and then find that what is offered either in terms of the course itself or what it is necessary to achieve in order to complete it successfully, is not what was bargained for. Clive Lewis[175] described such a case arising in Canada: *Doane v Mount Saint Vincent University*[176] in which a change in assessment arrangements was communicated to the student after she had registered. Although Morrison J was not prepared on the facts to allow a contractual remedy, Lewis suggested that his preference for the possibility of the use of prerogative writs (ie judicial review) might be explained by the fact that post-registration variation of the contract should in theory require both the consent of the student and consideration, neither of which was evident. However, it is clear from this case and *King v University of Saskatchewan*[177] that where the requirements of a course are adequately conveyed to a student who then fails to complete successfully, the Canadian courts will not intervene unless the student can show fraud, malice or bad faith on the part of the institution, or a denial of natural justice.[178] The same applies in the US[179] and it is suggested that the UK courts would take the same view.

4.85 The difficulty to which Clive Lewis draws our attention might be overcome, as he suggested, by the presence in the contract of matriculation of an implied term giving the institution freedom to alter its rules without consent or consideration. In practice in the UK

---

175 C B Lewis 'The Legal Nature of a University and the Student-University Relationship' (1983) Ottawa Law Review xv.
176 (1977) 74 DLR (3d) 297: *Re Polten and Governing Council of the University of Toronto* (1975) 59 DLR (3d) 197 was referred to.
177 (1969) 6 DLR (3d) 120.
178 There was heavy reliance in the 1970s Canadian cases on the article by G H L Fridman 'Judicial Intervention into University Affairs' (1973) xxi Chitty's Law Journal 181.
179 *Mahavongsanan v Hall* 529 F2d 448 (1976).

most higher education institutions provide clear notice in prospectuses and other documents that courses, etc may be changed both before and after a candidate's admission, implicitly without either consent or consideration. It is suggested that this is an express term of the contract of matriculation and this is what some of the disclaimer clauses attempt to be. No doubt such a clause would have prevented the result in *University of Texas Health Science Center at Houston v Babb*[180] where the student was entitled to rely on the catalogue at the time of matriculation and was not bound by subsequent changes by the University. By contrast in *Doherty v Southern College of Optometry*[181] the court held that a change of course requirements during D's time on the course was not an exercise of bad faith on the College's part and therefore was not a breach of contract. In the US, the generally held view is that rigid application of contract principles is not appropriate to the university-student relationship.[182] However, in the UK the effect of section 5 Unfair Contract Terms Act and the Consumer Contract Regulations might be to render terms allowing significant changes unfair and therefore not binding on the student although the institution may argue that provision for changes in the contract are necessary and in good faith. Schedule 3 of regulation 4(4) of the 1994 Regulations is an illustrative list of terms which may be regarded as unfair. These include: making the contract binding on the consumer whereas provision of services by the supplier depends on the supplier's will alone (freedom to change class or examination times at will?); and irrevocably binding the consumer to terms which the consumer had no real hope of becoming acquainted with before contracting (most of the contents of an institutional rulebook?).

4.86 A comprehensive disclaimer clause is that used by the University of Stirling for its modular MBA degree programme. This clause is designed for specific circumstances and it is more likely to be acceptable for general use if it is adapted to include some requirement for 'reasonableness' on the part of the institution. For example, one could contemplate the hypothetical situation of an institution which decided to close down all arts courses, thus compelling all students to take science courses.

> The University's courses are subject to a continuous process of review ... The University reserves the right in every case at its discretion to vary the contents of courses, to discontinue existing courses and to cancel courses in the event of low enrolments ... On registration for

180 646 SW 2d 502 (1982).
181 862 F 2d 570 (1988).
182 See eg *Abbaraio v Hamline University School of Law* 258 NW 2d 108 (1977).

any course covered by this brochure this notice shall constitute a term of any contract between you and the University and your acceptance of a place is subject to this express condition.

Course structure permitting variation

4.87   There is a wide variety of practice among institutions as to the precise nature of registration and for what the student has registered. This is dictated by the academic structure and ethos of the institution. In some the student registers to take a 'course in A' or 'subject A' for the entire 3–4 years of an undergraduate course, normally in stages each of which must be completed successfully in order to proceed to the next. These may or may not involve the additional study of subjects B, C etc as an essential or optional element in the course. In others the student has a wide, not usually completely unfettered, choice or menu from which to choose a degree programme. That menu and the optional elements in courses of the first type may change from year to year as the subject develops or as there is turnover in teaching staff. The prospect of such changes is, as indicated earlier, normally made clear to students at an early stage, both in the prospectus before admission and in the calendar or similar document after admission.

4.88   As we have seen, Morrison J in *Doane v Mount Saint Vincent University*[183] found some difficulty in reconciling with a true contractual relationship the absence of any obligation to consult those who might be affected by changes before putting them into effect. The institution always has power in its charter or instrument of government to provide instruction in the way in which it sees fit. Likewise there is no obligation to renew the contract from year to year unless this can be implied as a condition of the initial contract of admission which has been incorporated in the subsequent contract of matriculation. Whether it could be implied is a question of fact; the UCAS Handbook uses the word 'course' throughout implying some liability as agent on the part of its principals. And it must surely be an implied term of a contract for registration as a research student that subject to satisfactory progress and fee payments, the contract will endure for at least the minimum specified period for the degree.

183   (1977) 74 DLR (3d) 297.

The Casson case

4.89   In *Casson v University of Aston in Birmingham*[184] the university denied the existence of a contract to provide instruction in accordance with the terms of the original prospectus.

> Admission to a course in one subject having been offered and accepted, it was open to the applicants to sue for breach of contract when the university subsequently withdrew the offer, replacing it by an offer of a place to read a related subject, which the applicants accepted. They then registered and commenced their studies but were unhappy with the new course. They sued the university in the county court.

The court ruled that it had no jurisdiction in disputes of this kind which were matters for the Visitor. The Visitor held that the county court was wrong, as the dispute arose before the applicants achieved the status of corporator, despite a suggestion by John Bridge[185] that the jurisdiction of the Visitor might extend to persons who claim to be corporators, as rejected candidates for fellowships and scholarships at the ancient universities had been held to be within that jurisdiction. The contractual issue remained undecided.

Credit accumulation and transfer

4.90   The contract between a student and the institution must specify clearly what it is that the parties are contracting for. Admission to a 'course' is not appropriate in a credit transfer scheme such as the national CATS or SCOTCATS (or the EU credit transfer scheme ECTS) which envisage the possibility of some credits being obtained from other institutions, when the student will be party to separate contractual arrangements either with them or with a co-ordinating authority or both. It will, however, be possible to allow for credit accumulation within an institution. Naturally, transfer of credit at a later date may not be foreseen when the student registers initially and therefore the most appropriate contractual arrangement would appear to be one which allows variation by consent.

184   [1983] 1 All ER 88.
185   (1970) lxxxvi Law Quarterly Review 531.

Academic progress

Need for effective guidance

4.91 Once matriculated, a student's progress is governed by the regulations pertaining to the course or degree programme which is being followed. These are often complex and institutions differ as to the extent to which they expect students to find their way round the system unaided or offer advice or direction. There are no reported cases in the UK of students taking legal action against an institution or a member of its staff for 'bad' advice or professional negligence in relation to guidance but the more complex the system, the more necessary it becomes for administrators and others to maintain a checking system to try to avoid a student going too far astray. Even if strict legal liability could be denied, a situation in which a student could demonstrate a reasonable case might lead to an institution recognising some right to compensation.

Academic failure

4.92 Clearly the area in which legal action is most likely is that of academic failure. Regulations will spell out what a student is required to do should he or she fall ill or suffer some other extraneous mishap at a crucial stage in assessment or examination and generally speaking there should be no problem if these regulations are adhered to. But where there is failure which is not for disciplinary reasons (such as plagiarism or cheating) the student will almost certainly have an internal right of appeal on specified grounds.

Academic appeals

4.93 Janaki Vijayatunga's case[186] was an unsuccessful attempt to involve the courts in an academic appeal.

A student submitted a PhD thesis and two professors were appointed to examine it. She complained that they were unsuitable on academic grounds. She was unsuccessful in both her initial examination and a re-examination. She petitioned the Visitor to set the appointments aside or alternatively to declare that the professors were not proper or

186 R v Committee of the Lords of the Judicial Committee of the Privy Council acting for the Visitor of the University of London, ex p Vijayatunga [1988] QB 322.

competent to examine her. When the Visitor declined to interfere with
the appointments, she attempted to impugn that decision in the courts.

The court upheld the exclusive jurisdiction of the Visitor, who would
not interfere with 'academic judgment' a principle upheld by the
courts in England following the emergence of universities without
Visitors as in *R v University of Humberside, ex p Cousens*,[187]
Thirunayagam v London Guildhall University[188] and *Madekwe v
London Guildhall University*.[189] This is true throughout the common
law jurisdictions, including Scotland,[190] Australia[191] and the United
States.[192] The question is not whether the decision was 'right' or
'wrong' but whether the institutional bodies acted fairly and
reasonably and no reviewing authority including an Ombudsman[193]
or Administrative Tribunal[194] will intervene otherwise. The attitude
of the courts is perhaps best illustrated in a quotation from the United
States Supreme Court:

> The determination whether to dismiss a student for academic reasons
> requires an expert evaluation of cumulative information and is not
> readily adapted to the procedural tools of judicial or administrative
> decision-making ... Courts are particularly ill-equipped to evaluate
> academic performance.'[195]

187 [1995] EdLM 2(6) 11, CA.
188 (13 March 1997, unreported), CA.
189 (5 June 1997, unreported), CA.
190 Eg *Saleh v University of Dundee* (1992) Times, 23 December; *Carleton v Glasgow
     Caledonian University* (1993) unreported.
191 Eg *Re University of Sydney, ex p Forster* (1963) 63 SRNSW 723: the court at
     730 put faith in 'the good sense and wisdom of the Senate acting as a responsible
     body charged with an important public function, exposed to public criticism and
     subject to the measure of public control.'
192 See eg *Susan M v New York Law School* 557 NYS 2d 294 (1990). Generally on
     the US attitude see T A Schweitzer (1992) 'Academic Challenge Cases: Should
     Judicial Review extend to Academic Evaluations of Students?' The American
     University Law Review, Winter, 264.
193 See Annual Report of the Tasmania Ombudsman 1992, p 33 where it is made
     clear that the Ombudsman will not seek to substitute his own opinion for that
     of the institution concerned where it is clear that decisions taken have been a
     matter for professional judgment, properly applied.
194 Eg *Redfurn v University of Canberra* No A/94/91 and A95/57 Administrative
     Appeals Tribunal (General Administrative Division), Australian Capital Territory
     emphasising the finality of examiners' decisions.
195 *Board of Curators of University of Missouri v Horowitz* 435 US 78 at 83,84
     (1978). For cases of successful petitions see *Keller v Hewitt* 109 Cal 146(1895);
     Baltimore University of Baltimore City v Colton 98 Md 623 A14 (1904); *Russel
     v Salve Regina College* 646 SW 2d 502 (1982).

Where it has been attempted, as in *State, ex rel Nelson v Lincoln Medical College*,[196] the expert witnesses awarded grades ranging from 57% to 94% for the same piece of work.

The Supreme Court also took the view that there are distinct differences between a decision to suspend or dismiss a student for disciplinary purposes and similar actions taken for academic reasons: the former may call for hearings but not the latter.[197]

4.94   In *Cousens* the student failed an examination in the first semester. It was the University's policy not to allow candidates to proceed from the first semester unless all examinations were passed, but the examination board had a discretion to condone the failure on one module if satisfied that at that stage the student's overall performance merited that decision. When the board did not do so, C sought judicial review on grounds of irrationality and procedural unfairness. C had refused to submit coursework to demonstrate that although he had failed the examination he was fit to proceed with the course. The court held that it was not 'irrational' to ask him to do so; the board had considered all relevant circumstances and its views were adequately conveyed in a letter to C. In *Saleh v University of Dundee*[198] the court would not interfere with a decision of the University Senate, acting in accordance with procedure over the examination for a higher degree of Ahmed Saleh. In *Carlton v Glasgow Caledonian University*[199] a petition against the non-award of an honours degree was both barred by delay in bringing the case (some two years in all) and again the court would not interfere with the decision of a duly-appointed committee of academics.

4.95   It is now fairly common for institutions to be faced with appeals of this kind which allege either breach of contract by failure to provide the course offered, or more commonly through some lack of professionalism in teaching or supervision or alleged bias by examiners. Universities responded in the late 1980s to the message of a number of cases heard by Visitors by producing through the CVCP a Code of Practice governing appeals procedures at postgraduate research degree level. Individual universities have either adopted the provisions of the Code or made equivalent provision in their regulations. The CVCP drew a distinction between appeals procedures at this and other levels, on the basis that the relationship between a research student, his or her supervisor and examiners is

196   81 Neb 533, 116 NW 294.
197   *Horowitz* (n 193) at 84.
198   (1992) Times, 23 December, Ct of Sess.
199   (1993) unreported, OH.

inevitably different to that between a student on a taught course, academic staff and examiners: the case for a code of good practice for research supervision appears to be overwhelming.[200] However there are well-documented appeals procedures at both undergraduate and postgraduate level, deriving from the work of the CVCP and also the arrangements put in place in the pre-1992 non-university sector by the Council for National Academic Awards (CNAA).[201]

Grounds of appeal

4.96 Typically such procedures provide for appeal on grounds similar to those set out in paragraph 4 of the CVCP Code.

Grounds for Appeal
(1) That there exist circumstances affecting the student's performance of which the examiners had not been made aware when their decision was taken.
  (2) That there were procedural irregularities in the conduct of the examination (including administrative error) of such a nature as to cause reasonable doubt as to whether the result might have been different had they not occurred.

The institution's rules should make it clear that normally circumstances under (1) should be drawn to the institution's attention before the results are published. Although there is no reported case of challenge to an academic authority's assessment of medical evidence on the basis of lack of professional competence to do so, the risk when such evidence may be interpreted differently by separate bodies in the same institution must be a real one.

4.97 Indeed, it may be argued that in an academic community there can be no 'right of appeal' against an examination result as such. The findings of examiners, where examinations are properly conducted, are final and that must be an express term of the contract of matriculation. If one of the grounds listed above is established, the examiners' finding will be a nullity, any review committee will consider it to be quashed and a new, properly constituted board of

---

200 See C Hole (1997) *Research Supervision: The Case for a Code of Good Practice* Universities and Colleges Staff Development Agency Briefing Paper 47; National Postgraduate Committee (1992) *Guidelines for Codes of Practice for Research Students;* M Harris (1996) *Review of Postgraduate Education* HEFCE.
201 See *CNAA Handbook* (1990–91) paragraphs E2.11(N), G3.8 and Appendix III.

examiners will have to be formed to undertake the proper conduct of that part of the examination process shown to have been defective.

Extraneous matters

4.98   In *R v Aston University Senate, ex p Roffey*[202] Derek Roffey and Michael Pantridge had failed their examinations and sought judicial review of the Senate's decision to exclude them since they had not been given the opportunity to comment on a number of matters taken into account by the examiners. As the court put it in 1993 in *R v Higher Education Funding Council, ex p Institute of Dental Surgery*[203]

> A mark ... awarded at an examiners' meeting where irrelevant and damaging personal factors have been allowed to enter into the evaluation of a candidate's written paper is something more than an informed exercise of academic judgment. Where evidence shows that something extraneous has entered into the process of academic judgment, one of two results may follow depending on the nature of the fault: either the decision will fall without more, or the court may require reasons to be given, so that the decision can either be seen to be sound or can be seen or (absent reasons) be inferred to be flawed.

Although widely known as the Roffey case, in fact Derek Roffey's case was not proceeded with; it was Michael Pantridge's case which was considered by the court.

> Michael Pantridge was admitted to the University of Aston in 1966 to read behavioural sciences. In June 1967 he passed examinations in major subjects but failed in the subsidiary subject of social and economic history. He failed again in the September re-examination and was required to withdraw. In July 1968 he sued the University on the ground that the decision to exclude him was unreasonable, capricious and contrary to natural justice. A number of bodies had considered the matter: some of them had agreed to let Mr Pantridge have the benefit of doubt expressed as to certain statements alleged to have been made by members of staff and consideration of his general academic and personal history on which he had not been allowed to comment. Ultimately it was the Senate which decided to exclude him, on the basis that there was no substantial cause for overruling the provisions of the regulations.

---

202   [1969] 2 QB 538, 543, 556: it is unclear how the action came to be raised against the Senate which was not a legal entity.
203   [1994] 1 WLR 242.

4.99   It is clear now, as Megarry VC stated in *Patel v University of Bradford Senate*[204] that the court had no jurisdiction to entertain this application since it was within the exclusive jurisdiction of the Visitor of the University of Aston in Birmingham.[205] Nevertheless, the court did assume jurisdiction and did not give Mr Pantridge the relief he sought, since he had allowed too much time to elapse before bringing his case: in the words of Blain J 'This court should not be used for the creation of a real life counterpart to Checkhov's perpetual student ...'. To allow the students to comment on the extraneous issues would, in any event, as David Foulkes says, have probably been a useless formality since the examiners would have reached the same decision.[206]

4.100   Even though the court acted outside its jurisdiction, there are some interesting points about the Roffey and Pantridge case. Counsel for the University of Aston conceded that the rules of natural justice were applicable, bringing the case within the ambit of administrative law. As has been shown, that does not mean that the right to a hearing would be automatic. Counsel was adopting the opinion of the Judicial Committee of the Privy Council in *University of Ceylon v Fernando*[207] where a declaration (a remedy suited to both statutory and contractual cases in which the court states the rights or legal position of the parties) was refused.

The Fernando case

Mr Fernando, a zoology student, had taken an examination, part of which consisted of a passage in German. During the examination another student looked in his notebook while he was out of the room and found it contained a number of German words which appeared in the same order as in the passage. Mr Fernando was suspended from further examinations by a board which did not invite him to be present

---

204 [1978] 3 All ER 841, 852: Bradford's Senate was in the same position as Aston's, ie not a legal entity.

205 The court is of course able to ignore the existence of a special jurisdiction if it is not drawn to its attention: *Dr Walker's Case* (1736) Cas Lee temp Hard 212, 218 per Lord Hardwicke CJ. There are numerous examples of the jurisdiction being overlooked: eg *Glynn v Keele University* [1971] 1 WLR 487; *Tubbs v Auckland University College Council* (1907) 27 NZLR 149. Why Aston and Bradford overlooked it is unclear.

206 D L Foulkes *Administrative Law* (5th ed, 1982) p 241: the same principle held in *Glynn v Keele University* [1971] 1 WLR 487 since nothing the student could have said could have affected the disciplinary penalty.

207 [1960] 1 WLR 223.

at the examination of witnesses, including the student who had looked in the book. He sought judicial review of the decision.

4.101　Mr Fernando had not sought an opportunity to be present, and the Judicial Committee found that there was no ground for supposing that if he had made such a request it would not have been granted. They cited with approval the statement by Harman J in *Byrne v Kinematograph Renters Society*[208]

> What then are the requirements of natural justice in a case of this kind? First, I think that the person accused should know the nature of the accusation made; secondly, that he should be given an opportunity to state his case, and thirdly, of course that the tribunal should act in good faith. I do not myself think that there really is anything more.

It may be argued however that this case arose before the development of administrative law later in the decade and as S A de Smith pointed out[209] there are doubts about the procedure employed in the original hearing of the case.

4.102　Naturally, a reviewing authority, whether it be a Visitor or a court, will be prepared to intervene in appeals where there was no evidence logically supporting the decision reached by the appeal body.[210] It has the power to intervene to secure release of 'confidential' minutes of meetings or correspondence where these have been unreasonably withheld from the appellant and where the appellant's case has been seriously disadvantaged as a result. It does not matter particularly that the issue is seen as a contractual one but in *R v Post Office, ex p Byrne*,[211] concerned with the dismissal of a Post Office employee, Bridge J commented on the University of Aston's concession of the relevance of administrative (or, as we would now say, public law). The majority judgments of Donaldson J and Blain J in the *Roffey* case had been the subject of criticism by Sir William Wade[212] 'not least by reason of the fact that the relationship between the [students] and the university was one of contract.' In *Herring v*

208　[1958] 1 WLR 762, 784.
209　(1960) Modern Law Review 428, 431, 432.
210　See eg *Re McInnes and Simon Fraser University* (1982) 140 DLR (3d) 694; and see in the context of a disciplinary appeal *Hossack v General Dental Council* (1997) Times, 22 April where the Judicial Committee of the Privy Council held that a finding of fact by a committee was out of tune with the evidence to such an extent that members must have misunderstood the evidence: see also in the same vein *Libman v General Medical Council* [1972] AC 217.
211　[1975] ICR 221, 225.
212　(1969) lxxxv Law Quarterly Review 468.

Templeman[213] Russell LJ supported this view, saying '... no-one appears to have examined what the precise contractual relationship between the [students] and the university was ...' In the *Byrne* case, the argument advanced by counsel appeared to turn on whether the Senate of the University of Aston in Birmingham could be held to be a public body, to which certiorari might lie. In view of the criticisms of the *Roffey* case the court hearing the *Byrne* case felt that *Roffey* could not be of assistance.

4.103 Nevertheless, for all its faults and the strange position taken by the University of Aston, there are some pointers emerging from the Roffey and Pantridge case. The view taken by Donaldson J supported by Blain J was that the students should have been given the opportunity to be heard, orally or in writing, before examiners reached a final decision on the termination of their course, particularly since they took into consideration the extraneous matters. Lord Parker CJ had 'considerable doubts' about establishing such a principle and reached the conclusion that there had been a breach of natural justice only on the particular facts of the case: the precise wording of special regulations and the fact that the examiners, in exercising discretion given to them by the regulations, were prepared to take into consideration the personal difficulties and problems of each student. Indeed, it may be that a hearing is an unnecessarily adversarial way of dealing with technical matters: in *Board of Curators of the University of Missouri v Horowitz*,[214] the US Supreme Court considered that a review of a student's performance by seven outside physicians was better than a formal hearing. The Court considered that the educational process is non-adversarial and was concerned that an expansion of judicial intervention may harm this position. It also concluded that an academic dismissal may require less 'due process' than one based on misconduct.

4.104 The special regulation which gave rise to the problem in *Roffey* stated:

> Students who fail in more than one major subject, or who fail in a referred examination, may at the discretion of the examiners, re-sit the whole examination or may be required to withdraw from the course. Students who are successful in such re-sit examinations shall normally be eligible to proceed to the pass degree only.

213 [1973] 3 All ER 569, 585.
214 435 US 78 (1978).

Innocuous enough at first sight, but the fact that the examiners could require withdrawal in the circumstances described persuaded the court that, once the University of Aston conceded that the rules of natural justice were applicable, the students should have the opportunity to put forward a statement in explanation or mitigation. The importance of a clear understanding of the rules for 'compensation' and for training staff to reach consistently secure decisions, have been stressed by inter alia HEQC.[215]

Conclusion on the rights of students

4.105 The discussion of *Roffey* and the other cases brings us back to the position that so far as is relevant and appropriate, the institution-student relationship should be seen as contractual.

Student discipline

A compendious text

4.106 The subject of student discipline has occupied a disproportionate number of pages of text in books, articles and law reports relating to the law applicable to higher education.[216] Much of this was due directly to the rapid development of administrative law in England from the mid-1960s onwards at a time of great student unrest. Here the application of principles of justice and fairness in student disciplinary matters was seen to be of importance, just as in other areas of interaction between the citizen and public or quasi-public bodies. Once 'natural justice' principles were seen to be satisfied, there was little more for administrative law to contribute. Since the early 1970s and until very recently there has been relatively little activity in this area, other than the continuing saga of the jurisdiction of the Visitor and the excitement among right-wing English politicians which led to the enactment in England and Wales only of the free speech provisions of E(2)A86.

---

215 HEQC (1996) *Improving Institutional Capacity for Self-Regulation* Part II section 9.
216 Recent examples: M H Whincup 'The exercise of university disciplinary powers' (1993) 5(1) Education and the Law 19; J W Parlour and L R V Burwood 'Students' Rights' (1995) 7(2) Education and the Law 79; A Carroll 'The abuse of academic disciplinary power' (1994) New Law Journal 729.

4.107 In fact, as has been explained in the context of academic appeals, the relevance of administrative law in this area, and hence much of the material from the 1960s and 1970s has been questioned on the basis that the relationship of the student to the institution is contractual and hence (in England at least) based in private rather than public law.

Disciplinary procedures

4.108 It is in the area of discipline of the individual that attention has recently been focused. Disciplinary procedures are designed to deal with offences against the good order and discipline of the institution. They are not designed to intrude upon or replace the generally applicable rules of the criminal law in such areas as sexual offences, serious assault or theft.[217] There will always be the student who falls foul of institutional regulations, whether by cheating in examinations, parking a car incorrectly, failing to return a library book or playing music too loudly in a hall of residence. All these can safely be dealt with internally and institutions are free within the terms of the contract to set up as few or as many procedures as they wish. Most institutions take such issues very seriously when there is a possibility that the student may be excluded or fail: the meticulous care taken by the university in the long-running case of *Foecke v University of Bristol*[218] is an example.

4.109 It must be remembered that most pre-1992 universities' procedures were actually designed for a completely different purpose: that of dealing with collective indiscipline. The period between 1968 and 1974 saw student mass action causing disruption and wholesale breach of regulations on a large scale for the first time, on several fronts, principally to secure improved representation for students in the governance of higher education (largely conceded) and to effect a political revolution and secure workers' control (unsuccessfully). The new universities of the 1960s experienced a disproportionate amount of this trouble and had relatively inexperienced Vice-Chancellors and administrative staff to deal with it. Universities' disciplinary procedures had been drawn up as a cross between the rules which might be applied in loco parentis and the rules of a gentleman's club. Neither was suited to the revolution of the late 1960s: most students became adults on the passing of the Family Law

217 See the Report of the CVCP Task Force on Student Disciplinary Procedures 1994.
218 Unreported.

Reform Act 1969: those who participated in the violence, destruction and intimidation of the time could certainly not be regarded as gentlemen. So the procedures were unable to cope. Vice-Chancellors unable to solve their problems internally rushed to the courts for help when buildings were occupied and work disrupted. The general law relating to dispossession from property was found to be procedurally cumbersome and in Scotland wholly ineffective. Lord Devlin echoed the feeling of the time when as High Steward he reported on a sit-in in the University of Cambridge:[219]

> It is really only the threat of Direct Action that keeps university discipline going. It has to be remembered that most societies when they find themselves in peril from groups organised to disrupt, have had to resort to sterner procedures.

4.110 Revisions to disciplinary procedures were carried out, some more hastily than others, and the legacy of that period is a set of usually lengthy codes of discipline which attempt to preserve a balance between the rights of individuals and those of the community, incorporating the rules of natural justice, due process and rights of appeal. According to Graeme Moodie and Rowland Eustace[220] the formalisation and institutionalisation of disciplinary procedures was possibly the most important outcome of the 1960s challenges to the rights of universities to regulate the private lives of students. Although there was some resurgence of the 1960s behaviour in the mid-1980s, this time directed towards the effects of public expenditure cuts and their consequences for students, little has been heard of mass protest in higher education institutions for some time. Even the reform of student unions, which would have caused apoplexy in the 1970s, passed relatively unnoticed. The demand for increased representation which was conceded at a fairly early stage in the 1960s–1970s troubles is now actually slightly difficult to reconcile with student status as customers. Recently, institutions have been turning their attention towards procedures designed to deal with offensive and intimidating behaviour, including that exhibited on widely-used

219 *Report of the Sit-In in February 1972 and its consequences* (Devlin Report), Vol C111, *Cambridge University Reporter*, Special, No 12, 14 February 1972 p 54. See also L N Brown 'Student Protest in England' (1969) 17 American Journal of Comparative Law 395; L A Sheridan 'Sacking Professors and Sending Down Students – Legal Control' in *Law, Justice and Equity* (1967) 43.
220 (1974) *Power and Authority in British Universities* 197–8.

electronic mailing systems,[221] and inter-personal issues such as racial and sexual harassment, unless these are purely private disputes which do not impinge on the institution's community.

Purpose of disciplinary codes

4.111   The overt purpose of disciplinary codes is retributive rather than restorative in character. Codes are not normally expressed in terms of being part of the support offered to students, although it may be argued that the institution's role when aberrant behaviour occurs should be restoration of the status quo and reconciliation rather than retribution. This may better be achieved through mediation and discussion than through adversarial hearings. If as is indicated here the institution-student relationship rests on a contract, then conflict resolution within the terms of that contract may be a better goal to aim for than identifying a 'guilty' party and winners and losers in a formal tribunal. There is as yet little evidence that institutions are moving in this direction.

Source of disciplinary authority

4.112   The formal source of authority is normally the Charter and Statutes or its equivalent. In the ancient Scottish universities the effects of the Universities (Scotland) Acts 1858–1966 have been to place the jurisdiction on a statutory basis.[222] Primary responsibility for discipline is normally vested in the Senate or equivalent and appellate functions in the Council (Court in Scotland) or other governing body. By matriculating or enrolling as a student, a person becomes subject to institutional discipline whether or not the student expressly agrees to be bound by it and whether or not he or she is aware of the substance of the disciplinary rules. The legal basis of disciplinary power rests in the voluntary subscription of the individual, whether as a member of a chartered institution or simply as a student, to the rules of the institution. A form of undertaking to observe these rules

---

221   See Interim Report of CVCP Working Group on Extremism and Intolerance on Campus (1997) which suggested amendments to the list of disciplinary offences proposed by the 1994 CVCP Task Group on Student Disciplinary Procedures (the Zellick Report).

222   The Universities (Scotland) Act 1966 empowers the Court by resolution 'on the recommendation of the Senatus to prescribe the procedure to be followed in the case of alleged breaches of discipline within the University where the alleged breach is one which might be punished by expulsion or rustication.'

as made by the competent authorities of the institution is commonly executed. Separate undertakings are given in respect of admission to residential accommodation, use of library and computing facilities and safety requirements of laboratories. Such undertakings form part of the contracts, whether of matriculation, of lease or licence or of membership of the library. They are unaffected by any status which the student may have as a corporator in chartered institutions; this becomes of importance only when considering the means of enforcing the terms of the contract and the penalties for breach of those terms.

Essential elements of a disciplinary code

4.113   Prior to the implementation of the guidelines suggested by the Report of the CVCP Task Force in 1994, disciplinary procedures in the pre-1992 chartered institutions could be cumbersome, tedious and expensive to operate. In many instances they were more sophisticated than the disciplinary procedures applying to non-academic staff. This was not necessarily the case in the post-1992 universities and other higher education institutions, where students are not members of the corporation.

4.114   Disciplinary codes of all kinds with some legal force have certain similar characteristics. They should be expressed in clear language, enable the speedy determination of complaints, be procedurally fair – which means that the basic rules of natural justice should be followed[223] – and ensure that any findings of guilt and penalties imposed should be subject to appeal. In *R v Sheffield Hallam University Board of Governors, ex p R*[224] one element of fairness, the requirement to give a student prior warning of the charges against her, had not been met in full. It seems inappropriate to hold disciplinary hearings in public[225] but to avoid arguments over the evidence, a clear record should be kept: the suggestion by a Visitor that proceedings be tape-recorded is worth serious consideration.[226]

---

223 This is the basic requirement in other common law jurisdictions; see eg *Knapp v Junior College District of St Louis County* 879 SW 2d 588 (1994).
224 [1995] ELR 267.
225 But see *Diennet v France* (1995) 21 EHRR 554, E Ct HR.
226 See *Times Higher Education Supplement*, 12 September 1997 relating to the conduct of a disciplinary case at the University of Warwick which attracted criticisms from the Visitor.

4.115 The reasons for having a fair disciplinary procedure are obvious without recourse to legal explanations. As Clive Lewis said,[227] the interests of a student lie in being part of the institution and in obtaining an academic qualification. The extent to which the courts and Visitors will expect institutions to go in demonstrating fairness depends to some extent on the seriousness of the potential consequences: will the decision influence the livelihood or reputation of the student? In the 1990s it is an understatement to repeat Blain J's observation that students are 'potential graduates and potential holders of degrees which could prove advantageous in professional or commercial life.'[228] The message of the 1969 Report on Student Relations[229] thus assumes even greater importance:

> Disciplinary matters have in one sense assumed increasing importance as the value of a degree as a starting point has grown, and a decision to suspend or even in some cases to send down a student is regarded in a much more serious light than it would be a generation ago.

There is, as Clive Lewis pointed out, nothing inherently different about student discipline for non-academic offences than discipline in any other organisation or in society in general. It may be argued that theft, assault and traffic offences are not related to the academic nature of a higher education institution whereas cheating, plagiarism and general conduct in a hall of residence are.

Criminal offences

4.116 There is a point at which an internal disciplinary matter becomes one which is more suited to the procedures of the criminal law: the jurisdiction of the authorities of the *studium generale* is inappropriate.[230] The medieval universities exercised considerably more disciplinary authority over their members than do modern institutions; the language of the time suggests that many of the charges heard then would today be handed over to the local police: housebreakers, footpads and those carrying arms were outlawed. So

227 C B Lewis 'Procedural Fairness and University Students: England and Canada Compared' (1985) 3 Dalhousie Law Journal 313.
228 *R v University of Aston Senate, ex p Roffey* [1969] 2 QB 538, 556.
229 *Report of Vice-Chancellors and Principals and the National Union of Students*, reproduced in Vol 11 of *Report on Student Relations* Select Committee on Education and Science (1969) p 83 para 13.
230 Students are not 'above the law': '... an adult student ... cannot, by virtue of his (sic) education, claim preferential treatment': *R v Caird* (1970) 54 CrAppRep 499 per Sachs LJ.

too were 'assaulters of women' which we would today describe as sexual assault or harassment. The 1994 CVCP Guidelines suggest where the line should be drawn between offences which can reasonably be dealt with internally and those which cannot. It is clear that not all institutions have followed the guidelines. As the Visitor remarked in a case reported only in the press against the University of Warwick in 1997[231] institutions should not attempt to deal with serious offences under the criminal law which are more properly dealt with by the courts. Admission of evidence of criminal offences with which a student is not charged is manifestly unfair. Where an institution reasonably apprehends that a criminal offence has been committed, and nevertheless proceeds with an internal enquiry, it would be well advised to consider the issues raised by the court in *Joy v Federation Against Software Theft (FAST) Ltd.*[232] In the parallel case of a prosecution brought against an employee it was held that management wishing to introduce into the criminal procedure evidence collected for internal purposes should ensure that the evidence is obtained following the guidance given in the relevant code of practice issued under the Police and Criminal Evidence Act 1984 or its equivalent in Scotland and Northern Ireland.

4.117   Among the categories of offences which the 1994 Task Group recommended should be handed over to the police are those involving illegal drugs.[233] The Guidelines also suggest that 'bringing the institution into disrepute' may be an appropriate disciplinary offence: this is a difficult area, as evidenced by the reported intention of a Cambridge college to take action on this ground against students accused of pelting noisy tourist buses with tomatoes when their examination revision was disturbed.[234]

4.118   One problem facing institutions in applying the rules of natural justice is that of staff members potentially being, at different stages in the hierarchy of committees and tribunals, prosecutor, judge and jury. There is no independent prosecution service and in some cases it is very difficult for administrators to find persons qualified

---

231 *Times Higher Education Supplement*, 12 September 1997.
232 [1993] Crim LR 588.
233 Further guidance on this subject was published by CVCP in conjunction with the Association of Managers of Student Services in Higher Education (AMOSSHE) in May 1997.
234 The issues were rather more complex: possible infringement of environmental pollution and anti-noise legislation by the bus operators, potential failure of the college authorities to provide reasonably peaceful enjoyment of student accommodation are just two avenues for litigation.

under the institution's rules who are both willing and able to act as 'judge and jury' and are not disqualified by some previous connection with the accused. This is obviously particularly difficult in cases of mass disruption of a Senate meeting, for example. A decision-making body should, by analogy with the position in *R v Secretary of State for Education, ex p Prior*[235] be properly constituted, but as in *R v Hereford and Worcestershire County Council, ex p Wellington Parish Council* [236] some overlaps in committee membership seem inevitable. The fact that members sit on more than one committee dealing with the same problem does not automatically mean they are incapable of acting fairly.

Academic discipline

4.119 The law in general is much less suited to intervention in cases which are wholly related to the academic nature of an institution. To quote the Annan Report:[237]

> There are actions, such as cheating in examinations ... which destroy ... the relationship between teachers and students on which good teaching depends. They are not crimes but they cannot be tolerated because they destroy the raison d'etre of a university.

There is likely to be a considerable element of subjective judgment, particularly where charges such as plagiarism are invoked.

4.120 Disputes arising from alleged plagiarism (L, *plagiarus*, kidnapper) are a frequent source of litigation in the US[238] being part of a larger problem of academic fraud, by no means confined to students.[239] There is less evidence of this in the UK where such matters tend to be disposed of internally, although the consequences for the offender can be serious, possibly leading to deprivation of a degree.[240] Those that come to court or to the Visitor usually arise because of some alleged procedural defect. In *R v South Bank University, ex p*

235 [1994] ELR 231.
236 (1995) 160 LG Rev 161.
237 *Annan Report* University of Essex 1974.
238 See discussion in W C A Kaplin and B A Lee (3rd edn, 1995) *The Law of Higher Education* (Jossey-Bass) Chapter 4, section 8.
239 R D Mawdsley *Legal Aspects of Plagiarism* (1985) and *Academic Misconduct: Cheating and Plagiarism* (1994) (Kansas, NOLPE, Topeka).
240 G Parry and D Houghton 'Plagiarism in UK Universities' (1996) 8(3) Education and the Law 201.

Ifediora[241] the University allowed the student to resubmit a project alleged to have been significantly plagiarised after it agreed, at the stage of leave to apply for judicial review, to reconsider the matter. *Jones v University College Aberystwyth*[242] was a Visitorial judgment holding that the handling of allegations by the College was procedurally defective. It may be possible to distinguish cheating and plagiarism from 'attempting to gain an unfair advantage' as in *R v Manchester Metropolitan University, ex p Nolan*[243] and a comprehensive list of various kinds of academic misconduct can as HEQC stated[244] be drawn up and clearly promulgated to students. Whatever is provided in the regulations, which should themselves be clear and unambiguous, should be made known to all those likely to be affected by them.

4.121 A potential problem lies in determining whether plagiarism and other academic fraud is an academic or a disciplinary issue, requiring different procedures. It is important to ensure that separate procedures do not become so entwined or are so inconsistent as to raise the possibility of unfairness, as appears to have happened in *R v Manchester Metropolitan University, ex p Nolan*.[245] In the US plagiarism as a species of academic fraud is not considered under the same procedures as general misconduct and not therefore subject to the same detailed requirements of due process, whether implied from constitutional law or from the contract in private institutions.[246] However in *Flanagan v University College Dublin*[247] the Irish High Court considered that the appeal procedures where a student was accused of plagiarism and cheating should be close to those of a court hearing. In that case procedures were seriously flawed, in that the student was not given full information about the 'charges' nor the opportunity properly to present her evidence. Furthermore the Registrar, who presented the case to the disciplinary committee, was present while the committee reached its decision, an action which was clearly wrong in principle. Certainly in the *Nolan* case it is clear that Sedley J expected the normal rules of fairness applicable to a disciplinary procedure to be observed.

241 (1996) unreported.
242 (1995) unreported, Visitor.
243 [1994] ELR 380.
244 HEQC (1996) *Improving Institutional Capacity for Self-Regulation* Part II paragraph 6.2.
245 [1994] ELR 380.
246 See eg *Napolitano v Trustees of Princeton University* 453 A 2d 263 (1982); *Board of Curators of University of Missouri v Horowitz* 435 US 78 (1978).
247 [1988] IR 724.

The naked sunbather (2)

4.122 In *Glynn's* case, where the court exceeded its jurisdiction by admitting an application for judicial review in a chartered institution with a Visitor, the student concerned was one of a number who appeared naked on campus. The Vice-Chancellor had, in the exercise of his general authority for good order, excluded Simon Glynn from residence and fined him £10 (which he paid). Since the incident occurred near the end of the academic year it had not been possible to convene a disciplinary panel, which would have been the normal procedure, although the court accepted that the Vice-Chancellor possessed all the necessary powers to deal with the matter. The court held that the Vice-Chancellor's powers were so fundamental that they were quasi-judicial in nature rather than merely matters of internal discipline. The Vice-Chancellor had failed in his duty by not giving Mr Glynn an opportunity of being heard before the penalty was imposed. An injunction was refused in discretion (the judge commenting that discretion should be very sparingly exercised against a plaintiff in these circumstances)[248] since Mr Glynn did not dispute the facts, there could have been no more than a plea in mitigation and the penalty inflicted was intrinsically a perfectly proper one for a 'serious offence.[249] Moreover Mr Glynn had failed to make the necessary arrangements to enable him to attend the hearing of an appeal of which the university had taken all reasonable steps to notify him. He had therefore not been deprived of his right to appeal and, as he had not applied for a rehearing the decision of the appeal committee to uphold the Vice-Chancellor's decision was still effective. A flaw in an original hearing can be corrected at the appeal stage.[250] Sir William Wade criticised the outcome of Simon Glynn's case in

248 Discretion can be exercised against a plaintiff where there is no material advantage to him or her in granting the order sought, as explained by Turner J in *R v Governors of St Gregory's RC Aided High School, ex p M/Roberts* [1995] ELR 290, where the application to overturn an expulsion order was refused anyway.
249 There are some paternalistic overtones in the judgment of Pennycuick VC who spoke of the unique relationship of tutor and pupil and the responsibility borne by the University for the pupil's upbringing, possibly out of touch with reality even in 1971. What constitutes a serious offence is of course highly subjective although guidance is now given in the CVCP Guidelines (1994). Modern Vice-Chancellors at least do not run the risk of having their actions quashed by writ of habeas corpus, as did the Vice-Chancellor of the University of Cambridge when he committed one Daisy Hopkins to detention for 'walking with a member of the University,' an offence which the court held was unknown to law: *Ex p Hopkins* (1891) 61 LJQB 240.
250 See eg *R v Governors of St Gregory's RC Aided High School, ex p M/Roberts* [1995] ELR 290.

an article 'Nudism and Natural Justice'[251] based on the failure of the university to observe the principles of natural justice.

4.123 The nature of a Vice-Chancellor's powers were discussed earlier. In the pre-1992 universities they are often expressed in vague terms, including the maintenance of good order, which must imply a power to do something if good order is threatened. In so far as the contract between the institution and the student is concerned, it is more than likely that unless great care is taken, these powers in respect of student discipline will be attenuated or entirely excluded by express provision for a disciplinary procedure.

4.124 It may be gathered from Simon Glynn's case that a student has a right to a fair hearing, although it is suggested that that right is conferred by the contract and not imported from administrative law. In other cases dating from 1969–1971 the courts upheld the concept while denying the remedy. For example in *R v Oxford University, ex p Bolchover*[252] where a student claimed that the university's Proctors (officials exercising disciplinary authority) had acted unfairly Lord Parker CJ is reported to have said:

> At the end of the day we remain unconvinced that the conduct of the hearing before the Proctors offended against such rules of natural justice as were applicable in the circumstances. To put it more simply we are not satisfied that the hearing was unfair.

But even if the hearing had been unfair that would not necessarily have assisted Mr Bolchover:

> But it is only right to add that even if the court felt there might be something to be enquired into, nevertheless as a matter of discretion they would, having regard to the appeal, refuse you leave.

Relationships between staff and students

4.125 The extent to which a member of staff owes a duty of care towards students in terms of standard of professionalism has been

---

251 (1971) lxxxvii Law Quarterly Review 320; see also B A Hepple 'Natural Justice for Rusticated Students' (1969) Cambridge Law Journal 169.
252 (1970) Times, 7 October (it will be recalled that as a civil corporation the University of Oxford has no Visitor); see also *University of Essex v Ratcliffe* (1969) Times, 28 November (in excess of jurisdiction as the University of Essex has a Visitor) and *Ward v Bradford Corpn* (1971) 70 LGR 27.

discussed. This encompasses the extent of staff liability for statements made about students and former students in references, testimonials and assessments. Personal relationships are not a matter for the law unless they transgress accepted codes of behaviour, in which case they become a matter either for the student discipline procedures outlined here or staff discipline procedures. Advice given to students should be given within the framework of the professional standard of competence to be shown by a person giving the advice in question.

References

4.126   Following the settlement out of court of an action brought against the University of Glamorgan by a student who suffered financial loss as a direct result of a reference negligently provided by a member of academic staff, there has been renewed interest in the law relating to references and heightened fear of litigation. The university accepted that the principles set out by the House of Lords in an employment case *Spring v Guardian Assurance plc*[253] applied to this particular non-employment setting. The opinions of the majority of the House are lengthy and complex.[254] The courts are developing an implied right of an employee to a reference from his/ her employers and at the same time allowing the possibility of a claim in negligence for information wrongly given. It is the latter, confirming the trend in both England and Scotland to impose a duty of care *to the subject of the reference* to give accurate statements in 'special relationships' independent of contract[255] and extending beyond purely fiduciary ones,[256] which forms the basis of the view taken in Wales that the case would succeed.

4.127   It may be possible to avoid liability for negligent misstatements if the giver of the reference (G) makes it clear to the subject of the reference (S) that G will only give one if S accepts that there will be a disclaimer of liability to S and to the recipient of the

253 [1995] 2 AC 296, [1994] 3 All ER 129.
254 D Brodie *Protecting Reputations* 1994 SLT (News) 365.
255 Although it is now fairly well established that there is a contract between a student and a university, it is not clear that, in the absence of anything expressly stated in the prospectus, Calendar or elsewhere, this includes an implied term requiring the university to provide a reference. Occasionally there may be a contractual commitment implied from the nature of the employment.
256 *Robinson v National Bank of Scotland* 1916 SC (HL) 154; *Hedley Byrne & Co v Heller & Partners* [1964] AC 465; *Kenway v Orcantic* 1979 SC 422.

reference (R).[257] Such a disclaimer may well be valid at common law, but must be fair and reasonable to escape the application of the Unfair Contract Terms Act and the Consumer Contracts Regulations 1994 (which do not apply to employment contracts but probably do apply to the university-student contract). Although untested, the argument may well be that as an accurate reference is, to use a conservative description, of considerable importance to S, a disclaimer which sought to exclude G's liability in this area would not be allowed to operate. It is possible that a disclaimer might protect a statement of opinion honestly given. On balance, it seems sensible to include a broadly based disclaimer, such as

> While pleased to provide this reference, it is given on the understanding that this is done without legal responsibility, and with the exclusion of legal liability, on the part of, and in respect of, the University and the author of the reference, and without legal liability to the subject of it and the recipient of it.

4.128   Prior to the *Spring* case the dissatisfied former employee S could only have proceeded in an action for defamation against the giver of the reference G. Such actions are difficult, do not attract legal aid, and are subject to the defence of qualified privilege. To overcome this defence S would have to prove malice on the part of G. Simply telling lies (as happened in the *Spring* case) is not sufficient to demonstrate malice. The same general principles would apply in a university-student setting. Similarly, actions for verbal injury (malicious falsehood) have to show not only that G's statements were untrue but also that there was a deliberate intent on G's part to injure S or at least there was such reckless disregard of injury as to yield the inference of such intent.[258] This is most unlikely to arise in a higher education setting. It would undoubtedly attract disciplinary sanctions.

4.129   The obligation is to take reasonable care in the compilation of the reference and failure to do so is the essential element of a successful claim. The standard of care required in English and Scots law is that of the reasonably careful, ordinary, prudent person in all the circumstances of the case, 'free from both over-apprehension and from over-confidence.'[259] Any factual statement made should be accurate based on verifiable data. Obviously if a student has been awarded a second class honours degree (lower division) it would be

257 See *Spring* at 162h, per Lord Slynn of Hadley and *Lawton v BOC Transhield Ltd* [1987] ICR 7.
258 See eg *Steele v Scottish Daily Record* 1970 SLT 53.
259 *Muir v Glasgow Corpn* 1943 SC (HL) 3, per Lord Macmillan at 10.

a negligent misstatement to say that the award was anything other than that. An expression of opinion about the likelihood of a student achieving a particular class of degree in future based on the proper exercise of academic judgment of a member of staff *with knowledge of the student's performance and backed up by facts* would not be a negligent misstatement if in the event the student performed otherwise than reasonably expected.

4.130 It would be too much to expect all predictions to be wholly accurate. But in the Welsh case the reference which suggested that the student would perform less well than she did in fact perform, resulting in the withdrawal of a job offer, was not based on sound academic judgment of verifiable facts. Therefore references should normally only be given where the student has asked the member of staff concerned to act as a referee. This gives the member of staff the opportunity to decline if they have insufficient knowledge, or (with the consent of the student) to pass on the request to a colleague who is better placed to deal with it. It is the responsibility of the person providing the reference to ensure that what is stated in the reference is true and fair. The writer should stick to the facts, wherever possible, rather than opinions. Facts for these purposes may be gleaned from a variety of sources provided these are not inconsistent. Where an expression of opinion is sought, eg about the likely future achievement of the student, the writer should ensure that he or she has sufficient information on which to base a judgment. Questions related to the character or integrity of the individual can only be answered within knowledge which is unlikely to extend beyond the Department: this should be made clear and any points of interpretation checked with colleagues.

Finance

Payment of fees and other charges

4.131 Matriculation or enrolment normally requires the payment of tuition fees which until the autumn of 1998 for the great majority of full-time home undergraduate students on higher education courses are paid automatically by the local education authority or equivalent and for many postgraduate students by government departments or other agencies. Part II Teaching and Higher Education Bill 1997 (THEB) makes new provision for financial support for home/EU undergraduate student entering higher education in 1998 and requires Funding Councils (through the Financial Memorandum) to require governing bodies of higher education institutions to impose prescribed fees on new students. For most overseas students and other categories of home students institutions have devised schemes for payment by instalments, provisional registration pending payment or deposit-taking on acceptance of offer of admission, to ensure that fees paid by these categories are forthcoming and such arrangements will no doubt be modified to reflect the new funding position. In all cases the fee regulations will form part of the contract of matriculation (a promise to pay fees having been part of the contract of admission) and should therefore spell out clearly what will happen to a person who does not pay the fees by the time required. For obvious reasons institutions are anxious to do everything in their power to avoid expulsion of a non-registered student; although other reasons can be adduced, one natural consequence is that the fee is lost with little prospect of filling the vacant place. These principles apply whether or not the student is paying the whole or part of the fee. Payment of other charges (for example graduation fees) is normally required as part of the contractual terms agreed at registration or matriculation.[260]

Discretion as to late payment

4.132 The exercise of discretion by the Vice-Chancellor, Registrar or Finance Officer as spelt out in the regulations has to be reasonably consistent if potential legal problems are to be avoided. Claims of discrimination on grounds of race or nationality are possible where a more liberal approach is taken with certain groups of potential students. While the non-matriculated student in a chartered corporation would appear to have no redress before the Visitor, a claim of discrimination might be brought before the ordinary courts under the terms of RRA.

4.133 Where some time has been granted for late payment of fees, the non-matriculated student in a chartered corporation is in a curious position. By definition this person is not a member of the university unless its domestic legislation confers that status. It is possible to envisage an overseas student passing through a one-year Master's course or a nine-month diploma course without ever having attained

---

260 The introduction of a graduation fee at one Scottish university in 1994 led to small claims action being issued for 'implementation of obligation' although apparently the students had agreed to it on registration at the start of the academic session.

the status of matriculated student at all.[261] Institutions should be wary of students who enrol for a course lasting more than six months simply to avoid losing immigration appeal rights under the Asylum and Immigration Appeals Act 1993. Most institutions provide that such a person may not have a degree or diploma formally conferred but that may be insufficient threat to produce payment at a time to suit the institution's cashflow. Here there is an important interaction between law and practice. Powers do exist in a number of institutions for the responsible administrative officer to refuse to allow a person who has failed to complete registration to sit examinations on a course, to impound the examination papers written and not release them to the examiners until the fees are paid, or for the examiners to be instructed not to disclose a result to a person who has not completed registration. This should be set out expressly in the contract not only to avoid a decision of this kind being overturned as in *Keller v Hewitt*[262] but also falling foul of the requirements of the Unfair Contract Terms Act 1977 and the Consumer Contract Regulations 1994.

Overseas fees

4.134 In accordance with the Education (Fees and Awards) Regulations,[263] higher (overseas) levels of fee are payable by students who do not have a 'relevant connection' with the UK.[264] The Regulations post-date the issues which gave rise to *Orphanos v Queen Mary College*[265] where the House of Lords held that an overseas student had been the subject of unlawful racial discrimination but awarded him no compensation. 'Relevant connection' requires firstly that the student has been ordinarily resident throughout the three-year period preceding the start of the course and secondly that the

---

261 Arguably neither student in *Joobeen v University of Stirling* 1995 SLT 120n or in the parallel case *Naik v University of Stirling* 1994 SLT 449 was ever a matriculated student since neither paid the full fees.
262 109 Cal 146 (1895).
263 See Education (Fees and Awards) Act 1983; Education (Fees and Awards) Regulations 1997; Education (Mandatory Awards) Regulations (annual; 1997: SI 1997/431); Education (Areas to which Pupils and Students Belong) Regulations 1996/615 and the corresponding Scottish and Northern Irish regulations. The Education (Fees and Awards) Act is an example of legislation which pursuant to section 41 RRA renders lawful what would otherwise be unlawful discrimination.
264 There is considerable discretion over the actual amounts of overseas fees.
265 [1985] 2 All ER 233; see also *Kent v University College London* (1992) 156 L G Rev 1003, CA.

student has not been resident therein, during any part of the three-year period, wholly or mainly for the purpose of receiving full-time education. There are also certain categories of excepted students, including nationals and children of nationals of the European Union,[266] certain persons granted asylum or refugee status, students on fully-reciprocal exchanges, and recently-arrived immigrants who are also liable to pay only the lower (home) fee.

4.135 The meaning of 'ordinary residence' was considered in *Shah v Barnet London Borough Council*[267] where it was held that the question was whether the appellant had habitually and normally resided in the UK from choice and for a settled purpose throughout the prescribed three-year period, apart from temporary or occasional absences. In a case distinguished by its unusual facts *University College London v Newman*[268] the Court of Appeal held that a New Zealand national who had spent three years travelling around Europe should be treated as an EU student for fee purposes. Evidence of intention to settle was sufficient to grant a student home status in *Kent v University College London*.[269] A person who acquires EU nationality during a course becomes entitled to pay the lower rate of fee from the next payment period[270]. Judgments of the European Court of Justice,[271] ruling on the interpretation of Article 7 of Council Regulation (EEC) No 1612/68 on freedom of movement of workers within the European Union, have further extended the categories of student which are eligible for mandatory awards under the annual Mandatory Awards Regulations.

Benefits

4.136 There has been a spate of litigation surrounding the availability of social security benefits which are not normally awarded

---

266 Extended to EFTA countries in 1994. The British Islands (Channel Islands and the Isle of Man) are not within the European Union and fees for students from them are negotiated between the governments.
267 [1983] 2 AC 309.
268 (1986) Times, 8 January.
269 (1992) 156 L G Rev 1003, CA.
270 UKOSA Briefing August 1993 p 4.
271 *Centre Public d'Aide Sociale de Courcelles v Lebon*: Case No 316/85 [1987] ECR 2817; *Lair v University of Hanover*: Case No 39/86 [1988] ECR 3161; *Brown v Secretary of State for Scotland*: Case No 197/86 [1988] ECR 2305; *Blaizot v University of Liège*: Case No 24/86 [1988] ECR 379; Education (Fees and Awards) (Amendment) Regulations 1988 (SI 1988 No 1391).

to full-time students. In *Chief Adjudication Officer v Webber*[272] a person who embarked on a three-year course of study as a full-time student but in his second year continued the course as a part-time student was not excluded from entitlement to income support by virtue of being deemed not to be available for and actively seeking employment. The cases of *Chief Adjudication Officer v Clarke and Faul*[273] and *Driver v Chief Adjudication Officer*[274] together with the Social Security Benefits (Miscellaneous Amendments) Regulations 1995[275] clarify that simply intercalating a year is insufficient to qualify for benefit as the student remains a student: it is the latter which is important in determining status at any relevant stage.

Development of the contract of matriculation

The case for a written statement

4.137 There is obviously a strong case for a written statement of the respective rights and obligations of an institution and its students and this appears to be in line with the requirements of the CCI Charters. The student must know what he or she has enrolled for and what he or she has the right to expect from the institution, what is expected from him or her in order to succeed and under what circumstances the contract may be varied or terminated by the institution. As higher education increases in complexity, so does the nature of the contract. The institution must have enforceable rights to fees and other charges and the ability to maintain discipline in academic matters and in personal conduct.

4.138 Although it is not possible to draw exact parallels, the closest analogies appear to be the contract of employment and the contract of apprenticeship. The principal terms of a contract of employment are required to be given to employees in a statutory statement[276] although some of the fundamental terms of the employment relationship are implied from common law and some others from collective agreements. Employers are specifically required to inform employees of disciplinary and grievance procedures, many of which in practice are considerably less complex than those adopted by some of the pre-1992 universities for dealing with student discipline.

272 [1997] 4 All ER 274, CA.
273 [1995] ELR 259, CA.
274 [1997] ELR 145, CA.
275 SI 1995/1741.
276 Section 1 EmpRA.

4.139 The contract of apprenticeship between master and apprentice, which has medieval historical origins like the master-scholar relationship of the *studium generale*, is perhaps closer to the institutional-student relationship than that of employer to employee, as it combines elements of a contract of service with education and training. It is however essentially a common law concept with relatively little statutory intervention since its heyday in the nineteenth century.[277]

The content of the statement

4.140 A statement embodying the following, some of which is adapted from the statutory statement of terms of employment, probably represents all that is required in a contract of matriculation:
(i) identification of the parties;
(ii) statement of the course or programme which the institution has agreed to provide and the resources available to support it including a safe working environment supportive of study;
(iii) academic and financial obligations of the student in respect of that course or programme;
(iv) circumstances under which the course, the programme and (if relevant) its location may be varied by the institution or under which the student may apply to vary the course or programme;
(v) the disciplinary rules applicable to the student both in relation to academic and non-academic activities;
(vi) arrangements, if any, for appeals against failure to meet specified academic or non-academic obligations or penalties imposed for breach of discipline.

4.141 There are a number of subsidiary issues, such as health and safety, equal opportunities and similar policies, which could be added. Just as certain terms of employment may be included in a readily accessible document to which the employee may make reference, it is obviously more practicable if the student is able to refer to a published volume of regulations for the details of these policies and for details of programmes, disciplinary procedures and so on. What should be avoided, however, is a plethora of material which is ill-co-ordinated, supplemented by oral statements made by individual members of staff. The statement should state clearly that its provisions prevail over any conflicting material.

---

277 The legislation is not surprisingly rather old: Apprentices Act 1814, Employers and Workmen Act 1875. See now section 295(1) TULRCA and section 230 EmpRA.

International students

4.142 When staff and students are on the premises, at least the respective rights and obligations of institution and individual are clear, or ought to be so, and it is possible for administrators to be reasonably confident that issues which could lead to litigation are kept under control. However, institutions, staff and students engage in a variety of activities off-site, some within the UK, others abroad. Keeping track of those legal rights and obligations in those circumstances is much more difficult. In all cases it requires careful thought before such activities take place and a regular 'audit' of arrangements to ensure that they remain legally watertight.

4.143 There is a long list of activities which require attention. They include arrangements for validating courses elsewhere, franchising courses, exchange programmes, study abroad, placements for language training, professional experience, field trips, participation in international research and consultancy programmes, etc. Different considerations will apply when the activities take place within the UK, although even within the UK there are different legal jurisdictions, and when they take place 'overseas' where the number of potential jurisdictions with different rules runs into hundreds. It is the practice of some foreign courts to award much larger damages for injury to persons, reputation and property than would be the case in the UK. But in some countries there are procedures in place which are quite different to those with which UK institutions are familiar. Likewise of course there are procedures in place in the UK with which foreign students will be unfamiliar, as for example the prohibition on non-EU students taking public authority housing except where arranged through the institution.[278]

4.144 Many institutions participate in bilateral exchanges of students with institutions in other countries and/or provide facilities for overseas students, primarily but not exclusively from the US, to follow credit-bearing courses as part of their home programme. Where exchanges are not conducted within a framework imposed from outside the system (eg by the various European programmes) the precise nature of the inter-institutional and institution-student relationships will depend upon the terms of bilateral agreements, the validity enforceability and interpretation of which depend upon the operation of law.

---

278 Housing Accommodation and Homelessness (Persons subject to Immigration Control) Order 1996 (SI 1996/1982).

4.145   There are a number of important principles to have in mind when negotiating the terms of the inter-institutional agreement and when offering a place on an exchange or study abroad programme to an intending student. There are also issues to be considered when placing a home student onto an international exchange programme or sending a student to an overseas institution on a credit-bearing placement.

4.146   One area which concerns US and Australian institutions in particular is the extent to which they may be held liable for academic advice given to their students about the suitability of courses taken elsewhere. It is clear that there can exist a special relationship between a person giving advice who might reasonably be expected to be knowledgeable about the subject-matter and the person receiving advice. Of course this relationship does not just exist in international studies and liability for negligent statements in giving of 'domestic' advice may arise in accordance with the principles developed in the leading case *Hedley Byrne & Co Ltd v Heller & Partners Ltd*.[279] That case was concerned with a gratuitous but negligent bank reference. The House of Lords held that a negligent, though honest, misrepresentation may give rise to an action for financial loss caused by it, even though there is no contractual or fiduciary relationship. The law will imply a duty of care when one party A seeks information from party B possessed of a special skill, trusting B to exercise due care, and B knew or ought to have known that reliance was being placed on his or her skill and judgment. So far this question has not arisen directly in the UK.

4.147   However, Gordon King[280] has shown how recent cases in the Australian courts, developing the *Hedley Byrne* principles, lead to the possibility of litigation in the area of educational advice. The nature of the advice given has been extended from answers to a specific enquiry to more general advice. The adviser assumes responsibility for advice either expressly or by implication and liability may arise so long as (s)he knows that someone, not necessarily the enquirer, can reasonably be foreseen to rely on the advice. A disclaimer can be effective, so long as it is made known to the enquirer, and in the US, where an 'informed person' may be held to be liable in negligence for advice given in an educational setting, some

279 [1964] AC 465.
280 G King *Negligent Advice Giving in Educational Contexts: Some Possible Risks* (1994) Proceedings of the 3rd Annual Conference of the Australia and New Zealand Education Law Association p 85.

universities use an express waiver to attempt to avoid responsibility for warranting the content of any material from overseas; eg one institution affixes a sticker with the following wording to every overseas institution's prospectus or calendar:

> 'U is not an agent for this program. U does not guarantee its quality or that academic credits earned in this program may be transferred to U. This brochure is provided for your information only.'

There is nothing to be lost by institutions in the UK adopting express disclaimers of this kind.

4.148   If the student is registered with the receiving institution then a contract will be created between the student and the institution, the terms of which will depend upon the correspondence, the University's own rules and regulations, etc. The standard 'student contract' may be adjusted by reference to the inter-institutional agreement, any relevant terms of which should be drawn specifically to each student's attention. In accordance with the terms of relevant international conventions and UK domestic law (eg the Contracts (Applicable Law) Act 1990), any action brought by or against the student will normally be decided in accordance with the law of the jurisdiction in which the contract is to be performed. This implies that any appeal, grievance, complaint or disciplinary matter not resolved internally will be litigated there or subjected to any alternative special procedure such as the Visitor, an arbitrator, or an ombudsman. It is incumbent on institutions sending students abroad to ensure that they are properly advised about this and about any significant differences in what is permitted or prohibited by the law of the jurisdiction into which they are being sent. For example, the different restrictions on purchase and consumption of alcohol.

4.149   Obligations for the health and safety of international students will fall on the receiving institution and normally any issues will be decided according to the law of the jurisdiction in which they arise.[281] It is particularly important to clarify what obligations may arise on visits made as part of the course to another jurisdiction. Of course this is true if the party is made up entirely of home students but may become more complicated where the party is of mixed nationality or domicile. Sending and receiving institutions should make it

---

281   Convention on Jurisdiction and the Enforcement of Judgments in Civil and Commercial Matters 1968; Civil Jurisdiction and Judgments Act 1982.

absolutely clear to students what their rights and obligations are as visitors to other jurisdictions and should be particularly careful to advise on relevant and sufficient insurance cover; in this respect the domicile of the international student may be important. Under no circumstances, deliberately or by default, should the sending institution take upon itself any liability for warranting the safety of the environment into which its students are sent.

Student unions

Historical origins

4.150 Student unions were first formed as Student Representative Councils (SRC) in Scotland[282] and given statutory recognition in section 3 Universities (Scotland) Act 1889.[283] The 'Scottish influence' led some of the then new English universities of the early twentieth century to accord recognition to the student body, beginning with the University of Birmingham Guild of Students in 1900. Others started out as social and/or athletic clubs and their current constitutions reflect that origin. In its Report for 1923–24[284] the University Grants Committee encouraged universities to establish unions to develop 'athletic and social clubs and societies and to foster the growth of a corporate life' when many students lived at home. Following the development of unions as political pressure groups in the 1950s and 1960s, the 'Robbins' universities experimented with new constitutional forms. In the former public sector, student unions became formalised in about 1970, when the then Department of Education and Science included provision for student unions in its model articles of government.[285] 'Student representation' has been widened from catering, accommodation, etc issues into academic areas.[286]

---

282 The earliest recorded form of student organisation was in 1834 at Edinburgh University where the Dialetic, Scots Law, Diagnostic, Hunterian Medical and Plinian Societies jointly formed the Associated Societies with an elected representative council. By 1884 there was a Student Representative Council.
283 Regulated by Ordinance No 60; General No 22 of 4 February 1895.
284 HMSO 1924.
285 DES Circular 7/70.
286 For international comparisons, including a critique of EA94, see L Giesecke (1995) 'Blick über den Zaun' Forschung und Lehre, August, 440.

Meaning of student union

4.151 Until the Government published its proposals in 1993 to legislate in respect of student unions there was no attempt to define what is meant by the term. Fundamentally they are associations formed as part of the representative democratic structure of higher education institutions for the principal purpose of representing students' interests and for providing student-run sporting, cultural and social activities. Holding an office in a student union has always attracted a certain cachet and many successful people effectively started their careers in this way. In attempting a definition for the purposes of their Education Bill, the Government concentrated on the representational role. In a number of institutions, particularly in Scotland, the body which they wished to bring within the ambit of the legislation is a Student Representative Council, while a separate student union or association runs commercial activities. In some institutions the student union or association has contracted to provide commercial services such as catering which have in the past been run by the institutions themselves.

The Education Act 1994 (EA94)

4.152 Part II EA94 defines 'student union' as

(a) an association of the generality of students at an establishment … whose principal purposes include promoting the general interests of its members as students; or

(b) a representative body (whether an association or not) whose principal purposes include representing the generality of students at an establishment … in academic, disciplinary or other matters relating to the government of the establishment.

The definition is extended to include bodies which represent undergraduate students or graduate students as students 'at a particular hall of residence.' It also extends to bodies which consist either (i) of constituent or affiliated associations or bodies which are themselves student unions; or (ii) representatives of such constituent or affiliated associations, which fulfil the functions of student unions within the definitions above in respect of any establishment. While the Act extends to unions which relate to more than one establishment, it does not extend to bodies which relate to establishments generally in the UK or part of the UK. Hence it does not extend directly to the National Union of Students (NUS), founded in 1922, nor to sub-sections of the NUS.

4.153   The genesis of this part of EA94 was the Conservative Government's often stated intention to legislate to require student unions to be voluntary bodies which students might join at will. This concept was included in the Adam Smith Institute's proposal for a Student Charter.[287] It is either an express or an implied term of the contract of matriculation that students automatically become members of the relevant union, enjoy the privileges and are subject to the rules of that body, whether they wish to belong or not. It was decided not to proceed to voluntary membership: in summer 1993 the Government published an outline of its proposals, due to be enacted as regulations made by the Secretaries of State under the forthcoming Education Act, for (i) restricting public funding (either in cash or cash equivalent) of unions to specified 'core' services and (ii) prohibiting the use of public funds for affiliation to external organisations such as the NUS. In fact, the proposal to provide for voluntary membership was changed during consideration of the draft to one of allowing students to withdraw from membership if they wished, without thereby suffering any detriment. This provision in section 22 EA94 among others has forced institutions to develop mechanisms for voluntary withdrawal; press and other reports suggest that in the period 1994 to 1997 fewer than 10 students in total in the UK as a whole had chosen to withdraw.

4.154   Section 22 EA94 requires the governing body of an institution to take such steps as are reasonably practicable to secure that any union operates in a fair and democratic manner and is accountable for its finances.[288] In particular,[289] the governing body must take such steps as are reasonably practicable to ensure that:
(i)   the union has a written constitution;
(ii)   it approves and regularly reviews the constitution;
(iii)   secret ballots are held for elections to major union offices;
(iv)   union elections are fairly and properly conducted;
(v)   no student holds a union office for more than one year, or more than one office while a student;
(vi)   financial affairs of the union are properly conducted and proper arrangements exist for their scrutiny;
(vii) regular financial reports are published and made available to all students and the governing body;

---

287 B Davey *The Student Charter Project Report* University of Kent (1992) p 15.
288 Section 22(1).
289 Section 22(2).

(viii) the procedure for allocating resources to groups or clubs is fair, set down in writing and freely accessible to all students;
(ix) affiliation to external organisations [eg the NUS] is decided upon annually by secret ballot;
(x) there is a complaints procedure, with effective remedies, available to students dissatisfied in their dealings with the union;
(xi) complaints are dealt with promptly and fairly.

4.155 The governing body is also required to draw up a code of practice governing the operation of unions within these specific principles[290] and both applicants[291] and students must be informed about the arrangements made for compliance with the Act. Existing students must be so informed 'at least once a year.'[292] The penalties for failure to abide by these requirements are not specified in the Act, but presumably the alleged failure to comply might render the governing body or the institution susceptible to an action for judicial review.

4.156 According to Sedley J in *R v Thames Valley University Students Union, ex p Ogilvy*[293] the essential private law character of the union, (in that case held to be a voluntary association with a free-standing constitution, not incorporated into the University's structure) was not affected by EA94. Section 20 merely defines a union and then 'grafted on to the rules [of the union] the requirements of Parliament.' In the view of Sedley J 'that does not invest a students union … with a public law or statutory character.' It was, in essence a private members' club and not amenable to judicial review on the basis of the reasoning in *R v Disciplinary Committee of the Jockey Club, ex p Aga Khan*[294] even though its decisions had major consequences for individuals. It might however possibly be argued that because EA94 exists, and the fact that a student union, while a voluntary organisation, has automatic membership unless this is renounced, the public interest element would be sufficient to allow judicial review.[295] However, Mr Ogilvy appeared in person and no arguments were put by counsel.

---

290 Section 22(3).
291 Presumably in the prospectus.
292 Section 22(5).
293 (1997) 4(8) ELM 6.
294 [1993] 2 All ER 853, CA.
295 See *R v Legal Aid Board, ex p Donn & Co* [1996] 3 All ER 1 and *R v BBC, ex p Referendum Party* (1997) Times, 29 April, DC.

Types of association

4.157 For simplicity the title 'student union' will be used to describe the students' organisation in each institution. There is however, a range of names including Union, Guild, Association and Assembly. Sometimes the 'Union' is a building or the social part of a larger organisation, particularly in Scotland where the Union is often a club within the meaning of the licensing laws: it is important not to confuse the terminology. For the purposes of this part of the chapter, the relevant body in the ancient Scottish universities is the Students' Representative Council (SRC), which may be part of a larger Association or Assembly. In one case the officially-established body (the SRC) is part of the union and in some institutions there is a separate Sports Union or athletic association. Some unions are conglomerate with functions ranging outside the institution, requiring fairly complex constitutional provision.

4.158 There are a number of general issues relating to student unions: status of the union in the institution of which it forms part; objectives and charitable status; relationship with the institution; internal government and discipline; freedom of speech and disruptive activity.

Establishment and control

4.159 Constitutionally, we may group student unions in two ways, either by the form of their establishment or by the controls which the institution exercises over their government and management. Almost all unions are established either by the charter, by statute or by some process under the equivalent articles of government, in some cases carried on from former existence as a polytechnic or CI.[296] An example from a post-1992 constitution is that of the University of Greenwich:

> There shall be a Students' Union ... [it] shall conduct and manage its own affairs and funds in accordance with a constitution approved by the Court and shall present audited accounts annually to the Court. No amendment to or rescission of its constitution, in part or in whole, shall be valid unless and until approved by the Court.

---

296 Eg at Napier University the former students' union under the Napier College of Commerce and Technology (No 2) Regulations 1985 was continued under the Napier University (Scotland) Order of Council 1993 (SI 1993/557) Article 7.

and from the pre-1992 sector, the University of Hull:

> There shall be ... a Union of Students (Charter); There shall be a Union of Students ... Ordinances shall prescribe the constitution, functions, privileges and other matters relating to [it] (Statute); As part of the University there shall be a Union of Students ... to serve the interests of the students ... Regulations shall be prepared by the Union for the furtherance of the objects of the Union ... receiving the approval of the Senate and the Council ... (Ordinance).

However, as we have seen in *R v Thames Valley University Students Union, ex p Ogilvy*,[297] the court held that the Union in Thames Valley University was a voluntary association with a free-standing constitution, albeit one which required approval by the university's governing body under EA94. There was no mechanism by which the Union had been incorporated within the University's structure.

4.160   In the pre-1992 universities there appear to be only three universities whose student unions are not established by the Charter and Statutes: Cambridge,[298] Essex and York. In the last two the relevant instrument is an Ordinance. The practical effect of the difference is that if established by Ordinance the union's existence may be terminated by act of the institution without the requirement for consent of the Privy Council. Where the union is constituted by charter, statute, instrument or articles of government detailed constitutional provision is then made by the governing body:[299] this may be by Ordinance in the older institutions. Although there may be a provision for constitutional amendments to originate with the union, there can really be no doubt that the governing body always has the ultimate authority: it must in any event take responsibility for financial control under the Financial Memorandum with the Funding Council and for ensuring proper conduct of the union's financial affairs under section 22(2) EA94.

4.161   The extent to which the rules/regulations are spelt out in the Ordinances or similar instruments varies considerably, reflecting local circumstances and problems which have arisen in past years: in most cases only the principal rules are set out and the union is permitted to adopt subsidiary rules which do not conflict with the principal rules. The question of control is complicated to some extent by the

297   (1997) 4(8) ELM 6.
298   Grace 1 of 16 May 1984, amended by Graces 2 of 30 January and 9 of 24 April 1985.
299   Eg Article 53, Articles of Government of the University of Greenwich.

existence of joint institution-union boards, eg the Aston Guild Board, established by the Council of the University 'to have general oversight of the affairs of the Guild' with powers inter alia to approve the constitution of the Guild of Students, approve estimates and authorise expenditure and the Liverpool Joint Union Management Committee which is responsible to the University of Liverpool for the good order and management of the Union, ie the building.

Financial control

4.162   In some cases the institution participates in the financial control of the union either by the appointment of a Senior Treasurer or a Financial Adviser. *In Baldry v Feintuck*[300] the court noted that the University of Sussex Union had a Treasurer nominated by the Senate, but the office was vacant at the time.

Objectives

4.163   The NUS was founded in 1922 mainly by ex-servicemen, not only as a national student representative body but also as a means of promoting international peace and understanding. The list of objects or functions of individual unions now ranges in size from one sentence to a page of detailed clauses. Several include among their objectives or as an overriding clause the requirement for equal treatment of members, etc, in terms of sex, race, political belief, etc and to uphold freedom of speech. The most common objectives are to act as a recognised means of communication between students and the institution authorities, to foster and develop a corporate spirit, including athletic, cultural and social activities (including provision of bars, etc), to provide information and welfare services to students, to support student societies, to liaise with other student unions, locally and nationally and to represent the interests of students. These objectives are broadly consistent with the definition in section 20(1) EA94, ie promoting the general interests of members and representing them both collectively and individually in relationships with the institution. The CCI Charters' emphasis on the rights of individual students may in due course have an adverse effect on student unions' ability to represent the interests of students by taking collective action.

---

300 [1972] 2 All ER 81; see also *Harrison v Hearn* [1972] 1 NSWLR 428.

Charitable status

4.164 As explained earlier, charitable status is granted to those bodies which have charitable objects according to the law, which can be traced back to a Statute of Elizabeth.[301] Where a union is part of the institution, then it falls under the 'umbrella' of the institution as an educational charity under the provisions of the Charities Acts 1960–93 in England and Wales. It exists for the public benefit to further the educational purposes of the institution. So far as is known, only one English chartered university seeks by Ordinance to distance the union by a disclaimer of liability for debts clause:

> The Council of the University is not responsible financially or in any other way for any act or contract engaged in by the Students' Union ... a note to this effect shall appear in all contracts, undertakings or legal agreements entered into by the Students' Union. (University of Kent at Canterbury)

In practice where unions are constituted by charter, statute, articles of government or ordinance they are likely to be treated as creatures of the institution. As Lord Annan said in his report:[302]

> The Students' Union, like any other constituent part of a university, is subject to the Statutes, Ordinances and Regulations of that university. Lord Devlin made this clear in his Report.[303]

And it is unclear how the university could escape liability.

4.165 The Attorney-General (Lord Advocate in Scotland) issues guidance on expenditure by student unions. This makes it clear that a student union has charitable objects if it exists to represent and foster the interests of the students at an educational establishment in such a way as to further the educational purposes of the establishment itself. It is not open to a union to adopt objectives which conflict with the charitable educational purposes of the institution.[304]

4.166 The charitable status of student unions has been considered by the courts in a number of cases. The first two were heard by the

301 43 Eliz cap 4.
302 Annan Report, University of Essex, 1974, p 16.
303 *Report of the Sit-In in February 1972 and its Consequences (Devlin Report)*, Vol C111, *Cambridge University Reporter*, Special, No 12; 14 February 1972, p 54.
304 See *Student Unions: A Guide* (1995); *Political Activities and Campaigning by Charities* (CC9), Charity Commissioners.

same judge, Brightman J. In *Baldry v Feintuck*,[305] where support by a students' union for a campaign of protest against the then government's policy of ending free milk for schoolchildren was held to be a non-charitable application of funds, the case proceeded on the basis that the student union of the University of Sussex was a charity and the point was not argued. In the words of Brightman J[306]

> The union [of the University of Sussex] is, clearly, an educational charity and the officers of the union who have power to dispose of the union's funds are, clearly, trustees of those funds for charitable educational purposes.

Lord Annan's conclusion was also assumed in *Baldry v Feintuck*, where Brightman J held that the constitution of the relevant union

> ... must by necessary implication, be construed in the context of the educational purposes of [the] University ...[307]

4.167 In *London Hospital Medical College v IRC*,[308] Brightman J came to the considered view that the college union was charitable. The union had been established and existed for the sole object of assisting the college in its charitable purpose of teaching medicine, by providing those physical, cultural and social outlets for students which were needed, or at any rate were highly desirable, if the college was efficiently to perform its charitable purpose. Relying inter alia on the decision in *Re Mariette*[309] he held that the union was itself a charity. In *A-G v Ross*[310] Scott J was faced with the preliminary point of determining whether the students' union of the then North London Polytechnic was established for charitable purposes. It was formed and existed for the purpose of furthering the educational interests of the polytechnic (and of the local authority which funded it) and was therefore established for charitable purposes. There was nothing inconsistent with that charitable purpose that the polytechnic in the furtherance of its educational function encouraged its students, through the union, to develop political awareness and to form views

---

305 [1972] 1 WLR 552.
306 [1972] 2 All ER 81, 84. See also *Harrison v Hearn* [1972] 1 NSWLR 428, where it was held that the funds of the Students' Council of Macquarie University approximated to trust funds and that in using these funds the members of the Council owed a fiduciary duty to the persons whom they represented.
307 [1972] 2 All ER 81, 84.
308 [1976] 1 WLR 613.
309 [1915] 2 Ch 284.
310 [1986] 1 WLR 252.

on political issues. In *Webb v O'Doherty*[311] support by a student union for a campaign against the Gulf War was held to be a non-charitable application of funds, as was affiliation to bodies carrying out a similar campaign. The student union was assumed to be charitable from the start.

4.168   In Scotland charitable status is also dependent on the statute of Elizabeth.[312] There is no charities legislation as such, but recognition by the Inland Revenue for tax purposes for the purposes of section 505 Income and Corporation Taxes Act 1988 and other legislation achieves the same practical effect. Provision for the regulation of charities is made in Part I Law Reform (Miscellaneous Provisions) (Scotland) Act 1990 and associated regulations.[313] The Lord Advocate's powers under the Act are exercised on his or her behalf by the Scottish Charities Office (SCO) which is a division of the Crown Office and advice on the charitable status of students' unions has been issued by the SCO.[314] However, following on that advice, it has been accepted by SCO that if a students' union is part of the institution itself it may not have a separate legal personality and is such cases will not be a separately recognised charity.[315]

4.169   The status of the Student Representative Councils of the four ancient universities is secured by the nineteenth century statutes: the student unions are essentially buildings administered by students' associations. In the 1960s chartered institutions, the students' associations are established by the Charter. Dundee and Stirling both exclude liability for debts, and charitable status has been secured for their associations. The post-1992 universities established student associations under statutory powers[316] continued in being by the 1993 Orders of Council establishing the new institutions. The functions of such associations are 'to advise, assist and represent the students, to provide a channel of communication between the students and the authorities of the University, to provide social and recreational services and facilities for the students and to enable its members to co-operate with members of other institutions for their mutual benefit.'[317]

311 (1991) Times, 11 February.
312 *Trustees for the Roll of Voluntary Workers v IRC* 1942 SC 47; *Williams' Trustees v IRC* [1947] AC 447.
313 Charities Accounts (Scotland) Regulations 1992 (SI 1992/2165).
314 *Charity Law and Scottish Student Bodies* (1996).
315 Letter from Director, SCO, to author, 11 October 1996.
316 Eg The Napier College of Commerce and Technology (No 2) Regulations 1985.
317 Article 7, Napier University (Scotland) Order of Council 1993 (SI 1993/557).

4.170 It is incumbent on institutions to ensure that student unions or Representative Councils recognised as charities or part of an educational charity restrict themselves to educational charitable purposes. These would include representation of students on governing bodies and academic bodies, giving educational and related advice to students and providing support for student activities directly related to the provision of education, including sport, culture, promotion of international understanding, etc. Although it is unlikely that any of these standing alone would justify charitable status, linking them directly to the support of education is a different matter. VAT legislation clearly identifies which are 'business purposes' and these might be undertaken by a wholly-owned subsidiary company limited by guarantee, which covenants back a proportion of its surplus to the union. As mentioned above, a small number of universities have sought to exclude the possibilities of being held liable for the actions and debts of their unions but it remains a matter for decision whether such a provision would have the desired effect. The only certain way for the university to avoid the prospect of suit for damages for breach of contract by the union would appear to be to incorporate the union itself, a step taken by the University of Central England, thereby creating limited liability status for the union.[318]

Internal relationships

4.171 This treatment of students' unions is important in two aspects: in the internal relationship between the institution and the union, in contractual relationships with third parties and in alleged breaches of statutory obligations. In the chartered universities outside Scotland, student unions have the right to petition the Visitor on 'domestic' matters: in *Re Students' Union of Brunel University, John Flanagan, Andrew Gale and Brunel University*[319] Lord Hailsham LC, the Visitor, found it unnecessary to decide on a challenge by the university to the locus standi of the union in a case concerning the termination of a course. He went on to say:

> ... I must make it clear that I do not necessarily consider that the Students' Union has a locus standi except in cases which actually or potentially involve existing students.

318 See I Leedham *Incorporation of Students' Unions* (1997) UCELNET Reporter No 4.
319 (1985), unreported.

This would probably exclude the union from making valid representations to the Visitor about changes in the academic structure of the institution which did not affect existing students.

Interrelationship between student office and student membership of the institution

4.172 In *Shuttleworth v Fox and Brain and Imperial College of Science and Technology*,[320] a student elected as editor of the student newspaper failed his examinations and was required by the College to withdraw. He sought an interlocutory order that his subsequent removal from the editorship by the union was invalid: Fox and Brain were sued as representing the union. Neill J held that the proper construction of the relevant regulations required the editor to be a 'student' and that as he had ceased to be a registered student his application failed. However, a reading of the judgment confirms that the union's byelaws had not been amended, as intended by the College, to deal with the issue of students elected to union office subsequently being deregistered. While the judgment did not turn on that point, it is clear that if an institution enters into arrangements with its union which require some constitutional action, it should take steps to ensure that the action is carried through.

Relationship with third parties

4.173 Even in cases where the union is expressed to be part of the institution, unless it is separately incorporated it is at law an unincorporated association of persons; it is not a legal person.[321] The relevant officers or committee have power to sue and be sued and to enter into contracts as representatives of the membership, but the union itself has no legal personality, despite the fact that in many institutions it appears to third parties to employ staff and hold property. In the *Re Visitor of the University of Hull*,[322] the amenity fee dispute already referred to, Lord Roskill appeared to countenance the prospect of a legally binding agreement between the university and the union. It is difficult to imagine a situation in which one part of a corporation can enter into a legally binding agreement with

---

320 (1979), unreported.
321 Such bodies apparently exist and carry on their activities as separate units, but are not incorporated: common examples outside higher education are members' clubs, friendly societies and trades unions.
322 May 1983, p 7.

another. How could the terms of such an agreement be enforced? It can only be argued that some form of legal identity has been created for student unions by the practice of naming their officers in representative actions (for example, when an institution seeks to recover possession of occupied buildings) but there is no authority to this effect.

4.174 The question of status of the student union is equally important in relation to third party contracts for the employment of staff or for the supply of goods or in cases involving torts or breach of statutory liability. A third party might reasonably expect for example that he or she would have redress against the institution for failure to meet lawfully-incurred debts or for wrongful or unfair dismissal. If a 'stand-alone' unincorporated association, a student union could not itself be sued by those aggrieved. Equally, an aggrieved member of the union might attempt redress against the university for alleged invalid acts by the union. The action in *Baldry v Feintuck* against the Chairman of the Council and a university employee was withdrawn, it being accepted by counsel for the plaintiff student that neither was responsible for disputed payments 'since ... [the payments] ... were the subject-matter of a resolution of the union in general meeting.'[323]

4.175 There are two issues of considerable importance. The first is potential liability for breach of health and safety legislation, or the common law duty of care, in activities organised and supervised by the union or its subsidiary bodies (eg a climbing accident, a minibus crash or a sports injury).[324] Section 3 HASWA may be prayed in aid in requiring institutions to take all reasonably practicable steps, when approving the union constitution under EA94, to ensure that the safety and well-being of participants is maintained in just the same way as if those taking part were employees, where section 2 HASWA applies. The second area is that of liability for defamation arising from material published in a student newspaper or an official union website (as opposed to a personal website) where it is impossible to establish a recognised defence. Institutions could insist that publications issued in the name of the union, or by a union club or society, are professionally vetted to ensure that, as far as possible, they do not put the union, the institution or the authors and editors

---

323 [1972] 2 All ER 81, 85.
324 See *Smoldon v Whitworth* [1997] ELR 249, CA on the liability of a referee; *Sport in Higher Education* (1996) CVCP; *Safe Sport in Universities* (1996) BUCPEA.

personally at risk. Commercial printers of such publications may put up a defence based on the 'innocent publication' principle established in section 1 Defamation Act 1996, although this is by no means a carte blanche for them.

4.176 The position of union staff varies but generally speaking they are appointed by and are responsible to the relevant officers or committee of the union: they owe no direct allegiance to the university. Occasionally this might put them into a situation of conflict and it is wise to spell out their responsibilities clearly in their contract of employment. The corollary is that institutions may not be vicariously liable for acts committed by union staff in the course of their duties, for example where a steward employed by the union uses unreasonable force to eject someone from union premises and is later sued for damages. There have been a number of cases arising under employment legislation, eg *Hadden v University of Dundee Students' Association*[325] and *Leicester University Students' Union v Mahomed*[326] where clearly the bodies in question must have had some form of legal personality in order to be sued.

Internal structure of unions – (i) policy-making

4.177 The internal structure of unions reflects to some extent that of the institutions of which they are part, although unlike the English Court, the General Meeting of union members often exercises supreme power in a genuine sense. The General Meeting can prescribe policy which other bodies and office-holders are 'mandated' to apply on pain of loss of position or office. Obviously a minority can effectively prescribe the policy for the majority. The Conservative Government was particularly concerned about the influence of bodies such as the National Union of Students (NUS) and this is why EA94 makes particular reference to procedures to be followed for affiliation to external organisations so that affiliation does not go through by default.[327]

4.178 The general principles in relation to the conduct of meetings will apply and it is important that the quorum rules for each category of meeting (ordinary, special, extraordinary, etc) are clearly set out. Arguably these should be more stringent when action is contemplated

325 [1985] IRLR 449.
326 [1995] ICR 270.
327 Sections 22(2)(j–l)

which will affect the relationship between the union and the institution. In practice we find that the quorum for special meetings ranges from nothing specified (in which case the common law rule is that it should be a majority of the members) through a specified range of between 1% and 20% of the full membership. The absolute number of students needed for special meetings (ordinary meetings where there is no special quorum) is remarkably similar, commonly in the range 200–300, excluding very small institutions, with only two large institutions requiring a quorum in excess of 500. There is no direct correlation between size of institution and number of students able to authorise 'direct action.' Although there seems to be a tradition that students will not entertain such action unless this has been 'legitimised' in some way by a quorate meeting, there is in fact no possibility of action which is otherwise unlawful being rendered lawful simply by reason of approval by a quorate meeting. This is a political rather than a legal advantage.

Internal structure of unions – (ii) policy implementation

4.179   Below the level of General Meeting it is common to find two further tiers of government and numerous sub-committees of various kinds. Depending on the nature, size and geographical layout of the institution, it is common to find a representative Council with policy-making powers (usually subject to the direction of the General Meeting) and an Executive Committee with day-to-day control of the union's affairs, including the appointment of staff. The Executive Committee normally includes among its members a number of full-time sabbatical student officers as well as permanent staff. The number of sabbatical officers allowed by the institution depends on its size and in some cases on its geographical layout. The *Shuttleworth* case concerned a sabbatical officer who ceased to be a registered student and it is essential that the institution's rules prescribe what happens to the individual in this eventuality.

Internal discipline

4.180   Most unions reserve the right to discipline members, generally in relation to misconduct on union premises, in union meetings or in relation to elections. Some appoint a special Judicial or Disciplinary Committee, others act by the Executive Committee or its equivalent. In all cases the rules of natural justice apply, and in some cases are spelt out in elaborate detail. Typical penalties would include suspension from the use of union facilities for a period, restoration of damaged property or moderate fines. Institutions generally have by the act of approval of the unions' constitutions delegated such disciplinary power in respect of union offences although the position varies considerably between them. In all cases institutions should ensure that procedures are fair. In particular institutions need to satisfy themselves that 'automatic' reciprocal penalties imposed on students by other unions are themselves fair.

4.181 As a consequence of the status of unions as unincorporated associations, any member with a grievance which could not be settled otherwise would have to sue the committee and could bring a representative action, as in the *Baldry* and *Shuttleworth* cases. EA94[328] obliges the governing body of the institution to ensure that there is an effective internal complaints procedure including an external, independent final stage, a role which in the chartered universities outside Scotland would be filled by the Visitor.

Application of section 43 E(2)A86 to students' unions

4.182 As already explained, section 43 E(2)A86, which does not extend to Scotland or Northern Ireland, imposes certain duties on individuals and bodies concerned in the government of higher education institutions ('establishments') in relation to freedom of speech within the law on their premises.[329] Section 43(8) brings the premises of student unions which are not premises of the institution within the definition of 'premises of the establishment.' The Act does not define 'student union' nor does it tackle the problem of the wholly independent union, one occupying its own property or a 'conglomerate' union which serves students from a number of local institutions. According to the CVCP in a letter to the Secretary of State for Education and Science,[330] 'The practical difficulties ... [of the legislation] ... are greatly increased by subsection 8 which brings into the net the premises of students' unions.'

4.183 Is a student union a body 'concerned in the government' of an institution? The DES view was that it is, where it is part of the institution under the charter, statutes, etc. Even where it is not:

---

328 Section 22(2)(m)
329 See *Extremism and Intolerance on Campus* Interim Report of a CVCP Working Group (1997).
330 Attachment to letter of 15 October 1986.

The purpose of subsection (8) was to bring the premises of a legally separate students' union within the scope of subsection (2) which seeks to prevent discrimination in the use of university ... premises. Given that in most cases the premises of a students' union would be 'premises of the establishment' within the meaning of subsection (2), it was not considered that the definition of a students' union was critical.

The provisions were drafted 'in such a way as to avoid the risk of accidentally excluding any bodies we wished to include.'[331] It seems clear that some unions are not 'concerned in the government' of the institutions they serve, as in *R v Thames Valley University Students' Union, ex p Ogilvy*.[332] In that case Ogilvy, a student employed as a counsellor by the Union, had been excluded from the premises for alleged misconduct. Sedley J held that his exclusion did not inhibit his right to freedom of speech under section 43, nor penalise him for his views and beliefs.

4.184   E(2)A86 also obliges institutions of higher education in England and Wales to prepare a code of practice relating to free speech.[333] Institutions have approached this duty in a number of ways and it is only one weapon in the armoury of an institution facing disruptive behaviour against unpopular speakers by students or other groups on its premises. For example the common law provides a remedy against actions likely to cause a breach of the peace. The various main types of unlawful speech are set out in the Public Order Act 1986, as amended, which provides for a number of criminal offences.

---

331 Letter dated 19 August 1987 to the author from Further and Higher Education Branch III, DES.
332 (1997) 4(8) ELM 6.
333 For an example of the exercise of an institution's duty under the Act see *R v University of Liverpool, ex p Caesar-Gordon* [1991] 1 QB 124 where it was held that the university was not entitled to take account of threats of public disorder outside university precincts by persons not within its control; the university was not acting ultra vires by imposing necessary conditions relating to security, charges and admission to a meeting.

Direct Action

4.185 A number of institutions have from time to time taken steps in the English courts to restrain students from disruptive activity of various kinds or to regain possession of buildings unlawfully occupied, usually following a resolution of the students' union.[334] Such actions are normally taken against named officers of the union as representative of the students. The union itself, as an unincorporated association and as part of the university, cannot be sued. After some early difficulty with identification the Court of Appeal in *Warwick University v De Graaf*[335] was prepared to act on the basis that the institution took all reasonable steps to identify those causing the disruption. A permanent injunction against students cannot be granted since it is an equitable remedy equity acts in personam and successors in title are not bound.[336]

4.186 In Scotland it is not possible to secure interdict (the equivalent of injunction) against unidentified persons nor to obtain an interim order of ejection. Advice to institutions has been that the most effective procedure to secure the removal of persons from occupied buildings is the use of the criminal law of trespass under the Trespass (Scotland) Act 1865.

---

334 The procedure used in England and Wales depends upon whether disruptive activity is apprehended, in which case an interlocutory injunction may be sought ex parte from a judge of the High Court, or when repossession of premises unlawfully occupied is sought, in which case the institution may proceed under RSC Order 113.

335 [1975] 3 All ER 284. See also *University of Essex v Djemal* [1980] 2 All ER 742, applied in *Ministry of Agriculture, Fisheries and Food v Heyman* (1989) 59 P & CR 48.

336 *A-G v Birmingham Tame and Rea Drainage Board* (1881) 17 ChD 685.

Appendix A

A model contract

THIS IS AN AGREEMENT between [......] (hereinafter called 'the Institution') and ....(hereinafter called 'the student').

The Institution undertakes that in consideration of the payment of its stipulated tuition fees by or on behalf of the student and the due observance by the student of the provisions of [the Institution's Charter and Statutes/Instrument and Articles of Government, Ordinances/Byelaws, Regulations and Rules] as are current during the period of this Agreement [and are set out in the Calendar] it will provide adequate tuition and supervision of professional quality in respect of a programme of study leading to the degree or other qualification for which the student has been admitted and has registered subject to the following conditions:

(i) the student must achieve and sustain such standards of academic performance as are stipulated by the Institution from time to time in respect of the programme being followed and the Institution undertakes not to change such standards unilaterally without prior consultation with elected student representatives:

(ii) the Institution reserves the right upon giving notice which is reasonable in all the circumstances to make changes in the programme of courses being offered for reasons of changes in funding in staffing or for any other reasonable cause;

(iii) the student submits to the jurisdiction of the Institution in all matters connected with academic progress and discipline while on Institution premises or engaged in Institution activities and the

Institution agrees that the exercise of that jurisdiction shall be subject to standards of reasonableness and fairness.

The Institution and the student agree that the terms of this Agreement shall prevail over the content of any prospectus or other similar marketing material, or any written or oral statement made by either party or by the Institution's employees or agents.

Any disputes arising from the interpretation or performance of this Agreement and which cannot be resolved by negotiation between the parties shall be referred for decision by [the University's Visitor] [an arbitrator to be appointed on a standing basis by the Institution and the Students' Association] and such decision shall be final and binding on both parties.

Signed

Addition for validation/franchise arrangements:

I agree that by registering with 'A' College I am bound by the regulations of the College as set out in [the College Calendar.] I further agree that my registration with 'B' University is for formal record purposes only and that I am not thereby accorded the status of a student of that University in terms of its [Charter and Statutes].

Chapter 5

The employment of staff

'New look' staffing policies

5.1 Approximately 380,000 people are employed by higher education institutions in the UK[1] with about 40% employed as teachers or researchers.[2] Higher education is by any measure a major employer of labour and spends over three-quarters of its income on wages, salaries, national insurance and superannuation contributions. Like all employers, higher education has responsibilities to its staff, many of which are statutory. In the past, most attention has been paid in the media, in Parliament and in the academic press to the affairs of a minority of such staff, the academic staff working for the English chartered universities. Now, with the 1992 changes in the structure of higher education well entrenched, and moves even in the English chartered sector towards single status employment, we may cast the net rather wider and seek to describe the relationship of all staff to all institutions. Inevitably, we begin with the academic staff, but start to see the first signs of the 'new look.'

5.2 One of the most interesting and perceptive observations on the 'new look' in higher education staffing policies was that of Dillon LJ in *Pearce v University of Aston in Birmingham*[3] where his Lordship contrasted the old style 'good cause' statute which had been designed to protect university academics' independence in the light of how their

1 Census of Employment, 1995. This represents 1.8 per cent of the total UK workforce in employment. Quoted in paragraph 3.29, Main Report, NCIHE, July 1997.
2 Paragraph 3.13 Main Report, NCIHE, July 1997 based on a CVCP survey undertaken in 1996/7.
3 [1991] 2 All ER 461, discussed by P H Pettit in (1991) 54 MLR 137.

counterparts had been treated in totalitarian states,[4] with new style 'managerial interest' in the pursuit of economy in the use of public funds. We have seen the distinction between the procedures adopted by the old UGC and those adopted by the Funding Councils and the increasing intervention by government in the academic and financial affairs of the traditional universities, intervention which was no stranger to the rest of the higher education system.

5.3 Despite the theoretical equality of the 'Masters and Scholars' in the congregation of the University, academic staff of the pre-1992 universities always enjoyed quite different terms of employment from the majority of employees and indeed from the majority of university staff who are not academics. In recent years considerable changes have taken place, as a direct consequence of the difficulties which faced universities in the aftermath of the public expenditure cuts of the early 1980s. The result is that a member of academic staff of the older universities appointed or promoted on to a higher salary scale after 20 November 1987 is in practice in no better position than any other employee, save possibly that an academic employed by one of these institutions may not be dismissed for holding and expressing individual views on academic issues, the so-called 'academic freedom' which the traditional universities fought hard to protect during the passage of ERA.

The redundant lecturer

5.4 The precise contractual position of a member of the academic staff can only be found by a careful study of a number of documents:
(i) the contract of employment;
(ii) the relevant governing instrument, whether it be charter and statutes, Act of Parliament, instrument of government or the Articles of Association of a company limited by guarantee, plus all the subordinate legislation (ordinances, regulations, rules) enacted in accordance with the provisions of the governing instrument;
(iii) the terms of any collective agreement relevant to academic staff, which in the case of the older universities is usually one between the individual institution and the local branch of the Association of University Teachers (AUT) and in the case of the newer

4   This protection 'should be written in gold in every university's statutes': A N Khan and A G Davison 'University Visitor and Judicial Review in the British Commonwealth (Old) Countries' (1995) 24(3) Journal of Law and Education 457.

institutions is more likely to have been arrived at by national negotiation between representative bodies of the employers and a number of different trades unions.

5.5 The importance of the terms of the contract of employment was demonstrated in a lengthy dispute involving Edgar Page, formerly a member of the academic staff of the University of Hull.

In 1966 Edgar Page was appointed as a lecturer in the University of Hull. His letter of appointment provided for termination of the appointment by either the University or the appointee giving three months' notice. The University Statutes provided that 'subject to the terms of his appointment' no member of staff of his grade could be removed except for good cause. In 1988 the University gave notice of termination on grounds of redundancy. Mr Page claimed that this termination was ultra vires the University's powers and therefore invalid. He appealed to the Visitor.

5.6 In the course of proceedings before the Visitor and subsequently the higher courts, Edgar Page argued that according to the university's statutes his contract of employment could not be terminated before his normal retiring age (67) except on the limited grounds of good cause set out in the statute, those grounds being (the ellipses referring to procedure):

(a) Conviction of any felony or misdemeanour which the Council ... shall deem to be of an immoral, scandalous or disgraceful nature.

(b) Actual physical or mental incapacity which the Council ... shall deem to be such as to render the member of the Staff unfit for the execution of the duties of his office.

(c) Conduct of an immoral, scandalous or disgraceful nature which the Council ... shall deem to be such as to render the member of the Staff unfit to continue to hold his office.

(d) Conduct which the Council ... shall consider to be such as to constitute failure or inability to perform the duties of his office or to comply with the conditions of the tenure of his office.

5.7 Termination of employment on grounds of good cause required a specified formal procedure, which had not been followed in this case. Mr Page's dismissal had been intimated to him by a letter from the University Registrar and Secretary indicating that his services were no longer required by reason of redundancy. The University's argument was that the statute contained the additional clause:

Subject to the terms of his appointment no member of the teaching ... staff of the University ... shall be removed from office save upon the grounds specified ... and in pursuance of the procedure specified ...

and that the terms of appointment, including the notice clause, provided the university with the option to terminate employment on giving notice for any lawful reason except where termination was on grounds of good cause. This interpretation was upheld by the Visitor and after a considerable period of time the House of Lords held by a majority that a Visitor's determination on a point of law was not normally amenable to judicial review. The minority view was that judicial review could be sought but that the original decision was correct.[5] Mr Page therefore lost his job. It should be noted that a total of seven judges had expressed a different opinion to that of the majority in the House of Lords, two in the Divisional Court, three in the Court of Appeal and two in the House itself.

5.8 An earlier Australian case *Orr v University of Tasmania*[6] had dismissed the argument that a notice clause as operated in Edgar Page's case was also invalid because a separate statute provided for appointment to terminate on a set date following the employee's 65th birthday. In the law of Scotland, a *tenure ad vitam aut culpam* like that in the Page case is confined to those who hold a *munus publicum*, an office involving duties to the public[7] and the *munera publica tenure ad vitam aut culpam* is qualified by the retirement provision. It is clear that professors of the ancient Scottish universities were considered to hold the *munus publicum* but how this came to be generally applicable to lecturers etc is unclear. At least one of the 1960s chartered Scottish universities had 'cast-iron' tenure written into its original statutes in 1967, ie without the 'Hull phrase'- 'subject to the terms of his [sic] employment' which the Privy Council had otherwise insisted upon since the early 1960s – for example when the consultations on the draft charter of the Loughborough University of Technology were taking place, the Association of University Teachers objected to its inclusion. It seems that all parties realised from at least that point that this phrase had some legal meaning. Therefore it may reasonably be argued that a member of staff of those institutions with a 'Hull phrase' appointed or promoted before 30 November 1987 would be in the same position as Edgar Page if the institution decided to follow a similar course to that of Hull. At least one university had taken the further step of enacting an ordinance setting out procedures to be followed when redundancy was contemplated, procedures which are now required in the statutes of all the pre-1992 universities.[8] Most universities, however, either

---

5   *R v Lord President of the Privy Council, ex p Page* [1993] AC 682.
6   (1957) 100 CLR 526.
7   *Hastie v McMurtrie* (1889) 16 R 715; see also *Stewart v Secretary of State for Scotland* (1998) Times, 28 January.
8   Section 204 ERA.

considered that they were not in a position to declare redundancies among academic staff prior to the determination of the *Page* case, or did not wish to think they could.

5.9   In the period following the cuts in public expenditure of 1981, a number of universities were forced to shed substantial numbers of staff posts. As the majority considered that they were not in a position to effect these cuts by redundancy, the University Grants Committee, which accepted this view, had to make available very substantial sums in restructuring funds to enable universities to purchase premature retirement compensation from the superannuation schemes for those over the age of 50, and to provide a generous redundancy package for those under 50. If these funds had not been made available, then it was argued that the compensation likely to be awarded by the courts, particularly to academic staff who could not reasonably be expected to secure alternative employment at a comparable salary, would be likely to bankrupt some institutions. Following the *Page* case, it is now clear that view was mistaken in respect of all but a relatively few institutions with 'cast iron tenure,' although that concept was not tested in the higher courts.

5.10   Most universities treated premature retirements as redundancies, enabling the staff to receive additional compensation, part of which could at the time be reclaimed from the Department of Employment. The University of Liverpool, however, refused to make redundancy payments and, some three years after the event, the Court of Appeal agreed in *Birch and Humber v University of Liverpool*[9] that cases such as this were not 'dismissals' but 'termination by mutual consent' so that there was no entitlement to a statutory redundancy payment.[10] It is now clear that at least the University of Hull, and other institutions with comparable statutes, could have effected these redundancies without resort to the UGC restructuring funds. It is also clear that a number of institutions used these funds without adequate staff or manpower planning to support the reductions.[11]

---

9   [1985] IRLR 165.
10   Volunteers for redundancy, rather than for early retirement, are volunteering for dismissal and will be entitled to a redundancy payment: *Burton, Allton and Johnson Ltd v Peck* [1975] ICR 193.
11   See Report of the National Audit Office: *Department of Education and Science: Redundancy Compensation Payments to University Staff*, 23 October 1985.

The Visitorial jurisdiction

5.11 In fact *Page's* case was the last in a series in which the courts confirmed the 'final' nature of the Visitor's jurisdiction in non-Scottish chartered institutions: other cases falling within that jurisdiction include *Hines v Birkbeck College*,[12] *Thomas v University of Bradford*[13] and *Pearce v University of Aston in Birmingham*.[14] Such cases are no more. ERA removed the exclusive jurisdiction of the Visitor in relation to wrongful dismissal once the new procedures to be established by the University Commissioners were in place. Section 206(1) ERA provides: 'The visitor...shall not have jurisdiction in respect of any dispute relating to a member of the academic staff which concerns his appointment or employment or the termination of his appointment or employment' except where the Visitor is asked to hear or determine appeals or hear or redress grievances under the terms of the statutes to be made by the University Commissioners. The latter proviso would presumably allow the Visitor to redress the grievance of a member of the academic staff who maintained, for example, that he or she had been subject to discriminatory treatment in relation to promotion;[15] the applicant could also proceed against the institution under the anti-discrimination legislation. The Visitor could also hear any matter relating to a person 'on the foundation' other than a member of the academic staff.

5.12 The *Pearce* case raises another issue of more general importance: the right of an employer, like the right of any party to a contract, to break the contract and take the consequences. That issue lies at the heart of any discussion of the contract of employment and will be further examined later.

Tenure and the Education Reform Act 1988

The University Commissioners

5.13 Substantial powers to change the nature of tenure were included in ERA and by 1995 University Commissioners provided for in the Act had completed their task of ensuring that all the pre-

---

12 [1985] 3 All ER 156.
13 [1987] 1 All ER 834.
14 [1991] 2 All ER 461.
15 In 1997 Gillian Evans, a member of the academic staff of the University of Cambridge, had such a case considered by the nearest equivalent of the Visitor, the Vice-Chancellor's Commissary, Lord Oliver of Aylmerton.

1992 universities are able to declare redundancies among academic staff and have effective disciplinary and grievance procedures covering these staff. The powers of the Commissioners in relation to redundancy provisions were to amend the statutes of universities as necessary so as to enable any appropriate body or section thereof to dismiss any member of the academic or equivalent staff for redundancy defined as in the principal employment protection legislation, now EmpRA.

5.14   Section 204 ERA gave the Commissioners power to make modifications to statutes in respect of matters set out in section 203(1) – inter alia the dismissal or removal from office of a member of academic staff for 'good cause' which includes reasons now set out in section 98 EmpRA. Section 203(4) extends that power to other university posts with equivalent conditions, but does not give the Commissioners power to make modifications in respect of any other employment or office. The result is that appointment to other 'offices' (Dean, Warden, Radiation Protection Officer, etc) is not covered by the statutes. There may be two separate contracts of employment in such cases.[16] Section 204(6)(c) ERA recognises the common practice in universities of making honorific or temporary additional appointments. Removal from one of these offices may be covered by some other procedure where some right to be heard by the appropriate appointing body is normally provided, according to the principles in *Malloch v Aberdeen Corpn*.[17]

5.15   During the discussions leading up to the Commissioners' publication of a 'model statute' there was debate as to whether ERA empowered the Commissioners to act in respect of the ancient Scottish universities. The question was whether the meaning of 'statutes' in section 203(8) ERA included Acts of Parliament; if not then the argument runs as follows: the ancient Scottish universities' equivalent of 'university statutes' are Ordinances but none had been enacted on the subject-matter of ERA; since sections 204(1) and 235(1) ERA empowered the Commissioners to make 'modifications' and there was nothing for them to 'modify' then they could not proceed. These issues were not tested in the courts.

5.16   The Statutes as amended by the action of the Commissioners now apply to all appointments made or contracts of employment

---

16   See eg *Throsby v Imperial College of Science and Technology* [1978] 2 All ER 465.
17   [1971] 1 WLR 1578.

entered into after 20 November 1987, other than, according to the Northern Ireland Court of Appeal in *Deman v Queen's University of Belfast*,[18] probationary appointments. The powers are restricted in such a way in order to safeguard the position of staff already in post in November 1987.

Other institutions

5.17 The post-1992 universities and other institutions of higher education are not covered by these provisions and academic staff enjoy such protection from redundancy or dismissal as is provided by the general law, section 221 ERA,[19] the requirements of the articles of government of their institution and their contract of employment.[20]

Coverage of this section

5.18 As this is not a textbook on the law of employment generally,[21] it will be selective in its coverage, relating a number of areas covered by this branch of the law to the specific requirements of higher education. The law of employment is in fact a mixture of common law principles and statutory legislation, most of the latter being relatively recent. Apart from the Visitorial cases there have been about 40 reported cases[22] involving higher education institutions in industrial tribunals (and appeals from their decisions) since 1973, all of which have been concerned with rights arising from the recent employment legislation. There have also been a number involving further education lecturers and other staff at colleges of further and higher education. Of the 40 or so in the higher education field, 11 have alleged sex discrimination or failure to abide by equal pay legislation, three have been about redundancy, two about the rights of non-members of trades unions, one about the consequences of industrial action and the remainder about unfair dismissal, mainly technical and procedural aspects of the law. The latter have made a

18 [1997] ELR 431, NI CA. The changes were made to the statutes by SI 1993/1259 under provisions corresponding to those in ERA.
19 Amended by Schedule 8 paragraph 52 FHEA.
20 See R Lewis 'Disciplinary dismissals and redundancies in higher and further education' (1997) 7(4) Education and the Law 211.
21 Reference should be made to an up-to-date textbook such as N Selwyn *Selwyn's Law of Employment* (9th ed, 1996).
22 Most industrial tribunal cases are not reported but those of significance are notified to institutions by their respective representative bodies (CVCP, etc).

particular contribution to the general development of the law in relation to non-renewal of fixed-term contracts. There has also been a handful of cases in the ordinary courts, for example *Educational Institute of Scotland v Robert Gordon University*[23] concerning the Institute's (trade union's) title to sue as a representative body where the University was alleged to have made an unlawful decision in breach of statutory requirements. Some unreported cases have dealt with the inevitable problems arising on transfer of employing authority from local authority to independent corporation.[24]

Management and staff

5.19 As examples of Charles Handy's 'organisations of consent'[25] higher education institutions have not been thought of as experiencing the same clear distinction between management and staff as many other large employers. That view is restricted to limited categories of staff, notably academic and, in most universities, senior academic-related staff. The distinction was better defined in the 1970s and 1980s in the former public sector institutions and has been creeping into the traditional universities since the mid-1980s. It is however a factor to be borne in mind that the traditional negotiation between management and workers can, in the context of a university's negotiations with its academic staff in particular, be almost indistinguishable from a meeting of the management itself. This is obviously a factor in the Privy Council insistence that in all but the oldest English universities there must be a 'lay' majority on governing bodies which have responsibility for employment matters.

5.20 Traditionally, the salaries and superannuation arrangements of academic and equivalent staff have been settled nationally, whereas other conditions of service have been fixed locally or nationally depending on which side of the 'binary line' the institution fell before 1992. For example, pre-1992 university academic staff traditionally have had contracts of employment with no set hours of work and no fixed holiday entitlement, whereas the contracts of academic staff

---

23 [1997] ELR 1, Court of Session, OH.
24 Eg *Crowley v Hatfield Polytechnic Higher Education Corpn* Case No 11664/90/LN, an unsuccessful claim for £11.87 of disturbance mileage allowance, the corporation having adopted a lower rate than that previously paid by the Hertfordshire County Council.
25 C Handy 'The Organisations of Consent' in D W Piper and R Glatter (eds) *The Changing University* (1977).

in the other institutions include a degree of control over both.[26] While the academic staff and to some extent the senior academic-related staff of institutions have a special status of one kind or another, the majority of staff working in higher education are employed on terms which are similar to those of any public sector organisation. In the pre-1992 universities, the pay and main conditions of service are negotiated nationally, whereas the superannuation arrangements are based on a variety of local schemes, in some cases on the teachers' or local government schemes on which the arrangements for the staff of the remaining institutions are based. UCEA (Universities and Colleges Employers Association) is the employer's organisation for the whole sector. It is an agency of CVCP, CUC and SCOP. The Conference of Scottish Centrally-Funded Colleges (CSCFC) also participates. Individual institutions retain powers to make local enhancements, eg using tax-efficient pay schemes.

The contract of employment

Master and servant

5.21 The law of employment is based on the concept of 'master and servant' ie there must be a degree of control of the work of one individual by another individual or artificial person such as a company. This distinguishes the contract of employment or 'contract of service' from a contract for the engagement of an independent contractor or 'contract for services.' Such terminology is somewhat out of step with modern concepts of co-operation and teamwork, particularly in a public service environment, and it may be more appropriate to think in terms of the 'employment relationship.' An employer normally has liability (vicarious liability) for the acts of an employee carried out in the course of employment, where such acts are within the employee's actual or ostensible authority.[27]

---

26 For a full account of the (then) differences between the sectors, and the Government's involvement, see Chapter 7 *Higher Education – A New Framework* Cm 1541 (1991).
27 See *Generale Bank Nederland NV (formerly Credit Lyonnais Bank Nederland NV) v Export Credits Guarantee Department* (1997) 141 Sol Jo LB 194, in respect of exclusion of vicarious liability for an employee assisting in the fraudulent scheme of a third party. The rules relating to liability for the dishonest acts of an employee differ from those relating to acts of negligence and trespass: *Armagas Ltd v Mundogas SA* [1986] AC 717.

Independent contractors distinguished

5.22 In a higher education institution it should not be difficult to distinguish employees from independent contractors, although the distinction may become clouded when members of staff take on work for outside agencies in the capacity of independent contractor and it may then become difficult to determine whether a particular act of the member of staff in question has been carried out 'in the course of employment' which affects the liability of the employer. Other common examples of independent contractors working for higher education institutions are window cleaners, designers, and, sometimes, medical practitioners. The question is one of fact for a tribunal or court to decide.[28] In determining whether a contract of employment exists, the courts have adopted the principle of examining the facts of the case and not necessarily accepting what the parties might have considered to be the nature of their relationship as evidenced by what they have said or done,[29] explained by the Court of Appeal in *McMeechan v Secretary of State for Employment*[30] as a careful weighing and balancing of the various *indicia* as interpreted according to the particular context. Because independent contractors do not enjoy the same legal protection as employees over a wide range of aspects of the contract, the courts are reluctant to find that the relationship is one of independence. Paradoxically this may work against the interests of the individual, who might otherwise be able to enjoy some fiscal advantage. CVCP notes[31] that external examiners for first degrees (and some taught higher degree programmes) are treated as employees by the Inland Revenue (despite the requirement for them to be independent) and their fees are therefore subject to deduction of income tax under PAYE. Those for higher degrees are not. The reason for this difference appears to be that external examiners for first degrees are normally appointed for a period of years, whereas those for other degrees are appointed ad hoc. This has relevance for the application of the rules relating to employment of non-EU nationals in the Asylum and Immigration Act 1996.

---

28 *Lee Tin Sang v Chung Chi-Keung* [1990] ICR 409, PC; and see also *Market Investigations Ltd v Minister of Social Security* [1968] 3 All ER 732; *Ready-Mixed Concrete (South-East) Ltd v Minister of Pensions and National Insurance* [1968] 1 All ER 433 and (in Scotland) *MacDonald v Glasgow Western Hospitals Board of Management* 1954 SC 453.
29 See *O'Kelly v Trusthouse Forte* [1983] IRLR 369.
30 [1997] ICR 549, CA.
31 CVCP Advice, June 1997.

Consultancy

5.23 As the 1992 CVCP paper *Sponsored University Research: Recommendations and Guidance On Contract Issues*[32] points out, consultancy is an important mechanism for university/industry collaboration. The first point to discuss in relation to consultancy contracts is whether the contract is between the institution and the client – although in practice the consultancy will be carried out by a member or members of staff – or is a private arrangement between a member or members of staff and the client. If the former then the corporate body is contractually liable in all respects for the performance of the contract according to its terms, and also is liable in tort or delict or for any other breach of the civil or criminal law relevant to the work being carried out on its behalf.

5.24 On the other hand, provided the institution, in authorising a member or members of staff to undertake private consultancy, ensures that it distances itself fully from the contract, it can avoid any liabilities of this kind. As a corollary, it allows the member or members of staff to retain any moneys received. If of course it chooses to require the staff to pay over a proportion of their income, then it may by so doing become involved in the contract. It is for the member or members of staff to ensure that they are fully protected in terms of the insurance which, if they were carrying out the work on behalf of the institution, it would normally provide.

5.25 Some 25 years ago the Committee of Vice-Chancellors and Principals urged the then universities to ensure that staff were forbidden to undertake consultancies without express permission of the university and that the university should ensure that any third party dealing with a member of staff understood the position: either that the member of staff was acting on behalf of the institution or privately.[33] It was suggested, and reiterated in 1979[34] that an institution, in granting permission to the staff member to undertake the consultancy, should write to the third party concerned, before the work commenced. It was considered that staff should be made aware of the liabilities they were taking on by acting in a personal capacity and that universities should not provide legal or commercial advice to staff in such circumstances, as to do so would make it more difficult to argue that they were not concerned in the consultancy.

32 CVCP (1992) paras 11–14.
33 CVCP CIRC/74/27.
34 CVCP N/79/40.

Although by the end of 1997 no further advice in this area had been forthcoming, the natural extension of this to a complete barrier between the institution and the private contractor has much to commend it if the institution is to avoid product and professional liability.

A model consultancy agreement between an institution and a member of staff

5.26 An agreement of this kind should have the following specific features:
(i) the employee should be granted permission to undertake work for a specified period, number of days or hours and required to notify the institution (Head of Department or equivalent) when he or she is utilising this permission;
(ii) there should be a prohibition on the use of institutional notepaper, telephone, facsimile, electronic mail or other forms of address;
(iii) no institutional services, including accommodation, whether paid for or not, may be used;
(iv) the employee should be required to inform the tax and social security authorities of the private work;
(v) there should be an express statement that the employee is not covered by the institution's liability and personal insurances.
A suggested model is given in Appendix A.

Notice to be given by an institution to a third party client

5.27 This notice should contain the following elements:
(i) an express statement that the member of staff is not acting on behalf of the institution;
(ii) a statement in relation to insurance cover.
A suggested model is given in Appendix B.

Special cases

5.28 It is possible for a member of staff to be employed in two capacities simultaneously – in *Throsby v Imperial College of Science and Technology*[35] Phillips J said

---

35 This case was considered together with *Dixon v BBC* and other cases [1978] 2 All ER 465.

... we see no reason in principle why a man should not have two quite separate contracts of employment with the same employer, or why it is not possible to terminate one only ...

Peter Throsby was employed as a lecturer and also held an appointment as warden of a hall of residence. The Court did not decide whether there was one contract or two: if called upon to do so they would have to have decided whether his service as warden, for which he received an honorarium, was as employee or office-holder.[36]

5.29 It is also possible for employees to be employed by different legal entities (trading companies, for example) operating under the general umbrella of the institution or by a student union or association. *Hadden v University of Dundee Students' Association*[37] and *Leicester University Students' Union v Mahomed*[38] are cases in point. A students' union can be sued in its own name where it has independent legal status, as in *R v Thames Valley University Students' Union, ex p Ogilvy.*[39]

5.30 It is also common in the public service to find employees working on probationary contracts where the employer retains the right not to confirm the employment when the probationary period ends, and indeed to give notice during that period in certain circumstances.[40] Employees on probation are treated like other employees for the purposes of statutory employment protection, although they may be subject to a different contractual regime.[41]

5.31 Finally as a special case we find that in some instances students are taught or supervised by professional staff who are paid by and contracted to other organisations, for example in social work, teacher training, medical and para-medical areas and veterinary medicine. Such staff may or may not be 'vetted' at institutional level eg by the award of recognised teacher status, but may have no direct contractual or financial relationship with the institution. In such cases it is necessary for detailed procedures to be drawn up to deal with disputes, failure to observe common law or statutory duty of care, etc.

---

36 See *102 Social Club v Bickerton* [1977] ICR 911.
37 [1985] IRLR 449.
38 [1995] ICR 270.
39 (1997) 4(8) ELM 6.
40 *Dalgleish v Kew House Farm Ltd* [1982] IRLR 251.
41 As in *D v Queen's University of Belfast* [1997] ELR 431, NI CA.

Statutory definition of 'contract of employment'

5.32 Section 295 TULRCA and section 230 EmpRA define 'contract of employment' and 'employee' for the purposes of employment protection legislation, and as relevant to the law of higher education, as follows

> 'contract of employment' means a contract of service or of apprenticeship;

> 'employee' means an individual who has entered into or works under (or, where the employment has ceased, worked under) a contract of employment;

subject to the sections of the Act which relate to requirements for ballots before industrial action in which

> ... references to a contract of employment include any contract under which one person personally does work or performs services for another ...

and also subject to

> ... other provisions conferring a wider meaning on 'contract of employment' or related expressions.

The expression 'worker' which has a wider usage in employment law, is defined as meaning

> an individual who works, or normally works or seeks to work–
> (a)   under a contract of employment
> (b)   under any other contract whereby he undertakes to do or perform personally any work or services for another party to the contract who is not a professional client of his ...

and in relation to a trade dispute with an employer as extended to include

> (a)   a worker employed by that employer; or
> (b)   a person who has ceased to be employed by that employer where
>   (i)   his employment was terminated in connection with the dispute; or
>   (ii) the termination of his employment was one of the circumstances giving rise to the dispute.[42]

---

42   Section 244(5) TULRCA.

Statement of terms and conditions

5.33 The terms of employment are bilateral in that they are part of the employer-employee agreement, whereas conditions are unilateral instructions on the part of the employer.[43] Rather as in the contract of matriculation of students, the full terms of a contract of employment can be found only from a variety of sources. Naturally, there is now a considerable degree of formality associated with this: since the 1960s most employees[44] have been entitled after no more than two months of employment to a written statement of its principal terms, an employer's duty now governed by Part I EmpRA. The Act requires that certain basic details are given in one document (the principal statement) and the others may be given in instalments to be completed within the two-month time limit.

5.34 The terms to be included in the principal statement are:
(a) the names of the employer and the employee;
(b) the date when the employment began;
(c) the date on which the period of continuous employment began, taking into account any employment with a previous employer which counts towards that period;
(d) the scale, rate or method of calculating remuneration (including overtime pay, bonus payments, etc);
(e) the intervals at which remuneration is paid;
(f) any terms and conditions relating to hours of work (including normal working hours and contractual overtime);
(g) any terms and conditions relating to holiday entitlement (including public holidays) and holiday pay, including any entitlement to accrued holiday pay on the termination of employment;
(h) the title of the job which the employee is employed to do or a brief description of the work for which the employee is employed;
(i) either the place of work or, where the employee is required or permitted to work at various places, an indication of that and of the address of the employer.

5.35 Details must also be provided of
(i) disciplinary rules;
(ii) grievance procedures;
(iii) contracting-out certificates in force;
(iv) any collective agreements directly affecting the employment; and

43 N Selwyn *Selwyn's Law of Employment* (9th ed, 1996) p 74.
44 Gradually extended to virtually all employees.

(v) of the following matters, for which reference may be made to a collective agreement which the employee has reasonable opportunities of reading in the course of employment or which is readily accessible to the employee in some other way:
  (a) provision for sickness absence and sick pay;
  (b) information about pensions and pension schemes;
  (c) the length of notice required to be given or received on termination of the employment.

As an alternative to referring the employee to the terms of a collective agreement for information about periods of notice, the employer may refer the employee to the law.

5.36 These details are so important not only because they provide both the basis for employment protection of the employee, which will be discussed in detail later, but also because they can assist the employer when it comes to discipline, dismissal and so on. One aspect which is frequently overlooked is the requirement for the employee to give notice. While in many cases employers will readily waive notice periods, if only to save money, this may not be appropriate when the employee has received expensive training and development to equip him or her for the work. A recent example of this in the computing field arose in *Hubble v EDS*[45] in which a member of staff had given an undertaking not to leave before a certain date, having received considerable training including a ten-week course at the company's US headquarters. He was successfully sued for a four-figure sum to compensate the employer when he left before the contractual date.

Other terms

5.37 However, the Act does not provide the full picture. Some terms in a contract of employment may be imported from the law, eg minimum statutory periods of notice, the statutory duty of employers for health and safety and the rights of an employee whose invention generates a 'substantial benefit' for the employer when patented. A particular difficulty may arise in relation to academic freedom. In England and Wales, as we have seen, section 43(1) E(2)A86 imposes a duty on the governing body of every institution to secure freedom of speech within the law for its staff, who are entitled to rely on the governing body so to do. If a case arose in which the exercise of this duty was in question, it would be a mixed issue of public and private

45 (1992) unreported.

law. On the one hand the courts insist that private contractual rights are not amenable to judicial review, whereas on the other hand a failure by the governing body to carry out its statutory duty is clearly so amenable. The Visitor would not have jurisdiction over the latter since the visitorial jurisdiction extends only to interpretation of the institution's internal rules.

5.38 In a higher education institution in which members of staff are members of the body corporate many of their rights and privileges derive from the governing instrument and subordinate legislation made by the relevant body. In a chartered university, this starts with the charter and statutes, through ordinances to regulations and rules of various kinds, all of which will be either expressly incorporated into the contract or can be implied. Questions concerning the mutual rights and obligations of corporators, members and officers of a corporation can be complex in the employer-employee relationship: the old cases *Ex p Berkhampstead Free School*[46] and *A-G v Crook*[47] still provide useful guidance, and dicta of Hoffmann J in *Hines v Birkbeck College*[48] are also relevant. However it is also clear that failure to follow the provisions of the articles of government of a higher education corporation could have serious consequences.[49]

5.39 Express terms derived from domestic legislation and the contract of employment itself were minutely dissected by those advising the pre-1992 universities at the time of the threatened industrial action by academic staff members of the Association of University Teachers in 1989: fortunately it did not become necessary to attempt to rely on what were and remain extremely complex questions of interpretation. Those institutions belonging to the PCEF and admitting students through PCAS adopted a form of disclaimer clause in prospectuses covering industrial action, now translated into the UCAS handbook and apparently applying to all institutions admitting through UCAS – ie undergraduate students only. These issues are discussed elsewhere in connection with the institution-student relationship.

---

46 (1813) 2 Ves and B 134.
47 (1836) 1 Keen 121.
48 [1985] 3 All ER 156 at 165.
49 See O Hyams 'Higher and Further Education dismissals and redundancies – problem areas and their consequences for corporations and governors' (1996) 8 Education and the Law 2; citing *R v Secretary of State for Education, ex p Prior* [1994] ICR 877 as establishing principles which would apply equally to a dismissal by a higher education corporation as to the grant-maintained school in that case.

5.40   One issue which is of increasing concern is the extent to which institutions may hold employees to an express term that a contract of employment is 'whole time' or equivalent, particularly in relation to the operation of the European Council Directive 93/104/EC 'Concerning Aspects of the Organisation of Working Time' which it is considered applied directly to publicly-funded higher education institutions with effect from 23 November 1996.[50] In theory, in the pre-1992 universities, staff have, generally speaking, no fixed hours of work and in many they have no specified holiday entitlements. The position is somewhat different in the former public sector institutions where specified hours for teaching etc are common and where holiday entitlements are very specific. Nevertheless, employees are still technically 'whole time.' It is in principle difficult to reconcile this concept with the common position in which a member of the academic staff on a whole-time contract is simultaneously employed in the same institution as a warden as in *Throsby v Imperial College of Science and Technology*.[51] Given this widespread practice in many institutions, those which now seek to argue that they may control the work of staff outside the institution are on difficult ground.

5.41   In the absence of express terms, the process by which domestic rules and regulations can be implied applies also to certain fundamental common law attributes of the contract of employment, the most important of which are
(i)   the existence of a relationship of confidence and trust between employer and employee (it is the breakdown of this relationship which, as we shall see, is a frequent cause of so-called 'constructive dismissal' in the law relating to unfair dismissal): an example of this is the case in which a senior officer described his personal secretary as 'an intolerable bitch on a Monday morning',[52] and sexual harassment may fall into this category;[53]
(ii)   the duty of fidelity by the employee towards the employer, which includes the duty not to disclose confidential information after the employment ends[54] (which we shall discuss under the heading of obligations of academic staff in particular) and the duty not to disrupt or endanger the employer's business – 'lawful' industrial action being no exception, since any form of

50   See E Adams and J Nazerali 'Working Time Directive – a Storm in a Teacup?' (1996) 17 Business Law Review 12.
51   [1978] 2 All ER 465.
52   *Isle of Wight Tourist Board v Coombes* [1976] IRLR 413.
53   See section 3 of the European Union Code of Practice *Protecting the dignity of women and men at work* 1990.
54   *Faccenda Chicken Ltd v Fowler* [1986] ICR 297.

withdrawal of labour is a breach of contract. Although an employee is not in a fiduciary relationship with the employer and therefore does not have to report his own breach of contract,[55] a manager has a duty to report misconduct of subordinate staff even if it reveals his own breach of contract;[56]

(iii) the entitlement of an employee to reasonable support from the employer in carrying out the job: this is particularly important in managerial or supervisory posts:[57] the natural corollary is that managers will serve their employers faithfully, so that withdrawal of goodwill may be a breach of contract;[58]

(iv) the duty of an employer to take reasonable care not to injure the employee's health or safety, including a requirement to engage reasonably competent fellow employees;[59]

(v) custom and practice in the employment concerned: in higher education institutions where annual leave is not specified, the practice of the institution would be an important factor in determining whether an individual member of staff has breached the contract of employment by taking holidays at a certain time.

Implied terms subject to express terms: health and safety

5.42 These implied terms and others are deemed to be incorporated because they give 'business efficacy' to the contract of employment, either because the parties, if asked, would have immediately agreed that the term was obvious or, where that agreement was not forthcoming, if to imply the term would be a reasonable course of action for a court to take.[60] However, in 1991 in *Johnstone v Bloomsbury Health Authority*,[61] a majority of the Court of Appeal took the view that an implied contractual duty on an employer (such as that to take reasonable care of the health and safety of employees) is subject to any express term requiring an absolute duty on the part of employees to work certain specified hours. This was an action brought by a junior doctor who alleged that his contractual commitment to work a very large number of hours each week was both a breach of this implied term and contrary to section 2(1) Unfair

55 *Bell v Lever Bros* [1932] AC 161.
56 *Sybron Corpn v Rochem Ltd* [1983] IRLR 253.
57 Eg *Wigan Borough Council v Davies* [1979] IRLR 127.
58 *British Telecommunications plc v Ticehurst* [1992] ICR 383.
59 *Hudson v Ridge Manufacturing Co Ltd* [1957] 2 All ER 229.
60 *Howman & Son v Blyth* [1983] IRLR 139; the 'business efficacy' test is that laid down in *The Moorcock* (1889) 14 PD 64.
61 [1991] 2 All ER 293, CA.

Contract Terms Act 1977. The reported hearing in this case, however, was concerned only with procedural issues. The court adopted the view of the Judicial Committee of the Privy Council in 1985 in *Tai Hing Cotton Mill Ltd v Liu Ching Hing Bank Ltd*[62] that as in a contract of employment the parties have, subject to a few exceptions, the right to determine their obligations to each other, there is no advantage in searching for a liability in tort. The Court of Appeal allowed Dr Christopher Johnstone also to pursue his complaint that his contractual commitment to work long hours was in breach of section 2(1) Unfair Contract Terms Act 1977, which provides that a term of a contract cannot exclude or restrict a person's liability for death or personal injury resulting from negligence. An employer may be held responsible for an employee's psychiatric illness[63] and higher education institutions need to have measures in place to prevent cases of overwork and stress.

5.43 The Court of Appeal in its consideration of the *Johnstone* case was referred to *Ottoman Bank v Chakarian*[64] which, together with the decisions in *Cook v Square D Ltd*[65] and *Morris v Breaveglen Ltd (trading as Anzac Construction Co)*[66] offers some useful guidance to institutions who send staff to work for another employer or overseas as part of the contract of employment.[67] In the first case the employee was contractually bound to serve in the bank in Turkey or elsewhere. He was ordered to serve at a branch where, as his employers recognised, he would be at personal risk and refused to do so, whereupon he was dismissed. The Privy Council held that 'the risk to [the employee] was such that he was not bound to obey the order, which was therefore not a lawful one.'[68] This was therefore a case in which an express agreement to serve in Turkey was overridden by an implied duty of care.

5.44 In the *Square D* case, the employee was working abroad in a sub-contracted capacity for what was evidently a reputable employer when he suffered injury by falling through a manhole left open for

62 [1985] 2 All ER 947, PC.
63 *Walker v Northumberland County Council* [1995] 1 All ER 737; cf *Woodrow v Commonwealth of Australia* (1993) Aust Tort Rep 81-260, a case of an 'abnormally sensitive' employee.
64 [1930] AC 277.
65 [1992] ICR 262.
66 [1993] ICR 766, CA.
67 See also the Health and Safety At Work Etc. Act 1974 (Application outside Great Britain) Order 1995 (SI 1995/263).
68 [1930] AC 277, 285. Another case in a similar vein was *Turner v Mason* (1845) 14 M & W 112, 117–115.

access to wiring. The court held that his UK employer was not liable under the Health and Safety At Work etc Act for failing to secure safe working conditions, but it is clear that that decision was reached on the court's interpretation of what was reasonable in the particular circumstances. In the *Morris* case, the employer was held liable when it sent the employee to work for another firm within the UK and he was injured in the process. The implied duty of care, reinforced by the statutory requirements of the 1974 Act, is a difficult one to avoid; in the words of Lord Brandon of Oakbrook in 1987 in the House of Lords case *McDermid v Nash Dredging and Reclamation Co Ltd*[69] it is 'non-delegable.' It is obviously a sensible precaution for an institution to take, where it sends a number of employees away either in the UK or overseas, or one or two employees for a lengthy period, to have the workplace inspected by its own qualified staff and to satisfy itself that the occupiers of that workplace are aware of their obligations to secure the health and safety of staff working there. The EC Posted Workers Directive, due to be implemented by September 1999, guarantees certain workers posted abroad certain conditions whether the matters covered in the Directive are laid down by law, regulation, collective agreement or arbitration awards. These include health and safety measures as well as protection against discrimination.

Collective agreements

5.45   There may also be implied the terms of any collective agreements made between the employer and a trade union representing the member of staff, or deemed to represent him or her if a non-member, other than those rendered void by statute as discriminatory.[70] Collective agreements are not legally binding between the parties unless there is an express provision to the contrary.[71] The importance of collective agreements was diminished considerably by legislation first enacted in 1993 which (i) enables employers to induce employees to abandon collectively-agreed terms and conditions and the right to have these negotiated by a union and

---

69   [1987] ICR 917, 930; see also *Wilsons and Clyde Coal Co Ltd v English* [1938] AC 57.
70   Section 6 Sex Discrimination Act 1986, section 77 SDA, section 1 Equal Pay Act 1970; section 137 TULRCA in relation to attempted operation of 'closed shops.'
71   Section 179 TULRCA. This provision dates from 1974 and repealed a provision of the Industrial Relations Act 1971 with precisely the opposite effect and which resulted in a proliferation of TINALEA clauses (This Is Not A Legally Enforceable Agreement).

(ii) limits the right of employers to refer employees to collective agreements for specific terms and conditions in the written statement to which they are entitled.

5.46 These changes do not resurrect precisely the anti-discrimination provisions designed to protect non-members in section 5 of the short-lived Industrial Relations Act 1971, under which two institutions, Royal Holloway College[72] and the Imperial College of Science and Technology,[73] were sued when a restructuring scheme for technical staff was introduced in the early 1970s. Both claimed that different aspects of the procedure adopted discriminated against them as non-members of the relevant trade union. Mr Mucci of Imperial College was successful in an industrial tribunal, Mr Mason of Royal Holloway College was unsuccessful in the National Industrial Relations Court (the predecessor of the Employment Appeal Tribunal).

5.47 Collective agreements can relate to matters other than those specified in Part I EmpRA. The extent to which the terms of a collective agreement can be incorporated into individual contracts was clarified (before the enactment of the 1993 legislation) in *National Coal Board v National Union of Mineworkers*.[74] The court accepted the argument of counsel as follows:

> There is a distinction to be drawn between terms of a collective agreement which are of their nature apt to become enforceable terms of an individual's contract of employment and terms which are of their nature inapt to become enforceable by individuals. Terms of collective agreements fixing rates of pay, or hours of work, would obviously fall into the first category. Terms which deal with the procedure to be followed by an employer before dismissing an employee also would fall into the first category. But conciliation agreements setting up machinery designed to resolve by discussions between employers' representatives and union representatives, or by arbitral proceedings, questions arising within the industry, fall firmly into the second category. The terms of conciliation schemes are not intended to become contractually enforceable by individual workers whether or not referred to in the individuals' contracts of employment.

5.48 The Court of Appeal has held that those terms of a collective agreement which are incorporated into an individual's contract of

---

72 *Mason v Royal Holloway College* [1974] IRLR 42.
73 *Mucci v Imperial College of Science and Technology* [1973] IRLR 130.
74 [1986] IRLR 439.

employment can survive a unilateral abrogation or withdrawal or variation to which the other party to the agreement does not agree.[75] Changes in the relevant terms of employment of existing employees may be achieved by means of collective agreements, if provision is so made in the original contract of employment or if the negotiating arrangements with unions are such that the terms of collective agreements are binding on both employer and current as well as prospective employees.

5.49 The collective agreement approach could, in theory, be abandoned in favour of individual negotiation of terms and this approach is one increasingly taken with senior staff, the terminology used being 'personal contracts'. Section 146 TULRCA permits this provided it is not done with the purpose of preventing, deterring or penalising trade union membership.[76] This opens the door to moves away from collective bargaining with trade unions who although recognised by the employer may be unrepresentative of the workforce. Statistics on union membership in higher education are difficult to analyse. There is believed to be a high proportion of members among those eligible in manual, technical and clerical grades and this is also true of research staff employed on insecure contracts. While a majority of academic staff may be in membership, there are probably far fewer union members among directing, managerial and administrative staff, where the scope for personal contracts seems greater.

Breach of contract

5.50 The mutual undertakings which give rise to a contract of employment, like any other contract, can be broken. A breach of contract is committed when a party without lawful excuse refuses or fails to perform, performs defectively or incapacitates himself or herself from performing the contract. A contract of employment may be broken by either party:
(i) by the employer by wrongful dismissal, as in the further education case *Gunton v Richmond upon Thames London Borough Council*,[77] where the council failed to carry out correctly the terms of its disciplinary procedure and in the equally relevant case

---

75   *Robertson and Jackson v British Gas Corpn* [1983] IRLR 302.
76   This section prohibits a practice earlier upheld by the EAT
77   [1980] 3 All ER 577: as in this case, wrongful dismissal does not mean that the plaintiff or pursuer gets his or her job back, but compensation may be awarded according to generally established principles of the law of contract.

Stubbes v Trower, Still and Keeling[78] where the employer, a firm
of solicitors, wrongfully terminated the appointment of an
articled clerk who had been offered the job before the results of
the Law Society examinations were known and who failed part
of them and had no definite plans to resit;
(ii) by either party breaking express terms of the contract or the
fundamental terms implied at common law; or
(iii) by the employee by taking industrial action.
In the normal course of events there are remedies: the most common
breach of contract is undoubtedly industrial action by the employee,
which will be discussed later. And for wrongful dismissal there is the
possibility of monetary damages being awarded. In the pre-1992
universities the threatened dismissal of academic staff following the
1981 and subsequent reductions in grant gave rise to the possibility
of breach of contract actions for wrongful dismissal in breach of the
express terms of the contract as laid down in the university statutes
and the prospect of an employer being ordered by the Visitor or the
courts to continue to employ the employee, which is a departure from
normal principles of the employment contract. The questions posed
as a result of the events in *Pearce v University of Aston in
Birmingham*[79] are
(i) whether the University of Aston could have decided unilaterally,
like any other employer, to break the contract, and suffer
whatever financial consequences the Visitor determined; or
(ii) whether it was actually prevented from taking such action by
the statutes.

5.51 Specific performance of a contract of employment (in Scotland
a decree *ad factum praestandum*)[80] is not normally ordered, even in
the exceptional circumstances of an ultra vires act by a public
authority. In *Francis v Municipal Councillors of Kuala Lumpur*[81]
(which arose after the frequently-cited case *Vine v National Dock
Labour Board*)[82] the Judicial Committee of the Privy Council said:

> ... when there has been a purported termination of the contract of
> service a declaration to the effect that the contract of service still
> subsists will rarely be made. This is a consequence of the general
> principle of law that the courts will not grant specific performance of

78 [1987] IRLR 321.
79 [1991] 2 All ER 461.
80 *Mortimer v Beckett* [1920] 1 Ch 571; *Rose Street Foundry Co v Lewis* 1917 SC
341.
81 [1962] 3 All ER 633, 637, PC.
82 [1956] 3 All ER 939, HL.

contracts of service. Special circumstances will be required before such a declaration is made and its making will normally be in the discretion of the court ...

5.52 This, the *Vine* and other cases were examined by Buckley LJ in *Gunton v Richmond upon Thames London Borough Council.*[83] Norman Gunton was dismissed from his post as Registrar of the Twickenham College of Technology. His dismissal was held to be wrongful since the council, although it had the power to terminate his contract on a month's notice on other than disciplinary grounds, had dismissed him on such grounds without carrying out all the steps of the agreed disciplinary procedure. It was held by a majority of the Court of Appeal that the wrongful dismissal did not immediately terminate his contract of employment; in particular it did not destroy his right under his contract not to be dismissed on disciplinary grounds until the agreed procedures had been completed and to be compensated accordingly if they were not. Although there have more recently been cases in which injunctions have been granted continuing employment unless or until it is validly terminated,[84] it is clear from *Marsh v National Autistic Society*[85] that the remedy for wrongful termination of a contract is damages, probably restricted to the salary which the employee would have been paid if given proper notice; an interlocutory injunction is not appropriate. The same principle appears to have been applied in Scotland since at least 1884 in the case of *First Edinburgh Building Society v Munro.*[86]

5.53 In the course of the judgment in the *Gunton* case, Buckley LJ made it clear that Mr Gunton's relationship to the council was purely contractual: 'They were not entrenched by any statutory or other extra-contractual provisions.'[87] Indeed in the great majority of today's higher education institutions that relationship is the one enjoyed by staff. But in the *Pearce* case the University's statutes gave the academic staff a special status. This issue was fully discussed by Professor Sir Frederick Crawford in his university internal bulletin.[88] The basis of the argument accepted by the Visitor was that any action of the university contrary to its statutes was not ultra vires or void against

83 [1980] 3 All ER 577.
84 Cases cited in *Wadcock v London Borough of Brent* [1990] IRLR 223 and *Jones v Gwent County Council* [1992] IRLR 521 (a grant of a permanent injunction under the then new Order 14A RSC).
85 [1993] ICR 453.
86 (1883) 21 SLR 291.
87 [1980] 3 All ER 577, 590(i).
88 *Vice-Chancellor's Report to Council on Visitor's judgment relating to overstaffing – Aston Fortnight* Special Issue Vol 10 No 1, 20 September 1989, p 25.

the outside world, but would be as between those subject to its domestic laws: the members of the University of Aston in Birmingham were entitled to insist on its administration being lawful in that sense. That opinion is by no means a new one, nor confined to Aston. A number of universities took legal advice and received opinion to the same effect at the time of the major reductions in funding by the University Grants Committee in the early 1980s.

Variation of terms

5.54 Like other forms of contract, the terms of the contract of employment can also be varied. Normally this will be provided for within the contract terms, either through the implication of the terms of a collective agreement or in some other agreed way. However, employers may decide to vary the terms unilaterally and this may lead to difficulty. In *Rigby v Ferodo*,[89] the courts supported Harry Rigby and his workmates when the employers unilaterally imposed a reduction of wages. However, in *Cresswell v Board of Inland Revenue*[90] the Court of Appeal dismissed claims by Michael Cresswell and seven other staff whose duties changed from manual processing of tax documents to a computerised system that this was a variation of their contract which they were not obliged to accept. The court held that employees were expected to adopt to new methods provided appropriate training was arranged and the duties did not alter so radically that they lay outside the employee's contractual obligations.[91]

Employment legislation

Individual and collective

5.55 There are two principal types of employment legislation, although there is inevitably some interaction between the two:
(i) that governing the rights of individual employees;
(ii) that governing the collective organisation of labour: trades unions and their members, trade disputes, etc.

---

89 [1987] ICR 457; see also *Lee v GEC Plessey Telecommunications* [1993] IRLR 383.
90 [1984] ICR 508, CA.
91 The employers were held to have been justified in withholding payment of salary for the employees' refusal to operate the new system.

Most of this law is in the form of statutes enacted since 1971: the Contracts of Employment Act 1964 and the Redundancy Payments Act 1965 have now been consolidated. The statutory framework applies throughout Great Britain: in Northern Ireland similar provision has been made by Order under the 'temporary' arrangements for the government of the province. The fair employment legislation, which is unique to Northern Ireland, will be discussed later.

5.56 The principal statute governing individual rights, other than those in relation to trade union membership, is EmpRA, a consolidating statute which includes the law on unfair dismissal, which it is often forgotten was first introduced by the Conservative Government's Industrial Relations Act 1971. It also includes provisions for maternity leave and the right to time off work for certain public duties and trade union activities. Amendments to EmpRA are proposed in the Employment Rights (Dispute Resolution) Bill before Parliament in late 1997. Other relevant statutes are the Equal Pay Act 1970, the Sex Discrimination Acts 1975 (SDA) and 1986 (and the unconsolidated sections of the Employment Act 1989 relating to sex discrimination), the Race Relations Act 1976 (RRA) and the Disability Discrimination Act 1995 (DDA) (and unrepealed sections of the Disabled Persons (Employment) Acts 1944 and 1958 and the Chronically Sick and Disabled Persons Act 1970.) DDA is the first UK statute to address the issues of discrimination against an estimated 6.5m disabled people; previous legislation was originally a response to the problems caused by war disablement. The sex discrimination and equal pay legislation originated in proposals of the European Union (European Community). The statutory protection for employees, which has only recently been extended to part-time employees,[92] was intended to be a minimum and, indeed, many higher education institutions operate schemes for parental leave etc well in excess of the statutory provision. Section 110 EmpRA provides that employees may 'contract out' of the unfair dismissal procedures, provided that the Secretary of State has approved an 'exempted dismissal procedure agreement' giving at least equal protection.

5.57 The principal statute governing collective issues is TULRCA which also covers the rights of individuals in relation to trade union membership and activities and, somewhat hidden away in section 236

---

92 See R Upex 'Part-time employees: the new régime' (1996) 8(4) Education and the Law 307.

TULRCA, restates the long-standing prohibition on a court ordering an individual to work. The Act consolidates provisions dating back to 1861, but its principal achievement was to marry together the remaining parts of the Labour Government's trade union and labour relations legislation of the 1970s with that of the Conservative Government of the 1980s, which respectively stress the rights of trades unions and the rights of employers and individuals. The Trade Union Reform and Employment Rights Act 1993 (TURERA) introduced a number of new measures and amended existing arrangements.

The Advisory, Conciliation and Arbitration Service (ACAS) and other central bodies

5.58 Legislation has over time established a number of bodies to carry out functions in relation to both individual and collective issues. These are continued in existence by the recent consolidating legislation. The first, and arguably the most important, of these is the Advisory, Conciliation and Arbitration Service (ACAS) established in the mid-1970s to take the process of conciliation and mediation out of central government departments.[93] Its functions, as befits its title, are persuasive rather than directory. They are set out now in Part VI TULRCA as amended by TURERA and include

(a) providing conciliation or other assistance in trade disputes including arranging arbitration with the consent of the parties
(b) providing conciliation officers for the settlement of matters which could be the subject of proceedings in industrial tribunals
(c) offering and publishing advice on industrial relations and employment policies
(d) issuing Codes of Practice containing practical guidance on a range of industrial relations issues.

Part II Employment Rights (Dispute Resolution) Bill 1997 enables ACAS to provide, fund and promote a scheme for the arbitration of unfair dismissal disputes, accessible either by a compromise agreement or an agreement promoted by a conciliation officer.

5.59 The Codes of Practice issued by ACAS are *Disciplinary Practice and Procedures in Employment, Disclosure of Information to Trades Unions for Collective Bargaining Purposes* and *Time Off for Trade Union Duties and Activities.* Rather like the Highway Code,

---

93 The equivalent in Northern Ireland is the Labour Relations Agency, established by the Industrial Relations (Northern Ireland) Order 1976 (SI 1976/1043).

these codes do not have the force of law but are required to be taken into account by industrial tribunals and are therefore of considerable persuasive authority. The University Commissioners took the ACAS Code of Practice on disciplinary issues into account when formulating their proposals for changes in university statutes under ERA and higher education institutions generally have based their procedures on the principles of the Code. ACAS advisory booklets cover a range of subjects including job evaluation, payment systems, personnel records, absence and labour turnover, recruitment and selection, induction procedures, appraisal, handling redundancies and effective organisation. All of these are relevant to staff management in higher education. ACAS charges for conferences, seminars, self-help clinics for small business and for some advisory publications; otherwise its services are free.

5.60 Other bodies include the Central Arbitration Committee (CAC) first established in 1975 as a successor to the Industrial Arbitration Board, itself a successor to the Industrial Court (not to be confused with the short-lived National Industrial Relations Court established under the Industrial Relations Act 1971). Its functions are now prescribed in section 183 TULRCA. It conducts arbitrations on matters referred to it by ACAS with the consent of the parties to a dispute. It also has certain functions in which its awards are binding (eg in relation to the implementation of equal pay in collective agreements). Although independent, the Committee's links with ACAS are necessarily very close. The equivalent of the Committee in Northern Ireland is the Northern Ireland Industrial Court. Although a court rather than a committee, its functions are essentially the same. There is also a Certification Officer responsible for maintaining lists of trades unions (and employers' associations), determining their independence of employers[94] and overseeing the requirements of legislation in relation to accounts, the operation of the political fund and superannuation schemes.[95] Individual members of trades unions have the right to complain to the Certification Officer about alleged procedural deficiencies in the process of amalgamation of trades unions and related matters. Finally there are two Commissioners, the first of which is the Commissioner for the Rights of Trade Union Members, who has the function of providing assistance to individual trade union members who are pursuing or intend to pursue certain proceedings against the union. These include

---

94 Ie not liable to domination or interference by the employer as in *Government Communications Staff Federation v Certification Officer* [1993] ICR 163.
95 The CO no longer provides financial support for secret ballots.

allegations of failure to comply with the rules relating to secret ballots before industrial action, defects in election procedures, misapplication of funds for political purposes and breach of rules over a wide range of issues. The second Commissioner is for Protection Against Unlawful Industrial Action who has the function of assisting persons in court proceedings to obtain orders restraining unlawful industrial action.

Anti-discrimination bodies

5.61   Unlike some other jurisdictions, the UK has no single Rights Commission but different Commissions dealing with different rights issues. The Equal Opportunities Commission (EOC), the Equal Opportunities Commission (Northern Ireland), the Commission for Racial Equality (CRE), all established in the mid-1970s, and the Fair Employment Commission (Northern Ireland) (FEC), established in 1989,[96] are bodies set up to deal with alleged unlawful discrimination on grounds of sex, race (and related issues) and, in Northern Ireland only, religious belief.[97] The EOC and its Northern Ireland counterpart have the duty of working towards the elimination of sex discrimination, in particular but not solely, in employment and related spheres. The EOC has published a Code of Practice on the elimination of discrimination on the grounds of sex and marriage. The Equal Opportunities Commissions have power themselves to initiate action before a court (eg in relation to discriminatory advertisements) and may assist a tribunal complainant with the preparation and conduct of a the case.[98] The CRE has a very similar role in relation to racial discrimination and has published two Codes of Practice, the second following the enactment of the Asylum and Immigration Act 1996. The FEC was established as a successor body to the Fair Employment Agency established in 1976: the Commission is a pro-active body with significant powers to enforce fair treatment of employees and potential employees.

---

96   Succeeding the Fair Employment Agency established under an Act of 1976.
97   There is some interface between religious belief and racial discrimination, in particular that relating to turban-wearing Sikhs, discussed in relation to racial discrimination below.
98   See also *R v Secretary of State for Employment, ex p Equal Opportunities Commission* [1995] 1 AC 1 where EOC was held to have standing to bring a case against the government in respect of alleged indirect discrimination against women as employment protection laws as they then stood did not extend to part-time workers.

Employment (formerly Industrial) Tribunals and the Employment Appeal Tribunal

5.62   Industrial tribunals were first established throughout the UK in 1964, initially to deal with appeals relating to levies under industrial training legislation. Their remit was extended in 1971, as an informal or semi-formal mechanism for dealing on a pragmatic basis with issues related to individual employment. It was felt that a three-person tribunal with a legally-qualified chairman but otherwise consisting of experienced employer and union representatives, would provide a faster, cheaper and less technical approach than the courts to resolving individual claims of unfair dismissal. Changes in procedures introduced in the mid-1990s helped to speed up the hearing process. The remit of the tribunals and the Employment Appeal Tribunal is now governed by the Industrial Tribunals Act 1996 (ITA) and procedural regulations;[99] administrative support to them is given by an executive agency. The Employment Rights (Dispute Resolution) Bill before Parliament in December 1997 proposed renaming of Industrial Tribunals as Employment Tribunals and makes procedural amendments. For the rest of this Chapter, it is assumed that the tribunals will be renamed.

5.63   The law which these tribunals were required to apply from 1971 on was, like any other statutory legislation, quickly the subject of appeal and interpretation by the higher courts and the area of industrial relations law became a new source of income for lawyers and for authors. There are a number of instances in which the higher courts have commented on the move from informality and the introduction of unnecessary legalism: one such case was *White v University of Manchester*,[100] where the balance to be kept between avoiding unnecessary legalism and doing justice to the claimant was discussed. The EAT suggested that 'commonsense and goodwill' involved, in most cases, giving reasonable detail about the nature of the complaints to be made to a tribunal. The law as it stands today is complex and still subject to a continuous process of interpretation: this book will attempt to bring out issues which are relevant to higher education staff and institutions.

---

99   The Industrial Tribunals (Constitution and Rules of Procedure) Regulations SI 1993/2687 and SI 1994/536 and their equivalents in Scotland SI 1993/2688 and SI 1994/535. These procedures will be streamlined following the enactment of the Employment Rights (Dispute Resolution) Bill.
100   [1976] IRLR 218.

5.64 Employment tribunals are empowered to deal with cases of alleged unfair dismissal, discrimination on grounds of sex and race and certain other issues: the legislation allows actions related to other employment contractual matters to be heard in certain circumstances,[101] something 'long since suggested' by the Employment Appeal Tribunal, according to Wood J in *Sunderland Polytechnic v Evans*.[102] In cases of alleged unfair dismissal, ACAS has a statutory duty to attempt to conciliate on request and if agreement is reached (a COT3 agreement), the employee is precluded from pursuing the claim further. Section 203 EmpRA provides that a settlement made by an employer and employee, where the employee has been advised by a solicitor on the question of employment rights, known as a compromise agreement, has the same effect as a COT3 agreement. Part II Employment Rights (Dispute Resolution) Bill 1997 extends the arrangements for compromise agreements.

5.65 Tribunal decisions (other than those relating to breach of contract claims, where ITA failed to re-enact earlier provisions[103]) may be appealed on a point of law only to the Employment Appeal Tribunal (EAT) in the first instance and thereafter to the Court of Appeal or Court of Session (Inner House) as appropriate. In Northern Ireland appeals from employment tribunals are heard by the Northern Ireland Court of Appeal. A number of important cases have been referred to the European Court of Justice for a ruling on the application of the various European Treaties and Directives. Ultimately, if leave to appeal is granted, a case may, after several years, reach the House of Lords, with or without the benefit of a ruling from the European Court. The higher bodies may refer cases back to the employment tribunals for further consideration in the light of decisions on points of law. They may also refer matters for interpretation to the European Court of Justice. The EAT is also tripartite, with a High Court judge or judge of the Court of Session as chairman. The other two members, who have special knowledge or experience of industrial relations, have equal status with the judge and dissenting opinions are not uncommon. The law allows the judge to sit alone in cases involving appeals from a chairman of employment tribunals sitting alone in the circumstances provided for in Rule 6 of

101 Industrial Tribunals Extension of Jurisdiction (England and Wales) Order 1994 (SI 1994/1623). The equivalent Order for Scotland is SI 1994/1624. A tribunal may hear a claim under this provision where a person has contracted to work for an employer but the contract was terminated before work commenced: *Sarker v South Tees Acute Hospitals NHS Trust* [1997] ICR 673.
102 [1993] ICR 392, 395.
103 *Pendragon plc v Jackson* [1998] IRLR 17, EAT. This omission is being corrected in the Employment Rights (Dispute Resolution) Bill.

the Industrial Tribunals (Constitution and Rules of Procedure) Regulations 1993[104] as prospectively amended by the Employment Rights (Dispute Resolution) Bill. Appeals to the EAT have been numerous and over a quarter-century a considerable body of relevant case law has built up, since EAT rulings on points of law are binding on tribunals. As a consequence, inevitably tribunal proceedings have become rather more technical and formal than was the original intention. In order to discourage repeated and worthless claims, section 33 ITA allows the EAT to restrict vexatious proceedings before employment tribunals.

5.66   Although applicants may appear in person at all stages under the statutory procedures, it is common for them to be represented by trade union officials or by lawyers. In *Harber v North London Polytechnic*[105] a representative had by mistake (attributed to a variety of factors) withdrawn a complaint of unfair dismissal by a long-serving part-time lecturer, Eric Harber, during the hearing. The Court of Appeal held that although a litigant is normally bound by what his or her representative does,[106] if a mistake is made by the litigant's representative, it is not conclusive. An employment tribunal has a discretion to grant a review if the interests of justice so require, on certain well-established principles. In an earlier case involving the same institution *Dean v Polytechnic of North London*[107] a technical error was made in that the Polytechnic, which had originally claimed that Saifud Dean's dismissal was fair because he was temporary, introduced new evidence of lack of capability to which Mr Dean did not object; neither did he seek an adjournment (as he probably should have done). The National Industrial Relations Court held that his case was not prejudiced by this mistake on his part.

5.67   It is quite clear from the number of cases heard that the statutory jurisdiction of the employment tribunals and EAT, unlike the common law jurisdiction of the ordinary courts dealing with contractual disputes, is not ousted by the exclusive jurisdiction in the chartered universities (outside Scotland) of the Visitor over 'domestic' disputes. The Visitor's jurisdiction was only removed from 'any dispute relating to a member of the academic staff which concerns his (sic) appointment or employment or the termination of his appointment or employment,' so that other grades of staff employed

104 See *Tsangacos v Amalgamated Chemicals* [1997] ICR 154.
105 [1990] IRLR 198.
106 On the basis of the decision of the House of Lords in *Al Mehdawi v Secretary of State for the Home Department* [1990] 1 AC 876.
107 [1973] ICR 490.

in chartered institutions with a Visitor still have recourse to both routes simultaneously, although it is normal for the Visitor to deal with the matter first.[108] This applies to both unfair dismissal and discrimination claims. *Criper v University of Edinburgh*[109] is an example of a case in which it was held that 'contractual' issues which are now outside the Visitorial jurisdiction or judicial review in England and Wales are also outside the scope of judicial review in Scotland.

General principles of law governing individual disputes and grievances

The 'rules of natural justice'

5.68 The principal consideration at all times in employers' dealings with individual employees must be that of acting fairly, not just in the technical sense of the word when used to justify a fair dismissal under the terms of EmpRA, but also more widely. In ERA, the University Commissioners were charged with certain functions and given three principles to which they had to have regard. The third of these was the need 'to apply the principles of justice and fairness.' This introduces the concept of the rules of natural justice. As Lord Bridge said in *Lloyd v McMahon*,[110] 'the so-called rules of natural justice are not engraved on tablets of stone.' His Lordship went on to say

> To use the phrase which better expresses the underlying concept, what the requirements of fairness demand when any body, domestic, administrative or judicial, has to make a decision which will affect the rights of individuals depends on the character of the decision-making body, the kind of decision it has to make and the statutory or other framework in which it operates. In particular, it is well-established that when a statute has conferred on any body the power to make decisions affecting individuals, the courts will not only require the procedure prescribed by the statute to be followed, but will readily imply so much and no more to be introduced by way of additional procedural safeguards as will ensure the attainment of fairness.

108 See P M Smith 'Visitation of the Universities: a Ghost from the Past' (1986) 136 New Law Journal 665.
109 1991 SLT 129n, OH.
110 [1987] AC 625, 702–3.

5.69 The most common expression of the principles of justice and fairness lies in the phrase 'natural justice' which as generally understood in both English and Scots law encompasses two Latin maxims:

(i) 'audi alteram partem' -'hear the other side' ie give a fair hearing to the appellant; and

(ii) 'nemo judex in causa sua potest' – 'no one can be judge in his own cause' ie the rule against bias.

What this means is that any disciplinary or grievance procedure should so far as is reasonably practicable be conducted by an individual or group who or which has not been involved in the issues previously and that this body should give to the relevant parties the opportunity fully to state their case and answer any charges or criticisms before a decision is reached. Failure to allow a person accused of a disciplinary offence the right to challenge by question or by evidence the factual basis of the allegations against him or her is almost certain to be fatal to the fairness of disciplinary procedures.[111]

5.70 The right to a hearing was established in the early seventeenth century, notably in *Bagg's Case*[112] in which a freeman of the borough of Plymouth, disenfranchised for publicly, 'contemptuously and uncivilly' inviting the mayor to kiss his backside, was reinstated on mandamus. It was extended to higher education in 1723 in *R v University of Cambridge*,[113] where Dr Bentley, deprived of his degrees for insulting the Vice-Chancellor's Court, was reinstated on mandamus partly because he had not been given the opportunity to defend himself as required by 'the laws of God and man.' Fortescue J illustrated the requirement for giving the accused such rights by saying that God gave Adam the right to make a defence before passing sentence on him for eating the forbidden fruit.

5.71 That complying with such rules can be difficult in some

---

111 See eg *Kanda v Government of Malaya* [1962] AC 322; *Chief Constable of the North Wales Police v Evans* [1982] 1 WLR 1155; in *Jones v Welsh Rugby Football Union* (1997) Times, 6 March: the argument that a committee has always acted in a particular way was held to be no defence.

112 (1615) 11 Co Rep 93b. The writings of Seneca (*Medea* 199-200) were cited both in this case and the earlier *Boswel's Case* (1605) 6 Co Rep 48b: 'quicunque aliquid statuerit parte inaudita altera, aequum licet statuerit, haud aequus fuerit,' cited in English in *Earl v Slater and Wheeler (Airlyne) Ltd* [1973] 1 WLR 51.

113 (1723) 1 Stra 557. Seneca was also quoted in this case and the later *R v Archbishop of Canterbury* (1859) 1 E & E 545.

instances is recognised by the courts. The most celebrated judicial comment is that of Lord Denning MR in *Ward v Bradford Corpn*:[114]

> We must not force these disciplinary bodies to become entrammeled in the nets of legal procedure. So long as they act fairly and justly, their decision should be supported.

This is supported by dicta of Lord Wilberforce in the Opinion of the Judicial Committee of the Privy Council in the Australian Jockey Club case *Calvin v Carr*:[115]

> ... it is undesirable in many cases of domestic disputes, particularly in which an inquiry and appeal process has been established, to introduce too great a measure of formal judicialisation. While flagrant cases of injustice, including corruption or bias, must always be firmly dealt with by the courts, the tendency in their Lordships' opinion in the matters of domestic disputes should be to leave these to be settled by the agreed methods without requiring the formalities of judicial processes to be introduced.

Citing *Pillai v Singapore City Council*[116] as an example of this in practice, his Lordship concluded:

> What is required is examination of the hearing process, original and appeal as a whole, and a decision on the question whether after it has been gone through the complainant has had a fair deal of the kind that he bargained for.

At least one university case *Harelkin v University of Regina*[117] has been held to be consistent with the *Calvin* principles, cited by Kelly LJ in a case involving Queen's University Belfast, *Re Wislang's Application*.[118]

5.72 In a higher education institution the parties to an individual case will normally be the institution itself and a member of staff or an unsuccessful candidate for appointment. If a member of staff, the person concerned may be the subject of disciplinary proceedings (or an appellant from an earlier stage of disciplinary action) or may be mounting a grievance, for example in respect of an unsuccessful

---

114 (1971) 70 LGR 27, 35.
115 [1980] AC 574, 593.
116 [1968] 1 WLR 1278.
117 (1979) 96 DLR (3d) 14.
118 [1984] NI 63; see in similar terms *Re Elliot and Governors of the University of Alberta* (1973) 37 DLR (3d) 197.

application for promotion. On occasion it may be that a grievance will lie not against the institution but against another member of staff, a head of department or officer[119] or an appraiser. At least the second maxim of natural justice may be difficult to fulfil, as Robert Seaton[120] explained:

> ... because of the relatively closed nature of the institution and the difficulties officers or committee members may have in excluding prior knowledge and bringing a genuinely open mind to an issue. The hierarchical nature of institutional government may also present problems in that certain key individuals may ... be entitled to have significant involvement at several levels and since appeals necessarily move from level to level the question will arise whether an individual may properly be involved at more than one level.

Related issues were raised in *Re Wislang's Application*[121] where the applicant complained that the identity of some members of the Board of Visitors revealed an interest. The question to be addressed in such cases is whether a reasonable person would think it likely or probable that there would be bias.[122] This view goes back at least 100 years.[123] In higher education conducted by a statutory body, the case of *King v University of Saskatchewan*[124] (which was not an employment case) establishes that duplication of membership of internal domestic tribunals does not in itself amount to a denial of natural justice. In *Westminster City Council v Cabaj*[125] the contractual requirement for an appeal panel of three councillors was not satisfied when the panel which confirmed C's dismissal only comprised two councillors. However, the failure of the Council to fulfil its contractual obligation did not make C's dismissal unfair. The effect of the failure was a matter for the employment tribunal to consider.

5.73   A further question facing higher education institutions is the speed at which a case can be heard and determined. The University

---

119 As in *Humberstone v MacFadyen and the University of Southampton* (1997, unreported) and *Qureshi v Victoria University of Manchester and Brazier* [1997] IRLB 11.

120 R Seaton 'University Staff and Employment Law' in D J Farrington and F T Mattison (eds) *Universities and the Law* CUA/CRS (1990).

121 [1984] NI 63.

122 *R v London Rent Assessment Panel Committee, ex p Metropolitan Properties Co (FGC) Ltd* [1969] 1 QB 577, 599 per Lord Denning MR.

123 *Allinson v General Council of Medical Education and Registration* [1894] 1 QB 750.

124 (1969) 6 DLR (3d) 120.

125 [1996] ICR 960, CA.

Commissioners' Model Statute requires Ordinances to be made which will ensure that matters are dealt with as expeditiously as possible. In *Re Wislang's Application*[126] one of Dr Miles Wislang's complaints was that there was delay on the part of the Board of Visitors, thereby in some way depriving them of jurisdiction. While this complaint was rejected by the court, reference was made to *R v Central Professional Committee for Opticians, ex p Brown*[127] in which the applicant sought a court order requiring the Committee to consider and determine an application for approval of his professional qualifications to entitle him to provide ophthalmic services. The order was refused on the basis that there was no evidence of wilful or unreasonable delay, but the issue remains open if there is such evidence.

5.74 In the pre-1992 universities, the University Commissioners' model statute which has been adopted in all institutions (the precise detail differing to some extent) attempted to obviate these problems by setting out a clear hierarchy of officers who could deal with disciplinary and grievance issues. The most serious allegations are to be heard by a disciplinary tribunal with power to determine whether or not the charge has been made out and recommend dismissal to the 'appropriate officer' (normally the Vice-Chancellor or Principal). Lesser offences, and earlier stages in a procedure which might lead to dismissal, are dealt with by departmental and intermediate officers, apart from the preliminary enquiries which could lead to suspension and/or commencement of formal procedures, where the principles set out by Lord Slynn of Hadley in *Rees v Crane*[128] apply. It would be expected that in large institutions it should be possible to find sufficient senior staff who could exercise dispassionate judgment: the courts have however been prepared to take a realistic attitude in balancing fairness against the resources of the employer,[129] so that 'impossible burdens' are not imposed.

5.75 The latest statutes, ordinances and corresponding regulations normally provide for an oral hearing and for the possibility of legal representation in serious cases, although it is clear that neither are required by the general law.[130] If a body decides it will not allow an

---

126 [1984] NI 63.
127 [1949] 2 All ER 519.
128 [1994] 2 AC 173, 189F–196F, esp 191G–192A and 192F–G.
129 See eg *Rowe v Radio Rentals Ltd* [1982] IRLR 177.
130 See *R (Hennessy) v Department of the Environment* [1980] NI 1; *R v Melbourne, ex p Whyte* [1949] VLR 257; *Selvarajan v Race Relations Board* [1976] 1 All ER 12.

oral hearing nor legal representation then this is in accordance with the rules of natural justice provided it reaches this decision honestly and in good faith.[131] The question whether a body should give reasons for its decisions was fully discussed by Sedley J in *R v University of Cambridge, ex p Evans*.[132] In *R v Higher Education Funding Council, ex p Institute of Dental Surgery*[133] the court (Mann LJ and Sedley J) took the view that the categories of case in which reasons *must* be given were closed[134] although the class of apparently aberrant decisions did not include those which could be challenged by reference only to the reasons for them, such as a pure exercise of academic judgment. In *R v City of London Corpn, ex p Matson*[135] it was held that a decision of the Court of Aldermen to reject M's candidature for election, following a full interview, carried with it a duty to give reasons. As in the *Institute of Dental Surgery* case, it was considered that it was not unduly difficult or arduous for the decision-making body to give a collective reason for its decision. In *Evans* the applicant was granted leave to apply on this ground for judicial review of the University's decision not to select her for promotion but proceedings were stayed to enable the University to refine its procedures.

Discrimination on grounds of sex, race, disability, criminal record and religious belief

Provisions of charters, etc

5.76 Royal Charters have for many years normally contained provisions against discrimination on grounds of sex, race, religion or political belief. These provisions are unrelated to the anti-discrimination legislation enacted since the 1960s, but reflect the opening up of university education and work to all sections of society in the nineteenth and early twentieth centuries. The provisions of Charters are directly enforceable by members of the corporation against institutions before the Visitor or, in Scotland, before the courts as they form part of the contract of employment of members of staff. However, they are normally rather vague and there is no reported case of their having been used successfully to secure the sort of outcome which may be achievable under the anti-discrimination

---

131 *Maclean v Workers' Union* [1929] 1 Ch 602.
132 (1997) CO/1031, 22 August 1997.
133 [1994] 1 WLR 242.
134 Eg where statute blocks the giving of reasons, as in *R v Secretary of State for the Home Department, ex p Fayed* [1997] 1 All ER 228.
135 [1997] 1 WLR 765, CA.

legislation. It is clear, however, that higher education institutions do take such issues seriously, as evidenced by the publication of the *Equal Opportunities Guide for Higher Education* by CVCP in 1997.

Equal pay

5.77   The first modern statute to be passed with the objective of removing discriminatory treatment on grounds of sex was the Equal Pay Act 1970, which was amended by SDA and took effect at the end of 1975 following the UK's accession to the European Communities in 1973. It now appears as Schedule 1 to SDA, and was further amended in 1983 by the Equal Pay (Amendment) Regulations which were passed as a consequence of a decision of the European Court of Justice in *EC Commission v United Kingdom*:[136] they enable a woman to claim equal pay on the grounds of her work being of 'equal value' to that of a man, and vice versa. The Equal Pay Act was a first attempt in the UK to implement the general principle of Article 119 of the Treaty of Rome that men and women should receive equal pay for equal work. Supporting Article 119 is EC Directive 75/117. Following a period of considerable uncertainty, 'pay' was subject to a detailed definition by the European Court of Justice in *Barber v Guardian Royal Exchange Assurance Group*[137] and it is clear that where necessary Article 119 overrides the domestic legislation. In *R v Secretary of State for Employment, ex p Seymour-Smith*[138] the House of Lords referred to the ECJ questions about the applicability of Article 119 to compensation for unfair dismissal, and in *Levez v T H Jennings (Harlow Pools) Ltd*[139] the issue of arrears of remuneration or damages being limited to a two-year period before the tribunal claim was referred by EAT to ECJ. The Act introduced the concept of the 'equality clause' which is included in every contract of employment, whether expressly or by implication. This covers 'like work,' 'work rated as equivalent' and 'work of equal value.' The meaning of 'equal' has also been defined by the European Court of Justice in *Murphy v Bord Telecom Eireann*[140] so that work of unequal but higher value is also included. A Code of Practice on Equal Pay was issued by EOC in March 1997. An employment tribunal may

136   61/81: [1982] ICR 578.
137   C-262/88: [1990] IRLR 240.
138   [1997] 2 All ER 273, HL.
139   [1996] IRLR 499.
140   157/86: [1988] ICR 445.

refer an equal pay claim to an independent expert.[141] It is not necessary to show that the comparators have the 'same' terms and conditions, only that they are 'broadly similar.'[142]

5.78 The issues have become extremely complicated as the jurisprudence of the European Court of Justice has developed. Of considerable importance in higher education is the decision in the *Danfoss* case[143] which stresses the importance of the transparency of a pay system: if this is not the case, an employer may find it difficult to prove a lack of discrimination when the average pay of women is lower than that of men in the same employment.[144] It is also clear from *Enderby v Frenchay Health Authority and Secretary of State for Health*,[145] a case involving a speech therapist, that the employer must show that statistically significant pay differences are based on objectively justified factors. Section 1(3) EqPA requires the employer to prove that any variation between the woman's contract and that of the comparator man[146] is 'genuinely due to a material factor which is not a difference in sex.'[147] In a series of cases the ECJ has ruled on the applicability of Article 119 to occupational pension schemes.[148]

5.79 Cases which arose under the Act pre-dating *Danfoss* and *Enderby* were *Pointon v University of Sussex*[149] and *Benveniste v University of Southampton*,[150] both of which went to the Court of Appeal. In the first of these cases Dr Marcia Pointon, supported by the Equal Opportunities Commission, failed to prove that her university had discriminated against her by failing to pay her more because of her age – the so-called 'age-wage norm' was not a contractual term. In the second case, however, while accepting that the University of Southampton had appointed Dr Regina Benveniste at a lower salary point than might otherwise be the case at a time of

141 Section 2A(1) EqPA as amended.
142 *British Coal Corpn v Smith* [1996] IRLR 404, HL.
143 *Handels-og Kontorfunktionaererernes Forbund i Danmark v Dansk Arbejdsgiverforening (acting for Danfoss)*: 109/88 [1989] IRLR 532.
144 See also *Reed Packaging Ltd v Boozer* [1988] ICR 391 and *Hayward v Cammell Laird Shipbuilders Ltd* [1988] IRLR 257.
145 C-127/92: [1993] IRLR 591, ECJ.
146 Who may be a successor employee: *Diocese of Hallam Trustees v Connaughton* [1996] IRLR 505.
147 See *Tyldesley v TML Plastics Ltd* [1996] ICR 356; *Strathclyde Regional Council v Wallace* [1998] 1 All ER 394, HL.
148 See *Van den Akker v Stichting Shell Pensioenfonds* C-28/93: [1994] IRLR 616; *Coloroll Pension Trustees Ltd v Russell* C-200/91: [1995] ICR 179; Protocol No 2 to the Maastricht Treaty.
149 [1979] IRLR 119.
150 [1989] IRLR 122.

severe financial constraint in 1981–1982 (a 'material difference' for the purposes of the legislation), the Court of Appeal held that once this constraint was at an end, failure to remunerate her at the same level as her direct male comparators constituted a less favourable term in her contract of employment. To justify a 'material difference' the institution would need to show a real need on its part, objectively justified, possibly on grounds other than economic or administrative efficiency.[151] This gives a clear guide to institutions experiencing financial restraint as to the careful steps they should take to avoid suggestions of discrimination on grounds of sex in setting starting salary. While cases continue, as evidenced by *Young v University of Edinburgh*,[152] higher education institutions have responded to the case law, particularly *Enderby*, by establishing a process called Higher Education Role Analysis (HERA) to assist them in ensuring that they comply with the law.

5.80   Both the *Pointon* and *Benveniste* cases could have been brought before the relevant Visitor on the basis of contravention of the equal opportunities section of the respective university Charters and an 'internal' settlement arrived at. This would not have excluded the jurisdiction of the employment tribunal, provided the relevant time-limit for bringing cases before the tribunal had not been exceeded. A Visitor has power to award monetary compensation and there appear to be no limits to that power.

Sex discrimination

5.81   The Sex Discrimination Acts 1975-1986 (as amended by the Employment Act 1989) make discrimination on grounds of sex or marriage unlawful in, inter alia, employment, and training.[153] The legislation covers discrimination against both sexes and against married people although the great majority of cases have concerned alleged discrimination against women. The text hereafter should

---

151 *Hampson v Department of Education and Science* [1989] ICR 179, following *Singh v Rowntree Mackintosh Ltd* [1979] IRLR 199, *Rainey v Greater Glasgow Health Board* [1987] ICR 129, *Tyldesley v TML Plastics Ltd* [1996] IRLR 395 and *Strathclyde Regional Council v Wallace* [1998] 1 All ER 394, HL; see also the decisions of the European Court of Justice in *Bilka-Kaufhaus GmbH v Weber von Hartz* 170/84: [1987] ICR 110 and *Enderby v Frenchay Health Authority and Secretary of State for Health* C-127/92: [1993] IRLR 591.
152 [1995] 23 DCLD 10.
153 Action may be taken even if there is illegality in the fact of, or in the performance of, a contract of employment: *Leighton v Michael* [1995] ICR 1091.

therefore be interpreted as applying to all categories. Sex discrimination claims make up the largest single group of reported cases against higher education institutions.

5.82 There are two kinds of discrimination – direct and indirect. Direct discrimination is easily defined: on grounds of sex treating a woman less favourably than a man is or would be treated, the motivation being irrelevant.[154] Examples occur in higher education from time to time, as in *Cooke v University of Nottingham and Iacovetti*[155] where unlawful discrimination arose when the success of an application appeared to turn on whether C had children. Indirect discrimination is more problematic: it arises where a person applies to a woman a requirement or condition which is applied or would apply equally to a man but

(i) which is such that the proportion of women who can comply with it is considerably smaller than the proportion of men who can comply with it, and

(ii) which cannot be shown to be justifiable irrespective of the sex of the person to whom it is applied, and

(iii) which is to her detriment because she cannot comply with it.

5.83 In certain circumstances it may be a 'genuine occupational requirement' (GOQ) for a job that the person employed is of a particular sex. The EOC's code of practice makes it clear that GOQs will only apply where considerations of privacy and decency (eg lavatory attendants) or authenticity (eg actors/actresses) are involved. The only cases likely to arise in higher educational institutions apart from these are those in which postholders provide individual welfare services such as student counsellors, where probably the best policy is to try to ensure that there is at least one of each sex. This exception might possibly also apply to a warden of a single-sex hall of residence. It may also on occasion be the case that a married couple will be appointed to domestic posts and that is permitted. Unless a GOQ can be established, it is unlawful for an employer on grounds of sex or marital status to discriminate against a person in advertising a post, in determining who should be offered employment, in the terms of employment offered, in affording access for promotion, transfer or training, or in dismissing her or him subjecting her or him to any other detriment.

---

154 See *Birmingham City Council v Equal Opportunities Commission* [1989] IRLR 173, HL.

155 [1995] 23 DCLD 6.

5.84   One of the most interesting issues to arise in higher education has been whether or not the law should permit discrimination in appointments to single-sex educational establishments, such as some of the Oxbridge colleges. The leading case in this area was *Hugh-Jones v St John's College, Cambridge*,[156] where the EAT held that refusal to consider a woman for the award of a research fellowship, which was prima facie unlawful under the 1975 Act, was nevertheless rendered lawful by the earlier statutes of the College as a charitable body. Section 5 Employment Act 1989 effectively reversed this decision insofar as mens' colleges are concerned, but specifically excludes the reverse situation so that discrimination against men who apply for employment in womens' colleges remains lawful where it is necessary 'to comply with any requirement of any instrument relating to the college or institution that the holder of the position in question should be a woman.' It appears from press reports that there may be some difficulty fitting persons who have changed their gender within this rather traditional classification.

5.85   Most cases involving higher education institutions allege indirect discrimination. A reported case was that of *University of Manchester v Jones*[157] on appeal by the University to the Employment Appeal Tribunal. Forty-four-year-old Mary Jones alleged that the selection procedure for the post of careers adviser, seeking appropriately experienced people 'preferably aged 27-35 years' discriminated against mature graduates who were, according to published statistics, be more likely to be women than men. The EAT by a majority held that a tribunal had erred in reading into an advertisement a requirement for a graduate who had undertaken a degree as a mature student rather than for someone from the general graduate population to whom the advertisement was addressed. The tribunal had also erred in failing to effect an objective balance between the reasonable needs of the University and the discriminatory effect of the condition complained of: they had applied a subjective test to the particular circumstances of Miss Jones.

5.86   A similar issue arose in *Conway v Queen's University of Belfast*[158] in the Northern Ireland Court of Appeal. Mr Conway applied unsuccessfully for a post in a computer centre where all the other incumbents were female. He claimed he had the requisite qualifications and experience, although evidence showed that his

---

156 [1979] ICR 848.
157 [1992] ICR 52.
158 [1981] IRLR 137.

experience was less than that required. Although the court found that the tribunal hearing the case had erred in their view of the meaning of discrimination (which the court held was that enunciated by the EAT in inter alia *Moberley v Commonwealth Hall (University of London))*,[159] Mr Conway was not in fact discriminated against. Lord Lowry LCJ said:

> [Counsel for Mr Conway] has pressed upon the court what Kilner Brown J said in [*Moberley*] and what, adopting his dictum, I said in *Wallace v South Eastern Education and Library Board*[160] to the effect that once discrimination is proved between members of different sexes, there is a case to answer. But discrimination there means an unfair, or at least prima facie unfair, preference, and the appellant's difficulty, on the unchallenged evidence in this case, is that his exclusion from the list of candidates for interview was prima facie not unfair. Accordingly, the case for discrimination never got off the ground.[161]

5.87 The *Moberley* case concerned a female student, Miss Sheila Moberley, employed as a part-time relief porter. A master key was lost while she was on duty and a decision taken that the main porter on duty would keep it in future. She failed in her contention that this was unlawful discrimination on ground of sex, since the tribunal accepted that the decision was related to her competence and sense of responsibility, not her sex and the EAT were not prepared to hold that the tribunal had erred in law in reaching that conclusion. Other cases alleging indirect discrimination are *Dick v University of Dundee*,[162] where the University was held to have indirectly discriminated on grounds of sex by reviewing part-time lecturers on fixed-term appointments for redundancy in advance of reviewing all relevant staff, full time and part time, and *Huppert v University Grants Committee and University of Cambridge*[163] where the UGC was held to have discriminated indirectly against a 39-year-old female candidate for a 'New Blood' lectureship in setting and adhering to an upper age limit of 35. It was held that a smaller proportion of women than of men were able to satisfy the age limit of 35 because family and maternal duties interfered with career pathways.[164] The rights of female employees in certain circumstances to be allowed to return to work part time after maternity leave were first raised in

159 [1977] IRLR 176.
160 [1980] IRLR 193.
161 [1981] IRLR 137, 140.
162 (1982) unreported.
163 (1986) unreported.
164 The rules were changed as a result of Dr Huppert's action.

Home Office v Holmes.[165] In that case the EAT declined to interfere with the decision of an employment tribunal that the employer had unlawfully discriminated against Sara Holmes on grounds of sex by refusing her request to return part-time. However, the EAT stressed that such rights could not always be exercised and a requirement for staff to work full-time will be justified. Arguments which could be used to justify this might include administrative and practical difficulties and the effect on other employees. In practice, higher education institutions have been in the forefront of efforts to provide as many women as possible with part-time work in these circumstances, since the nature of most jobs is such that part-time working or job sharing can be accommodated.

5.88 Indirect discrimination is very difficult to prove as the claimant will have to produce detailed and often sophisticated statistics, as Mary Jones did in her case against the University of Manchester. There are regulations under SDA[166] which enable a complainant to ask certain standard and useful questions of an employer. The replies to these questions are admissible in evidence and a refusal or failure to reply are liable to be regarded adversely by the tribunal.

5.89 Other cases include those of *University of Reading v MacCormack* and *Busfield v University of Essex*, both heard on appeal by the EAT[167] on the preliminary point of an order for discovery of confidential references and documents submitted by other candidates for posts for which the complainants had unsuccessfully applied, the purpose being to assist the complainants in bringing allegations of discrimination in the making of appointments. The EAT applied the Court of Appeal's decision in two cases *Science Research Council v Nassé* and *Leyland Cars v Vyas*,[168] which held that confidential reports or references or assessments by independent assessors to whom candidates' qualifications have been referred normally ought to be treated as sacrosanct and not looked at, except in very rare cases where the employment tribunal Chairman might inspect the documents before giving a ruling.

5.90 Another possible ground of complaint under SDA is one of victimisation, where the complainant has brought a complaint of

165 [1984] ICR 678.
166 SI 1975/2048: similar arrangements apply in cases of alleged discrimination on grounds of race or disability.
167 [1978] IRLR 490.
168 [1978] IRLR 352.

unlawful discrimination under the Act or under the Equal Pay Act and that as a consequence the person complained of (typically the employer) has treated the complainant less favourably than [he] treats or would treat other persons. Two cases have been reported in higher education. In *Humberstone v MacFadyen and the University of Southampton*[169] H, in 1989, made an unsuccessful complaint of gender discrimination through the University's internal grievance procedure. In 1990 she took voluntary severance, but in 1994 applied for another post. She was not shortlisted, ostensibly on academic grounds. However, her application was not fully considered as it had been intercepted by an officer who thought it inappropriate that she be considered for the post in view of the large severance payment she had received. H complained of unlawful discrimination, the tribunal upholding her complaint, finding that the officer had not been solely motivated by the size of the payment but also that in her previous employment H had made an allegation of an act which contravened SDA.

5.91   In the earlier case *Cornelius v University College of Swansea*[170] which was a decision of the Court of Appeal, the original (unproved) allegation by Mrs R M Cornelius was one of unwelcome sexual attention by another employee and, after a transfer, she complained of sex discrimination in her treatment by the College. That application was made outwith the permitted time limit for complaints and was dismissed both by a tribunal and by the EAT. Subsequently she issued further complaints alleging victimisation by the College in their subsequent actions in refusing a further transfer and after the College refused to hear her grievances while her case was pending before the tribunal, she issued further complaints. The point before the court was a true interpretation of the relevant section of the 1975 Act. The Court of Appeal held that discrimination under this section is not discrimination on grounds of sex but on grounds of conduct of the kind described in the section. In the case before it, such discrimination could not be shown to have occurred. In an interesting obiter dictum, Bingham LJ said:

> If a woman were to be unfavourably treated as an employee because her sex had led a male fellow-employee to behave improperly towards her, I would for my part have no doubt that a claim under the Act would lie ...

169 [1996] 30 DCLD 3.
170 [1987] IRLR 141.

This conveniently introduces us to one of the most controversial areas of the law of sex discrimination, that of sexual harassment.

Sexual harassment

5.92 While harassment in general is in defined circumstances protected by the criminal law,[171] section 6(2) SDA provides that it is unlawful for a person to discriminate against an employee by subjecting him or her to a detriment. Section 41(1) SDA extends this to cover anything done in the course of a person's employment as being done by the employer as well. In *Strathclyde Regional Council v Porcelli*,[172] the EAT and the Court of Session, reversing the original tribunal's decision, held that suggestive remarks and conduct by two male school laboratory technicians against Mrs Jean Porcelli, a fellow technician, with the intention and result that she applied for a transfer to another school, while not in itself amounting to sex discrimination under the Act, in fact constituted a detriment within her contract of employment and this case formed the basis for court intervention in this area.

5.93 Sexual harassment of women by men or (rarely) vice versa is nowadays considered by employers, if sufficiently serious in nature, to be a valid and fair reason for dismissal. For the purposes of this section, reference may be made to the EC Code of Practice on measures to combat sexual harassment ('Protecting the dignity of women and men at work') adopted in 1990. It defines sexual harassment as meaning 'unwanted conduct of a sexual nature, or other conduct based on sex affecting the dignity of women and men at work. This can include unwelcome physical, verbal or non-verbal conduct' – a wide-ranging definition indeed. It is perhaps worth considering how the Code amplifies the definition:

> The essential characteristic of sexual harassment is that it is unwanted by the recipient, that it is for each individual to determine what behaviour is acceptable to them and what they regard as offensive. Sexual attention becomes sexual harassment if it is persisted in once it has been made clear that it is regarded by the recipient as offensive, although one incident of harassment may constitute sexual harassment if sufficiently serious. It is the unwanted nature of the conduct which distinguishes sexual harassment from friendly behaviour, which is welcome and mutual.

171 Eg Protection from Harassment Act 1997.
172 [1986] IRLR 134, Court of Session.

5.94 The definition of sexual harassment in the Code was referred to by the EAT in *Wadman v Carpenter Farrer Partnership*[173] where it was suggested that it might help tribunals when considering allegations of this type. The Code makes a number of recommendations for employers and trades unions. In practice, following guidance from the CVCP, most of the pre-1992 universities adopted codes of practice and guidelines on dealing with sexual harassment in the early 1990s, and similar action has been taken in the rest of the higher education system. The Equal Opportunities Commission for Northern Ireland published separate guides for both employers and employees in 1993 and the EOC published a guide *Consider the cost ... Sexual Harassment at Work* in 1994. It has been suggested that an employer may be in breach of its contractual duty to employ safe and competent employees if it fails to take action to prevent sexual harassment.[174]

5.95 The mere holding or expressing a view cannot amount to sexual harassment or sex discrimination unless it consists of telling jokes or stories over a period of time, deliberately to embarrass a female colleague.[175] Placing advertisements for underwear in the cabinet of a female employee with the message 'Try this and it might improve your bust' did not justify a complaint as it was not established that she resented or was offended by 'banter.'[176] On the other hand, unwanted squeezing of the breasts of a female member of staff at a Christmas party, at which other female staff had given chocolate penises to the male staff, constituted sexual harassment,[177] as did a remark by a young man to an older woman in a meeting 'Hiya, big tits.'[178] An employer may be liable for sexual harassment of an employee by a third party.[179]

Complaints of sex discrimination

5.96 Complaints of discrimination in employment matters on grounds of sex should always be properly investigated by the

---

173 [1993] IRLR 374.
174 S Middlemiss (1997) SLT (Note) 37, referring to inter alia *Hudson v Ridge Manufacturing* [1957] 2 QB 348.
175 *Stagg v Property Services Agency Ltd* COIT 7313/90.
176 *Cann v Unilift Ltd* COIT 9197/92.
177 *Van Den Berghen v Nabarro Nathanson* COIT 29779/91.
178 *Insitu Cleaning Co Ltd v Heads* [1995] IRLR 4.
179 *Go Kidz Ltd v Bardouane* EAT 1110/95.

employer.[180] If the employer does not satisfy the employee, cases may be taken to employment tribunals. A tribunal may, where it finds the complaint well-founded, take one or more of three courses of action:[181]

(i) make an order declaring the rights of the parties;
(ii) make an order of compensation of an amount corresponding to the damages which the complainant would have received from the courts had the matter been one falling within that part of SDA which deals with discrimination in other fields;
(iii) make a recommendation for action by the respondent to obviate or reduce the adverse effect on the complainant of the act of discrimination.

5.97 The compensation which may be awarded for unlawful sex discrimination was restricted by SDA to the maximum payable under the employment protection legislation. However in *Marshall v Southampton and South West Hampshire Area Health Authority*[182] the ECJ held that Article 5(1) of Council Directive 76/207/EEC was to be interpreted as meaning that a general policy of termination of employment whereby a woman's employment was terminated solely because she had attained or passed the qualifying age for a state pension, that age being different under national legislation for men and for women, constituted discrimination on ground of sex contrary to the Directive. Following this through, in *Marshall v Southampton and South-West Hampshire Area Health Authority (No 2)*,[183] the ECJ held that the proper application of the relevant Council Directive[184] required that compensation should not be limited a priori and should be related to the circumstances of the case. The Sex Discrimination and Equal Pay (Remedies) Regulations 1993[185] gave effect to this change. The first subsequent case was *Holden v Wirral Hospital Trust*[186] where Kathleen Holden, a part-time medical laboratory scientific officer was awarded £17,127 compensation following the alleged failure of the Trust to transfer her to full-time work. In 1996

---

180 *Edmondson v BRS Southern* COIT 5877/91.
181 Section 65 SDA (as amended).
182 152/84: [1986] ECR 723.
183 C-271/91: [1993] IRLR 445, ECJ.
184 Council Directive 76/207/EEC 9 February 1976 (*Official Journal* 1976 L39 p 40) on the implementation of the principle of equal treatment for men and women as regards access to employment, vocational training and promotion, and working conditions.
185 SI 1993/2795.
186 (1993) unreported.

employment tribunals' powers to award compensation was extended to indirect discrimination claims.[187]

Discrimination on grounds of sexual orientation and gender re-assignment

5.98 UK law does not provide a remedy for discrimination on grounds of sexual orientation. In *Smith v Gardner Merchant*[188] EAT held that discrimination on grounds of sexual orientation is not discrimination on grounds of sex and thus not contrary to SDA. But in *P v S and Cornwall County Council*[189] the dismissal of a transsexual for a reason related to a gender re-assignment was held by ECJ to be in breach of the Equal Treatment Directive 76/207/EEC.

Discrimination on grounds of race, nationality, etc

5.99 The prevention of racial discrimination is covered by RRA, the provisions of which are mutatis mutandis very similar to those of SDA. As with SDA, there is well-developed case law on the application of requirements or conditions justifying discrimination.[190] RRA is however a development of earlier legislation (the Race Relations Act 1968) and does not originate in the European Union. It does not yet extend to Northern Ireland. A new article in the Treaty of Rome designed to combat racial, religious and other forms of discrimination was agreed by member states at the Amsterdam Summit in June 1997 but is not expected to be ratified before 1999 and will not have direct effect.

5.100 The provisions of the Act are enforced by mechanisms parallel to those for sex discrimination and previous limits on compensation were removed by the Race Relations (Remedies) Act 1994. As explained by the Court of Appeal in *Majid v London Guildhall University*,[191] where Amir Majid alleged discrimination and victimisation, the right not to be discriminated against is a private law matter and thus not amenable to judicial review. Direct and

---

187 Sex Discrimination and Equal Pay (Miscellaneous Amendments) Regulations 1996 (SI 1996/435).
188 [1996] IRLR 342.
189 [1996] IRLR 347.
190 See *St Matthias Church of England School (Board of Governors) v Crizzle* [1993] IRLR 472.
191 (1993) The Higher, 12 November.

indirect discrimination and victimisation are defined in virtually
identical terms, mutatis mutandis, to those used in SDA. The Act
refers to the concepts of 'racial grounds' and 'racial group.' 'Racial
grounds' is defined to include colour, race, nationality or ethnic or
national origin. 'Racial group' means a group of persons defined by
reference to these characteristics. In both cases, 'nationality' includes
citizenship. A person may be included in more than one racial group
and may have different nationality and citizenship. So it would be
unlawful to discriminate against a black Irishman or to accord less
favourable treatment to a British national who is a Spanish citizen.
According to the tribunal in *Griffith v Reading University Students'
Union*[192] the Welsh people are a distinct racial group. In *Bryans v
Northumberland College of Arts and Technology*[193] the same was
held to be true of the Irish. In certain circumstances, notably in the
case of turban-wearing Sikhs, indirect discrimination under the Act
may arise on grounds which are a composite of racial and religious
discrimination.[194] The Act also refers to discrimination on the ground
of ethnic origin which has a wider meaning than 'race.'[195]

5.101   The principle enunciated by the EAT in *Commission for
Racial Equality v Imperial Society of Teachers of Dancing*[196] is
important to higher education institutions. In that case, it was found
that on the balance of probabilities a secretary acting for the Society,
in the course of asking a careers teacher to provide a candidate for a
junior post, said that she would rather that the school did not send
anyone coloured, the reason being that that person would feel out
of place as there were no other coloured employees. That was held
to be an unlawful inducement of the careers teacher to discriminate,
since the word 'induce' means 'to persuade or to prevail upon or to
bring about.' It is clear from this case that anyone involved in
recruiting at any level requires clear instructions on language to be
used.

5.102   Another interesting case is *Karia v Reliance Security Services
Ltd*[197] where the employer dismissed the employee on the pretext of
being unable to obtain a reference when in fact he had never taken
one up. The tribunal held that the employer's failure to do so or to

192 [1997] 31 DCLD 3.
193 [1995] 26 DCLD 5.
194 Sections 11 and 12 Employment Act 1989 deal with the wearing of safety helmets
     by turban-wearing Sikhs on construction sites.
195 *Mandla v Dowell Lee* [1983] 1 All ER 1062.
196 [1983] IRLR 315.
197 COIT 1917/212.

discuss the matter with the employee amounted to direct racial discrimination.

5.103 The circumstances in which a complaint of racial discrimination may be upheld are numerous. In *Riedel v Wolverhampton Polytechnic*[198] R, a part-time lecturer, was discriminated against by being excluded from the campus for accusing some students of racist behaviour following a complaint by a fellow member of staff. Harassment on grounds of race may occur in much the same way as sexual harassment and these are normally dealt with together in regulations and codes of practice made by higher education institutions. In some circumstances employers can be held liable for harassment by third parties[199] and individual employees can also be made liable alongside their employer.[200] An employer may be liable for an employee's actions even though they are not 'in the course of employment.'[201] As explained by the EAT in *Qureshi v Victoria University of Manchester and Brazier*,[202] a claim alleging discrimination and victimisation, it is not permissible for a tribunal to take a 'piecemeal' approach to determining the issue before them. The tribunal's finding that while the University had not discriminated against Q but B, Dean of Faculty, had discriminated by way of victimisation on one occasion, was 'fatally flawed.' It is unlawful discrimination to discipline an employee for bringing an action for racial discrimination which in the event was unfounded, where the complaint is brought in good faith.[203]

The free movement of workers and the Asylum and Immigration Act 1996

5.104 EU nationals benefit from the 'freedom of movement of workers' provisions of the Treaty of Rome. Article 48(4) of the Treaty (which was unaffected by the Single European Act) qualifies the general provision by stating that it does not apply '... to employment in the public service ...' In the domestic law of the UK, there is no

---

198 COIT 10782/92.
199 *Burton and Rhule v De Vere Hotels* [1996] IRLR 596.
200 For the circumstances in which this may arise see *Barker v Shahronki* [1996] 28 DCLD 11; *Bryans v Northumberland College of Arts and Technology* [1995] 26 DCLD 5.
201 *Jones v Tower Boot Co Ltd* [1997] ICR 254, CA.
202 [1997] IRLB 11; it was reported subsequently that following a rehearing, Q's claim of racial discrimination against the University had been upheld.
203 *Sandhu v Customs and Excise Comrs* COIT 33959/91.

bar to nationals of other EC states holding posts in higher education.[204] But this is not automatically a two-way process, as illustrated by the case of *Lawrie-Blum v Land Baden-Württemberg*.[205] A national of the UK was refused access to a teacher-training course in Germany, where that course included teaching practice in a state school. The ECJ ruled that teacher-training was not 'employment in the public service' within the meaning of Article 48(4) and that the principle of free movement of workers applied. In 1988, the European Commission published a statement on a strategy for eliminating restrictions on grounds of nationality to access to a range of non-sensitive posts in the public sector, including teaching in state educational institutions and research for non-military purposes.[206] As has been pointed out,[207] a guarantee of 'access' does not necessarily guarantee equal of opportunity once appointed. It remains the case that states are entitled to require the possession of specific national occupational or professional qualifications for certain occupations, particularly at a senior level and may be entitled to insist on linguistic qualifications where these are essential for the work.

5.105 The Asylum and Immigration Act 1996 is part of a network of legislation adopted by EU member states to tighten immigration controls. Treaties concluded prior to the Single European Act set mutually reinforcing obligations for member states to restrict entry of immigrants and asylum seekers into the EU. The Act provides for new immigration offences further to those contained in the Immigration Act 1971, and stringent provisions against the employment of immigrants who are not in possession of a work permit. Under section 8 it is a criminal offence to employ a person aged 16 or over who is subject to immigration control unless either there is appropriate consent or permission or the person falls into a category where such employment is allowed.

Disablement

5.106 The Disability Discrimination Act 1995 (DDA),[208] as brought into force in stages, replaces most provisions of the Disabled Persons

---

204 Except perhaps where considerations of national security affected particular posts but this should be rare.
205 66/85: [1986] ECR 2121.
206 *Official Journal* 18 March 1985.
207 J Handoll 'Article 48(4) EEC and Non-national Access to Public Employment' (1988) European Law Review No 4 p 223.
208 See B Doyle 'The DDA: Enabling legislation or dissembling law?' (1997) 60 MLR 64.

(Employment) Acts 1944–58, which established a voluntary register of disabled persons, open to employed an unemployed people alike. There were certain eligibility conditions to be satisfied before a name could be entered on the register, abolished by DDA.

5.107 In broad terms, if in the employment setting a person is to be protected by DDA, there must be a 'physical or mental impairment' which must affect the individual's 'ability to carry out normal day-to-day activities' and the adverse effect must be 'substantial' and 'long term.' Discrimination in employment is defined by Part II DDA in terms of (i) according unjustified less favourable treatment to a person for a reason related to the disability and (ii) an unjustified failure to provide such reasonable adjustment to the working environment as is required by section 6 DDA. Section 4(2) DDA makes it unlawful to discriminate against a disabled person by dismissing that person or subjecting him or her to any detriment. Dismissal, including compulsory premature retirement, must be justified by the employer and the reason has to be one which cannot be removed by 'reasonable adjustment.' By contrast with SDA and RRA, positive discrimination is not restricted by DDA, so that it is lawful to treat a non-disabled person in a less favourable way than a disabled person. Employers can therefore advertise posts available only to disabled persons.

5.108 The crucial issue in cases arising under DDA will be whether the treatment, or failure reasonably to adjust, can be 'justified.' To justify less favourable treatment an employer must show that the reason for the treatment was both material to the circumstances of the case and substantial. It is suggested that 'material' may be defined as 'significant and relevant'[209] and 'substantial' means 'considerable, solid or big.'[210] Section 59 DDA provides that where there is a conflict with statutory provisions governing health and safety, the latter take precedence. Section 6 DDA provides an illustrative list of steps which it may be reasonable for an employer to take to adjust the working environment including transfers, alterations in hours of work, time off, training, acquiring or modifying equipment, instructions or reference manuals, modifying testing or assessment procedures, providing a reader or interpreter, and supervision. Alterations to premises under lease are covered by section 16 DDA.

---

209 *Rainey v Greater Glasgow Health Board* [1987] IRLR 26, HL.
210 *Palser v Grinling* [1948] AC 291.

Rehabilitation of offenders

5.109   The Rehabilitation of Offenders Act 1974 is of importance only when considering applications for exempted occupations as defined in the Act, which in higher education institutions would include medical practitioners, dentists, lawyers and social workers and

> Any office or employment concerned with the provision to persons aged under 18 of accommodation, care, leisure and recreational facilities, schooling, social services, supervision or training, being an office or employment of such a kind as to enable the holder to have access in the course of his [or her] normal duties to such persons, and any other office or employment the normal duties of which are carried out wholly or partly on the premises where such provision takes place.

Persons applying for such posts must disclose all convictions, regardless of the nature or length of sentence, if told that they must do so because of the effect of the Rehabilitation of Offenders Act 1974 (Exemptions) Order 1975.[211] The onus is on the employer to inform them.[212] Otherwise it is legitimate to ignore all convictions for offences for which the sentence has been less than 30 months' imprisonment (or its equivalent) once the rehabilitation period, which varies according to the nature and length of sentence, has expired. Most higher education students are aged over 18. Nevertheless there are some who are not, and institutions should consider carefully whether to seek information on past convictions to anyone (academic, administrator, cleaner or other employee) who may come into contact with the under-18s.

Fair employment

5.110   The Fair Employment (Northern Ireland) Act 1976 was an attempt to tackle discrimination in employment among those belonging to different Christian denominations. It was replaced by the Fair Employment (Northern Ireland) Act 1989 (FEA) which introduced stronger machinery for monitoring the workforce and powers to promote equality of opportunity. The definition of direct and indirect discrimination in FEA parallels that in SDA and RRA.

---

211 SI 1975/1023.
212 Rehabilitation of Offenders Act 1974 (Exemptions)(Amendment) Order 1986 (SI 1986/1249).

In *McCausland v Dungannon District Council*[213] the Northern Ireland Court of Appeal ruled on the definition of indirect discrimination for the purposes of the Act: the definition was wider than that so far associated with sex and race discrimination and may have wider application. The Fair Employment Commission (FEC) established by FEA has as its main tasks promoting affirmative action and maintaining a quasi-statutory code of practice for the promotion of equality of opportunity. Employers, other than very small ones, are required to register with FEC, which may require them to give an undertaking to promote such equality of opportunity. Penalties may be imposed where this undertaking is not honoured within a reasonable time.

5.111 'Affirmative action' for the purposes of FEA is defined as:

> ... action designed to secure fair participation in employment by members of the Protestant, or members of the Roman Catholic, community in Northern Ireland by means including (a) the adoption of practices encouraging such participation; and (b) the modification or abandonment of practices that have or may have the effect of restricting or discouraging such participation.

The Act has no relevance to, nor does it promote affirmative action in respect of, adherents of other religious belief or those of no religious belief. It is therefore in principle possible for employers to discriminate against these groups.

5.112 A Fair Employment Tribunal established by FEA to replace the Fair Employment Appeal Board has jurisdiction reflecting that of employment tribunals in cases under the sex discrimination legislation. Just as an employment tribunal can withhold publicity in cases involving elements of sexual misconduct, FEA allows the Tribunal to sit in private to receive information from any person which would create a substantial risk that he or another individual would be subject to physical attack or sectarian harassment and to prohibit disclosure of specified information.

Discrimination against women returning after maternity

5.113 Only women can be discriminated against in the terms on which they are accepted back into the workplace after maternity. The statutory entitlements to maternity leave and the right to return are

213 [1993] IRLR 583.

set out in sections 68-74 EmpRA and the latter right is subject to certain restrictions imposed under health and safety legislation (eg Maternity (Compulsory Leave) Regulations 1994[214]) and to risk assessments under regulations 13A–C of the Management of Health and Safety At Work Regulations 1992.[215] Recent cases have concentrated on the technicalities of time limits for notification and bringing actions whether under these provisions or for discrimination under SDA[216] and the requirement physically to present oneself for work at the due time.[217]

The TUPE (Transfer of Undertakings (Protection of Employment)) Regulations

5.114   The TUPE Regulations 1981[218] implement the EC Acquired Rights Directive, the object of which is to ensure that employees' rights are safeguarded in the event of a change in employer. The Regulations require the new employer to apply to the employees the same conditions of employment as agreed with the old employer. The requirements of the Directive have been spelt out by the European Court of Justice in a number of cases and the area continues to develop rapidly. Examples of leading cases are *P Bork International A/S v Foreningen af Arbejdsledere i Danmark*[219] and *Dr Sophie Redmond Stichting v Bartol*.[220] In *Rask & Christensen v ISS Kantineservice A/S*[221] it was held that these provisions may apply in cases where a service previously provided directly by the employer is contracted out, eg provision of a staff canteen. In *Hadden v University of Dundee Students' Association*[222] the Association had first contracted out its catering service to a private firm, which employed Mrs Hadden and other staff previously employed by the Association. When the contract with the private firm was terminated, the Association did not re-employ Mrs Hadden, who claimed a remedy

214 SI 1994/2479.
215 SI 1992/2051 as amended by SI 1994/2865.
216 *McPherson v Drumpark House* [1997] IRLR 277; *Hilton International Hotels (UK) Ltd v Kaissi* [1994] IRLR 270; *Institute of Motor Industry v Harvey* [1992] IRLR 343; *Cast v Croydon College* [1997] IRLR 14.
217 *Crees v Royal London Insurance* [1997] IRLR 85; *Kwik Save Stores v Greaves* [1997] IRLR 268; *Lewis Woolf Griptight Ltd v Corfield* [1997] IRLR 432, EAT.
218 SI 1981/1794; amended by the Collective Redundancies and Transfer of Undertakings (Protection of Employment) Regulations 1995 (SI 1995/2587).
219 101/87: [1989] IRLR 41.
220 C-29/91: [1992] IRLR 366.
221 C-209/91: [1993] IRLR 133.
222 [1985] IRLR 449.

under TUPE. The EAT held that she had no remedy of this nature, but might possibly have a common law (breach of contract) remedy for breach of an undertaking apparently given to her that she would be re-employed if the contract with the private firm was terminated.

Termination of employment

The main employment protection right

5.115   The law relating to dismissal, for whatever reason, is that which most people identify as 'the law of employment' or 'employment protection' and indeed the introduction in 1971 by the Heath Government of the concept of unfair dismissal was by far the most important innovation in employment law to date.

Mutual agreement distinguished

5.116   Before considering termination of employment by the employer, we should recognise that the majority of terminations are by the giving of notice by the employee (resignation)[223] or the efflux of time (retirement, the end of a fixed-term contract[224] or death in service). There may also be termination by agreement (premature retirement, voluntary redundancy or just an agreement to part company) or agreement on an offer by an employee to be selected for redundancy.[225] There may be a fine line between an agreement to part company and a dismissal; an employer cannot claim to have dismissed an employee if the employer uses words which are vague and unspecific.[226] In *Mallinson v University of Bournemouth*,[227] the tribunal found that Dr Mallinson's contract had been terminated by mutual agreement after he had accepted an offer of a cash settlement negotiated by his trade union representative and approved by a solicitor: under section 203 EmpRA a 'compromise agreement' accepted after a solicitor's advice would now prevent such a case from proceeding. Guidance on how to establish whether there is dismissal

---

223 Even giving notice of intention to resign may be treated for the purposes of employment protection law as a dismissal: *Ely v YKK Fasteners (UK) Ltd* [1993] IRLR 500, CA.
224 Although technically this is a dismissal as discussed below.
225 Again, technically, a dismissal.
226 *International Computers Ltd v Kennedy* [1981] IRLR 28.
227 (1993) unreported.

or a mutual parting of the ways was given by the EAT in *Lambert v Liverpool City Council.*[228]

Wrongful dismissal

5.117 A dismissal may be wrongfully effected by the employer, acting in breach of the contract of employment, in which case an action may lie for breach of contract before the courts, extended in certain cases to employment tribunals. In *R v East Berkshire Health Authority, ex p Walsh*[229] Sir John Donaldson MR said

> The ordinary employer is free to act in breach of his contracts of employment and if he does so his employee will acquire certain private law rights and remedies in damages for wrongful dismissal, compensation for unfair dismissal, an order for reinstatement or re-engagement, etc.

5.118 As we have seen, chartered universities in England are not 'ordinary employers' for the Visitor (prior to 1989 for academic staff) or the courts as appropriate may restrain these bodies from attempting to act in breach of their charter and statutes. If they attempt to do so, any such action will be void. In the case of academic staff governed by the 'Model Statute' or equivalent provisions, the grounds for dismissal will have to be brought within the 'good cause' reasons which taken as a whole are broadly similar to those set out in EmpRA. They are:

(i) conviction for an offence which may be deemed by a Tribunal ... to be such as to render the person convicted unfit for employment as a member of the academic staff; or

(ii) conduct of an immoral, scandalous or disgraceful nature incompatible with the duties or employment; or

(iii) conduct constituting failure or persistent refusal or neglect or inability to perform the duties or comply with the conditions of employment; or

(iv) physical or mental incapacity ...

5.119 These provisions are subject to criticism on a number of grounds. In particular dismissal for misconduct which does not arise as a result of a criminal conviction (that is, where the criminal court has found the charge proved beyond reasonable doubt) has to be brought under the heading of 'immoral, scandalous or disgraceful'

228 (1997) unreported.
229 [1985] QB 152.

conduct. If the ground for dismissal would if proved amount to an action on which a criminal charge could be instituted, then it is arguable that action must be brought under (i) above and a conviction secured with all the protection for the individual that the higher standard of proof in criminal proceedings requires. Assessing the matter on the lower standard of proof 'on the balance of probability' while adequate for the purposes of fairness in case of a challenge for unfair dismissal, to be discussed later, seems inadequate for the purposes of an action for wrongful dismissal, since the employee is entitled to rely upon the terms of the Statute.

5.120 Care must also be taken that proceedings for misconduct, inability etc do not offend against the principles of academic freedom described earlier, in particular in England and Wales the provisions of section 43(1) E(2)A86. Although recent research shows a remarkably low incidence in the UK,[230] in principle academic fraud presents a particular difficulty: It 'presents a unique legal problem because although plagiarism generally occurs in an academic setting it may involve penalties comparable to those awarded for disciplinary misconduct violations, such as theft or vandalism.'[231] As has been pointed out[232] plagiarism charges against a scholar can divide experts, perplex scholarly societies and raise intractable questions such as who should investigate: the institution, a learned society or professional body or an aggrieved publication?

The law of fair and unfair dismissal

5.121 Quite separately from the individual's contractual right not to be *wrongfully* dismissed, or to be compensated if such dismissal in fact takes place, section 94 EmpRA provides that every employee has the right not to be *unfairly* dismissed. The major points considered to be important in the application of the law of unfair dismissal to the higher education environment are described in this section. A full description of the complexities of the subject is outside the scope of this work.[233]

---

230 G Parry and D Houghton 'Plagiarism in UK Universities' (1996) 8(3) Education and the Law 201.
231 R D Mawdsley *Legal Aspects of Plagiarism* (1985) and *Academic Misconduct: Cheating and Plagiarism* (1994) (Kansas, NOLPE, Topeka). Relevant US cases include *Newman v Burgin* 930 F2d 955 (1991); *Yu v Peterson* 13 F3d 1413 (1993).
232 C J Mooney *The Chronicle of Higher Education* (1992).
233 For a full guide see F Walton (ed) *Encyclopaedia of Employment Law and Practice*, Professional Publishing: this is a subscription volume updated quarterly.

The meaning of 'dismissal'

5.122 The meaning of dismissal is set out in Part X EmpRA as follows:

> an employee shall be treated as having been dismissed by his employer if, but only if,
> (a) his contract is terminated by the employer with or without notice;
> (b) where a fixed-term contract expires without being renewed under the same contract;[234] or
> (c) where the employee himself terminates the contract with or without notice in circumstances such that he is entitled to terminate it without notice by reason of the employer's conduct.

5.123 To pursue a claim of unfair dismissal before a tribunal an employee has to show that he or she was in fact dismissed in terms of the Act. This covers both dismissal on due notice, as provided for in the contract, and summary dismissal which can be carried out without breach of contract only if the employee has been guilty of repudiation of the contract or has breached the contract fundamentally, for example by gross misconduct. Whether or not the summary dismissal is possible without breach of contract is not a matter for the tribunal to consider when examining the fairness of the dismissal.

Restrictions on right to claim unfair dismissal

5.124 There are three other points which must be satisfied before the tribunal has jurisdiction to hear a case. First, pending resolution of whether a qualifying period is compatible with EU law, referred to the ECJ by the House of Lords in *R v Secretary of State for Employment, ex p Seymour-Smith*,[235] the employee must have been employed for a continuous period of two years or more[236] and if unchallenged evidence to that effect is presented, as in *Leicester*

---

234 In the particular case of a fixed-term contract, which would normally expire on efflux of time, an employee who is allowed to continue working and is paid by the employer on the previous contractual terms is assumed to have an indefinite contract of employment terminable on a reasonable period of notice.
235 [1997] 2 All ER 273.
236 The period has been progressively increased from 26 weeks in 1971 to two years in 1990, now set out in section 108(1) EmpRA. A case on what constituted '26 weeks' under the legislation in force in 1976 was *Coulson v City of London Polytechnic* [1976] IRLR 212.

University Students' Union v Mahomed [237] the tribunal must accept it. The effective date is defined (with some qualifications which are not relevant here) in EmpRA as follows:

(a) where notice has been given by either the employer or the employee, the date on which that notice expires; or

(b) the date of termination of employment where the employee's contract is terminated without notice; or

(c) the date on which a fixed-term contract expires without being renewed; or

(d) in the case of a woman who has been absent for pregnancy and confinement and who has expressed her intention to return to work but who has not been allowed by her employer to return, the date which she notified to the employer as her expected date of return.

5.125   Secondly, service must have been 'continuous' ie without gaps, for two years of employment for the minimum number of hours per week. Hours spent on-call, on standby, or even off-duty hours spent working at home without obligation or requirement by the employer, do not count. [238] Absence from work because of a 'temporary cessation of work' as defined in the Act does not break continuity as long as the contracts are 'in the same series' [239] and in *University of Aston in Birmingham v Malik* [240] the distinction was drawn between 'work' and 'paid work' for the purposes of the legislation.

5.126   Thirdly, the claim must be presented within a prescribed time limit. Section 94 EmpRA provides that an employment tribunal shall not consider a complaint unless it is presented to the tribunal before the end of a period of three months beginning with the effective date of termination. To calculate whether an individual falls within this requirement, the effective date of termination of the contract must be ascertained in, according to the EAT in *Newman v Polytechnic of Wales Students' Union*, [241] a practical and commonsense way. In that case N was dismissed by an invalid decision of the officers of

---

237 [1995] ICR 270, EAT.

238 *Lake v Essex County Council* [1979] IRLR 241; *Nottinghamshire Area Health Authority v Gray* EAT 163/81.

239 *Ford v Warwickshire County Council* [1983] ICR 273; *Lewis v Surrey County Council* [1987] IRLR 509.

240 *University of Aston in Birmingham v Malik* [1984] ICR 492, applying *Fitzgerald v Hall, Russell & Co Ltd* [1969] 3 All ER 1140, HL and *Ford v Warwickshire County Council* [1983] ICR 273, HL.

241 [1995] IRLR 72.

the Union, later retrospectively validated by the executive committee. The effective date was the date of the technically invalid decision. Even one day's delay is fatal, as was the case in *University of Cambridge v Murray*.[242] Alison Murray was dismissed on 30 April 1991 and her complaint was presented on 30 July 1991, held by the EAT, some 18 months later, to be one day too late. The only exemption is where it was 'not reasonably practicable' for the complaint to be presented before the end of the three-month period, eg where the staff of the tribunal give erroneous advice to the applicant.[243]

Fixed-term contracts: efflux of time

5.127 Dismissal by termination of fixed-term contracts is of major significance in higher education institutions: in the case of the pre-1992 universities the statutes made by the University Commissioners extend the protection of the right of appeal against dismissal to all such contracts made with persons covered by the statute (normally academic and research staff). They use the language of EmpRA but, unlike the Act, make no provision for waiver of rights, as described later. This is because they make provision for the giving of notice of appeal against dismissal within a specified, short, period from the notice of dismissal which is, in effect, contained in the letter of appointment. The argument then is that the member of staff not only has full knowledge from the start that the appointment is for a fixed term but also knows that he or she can appeal against that dismissal, even though that appeal has to be entered very shortly after taking up the post. There is no reported case relating to this ingenious provision.

5.128 The law relating to fixed-term contracts in unfair dismissal claims is now very complicated. Provisions for unfair dismissal are different to those for redundancy, which will be discussed later. Fixed-term contracts, or renewal of such contracts, are not in practice used where there is a defined task to be done with a definite end in sight. Many higher education institutions use fixed-term contracts as a 'management tool' to provide flexibility in the workforce, regardless of whether the post concerned is qualitatively different from one to which they might otherwise appoint on a 'permanent' basis. In so doing their policy, apart from exposing them to risk of action for

---

242 [1993] ICR 460.
243 *London International College v Sen* [1993] IRLR 333, CA.

discrimination or equal pay, runs contrary to the clear description of such arrangements in case law as contracts which are 'to endure for a maximum definite period, not for a stated minimum period with provision for future extensions.'[244] As *Dean v Polytechnic of North London*[245] illustrates, the issue has been current in higher education for at least 25 years. Institutions insist that as a condition of taking a fixed-term appointment, the member of staff waives the right to complain of unfair dismissal on expiry of the contract as permitted by section 197(1) EmpRA for contracts of one year or more (two years up to 1980). The waiver must be in writing, though not necessarily in the original contract, and must be made before the expiry date. In some cases the courts will treat the use of fixed-term contracts as a sham, and the employment relationship will be regarded as a continuing one, so that a waiver clause is invalid.[246] The position at the end of 1997 is as set out in *BBC v Kelly-Phillips*.[247] Contracts with fixed beginning and ending dates are contracts for fixed terms regardless of their terminability by notice, as established in *Dixon v BBC*,[248] and *Wiltshire County Council v NATFHE and Guy*.[249] When a contract ends because funding ceases, there should be no problem.[250] When establishing whether the relevant employment is for one year or more, the tribunal should look at the last contract in force, which is the one that matters[251] as in *Open University v Triesman*[252] although unfortunately for T, it was held that her claim was 'out of time' and therefore the employment tribunal lacked jurisdiction to hear it. EAT specifically rejected the contrary interpretation of the Northern Ireland Court of Appeal in *Mulrine v University of Ulster*.[253]

Constructive dismissal

5.129 Section 95(1) EmpRA covers what is normally termed constructive dismissal, that is to say where there is no actual dismissal by the employer – there may even be a resignation by the employee

---

244 *Warren v D Ferranti Ltd* (1968) 3 ITR 286.
245 [1973] ICR 490.
246 *Richards v BP Oil Ltd* (unreported), referred to in *Mulrine v University of Ulster* [1993] IRLR 545.
247 EAT 1397/96: see also *Bhatt v Chelsea and Westminster Health Care Trust* [1997] IRLR 660.
248 [1979] ICR 281.
249 [1980] IRLR 198.
250 *Brown v Knowsley Borough Council* [1986] IRLR 102.
251 *BBC v Ioannou* [1975] ICR 267.
252 [1978] IRLR 114.
253 [1993] IRLR 545.

– but the Act treats certain acts of the employer as tantamount to dismissal. The key criterion for establishing constructive dismissal is whether there has been a material breach of contract by the employer. It is not sufficient for the employee merely to establish that the employer had acted in what the employee considers to be an unreasonable way. The employee has to show that the employer's conduct entitled him or her to leave and that this entitled him or her to terminate the contract of employment without notice, whether or not (s)he gave notice, and that there has been an unambiguous repudiation of the contract by the employer and an unambiguous acceptance by the employee of that repudiation, a position originally set out in 1978-80 in *Western Excavating (ECC) Ltd v Sharp*[254] and *Spafax Ltd v Harrison.*[255] Although the contractual test is now well established, it is not necessary for the employee to point to a specific term of the written contract – as, for instance, a failure to pay salary at the agreed rate or to bar the employee from benefits to which there is a contractual entitlement. The employee can found on the breach of an implied term of the contract provided that he or she can show the term to be of such importance that breach of it by the employer indicates an intention not to be bound by the contract. The implied term which is most commonly founded on in constructive dismissal cases is the obligation not to act in such a way as to destroy or seriously damage the relationship of mutual trust and confidence between employer and employee. Whether the employee will succeed before the tribunal will depend in showing that it was the institution as the employer which had undermined the employee's authority or withdrawn support from him or her in such a way as to drive the employee to the decision rather than, for example, inter-personal difficulties with other members of staff.

5.130 Examples include *Jones v F Sirl & Son (Furnishers) Ltd*[256] where a female employee of 30 years' standing was treated to a succession of breaches of contract by the employer, including cuts in allowances and pension provision, appointment of a manager without consultation and removal of a significant part of her duties. A clear link was established between these acts and her resignation and she was found to have been constructively dismissed. And in *Lewis v Motorworld Garages Ltd,*[257] after a demotion accepted by Mr Lewis, which involved loss of his sole use of an office, there was a series of

254 [1978] IRLR 27.
255 [1980] IRLR 442.
256 [1997] IRLR 493, EAT.
257 [1985] IRLR 465.

criticisms by senior management culminating in a final warning. Mr Lewis felt that this criticism and the earlier demotion were unjustified and resigned. The series of actions complained of cumulatively amounted to a breach of the implied term of confidence and trust in the contract.

5.131 There is obviously a range of circumstances in which employees might justifiably claim a fundamental breach of contract by the employer. Possibly the most likely to occur in an academic community is a breach of the essential elements of confidence and trust. Although this can arise by a steady erosion, as in the cases of Mrs Jones and Mr Lewis, it can also happen simply as a result of an ill-judged action or statement by an employee in a management or supervisory position. A clear case of this was *Courtauld's Northern Textiles v Andrew*,[258] where an assistant manager told the employee concerned that '... [you] can't do the bloody job anyway.' This statement was held to be sufficient to 'destroy or seriously damage the relationship of confidentiality and trust between employer and employee' which was conduct 'which goes to the root of the contract.' Against this, it may be argued that academic freedom includes freedom of speech within the law as previously discussed. To what extent the courts might accept that the academic equivalent of the words used on the building site would be insufficient to cause a breakdown in trust and confidence has yet to be determined. It is however clear that some language used in academic interchange may be actionable in defamation and therefore may not be considered to be 'within the law'.[259]

5.132 An example of a different kind, but with relevance to staff employed in laboratory or trades work, is *British Aircraft Corpn v Austin*,[260] where an employee who used spectacles and who needed to wear eye protection for her work found she could not wear the goggles provided. She stopped using them and asked for safety glasses incorporating her own prescription, to be provided at the employer's expense. The safety officer undertook to investigate the employer's reaction to this request. When she heard nothing more, she resigned and successfully claimed constructive dismissal. The employer's failure to investigate the employee's complaint was a fundamental

---

258 [1979] IRLR 84.
259 As in the long-running dispute involving the late Dr Rindos, the facts of which may be found in *University of Western Australia v Rindos* (1995) 76 WAIG 736.
260 [1978] IRLR 332.

breach of the contractual duty to take reasonable care for the safety of employees.

5.133 A case which should be noted in these days of continuous restructuring and reorganisation of work is *Robson v Cambion Electric Products*[261] in which the secretary to the company accountant was promoted by being simultaneously appointed personnel officer with her own secretary. There was then a further reorganisation and she was told that she would revert to being only secretary to her initial superior (by then company secretary), at the same rate of pay, except that an expected 10% increase would not be implemented. She resigned and the tribunal accepted that there had been constructive dismissal.

5.134 In cases of alleged constructive dismissal, it is for the employee to show that this has taken place. The employee must also act reasonably promptly if he or she wishes to use a breach of contract as the basis of a claim for unfair dismissal; otherwise there is a risk that he or she will be regarded as having chosen not to treat the contract as terminated and therefore will not be able to claim constructive dismissal. In *Brown v J B D Engineering Ltd* [262] the EAT held that constructive dismissal may occur even if the employer acts to the employee's detriment (as in this case by filling Brown's post) in a genuine though mistaken belief that the employee has resigned.

Unfairness of dismissals

5.135 The concept of unfair dismissal dates from 1971 and it is now governed by section 94 EmpRA. As every employee has the right not to be unfairly dismissed, the onus is on the employer to show that the dismissal was fair. Section 98 EmpRA provides:

> (1) In determining for the purposes of this Part [of the Act] whether the dismissal of an employee was fair or unfair, it shall be for the employer to show:
> (a) what was the reason (or if there was more than one, the principal reason) for the dismissal, and
> (b) that it was a reason falling within subsection (2) or some other substantial reason of a kind such as to justify the dismissal of an employee holding the position which that employee held.
> (2) A reason falls within this subsection if it–

261 [1976] IRLR 109.
262 [1993] IRLR 568.

(a) relates to the capability or qualifications of the employee for performing work of the kind which he was employed by the employer to do; or
(b) relates to the conduct of the employee; or
(c) is that the employee was redundant; or
(d) is that the employee could not continue to work in the position which he or she held without contravention (either on his or her part or on that of the employer) of a duty or restriction imposed by or under an enactment.

One or more of these reasons must be shown even where the employment is described as probationary (and lasts for more than two years).[263]

Multiple reasons

5.136 If more than one reason is given for dismissal, the employer must show not only which was the principal reason but also how each reason formed part of the principal reason. In *Smith v City of Glasgow District Council*,[264] the employer failed to show which of four reasons given was the principal reason and whether or not the allegations made against the claimant formed part of the principal reason. It is therefore of crucial importance that a higher education institution should form a clear view as to the reason for a dismissal and stick to it.

5.137 Section 98(4) EmpRA provides:

Where the employer has fulfilled the requirements of subsection (1), then, subject to sections 99 to 106, the determination of the question whether the dismissal was fair or unfair, having regard to the reason shown by the employer, shall depend on whether in the circumstances (including the size and administrative resources of the employer's undertaking), the employer acted reasonably or unreasonably in treating it as a sufficient reason for dismissing the employee; and that question shall be determined in accordance with equity and the substantial merits of the case.

Ie 'Did the employer act reasonably or unreasonably in treating the real reason as a sufficient reason for dismissing the employee?' Guidance as to how the tribunal should approach this question was

263 *Weston v University College Swansea* [1975] IRLR 102.
264 [1987] IRLR 326.

set out by the EAT in *Iceland Frozen Foods Ltd v Jones*[265] and in *Post Office (Counters) Ltd v Heavey*.[266] In deciding on the reasonableness of a dismissal, a tribunal may also take into account Codes of Practice, such as that published by ACAS on Disciplinary Practices and Procedures in Employment. There is no particular 'burden of proof' to be discharged. This is important, since many of the decisions in cases prior to 1980 depended on that factor. In *Polkey v A E Dayton Services Ltd*[267] the House of Lords made it clear that the tribunal is concerned with whether the employer's actual action was reasonable, not what might have been the case had the employer acted differently. Just because a rule states that a breach of disciplinary regulations will result in dismissal does not necessarily mean that the dismissal will meet the statutory test of fairness. The test of reasonableness requires the employer to consider all the facts relevant to the breach, including the extent of its gravity.[268]

Reason (i) – Capability and qualifications

5.138 The first reason for dismissal to be considered is that relating to capability and qualifications. 'Qualifications' can be disposed of quickly: if it is a condition of continued employment that an employee must obtain a specified qualification within a set time period (which is likely in any event to be less than the two-year qualifying period) and this is not achieved, it is likely to be a fair dismissal if employment is terminated as a consequence. There are a number of cases in which this situation might arise in higher education, in relation not only to academic staff ('You must obtain your PhD within two years') but also in relation to support staff: part-qualified accountants, medical and nursing staff required to obtain further qualifications, trainee librarians, etc.

5.139 At common law an employee must perform his or her duties with reasonable care;[269] where he or she is engaged in a professional capacity then the employer is entitled to a degree of skill reasonably expected from an ordinary member of that profession.[270] The question

265 [1982] IRLR 439.
266 [1989] IRLR 513.
267 [1987] IRLR 503.
268 *Ladbroke Racing Ltd v Arnott* [1983] IRLR 154; *Marks & Spencer plc v O'Connell* EAT 230/95; *Scottish Daily Record and Sunday Mail (1986) Ltd v Laird* 1997 SLT 345.
269 *Lister v Romford Ice and Cold Storage Co* [1957] AC 555; *Janata Bank v Ahmed* [1981] IRLR 457.
270 Eg in medicine *Hunter v Hanley* 1955 SC 200.

of what constitutes reasonable standards in academic work has been considered separately: it is a difficult one and is tied up with questions of quality assurance and assessment. Capability obviously relates to performance and can become entangled with conduct where there is an element of wilful failure to perform. Where failure to perform is not wilful, in most cases it ought to be possible to identify the problem within two years of a new appointment and in this case no question of an unfair dismissal claim can arise. Problems are more likely to arise when existing staff are promoted to a new role, where there are changes in working techniques to which a longer-serving employee is unable to adapt, or in cases of ill-health which will be considered separately below.

5.140   The guidelines which have been laid down by the courts for dealing with alleged lack of capability are clear:

> An employer may have good grounds for thinking that a man is not capable of doing his job properly, but in the general run of cases it will not be reasonable for him to regard that lack of capability as a sufficient reason for dismissing him until he is given a warning so that the man has a chance to show if he can do better.[271]

The employee must know what is expected of him or her.[272] In *Williams v Southampton Institute of Higher Education*[273] the tribunal was satisfied that the dismissal of Mrs Williams, a lecturer in law, was fair, in that the Institute had an 'honest belief' in her lack of capability.

5.141   The nature of the 'warnings' to be given will naturally depend on the nature of the work being done and the seniority of the employee. In some cases a specific warning may be unnecessary where it is clear that the employee knew that his or her job was at risk. Eg in *A J Dunning & Sons (Shopfitters) Ltd v Jacomb*[274] the applicant's inability to co-operate with the company's clients, which seemed to be an irredeemable incapability, was well-known without the need for a specific warning to be given. In the new era of 'customer care' it may not be safe to assume that all staff whose duties require them to be in contact with the institution's 'customers' are suited to the task. This was true even in 1976: in *White v University of*

---

271 *Vokes Ltd v Bear* [1973] IRLR 363, approved by the House of Lords in *Polkey v A E Dayton Services Ltd* [1987] IRLR 503.
272 *Cresswell v Board of Inland Revenue* [1984] IRLR 190.
273 COIT 45730/95.
274 [1973] ICR 448.

Manchester,[275] one of the reasons for dismissal of Lorna White, a typist, was 'her [alleged] attitude to and treatment of students and other university employees.' It would not be fair to dismiss such employees if they had not been warned about their lack of capability in this area and given the opportunity, including the offer of suitable training, to improve. Senior staff may be assumed to have a good understanding of what is required of them[276] and no specific warning may be required: it will have become clear what the problem is and whether it is capable of being resolved.[277] In all these cases, a properly organised and conducted appraisal scheme should be able to identify weaknesses and recommend action to deal with them. It is, however, vital that if evidence of formal assessment is used to justify the fairness of a dismissal, the assessment has been carried out in a fair and proper manner and, if appropriate, the necessary follow-up action taken. In *Jacomb v British Telecommunications*,[278] BT were able to demonstrate this and a complaint of unfair dismissal failed.

5.142   Naturally, there are some circumstances in which it is justified to dismiss on capability grounds after only one failure to display competence, as where an airline pilot was dismissed following investigation by a Board of Enquiry after an incident involving a passenger-carrying aircraft.[279] Such cases are unlikely to arise in higher education: issues such as the loss of a necessary driving licence or Home Office animal experimentation licence are dealt with separately below.

5.143   Dismissal on grounds of ill-health is a particular aspect of capability and one which requires to be handled with great sensitivity on the part of the employer. The important point is that the decision to dismiss or not is that of the employer, who is entitled to take medical advice and come to a decision in the light of that advice and other relevant circumstances. Except in the most extreme circumstances, the employee should be consulted: the employee may wish to produce medical evidence on his or her own account, which should then be considered by the employer as well.[280] In cases of

275 [1976] IRLR 218.
276 The obligations of professional employees may be defined by reference to the profession *Sim v Rotherham Metropolitan Borough Council* [1986] ICR 897.
277 *Winterhalter Gastronom Ltd v Webb* (1973) 8 ITR 313; *Cook v Thomas Linnell & Sons Ltd* [1977] IRLR 132.
278 COIT 24397/82.
279 *Alidair Ltd v Taylor* [1978] ICR 445.
280 General principles have been laid down by the EAT in such cases as *East Lindsey District Council v Daubney* [1977] IRLR 181, *Lynock v Cereal Packaging Ltd* [1988] ICR 670 and *Ford Motor Co Ltd v Nawaz* [1987] ICR 434.

frequent absences for what may be considered as minor ailments, a requirement to take formal medical advice may be an unreasonable burden on the employer and the EAT has stated that the procedure required should be:

- a fair review by the employer of the attendance record and the reasons for it; and
- appropriate warnings after the employee has been given an opportunity to make representations; and
- if then there is no adequate improvement in the attendance record, it is likely that in most cases the employer will be justified in treating the persistent absences as a sufficient reason for dismissing the employee.

Indeed, the medical adviser if consulted in such cases may be unable to give an opinion: in *International Sports Co Ltd v Thomson*,[281] Mrs Thomson suffered from a series of minor problems, all certificated, including dizzy spells, anxiety and nerves, bronchitis, virus infection, cystitis, althruigria of the left knee, dyspepsia and flatulence. The employer's medical adviser was unable to verify this, nor was he, as a matter of ethics, prepared to contradict the certificates provided by the employee's own doctor.

5.144 Dealing with mental health problems can be much more difficult. In some instances the behaviour of employees manifesting mental ill health can result in dismissal for misconduct and if this is the reason given for dismissal it may in some cases be upheld as fair.[282] Examples of such behaviour might include frequent unexplained absences, insistence on doing work other than that required or making accusations against colleagues without any reasonable ground for doing so.

Reason (ii) – Conduct

5.145 'Misconduct' in a higher education institution can be of very many kinds, ranging from the trivial practical joke (which can still have serious consequences) to the most serious assault, embezzlement or fraud. Practice varies, but it is common to find in disciplinary procedures for support staff a detailed list of offences which will be considered serious enough to warrant summary dismissal, those

---

281 [1980] IRLR 340.
282 In *Thompson v Strathclyde Regional Council* EAT 628/83 the EAT hinted that this might be a better and indeed more sensitive course of action for an employer to adopt than to proceed along the capability route.

considered less serious but still rendering the employee liable to dismissal procedures and those which will normally lead to a disciplinary warning. Such distinctions are not often spelt out so clearly for more senior grades of staff, but in the new statutes drawn up by the University Commissioners for the pre-1992 universities and applying to academic staff only, the distinction is made, although the offences classified as 'serious' are not defined, it being left to the institution to do so if it wishes. In these statutes, which in this aspect are based on the procedures set out in the ACAS Code of Practice on Disciplinary Practice and Procedures in Employment,[283] a procedure for dealing with disciplinary issues is laid down: in those cases which do not justify summary dismissal, the employer should proceed through a series of oral and written warnings.

5.146 If the circumstances in which summary dismissal for misconduct (subject to whatever procedures are laid down in the contract of employment whether expressly or by implication from, eg, the statutes referred to) are not spelt out, then the general principle of law is that the conduct must be such as to fundamentally repudiate the contract of employment. In this sense it mirrors the behaviour by the employer which may lead the employee to claim constructive dismissal. It is for the employer to decide whether to accept the employee's conduct as repudiation, just as in the case of constructive dismissal it is for the employee to decide whether to accept the employer's conduct as repudiation. If the employer elects not to treat the conduct as such, there may be substituted some lesser disciplinary penalty: it is in the institution's interests that it (its designated officer) decides the matter quickly, following such procedures as are set out in the relevant disciplinary code or statute. Some examples of conduct which might be considered to be repudiation are obvious : they include theft, sexual offences, assault, malicious damage to the property of the employer. But these will not automatically lead to dismissal: it is for the employer to decide in all the circumstances and with the employee given an opportunity to put his or her case at the level at which the decision is taken. In principle it would appear to be highly unlikely that criticism of the employer, which might well be held to be misconduct in other settings, would be a fair reason for dismissal of a member of academic staff given the protection of freedom of expression. As evidenced by *University of Glasgow v Gow*,[284] care must be taken when dealing with similar misconduct

---

283 Employment Protection Code of Practice (Disciplinary Practice and Procedures) Order 1977 (SI 1977/ 867).
284 EAT 118/83; see also *Harrow London Borough v Cunningham* [1996] IRLR 256.

by two or more employees. In any event, investigations must be conducted with proper enquiry.[285]

5.147 Misconduct does not have to take place in the course of the actual work, or at the place of work, since the definition in the Act is of a reason which 'related to the conduct of the employee.' The conduct must in some respect or other affect the employee, or could be thought to be likely to affect the employee, when the employee is doing his or her work.[286] This is a very useful negative definition of what constitutes misconduct since, in the case of academic staff at least, it is difficult if not impossible to define precisely whether an employee is at work, or what is the place of work. So long as the conduct affects him or her in carrying out the work, it may be brought within the statutory reason.

5.148 There are few reported tribunal (or higher) decisions on misconduct in higher education establishments, although it is possible to overlook cases brought against the local authorities which formerly were the legal employers of many staff in the former public sector of higher education.[287] One which illustrates how the tribunals may be prepared to hold that a warning is unnecessary before dismissal was Robert Farnborough's case against the Edinburgh College of Art.[288] Mr Farnborough did not agree with the allocation of teaching duties and refused to obey legitimate instructions from his head of department, posting a notice to students to the effect that he did not have time to undertake the specified duties. In his claim for unfair dismissal, he said that he should have received an express warning of the possibility of dismissal. The National Industrial Relations Court decided that the tribunal were entitled to hold that in the circumstances a warning to Mr Farnborough of possible dismissal, as the result of his conduct, was unnecessary. He was

> ... an educated man in a responsible academic position [and] must, or at least certainly ought to, have appreciated ... that his failure to co-operate in the work of the Department as directed by the Head of Department must put his employment at risk.

---

285 *Chamberlain Vinyl Products Ltd v Patel* [1996] ICR 113.
286 *Singh v London Country Bus Services Ltd* (1976) 11 ITR 131.
287 The case most quoted in the FE sector is *Gunton v Richmond-upon-Thames London Borough Council* [1980] 3 All ER 577, CA but that was an allegation of wrongful rather than unfair dismissal.
288 *Farnborough v Governors of the Edinburgh College of Art* [1974] IRLR 245, heard by the National Industrial Relations Court, the predecessor of the EAT.

5.149 Where the conduct for which the employee is dismissed is also potentially the subject of criminal proceedings, the courts have made clear that provided the employer acts reasonably in believing the employee to be guilty of the offence, it is not for the tribunal to decide whether he or she is in fact guilty. If a criminal charge is being pursued simultaneously with the procedure which may ultimately lead to dismissal, it will still be for the employer to take such action as is reasonable in all the circumstances.[289] *Boys and Girls Welfare Society v McDonald*[290] provides a helpful formulation of the way employment tribunals should approach this matter. The starting point is the words of section 94 EmpRA. The tribunal must consider the reasonableness of the employer's conduct, must not substitute its decision for that of the employer and should consider whether the employer's action falls within a band of reasonable responses.[291] This might include dismissal, or suspension pending the outcome of the criminal proceedings (or a decision by the Crown Prosecution Service or procurator-fiscal not to proceed). The courts will only interfere where there is a real danger that there would be a miscarriage of justice in the criminal proceedings if the internal procedure continues.[292]

5.150 In England and Wales, one factor influencing the decision to prosecute or not will be whether it is intended to rely on the evidence of management obtained at the time and if so, whether there has been compliance with the relevant code of practice issued under the Police and Criminal Evidence Act 1984.[293] If it is the manager's contractual duty to investigate, it is likely that the court will require compliance at least so far as the accused's right to legal representation and the giving of a caution are concerned.[294] The Criminal Procedure (Scotland) Act 1995 makes provision of a similar nature to the Police and Criminal Evidence Act; corroborative evidence is required in criminal proceedings. Strict evidential procedures do not apply in any of the UK legal jurisdictions to the internal consideration of a

---

289 *British Home Stores v Burchell* [1978] IRLR 379, approved in *Morgan v Electrolux Ltd* [1991] IRLR 89 and see also *Maclay & Co Ltd v Clark* (1997, unreported), Court of Session, First Division.
290 [1996] IRLR 129.
291 *Iceland Frozen Foods v Jones* [1982] IRLR 439.
292 *R v BBC, ex p Lavelle* [1982] IRLR 404.
293 Code C (revised edition 1991); see also section 67 Police and Criminal Evidence Act 1984, and section 78(1) in relation to the court refusing to allow evidence: *R v Thwaites and Brown* (1990) Daily Telegraph, 11 May, CA. See also Criminal Procedure and Investigation Act 1996.
294 *Joy v Federation against Copyright Software Theft (FAST) Ltd* [1993] Crim LR 588, DC.

disciplinary offence nor to proceedings before employment tribunals. Thus in *Dick v University of Glasgow*[295] it was not fatal to fairness that the employer had failed to have regard to material, when that material was not placed before the employer but was only adduced in evidence before a tribunal. In this case David Dick and Henry Corbett, two members of the University's staff, were dismissed when a recorded delivery packet went missing. Evidence of mistaken identity, which was not put before the University when a decision to dismiss them was taken, was first raised at the tribunal, which found the dismissals to be unfair. The EAT and Court of Session reversed this finding.

5.151 In the event of conviction carrying a lengthy immediate custodial sentence, the contract of employment may be ended by the common law doctrine of frustration (ie it is no longer possible for it to be performed). If a lesser sentence is imposed, the employer will still have to decide whether or not to dismiss and, in the case of serious misconduct such as theft or sexual assault, there should be no real difficulty. In less serious cases the employer will have to give very careful consideration to the circumstances, not just the position of the convicted employee, but also the effect on other employees and customers of a decision to retain the employee's services. In the event of acquittal, it will even then be open to the employer to dismiss, since the burden of proof in civil cases is on the balance of probabilities rather than the stricter 'beyond all reasonable doubt' required for a criminal conviction. An example is *Norfolk County Council v Bernard*[296] where a drama teacher, convicted of possession and cultivation of cannabis, was ruled to have been unfairly dismissed on evidence that he was not an habitual cannabis smoker; there is no rule that a teacher so convicted must automatically be dismissed or that such a dismissal will be fair. And in *University College at Buckingham v Phillips*[297] the college's evidence was that Alan Phillips, a van driver, at first confessed but later retracted his confession to stealing petrol. He denied that he had ever confessed. Overturning an employment tribunal finding of unfair dismissal, the EAT held that in cases where there is a confession and then a retraction, it was for the tribunal to determine whether, in all the circumstances of the case, the employer was reasonable in continuing to rely on the confession. The case was remitted to a different tribunal for determination of exactly what happened at the crucial meeting

295 [1993] IRLR 581, Court of Session, Inner House.
296 [1979] IRLR 220.
297 [1982] ICR 318.

between the college staff and the employee.[298] The lesson here is that where there is a dispute, a clear and careful record should be kept and if possible agreed by the parties.

Reason (iv) – Contravention of a statutory duty or restriction

5.152   Suspension of or loss of a driving licence where this is essential for the job is the most widely cited example under this heading and may arise in certain areas of higher education (Vice-Chancellor's chauffeur, perhaps?) But there are other areas as well: loss of the Home Office licences for animal experimentation; inability to secure a work permit; being struck off the medical or dental register. In deciding whether to dismiss a chauffeur, for example, it is necessary for the employer to consider whether the chauffeur might be redeployed to other duties pending the reinstatement of the driving licence. Alternatively the employee might be discharged but offered re-employment when the licence is reinstated. In every case the issue and the alternatives should be fully discussed with the employee. It is not sufficient merely for the employer to believe that to continue the employment would break the law.[299]

Reason (v) – Some other substantial reason

5.153   EmpRA does not define what is described as 'some other substantial reason' for dismissal, although dismissal of an employee who has been taken on to cover the duties of another employee suspended on statutory or related medical grounds, and who is informed that the employment will be terminated when the suspension ends, is specifically included within the definition.[300] Apart from that, to fall within the provision of the Act the reason has to be 'substantial' and it must be substantial enough to '... justify the dismissal of an employee holding the position which that employee held.' It must not be 'trivial or unworthy.'[301] The operative words are 'an employee holding the position' so that the reason must not be specific to the individual employee dismissed. The Court of Appeal pointed this out in *Dobie v Burns International Security Services (UK)*

---

298 '[The bursar's] evidence on certain points was found to be unreliable by the tribunal': [1982] ICR 318, 321.
299 *Bouchaala v Trusthouse Forte Ltd* [1980] ICR 721.
300 Section 106(1) EmpRA.
301 *Kent County Council v Gilham* [1985] IRLR 18, CA per Griffiths LJ at 21.

Ltd:[302] '… different types of reason could justify the dismissal of the office boy from those which could justify the dismissal of the managing director.' Except where a material disadvantage is shown to be caused to the employee, the tribunals are willing to accept 'some other substantial reason' as the reason for dismissal where, as a matter of law, the reason originally relied upon cannot be sustained. The EAT so held in *Hannan v TNT-IPEC(UK) Ltd*,[303] applying the doctrine established by the Court of Appeal in *Murphy v Epsom College*[304] to a case in which no disadvantage to the employee could be shown when the employment tribunal substituted 'business reorganisation' for 'redundancy' as the true reason for dismissal. A somewhat controversial case was *Ely v YKK Fasteners (UK) Ltd*.[305] In this case Mr Ely had intimated his intention to resign, although he did not actually do so and the employer had appointed a replacement. Mr Ely then changed his mind. He was dismissed and claimed unfair dismissal. The Court of Appeal held that the employment tribunal was entitled to have resort to a state of facts known to and relied on by the employer, for the purpose of supplying him with a reason for dismissal which, as a consequence of his misapprehension of the true nature of the circumstances, he was disabled from treating as such at the time.

5.154 Apart from this, the special cases of genuinely mistaken belief about work permits and the dismissal of forewarned temporary staff hired for specified purposes, there is a wide range of reasons which have been held to fall into the category of 'some other substantial reason.' Those relevant to higher education institutions include:
(i) various aspects and consequences of reorganisation;
(ii) failure to disclose relevant information in job applications;
(iii) irreconcilable clash of personalities;
(iv) imprisonment of the employee.

Reorganisation and restructuring

5.155 Reorganisation or 'restructuring' (to use an expression which found favour with government and government agencies during the 1980s) can and often does give rise to redundancies, whether voluntary or otherwise, and this is treated separately below. But where the reorganisation does not fit the statutory definition of

302 [1984] IRLR 329.
303 [1986] IRLR 165.
304 [1984] IRLR 271.
305 [1993] IRLR 500, CA.

redundancy,[306] a dismissal of an employee who does not co-operate, even where there is no 'proper consultation' as in *Leicester University Students' Union v Mahomed*[307] but is for 'some sound, good business reason,' may be for 'some other substantial reason'[308] although quite separately it may be a breach of contract by the employer. Neither the wording of section 95 EmpRA (meaning of dismissal) nor that of section 98(4) (the 'reasonableness' test) contain any mention of breach of contract, or proposed breach of contract by an employer, as being a factor rendering a dismissal unfair. In the leading case, *Hollister v National Farmers' Union*,[309] Lord Denning MR pointed out again that refusal to co-operate in a reorganisation would be a substantial reason of a kind sufficient to justify dismissal: whether the actual dismissal was justified would depend upon all the circumstances of the case. In determining whether a reorganisation is necessary, the EAT has approved the employment tribunal's statement in *Ladbroke Courage Holdings Ltd v Asten*:[310]

> In deciding whether a dismissal is fair or unfair, we consider it very material to know whether the employer was making profits or losses. We do not consider that an employer can satisfy a tribunal that it was fair to dismiss an employee merely by proving that a ... [manager] ... had instructions to reduce his wages bill, without any evidence as to the reason why the instructions were given.

Where there are sound economic reasons, such as reductions in government funding which lead to reorganisation, as in *Dorney v Chippenham College*[311] dismissals may be fair.

Job applications

5.156 Although the recruitment practices of institutions vary, all will have in place some process by which people apply in writing for jobs. The safest way to ensure that at this stage the employer obtains all the information required to process the application is to use a standard application form. Many institutions, particularly the pre-

---

306 Which is also used in the statutes prepared by the University Commissioners for the pre-1992 universities.
307 [1995] ICR 270.
308 *Ellis v Brighton Co-operative Society Ltd* [1976] IRLR 419; adopted by the Court of Appeal in *Hollister v National Farmers' Union* [1979] IRLR 238.
309 [1979] IRLR 238.
310 [1981] IRLR 59.
311 COIT 61591/95.

1992 universities, adopt the practice of applications, for academic and other senior posts in particular, being by letter and non-standard curriculum vitae. This alone makes it difficult to justify taking action against an employee who has failed to disclose material information, if it was not asked for, particularly if it was not sought at interview either. The general principle is that there is no duty on the prospective employee to disclose information unless asked directly.[312] Examples might include treatment for medical conditions (including mental health problems)[313] or convictions (subject to the provisions of the Rehabilitation of Offenders Act 1974). In *Langdon v Henlys of Barnes*[314] there was a fair dismissal when references, essential for insurance purposes, arrived 18 months after employment started and were considered to be unsatisfactory.

Clash of personalities

5.157   Clashes of personalities seem inevitable in academic life and can normally be resolved by the processes of discussion and mediation. Sometimes, however, they are irreconcilable and in such cases, provided that they are having a seriously adverse effect on the organisation and no alternative employment is available, this may constitute a substantial reason for dismissal[315] rendering it fair, although the dismissal might be wrongful in terms of the procedures set out in the 'Model' statute where this applies.

Imprisonment

5.158   For convictions unrelated to the employment and which might therefore not fall under the 'conduct' reason for dismissal, a substantial period of imprisonment may frustrate the contract so that it is no longer in being. In any case a shorter period might be considered sufficient reason for dismissal, particularly where, as in the case of *Kingston v British Rlys Board*,[316] the absence of the employee meant that the normal disciplinary procedures could not be followed.

---

312 *Walton v TAC Construction Materials Ltd* [1981] IRLR 357.
313 This occurred in a university in the 1980s and the member of staff, who had tenure, was not sufficiently ill to justify ill-health retirement. The only option was a negotiated financial agreement to part company.
314 COIT 1849/91.
315 *Treganowan v R Knee & Co Ltd* [1975] IRLR 247.
316 [1984] IRLR 146.

Other reasons for dismissal

5.159 Dismissal of a female employee on grounds that she is pregnant constitutes direct discrimination on grounds of sex, contravening the EC Equal Treatment Directive (76/207), as does refusal to recruit a pregnant woman,[317] and is automatically unfair under section 99 EmpRA. Section 100 EmpRA protects employees dismissed or otherwise suffering detriment for specified activities relating to health and safety. These include carrying out health and safety work as designated by the employer or as a safety representative or, where there is no safety representative, bringing matters to the employer's attention. They also include taking emergency action in cases of danger to the employee or other workers, unless the employer could reasonably treat this behaviour as negligent, reasonableness to be assessed in the usual way. The two-year qualifying period of service does not apply. Section 104 EmpRA provides protection against dismissal for assertion of a range of statutory rights, whether or not the employee actually has the right in question and whether or not it has been infringed,[318] subject only to the employee acting in good faith. The statutory rights concerned include any right conferred by EmpRA and which may be the subject of a complaint to an employment tribunal and rights in relation to deductions from pay, union activities and time off conferred by EmpRA. The two-year qualifying period of service does not apply. Section 238 TULRCA relates to unfair dismissal of employees taking part in industrial action.

Redundancy

5.160 The present law relating to redundancy is contained in section 188 TULRCA and Part XI EmpRA. These relate, respectively, to the requirement for consultation with appropriate representatives of employees before redundancies are effected (which in respect of recognised trades unions dates from 1975) and to the rights of individuals who may be made redundant (which, in respect of redundancy payments, dates from 1965). Section 139 EmpRA defines a dismissal as being by reason of redundancy if, wholly or mainly, it is attributable to the fact either

---

317 *Handels-og Kontorfunktionaerernes Forbund i Danmark (for Hertz) v Dansk Arbejdsgiverforening (for Aldi Marked K/S)*: C-179/88 [1991] IRLR 31.
318 See *Mennell v Newell & Wright (Transport Contractors) Ltd* [1996] IRLR 384.

that the employer has ceased, or intends to cease, to carry on the business for the purposes of which the employee was employed by him or ... to carry on that business in the place in which the employee was so employed[319] or

that the requirements of that business for employees to carry out work of a particular kind ... have ceased or diminished.[320]

Such cessation or diminution may arise from whatever cause and encompass a temporary cessation or diminution.[321] A reduction in the number of employees required to carry out an undiminished volume of work, giving rise to redundancy, may arise through technological change,[322] where employees are replaced by outside contractors,[323] where posts are abolished and duties redistributed[324] or two posts merged into one.[325] A redundancy will not arise where the employer seeks to replace an employee with someone with different personal characteristics[326] or at a lower grade[327] or changes terms and conditions, eg shift hours[328] or if the employer seeks to reassign the employee to other contractual duties.[329] Statutes made by the University Commissioners under section 203 ERA use a definition closely based on the statutory wording. The employer does not have to justify its decision to make redundancies or explain the economic or commercial reasons which prompted that decision.[330] So a higher education institution will not have to show that it acted reasonably in creating a redundancy situation. The tribunal would be concerned to see that it was a genuine redundancy situation and not a 'front' for dismissal for some other reason.

319 To be determined on the basis of a factual rather than a contractual test: *Bass Leisure Ltd v Thomas* [1994] IRLR 104; *Safeway Stores plc v Burrell* [1997] IRLR 200; *High Table Ltd v Horst* [1997] IRLR 513, CA.
320 As in *Association of University Teachers v University of Newcastle Upon Tyne* [1987] ICR 317 where EAT held that there was a redundancy situation when a course was discontinued following the withdrawal of external funding even though there had been no decrease in the demand for the course.
321 *Gemmell v Darngavil Brickworks Ltd* (1967) 2 ITR 20.
322 *Scarth v Economic Forestry Ltd* [1973] ICR 322.
323 *Bromby & Hoare Ltd v Evans* [1972] ICR 113: where employees are transferred to the outside contractor the Transfer of Undertakings (TUPE) Regulations will apply.
324 *Sutton v Revlon Overseas Corpn Ltd* [1973] IRLR 173; *Delanair v Mead* [1976] ICR 522 (even where other employees had to work overtime as a result).
325 *Carry All Motors Ltd v Pennington* [1980] ICR 806.
326 *Vaux and Associated Breweries Ltd v Ward (No 2)* (1970) 5 ITR 62.
327 *Pillinger v Manchester Area Health Authority* [1979] IRLR 430.
328 *Johnson v Nottinghamshire Combined Police Authority* [1974] ICR 170.
329 *Nelson v BBC* [1977] IRLR 148; *Same v Same (No 2)* [1979] IRLR 346.
330 *James W Cook & Co (Wivenhoe) Ltd v Tipper* [1990] IRLR 386.

5.161 The requirement for employers to consult appropriate representatives when redundancies are proposed (except where there are special, unforeseen circumstances)[331] is now set out in TULRCA[332] implementing a European Directive.[333] This was formerly known as a 'section 99' requirement since it was introduced in a slightly different form by section 99 Employment Protection Act 1975. Where the employees are of a description in respect of which an independent trade union is recognised by the employer, the appropriate representatives will be those of the trade union, whether or not the employees are actual members.[334] Consultation must begin 'in good time' and must in any event begin within a specified period depending on the number proposed to be dismissed. For the purposes of the consultation the employer must provide the representatives, in writing,[335] with the reasons for the redundancies, the numbers and descriptions of employees whom it is proposed to dismiss, the total number of employees employed, the proposed method of selecting those to be made redundant and the proposed method of carrying out the dismissals. The objective is to reach agreement with the representatives.[336] Failure to comply may result in an award being made by an employment tribunal to the affected individuals.[337] Separately, under section 193 TULRCA, the employer must notify the Secretary of State when it is proposed to make 20 or more employees redundant. A form (HR1) is available for this purpose. Failure to comply is a criminal offence.

5.162 It has also been held that a reasonable employer will at least discuss the possibility of alternative employment with an employee, even if consultation with the representatives has resulted in an agreed

---

331 A deteriorating financial situation does not fit this description: *Clarks of Hove Ltd v Bakers' Union* [1978] IRLR 366; but a sudden financial crisis might: *General Municipal and Boilermens' Union v Rankin* [1992] IRLR 514.

332 Sections 188-194 TULRCA as amended by the Collective Redundancies and Transfer of Undertakings (Protection of Employment)(Amendment) Regulations 1995 (SI 1995/2587) following the decision of the ECJ in *EC Commission v United Kingdom*: C-382/92 [1994] ICR 664 relating to the implementation of the EC Collective Redundancies Directive 75/129/EEC.

333 If a higher education institution is an 'emanation of the state' as discussed earlier, the Directive is directly enforceable.

334 *Northern Ireland Hotel and Catering College v National Association of Teachers in Further and Higher Education* [1995] IRLR 83, NI CA.

335 *Transport and General Workers' Union v Nationwide Haulage* [1978] IRLR 143.

336 Section 188(6) TULRCA.

337 In a case concerned with unfair dismissal, not of alleged failure to consult, the EAT spelt out what it would expect of a reasonable employer carrying out the 'section 99' consultation: *Dyke v Hereford and Worcester County Council* [1989] ICR 800.

procedure which would lead to that employee being dismissed.[338] It does not matter that the employer believes that the redundant employee was the only person who could be made redundant: there are other good reasons why consultation should take place.[339] It is a question of fact and degree for the tribunal to consider whether consultation with the individual and with the representatives was so inadequate as to render the dismissal unfair.[340] The tribunal can take into account that consultation in reality would have made no difference and limit any award to the period by which the dismissal would have been postponed if consultation had taken place[341] or reduce compensation by an appropriate percentage to reflect the chance that the employee would have been dismissed in any event[342] unless the unfairness related to criteria for selection.[343]

5.163   The last occasion on which many of the pre-1992 universities had to undertake a general section 99 consultation was in the aftermath of the 1981 reductions in recurrent grant imposed by the University Grants Committee as a consequence of cuts in public expenditure.[344] Now the issues largely concern expiry of fixed-term contracts. Even one proposed redundancy attracts the duty to consult, as in the case of *Association of University Teachers v University of Newcastle-Upon-Tyne*[345] which involved dismissal for redundancy of a temporary lecturer. As explained in *University of Glasgow v Donaldson*[346] the employee should be consulted and the employer should consider whether there are vacancies to which the potentially redundant employee could be appointed. In respect of waiver clauses, the position is that if the original fixed-term contract is renewed for a further term of two years or less and during that extended term the parties enter into a waiver agreement, dismissal arising out of the expiry of the original fixed term as extended will not give rise to a claim for a redundancy payment.[347] In *Pfaffinger v City of Liverpool*

---

338 *Huddersfield Parcels Ltd v Sykes* [1981] IRLR 115.
339 *Heron v Citylink-Nottinghm* [1993] IRLR 372.
340 *Mugford v Midland Bank* [1997] IRLR 208.
341 *Mining Supplies (Longwall) Ltd v Baker* [1988] IRLR 417.
342 *Dunlop Ltd v Farrell* [1993] ICR 885.
343 *Steel Stockholders (Birmingham) Ltd v Kirkwood* [1993] IRLR 515.
344 It should be recalled that at least one institution treated the departure of staff under premature retirement arrangements as termination of contract by mutual agreement, not by redundancy, and that this was upheld by the Court of Appeal – *Birch and Humber v University of Liverpool* [1985] IRLR 165.
345 [1988] IRLR 10.
346 [1995] 522 IRLB 13, EAT.
347 *Housing Services Agency v Cragg* [1997] IRLR 380.

Community College; Muller v Amersham and Wycombe College[348]
it was held that expiry of contracts at the end of a course or academic
year is by reason of redundancy, requiring advance consultation with
representatives and entitling the employees to a redundancy payment;
continuity of employment is not broken if the employee is re-engaged.

5.164   Actual selection for redundancy will depend upon the agreed
procedure or customary arrangement which is reasonably certain:[349]
if there is an agreed procedure or arrangement and the employer seeks
to depart from it, some objective criteria will have to be demonstrated
to justify that course of action.[350] In *Rolls-Royce Motor Cars Ltd v
Price*[351] the employers were justified in departing from an agreement
based on LIFO (Last In, First Out) because this would have defeated
the objective of 'carrying the business forward in difficult times.'
Otherwise, the employer will be obliged to select objective criteria
such as length of service like LIFO (unlikely to be desirable in an
educational redundancy situation), experience or attendance
record.[352] If experience equates to seniority, that may be
discriminatory on grounds of sex if used as a criterion,[353] as in some
circumstances may 'flexibility' in terms of mobility or hours of
work[354] or attendance when absences due to pregnancy and maternity
are involved.[355] 'Attendance' as a criterion should be used only where
there has been an examination of the reasons for absence[356] but
employees do not have to be warned in advance that a poor
attendance record would render them vulnerable to selection for
redundancy.[357] Performance is obviously an area in which subjective
judgment is likely to influence objectivity, unless extremely careful
steps are taken as in *Anderson v Potterton Myserson Radiators*[358]
where a complex assessment scheme run along something resembling
military lines was accepted as being sufficiently objective, particularly
as it was one of a set of criteria including wholly objective details of

348 [1996] IRLR 508.
349 *Suflex Ltd v Thomas* [1987] IRLR 435.
350 *Tilgate Pallets Ltd v Barras* [1983] IRLR 231.
351 [1993] IRLR 203.
352 Guidelines were laid down by the EAT in *Williams v Compair Maxam Ltd* [1982]
     IRLR 83.
353 *Nimz v Freie und Hansestadt Hamburg* C-184/89 [1991] IRLR 222.
354 *Handels-og Kontorfunktionaerernes Forbund i Danmark v Dansk
     Arbeijdsgiverforening (acting for Danfoss)*: 109/88 [1989] IRLR 532.
355 *Dekker v Stichting Vormingscentrum voor Jong Volwassenen Plus*: C-177/88
     [1991] IRLR 27.
356 *Paine and Moore v Grundy (Teddington) Ltd* [1981] IRLR 267.
357 *Gray v Shetland Norse Preserving Co Ltd* [1985] IRLR 53.
358 COIT 27786/90.

each employee's position in the company. In the *Page* case, the criterion used for selecting Edgar Page from among the staff of the Department of Philosophy at the University of Hull was age. That at least can be determined objectively. Criteria considered by the courts to be too subjective include 'attitude to work'[359] and 'personnel less suited for the needs of the business under the new operating conditions.'[360] Where a criterion for selection is in fact applied unfairly, the tribunal will consider whether in practice it would have made any difference if the criterion had been applied fairly, and set compensation accordingly, on the test of whatever is 'just and equitable' in terms of the Act.[361]

5.165 Dismissal for redundancy does not occur if the employer makes the employee an offer of suitable alternative employment which the employee unreasonably refuses. Suitable vacancies should be offered to the employee if they arise during the notice period.[362] EmpRA provides for employees to have a period of four weeks in which to try another job without losing their entitlement to redundancy payments. If a redundant employee is offered alternative employment which is 'suitable employment in relation to the employee'[363] and he or she unreasonably refuses it either before or during the trial period, entitlement to redundancy payments is lost. In 1993 the EAT defined 'suitable alternative employment' as being not only suitable in the objective sense – ie that it is substantially equivalent to the previous employment in terms of earnings and status, but also in the employee's personal perception.[364] Unsuitable offers may include those involving a drop in status[365] or reduction in pay.[366] The tribunal must decide as a matter of fact the reasonableness of the employee's attitude in terms of his or her behaviour and conduct.[367]

359 *Graham v ABF Ltd* [1986] IRLR 90.
360 *Smith v Haverhill Meat Products Ltd* (unreported).
361 *Pickrose Co Ltd (t/a Long Airdox (Cardox) Ltd) v Jones* (1993) unreported, EAT.
362 *Stacey v Babcock Power Co* [1986] ICR 221.
363 Sections 138, 141 and 144 EmpRA .
364 *Cambridge and District Co-operative Society v Ruse* [1993] IRLR 156.
365 *Taylor v Kent County Council* [1969] 2 QB 560.
366 *Kennedy v Werneth Ring Mills Ltd* [1977] ICR 206.
367 *Executors of Everest v Cox* (1993) unreported.

Remedies for unfair dismissal or selection for redundancy

5.166 As might be expected of a system which is meant to be a statutory minimum protection against unfair actions by employers, the remedies available are limited in scope and quantum. Where a tribunal decides a claim for unfair dismissal is well-founded, the outcome can be
(a) an order for reinstatement (ie to the same job); or
(b) an order for re-engagement (ie to a comparable job); or
(c) an award of compensation.

5.167 The tribunal must ask the claimant whether he or she wishes an order for reinstatement or re-engagement be made; if that is not the case, or if the tribunal decides not to make one – for example, if it is considered impracticable for the employer to comply or if it seems inequitable because there has been contributory fault on the part of the employee – then an award of compensation can be made. If an employer fails to comply with an order for reinstatement or re-engagement, then the tribunal will award additional compensation, ie over and above the basic sum under (c). This is an option not infrequently taken by employers who prefer to make larger payments in order to avoid taking an employee back into employment. To this extent the remedies open to tribunals may be regarded as ineffective but, in fact, in successful wrongful dismissal cases it is usual for monetary compensation (of somewhat larger sums) to be awarded and the wrongfully dismissed employee rarely gets the job back. Section 124(3) EmpRA allows tribunals to exceed the statutory limits to the extent necessary to enable the award to fully reflect the amount specified as payable when reinstatement or re-engagement is ordered.

5.168 There are four types of award for compensation for unfair dismissal:
(i) a basic award calculated by reference to length of continuous service and age and expressed in terms of a week's pay up to a maximum which is revised from time to time;
(ii) a compensatory award to reflect the employee's loss;
(iii) an additional award if the employer fails to comply with a reinstatement or re-engagement order: if the dismissal was in contravention of SDA or RRA, the maximum award under this head is doubled: the current limits may in certain circumstances be exceeded;
(iv) a special award for dismissal relating to trade union membership or activities or victimisation attributable to the employee's health and safety activities: this is in lieu of an additional award: when

no re-engagement or reinstatement order is made the maximum award is smaller than when such an order is made but is not complied with.

Where the employee is considered as having caused or significantly contributed to the dismissal, the tribunal may reduce the calculated award. There may also be a reduction in respect of a separate statutory redundancy payment.

Grievances and complaints

5.169 The Model Statute sets out procedures for handling grievances, which if not resolved internally might otherwise be brought to the Visitor or (depending on their nature) the courts or employment tribunals. Following the second report of the Committee on Standards of Conduct in Public Life (the Nolan Committee) CVCP recommended that all institutions accept the principle that staff should be able to settle appeals and disputes by independent review. When considering this, the Nolan committee had in mind such issues as maladministration, financial and non-financial malpractice and cases concerning academic standards and academic freedom. CUC issued 'Advice on Whistleblowing' in October 1997. Personal grievances, matters connected with individual terms of employment or decisions of promotion boards were not at issue. Either the Visitor or a panel of independent members could deal with such cases.

Trade disputes

5.170 Disputes in higher education are usually about pay, whether it be the annual pay settlement or some element of pay such as discretionary sums awarded for performance. The right to strike or to take other industrial action is well established as part of collective bargaining and it is also established that withdrawal of labour by an employee is a breach of contract which the employer is entitled to treat as repudiating the contract of employment. In practice the employer normally allows the contract to continue but deducts payment for the period of the strike on the basis permitted by Part II EmpRA. Suspension without pay is a breach of contract unless justified by the terms of the contract.[368] In such circumstances, it was established by the EAT in 1993 in *Sunderland Polytechnic v Evans*,[369]

---

368 *McArdle v Scotbeef* 1974 SLT (Notes) 78.
369 [1993] ICR 392.

an employment tribunal has no jurisdiction under the provisions of what is now sections 14(8) and 16(3) EmpRA to hear claims of unlawful deduction. The case, in which Mrs Ann Evans claimed that the former polytechnic was wrong to deduct 1/365 of her annual salary when she took part in a half-day strike in November 1990, could only be heard in the courts. Precedent would suggest that the claim would be unlikely to succeed either in England[370] or in Scotland.[371] The *Sunderland Polytechnic* case is of wider interest since it is one of the first in which a court (the EAT) had used the authority given by the House of Lords in *Pepper v Hart*[372] to examine the words used by the relevant government minister in Parliament to ascertain the meaning of a phrase used in an Act of Parliament.

5.171 Industrial action short of strike is rather more difficult to deal with. A selective withdrawal from duties might take the form of a boycott of examining or other duties, as indeed came very close to happening in the pre-1992 universities in 1989 and 1996. In such circumstances, the employer must fall back on the contract of employment and determine whether the failure to carry out the particular duty is a breach of contract which would enable the employer to treat the contract as repudiated. In the case of 'whole time' contracts it seems obvious that the employer is entitled to withhold 1/365 (or 1/366 in 1996 as a leap year) of pay for a one-day strike, not 1/260 as was widely canvassed in 1996. Whether or not the whole time contract is compatible with the terms of the EU Working Time Directive has yet to be resolved. Some guidance on deductions is found in *Royle v Trafford Borough Council*[373] in which a teacher who on union instructions refused to add five extra pupils to his 'normal' class of 31 was in breach of contract, but the appropriate penalty was a 5/36 deduction in pay rather than a six months' pay deduction as 'damages' imposed by the employer who had impliedly affirmed the contract by accepting partial performance over the period in question. In *Henthorn v CEGB*[374] power station workers working to rule who had had pay stopped failed to recover it on application to the court, since it was held that the burden of proof was on them to show, as persons claiming money under a contract, that they were fully willing and able to affirm the contract.

---

370 *Miles v Wakefield Metropolitan District Council* [1987] AC 539; Apportionment Act 1870.
371 *Buchanan v Strathclyde Regional Council* (1981) unreported, OH.
372 [1993] ICR 291.
373 [1984] IRLR 184.
374 [1980] IRLR 361, EAT.

In *Wiluszynski v Tower Hamlets London Borough Council*[375] an estate officer, in furtherance of a NALGO dispute with the Council, refused to answer one or two enquiries a week from Council members but otherwise performed his duties normally. The Court of Appeal, reversing the judge's decision that he was entitled to be paid, ruled that he was in breach of contractual conditions in a small but constitutionally important respect and, therefore, the Council was entitled to refuse to pay him. And in *Ticehurst v British Telecommunications plc*[376] Mrs Ticehurst and a colleague were managers who participated in industrial action including half-day strikes (a 'rolling campaign' of strategic action designed to disrupt BT's business). In dismissing their claim for pay when BT sent them home for refusing to give an undertaking to work in accordance with their contracts, the Court of Appeal held that managers had to exercise their duties faithfully in the interests of the employer. If they failed to do so, by for example evincing an intention to participate in withdrawal of goodwill, the employers were entitled to refuse to let them remain at work, without terminating the contract of employment.

5.172 Naturally, institutions took legal advice in this area at the time of the threatened action in 1989 and 1996. They were particularly concerned since in many cases it appeared that failure to set, mark and communicate the results of examinations (and, in those institutions in which they formed an important part of assessment, periodic tests) would be a breach of the institution's contract with its students rendering the institution liable for damages.[377] Once again, the precise nature of the duties which academic staff could be required to undertake, and who could require them to undertake those duties, depended upon a detailed examination of the governing instruments of the institution, its domestic rules and, most importantly, the written terms and conditions of employment. In 1996 when withdrawal of co-operation from inspections by the Office for Standards in Education (OFSTED) on behalf of TTA was contemplated, a situation which might have led to withdrawal of accreditation, it was recognised that there might be a legitimate cause of action by trainee teachers against the institutions.

375 [1989] IRLR 259, CA.
376 [1992] IRLR 219.
377 Taking a pragmatic view, the Research Councils indicated that subject to certain safeguards they would accept academic judgment of candidates for postgraduate awards in lieu of actual results if it proved impossible to grant degrees due to industrial action.

Trade unions and their members

5.173 Trade disputes almost certainly involve trades unions, although the legal definition of a trade dispute is one 'between employers and workers, or between workers and workers.'[378] It is fair to say that the trend of employment legislation since 1980 has been away from granting special status to trades unions and their members, towards restricting the activities in which they may lawfully engage, granting statutory rights to members which previously existed, if at all, as incidents of the contract of membership and granting rights, in certain circumstances, to those affected by industrial action organised by trades unions. The political objective was to remove most of the incidents of the favourable position which trades unions enjoyed prior to the election of the Conservative Government in 1979, while permitting them to conduct their affairs on democratic lines, with due regard to the rights of their members ('returning the unions to their members') and those who may be affected by their activities. For example since 1982 any term or condition in a commercial contract is void if it requires that the whole, or some part, of the work to be done under the contract is to be done only be members of trades unions, or of a particular union, or non-members of either. The long-standing and wide-ranging 'trade disputes immunity' which has existed since 1906[379] namely

> An act done by a person, or a trade union if the act has been authorised or endorsed by a responsible person, in contemplation or furtherance of a trade dispute is not actionable in tort[380] on the grounds that:
> (a) it induces another person to break a contract or induces any other person to interfere with its performance; or
> (b) it consists in the person threatening that a contract (whether he is a party to it or not) will be broken or its performance interfered with, or that he will induce another person to break a contract or interfere with its performance.[381]

has been modified so that a number of types of dispute are excluded from the protection, namely:
(i) enforcement of union membership;
(ii) dismissal for taking unofficial industrial action;
(iii) secondary industrial action (other than lawful picketing);[382]

---

378 Section 218(1) TULRCA.
379 Trade Disputes Act 1906.
380 Delict in Scotland.
381 Section 219(1) TULRCA.
382 See Code of Practice on Picketing 1992.

(iv) pressure to impose union recognition.[383]
In order to be protected under the trade disputes immunity there must
have taken place a secret ballot held in the manner prescribed by
TULRCA[384] and trades unions must give employers at least seven
days' notice of industrial action[385] supplying a list of names.[386] In
Blackpool and Fylde College v NATFHE[387] a notice informing the
employer that all the union's members employed by the union would
take discontinuous industrial action was held not to be sufficiently
precise or specific. In *University of Central England v National and
Local Government Officers' Association*,[388] the High Court held the
legislation imposed no requirement that entitlement to vote in a ballot
must be restricted to the employees of one employer. Thus those
institutions represented by the Polytechnics and Colleges Employers'
Forum could be treated as one employer for this purpose.

5.174   Trade union officials and members retain some rights granted
by the Labour employment protection legislation of the 1970s, and
although the details have been subject to amendment, the principles
are the same. These are rights to time off for trade union duties and
activities and the right not to be penalised through being a member
of a particular union.

5.175   Under section 235(A) TULRCA anyone deprived of goods
or services because of unlawful industrial action has the right to take
court proceedings to stop this happening. Assistance may be sought
from the Commissioner for Protection against Unlawful Industrial
Action.

Confidentiality and post-termination restrictions

Confidentiality

5.176   It is one of the common law duties owed by an employee to
an employer that the former will keep the latter's trade secrets, which
would include customer contacts where there is a market place for
the product. The principles are set out in the judgment of the Court

383 Sections 220 -225 TULRCA.
384 Section 226 TULRCA.
385 Section 234(A) TULRCA: see also DTI *Code of Practice – Industrial Action
Ballots and Notice to Employers 1996.*
386 Section 226A TULRCA.
387 [1994] IRLR 227, CA.
388 [1993] IRLR 81.

498 ♦ The employment of staff

of Appeal in *Faccenda Chicken v Fowler*[389] as follows. The duty of fidelity owed by an employee during the currency of the contract of employment is contractual, whether as an express or implied term of the contract of employment. So an employee cannot lawfully disclose information or assist a competitor, whether in 'paid' or 'own' time. An ex-employee may be under a duty not to disclose confidential information such as trade secrets. Relevant factors in determining whether or not information is confidential for this purpose include the nature of the employment, the nature of the information, whether the employer regarded the information as being confidential and informed the employee of this and how easy it is to distinguish this information from that which the ex-employee is free to use.

5.177 In higher education, most academic staff are not in the position of possessing marketable secrets or contacts gained other than in the course of normal and indeed expected professional development. The particular case of ownership of copyright in course materials, etc, will be dealt with separately. A member of the administrative staff, such as one in possession of the institution's financial forecasts not yet in the public domain, or one who can predict major problems in student recruitment, may be in a position to embarrass the institution and possibly cause it harm. Where an employee does fall into the category in which protection is felt necessary, the model clause drafted in 1990 by the ACAS Working Party on Teaching Staff Contracts appears to offer an appropriate solution:

1. You shall not, except as authorised by [the institution] or required by your duties hereunder, use for your own benefit or gain or divulge to any persons firm company or other organisations whatsoever any confidential information belonging to [the institution] or relating to its affairs or dealings which may come to your knowledge during your employment. This restriction shall cease to apply to any information or knowledge which may subsequently come into the public domain other than by way of unauthorised disclosure.
2. All confidential records, documents and other papers (together with any copies or extracts thereof) made or acquired by you in the course of your employment shall be the property of [the institution] and must be returned to it on the termination of your employment.
3. Confidential information must be determined in relation to individual employees according to their status, responsibilities and the nature of their duties. However it shall include all information

389 [1987] Ch 117.

which has been specifically designated as confidential by [the institution] and any information which relates to the commercial and financial activities of [the institution], the unauthorised disclosure of which would embarrass harm or prejudice [the institution]. It does not extend to the information already in the public domain, unless such information arrived by unauthorised means.

4. Notwithstanding the above [the institution] affirms that academic staff have freedom within the law to question and test received wisdom, and to put forward new ideas and controversial or unpopular opinions, without placing themselves in jeopardy of losing their jobs and privileges they have at [the institution].

Post-termination restrictions

5.178 In certain circumstances it is permissible, and occasionally desirable even in a higher education institution, to make an appointment subject to a restrictive covenant or, as it is now more commonly known, a post-termination restriction. The example quoted by Robert Seaton[390] is of the medical school which wished to establish a teaching practice in an area where the local NHS committee responsible considered there was already a surfeit of general practitioners scraping a living. The compromise reached was that the senior lecturer who was to be one of the principals in the practice signed a restrictive covenant preventing him practising as a general practitioner in that area for a period of three years following his future departure from university employment.

5.179 There was no agreement in 1990 in the ACAS Working Party on Teaching Staff contracts on the issue of post-termination restrictions and, indeed, the chairman drafted a provision to deal with a problem which he thought would be self-solving, as such restrictions, which must be fully contractual, are normally invalid unless justified as necessary and reasonable. It is not possible, for example, to stop an employee taking away the skills and experience which the employer loses. The interests which the institution seeks to protect must be sufficiently essential to its business, as in *RS Components v Irwin*[391] where a company distributing electrical components introduced a new service agreement with a restrictive covenant preventing employees from competing in the same business

---

390 R Seaton 'University Staff and Employment Law' in D J Farrington and F T Mattison (eds) *Universities and the Law* CUA/CRS (1990).
391 [1973] IRLR 239.

in the same geographical area for a period of 12 months after leaving the company's employment. Mr Irwin refused to sign and was dismissed. It was held that the dismissal was fair, since the employer had a substantial reason for the restrictive covenant and was entitled to seek protection against competition. In *Office Angels v Rainer-Thomas*[392] two employees of a recruitment consultancy successfully challenged a restriction on working within 1,000 metres of their former branch: the area in question was the City of London and the Court of Appeal considered this to be unreasonable. In *GFI Group Inc v Eaglestone*[393] the issue was whether the employee could be held to a 20-week notice period, during which full salary and benefits would be paid by the employer, before starting work for a competitor. The court took into account the fact that Mr Eaglestone was a very highly paid employee with considerable experience and that his relationship with customers had been built up at the employer's expense. On the balance of convenience, a notice period of 13 weeks was enforced. Similarly in *Credit Suisse Asset Management Ltd v Armstrong*[394] an attempt to enforce a 12 month 'rest' was reduced to six months.

5.180 The chairman of the ACAS Working Party suggested the following clause which deals with teaching and training services:

> 1. You undertake that you will not (without the consent in writing of the [governing body] for a period of twelve months immediately following the termination of your employment either on your own account or in conjunction with or on behalf of any person, firm, company or other organisation, and whether as an employee, director, principal, agent, consultant, or in any other capacity whatsoever, in competition with [the institution] provide teaching or training services to any client of [the institution]:
> (i)   with whom you shall have had personal contact or dealings on behalf of [the institution] during the two years immediately preceding the termination of your employment; or
> (ii) with whom employees reporting to you have had personal contact or dealings on behalf of [the institution] during the two years immediately preceding the termination of your employment.
>
> 2. You undertake that you will not (without the consent in writing of [the governing body]) for a period of twelve months immediately following the termination of your employment either on your own account or in conjunction with or on behalf of any person, firm,

392 [1991] IRLR 214.
393 [1994] IRLR 119.
394 [1996] IRLR 450, CA.

company or other organisation whatsoever in competition with [the institution] solicit induce or procure any client: ...
   [(i) & (ii) as above] ...

to accept the performance or provision of teaching or training services by you whether as an employee, director, principal, agent, consultant or in any other capacity whatsoever.

3. For the purposes of this clause 'client' shall mean any person, firm, company or other organisation whatsoever to whom [the institution] has supplied teaching or training services for payment or other consideration, but excluding any person enrolled by [the institution] as a student.

5.181   Teaching and training is not defined, but would presumably include the preparation of distance learning material as well as the short courses and similar activities which are its prime target. The clause could be adapted to include research contracts, consultancies and other services in addition to teaching and training. It now seems unlikely that the 12 months would be enforceable on the basis of the *GFI* and *Credit Suisse* cases.

References

5.182   Most senior staff will be called upon to write references for subordinate staff seeking job moves or promotion, or former colleagues or peers seeking support in various ways. There is no obligation to do so, except in the unlikely event that it is an express term of the contract of employment.[395]

Extent of duty of care owed to employee

5.183   It is now clear from the decision of the House of Lords in *Spring v Guardian Assurance plc*[396] that a person giving a reference owes a duty of care in the tort of negligence to the subject of the reference. The duty of the referee to the subject of the reference is

---

395 *Moult v Halliday* [1898] 1 QB 125; *Gallear v J F Watson & Son Ltd* [1979] IRLR 306; in Scotland *Fell v Lord Ashburton* (12 December 1809, unreported), FC.
396 [1994] 3 All ER 129. See S D Migdal and A E M Holmes 'References – Beware Playing the Good Samaritan' (1993) Business Law Review 144; D Brodie 'Protecting Reputations' (1994) SLT 365.

not one exclusively governed by the tort of defamation.[397] Employers should note that if a favourable reference is given to an employee who then claims unfair dismissal, it will be difficult to argue that the employee had been fairly dismissed for incompetence.[398] There is no provision in the anti-discrimination legislation relating to former employees (as opposed to potential and serving employees) so no action under RRA can lie against an employer accused of giving an unfavourable reference on racial grounds.[399] However section 4(2) Rehabilitation of Offenders Act 1974 provides a statutory defence for failure to give accurate information in a reference relating to spent convictions.

Extent of duty of care owed to person seeking reference

5.184 The writer of the reference may owe a duty of care to the recipient on the basis of the judgment of the House of Lords in *Hedley Byrne v Heller & Partners Ltd*.[400] That case was concerned with a gratuitous but negligent bank reference. The House of Lords held that a negligent, though honest misrepresentation may give rise to an action for financial loss caused by it, even though there is no contractual or fiduciary relationship. The law will imply a duty of care when one party A seeks information from party B possessed of a special skill, trusting B to exercise due care, and B knew or ought to have known that reliance was being placed on his or her skill and judgment. In the case itself, an express disclaimer of responsibility had been given and so no such duty of care could be implied. An employer providing a false reference may also be committing a criminal offence under the remaining sections in force of the Servants' Characters Act 1792.[401] In Scotland an 'unduly laudatory' reference may make the employer liable to a third party who engages the employee relying on it.[402]

---

397 In Scotland, an averment of malice is necessary to the relevancy of an action: Bell *Principles* section 185.
398 *Haspell v Restron and Johnson Ltd* [1976] IRLR 50.
399 *Misra v Drew and Legal and General Assurance* COIT 2446/184.
400 [1964] AC 465.
401 *R v Costello and Bishop* [1910] 1 KB 28.
402 *Anderson v Wishart* (1818) 1 Murr 429.

The Warner Report

5.185 When references are relied on, there are circumstances in which errors in appointment can be made with far-reaching consequences. The Report of the Committee of Enquiry into the Selection, Development and Management of Staff in Childrens' Homes[403] makes some interesting general points about references and applications. Among them are:

(i) referees should be given more direction on questions needing answer, for example on disciplinary matters and on weaknesses as well as strengths;

(ii) the curriculum vitae should be full with no unexplained gaps;

(iii) the appointing body should reserve the right to approach all previous employers for references;

(iv) there should be more use of informal networks – since this would possibly raise issues of discrimination this is obviously restricted to the kind of appointment which was the subject of the inquiry.

The Police Act 1997 provides for a system of certification, under which anyone may apply to a Criminal Records Agency for a 'criminal conviction certificate' listing all convictions (other than those spent under the Rehabilitation of Offenders Act 1974 – except in the exempt categories described earlier, where a 'criminal record certificate' will be issued instead) or no convictions as appropriate. An 'enhanced criminal record certificate' will be relevant to those working with under-18s.

Assessments given for promotion and similar purposes

5.186 In principle the same rules ought to apply to the production of references and assessments for internal purposes: they will certainly apply to external referees. However, the employee called upon to provide a reference for a fellow employee for internal purposes also owes a common law duty to his or her employer to carry out his or her work in a professional manner and it is possible that disciplinary proceedings could be taken if there was defalcation in this respect. In *Slavutych v Baker*[404] the court held that the university could not use a faculty member A's confidential and highly critical assessment of a colleague B, as a basis for misconduct justifying dismissal of A. An absence of good faith could not be inferred simply because A made serious unsubstantiated charges against B. If A honestly believed his

403 *Choosing with Care* (The Warner Report) (1992) HMSO.
404 (1975) 55 DLR (3d) 224.

statement to be true he was not to be held malicious merely because the belief was not based on any reasonable grounds or because he was hasty, credulous, foolish in jumping to a conclusion, irrational, indiscreet, pig-headed or obstinate in his belief.[405]

5.187 In fact, the only ground upon which B could have challenged A, and anyone complaining of the content of such a reference or assessment could proceed, would be to sue for defamation, being convinced that malice could be proved, since otherwise the defence of qualified privilege operates. The first obstacle to overcome would be to secure a copy of the statement complained of. There is no principle in English law by which documents are protected from discovery by reason of confidentiality alone.[406] A subject of a reference may obtain access to it under the Data Protection Act 1984, if it is held on a computer system, or under an order of discovery issued by an employment tribunal to support an allegation of unlawful discrimination.

Disclaimer clauses

5.188 In *Lawton v BOC Transhield Ltd*[407] Tudor Evans J suggested that when giving a reference 'it is open to an employer to protect himself with a disclaimer of responsibility.' Disclaimer clauses could be framed so as to exclude a liability to the recipient and protect the actual writer of the reference. It has been suggested that as there is no duty to write a reference, the courts are likely to take the view that it is fair and reasonable to exclude liability within the meaning of the Unfair Contract Terms Act 1977.[408]

'Subject to references'

5.189 Appointments may be offered expressly 'subject to references.' In *Wishart v National Association of Citizens' Advice Bureaux*[409] a reference from the previous employer disclosed a record

405 Honest and genuine belief in the truth of a statement made in connection with the purposes for which it is required will override any suggestion of malice: *Horrocks v Lowe* [1975] AC 135.
406 *Nasse v Science Research Council; Vyas v Leyland Cars* [1979] IRLR 465, HL.
407 [1987] IRLR 404.
408 S D Migdal and A E M Holmes 'References – Beware the Good Samaritan' (1993) Business Law Review 144, 146.
409 [1990] IRLR 393.

of absence through sickness which the applicant had not previously revealed. The Court of Appeal, overturning injunctions granted by the High Court, established the principle that provided the prospective employer acts in good faith, it is for him or her to determine whether the references are satisfactory or not. The employer did not act in good faith in *Karia v Reliance Security Services Ltd*[410] when he made no attempt to take up a reference or to discuss the matter with the employee and the dismissal of the employee was held to constitute direct racial discrimination. By contrast in *Langdon v Henlys of Barnes*[411] an appointment offered subject to references was fairly terminated some 18 months after the employment started when references unsatisfactory for insurance purposes were received.

410 COIT 1917/212.
411 COIT 1849/119.

Appendix A

A model consultancy agreement between an institution and a member of staff

THIS IS AN AGREEMENT BETWEEN:

(1)   ('the Employee') and

(2)   ('the Institution')

WHEREAS: the Employee wishes to engage in personal consultancy services with [...] ('the Customer') on his or her own account and in consideration of granting permission for this purpose [in consideration of the payment of £ ... /x% of payments received] the Institution requires certain conditions to be observed

NOW THEREFORE IT IS HEREBY CONTRACTED AND AGREED BETWEEN THE PARTIES AS FOLLOWS:
1. The [Institution] permits the Employee to engage in personal consultancy services with the Customer for a period of [ten days per annum] [five days] [eight hours per week] commencing on ... ..19.. (which date shall not be earlier than the date on which the Institution accepts the documentation referred to in paragraph 4 below) and continuing until ... .20.. ('the Consultancy Period') unless previously determined by the Institution in writing.
2. During the Consultancy Period when engaging in consultancy services (which shall include any preparation, discussion, report-writing or any activity of any kind whatsoever associated with the consultancy services, whether carried out during the Consultancy Period or otherwise) the Employee shall not make use of any of the following facilities of the Institution viz
    (i) office accommodation, utility services and staff resources of any description;

     (ii) the institution's postal address, telephone number, facsimile number or electronic mail addresses.

3. The Employee will inform the relevant tax and social security agencies in writing of the consultancy services being undertaken and will provide copies of correspondence on request by the Institution.

4. The Employee will inform the Customer in writing that the consultancy work being undertaken is personal to him or her, that the Institution accepts no legal or other liability whatsoever for the consequences of any acts or omissions on his or her part and that the Institution's professional and public liability insurances do not extend to the consultancy services. A copy of the correspondence between the Employee and the Customer will be made available to the Institution before the Consultancy Period commences.

5. The Employee recognises that while engaged on consultancy services he or she is not engaged in the employment of the Institution, is not covered by the personal, professional and public liability insurances effected by the Institution and agrees that he or she will be entirely responsible for effecting such insurances on his or her own account.

6. The Institution recognises that while engaged on personal consultancy services the Employee is not engaged in its employment and that it therefore has no legal or other right to receive payment or to ownership or the proceeds of exploitation of intellectual property created by the Employee as a result of his or her acting in this capacity.

IN WITNESS WHEREOF this page and the preceding page are subscribed by the parties hereto on the   day   of 199 .

SIGNED by the Employee:

SIGNED on behalf of the Institution:

Appendix B

Notice to be given by an institution to a third party client

[To the Customer]

Dear Sirs

CONSULTANCY SERVICES PROVIDED BY [THE EMPLOYEE]

I am writing in connection with the proposed arrangement between yourselves and our employee .... in which he/she would provide personal consultancy services in connection with ....

As required by the [Institution's] rules, I am writing to inform you that while carrying out these services, or acting in any preparatory or other capacity whatsoever relating to them, ... will be acting as a private individual. The [Institution] will therefore accept no legal or other liability for the consequences of any acts or omissions on his/her part. While he/she is engaged in these activities he/she is not covered by the [Institution's] professional, public liability or personal insurances and I can confirm that he/she has been advised to effect such insurances on his/her own part.

It is a condition of his/her being granted permission to undertake these services that

> 'The Employee will inform the Customer in writing that the consultancy work being undertaken is personal to him or her, that the Institution accepts no legal or other liability whatsoever for the consequences of any acts or omissions on his or her part and that the Institution's professional and public liability insurances do not extend to the consultancy services. A copy of the correspondence between the

Employee and the Customer will be made available to the Institution before the Consultancy Period commences.'

The consultancy services cannot therefore commence until copies of the required correspondence are to hand.

Yours faithfully

[For and on behalf of the Institution]

Chapter 6

Information, higher education and the law

The importance of information in higher education

Introduction

6.1 We live in a society which is more and more dominated by the need for information. This chapter deals with information of all kinds, its creation, modification, recording and protection. There are many staff, students and others working in higher education for whom this area of the law remains as impenetrable as any other, and yet it is a vital part of the background against which they are working or studying. 'Intellectual property rights' (IPR) law covers a wider range of issues than patents alone and is only part of the law relating to information. It includes such issues as copyright and design protection: along with the law relating to protection of personal data it is complex and is one of the areas in which an institution is most likely to turn to expert and expensive outside advice. No general work of this nature can substitute entirely for that advice. In the case of patent law there is a whole profession, that of patent agent, which exists because of the need to be absolutely accurate in patent specifications when millions of pounds are involved. The aim will be to isolate and discuss those issues which are important to higher education generally and thus reduce the need to ask for help on simple matters.

6.2 All institutions of higher education are now keen to avoid losing out on protection of IPR and with government encouragement many have set up organisational structures to ensure that they do not, or at least to ensure that staff are aware of what is available to assist them in protecting intellectual property rights for the benefit of the

institution. The first formal recognition that patents could be of benefit to universities came with the establishment in 1975 of a Working Party
(i) to examine present practices within universities on patenting and the commercial exploitation of research results, and
(ii) to prepare guidance for universities on the legal, administrative and financial implications thereof.
As paragraph 1 of the Report of the Working Party states:

> ... The Comptroller and Auditor General ... made the observation that this was an area that could profitably be investigated and this in turn prompted the UGC to suggest that an examination of the issues might be appropriate with the aim of introducing greater uniformity into existing arrangements.[1]

6.3 The importance of protecting intellectual property in general was further recognised in 1991 in the CVCP paper *University-Industry Collaboration: Recommendations and Guidance for Universities on Contract Issues.*[2] Two recommendations are of a general nature:

(xiv) A university [should inform] its staff and students of its policy on intellectual property ownership;
(xv) Ownership of intellectual property arising from research projects should be vested in the university.

For 'university' we should now read 'higher education institution.' So institutions need to be aware of the nature of the legal imperatives and constraints on their policy and the mechanisms by which they may secure intellectual property rights.

6.4 Reference will also be made to the Report of the ACAS Working Party on Teaching Staff Contracts (in the pre-1992 polytechnics and colleges sector) published in 1990. This provides some valuable advice to institutions on a range of intellectual property rights issues related to the contract of employment: the advice is as relevant to the former UFC sector as to the former PCFC sector.

---

1 *Report of a Working Party on Patents and the Commercial Exploitation of Research Results* CVCP (1978).
2 CVCP Paper N/91/164.

Legislation governing IPR

6.5 IPR is an area in which the European Union has been very active: a number of changes in UK domestic legislation have resulted in the 1990s. There are fundamentally two types of intellectual property right, those which arise automatically on the creation of the work – copyright, design right – and those that arise at the option of the creator subject to statutory restrictions – patents, trade marks and registered designs. The Copyright, Designs and Patents Act 1988 (CDPA), as amended,[3] is a useful starting point for this discussion. Together with the Patents Act 1977 (PA), the Trade Marks Act 1994 and the Registered Designs Act 1949[4] it constitutes the basic law relating to the protection of IPR. Among other things CDPA restated the law of copyright, repealing the Copyright Act 1956 and made a number of amendments to the 1977 and 1949 Acts. It also introduced two new rights in UK law: the moral rights of authors and others, and design right. Significant amendments to CDPA came into effect on 1 January 1993 as a result of the implementation in the UK of the EC Directive 91/250/EC on the legal protection of computer programs.[5]

The law of confidence

6.6 Before the discussion on the well-known forms of IPR we should consider the common law relating to confidence. 'Breach of confidence' is the action used to protect trade secrets: equity will impose an obligation of confidence where it is just, in all the circumstances, to do so.[6] To be protected by the law information must have the necessary quality of confidence about it, must have been imparted in circumstances importing an obligation of confidence eg employment[7] or where the person receiving the information has expressly agreed to use it for limited purposes or where, as a 'reasonable person' it would have been clear to him or her that that was the case[8] and there must have been an unauthorised use of the information to the detriment of the party communicating it.

---

3   For example by Part IX Broadcasting Act 1990 and Part VII Broadcasting Act 1996.
4   Now Schedule 4 CDPA.
5   Copyright (Computer Programs) Regulations 1992 (SI 1992/3233).
6   *Seager v Copydex Ltd (No 2)* [1969] RPC 250.
7   *Faccenda Chicken v Fowler* [1986] 1 All ER 617.
8   *Coco v A N Clark (Engineers) Ltd* [1969] RPC 41; *De Maudsley v Palumbo* [1996] FSR 447.

Information ceases to be confidential when it falls into the public domain.[9]

Confidentiality agreements

6.7 It is likely that an industrial or commercial sponsor who is using the research or consultancy to promote his or her product will wish to invoke 'commercial confidence,' inconsistent with the wishes of academic staff and of the institution, in so far as commercial contracts are assessed for the research selectivity exercises. It may be that in view of the importance of the research selectivity exercise for funding, and the pressures of quality assessment of teaching, staff will not wish to be party to secretive commercial contracts at all. However this is approached, it is important that there is certainty on both sides. Both sponsors and institutions may wish to impose confidentiality agreements on the personnel of the other party. Sponsors may need to give institutional personnel access to material not protected by patents which is nevertheless commercially sensitive. Institutions may wish to ensure that potential sponsors, having been given such access to the institution's know-how and facilities as are necessary to enable them to decide whether to invest, do not pass on details to other institutions in what is a commercial market. In such cases they may call upon personnel of the other party to sign confidentiality agreements which bind them not to disclose what they have learned to any third party. In English law, unless made for consideration or under seal, such agreements are not enforceable as contracts. In any event institutional personnel (and indeed any other employee) may not be able to sign such agreements without the express permission of their employer, since any information to which they become privy during the course of employment will automatically belong to the employer.

Copyright

Introduction

6.8 The intellectual property right of copyright protects the expression of ideas. It is an international concept originating in the UK in a statute of Queen Anne (1709), but it is a national right

---

9   *O Mustad & Son v S Allcock & Co Ltd and Dosen* [1964] 1 WLR 109n, HL.

protected in the first instance by national legislation.[10] The differences in approach between countries following the Anglo-American common law tradition and those following civil law traditions adds to the complexity of the subject and it is an area in which the European Union is increasingly active.[11] Even in common law jurisdictions differences arise. For example in the US, the legal system attempts to draw clear distinctions between the protection of expressions of an idea (represented by copyright) and that of the idea itself (represented in certain circumstances by patents).[12] However, the boundary is not easily defined[13] and in the area of copyright in computer software it is particularly difficult. As UK law in this area, as in most, is not codified, the distinction is not drawn expressly but left to be covered by the separate legislation dealing with various kinds of IPR. For example the Copyright Act 1911 covers legal deposit, the right of the British Library Legal Deposit Office to receive copies of all published printed material within one month of publication.

The international law of copyright

6.9   The Berne Convention of 1886, amended on a number of occasions to 1971, is a multilateral copyright treaty which stipulates a set of minimum standards of copyright protection which signatory states must provide in their national legislation, and obliges them to grant equal protection to the nationals of other member states. In addition to the Berne Convention there is the Universal Copyright Convention (1952), the Rome Convention for the protection of performers, producers of phonograms and broadcasting organisations (1960), the Geneva Convention for the protection of producers of phonograms against unauthorised duplication of their work (1971) and the Brussels Convention relating to the distribution

---

10 A useful guide to copyright is D de Freitas *The Law of Copyright and Rights in Performances* (British Copyright Council, 1990).

11 For example, the Duration of Copyright and Rights in Performances Regulations 1995, SI 1995/3297 implemented Directive 93/98/EEC except Article 4; The Copyright and Related Rights Regulations 1996 (SI 1996/2967) implemented Directive 92/100/EEC and Article 4 of Directive 93/98/EEC; The Copyright (EC Measures Relating to Pirated Goods and Abolition of Restrictions on the Import of Goods) Regulations 1995, SI 1995/1445 relating to EC Regulation 3295/94 and other measures; European Commission Communication CON(95)282 on copyright and related rights in the information industry.

12 17 USC Sec 102(b).

13 See the dictum of Judge Learned Hand in *Nichols v Universal Pictures Co* 42 Fed 2d 119 (1930), 121: '... nobody has ever been able to fix that boundary, and nobody ever can.'

of programme-carrying signals transmitted by satellite (1974). The international law of copyright can be very complicated, notwithstanding the international conventions. An illustration of this is the problem which arose in 1988, when old Cliff Richard records, out of copyright in Denmark, were exported to Germany, where they were still in copyright.[14] Two new copyright and related rights treaties were concluded by the World Intellectual Property Organisation (WIPO) in 1996.

Application of non-discrimination provisions of the Treaty of Rome

6.10   In *Phil Collins v Imtrat Handelsgesellschaft mbH* and *Patricia Im-und Export Verwaltungsgesellschaft mbH v EMI Electrola GmbH*[15] the European Court of Justice held that copyright and related rights come within the scope of the Treaty provisions relating to non-discrimination, so preventing the legislation of a member state from excluding authors and performing artists of other member states from the right granted by the same legislation to nationals to prohibit the distribution on national territory of a phonogram manufactured without their consent, where the performance had been given outside the national territory. The general importance of this case lies in the finding by the Court that the principle of non-discrimination might be directly relied upon before a national court by an author etc in order to claim the benefit of the protection granted to national authors and artists.

How copyright protection arises

6.11   Ideas have to be 'recorded' to be protected.[16] 'Copyright' and 'copyright work' are defined in section 1 CDPA as follows:

> Copyright is a property right which subsists ... in the following descriptions of work–
> (a)   original literary, dramatic, musical or artistic works,
> (b)   sound recordings, films, broadcasts or cable programmes, and
> (c)   the typographical arrangement of published editions.
>
> ... 'copyright work' means a work of any of those descriptions in which copyright subsists.

14   *Clarion*, Newsletter of the Copyright Licensing Agency, Spring 1989.
15   (1993) Times, 19 November; joined cases C-92/92 and C-326/92 (ECJ).
16   Section 3(2) CDPA.

Copyright does not subsist in a work unless the requirements [of the Act] with respect to qualification for copyright protection are met ...

6.12   Copyright is an interesting, if intangible, concept in its own right but its true importance lies in its monetary value to those who own it. The income generated from copyright and its licensing is essential if there is to be sufficient incentive for the generation of new work.[17] Therefore the copyright laws of the UK and other countries provide considerable protection which, in the UK, extends to 70 years after the death of the author (50 years from the date of creation in the case of computer-generated works).[18]

6.13   The qualification requirements of the copyright sections of the Act relate to the citizenship or domicile of the author, the place of publication or broadcast. While the provisions of the Act extend in the first instance only to the UK, an Order in Council may extend it to the Channel Islands, Isle of Man and colonies and to other countries signatory to the Berne Convention in so far as like protection is afforded there to owners of copyright in the UK.

6.14   Certain types of work may be denied the protection of copyright, eg where there is a breach of confidence, as in the various books written by former members of the security services, or immorality, as in *Glyn v Weston Feature Film Co*.[19] On the other hand certain types of printing have been given special protection by the law as in *Universities of Oxford and Cambridge v Eyre and Spottiswoode Ltd*[20] in relation to the printing of bibles, *Basket v University of Cambridge*,[21] *Hills v University of Oxford* [22] and *Universities of Oxford and Cambridge v Richardson*[23] all concerned with printing of Acts of Parliament.

---

17   Copyright and related rights are said to account for an annual value of business representing 3–5% of the European Union's GDP.
18   Duration of Copyright and Rights in Performances Regulations 1995 (SI 1995/3297); Copyright subsists indefinitely in the case of *Peter Pan*: the proceeds go to the Great Ormond Street Hospital for Sick Children – section 301 and Schedule 6 CDPA; certain university copyright under older legislation is continued to 31 December 2039 – Schedule 1, para 13(1) CDPA.
19   [1916] 1 Ch 261.
20   [1964] Ch 736.
21   (1758) 1 Wm Bl 105.
22   (1684) 1 Vern 275.
23   (1802) 6 Ves 689.

Moral rights

6.15 In addition, CDPA introduced the concept of 'moral rights' which cannot be assigned. These originate in the Berne Convention as added to by the Rome Act 1928: there are three moral rights, those of paternity, integrity and freedom from false attribution and a separate special privacy right. Like copyright itself, moral rights fall within the anti-discrimination provisions of the Treaty of Rome.[24] The moral right of paternity is expressed in section 77 CDPA:

> The author of a copyright literary, dramatic, musical or artistic work, and the director of a copyright film, has the right to be identified as the author or director of the work in the circumstances mentioned in this section; but the right is not infringed unless it has been asserted
>
> ...

The circumstances include, as appropriate, commercial publishing, public performance or broadcast, sales of copies of sound recordings or photographs of works of architecture. The paternity right is asserted simply by the author giving notice to that effect. The integrity right does not have to be asserted. Moral rights cannot be asserted in relation to computer programs, computer-generated work or the design of a typeface. The rights do not apply to anything done by the author's employer where the employer owns the copyright. The moral right of integrity is the right of the author not to have his or her work subjected to derogatory treatment, but this right is also qualified where the employer holds the copyright. It may be a breach of the integrity right to omit photographs from text when copying. The separate special privacy right protects the privacy of a person who commissions a photograph or film for private or domestic purposes: there may be some circumstances in which an institution may wish to exercise this right. There is currently a proposal for an EU Directive on artists' resale rights or *droit de suite*.

Ownership of copyright in higher education institutions

6.16 As a general rule, copyright belongs to the person who originates the work. It is commonplace in common law countries to assign copyright to a publisher but in countries with *droit d'auteur* authors tend to retain their copyright, assigning publishers first

---

24 *Phil Collins v Imtrat Handelsgesellchaft mbH* and *Patricia Im-und Export Verwaltungsgesellschaft mbH v EMI Electrola GmbH* (1993) Times, 19 November; joined cases C-92/92 and C-326/92, ECJ.

publication rights by contract. The copyright in the original text of
a book belongs to the author unless he or she has assigned it to
another party or has produced it in the course of his or her
employment, in which case it belongs to the employer subject to any
agreement to the contrary. It is obviously important to know whether
or not it is an individual member of staff or student of a higher
education institution who owns the copyright in his or her work or
whether it is the institution which does so. This is true of the right to
assert moral rights as well. Section 11 CDPA provides:

> Where a literary, dramatic, musical or artistic work is made by an
> employee in the course of his employment, his employer is the first
> owner of any copyright in the work subject to any agreement to the
> contrary.

6.17 Where there is 'no agreement to the contrary' then plainly the
copyright in all work produced by members of the academic and other
staff of the higher education institution 'in the course of employment'
belongs to the institution. Some institutions have recognised that the
copyright in all textbooks and articles (and other material which can
be the subject of copyright) is included in this and, more importantly,
if there is no agreement to the contrary so do all the proceeds of
producing copyright work belong to them. The general practice
appears to be voluntarily to relinquish those rights in favour of the
staff member, eg

> Subject to any agreement to the contrary in any particular case, the
> University shall not be entitled to any copyright subsisting in any work
> or other material of which a member of the University is the author
> or the maker pursuant to the provisions of [CDPA 1988] ...

This is presumably a section 77 'agreement to the contrary' since
Ordinances are by implication normally part of the terms of the
contract of employment of members of staff.

6.18 Where students are members of the university, a clause like
this forms part of their contract of membership; where they are not,
some other explicit arrangement will be required. There are obvious
distinctions between types of material over which an institution may
wish to assert copyright: examination scripts may fall into this
category, whereas essays may not. So students may, by signing up to
the institution's regulations, voluntarily assign the copyright in their
examination scripts, but not other written work, to the institution
pursuant to section 77 CDPA. An undergraduate dissertation or

postgraduate dissertation or thesis based on sponsored work may be subject to specific agreements between the institution, the student and the sponsor.

6.19 The Report of the ACAS Working Party on Teaching Staff Contracts referred to the difficulty of formulating a contractual clause which would cover copyright in all of its possible permutations. The author of the report[25] recommended the following:

(i) Subject to the following provisions [the institution] and you acknowledge sections 11 and 15 of [CDPA].

(ii) All records, documents and other papers (including copies and summaries thereof) which pertain to the finance and administration of [the institution] and which are made or acquired by you in the course of your employment shall be the property of [the institution]. The copyright in all such original records, documents and papers shall at all times belong to [the institution].

(iii) The copyright in any work or design compiled, edited or otherwise brought into existence by you as a scholarly work produced in furtherance of your professional career shall belong to you; 'scholarly work' includes items such as books, contributions to books, articles and conference papers, and shall be construed in the light of the common understanding of the phrase in higher education.

(iv) The copyright in any material produced by you for your personal use and reference, including as an aid to teaching, shall belong to you.

(v) However, the copyright in course materials produced by you in the course of your employment for the purposes of the curriculum of a course run by [the institution] and produced, used or disseminated by [the institution] shall belong to [the institution], as well as the outcomes from research specifically funded and supported by [the institution].

(vi) The above sub-clauses (iii)–(v) shall apply except where agreement to the contrary is reached by you and [the institution]. Where a case arises, or it is thought that a case may arise, where such agreement to the contrary may be necessary, or where it is expedient to reach a specific agreement as to the application of the above sub-clauses to the particular facts of the case, the matter should be taken up between you and [your Head of department]. By way of example, this sub-clause would apply where any question of assignment of copyright or of joint copyright may arise; other examples and guidance may be contained from time to time in the Staff Handbook.

25 Ian Smith of the University of East Anglia.

6.20   It is a matter of policy, rather than of law, whether an institution takes the view that members of staff should be entitled to retain the profits of copyright work produced in the course of employment. In many cases such profits are small, even negligible, but in some cases they are an important element in the overall earnings of staff. On the other hand, the production of certain kinds of work is considered to be important for the institution in that it contributes to its output of research and scholarship, thereby having an effect on its overall funding.[26] The question must be, therefore, whether there should be a blanket waiver of the employer's rights, or whether a waiver should only be granted in circumstances in which the publication of a work is likely to enhance the reputation of the institution. Copyright in journal articles may be assigned to the journal, or alternatively first publication rights or rights to print may be granted, so that the author may then be free to place a copy on his or her website. The right to electronic publication may also be assigned to the institution. The National Academies Policy Advisory Group[27] took the view that 'it would be wrong for institutions to claim [copyright in the writings of academic staff] as a matter of general law, or indeed to take it by express contract, in a way which would deprive academic authors of essential powers to control how, when and where their work should or should not appear.' NCIHE has called for a review of the existing copyright law.[28]

Copyright in course material, brochures etc

6.21   Whatever the general position may be, problems may arise where an institution hires a third party to produce material for it, perhaps for a distance-learning programme, or where there is joint development of materials between institutions. In such cases institutions must ensure that the ownership of copyright is clearly defined in the contract, perhaps by adoption of the ACAS Working Party's model clause. It may be that the institution will wish to adopt different policies towards different academic areas where there are considerable disparities in the potential for financial reward, or between staff employed for different purposes. For example, someone employed specifically for the purpose of writing distance-learning material should presumably not be permitted to own copyright in

26   Paragraph 13.73, Main Report, NCIHE, July 1997, focussed on ownership of copyright in learned academic journals.
27   National Academies Policy Advisory Group *Intellectual Property and the Academic Community* (1995) p 56.
28   Recommendation 43, Main Report, NCIHE, July 1997.

the material. Institutions also have to ensure that where they permit members of staff to engage in consultancies, all parties are clear as to the ownership of copyright in whatever is produced (and, indeed the same applies to all other forms of intellectual property right).

6.22 An analogy can be demonstrated with *University of London Press Ltd v University Tutorial Press Ltd*,[29] where the University of London had appointed examiners (Lodge and Jackson) to set and mark examinations under the express condition that any copyright in the papers should belong to the University. It then assigned copyright in the papers to the University of London Press (ULP). The defendant then published papers including some of those produced by Lodge and Jackson. In this case, having established that the papers were copyright work under the Copyright Act 1911 (a predecessor of CDPA), the court held that the examiners were not (in modern terms) employees of the University and the copyright position was regulated by their contracts of appointment.

6.23 CDPA deals with joint authorship in section 10(1):

'Work of joint authorship' means a work produced by the collaboration of two or more authors in which the contribution of each author is not distinct from that of the other author or authors.

It may be possible in some circumstances to retain a discreet contribution to joint work. If that is the case, it is possible for each party to cross-license the other to use and copy the work or alternatively for the parties to enter into a contract for the use of the work in future.

6.24 It has already been pointed out that the principle that copyright in all work produced by an employee vests in the employer in the absence of agreement to the contrary conflicts with the general practice of institutions in respect of books and articles produced by members of academic staff in the course of employment. A different practice might arguably be adopted in respect of 'institutional' as opposed to 'personal' documents, particularly where it is sought to restrain staff moving from one institution to another in the course of career progression or otherwise from making use of their former employer's 'trade secrets.'[30] Obvious examples of the former include

29 [1916] 2 Ch 601.
30 As in *Faccenda Chicken v Fowler* [1987] Ch 117.

prospectuses, course leaflets and brochures and it is argued that it would be difficult for a member of staff to sustain a defence that such material was in fact his or her copyright.

6.25 The position would not be so clear cut in the case of teaching material produced either by a member of staff working alone, or by a team of staff each contributing part to the whole. Copyright practitioners distinguish between (i) 'know-how' – a term used to denote information that can be committed fairly straightforwardly to paper or other medium – and (ii) 'show-how' – which covers information which can only be transmitted through training. If the institution hiring a new member of staff expects access to either of these and the information is not such as might be expected from an employee displaying the ordinary skills of a skilled person in the field, then it must expect to pay the former institution for it. So where a member of academic staff who on taking up a new post sets up, markets and delivers a specified course indistinguishable from or even closely comparable to a course developed by him or her at the previous institution, it may be that the new institution is infringing the former institution's copyright. The infringement will be so much more blatant if the new institution deliberately hired the new employee to take business away from the former institution. Naturally, it is much more difficult to demonstrate that a breach of copyright has occurred if the new course is one on a well-known core subject such as Keynsian Economics than if it were in a highly specialised niche market such as a taught MSc in the Economics of Seafood Production. For the avoidance of doubt in this area it is important that the contract of employment contains, either expressly or by reference to another readily accessible document, provisions regulating the copyright position, as suggested in the ACAS Working Party report.

Copyright licensing schemes

6.26 Licensing made compulsory by statute would contravene the Berne Convention, so CDPA encourages the use of contractual licensing schemes, covering the work of more than one rights owner. In certain circumstances the Secretary of State or a Copyright Tribunal established under CDPA may override the rights of a copyright owner by granting licences against his or her will or by varying the terms of a licence, but consideration of this area is beyond the scope of this work.

6.27 Section 116 CDPA defines 'licensing scheme' and 'licensing body.'

... a 'licensing scheme' means a scheme setting out–
(a) the classes of case in which the operator of the scheme, or the person on whose behalf he acts, is willing to grant copyright licences, and
(b) the terms on which licences would be granted in those classes of case ...

... a 'licensing body' means a society or other organisation which has as its main object, or one of its main objects, the negotiation or granting, either as owner or prospective owner of copyright or as agent for him, of copyright licences, and whose objects include the granting of licences covering works of more than one author.

6.28 The effect of CDPA has been felt most in the academic community by the provisions for copyright licensing by a number of licensing bodies, principally the Copyright Licensing Agency (CLA) and the Educational Recording Agency (ERA) but also the Designers and Artists Copyright Society (DACS) and the Newspaper Licensing Agency (NLA). All these agencies contract with higher education institutions to permit specified copying of copyright works in books and periodicals (CLA), from terrestrial (not satellite) radio and television broadcasting (ERA), of artistic works (DACS) and from specified newspapers (NLA). CLA and ERA will be discussed in detail.

The Copyright Licensing Agency

6.29 CLA was established in 1983 prior to the enactment of CDPA. Its directors are appointed by its member organisations which include the Authors' Licensing and Collecting Society and the Publishers' Licensing Society. It is one of a number of Reproduction Rights Organisations (RROs) belonging to the International Federation of Reproduction Rights Organisations (IFRRO). As such, it has entered into reciprocal arrangements with other RROs, the most important of these to higher education institutions being that with the US Copyright Clearance Center (CCC). Among other RROs are the Copyright Collecting Agency (Ireland) Limited (CCAI), Agenzia Italiano dei diretti di Reproduzione della Opere e Stampa (AIDROS), CANCOPY (Canada) and Centre Français du Copyright. Interestingly, the US, which only signed the Berne Convention after

103 years in 1989, provides better protection to overseas authors than to its own, since US law restricts protection to books, etc, printed with the copyright symbol © and the date of publication, the requirements of the Universal Copyright Convention of 1952.

6.30 The copying which may be carried out under the terms of the CLA licence is limited in scope. With the objective of facilitating applications by higher education institutions for permission to make multiple copies for teaching purposes, which is not covered by the licensing scheme, CLA has established a Copyright Licensing Agency Clearing Scheme (CLARCS). This arrangement allows the institution, or such departments as it permits, to request clearance for the assembly of relevant material by telephone or fax by means of a system of passwords and then be invoiced for the licence fee later. The CLARCS system contains many of the essential elements of an Electronic Copyright Management System (ECMS). A prototype system to prevent illegitimate copying, COPICAT, is being developed with EU funding.

6.31 The CLA arrangements cover the following:

(i) up to 5% or one chapter from an original of a book;
(ii) published in the UK, Eire [sic], France, Germany, Norway, Spain, Sweden, Australia, Canada, New Zealand, South Africa and the US (certain publishers only);
(iii) the number of multiple copies of a single item of copyright material must not exceed the number needed to ensure that the tutor and each member of the class has one reproduction only.

The licence does not cover:

(iv) works published outside the countries listed in (ii);
(v) works specifically excluded by a notice issued by CLA;
(vi) printed music (including the words);
(vii) newspapers (except those published in France, Germany or Spain);
(viii) maps, charts, books of tables, separate photographs, illustrations and diagrams;
(ix) bibles, liturgical works, orders of service;
(x) public examination papers, privately prepared teaching material (eg correspondence courses), workbooks, industrial house journals; and unpublished material.

6.32 Many foreign publishers, then, are not within the CLA scheme and some domestic publishers exclude some works in particular subject disciplines, notably business. About 80 publishers appear on this list of exclusions. In these cases application to copy must be made to the publishers direct and the relevant fee paid. Licences are available separately from inter alia the British Standards Institution and the Ordnance Survey.

Excluded modes of copying

6.33 The CLA mandate from rights holders restricts it to licensing copying from paper on to paper. Section 17 CDPA defines copying as including storing work in any medium by electronic means and includes the making of copies which are transient or are incidental to some other use of the work. Using a fax machine falls into this category.[31] Reading a text into a computer by means of a scanner is copying, even if it is intended to be held in the computer's memory only long enough for a print to be made. This type of copying is not permitted under the terms of the CLA licence. With the exception of the loading of short extracts for personal use, which is permitted under the fair dealing exception of section 29 CDPA, such copying is an infringement of copyright and therefore in each case permission is required from the publishers (or from the author where the rights have reverted to him or her.) To reinforce this point, the Publishers' Association issued a statement *Electrocopying and Infringement of Copyright* in May 1992. This followed discussion documents on *Control of Electrocopying* (October 1991) and *Electronic Copying of Copyright Works* (January 1992). Particular problems arise with multimedia copyright. Advice was issued in 1997 on copying material from the internet. In principle copying starts when browsing starts, when copies are made into the computer's RAM, the browser's cache and possibly intermediate network caches. It is suggested that the act of allowing free access to a page implies that these copies are permitted, but the point is undecided. It is not safe to assume that copies may be printed unless it is so stated. Particular problems may arise if the material consists of proprietary information or JAVA applets. The law on hypertext links is unclear[32] and is discussed later.

---

31 Section 24(2) CDPA.
32 The only UK case was on an interim application: *Shetland Times Ltd v Wilts* 1997 SCLR 160 but it was settled before proof.

Restrictions on personnel covered by CLA licence

6.34 Another limitation imposed by the CLA licence relates to the individual undertaking the copying. The CLA has stated that its licensing arrangements do not extend to students on 'short courses' or to conference delegates if these categories are not receiving tuition from members of staff of the institution.[33] It is clear that legal responsibility in these cases is that of the organiser of the course or conference but, unless this is spelt out by the institution, it is likely to be the institution which is liable if, as is likely, its own staff are in any way involved with the arrangements. The CLA offers special licensing arrangements to cover courses and conferences not otherwise covered by the institutional licence.

Copying by libraries[34]

6.35 Prescribed (ie not-for-profit) libraries are able to make one copy of a periodical article or a reasonable proportion (defined by the British Copyright Council as 10% or one chapter) of a literary, dramatic or musical work for someone satisfying the librarian that it is required for research or private study.[35] The regulations prevent libraries from making copies for each member of a class: such copies must be made under the terms of the CLA licence or by permission of copyright holders who are not covered by the CLA scheme. Copyright owners of sound recordings, films and computer programs have the right to license the renting of their material by libraries. The act of electro-copying into a computer store is considered to be making multiple copies and so not permitted without specific licence.[36]

The Educational Recording Agency

6.36 The ERA Scheme[37] extends to all terrestrial broadcasting except programmes produced by the Open University and Open

33 CLA letter to institutions, 18 September 1990.
34 See S Norman *Copyright in Further and Higher Education Libraries* (1996) Library Association.
35 Sections 38 and 39 CDPA and The Copyright (Librarians and Archivists) (Copying of Copyright Material) Regulations 1989 (SI 1989/1212).
36 *Electrocopying and Infringement of Copyright* Publishers' Association May 1992; *Electronic Copying and Digital Use of Copyright Material* CLA (1997).
37 The Copyright (Certification of Licensing Scheme for Educational Recording of Broadcasts and Cable Programmes)(Educational Recording Agency Limited) Orders 1990 to 1993 (SI 1990/879) as amended.

College, which have separate arrangements.[38] The Educational Recording Licence issued to the institution by ERA as agent for the licensor members applies to specified types of works owned or controlled by the licensor members. It authorises the institution to record terrestrial broadcast or cable programmes and their contents or copy such recordings for the educational purposes of the institution. Recording or copying may take place either on the premises of the institution (in which case it must be under the direct supervision of a member of staff) or by a 'teacher' employed by the institution at his or her residence or, under certain conditions, by a third party authorised by the institution. 'Teacher' is not defined but presumably means any member of academic staff, thus preventing a technician or other employee from making recordings at home for use by academic staff on the premises of the institution. All recordings or copies must be marked with the date and title of the recording and a statement 'in clear and bold lettering' that 'this recording is to be used only for educational purposes.'

6.37 'Time-shifting' ie recording a programme for later use is specifically permitted by section 70 CDPA for private and domestic purposes. Broadcasts and cable programmes may be copied for adaptation by the National Subtitling Library for Deaf People designated by the Secretary of State under section 74 CDPA and archival copies may be made by the National Film Archive, the Scottish Film Archive, the British Library and the Music Performance Research Centre designated under section 75 CDPA.

Infringement of copyright

6.38 Copying of copyright work outside the terms of the CLA and ERA licences, or outside the special provisions for prescribed libraries, and without the permission of the copyright owner, is actionable by him or her under Chapter VI CDPA unless it is covered by the provisions for fair dealing for research or private study[39] which does not damage the economic interests of the copyright owner. The British Copyright Council has published a set of guidelines which set out what level of copying they will normally consider fair and non-infringing – in general terms one chapter or 5% of a book. Distinguishing between plagiarism and other types of misuse of other

---

38 The Copyright (Certification of Licensing Scheme for Educational Recording of Broadcasts)(Open University Educational Enterprises Ltd) Order 1990 (SI 1990/ 2008).
39 Section 29 CDPA.

people's copyright in publications can be difficult in practice; proving priority of authorship is one problem. Intent to deceive can be difficult to establish where disciplinary proceedings may follow.

6.39 Multiple copying is never considered 'fair dealing' and is what gives rise to most problems in the field of education. The owner may obtain 'all such relief by way of damages, injunctions, accounts or otherwise' except where the defendant did not know about the copyright, when damages may not be awarded. One of the earliest cases was *Copyright Licensing Agency and Publishers' Licensing Society v PS Don't Forget Stationery*,[40] where an interim interdict was issued requiring the defenders to cease copying complete textbooks which students had apparently borrowed from Glasgow University Library. The amount of damages which may be awarded will be increased if the infringement is particularly flagrant or the benefit accruing to the defendant is significant. Thus where a member of staff of an educational institution deliberately exceeds the copying restrictions imposed by the CLA licence with the objective of saving students the financial burden of buying copies of a text, the institution could be required to pay substantial damages to the copyright owner. There is also the possibility that the court could order the delivery up of the infringing copies and, in a particularly serious case, the equipment used to make them. Surrender of infringing copies was the remedy obtained by CLA, without court proceedings, against an information consultancy which had 300 copies of five articles taken from various journals printed illegally at a copyshop for the purpose of a training course in the Department of Health, and separately against a securities house some of whose employees had made copies of expensive reference books.[41]

6.40 It is also a criminal offence to make or deal with infringing copies of copyright work and the court may order a person charged with such an offence to deliver up the copies and the equipment used to make them. If a body corporate, such as a higher education institution, has committed the offence then if it is proved to have been committed 'with the consent or connivance of a director, manager, secretary or other similar officer of the body, or a person purporting to act in any such capacity', then that person, as well as the body corporate, is guilty of the offence and liable to be the subject of

---

40 (1990, unreported), Glasgow Sheriff Court (*Clarion*, the Newsletter of CLA, Winter 1990/91).

41 *Clarion* ibid. The position is less clear in the US: *Princeton University Press v Michigan Document Services Inc* 74 F2d 1528 (1996); cf *Basic Books Inc v Kinko's Graphic Corpn* 758 FSupp 1522 (1991).

criminal proceedings and punishment which may include imprisonment. Thus, apart from ensuring that steps are taken to prevent anyone in the institution from breaking the law, it is important that persons likely to fall within these categories take steps to ensure that they cannot be considered to have 'consented to or connived at' illegal activities.

Copyright licensing by institutions

6.41 Institutions may enter into agreements with commercial organisations to license their own copyright eg in archives. A licence of this type would normally be exclusive and limited in time and in geographical coverage and would specify precisely what the archives would be used for, consistent with its role as an educational institution. As CLA and ERA require copyright notices on licensed materials, so should the institution. The position of moral rights of authors should be clearly established and proper disclaimers of liability and warranties entered into.

The Directive on Rental Right, Lending Right and Neighbouring Rights

6.42 The EU Directive on Rental Right, Lending Right and Neighbouring Rights[42] is aimed at harmonising certain provisions of member states' copyright laws: the right to control lending of copyright work; the protection of the rights of performers, producers of phonograms and films and broadcasting organisations, was implemented by the Copyright and Related Rights Regulations 1996.[43]

Copyright in computer software

6.43 The copyright protection of computer software[44] is now governed by CDPA, as amended by the Copyright (Computer

42 92/100/EEC; OJ 1992 L346/61.
43 SI 1996/2967.
44 Two useful articles are D I Bainbridge 'Computer Programs and copyright – More Exceptions to Infringement' (1993) MLR 591 and L MacPherson 'The EC Directive on the legal protection of computer software: its effects on UK copyright law' (1993) Scots Law Gazette 45.

Programs) Regulations 1992.[45] CDPA had repealed the Copyright (Computer Software) Amendment Act 1985, which had clarified the position in relation to the Copyright Act 1956, itself repealed by CDPA. The principles of protection are basically the same as those that apply to other literary works, however recorded. Although the Act does not use the word 'software' it provides protection for computer programs, which neither it nor the 1992 Regulations define. The expressions 'computer-generated' and 'electronic' are defined.[46] The word 'software' is used only in the title of the 1985 Act, not in the main text.[47] The words 'computer,' 'program' and 'data' are also not defined in the Computer Misuse Act 1990, which provides criminal penalties for unauthorised access to and modification of software. The 1991 Directive which the 1992 Regulations are stated to implement[48] includes in its preamble the following:

> ... the term 'computer program' shall include programs in any form, including those which are incorporated in hardware, whereas this term also includes preparatory design work leading to the development of a computer program provided that the nature of such preparatory work is such that a computer program can result from it at a later stage ...

So we do not have a precise definition of what is meant by computer program.

6.44 However vague the definition of computer program may be (and it is argued that it is deliberately vague so as to try to avoid the rapid progress of technological developments giving rise to constant changes in the law), the definition of what is meant by 'copying' appears clear. This includes storing by electronic means so that loading a program onto a computer or network requires permission of the copyright holder: usually programs supplied to higher education institutions are accompanied by licences specifying the

---

45 SI 1992/3233. The most significant amendments for higher education include the automatic right to take back-up copies and permitting certain practices (eg decompiling).
46 Section 178 CDPA.
47 For cases on the 1985 Act see *M S Associates v Power* [1988] FSR 242; *Milltronics v Hycontrol* [1990] FSR 273, CA. Section 172 CDPA provides for the use of expressions in decisions on the earlier legislation to be used in the interpretation of the 1988 Act.
48 Council Directive on the Legal Protection of Computer Programs 91/250/EEC, 1991 OJ LI22/42.

extent of copying which is permitted, including the making of back-up copies.[49]

6.45 The problem to be addressed by the legislature is how to balance the rights of the originator of the program against those of other programmers who seek to build on and develop his or her work. Copyright in computer programs may be infringed by reproducing the 'look and feel' of a program, even where the code may be different from that of the original program, the lay person's analogy being perhaps where the plot of a film is plagiarised but not the actual script. The UK courts have tended to take a narrow view of the circumstances in which this could arise.[50] Recent decisions in the US[51] suggest that the view[52] that copyright protection extends beyond the literal code of the program to its structural aspects is outdated. The current approach of the US courts in dealing with alleged infringement of computer software is systematically to determine whether non-literal aspects of programs are 'substantially similar' and therefore whether copyright is infringed when one is derived from another.[53] It has been held that the process of linking several programs to create a new one does not create a 'compilation' within section 3(1)(a) CDPA which could then be protected by copyright as an original copyright work.[54] The EU Directive and the revised CDPA attempt to address the problem by permitting the original program to be studied and in certain circumstances to be decompiled to allow this to be done. Software houses usually protect their rights to improvements to licensed software. Preparatory design of computer software is specifically included in the 1991 Directive but not in the amended CDPA. It is considered that it falls within the general copyright protection afforded by CDPA to 'literary work.'

---

49 The 1993 amendments to CDPA by the 1992 Regulations allow lawful users to make back-up copies, which is a practice recommended by computer professionals.
50 Cases of this nature arise usually on application for an interim order pending trial of an action for infringement: see for example the case of *John Richardson Computers Ltd v Flanders* [1992] FSR 391.
51 *Computer Associates International Inc v Altai Inc* (1992) US App Lexis 14305; *Apple Computers Inc v Microsoft Corpn and Hewlett-Packard Co* (1992) US Dist Lexis 12216.
52 Taken in what has until recently been considered as the landmark decision in *Whelan Associates Inc v Jaslow Dental Laboratory Inc* 797 Fed 2d 1222 reported in the UK in [1987] FSR 1.
53 For a full analysis of these cases see P Groves and P Stone 'Computer Software – How Does that Look and Feel?' (1993) Business Law Review 87.
54 *Total Information Processing Systems v Daman* [1992] FSR 171 (Judge Baker QC).

CHEST™

6.46 The CHEST™[55] arrangements are particularly important. CHEST™ (Combined Higher Education Software Team) is a central body to negotiate with suppliers on behalf of the higher education and research communities. A considerable amount of software and database material is made available through the medium of its site licences. Unfortunately, it is not unknown for members of staff or students to abuse the terms of these licences either deliberately or unwittingly. It is therefore very important that institutions take steps to advise all staff and students of the licence conditions and to undertake audits of software in use. To facilitate this, the former UFC and PCFC drew up a *Code of Conduct for Use of Software and Datasets*.[56] The Federation Against Software Theft (FAST) exists to pursue offenders and enforce restrictions on illegal copying of copyright software.[57]

Databases

6.47 The contents of databases are literary works within the meaning of section 3 CDPA as 'a table or compilation.' The question is whether the database has been constructed or compiled with sufficient originality. An adopted EU Directive (96/9/EC) on the legal protection of databases, yet to be implemented in the UK, defines databases as 'a collection of independent words, data or other materials arranged in a systematic or methodical way and individually accessible by electronic or other means' which is a narrower definition than that in section 3. The Directive creates two new rights: a general database right protectable by copyright for 70 years and a sui generis right protectable for 15 years. The database must constitute the author's own intellectual creation and the sui generis right is designed to protect the investment in the work. An online database accessible via a telecommunications link is a cable programme service and downloading of such material without a licence will infringe copyright.[58] CD-ROMs are not available in this way and are therefore not treated as cable programme services: they are electronic copies

---

55 CHEST is a trademark of the University of Bath.
56 UFC/PCFC August 1992 (Issue 2).
57 Other representative bodies include the Entertainment Software Publishers' Association, the British Software Association and the Software Producers' Association.
58 Section 7 CDPA: The Cable and Broadcasting Act 1964 had amended the Copyright Act 1956 to make this clear.

of other material, which is itself protected by copyright. Hence a licence is required for downloading material from a CD-ROM other than where CDPA permits 'fair dealing' for the purposes of research or private study.

Code of Conduct for Use of Software and Datasets

6.48   The *Code of Conduct* is expressed to be 'not a legally binding document'[59] although it forms part of the contractual documentation which the institution accepts on acquiring software provided through the national arrangements. It is suggested that the terms of the Code should be incorporated into the institution's contracts with staff and students: so far as staff are concerned this is part of the general IPR clauses of the contract of employment. In the case of students, it would probably be adequate to refer to it as part of the regulations for the use of computers and the computing service. In all cases it is the institution which will be held liable for any illegal copying or illegal use of software and/or computer readable datasets by individual staff or students. This will apply also where an institution acts as intermediary between a supplier and another institution (perhaps an associated institution delivering franchised courses) or third party.

Moral rights of the authors of computer software

6.49   The moral rights of the author of computer software may also be infringed if the software is altered without the consent of the author. This is true even of shareware or freeware.

Lending computer software

6.50   Also restricted are the issue or renting of copies of computer software to 'the public' ie those persons not specifically licensed to receive, use and copy it. The owners of copyright have rights analogous to the Public Lending Right in books issued through public lending libraries, in that they are entitled to claim royalties. Likewise performances of computer programs on publicly accessible terminals

---

59   ISC Secretariat letter to Vice-Chancellors, etc reference 20/28/000 of 1 September 1992.

(but not demonstrations of computer-generated art) are subject to licensing.

Concessions relating to computer programs

6.51 There are certain concessions which apply to the use of computer programs which are not otherwise licensed. Since most programs used in higher education institutions will be licensed, this is of passing interest, but it should be noted that these concessions exist. Copyright is not infringed in these circumstances if

(a) the copying, adaptation or use is not of a 'substantial part' of the program: 'substantial' is not defined: however, in these cases it is likely to include the heart of the program, the peripheral elements being of no real interest;

(b) the copy or use is for the purposes of 'setting, communicating or answering' examination questions: 'examinations' is not defined and should therefore be given its dictionary meaning which is 'the process of testing knowledge or ability by questions:' on that basis it would include class tests which form part of periodical assessment, although that interpretation has not been tested in the courts;[60]

(c) the copying or use is for the purposes of research or private study in 'fair' circumstances, ie presumably where the copyright holder suffers no financial loss as a consequence.

New developments in technology

6.52 A number of potential problems will arise as technology continues to develop and the Act either has to be interpreted to cope with that development or amended. For example it is not clear whether the 'electronic means' specified in section 17(2) CDPA includes lasers (Light Amplification by Stimulated Emission of Radiation) since the definition of 'electronic' is 'actuated by electric, magnetic, electro-magnetic, electro-chemical or electro-mechanical energy' and arguably lasers are not included. If that is so, then copying by laser is not reproduction of work in any material form, and the protection of such work relies on the assumption that work is 'recorded' by such means within the coverage of section 3(2) CDPA.

---

60 The Library association maintains that the exemption does not apply in such cases: see S Norman *Copyright in Further and Higher Education Libraries* (1996) Library Association.

Imaging systems, both older analogue microform systems and digital optical disk systems are not covered by any CLA licence, neither is material posted on the internet, which in 1997 is estimated to have 50 million users world-wide. Reference has already been made to the problems associated with browsing and downloading material from the internet. The creation of a hypertext link to a web page without the consent of the page owner may constitute a breach of the latter's copyright.[61] There are numerous other non-copyright issues concerned with the internet, such as defamation,[62] obscenity, etc which are beyond the scope of this work.

Multimedia copyright

6.53   Multimedia copyright is a particularly difficult area, since it crosses the boundaries between the areas covered by the CLA and ERA schemes and other areas which are not, for example film and video. Difficulty in clearing multimedia copyright has serious implications for institutions involved in teaching and learning technology programmes (TLTP)[63] and for those which are connected to the SuperJANET broadband network, capable of providing multi-user access to a wide range of services, databases and courseware. Multimedia activities also risk infringing the moral rights of authors, artists and performers since often they consist in re-ordering, adding to, altering or incorporating work into other material. Moral rights must however be asserted and can be waived. Printing out, downloading, 'cut and paste' and networking from CD-ROM are governed by the specific terms of the CD-ROM licence agreement. Photocopying from CD-ROM printouts is not covered by the CLA licence. NCIHE called for an increase in the rate of use of copyright digital information.[64] In a typical application of Computer-Assisted Language Learning (CALL) a sentence may be scanned in and part of it (eg a verb) deleted. The student is then asked to complete the sentence. Such work is not covered by the CLA licence: if the work which is scanned in is the copyright of any person other than the institution, permission must be sought for its use. Extensive

61   *Shetland Times Ltd v Wilts* 1997 SCLR 160, action settled before proof.
62   The Defamation Act 1996 deals with exemption from liability for 'innocent' dissemination of defamatory material in certain circumstances.
63   The Information Services Committee (ISC) Courseware Development Working Party recommended in 1992 (*Beyond Lectures*) that the Funding Councils should address copyright issues.
64   Paragraph 17.34, Main Report, NCIHE, July 1997.

modification of work may also infringe the moral right of integrity of the author.

Computer-generated work

6.54 The author of a literary or other work which is computer generated is the person by whom the arrangements necessary for the creation of the work are undertaken ie most likely to be whoever paid for it, which includes employers. It is obviously essential that where there is more than one party involved the rights of the parties are spelt out in a contract.

Miscellaneous rights

6.55 The Performing Rights Society (PRS) administers applications for permission to perform a musical work in public or to broadcast it: institutions will be familiar with the annual assessments carried out by PRS in respect of live performances on their premises. The Mechanical Rights Performing Society (MCPS) administers the 'mechanical right' (the right to record music on to tapes or discs) and the 'synchronisation right' (the right to incorporate music in a film sound-track.) Phonographic Performance Ltd (PPL) administers public performances etc of rights in sound recordings, with corresponding rights in music videos being administered by Video Performance Limited (VPL). Individual record companies and film companies protect and administer their own rights. 'Rental right' is conferred by section 18 CDPA on sound recordings, films and computer programs, rental of which to the public is an act restricted by copyright.

The Copyright Tribunal

6.56 CDPA established a Copyright Tribunal[65] to hear and determine proceedings under the sections of the Act which allow the reference by affected parties of proposed licensing schemes, the refusal of licences or the terms of schemes considered to be unreasonable and a number of other issues related to licensing and royalties. The details of the Tribunal's jurisdiction will not be discussed here.

---

65 The Copyright Act 1956 had established a Tribunal called the Performing Rights Tribunal with more limited powers.

Patents

History of the patent

6.57 The second important form of intellectual, or industrial, property is the patent: a monopoly right to the exclusive use of an invention. One major difference from copyright is that a patent does nor arise automatically: it must be applied for and granted. The principal statute governing patents is the Patents Act 1977 (PA), which has been amended only slightly by CDPA. The word patent is derived from 'Letters Patent' – the grant of a monopoly right from the sovereign proved by the exhibition of open letters. Letters Patent are also used in the appointment of peers, certain officials and grants of other rights by the Crown. The earliest recorded patent in England was granted by Henry VI (1449) for the art of producing coloured glass: the first numbered patent was granted in 1617; in 1623 the Statute of Monopolies restricted the right of the Crown to grant monopolies except in respect of patentable inventions. A patent can now be considered as a form of contract between the Crown and the inventor. On the Crown's side, a monopoly is granted for a limited period. On his or her part the inventor must disclose to the Crown information necessary for the invention to be put into use. Although no doubt in the past the grant of a patent was a rather glamorous affair, patent protection in the UK is now administered by the Patent Office, an Executive Agency of the Department of Trade and Industry.

The Patents Rules and procedures

6.58 In addition to PA, the Patents Rules, amended from time to time, set out the detailed procedure, forms, charges levied etc.[66] Most important here is the 'priority date' which is the date of filing the application in the UK: under the terms of an international convention of 1883, filings in other countries may be made one year after the date of the initial application and retain the original priority date. The priority date is significant in relation to protection of the patent application and the existence of the invention as 'prior art.' The 1883 convention is the International Union for the Protection of Industrial Property, known as the Paris Union or the International Convention. There are a number of other international agreements: the Patent Cooperation Treaty (1970 – entered into force 1978) administered

---

66 Eg Patents Rules 1995, SI 1995/2093.

by the World Intellectual Property Organisation (WIPO)[67] provides a simplified system of search and examination by an International Searching Authority Examiner; the European Patent Convention 1973 which enables inventors to secure patents in signatory states in one application. A Community Patent Convention which allows a single application filed through the European Patent Office to mature into a single unitary indivisible object of property covering the whole of the EU, is yet to enter into force. An EC Commission Green Paper of 1997 raises questions about future development of EU policy on patents and the harmonisation of member states' patent laws. As Laddie J said in *Re European Patent (UK) No 189958 in the name of Akzo Nobel NV; Re a Petition by Fort Dodge Animal Health Ltd*[68] intellectual property litigation in general, patent litigation in particular in Europe, is in some disarray thanks to 'unedifying competition to secure jurisdiction over proceedings.'

Requirements of novelty, inventive step and industrial application

6.59 To be patentable a discovery must:
(i) be new;
(ii) involve an inventive step;
(iii) be capable of industrial application.[69]
An invention is *new* if it is not matter of any form which has been made known to the public by written or oral description, which includes material in a patent application having an earlier priority date.[70] It involves an *inventive step* if it is not obvious to a person skilled in the art and reading relevant published material.[71] It is the area of 'obviousness' which gives rise to most argument and litigation.[72] An invention must be *capable of being made or used in any industry.*[73] A product for medical or veterinary treatment is included if it is capable of industrial application, but not otherwise.

---

67 WIPO administers a wide range of treaties including the Paris Convention for the Protection of Industrial Property 1883 (revised seven times between 1900 and 1979), the Berne Convention, the Rome Convention for the Protection of Performers, Producers of Phonograms and Broadcasting Organisations 1961, the Washington Treaty on Intellectual Property in Respect of Integrated Circuits 1989, etc.
68 (1997) Times, 24 October.
69 See Strasbourg Convention on the Unification of Certain Points of Substantive Law on Patents for Inventions 1963.
70 Section 2 PA.
71 Section 1(1)(b) PA.
72 See eg *Chiron Corpn v Murex Diagnostics Ltd* [1996] RPC 535.
73 Section 1(1)(c) PA.

It is important to note that following the Agreement on Trade-Related Aspects of Intellectual Property (TRIPS) as part of the GATT negotiations, the US patent law was amended to include, from January 1996, provision for non-US inventors to establish 'invention dates' (the date of invention rather than the date of filing is the important date in the US) prior to that date, with an invention date of 1 January 1996 or the filing date whichever is earlier. Evidence of invention and proof of diligence in its reduction to practice are required.

Excluded categories

6.60 The following are not patentable:[74]
(a) a discovery, scientific theory or mathematical method;
(b) a literary, dramatic, musical or artistic work or any other aesthetic creation whatsoever;
(c) a scheme, rule or method for performing a mental act, playing a game or doing business, or a program for a computer;[75]
(d) the presentation of information.

Biotechnology and patents

6.61 Inventions which would encourage offensive, immoral or anti-social behaviour are also excluded. This aspect was in the forefront of the controversy over the patenting of the 'Harvard oncomouse,' a mouse genetically engineered to make it particularly susceptible to certain cancers. Although granted a European Patent in 1992, specific questions had been raised about the morality of the application. In addition to that, the application raised questions about the extent to which patents could be granted to categories long considered to be outside protection: animals, plants or biological processes. The oncomouse was considered to be a 'microbiological process.' NAPAG[76] recommend that this prohibition continues.

6.62 Processes for treating the human body for the prevention or cure of disease are not patentable in the UK. Schedule 2 PA makes

74 Section 1(2) PA.
75 VICOM/*Computer-Related Inventions* [1987] 2 EPOR 74; confirmed and applied by the Court of Appeal in *Re Patent Application No 9204956.2 by Fujitsu Ltd* (1997) Times, 14 March.
76 National Academies Policy Advisory Group *Intellectual Property and the Academic Community* (1995) Recommendation 3.

special provision for the treatment of micro-organisms[77] and there are proposals by the European Commission to establish a central Plant Variety Rights Office. New plant varieties can be protected under the Plant Varieties and Seeds Act 1964. A licensing scheme for farm-saved seed has been developed by the British Plant Breeders' Society. A draft European Directive on biotechnology patenting (not plant or animal varieties) was adopted by the European Parliament in 1997 in the light of the Biodiversity Treaty 1992 (the Rio Treaty) on access to and the exchange of technology and information, particularly in the biotechnology area. It appears likely that gene sequences will be patentable but it is clear that this could have an adverse impact on fundamental research, particularly the international *Human Geonome Project.*[78] Biotechnology patents can fail, as in *Biogen Inc v Medeva plc*[79] where a claim to an invention of a recombinant DNA molecule was too broad in that the same results could be produced by different means and no new principle had been established.

Requirement for confidentiality

6.63 The basic principle which must guide anyone thinking of applying for patent protection is that the invention or process for which protection is sought must not be disclosed to third parties, other than at International Exhibitions[80] (or unlawfully or in breach of confidence) not more than six months before the initial application is filed. Disclosure results in loss of protection. In *Re Bristol Myers Co's Application*,[81] Lord Parker LCJ expressed this rule thus '... if the information has been communicated to a single member of the public without inhibiting fetter that is enough to amount to a making available to the public ...' Conflict between this principle and the desire of academic staff to publish the results of their research is inevitable unless an institution has drawn up, and communicated to its staff, a clear policy on patent protection. This is one of the recommendations of the *Report of the CVCP Working Party on*

---

77 See Treaty on the International Recognition of the Deposit of Microorganisms for the purposes of Patent Procedure 1977 (The Budapest Treaty).
78 See M P Jackson 'The patenting of life' in *The Ivanhoe Guide to Chartered Patent Agents* (1993) Letts/CIPA.
79 [1997] RPC 1, HL.
80 Section 2(4) PA: certification is required by the applicant in a form prescribed in the Patent Rules 1995.
81 [1969] RPC 146.

Patents and the Commercial Exploitation of Research Results.[82] US law permits a grace period of 12 months during which publication of an inventor's own papers do not prejudice US patent applications. Under the EU system, publication is an immediate bar to patentability.

Ownership of patents

6.64 An invention made by an employee belongs to his or her employer if made in the course of employment or if the employee had an obligation to further the employer's interests. In *Greater Glasgow Health Board's Application*[83] a junior doctor, employed to treat patients, invented a new ophthalmic device. The court held that he and not his employer was entitled to the patent, Jacob J holding that it was a fallacy to assume on the basis that his duty was to diagnose and treat patients that it extended to devising new ways of doing so; his invention was a useful accessory to his contracted work but not really part of it. Duties can of course be assigned specifically and not be 'the standard or everyday duties on which a person is normally employed.'[84] 'Moonlighting' activities should not be assumed to fall outside the duties of an employee.[85] When an employee makes an invention where the patent is of outstanding benefit to the employer, the employee is entitled to reward to be determined by the Comptroller of Patents in the absence of agreement between employer and employee;[86] section 42 PA provides that contractual terms cannot restrict the employee's rights further than the Act already does. Today most higher education institutions will make regulations about the ownership of patents, as part of the contract of employment of those likely to be involved in inventions. The ACAS Working Party on Teaching Staff contracts recommended a clause which is adopted in Appendix A.

The patent application

6.65 Although in theory it is possible for anyone to file a patent application, in practice it is usual to engage the services of a patent agent to undertake the highly specialised work involved. The

82 CVCP 1978.
83 [1996] RPC 207.
84 *Secretary of State for Defence's Application* SRTS O/135/86.
85 *Missing Link Software v Magee* [1992] EIPR 361.
86 A rarely used provision: an example is *British Steel plc's Patent* [1992] RPC 117.

monopoly claimed must be delimited precisely. The Patent Rules specify the forms to be used and the manner in which the application must be set out. Part V CDPA amended PA in respect of the right to represent applicants at the Patent Office. No-one may describe themselves as a patent agent unless they are duly entered on the Register of Patent Agents kept by the Patent Office; registration is granted only to those who have passed qualifying examinations of the Chartered Institute of Patent Agents.[87]

6.66 A higher education institution will almost certainly wish to use the services of a patent agent and what follows is a simplified account of the agent's programme of action. The agent will wish to see a description of the invention including the following points:

(i)   the general character of the article or process involved;
(ii) details of and problems associated with previously known or used processes which are to be replaced or improved by the invention;
(iii) the inventive idea and its advantages over the processes described in (ii), together with the way or ways in which it can be put into effect;
(iv) a full description of the invention, illustrated if possible in the way shown in the Patent Rules.

6.67 Assuming the agent advises that the invention is patentable, it is then filed and then the remaining requirements for the first stage are completed (if not, the application lapses). A patent application may be filed in the UK alone or under the terms of the European Patent Convention of 1973 or the Patent Co-operation Treaty. Costs increase as territorial coverage increases. The remaining requirements are to file claims (brief definitions of the invention) and an abstract (a brief description of what the invention is and what it is for) and a request for preliminary examination and search. The latter must be filed within one year of the priority date. The examiner ensures that the requirements of PA and the Rules have been complied with (which one can assume if a patent agent has been engaged) and carries out a search to see what technical background the application will be judged against. As soon as practicable after 18 months from the priority date the Patent Office must publish the application papers as they were filed as a printed patent specification with a serial number. Further progress will depend on the results of the search. Assuming that the applicant wishes to proceed, as the search has disclosed nothing which makes the invention obvious or is so close to the invention as to make it unviable to proceed further, a request

87 Section 276 CDPA.

for substantive examination is made. The examiner may carry out an interactive process with the applicant (or agent) allowing amendment of the application to distinguish it from prior art: finally the examiner decides whether to grant the application or not. If granted, a patent is issued. If not, the applicant may appeal to the Patents Court, part of the Chancery Division of the High Court and further, with leave, to the Court of Appeal.[88]

Patent rights and infringement

6.68 Patent rights are negative in the sense that they forbid others to use the invention rather than giving the patentee positive clearance to use it, since the patentee may himself or herself be circumscribed in manufacturing activities by other patents. The grant of a patent does not necessarily mean that the invention will be produced, since this is a commercial decision based on other factors. Once granted, however, a patent lasts for 20 years and a patentee naturally hopes that he or she will be able to exploit it within that time. Developments in the 'art' during that time will, if the system is respected, result in negotiations between patent holders and inventors resulting in co-operative or licensing arrangements to their mutual benefit. The European Court of Justice has held that section 51 PA, which permits the Comptroller of Patents to order the grant of compulsory licences on the grounds that the invention was not being worked in the UK but could be, or that demand was being met by importation, is contrary to the Treaty of Rome.[89]

6.69 Assuming that such negotiations do not take place, are unsuccessful, or there is simply a blatant disregard of the patent, the aggrieved party may seek an injunction or interdict from the court restraining the infringing party from continuing with the infringement. If the infringer resists this, it will normally be because he or she argues that the patent is invalid and will seek its revocation. Cases are heard in the Patents County Court.[90] Section 289 CDPA permits transfer of cases between the High Court and the Patents County Court.[91] An EU Green Paper of 1997 raises the question

---

88 Sections 96–97 PA.
89 *EC Commission v United Kingdom*: Case C-30/90 [1993] FSR 1.
90 Section 287 CDPA; Patents County Courts (Designation and Jurisdiction) Order 1990 (SI 1990/1496).
91 Cases arising under this section include *Memminger-Iro GmbH v Trip-Lite* [1991] FSR 322; *GEC-Marconi v Xyllyx Viewdata Terminals Pte* [1991] FSR 319.

whether there should be jurisdiction at European level to determine disputes.

Registered designs and design right

Two different forms of IPR

6.70 It is very easy to confuse the two forms of intellectual property 'registered design' and 'design right.' Both of them are forms of copyright. The former requires formal action on the part of the owner of the design, the latter arises automatically on recording of the design in a design document or when an article has been made to the design. In July 1993 and January 1994 the EU published proposals for a draft Directive and Regulation on respectively harmonisation on the basis of a registered design system and a two-tier Community design system.

Registered designs

6.71 The Registered Designs Act 1949 as amended appears as Schedule 4 CDPA. The law relating to registered designs has been of only limited interest to higher education institutions except in relation to commercial activities. There are three requirements for a new design to be registrable:
(i)   it must relate to shape, configuration pattern or ornament;
(ii) it must be applied by an industrial process to an article (or part thereof if sold separately);[92]
(iii) it must appeal to and be judged by the eye.
The following are excluded from registration:
(i)   a method or principle of construction;
(ii) features of shape or configuration dictated solely by function;
(iii) features of shape or configuration dependent on the appearance of another article of which it is intended by the author of the design to form an integral part;
(iv) if the appearance of the article is not material, that is if aesthetic considerations are not normally taken into account by the purchaser or user and would not be if the design was applied to the article.[93]

---

92 There must be an 'article' – where there is not, there can be no registration, as in the thermostatic radiator valves case *Drayton Controls (Engineering) v Honeywell Control Systems* [1992] FSR 245.
93 Section 1 Registered Designs Act 1949 as it appears in Schedule 4 CDPA.

Registered designs last for five years, renewable to a maximum of 25 years.

Design right

6.72   Design right is a new right created in the UK by CDPA. Section 213 CDPA defines design right as 'a property right which subsists ... .in an original design.' 'Design' is then defined as '... the design of any aspect of the shape or configuration (whether internal or external) of the whole or part of an article.' The right does not subsist in a method or principle of construction, a surface decoration, or features of shape or configuration of an article which

(i)   enable the article to be connected to, or placed in, around or against, another article so that either article may perform its function, or

(ii) are dependent upon the appearance of another article of which the article is intended by the designer to form an integral part.

Furthermore, a design is not 'original' if it is commonplace in the design field in question at the time of its creation. There are special rules relating to semi-conductors.[94]

6.73   As in the case of copyright, there are qualifications on who may obtain design right and its territorial application. Design right only subsists in a design if the design qualifies by reference to the designer, his/her employer, the person commissioning the design or the person by whom and country in which articles made to the design were first marketed. The owner of design right where the design is commissioned, is the commissioner, not the person who created the design.[95]

6.74   Design right may be assigned or licensed in the same way as other intellectual property rights. It may run concurrently with registration under the Registered Designs Act for articles which incorporate the design. The rights and remedies arising on infringement of the holders of design right are very similar to those appertaining to the holders of copyright, other than the duration of design right, which is essentially 15 years from the end of the calendar year of recording or the date when an article was first made to the design, whichever occurs first or, where articles are made available

---

94 The Design Right (Semiconductor Topographies) Regulations 1989 (SI 1989/1100), implementing Directive 87/54/EEC.
95 Section 215(2) CDPA.

for sale or hire within five years from the end of that calendar year, 10 years from the end of that calendar year.

Trade marks

Law and definition

6.75 Trade mark registration dates from 1875:[96] the present law is governed by the Trade Marks Act 1994. The function of trade mark legislation is to protect the mark but not the article which is marked.[97] The recent legislation extended the protection afforded by the Trade Marks Act 1938 to marks used in relation to the provision of services ('service marks'). If registration is granted, it lasts for seven years in the first instance, renewable thereafter for 14 years at a time. The EU Council Regulation for the Community Trade Mark (CTM) came into force in 1994 and a CTM Office is situated in Alicante administered by OHIM (the Office for Harmonisation in the Internal Market (Trade Marks and Designs)). A CTM gives protection in all EU countries. The Madrid Protocol of 1989 to the original Madrid Agreement of 1891 provides a mechanism for registering trade marks in signatory countries through WIPO.

6.76 A trade mark is any sign that can distinguish the goods or services of one trader from the goods or services of another and can be represented graphically. A 'sign' includes words, devices, three-dimensional shapes and sometimes sounds and smells. A trade mark is used as a marketing tool so that customers can recognise the product of a particular trader but there are also numerous examples of celebrities registering their names and images under the Act.[98]

Trade marks and the internet

6.77 An Internet Ad Hoc Committee (IAHC) produced a report in 1997 on problems associated with international domain names and

---

96 Trade Marks Registration Act 1875.
97 Per Lord Templeman in *Re Coca-Cola Co* [1986] 1 WLR 695, 698, quoted by Lord Jauncey of Tullichettle in *Reckitt & Colman Products Ltd v Borden Inc* [1990] 1 WLR 491, 513.
98 See M Stephens 'I am a Trademark' *The Times*, 14 October 1997: examples include footballers Eric Cantona and Ryan Giggs.

the internet. WIPO is considering the conflicts between trade mark rights and internet domain names.[99]

Protection of institutional names and logos

6.78   Institutions of higher education have shown interest in protecting their names (in various forms such as 'The University of X' or 'X University') and their armorial bearings or logos for two main reasons:
(i)   to prevent their use by other bodies claiming to have a link with the institution;[100]
(ii) to be able to license their use on commercial goods – mugs, sweatshirts, keyrings, etc.
The controversy in 1993 over the use of the title 'St Catherine's College (University of Oxford) Kobe Institute' by an educational institution in Japan, is an example of the difficulties which can arise. The University of Oxford has made it clear that it has no 'branch campuses' other, possibly, than the University of Cambridge![101]

6.79   A number of institutions have made enquiries about, or formal application for, registration of their names and corporate identities under the legislation, either in class 16 (paper, stationery, teaching material, etc) or in class 41 (education and entertainment). The main difficulties in registering the name of an institution appear to be that (i) it is open to challenge on the basis of its descriptive, rather than distinctive, nature and (ii) so far as class 16 is concerned, could be deceptive if used on printed matter which did not relate directly to the institution. An examples of successful registration is Newcastle Law School.[102] The problem facing law schools is that the proliferation of the universities has left a number of cities and towns in England and Wales with more than one law school or faculty in separate institutions, leading to the possibility of confusion for clients and customers both at home and overseas.

6.80   Registration of a grant of arms would also be subject to any objection raised by the Kings of Arms. Registration of a specially-designed 'logo' would appear to be a possibility. If registration is granted, the possibility arises of an action similar to that in *Compaq*

---

99   See eg *Pitman Training Ltd v Nominet UK* [1997] FSR 797.
100 Such as the practice of offering fake degree certificates over the internet.
101 *New Straits Times* Singapore, 13 August 1993.
102 A Beale, N Bourne and R Geary 'What's in a Name? Protecting the Law School' (1993) Business Law Review 90.

Computer Corpn v Dell Computer Corpn[103] where injunction was granted to restrain the use of the plaintiff's name as a comparator in the defendant's advertisement. 'Our course is better than theirs' takes on a new significance. The possibility of protecting the corporate name by the simple expedient of claiming copyright in it as an original literary work within what is now the provisions of CDPA is effectively ruled out by the decision of the court not to allow this in *Exxon Corpn v Exxon Insurance Consultants International Ltd*.[104]

Data protection

Protection of personal data

6.81   The Data Protection Act 1984 (DPA) is concerned with the protection of personal data held on computer databases, which includes details held on computer about students and staff of higher education institutions. The DPA enabled the UK to ratify the Convention for the Protection of Individuals with regard to Automatic Processing of Personal Data established under the auspices of the Council of Europe. It introduced obligations on the part of computer and data users, established rights of individuals who are the subject of data held by data users and set up a system of registration of such users by a Data Protection Registrar. There is also a common law duty on an employer not to disclose to third parties confidential information about employees, unless this is specifically authorised by statute.[105] An EU Data Protection Directive due to be implemented in 1998 will make major changes in the law.

Definitions of 'data' and 'personal data'

6.82   The Act defines 'data' as

> ... information recorded in a form in which it can be processed by equipment operating automatically in response to instructions given for that purpose.

---

103 [1992] FSR 93.
104 [1982] Ch 119.
105 See eg *Dalgleish v Lothian and Borders Police Board* [1991] IRLR 422: interdict granted restraining the Board from releasing names and addresses for the purpose of identifying alleged community charge defaulters.

and 'personal data' means

> ... data consisting of information which relates to a living individual who can be identified from that information (or from that and other information in the possession of the data user), including any expression of opinion about the individual but not any indication of the intentions of the data user in respect of that individual.

So, an expression of opinion about a person (eg 'Mr A has a drink problem') is personal data but deductions from it ('credit refused because Mr A's health is unsound') is not. Under the Directive keeping certain types of data without consent will be unlawful. These include data which reveal religious or political beliefs, racial or ethnic origin.

The data protection principles

6.83 The Act applies only to data held on computers, not to data held in manual records, although implementation of the Directive will change this It establishes eight data protection principles, the first seven of which apply to personal data held by data users and the eighth applies in addition to personal data in respect of which services are provided by persons carrying on computer bureaux. These principles relate to the fair and lawful obtaining, use and disclosure of data and access by data subjects to personal information.

Registration

6.84 On registration a data user must give a description of and the purposes for which personal data are to be held and used, the sources of data or information contained in the data, the persons to whom disclosure of the data is intended and a list of the countries or territories outside the UK to which the data is intended to be directly or indirectly transferred. Some data is exempt, for example payroll, pensions and business accounting data if used solely for that purpose, data held only for the purpose of word processing, and data held solely for domestic and recreational purposes. Other exemptions include data held by incorporated members' clubs about their members, and data held only for distribution of articles or information to data subjects consisting only of names and addresses, provided the subjects have been asked and have not objected to this use of the data and restrictions on disclosure are complied with.

Rights of the data subject

6.85 A data subject has the right to inspect the register and to take copies, for a fee, of any entries of interest to him or her. An application may then be made to the data user for a copy of the records which contain information about the data subject. Assuming the application is bona fide, the data user must within 40 days supply a copy of all the records on the computer files which refer to the applicant. On receipt of the details, and if not satisfied with their contents, the data subject may request the data user to correct inaccuracies or may complain to the Registrar.

6.86 There are penalties for using personal data for unregistered purposes. These include issue of an enforcement notice or deregistration by the Data Protection Registrar. A data subject has the right to seek compensation through the courts, for damage or distress caused as a result of loss, destruction or unauthorised disclosure of particular personal data. A data subject also has the right to compensation for the holding of inaccurate data and may obtain a court order for access to the data so that it may be corrected or erased. Failure to register is an offence, as is contravention of the data protection principles. It is a criminal offence under the Act (as amended by section 161 Criminal Justice and Public Order Act 1994) to procure or sell personal data procured by persuading a data user to make a disclosure not covered by his or her entry on the register.

DPA registration in higher education

6.87 A typical Data Protection Act registration of a higher education institution would be divided between central administration, teaching departments, research and ancillary services, although there is a certain amount of overlap between each of these headings. 'Central administration' will include staff and student records, accommodation, procurement, public relations, marketing, alumni relations, and so on. The sources from which data is derived and the categories of persons or agencies to which it is disclosed will vary according to the subject-matter. 'Teaching departments' will record material on staff and students, at least in the case of students more detailed than appears on central records. 'Research' particularly social research will include details of subjects and clients. 'Ancillary services' will include commercial operations, consultancy and advisory services, library and computing services, all of which have a need to record some personal information about clients and users. Data

Protection registration is granted for three years at a time and it is necessary for institutions to check periodically that the registration required is up to date. This is particularly important where new lines of research work are developed for which access to personal data is necessary.

6.88 The Funding Councils are registered under the Data Protection Act; they are also subject to the *Government Statistical Service Code of Practice* which (inter alia) preserves personal confidentiality. The Councils have issued guidelines about the release of statistics. For example SHEFC '… has no wish to release any information from the statistical returns that violates personal confidentiality.'[106]

Data protection and the internet

6.89 Receiving data from the internet does not give rise to any particular difficulty, provided that existing procedures which govern response to requests for information are extended to include electronic mail, although it is possible that the setting of a 'cookie,' which catches audit trail information on a visitor to an internet site, infringes the Act. Personal data on screen while an individual is browsing are normally only displayed to see if it is of use. 'Use' in section 5(2)(b) Data Protection Act must mean more than just looking at the information.[107] Transmitting personal data, provided it is done within the Data Protection Principles, should be in order. All facets of the use of personal data obtained from, or transmitted via, the internet must be related to an appropriate purpose described in the data user's register entry.

Access to manually-held records

Access to personal files

6.90 The Access to Personal Files Act 1987 allows individuals access to a limited range of personal information held about them on manual files. The original intention was that this should extend to, inter alia, records kept by higher education institutions. However, the Act extends only to records held in connection with social services and

106 SHEFC *Guidelines governing the release by SHEFC of unpublished statistics about individual institutions* Circular Letter 59/93, 23 November 1993.
107 *R v Brown* (unreported), CA.

housing; regulations have been made to implement it in these areas.[108] During the passage of the Bill, ministers indicated that education would be brought within the framework of the Act by regulations made under section 27 Education Act 1980, but this has not been done and in any event section 27 does not extend to higher education. There are no corresponding powers in the higher education sector: even the powers given to the Secretaries of State to impose supplementary functions on the Funding Councils[109] do not extend to creating new functions which are not otherwise provided for by statute. It appears likely, however, that in due course access to higher education records will be granted. In practice, most of the records which are kept are available for inspection by the individuals to whom they relate, since they do not contain information not already known to or supplied by the individual member of staff or student, other than confidential references, disclosure of which would presumably be excluded from the regulations.

Access to medical reports

6.91 The Access to Medical Reports Act 1988 confers a right on the individual to have access to any medical report relating to him or her which is to be, or has been, supplied by a medical practitioner for employment purposes or insurance purposes. This is of significance to higher education institutions in cases involving premature retirement or dismissal on medical grounds. The employer requires the consent of the individual who may have access to the report before it is supplied. The individual has the right to request the medical practitioner to amend any part of the report which he or she considers is inaccurate or misleading. If the practitioner does not agree to this, the individual may request that a written statement of his or her views is attached to the report. There are exceptions to the right of access where in the view of the practitioner access would be likely to cause serious harm to the physical or mental health of the individual or would indicate the intentions of the practitioner in respect of the individual. There are also provisions to protect the confidentiality of the records of others.

---

108 Access to Personal Files (Social Services) Regulations 1989 and 1991 (SI 1989/ 206 and 1991/1587); Access to Personal Files (Housing) Regulations 1989 (SI 1989/503) and corresponding regulations for Scotland.
109 Section 69(5) FHEA and section 43(5) FHESA.

Access to health records

6.92   The Access to Health Records Act 1990 provides a right of access (subject to certain exceptions similar to those in the Access to Medical Reports Act) to information contained in manually held health records kept by medical practitioners and health authorities. This is likely to be of interest only to individual staff and students and to institutions employing medical practitioners.

Appendix A

Model contractual clause dealing with patents and inventions[110]

1. The provisions of sections 39, 40, 41, 42 and 43 of the Patents Act 1977 relating to the ownership of employees' inventions and the compensation of employees for certain inventions are acknowledged by [the institution] and by you.

2. You agree that by virtue of the nature of your duties and the responsibilities arising from them you have a special obligation to further the interest of [the institution.]

3. Any matter or thing capable of being patented under the Patents Act 1977, made developed or discovered by you either alone or in concert, whilst in the performance of your normal duties, duties specifically assigned to you or arising out of anything done by you to which paragraph 2 applies, shall forthwith be disclosed to [the institution] and subject to the provision of the Patents Act shall belong to and be the absolute property of [the institution][.

4. You shall (and not withstanding the termination of your employment) sign and execute all such documents and do all such acts as [the institution] may reasonably require:
4.1 to apply for and obtain in the sole name of [the institution] (unless it otherwise directs) patent registered design or other protection of any nature whatsoever in respect of the inventions in any country throughout the world and, when so obtained or vested, to renew and maintain the same;

---

110 Reproduced by permission of the Chief Executive of the Polytechnics and Colleges Employers' Forum.

4.2 to resist any objection or opposition to obtaining, and any petitions or applications for revocation of, any such patent, registered design or other protection;

4.3 to bring any proceedings for infringement of any such patent, registered design or other protection;

4.4 [the institution] hereby undertakes to indemnify you in respect of all costs, claims and damages, howsoever and wheresoever incurred, in connection with the discharge by you of any and all such requests under 4.1, 4.2 and 4.3.

5.1 [The institution] acknowledges sections 7 and 42 of the Patents Act. In respect of any invention which belongs to [the institution] by virtue of section 39 of the Patents Act, it shall be for [the institution] in the first instance to decide whether to apply for patent or other protection in law.

5.2 In the event that [the institution] decides not to apply for patent or other legal protection you have the right to be notified of that decision so soon as is reasonably practicable thereafter.

5.3 If, following such a decision by [the institution] you wish to apply for Patent either yourself or with another you must first inform [the institution] of your intention to do so. Within a reasonable period of time following such notification [the institution] must tell you whether it would object to your proposed application. The sole ground for such objection is that the patenting of the invention will involve or result in the disclosure to third parties of trade secrets or other confidential information belonging to [the institution] and that such disclosure may damage the interests of [the institution.]

5.4 Where [the institution] objects under 5.3 you hereby undertake in consideration of the payment of compensation to be determined under 5.5 below, not to proceed to apply for patent of the invention concerned nor to assist any other person to do so.

5.5 The calculation of compensation referred to above shall have regard to those factors set out in section 41 of the Patents Act. In the event that [the institution] cannot agree the amount of compensation, it shall be competent for either you or [the institution] to apply to the president of the Law Society to appoint an arbitrator under the terms of the Arbitration Act, whose decision shall be binding. [*This paragraph would require modification for use in Scotland.*]

Chapter 7

The future

Structure and governance

7.1   It appears unlikely in the short to medium term that the structure of the UK higher education system will undergo further upheavals of the kind experienced over the period 1988–1997. There may be a small increase in the number of universities and some mergers of existing smaller institutions with larger neighbours but the basic structure set out in Chapter 1 is unlikely to change significantly. The UK will continue to support a diverse range of higher education institutions. However developments in secondary and further education will influence the pattern and curriculum of higher education and we will see more evidence of a 'seamless transition' between the various forms of post-16 education. It is not impossible to contemplate a scenario in the longer term in which universities become essentially degree-awarding and validating bodies, with much of the actual teaching and learning being carried on by other providers using new technologies. Devolution to Scotland, changes in the school-leaving qualification system and the restriction of public funding for students from elsewhere in the UK wishing to study there may combine to make more radical changes in Scottish post-16 arrangements.

7.2   Changes in the student support system to be introduced in what will become during printing of this book the Teaching and Higher Education Act 1998 have more far-reaching consequences in terms of governance. The powers to be taken to require the Funding Councils to impose conditions on institutions relating to tuition fees are both a further attack on institutional autonomy and have the effect of bringing chartered institutions more into line with their non-chartered brethren. The unspecified power to 'demand and receive fees' which is a common feature of royal charters is attenuated by primary legislation which prescribes limits to those fees at least so far as full-time undergraduates are concerned.

7.3 Further external controls on governance seem inevitable in view of the number of problems in this area affecting individual institutions but having wider ramifications for the whole sector. In particular it is expected that there will be pressure to disentangle the supervisory role of independent members of governing bodies from their involvement in institutional management and executive decision-making. If, as is envisaged by the discussion in chapter 1, the legislative functions of the English chartered university's Court are abolished in favour of a direct link between the governing body and the Privy Council, at least the identity of the responsible authority will be clear in all higher education institutions. As all members of a governing body are technically equal, except where statute, instruments of government or procedural rules otherwise specify, then care has to be taken to specify what precisely is the additional role, if any, taken by the independent members who are always technically in the majority. It is also important to clarify the personal liability of each member of the governing body, not just that of the independent members.

7.4 Imposed codes of conduct may take over from voluntary arrangements. It is almost inevitable that one of the requirements of these codes, or of any voluntary arrangements which are acceptable to government as alternatives, will be the appointment of a properly qualified and independent adviser to the governing body, a role which many existing institutions may find it difficult to fill from within existing staff. The position of Secretary or Registrar, now generally a senior officer responsible for all or most of the administrative services, is not an independent one, since it is normal for this individual to be responsible in management terms to the chief executive. The independent adviser might also take on the role of monitoring officer in respect of services to the Audit Committee required by the Financial Memorandum, and possibly also in respect of equal opportunities, complaints and grievances monitoring, for example being the point of contact for those described somewhat inelegantly as 'whistleblowers' by the Nolan Committee, CUC and others.

7.5 Some problems which have arisen at institutions over the period 1993–1997 have been associated with alleged failures in procedures designed to monitor academic standards. A central monitoring officer might act as a 'back-stop' in such areas, and set up internal procedures to monitor and co-ordinate the institution's compliance with the vast array of legislation described in outline in chapter 2 and chapter 5.

Student issues

7.6   It seems to be accepted by all commentators that the more overt the contractual arrangements between students and institutions become, the more likely it is that complaints and grievances will be raised and that institutions will have to have proper procedures in place to deal with them. If all academic and disciplinary procedures are fair (and regular review is needed to ensure that that description fits contemporary standards laid down by the courts and Visitors) and they are fairly and consistently applied, institutions should survive any legal challenge. It remains unlikely that external bodies, whether they be courts, Visitors, arbitrators or regulatory bodies, will interfere in pure academic judgment properly exercised by adequately trained and experienced professional staff. As the area of educational malpractice develops in the various common law jurisdictions, institutions will have to be alert to what is required to satisfy external agencies that the staff resources being deployed are indeed properly qualified and trained for the purposes for which they are used. Issues such as liability for inadequately prepared references need to be addressed with due rigour.

7.7   The demographic changes in the student population over the last 20 years have been largely the result of improvements in equal opportunities for women and members of ethnic minority groups, improving access for mature students and more recently addressing the issue of disability in a coherent way (although the latter is far from being completed). Changes in student funding will almost certainly result in more students studying nearer home (although the fast-moving developments in information technology may pull in another direction) and either living at home or being more discerning about the type of residential accommodation they have to fund either immediately or longer term through loans. The effects of this change will be felt disproportionately by the largely residential 1960s Robbins universities and others situated away from major population centres. Disposal of, or changes in the use of, residential accommodation will require careful planning in terms of the law relating to the estate and the requirements of the Financial Memoranda. It may also result in a more pronounced consumer-provider relationship as students demand timetables geared to their availability as daily visitors rather than to the assumption that most students lived on site. The structure of the teaching week, semester or term, and academic year may also have to be reviewed as students pay more towards their education.

7.8 The abandonment of the Visitorial system for resolving student complaints in the minority of institutions which subscribe to it seems inevitable. In its place, and in place of direct access to the higher courts in the other institutions, should come an arbitration scheme based on widely-accepted principles. It may be that experiences with arbitration elsewhere, as in the planned arrangements for dealing with employment disputes in the Employment Rights (Dispute Resolution) Act 1998 (to be finalised as this book goes to press) will hasten this process. It may also be that institutions will themselves wish to establish mechanisms for alternative dispute resolution procedures based on best practice from other sectors. Whatever is the final outcome, it is inevitable that the system for handling student complaints, grievances and procedural aspects of appeals will be greatly improved. As it is improved, so it will be possible to avoid what has in the past seemed the inevitable 'opening of the floodgates' to successful litigation by dissatisfied students, a prediction which the author of this book has never shared.

7.9 The ever-increasing franchising, including international franchising, of higher education carries with it a range of issues concerned with the contractual arrangement between student and provider. Dispute resolution in internationally franchised programmes is fraught with problems about jurisdiction, applicable law, and the potential damages and other remedies which may be awarded by foreign courts. Institutions involved in such arrangements have to take expert advice before entering into, or even allowing their staff to explore entry into, such areas.

Staff issues

7.10 Equal opportunities in employment is the area in which most development is expected over the next few years. This encompasses all aspects of discrimination (sex, race and disability) and issues of equal pay and equality in contractual status. Serious efforts are being made to deal with the lack of any objective job evaluation in staff grading schemes. The use of continually renewed fixed-term contracts as a management tool for avoiding giving staff job security will probably be tackled in the European arena and will have a major impact on higher education institutions when there are no long-term funding plans.

7.11   The highly complex arrangements introduced into the pre-1992 universities by the University Commissioners under ERA are expected to come under scrutiny as part of a general trend to deregulate and simplify staff disciplinary and related procedures. As discussed in chapter 5 and in chapter 1 on the role and function of the Vice-Chancellor or equivalent, there are areas of the arrangements which leave room for doubt as to their fairness. It may be thought inconsistent that given the proposals for codes of practice to enable aggrieved staff to raise issues of concern, a system remains in place which places the Vice-Chancellor in the position of deciding, without further appeal, whether a grievance is to be taken forward or not. It is also not obvious that a power to decide whether to suspend a member of staff pending disciplinary investigation should be placed in the hands of the same individual who decides ultimately whether to dismiss that person. Finally it is somewhat at odds with modern concepts of teamworking and single status employment that only academic staff are subject to these procedures. Others can be dismissed without any special tribunal or appeal system.

Information

7.12   It is the area of information technology which above all others will influence the way higher education develops and the legal issues it generates will have far-reaching consequences. Copyright issues in electronic publishing is one area in which the law will have to develop; another is copyright in and liability for generation and use of information transmitted over the internet. As distance-learning develops, whether it be to local communities or across the world, it will be important to establish principles for handling copyright issues and methods by which intellectual property rights can be protected in practice.

7.13   The development of Europe-wide initiatives in the information area continues unabated, with the introduction not long after this book appears of new legislation in the fields of data protection, copyright in databases and protection of intellectual property rights in biotechnology. Institutions have to keep abreast of all these changes and take action to ensure that they take full advantage of the opportunities offered.

Legal audits

7.14   It is suggested that institutions can only hope to cope with all the ongoing developments in the law of higher education through regular legal audits of their policies and procedures carried out by experts in the different areas covered by this book. After all the discussion which has taken place in the system since the appearance of the first edition, the author has concluded that institutions have everything to gain and nothing to lose from a systematic examination and regular re-examination of their policies and procedures. If anything is to be commended to institutions for the future, this is it.

Index

Contracts—*contd*
model contract, 4. Appendix A
ostensible authority, 2.138-2.140
patents, model contractual clause
dealing with, 6. Appendix A
power to contract, 2.136
Public Works Contracts
Regulations, 2.53
Supplies and Works Directives,
2.141
Supply of Goods and Services Act
1982, 2.137
unfair contract terms, 4.28-4.33
variation of contract with student,
Casson case, 4.89
course structure permitting
variation, 4.87-4.88
credit accumulation and
transfer, 4.90
post-registration changes, 4.84-
4.86
Copying. *See* COPYRIGHT
Copyright
computer software,
CHEST, 6.46
code of conduct for use of
software and datasets,
6.48
concessions relating to computer
programs, 6.51
databases, 6.47
generally, 6.43-6.45
lending, 6.50
moral rights of authors, 6.49
computer-generated work, 6.54
copying,
excluded modes of, 6.33
libraries, by, 6.35
personnel covered by CLA
licence, restrictions on,
6.34
copyright work, meaning, 6.11
course material, in, 6.21-6.25
datasets, code of conduct for use of,
6.48
EU Directive on Rental Right,
Lending Right and
Neighbouring Rights, 6.42
Educational Recording Agency,
functions of, 6.36-6.37
freedom from false attribution, 6.15
how arising, 6.11-6.14
infringement of, 6.38-6.40
integrity, moral right of, 6.15

Copyright—*contd*
international law of, 6.9
lending computer software, 6.50
licensing by institutions, 6.41
licensing schemes, 6.26-6.28
meaning, 6.11
miscellaneous rights, 6.55
moral rights,
computer software, authors of,
6.49
concept of, 6.15
multimedia, 6.53
new developments in technology,
6.52
origins of, 6.8
ownership of, 6.16-6.20
paternity, moral right of, 6.15
time-shifting, 6.37
Treaty of Rome, application of non-
discrimination provisions of,
6.10
Copyright Licensing Agency
establishment of, 6.29
functions of, 6.29-6.32
Copyright Tribunal
establishment of, 6.56
Corporations. *See* HIGHER EDUCATION
CORPORATIONS
Council
non-university institution, 1.181
senate, separation of powers
between, 1.127-1.129
Courses
copyright in course material, 6.21-
6.25
structure permitting variation of
contract, 4.87-4.88
Court of Governors
responsibilities of, 1.162-1.164
Courts
legal issues and jurisdiction of. *See*
LEGAL ISSUES
Cranfield University
description of, 1.84
Criminal liability
nature of, 2.16
Criminal offences
students involved in, 4.116-4.118
Criminal record
discrimination on grounds of, 5.76
rehabilitation of offenders, 5.185
Crown
chartered corporations' relationship
to, 1.49

Quality—*contd*
  charters for higher education, 3.82-3.89
  exercise of professional duty,
    academic judgment, 3.98-3.100
    distinctions between
      professionals and others,
        3.95-3.97
    generally, 3.90-3.92
    reasonable skill and care, 3.93-3.94
  facilitating quality learning
    experience,
    change of emphasis, 4.4
    naked sunbather, 4.7-4.8
    quality of service, 4.5-4.6
    student, meaning, 4.9-4.11
  measurement, 3.68
  practical guides to meaning of,
    3.76-3.81
  professional and product liability,
    insurance cover, 3.105-3.108
  professional advice and services,
    3.101
  sale of goods, 3.102-3.104
  research. *See* RESEARCH
Quality Assurance Agency for Higher
    Education (QAA)
  academic audit conducted by, 2.85
  basic quality controls, 3.66
  fitness for purpose, meaning, 3.67
  governing instruments, commitment
    to quality in, 3.73-3.75
  legal entitlement to quality of
    provision, 3.72
  practical guides to meaning of
    quality, 3.76-3.81
  quality assessment, 3.69-3.71
  quality audit, 3.65-3.81
  quality measurement, 3.68
Quorum
  conduct of business, 1.203-1.204

Race discrimination
  educational reasons distinguished
    from racial grounds, 4.53-4.54
  students, relating to, 4.49-4.52
Radioactive substances
  premises on which kept, 2.49
Radiographers
  professional body, supervision by,
    3.106 n160

Real property
  easements etc., 2.155-2.156
  incumbrances, 2.159
  land. *See* LAND
  leases, 2.157-2.158
  ownership of land, 2.154
  personalty, realty and, 2.153
  registration of title, 2.159
  restrictive covenants, 2.156
Recognised bodies
  degrees, recognition of, 1.109-1.110
Records
  access to manually-held records,
    health records, 6.92
    medical reports, 6.91
    personal files, 6.90
  health, 6.92
Recruiting agencies
  conflict of laws, 4.41
  liability for acts of agents, 4.40
Rector
  role of, 1.226-1.227
Redundancy
  actual selection for, 5.164
  alternative employment, 5.162
    5.165
  appropriate representatives,
    requirement to consult,
    5.161
  consultation, 5.163
  present law relating to, 5.160
  redundant lecturer, 5.4-5.10
References
  staff,
    assessments given for promotion
      and similar purposes,
      5.186-5.187
    care, extent of duty of,
      employee, owed to, 5.183
      person seeking reference,
        owed to, 5.184
    disclaimer clauses, 5.188
    generally, 5.182
    subject to, 5.189
    Warner Report, 5.185
  students, relationships between staff
    and, 4.126-4.130
Registrar
  role of, 1.247-1.248
Registrary
  role of, 1.247-1.248
Registration
  data protection, 6.84 6.87

University Council. *See* COUNCIL
University Court
powers of, 1.136-1.145
University Grants Committee (UGC)
control of, 2.65
post First World War English
universities, role relating to,
1.78-1.79
university status, attitude to
requests for, 1.23
University Senate. *See* SENATE
University of Industry
proposals for, 1.6 1.85
Utilities
legal issues, 2.177

Value added tax
charitable status,
conferences, etc., 2.97
fund-raising, 2.95
generally, 2.89-2.94
inter-institutional supplies, 2.98
zero rating, 2.96
Veterinary surgery
professional body, supervision by,
3.106
Vice-Chancellor
Deputy Vice-Chancellor, 1.244-
1.246
Pro-Vice-Chancellor, 1.244-1.246
role of, 1.232-1.240
Victimisation
sex discrimination, 5.90-5.91
Video Performance Limited (VPL)
functions of, 6.55

Virtual University
proposals for, 1.6 1.85
Visitor
appointment of, 2.212-2.213
enforcement powers, 2.224
inspection, power of, 2.223
natural justice, standards of, 2.231-
2.232
origin of office of, 2.203-2.205
visitorial jurisdiction,
attenuation by ERA, 2.222
elsewhere in higher education,
2.221
exclusive nature of, 2.206-2.211
existence of, 2.202
extent of, 2.214-2.220
new look staffing policies, 5.11-
5.12
Scotland, 2.225-2.230
universities, in, 2.214-2.220
Voting
conduct of business, 1.209-1.210

Wales
universities, 1.95
Warner Report
references and applications, general
points on, 5.185
Wrestling
licensing of displays, 2.45

Zero rating
charitable status, and, 2.96